ART AND CULTURE
AROUND 1492

1992 Seville
Universal Exposition

ART AND CULTURE
AROUND 1492

Art and Culture
around 1492

Issued by

SOCIEDAD ESTATAL PARA
LA EXPOSICIÓN UNIVERSAL
SEVILLA 92, S.A.
Recinto de La Cartuja
41092 Sevilla, Spain
Tel. (5) 448 1992
Fax (5) 446 0427

Published by:
Centro Publicaciones,
Expo'92, S.A.

Publishers:
Raúl Rispa
María José Aguaza
César Alonso de los Ríos

Scientific editor.
Dr. Joan Sureda i Pons

English translation:
Oliver Strunk, l'Editora 02
(coordination)
Matthew Tree (corrections)
Pritchard & Witschey
y Asociados, Madrid
Paul Marshall, Charles
Dietz, Carleen Black,
William Notman, Stasa
Bailey, Sally Hine
(translations)

Editorial Production: Electa
Editorial coordination:
Franco Ambrosio
Francesca Brusa
Technical coordination:
Carlo Mion
Graphic design:
Marcello Francone
Dario Tagliabue

Cover

Graphic design:
Marcello Francone
Corporative visual design:
F. Medina, Triom Design Inc.,
Los Angeles,
© Expo'92, S.A.
Cartography:
Diseño y Comunicación, S.A.,
Sevilla

*Colour separation
and reproduction:*
Progreso Gráfico, Madrid
Printing and binding:
tf. Artes Gráficas, Madrid
Paper Gardamatt Brillante
gr. 135 **Cartiere del Garda**

Paperback
ISBN: 84-86925-70-3

Hard cover
ISBN: 88-435-4112-9

Depósito Legal: M-21353-1992

*The theme of Expo '92, the 1992 Seville Universal Exposition,
is the* Age of Discoveries, *i.e., the scientific, technological, and cultural
achievements of mankind over the last five hundred years, from the
voyages of Columbus to our own times.
All the participants have contributed to this celebration of man the
discoverer. However, the organisers have made a special effort to respond
to the motto decided by the International Exhibitions Office with a highly
ambitious exhibition plan. Thus, the global discourse implicit in the* Age
of Discoveries *is developed in a series of pavilions whose content form a
coherent whole: the 15th Century, Navigation, Nature, Energy,
Telecommunications, the Environment, and the Universe.
We decided that an exhibition of the state of the world at the beginning
of the* Age of Discoveries *would make its origins easier to understand.
The Pavilion of the 15th Century and the present exhibition are devoted
to this. Thus,* Art and Culture Around 1492 *responds to an aim which is
consistent with that of Expo '92 itself: universality. This represents a radical
revision of Eurocentric concepts of history. What was the cultural and
artistic state of the world at the time of the Discovery of America? The
fragmentary character of the world at that time and the real difficulties
in communication between different peoples do not negate the existence of
the different cultures of the 15th century, nor the influences, the
infections, or transmissions between them. And a knowledge of the
cultural background of 1492 is naturally of fundamental interest to
anyone who wishes to understand the world which began to take shape
from that year onwards. The richness of the contributions and the
relevance of the selection make this exhibition a cultural event which will
be of interest to both the general public and specialist.*

1992 Seville Universal Exposition

Art and Culture
around 1492

Organized by
Sociedad Estatal para
la Exposición Universal
Sevilla 92, S.A.

Building
Cartuja de Santa María
de las Cuevas, central area
of monastery
May 18th to
September 18th, 1992

Exhibition

Management
División de Exposiciones
Expo'92, S.A.

*Scientific director
and museum design*
Dr. Joan Sureda i Pons

General Advisers
Dr. Felipe Vicente Garín
Llombart
Dr. José Milicua Ilarramendi

Area Advisers
Dr. José Alcina Franch
(America)
Dr. Carmen García
Ormaechea y Quero
(Far East)
Dr. Purificación Marinetto
Sánchez
(Islam)
Dr. Joan Sureda i Pons
(Europe)

Exhibition design
Francisco Rodríguez
de Partearroyo
(management)

Production
Francisco Mínguez/
Grupo Entorno, S.A.

Transport and assembly
S.I.T., Transportes
Internacionales, S.A.

Insurance
T.A.I., Correduría de Seguros
La Equitativa

Sponsor:
BANCO CENTRAL HISPANO

Our thanks to the following museums, institutions and private collections which have contributed to Art and Culture around 1492:

Austria
Vienna, Museum für Völkerkunde.

Belgium
Antwerp, City of Antwerp, Etnografisch Museum.

China
Beijing, The Palace Museum; Shanghai, Shanghai Museum.

Colombia
Bogotá, Fondo de Promoción de la Cultura, Banco Popular; Bogotá, Instituto Colombiano de Antropología, COLCULTURA; Bogotá, Museo del Oro, Banco de la República.

Czechoslovakia
Prague, National Gallery Prague, Collection of Old Bohemian Art.

Denmark
Copenhagen, Nationalmuseet; Copenhagen, The David Collection.

Dominican Republic
Santo Domingo, Museo Arqueológico Nacional Altos de Chavón; Santo Domingo, Fundación García Arévalo; Santo Domingo, Museo del Hombre Dominicano.

Egypt
Cairo, General Egyptian Book Organization, GIBO; Cairo, Museum of Islamic Art.

France
Paris, Musée Cernuschi, Ville de Paris; Paris, Musée Guimet; Musée du Louvre, Département des Sculptures; Paris, Musée du Louvre, Département des Objets d'Art; Paris, Musée du Louvre, Département des Peintures; Paris, Musée du Louvre, Section Islamique; Sélestat, Bibliothèque Humaniste Sélestat.

Germany
Berlin, Museum für Islamische Kunst, Staatliche Museen Preussischer Kulturbesitz, Berlin; Cologne, Diözesanmuseum, Köln; Cologne, Schnütgen-Museum der Stadt Köln; Cologne, Schnütgen-Museum der Stadt Köln, Leihgabe Sammlung Ludwig; Leipzig, Grassimuseum/Museum des Kunsthandwerks; Munich, Bayrisches Nationalmuseum; Nuremberg, Germanisches Nationalmuseum.

Greece
Athens, Byzantine Museum of Athens.

Guatemala
Guatemala, Museo Nacional de Arqueología y Etnología.

Hungary
Budapest, Museum of Applied Arts; Budapest, Museum of Fine Arts.

India
Hampi, Vijayanagar Museum; New Delhi, Courtesy of the National Museum, Janpath.

Italy
Bologna, Biblioteca Universitaria di Bologna; Bologna, Museo Civico Medievale; Ferrara, Musei Civici di Arte Antica; Florence, Ente Casa Buonarroti; Florence, Galleria Palatina, Palazzo Pitti; Florence, Galleria degli Uffizi; Florence, Chiesa d'Ognissanti (Soprintendenza); Florence, Musei del Comune di Firenze; Museo Bardini; Florence, Musei del Comune di Firenze, Palazzo Vecchio, Collezione Loeser; Milan, Civica Pinacoteca del Castello Sforzesco; Modena, Galleria e Museo Estense; Parma, Galleria Nazionale; Perugia, Galleria Nazionale dell'Umbria; Pesaro, Museo Civico; Rome, Galleria Nazionale d'Arte Antica; Rome, Soprintendenza speciale al Museo Nazionale Preistorico Etnografico Luigi Pigorini; Turin, Museo Civico; Urbino, Galleria Nazionale delle Marche; Venice, Gallerie dell'Accademia; Verona, Museo di Castelvecchio.

Japan
Tokyo, Cultural Affairs Agency; Osaka, Masaki Museum of Art; Tochigi, Prefectural Museum of Tochigi; Tokyo, Idemitsu Museum of Art; Tokyo, Suntory Museum of Art; Tokyo, Fuji Art Museum; Tokyo, Japan Foundation.

Korea
Seoul, The National Museum of Korea; Seoul, Horim Museum.

Mexico
Mexico D.F., Instituto Nacional de Antropología e Historia, Consejo Nacional para la Cultura y las Artes.

Netherlands
Amsterdam, Rijksmuseum; Haarlem, Private Collection.

Nigeria
Lagos, Courtesy of Nigerian National Commission for Museums & Monuments.

Portugal
Aveiro, Museu de Aveiro; Lisbon, Museu Calouste Gulbenkian, Fundação Calouste Gulbenkian; Lisbon, Museu Nacional de Arte Antiga; Setúbal, Museu de Setúbal, Convento de Jesús.

Republic of Singapore
Singapore, Collection of the National Museum.

Spain
Avila, Museo Catedralicio; Barcelona, Museu Nacional d'Art de Catalunya; Barcelona, Museo de Cerámica, Ayuntamiento de Barcelona; Granada, Museo Nacional de Arte Hispanomusulmán; Madrid, Archivo Privado Conde de Bugallal; Madrid, private collection; Madrid, Colección de la Duquesa de Villahermosa; Madrid, Instituto Valencia de Don Juan; Madrid, Museo Arqueológico Nacional; Madrid, Museo Nacional de Artes Decorativas; Madrid, Museo de América; Madrid, Museo del Ejército; Madrid, Museo del Prado; Madrid, Patrimonio Nacional, Monasterio Descalzas Reales; Madrid, Patrimonio Nacional, Real Monasterio de San Lorenzo; Madrid, Patrimonio Nacional, Real Armería; Valencia, Museo de Bellas Artes San Pío V, Colección Real, Academia de San Carlos; Valladolid, Museo Nacional de Escultura.

Switzerland
Basel, Historisches Museum Basel.

Turkey
Istanbul, Archaeological Museum; Istanbul, Topkapi Sarayi Musezi.

United Kingdom
London, The British Library Board; London, the Trustees of the British Museum; London, the Trustees of the National Gallery; London, Percival David Foundation of Chinese Art; London, The Keir Collection; London, Trustees of the Victoria & Albert Museum; Oxford, the Warden and Fellows of New College.

United States
Los Angeles, The Paul and Ruth Tishman Collection of African Art, loaned by the Walt Disney Collection; New York, Collection of the Brooklyn Museum, Gift of Mrs. Evelyn Metzger; New York, The Metropolitan Museum of Art, Rogers Fund; Washington, The Arthur M. Sackler Gallery, Smithsonian Institution; Washington, National Gallery of Art, Widener Collection.

Vatican
Vatican City, Biblioteca Vaticana; Vatican City, Musei Vaticani.

We also wish to thank:
Conjunto Monumental del Monasterio de la Cartuja, Junta de Andalucía; Fuji Art Museum Tokyo; Idemitsu Museum of Art, Tokyo; Instituto para la Conservación y Restauración de Bienes Culturales, Junta de Andalucía; Japan Foundation, Tokyo; Masaki Museum of Art, Osaka; National Museum, Shanghai; Prefectural Museum of Tochigi, Tokyo; Vijayanagar Museum, Hampi-Hosp; the Imperial Palace Museum, Beijing; National Museum, New Delhi; Suntory Museum of Art, Tokyo; Juan Abelló Gallo, Colección Juan Abelló, Madrid; Myrtali Acheimastou-Potamianou, Byzantine Museum, Athens; Shah Alam, National Museum of Singapore; Daniel Alcouffe, Musée du Louvre, Département des Objets d'Art, Paris; José Angel Sánchez Asiain, Real Patronato del Museo del Prado, Madrid; Ibrahim Bakr, Museum of Islamic Art, Cairo; Xavier Barral, Museo de Art de Catalunya, Barcelona; Alberto Bartolomé Arraiza, Museo Nacional de Artes Decorativas, Madrid; Reinhold Baumstark, Bayerisches Museum, Munich; Milo Beach, Smithsonian Institution, Arthur M. Sackler Gallery, Washington; Jadranka Bentini, Galleria e Museo Estense, Modena; Marthe Bernus Taylor, Musée du Louvre, Section Islamique, Paris; Luciano Berti, Ente

Casa Buonarroti, Florence; Ingrid M. Bircann, Museo Arqueológico Regional Altos de Chavón, Santo Domingo; Deán Julián Blánquez Chamorro, Avila Cathedral, Avila; Marie-Thérèse Bobot, Musée Cernuschi, Paris; Prefect P. Leonard E. Boyle, Biblioteca Vaticana, Vatican City; Ana M. Brandau, Museu d'Arte Antiga, Lisbon; Christopher Brown, National Gallery, London; J. Carter Brown, The National Gallery, Widener Collection, Washington; Han Byung Sam, National Museum of Korea, Seoul; Paz Cabello, Museo de América, Madrid; Elvira Cuervo Jaranillo, Instituto Colombiano de Antropología, COLCULTURA, Bogotá; Marco Chiarini, Palazzo Pitti, Florence; Pedro Días, Instituto de Historiedades, Coimbra; Layla S. Diba, The Brooklyn Museum, New York; José Ramón Fernández de Bugallal, Colección Conde de Bugallal, Madrid; Lucia Fornari Schianchi, Galleria Nazionale di Parma, Parma; Eduardo Fresneda Padilla, Museo Nacional de Arte Hispanomusulmán, Granada; Mrs. Fugazzola, Museo Nazionale Preistorico Etnografico Luigi Pigorini, Rome; Jean-René Gaborit, Musée du Louvre, Département des Sculptures, Paris; Mercedes Garberi, Castello Sforzesco, Milan; Manuel Antonio García-Arévalo, Museo Fundación García Arévalo, Santo Domingo;

Carmen García Beneyto, Museo de Bellas Artes San Pío V, Valencia; Vittoria Garibaldi, Galleria Nazionale dell'Umbria, Perugia; Felipe Garín, Museo del Prado, Madrid; Yaro Gella, National Commission for Museums and Monuments, Lagos; Claudio Giardini, Museo Civico, Pesaro; María Teresa Gomes Ferreira, Fundação Gulbenkian, Lisbon; Renzo Grandi, Museo Civico Medievale, Bologna; Mgr. Dr. M.J. De Groot, Haarlem Kapel Bisschoppelijk Palais, Haarlem; Angela Grzesak, Museum des Kunsthandwerks, Leipzig; Ilmo. Julio de la Guardia, Patrimonio Nacional, Madrid; Dora Guerra De González, Museo Nacional de Arqueología y Etnología, Guatemala; John Guy, Victoria & Albert Museum, London; Frank Herreman, Etnografisch Museum, Antwerp; Eikichi Hayashiya, Japanese V Centenary Commission; Yoon Jang Sup, Horim Art Museum, Seoul; Jean-Françoise Jarrige, Musée Guimet, Paris; J.R. Knox, British Museum, London; Cafer Kocturr, Turkish Pavilion; Filedt Kok, Rijksmuseum, Amsterdam; Seyfettin Kustimur, Directorate General of the Ministry of Culture, Ankara; Michel Laclotte, Musée du Louvre, Paris; Liang Xinghua, General Commissariat of the Chinese Pavilion; María Lobato Guimarais, Museo de Aveiro, Aveiro; Jerry Patrick Losty, The

British Library, London; Peter Ludwig, Schnütgen Museum, Cologne; Luis Luna Moreno, Museo Nacional de Escultura, Valladolid; Torben Lundbaek, Nationalmuseet, Copenhagen; Hans Manndorff, Museum für Völkerkunde, Vienna; Sergio Marinelli, Museo di Castelvecchio, Verona; Balbina Martínez Caviró, Instituto Valencia de Don Juan, Madrid; Shozo Masuda, Japanese V Centenary Commission, Tokyo; Eduardo Matos Moctezuma, Museo del Templo Mayor, Mexico D.F.; Michael Meinecke, Museum für Islamische Kunst, Berlin; Ahmet Mentes, Topkapi Sarayi Musezi, Istanbul; Ahmet Morsi, Egyptian Pavilion; Hubert Meyer, Bibliothèque Humaniste, Sélestat; Miklos Mojzer, Szepmuveszeti Muzeum, Budapest; Philippe de Montebello, The Metropolitan Museum of Art, New York; Fernando Morban, Museo del Hombre Dominicano, Santo Domingo; Giovanna Nepi Sciré, Gallerie dell'Accademia, Venice; Masahiro Numa, Secretary of the Japanese V Centenary Commission, Tokyo; Mercedes Orihuela, Museo del Prado, Madrid; David Palfreyman, New College, Oxford; Antonio Paolucci, Soprintendenza per i Beni Artistici e Storici, Florence; Alpay Pasinli, Archaeological Museum of Istanbul; Fernando Antonio Baptista Pereira, Museo de Setúbal; Setúbal; Carmen Pérez,

Museo Arqueológico Nacional, Madrid; Anna Maria Petroli Toffani, Galleria degli Uffizi, Florence; Silvana Pettenati, Museo Civico di Torino, Turin; Carlo Pietrangeli, Musei Vaticani, Vatican City; Clemencia Plazas, Museo del Oro, Bogotá; Joachim Plotzek, Diözesanmuseum, Cologne; Paolo Dal Poggetto, Galleria Nazionale delle Marche, Urbino; Paolo Dal Poggetto, Soprintendenza della Regione Marche, Urbino; Picarda Quillice, Biblioteca dell'Università (Museo Aldrovandiano), Bologna; Pina Ragioneri, Ente Casa Buonarroti, Florence; Burkard Von Roda, Historisches Museum, Basel; Col. Rodríguez Del Cerro, Museo del Ejército, Madrid; Van A. Romans, The Paul and Ruth Tishman Collection, Los Angeles; Pierre Rosenberg, Musée du Louvre, Département des Peintures, Paris; Gyula Rozsa, Iparmuveszeti, Budapest; Saleh, Museum of Islamic Art, Cairo; María José Sampaio, Museo Machado do Castro, Coimbra; Trinidad Sánchez-Pacheco, Museo de Cerámica, Barcelona; Samir Sarhan, General Egyptian Book, Adab Farsi, Cairo; I.K. Sarma, Archaeological Survey of India, New Delhi; Vecdi Sayar, Turkish Ministry of Culture; Fiorenza Scalia, Museo del Palazzo Vecchio, Collezione Loeser, Florence; María del Carmen Serra Puche,

Museo Nacional de Antropología, Mexico D.F.; Alicia Eugenia Silva, Museo Arqueológico Banco Popular, Bogotá; Francesco Sisinni, Ufficio Centrale per i Beni Culturali, Rome; Lubomir Slavicek, National Gallery, Prague; Claudio Strinati, Galleria Nazionale d'Arte Antica, Rome; Rosa María Subirana, Conservación Técnica de los Museos de Barcelona, Barcelona; Edmund De Unger, The Keir Collection, London; Alfonso Urtáiz, Colección de la Duquesa de Villahermosa, Madrid; Duquesa de Villahermosa, Colección de la Duquesa de Villahermosa, Madrid; Anna Maria Visser Travagli, Palazzo Schifanoia, Ferrara; Kjield V. Folsach, The David Collection, Copenhagen; Wang Limei, The State Bureau of Cultural Relics, Foreign Affairs Division, Beijing; Watanabe, Agency for Cultural Affairs, Osaka; Oliver Watson, Victoria & Albert Museum, London; Hiltrud Westermann-Angerhausen, Schnütgen Museum, Cologne; Roderick Whitfield, Percival and David Foundation, London; Johannes Willers, Germanisches Nationalmuseum, Nuremberg; and all the Spanish embassies in the countries taking part, with special thanks to those in Egypt, Guatemala, the Holy See, India, Indonesia, Italy, Japan, Korea, Singapore and Turkey.

Photographic Credits:
Cultural Affairs Agency, Osaka; Ampliaciones y Reproducciones Mas, Barcelona; Araldo De Luca, Fotografie e Archivio d'Arte, Rome; M. Babey, Historisches Museum, Basel; Bayerisches Nationalmuseum, Munich; Sandro Bellu, Ripr. d'Arte, Perugia; Biblioteca de Catalunya, Barcelona; Biblioteca Nacional, Madrid; Biblioteca Universitaria di Bologna; Bibliothèque Humaniste, Sélestat; Bildarchiv Preussischer Kulturbesitz, Berlin; The British Library, Oriental and India Office Collections, London; The Trustees of the British Museum, London; The Brooklyn Museum, New York; Centro Documentazione Fotografica di Umberto Tomba, Verona; Civica Pinacoteca del Castello Sforzesco, Milan; Colección Conde de Bugallal, Madrid; Colección de la Duquesa de Villahermosa, Madrid; Colección Juan Abelló, Madrid; The David Collection, Copenhagen; Vicente del Amo Hernández; Ditta Quattrone Mario, Florence; Anna Elias; Ente Casa Buonarroti, Florence; Erzbischöfliches Diözesanmuseum, Cologne; Foto Roncaglia, Modena; Fundação Calouste Gulbenkian, Lisbon; Gabinetto Fotografico Soprintendenza, Palazzo Pitti, Florence; Galleria e Museo Estense, Modena; Galleria Nazionale delle Marche, Urbino; Galleria Nazionale, Parma; Germanisches Nationalmuseum, Nuremberg; Giovetti Fotografia & Comunicazioni Visive SNC, Mantua; Giraudon, Paris; Haarlem Kapel Bisschoppelijk, Haarlem; Mathias Hildebrandt, Museum des Kunsthandwerks, Leipzig; Iparmuveszeti, Budapest; Istituto Geografico De Agostini, Milan; Alfredo López; Moises Martínez Martínez; The Metropolitan Museum of Art, Rogers Fund, 1912; New York; Monumenti, Musei e Gallerie Pontificie, Vatican City; Musée Cernuschi, Paris; Musei Civici di Arte Antica, Ferrara; Musei Civici, Turin; Musei del Comune di Firenze, Museo Bardini; Musei del Comune di Firenze, Collezione Loeser in Palazzo Vecchio; Archaeological Museum, Istanbul; Museo Arqueológico Banco Popular, Bogotá; Museo Arqueológico Nacional, Madrid; Museo Arqueológico Regional Altos de Chavón, Santo Domingo; Museo de América, Madrid; Fuji Art Museum, Tokyo; Horim Art Museum, Seoul; Idemitsu Museum of Art, Tokyo; Masaki Museum of Art, Osaka; Suntory Museum of Art, Tokyo; Museo de Bellas Artes San Pío V, Valencia; Byzantine Museum, Athens; Museo Civico, Pesaro; Museo del Ejército, Madrid; Museo Fundación García Arévalo, Santo Domingo; Museo

del Hombre Dominicano, Santo Domingo; National Museum, New Delhi; National Museum, Shanghai; National Museum, Singapore; Museo Nacional de Artes Decorativas, Madrid; National Museum of Korea, Seoul; Museo Nacional de Escultura, Valladolid; Museo del Oro, Bogotá; Imperial Palace Museum, Beijing; Prefectural Museum of Tochigi; Museo de Setúbal-Convento de Jesús; Vijayanagar Museum, Hampi; Museu de Cerámica, Ajuntament de Barcelona; Museu Nacional d'Art de Catalunya, Barcelona; Museu Nacional de Arte Antiga, Lisbon; Museum of Fine Arts (reproduced by courtesy of the Board of Directors of the Budapest Museum of Fine Arts); Museum für Islamische Kunst, Staatliche Museen Preussischer Kulturbesitz, Berlin (photo by J. Liepe and P. Stüning); Museum für Völkerkunde, Vienna; Narodni Galerie, Prague; The National Gallery, London; National Gallery of Art, Washington; The National Museum of Denmark, Department of Ethnography; Nigerian National Commission for Museums and Monuments; Oronoz, Documentación Edición y Fotografía, Madrid; Patrimonio Nacional, Madrid (photographs by courtesy of the Patrimonio Nacional: cat. 33, 76, 77, 307); Percival David Foundation of Chinese Art, London (by courtesy of cat. 41, 249, 250, 252, 313); Francisco Petit; Philipe Photo Trade, Cairo; Photo H. Josse, Paris; Photocopy Estimate, London; Prisma Diseño, Granada; Réunion des Musées Nationaux, Paris; Rheinisches Bildarchiv, Cologne; Rijksmuseum-Stichting, Amsterdam; Arnold Robles Aguilar; The Arthur M. Sackler Gallery, Smithsonian Institution, Washington (photo by Jeffrey Crespi); Samy Mittry; Saporetti, Milan; Schnütgen Museum, Cologne; Serviprensa, Guatemala; Studio Professionale, C.N.B. & C., Bologna; Studios Dick Beaulieux, Historische Musea Etnografisch Museum, Antwerp; Szépmüvészeti Múzeum, Budapest; Thomas-Photos, Oxford; Umberto Tomba, Verona; Topkapi Sarayi Musezi, Istanbul; V & A Picture Library, London (courtesy of the Board of the Trustees of the V & A: cat. 42, 88, 232, 234); Walt Disney Imagineering, Los Angeles; Kit Weiss, Nationalmuseet, Copenhagen; Werner Forman Archive, London; Germán Zúñiga.

We wish to thank all the Museums, Institutions, and Private Collections who have made their photographic archives available to us.

This exhibition required a special effort in all fields by the Sociedad Estatal Expo'92, S.A. The exceptional quantity, quality and diversity of the 15th and 16th century works lent by 111 museums from all over the world meant that preparation of the exhibition continued until the very opening. The compilation of the texts, catalogue entries and information written by more than a hundred authors from four continents in a wide range of languages, and of the iconography for some three hundred works has entailed a quite extraordinary publishing programme, which accelerated after 5 June when the catalogue went to press with the present material. We have put the greatest care and effort into the publishing of these extremely varied materials – the content of which is the responsibility of the Scientific Director of the Exhibition – in order to publish a high-quality catalogue in record time (in normal circumstances it would have required months). The reader will thus be able to appreciate the diverse features of this catalogue, from a short bibliography which, in addition to a general bibliography, gives the author, year and page in each entry, to the rich documentation which will confer a permanent character on this unique exhibition after it closes on 18 September.

The Publishers

Contents

Art and Culture Around 1492:
The Exhibition

The night of Saturday, 31 December 1492 was a sad one for the dauntless lions that guard one of the Alhambra's loveliest patios; perhaps the moon was reflected in the water in the cup that, even today, their stone bodies appear to support; perhaps Boabdil, who, a few hours later, would hand over Muslim Granada to the Christian Kings of Spain, looked for the last time at the engraving which made the fountain gracing the patio more than just a fountain:

Liquid silver which slips between jewels, whiteness
and transparent beauty without equal.
Water and marble confound the gaze and we know not
which of the two is in motion.
Can you not see how the water flows to the sides and,
finding no obstacle, hides in the ducts?
Like a lover's eyelids flowing with tears, hidden
For fear of being surprised.
What is it, but a cloud that sheds its blessing
On the lions?
Like the hand of the caliph which is outstretched to pour
gifts over the lions of war.
Oh, you, who look to the caliph with respect, stop the lions
that are lying in wait from showing their ferocity!
Oh, direct descendants of the ansar,
inheritance of greatness that will permit you to destroy
those who come from above!
May the peace of God be eternally with you, in
The multiplication of joys,
In the grief of your enemies.

What the verses clamoured for never took place: the lions never showed their ferocity. On Monday, 2 January 1492 three banners waved in the breeze above the Alhambra of Granada's highest tower: one flaunting the cross of Cardinal Mendoza; one displaying the scallop shell of Santiago to the wind, and one emblazoned with the arms of Castile; the Church, the Crusades and political power had achieved, after centuries, the submission of a culture and the Christianisation of Europe.

The desire to submit men and cultures to one's will is a vain one; neither one nor the other will submit. They are like reeds that bend before the wind but never break because their freedom does not lie in the wings that would enable them to fly but in the roots that fix them to the earth.

In all cultures and through every age a sap common to all runs through these same roots: Art. What is Art? Man asks himself this question day after day without ever having ceased to create Art, as he has never ceased to live, yet still wonders what life is. We do not know and it matters little, because when we think we have discovered its secret it runs through our fingers like water trickling from a fountain.

How many times has man believed that Art was like the reflection of the moon in the river? How many times have cultures failed in attempting to embrace this reflection? We do not know this either, and that too, matters little. What is important is that men and cultures, in wanting to embrace the impossible, have discovered that that which appears to flee actually stays, and that Art is not a reflection of the world, but is the world itself.

Who, like the Chinese teacher, has not tried to step inside a painted landscape and not return from it? Who has not tried to escape from reality to take refuge in illusion? Paint or landscape? Reality or illusion? There is only Art.

Art takes man across the world and is capable of transporting him from today into past worlds, because the truth is that the world changes little, it remains the same. Its manifestations and expressions may vary, but its essence does not. When contemplating the art of any age we immerse ourselves in time and eliminate space; geographical, historical and cultural limits are of little use; the general imposes itself upon the particular and the essential upon the anecdotal. *Art and Culture Around 1492* endeavours to show that which is "common" and "essential" to the principal areas of culture that existed five hundred years ago, from the Islamic to the Oriental, from the European to the American, from the African to the Byzantine. None of these cultures was a "hortus conclusus", none was born at that time and none, despite the illusion of history, became extinct during it. The cultures of the world were not lost islands in a barren ocean; whether they made their presence felt or not, they were true neighbours because the characteristics of each fed the fantasies of the others. The Promised Lands, the El Dorados, the Edens, the Arcadias could equally well have been found in the West as in the East, in Africa or in America, because the place in which they were really to be found was in the mind of man.

Geographical proximity, or the lack of it, was not the only factor that fed these dreams of greatness, the desires for riches or mens' appetites for power also played their part. It was not only the geographical factor that incited men to leave their homelands to discover and conquer. Man had always created his own worlds, universes that helped make his own mortality bearable and acceptable, a cosmos that made him dream of a future as utopian as that of the land of Utopia itself. However, the gods and heroes that governed those worlds were as imperfect as the men that had created them and the latter, rebelling against their own creation, looked for other means to dominate that which they were incapable of understanding.

Faced with plagues and wars, injustice and the horrors of humanity, life and death, the gods could do nothing. The serpent of fire, whose powers should have brought victory to the defenders of Tenochtitlan succumbed before the fire from Spanish arquebuses. Religion and magic began to retreat in the face of technology, and Man, whether American, European, Asian or African started to feel helpless before his existence in the world and began to curse his inescapable destiny: "As soon as I, having escaped from prison, saw the light," wrote Camoens in one of his *Canzones*, "I was dominated by the fatal influence of the stars. They denied me the freedom to which I had a right. A thousand times destiny has shown me what is best, and in spite of myself, I have chosen for the worst. And, to ensure that my torments were in harmony with my age, when, as a child, I sweetly opened my eyes, they saw that before long an eyeless child would wound me."

The only thing remaining to Man from those unreal worlds was Art, an Art which had to be useful and effective, yet beautiful at the same time. What exactly is artistic beauty? What does a piece of Iznik pottery have in common with a Japanese figure, a Michelangelo drawing and a Nigerian head? Beauty.

Art and Culture Around 1492 also seeks to show this; the existence of a common beauty, whether beauty is considered more as the fruit of an emotional process or an intellectual one, whether it is understood that beauty should not be sought outside things but within the things themselves, in the aptness of these to their function and in the shape which their essence demands.

The thought expressed by the Sufi al-Gazzali in his treatise on the regeneration of religious sciences would be valid for all cultures: "Beauty does not lie within the perceptions of sight, nor in physiognomical harmony, nor in the mixture of white with red; we say: this a is a nice piece of penmanship and that is a nice voice, and this is a beautiful horse; but we also say that this fabric is lovely and that cup is beautiful; so where does the meaning lie in the beauty of the voice, of the penmanship and the rest of the things, if not in their very form?"

In *Art and Culture Around 1492* shape and form are understood as much in terms of their functional character, whether primary or symbolic, as in that of their beauty. This allows Shen Shou's landscapes to be compared with Leonardo da Vinci's portraits, African household articles with Islamic geometric arrangements. Even this last opposition, however, that of utility vs. abstract form, is more apparent than real. If it is true, for example, that a Muslim's conception of supreme beauty had to be the fruit of rational perception rather than of a sensual nature, it is also true that this man had to be capable of finding beauty in the things of this world, which, though transient, all aspire to the wholeness of the sublime.

The visitor who enters the Carthusian Monastery of Santa María de las Cuevas area to walk through the *Art and Culture Around 1492* exhibition will not be undertaking an imaginary journey into the past nor will he have to lose sight of the known horizon to begin walking down the path to discovery; his horizon will be Man himself, with his desire to triumph, his fears and anxieties in the face of life and death, his need to be accompanied on his journey by gods and heroes, his creative universes, his ways of looking at nature...

He will converse with objects that may be unknown and yet familiar to him, and his only means of getting close to them, and, through them, to the cultures that produced them, will be Art...and perhaps when he is alone with Art it may be useful to him to recall the Taoist fable which, like so many tales, could begin "Once upon a time..."

"Once upon a time, in Lungmen's Ravine, there was a kiri tree, a true king of the forest. Its head reached up to converse with the stars and its roots were buried deep in the ground...And it happened that a powerful magician made a wonderful harp out of this tree, whose stubborn spirit could only be dominated by the most gifted musicians. For a long time the Emperor of China kept the instrument, but the efforts of those who tried to wrest tunes from its strings were in vain. Finally Piewoh, the prince of musicians, arrived. With tender hands he caressed the harp, as if he were calming an untameable horse, and he touched the strings very gently.

Nature, the seasons, the high mountains and running water began to sing, and all the tree's memories bloomed! The sweet breath of Spring played among its branches once again... Suddenly the sleepy voices of Summer could be heard, with its ten thousand insects, the gentle falling of the rain, the lament of the cuckoo... Now it is Autumn; the moon, sharp as a sword, shines over the frozen grass. Now Winter reigns, and flocks of swans fly through the snow-filled air and hailstones bounce off the branches of trees with delicate ferocity.

Piewoh then changed his style and sang of love. The wood swayed to and fro like an ardent lover lost in his thoughts... the style changed once again; Piewoh sang of war, of the clash of steel and of charging steeds... in ecstasy, the Celestial monarch asked Piewoh where the secret of his victory lay.

"Lord," he replied, "The others failed because they sang for themselves. I let the harp choose its own theme, and I could not be certain whether the harp were Piewoh or Piewoh the harp".

We, it is clear, are the harp, and Piewoh, Art: a symphony played with our finest sentiments.

Joan Sureda i Pons
Scientific and Museum Director
Art and Culture Around 1992

A Look at 1492

20 *Art and Culture around 1492.* Clearly one discipline only cannot embrace the concepts and realities implied in this expression. Nor can one sigle exhibition, because it is clearly limited; it has to be arranged in a relatively small area and, above all, it inevitably has to dispense with works that allude to relevant concepts and realities. This renunciation is not imposed by the museums but by History. Even if our knowledge of the world in 1492 were exhaustive and the exhibition we envisaged became a reality, it would still remain incomplete and insufficient.

Today mankind has inherited immense treasures from five hundred years ago and our culture is rooted in that which shaped the "Age of Discoveries." Inevitably, however, mankind itself and time have ruined elements of this age which cannot be recovered. They have destroyed them as a consequence of the very laws of development either to eliminate or to create. Whatever the reasons, they are lost to the present and to posterity. Thus by using art to look at those cultures that thrived around 1492 we necessarily have to be selective. This look in fact will only give us a glimpse of the vastness of that cultural horizon. But a glimpse might suffice to provoke, in our senses and also in our mind, numerous evocations that draw us nearer to a remote and inaccessible culture.

Art and Culture around 1492 is therefore an opening that takes us towards a past that we have not lived but that is present in our lives. And it brings us closer to this past, half a millennium ago, not through imitation, not through the reproduction of all kinds of barriers that made the discovery of these cultures necessary.

Being both a part of and detached from these cultures of 1492 we can approach them with, if this is not too presumptuous, a Leonardesque perspective.

Just as Leonardo da Vinci, one of the supreme geniuses of that age, blurred the individual essence of the mountains, valleys and rivers to transform them, thanks to light and air, into an interdependent whole, so we search for this cultural essence where there are no limits.

The European, Asiatic, African and American cultures of around 1492 are given a place in this exhibition where they can fully reveal their essence and individuality but at the same time unite what is common to all. In *Art and Culture around 1492* time has ceased to exist and space has fused into a cultural *unicum.* The past has become the present.

José Milicua
Professor of History of Art,
Universidad de Barcelona

The Story of a Meeting

The world of 1492 was, in a way, a world in which dawn had still to break. Everything was to be hoped for in a Europe that was wise, but cloistered. To the south was the Mediterranean, in those days more of a moat than a bridge or path; North Africa, anchored in the Middle Ages and with a very different outlook, lay to the east; then there was the other East, the Far East. We scarcely knew of the Alexandrine Route until it was partially travelled by Marco Polo, the restless Venetian with an artist's soul whose many discoveries, including the Silk Route, along with a Cipango in which Xavier's print is still recognised today by the Japanese, helped the walls begin to break down. Also to the south was the to and fro of Islam and Christianity, which by this time was beginning to stabilise and would develop no further: they came to Europe, to Spain, they were fought, they were more or less tolerated and in the end they were expelled. To the west was geographic infinity, the "non plus ultra," the unknown. Not even mariners, alone or otherwise, Scandinavians – Erik, the Viking – or others that went but did not return to tell their tale, managed to convince those at home that there was something more...

And then came Columbus, the explosion the Old World needed to open up the seas. Columbus offered Europe the promise of that dawn referred to at the beginning, which would provide the West, its culture and its way of life, with new dreams. A romantic conscience – not because of the age but because of its sensitivity to the extraordinary – may have pondered, albeit insufficiently, on the wonderful adventure of these three boats, almost lost and with the crew mutinying, lacking in technique, or technology as we say these days, which reached some Neolithic islands that were little more than coral reefs. To add to the sailors' sense of wonder they found solidly structured states, extremely advanced in material terms, with everything but running water, that nonetheless performed human sacrifices. Three worlds, then: Castile, with plenty of drive, but with a tendency to haggle over financial means, saved by a half-Jewish, half-Aragonese Valencian – Lluis de Santàngel – who prepared the financing, and, on the other hand the human effort, the little boats whose Captain was a stubborn visionary who undoubtedly knew more that he admitted, and the Indians on whose beaches they arrived. Discoverer and discovered, both on the edge of history, and making history together.

The third nucleus or world, that of the Aztecs and Mayas who had a culture comparable with that of the Hélade or of Ancient Persia: this discovery would dazzle History itself. From there new materials and products would be brought – the potato, maize, the tomato, tobacco – and the sailors would take certain types of fauna away with them, including the horse, which the Greek Amazons and Holy knights of Asia Minor, St. George and others, had civilised and almost deified.

As a result of all this, the known world stopped being egocentric and opened itself up to learn, inevitably, of other cultures. It ceased being Ptolemaic and became Copernican. It was no longer the axis around which Creation turned, but a "slave" of the solar axis. The sun is the reference point; the Earth, its spherical shape now proven, is now just one more planet within its orbit.

The meeting of these cultures, so different in material terms yet less so in their approach to essential questions, is, undoubtedly, one of the key events of modern times. The world would never again resemble its old self-image. In Man's confrontation with his great problems – cosmic or close at hand – in the analysis of his relationships with superior beings or in his day-to-day activities in order to survive, every people and culture has reflected its genuine response through objects or by means of words. The good fortune to have inherited these across the centuries, these artefacts of life itself, be they cultural articles or items of symbolic value, enables us to confront them, to handle them, so as to be able to extract new and attractive hypotheses from them. They are, in short, dumb witnesses to an event which took place around 1492.

Felipe Vicente Garín Llombart
Director, Museo del Prado

Europe in 1492

Joan Sureda i Pons
University of Barcelona

As they alone believed, the unbelievable
happened: they travelled beyond the boundaries
of dreams, of the sea, of the impossible...
Captains of fantasy and chimera, they broke the horizon
once and for all, following the course of the sun...
And the sea, rising up to the heavens, is a mountain...
the only worthy singer of their heroic deeds.

With these lines, Sevillian poet Manuel Machado (1874-1947) usurped the seas prerogative of celebrating the feats of the men who, as the 15th century was drawing to a close, reached the New World in three caravels. But these new lands, which Martin Waldseemüller referred to as The Americas in *Cosmographie introductio* (1507), had already been discovered, in that they had always – at least within the bounds of human memory – been inhabited.

It is true that on Thursday, October 11, 1492, Christopher Columbus – later to become Admiral, Viceroy and Governor of all the lands he conquered for the Castilian Crown – was up against stormy seas. It is also true that on that same autumn day, the birds that wheeled above the ships and masts, and the reeds and branches that drifted up on the water, restored hope to those men who, whether or not they actually knew what they were looking for, had in any event lost faith. And it is true that on the following day, October 12, fantasy and chimera, not to mention vested interests, set foot on dry land.

But the true discoverers of a new reality, the men who forged a new vision of the world, did so not by sailing off into the unknown, but by extending the frontiers of thought. Toscanelli, Cusano, Ficino, Machiavelli, Erasmus, Moore, Nebrija, Ariosto, Dürer, Leonardo da Vinci, Gaffurio and many others like them cast off the leaden mantle of the waning Middle Ages and in doing so forged a new way forwards towards an infinity which man himself, through his fear of the unknown, had hitherto perceived as an horizon.

To be sure, 1492 was just a year like any other in Europe. Still, it is not a date that we are only inventing now five centuries later. Although the Europeans of that time could not possibly have seen that history was at a crucial juncture, it was they themselves who were propelling it towards this point.

Indeed, this shift was already evident at the beginning of the year when Queen Isabella of Castile ousted the Arabs from their stronghold in Granada, and when Valencias Rodrigo de Borja was made Pope. Change was in the air when the Jews were expelled from Spain's Christian territories, and when in Florence, financial and artistic capital, the still young Lorenzo de' Medici breathed his last.

What was this new Europe that came into being with the death of Lorenzo de' Medici? What was this Europe that the new Zeus of humanism had abducted from medieval shores to endow with the fruits of modernity?

Had a latter-day Icarus been able to fly towards the sun without melting his waxen wings, the mythological hero would have seen the earth as a sphere, as Martin Beham had imagined it in Nuremberg, and on it, Europe as a small patch of land, no more or less significant than any of the other patches on the globe. But the wax melted, and as the foolhardy Icarus plummeted into the sea, he no doubt mistook Europe for the intricate labyrinth built by his father, Daedalus.

The European Labyrinth

From the time when Christianity began to take root in the lands of Ancient Rome and others believed to be barbarian, Europe had become a *corpus christianum* led by two swords: the Popes and the Emperors. But their dominion had never been real, and if this was the case in the Middle Ages, it was even more so in the 15th century, during which Europe disintegrated into a thousand separate fragments of political power.

The scene portrayed in a miniature illustrating a prayer book dated 1493, now in the British Library in London, is as utopian as Amaurota, the capital of the half-moon shaped island that Thomas Moore called Utopia. The anonymous painter, whose work predates humanist Erasmus of Rotterdam's description in *Enchiridion Militis Christiani* (1503-1504), portrays the harmony of the *corpus christianum*. The rulers of Europe kneel before Saint George as they wait to receive communion: Charles III, king of France; the Hapsburg Emperor Frederick III; Ferdinand the Catholic, king of Aragon; Henry III of England, and Philip the Fair of Burgundy.

The scene translated onto a parchment in 1493 had been attempted in reality some years earlier by the poet Aeneas Silvius, better known as Pope Pius II (1405-1464). In 1459, he had summoned all the Christian monarchs to Mantua to fight against the Ottoman infidels who had just conquered Constantinople (1453). The summons was disregarded and the Pope, at once a champion of humanism, an admirer of the ruins of classical Rome, and a harsh critic of the great Federico de Montefeltro, could do nothing but hope for the conversion to Christianity of Mehmet II (1429-1481): "To the illustrious Mehmet, sultan of the Turks – wrote Pius II – kindly listen to these words... You and your forefathers have fought too many wars with the Christians; too much blood has been shed...(...). If you wish to extend your empire and make your name glorious... All you need is a little water with which to be baptised... were you to do this, there would be no sovereign on earth who could surpass or equal you in might. "Nos te graecorum el Orientis imperatorem appellabimus..." The era of Augustus would return... all ages would celebrate your name; and your praises would be sung in both Latin and Greek."

Mehmet never received this epistle. Indeed, he and his successors – above all the great Suleyman II, who led his troops as far as the gates of Vienna – maintained their expansionist zeal. But Europe was not over concerned with the movements of the Muslims, just as no great conflicts were engendered during the early years of the American adventure. The breeding ground for conflict was concentrated, rather, in the competing interests of the different Christian courts.

The Empire
The arbiters of these vying interests should have been the Hapsburgs, given that since 1440 they had occupied the imperial throne, and from 1516 on, the Spanish throne as well. But in the 15th century, the Emperor had no authority over the lands constituting his Empire, which was in any event simply a Germanic version of the old medieval ambition of reliving Roman unity. Even Maximilian I (1459-1519), who assumed the title of *Imperator electus*, and thus separated himself from the Popes guardianship, had to share his authority with the respec-

tive sovereigns of the Empires different territories.

Perhaps the only emperor to wield real power was Charles V, the man who believed himself to be Charlemagne's heir and representative – or, indeed, flail – of God. Thanks to the matrimonial policy of the Hapsburgs, Charles V inherited an empire which embraced most of Europe and was beginning to extend into the New World. Burgundy, the Franche-Comt, Luxembourg, the Netherlands, the possessions of the House of Austria, the territories of the Crown of Aragon, including Sicily and Naples, Castile and its overseas possessions, all came under the common standard of the two-headed imperial eagle for a few very decisive years.

Charles V was born with the century (1500) in Ghent, and died 58 years later in a simple palace that had been erected in the monastery of Yuste, Spain. This was not as strange as it might seem at first sight. Charles V believed that the Empire should cease to be a legal entity and become an ideological structure, a Christian enterprise. However, his wish came to nought, given that at the time new forms of government were emerging in Europe, heralded by powerful centralised states. Indeed, during his last years, Charles V undermined his own Empire to Spains advantage; upon abdicating in 1556, he passed the Empire on to his brother Ferdinand, while the Spanish, Flemish and Italian territories remained in the hands of his son Philip, his true heir.

When Charles V arrived in Spain in 1517, the country was very much the product of the reign of Isabella of Castile and Ferdinand of Aragon. The Catholic Monarchs had forged a modern confederate state, ruled by a Crown that respected the political institutions and conventions of the kingdoms that constituted it. The Crown of Aragon, represented by King Ferdinand, maintained its traditional Mediterranean policies. Castile, impelled by Queen Isabella, initiated Atlantic expansion, no doubt seeking alternatives to the Oriental and African trade routes which had been dominated by the Portuguese since the beginning of the 15th century.

Meanwhile, beyond the Empire, some nations, such as England, were heading in the direction of absolute monarchies, while others, such as Poland, where no middle class had evolved, retained the medieval definition of power, while Russia glorified a new Caesar in the form of Ivan the Great (1462-1505); only France had occasion to come into conflict with Charles V.

It is said that the Emperor, commenting on the aspirations of King François I of France (1494-1547), ventured: "Very soon, either I shall become a poor Emperor or he a poor king." Neither alternative quite came true, although the confrontation between the king and the Emperor over the Italian territories dominated the European stage for the first half of the 16th century.

Italy and Power

The monuments, paintings, and sculptures of the Renaissance could tempt us to think of Italy as the orchard of Europe, fed by the sap of the classical world; a country at once prosperous and peaceful, dedicated to philosophy, the arts, trade...

This arcadian vision of Italy is little more than a mirage of modern history. The recollection of one single event provides a clearer picture of how Italy really was at the time. During the Sack of Rome (1527), papal Rome was devastated by Spanish, German and Italian troops fighting a coalition of armies from various Italian cities organised by the French King François I and Pope Clement VII. The episode is significant, if not unique: Italy, despite the existence of various independent states whose independence was more formal than real, had been under foreign rule for some time.

The concept of the foreign in Europe at the dawn of the Modern Age was clearly quite different from todays. The immediate and the global, ones own village or city and Christendom, were the spatial coordinates in which people moved at the time. Despite language and geography, nationalism as we know it today had not yet engendered ideologies, but was rather a realm of philosophers and poets: "How much longer must we be condemned – oh cruel fate – to witness the barbarians being asked for help in subjugating Italy? And how much longer, oh people of Italy, will we continue to pay those who come to destroy us?"

Petrarch launched these words into the atmosphere of a country in which political fragmentation was the order of the day and where barbarians were often called on to settle internal issues and disputes. Even so, throughout the 15th century power became increasingly concentrated in ever larger geographical areas with flourishing cities as their nucleii. Their rulers, recognised by either Empire or Pope, created splendid courts, such as those of the Gonzagas in Mantua, the Estes in Ferrara and the Montefeltros in Urbino. They rivalled in splendour those of the peninsulas true political hubs: the kingdoms of Sicily and Naples, the Papal States, the Republics of Siena, Florence, Genoa and Venice, and the Duchy of Milan.

The history of these feudal states, republics and duchies was plagued not only with intrigues, conspiracies, political skirmishes and confrontations, but also with apocalyptic reformist voices clamouring for a drastic purge. One such voice was that of Dominican friar Girolamo Savonarola (1452-1498), prior of the Monastery of San Marco in Florence. Such accusatory voices were not well received by the ruling classes, and Savoranola, who had imbued all Florence with his fanatical reformist zeal, was hanged and burned. But although it was Florence and not Rome that underwent this process of reform, the same man who dreamt of a contemporary Cyrus who would reinstate order in Italy also directed accusations against Pope Alexander VI, whom he aimed to replace with a pope elected by a Universal Council called by the monarchs of Europe.

Church and Reform

The defects that Savoranola exposed in the papacy could equally have been found in any sovereign of the great European states, but the Pope was the figurehead of a religion that extended throughout Europe. For the papacy, 1492 represented the crux of a long period which had begun in 1417 when the two, and even three heads of the Church had given way to a unified Church led from Rome, and ended with Paul IV (1555-1559), when the Church stopped expending energy on direct participation in political life and focused itself instead on attaining a reunified universal Church.

This change of direction for the Church unquestionably came a little late: a need for reform had been latent throughout the 15th century. But despite the fact that reform was instigated from within the institution itself, it spread into the outside world at the beginning of the 16th century. Saxon theologian Martin Luther (1483-1546) was hailed as its main instigator.

Of all the reformers, Luther went the furthest in expressing the concerns of people who felt stifled by ecclesiastical hegemony, tired of a clergy which bought and sold preferment, of monasteries that accumulated ever more wealth and power, and of the courtly life of those who occupied the higher ecclesiastical echelons. It should be remembered that at the time the Churchs authority had already been threatened not only by reformist movements but also by the dissemination of the Bible. Thanks to the arrival of the printing press and of translations into vernacular languages, the faithful could find the

Reino de Francia

Condado
de Provenza
• Aviñón

• Génova

República
de Génova

Santiago de
Compostela

Reino
de Navarra

Rosellón

Córcega

Reino de Aragón •

Barcelona

Reino de Portugal

Toledo

Baleares

Menorca

Reino de Castilla

Mallorca

Cerdeña

Lisboa

Ibiza

M A R   M E D I T E R R A N E O

Sevilla

• Granada

Reino de Granada

M A R   M E D I T E R R A N E O

• Argel

Estados Berberiscos

true spirit of Christ for himself in the Bible; he could go back to the original source. Christianity consequently recovered its critical faculty and the people were thus emancipated from the power of Rome: "Spend no more of your money on Papal privileges – preached Luther in his *Adress to the Christian Nobility of the German Nation* – but affirm instead that the true Christian life lies in faith and charity. Let just two years go by, and you will see what remains of the Pope, the bishop, Mass, abstinences, robes, tonsures, and all the rules and statutes of the rotten papacy. It will all have vanished like smoke."

The Lutheran Reformation in 1517, when the Augustinian friar posted his ninety five theses on a church door in Wittenberg opposing the sale of indulgences, found immediate defenders and advocates among scholars, and even garnered support from among the princes who headed the independent German States on whose electoral support the Empire of Charles V depended.

Consequently, the Lutheran Reformation did more than simply pave the way for the individuals religious freedom. After a long period of struggle and attempts at conciliation, Emperor Charles V was obliged to consent to the Hapsburg Pact (1555), in which religious freedom was accorded to states, although not to subjects. With this pact, the unity of the Empire was ruptured, and Europe became divided between those who hoisted the banner of the Reformation, be it that of Luther, Zwingli, Calvin or Henry VIII, and those who sought to re-establish the authority of the Church and papacy by means of the Counter-Reformation.

Man: the Centre of the Universe
One should not, however, think that political disorder, institutional crises and philosophical rebellion brought about economic and social chaos in Europe during this period. Quite the contrary: in the late 15th and early 16th centuries, the European territories were thriving in all areas of human activity, from the demographic to the artistic – so much so that the thinkers of the time not only speculated but actually foretold that a new Golden Age was at hand. Indeed, in 1517, Erasmus wrote that he would love to be young again to be able to partake fully in the approaching new era. And four years later, Luther reflected that his times represented the pinnacle of human evolution: "A perusal of all the chronicles will make it clear that not since the birth of Christ has there been anything that can compare with what has been produced here among us in the past 100 years. Never in any country has there been so much construction and so much agricultural production! Never has there been so much to drink, and so much abundance and delicacy of food at our disposal. Clothes could not be more exquisite. Has trade ever been what it is today? It girdles the world, embracing the entire Earth. Painting, engraving, all the arts have flourished, and continue to do so."

For Luther, the preceding 100 years signalled the zenith of human accomplishment; for Erasmus, their spring-like promise was coming to fruition in the new century; for others, such as Pedro Canicio, whose perception mirrored that of papal Rome, the blessed beginning of the long-awaited renewal inspired declarations such as: "Viderunt oculi mei salutaria tempora". In their way, they were all right, and all, in one way or another, were products of their time and prisoners of their hopes.

But the longed-for Golden Age never arrived. What did happen, however, was that certain places, cities and individuals around Europe began to experience and see the world differently from the way it had been experienced and seen during the Middle Ages. Europe broke through its own philosophical frontiers, recovered its historical memory and in the process discovered, infiltrated by the lens of theology, Man and the Universe.

Classical Antiquity became the historical premise no longer of the past, but of the future; humanism discarded the Aristotelian principles that had guided Christianity, and embraced ever-present Platonism instead. Philosophers and humanists such as Pico della Mirandola, Politian, Lefèvre d'Etaples, Colet and Vives, without renouncing Christianity, sought in Plato the atlas upon which to construct a new conception of the world, a world in which man would occupy a privileged place among things temporal and eternal. Marsilio Ficino (1433-1499), translator of the works of Plato, perhaps expressed this most eloquently: "Human sovereignty is much like nature – wrote this Florentine priest – What God creates in the world by way of thought, the (human) spirit conceives for itself through the intellectual process, expresses it through language, and represents it in what man constructs of worldly matter... (Man) is the god of all the material things that he modifies and transforms... Who, then, could deny that he possesses creative genius? Who could doubt that he is capable of constructing the heavens if he found the necessary instruments and celestial matter at hand? Is he not doing so already in his own way, with other matter, but using the same principles?"

A New Status for Artistic Perception

One of the tools that man used to construct the heavens, to elevate mankind to the pinnacle of thought, and to explore Nature and the Universe, was science; another tool, in many aspects barely distinguishable from the first, was art. The art of humanism was generated in Italy during the 15th century, in a land whose people had grown up and lived among classical ruins, and in whose southern regions there still existed Greek-speaking communities. Architects, painters and sculptors all set out to achieve a consummate ideal of beauty by looking to the past as much as to the reality of the present. Art became an intellectual meditation on reality, a meditation on man's own belief that he could attain the absolute, be it the absolute of space or of the human body.

Since Petrarch, grammarians, writers and philosophers had found an invaluable goldmine of role models in the likes of Virgil, Cicero, Ovid and Seneca; artists found in the artistic and architectural remnants of the classical world the essential points of reference for the new art of the Renaissance. However, these classical presences were not seen so much as models to be imitated as sources of inspiration and, in any event, criteria for a representational method whose aim was to imitate reality.

In this Renaissance *dell'antichità*, art cast off medieval idealism and transcendentalism, which were seen as antiquated and removed from nature in the interests of replicating the visible world, the explanation of whose origins was no longer sought in the immaterial presence of a divine ideal, but rather in scientific knowledge and the authority of the Classical. Art, while continuing to be a means, began also to become an end in itself.

A New Status for Art

While medieval theologians hardly ever spoke of the arts – but rather of art as an abstraction and manifestation of divine beauty – and were even less concerned with artists, the 15th century began to feel pride in the skill of artists who could transform the mute walls and inert wood of altarpieces into works of art that seemed almost alive. Society began to echo Antiquity which, according to Pliny, had honoured its major artists, and Dante's admiration of the great Giotto became generalised. The ruling classes began to pride themselves on commissioning the best architects, painters or sculptors of the time to create the most diverse projects. Patrons protected artists in an almost paternal way, and entrusted them with everything from maintaining collections of antiques to inventing military contraptions, from designing country villas to drafting plans for an ideal city, from painting altarpieces to designing a costume for a special event.

But the ruling classes were not content simply to be patrons. Men such as Federico de Montefeltro and Cosimo de' Medici became moreover true arbiters in artistic questions. So high was the esteem in which art was held that even the influential Baldassarre Castiglione in his ideal depiction of the

INGLATERRA Y FRANCIA
EN TORNO A 1492

O C E A N O   A T L A N T I C O

M A R   D E L   N O R T E

Reino
de Escocia

Edimburgo

Irlanda

Duc. de
Lancaster

Pais de Gales

Reino de Inglaterra

Londres

La Haya

Brujas

Flandes   Gante   Aquisgrán

Artois   Lieja

Picardia

Duc. de Valois

Duc. de Normandia

Luxemburgo

Cond. del Maine

París

Duc. de Bretaña

Nancy

Duc. de Anjou

Basilea

Tours

Cond. de la Marche

Franco Condado

Duc. de Borgoña

Duc. de Borbon

Cond. de Angulema

Lyon   Duc. de
Saboya

Duc. de Auvernia

Delfinado

Reino de Francia

Cond. de Armagnac

Aviñon

Toulouse   Cond. de Provenza

Rosellón

diseño y comunicación s.a.

Urbino court *Il Cortegiano* (1528), recommended courtiers to study drawing to round off education in the liberal arts of *trivium* (grammar, rhetoric and dialectic) and *quadrivium* (arithmetic, geometry, astrology and music), even if only because drawing would be useful in their military campaigns.

But Castiglione's manual of courtly behaviour for the well-to-do was not the first reflection of the

place occupied by the mechanical arts of drawing and painting within the liberal spectrum. Indeed, throughout the 15th century, artists – who, despite often humble origins, rubbed shoulders with philosophers and literati, mathematicians and musicians – had believed their own particular branch as liberal as poetry and music.

Leonardo da Vinci saw painting as a sort of exact natural science, superior, if anything, to the sciences in the stricter sense of the term, since these were impersonal and could therefore be replicated. Pictorial art, on the other hand, was directly linked to the individual and his innate aptitudes. Indeed, around 1490, Leonardo himself, inspired as much by creative impulse as by scientific curiosity, started his anatomical drawings in which natural forms, men among them, appear life-like and even realistic, though they were in some cases imaginary. It is possible that Leonardo – and probably Raphael and Michelangelo also – had practised dissection, as many doctors were doing in Milan at the time. But painstaking exploration of human anatomy did not catch up with Leonardo's anatomical drawings until 1543, when the publication of the young Andreas Vesalius *De humani corporis fabrica* and the by then elderly Copernicus *De revolutionibus orbium coelestium* caused two concepts of science to converge and changed the world.

Art, Science and Invention

Leonardo da Vinci's quest for anatomical truth did not blind him to the fact that the beauty of forms was not simply a question of mimesis. Alberti, in his treatise *De pintura*, had already accused Demetrius, one of the great artists of Antiquity, of painting in a way that sacrificed aesthetics to realism. The artists mission was to go further than reflecting natural truth in search of a beauty never fully achieved in reality. This additional beauty, product of a *bellezza invenzione*, was born of both a chromatic and a proportional harmony. But this harmony could not be determined exclusively by the spirit or talent of the artist, but rather by the objective mathematical laws which had governed Classical statuary. Moreover, those mathematical and geometrical laws should guide the mind of the artist not only in portraying natural forms; when depicting space, he

should be guided by the laws of perspective.

The *perspectiva artificialis* of the Renaissance, in much the same way as its neo-Platonic philosophy, placed the spectator in the centre of the universe. Nevertheless, artists of the time recognised that the distance in relation to the eye of the spectator that caused not only the dimensions of figures to vary, so that they converged on the line of the horizon, but also their characteristics – substance, definition, colour – all varied depending on the space between them and the spectator. These principles of perspective, both artificialis and atmospheric, equipped Renaissance man with new eyes through which to view reality.

It was a new way of seeing. But it was not only in the Italian Renaissance that focus shifted from the realm of thought to the realm of sight. In the Netherlands, those painters who were less conditioned by tradition and intellectualism created a figurative universe in which realism acquired expressive force through choice of subject matter and a painstaking attention to detail.

The Real and the Fantastic

The concern with recreating the visible universe ran parallel to a new freedom to take reality to its extremes, going as far as to create worlds and forms that were completely alien to nature. The men who straddled the 15th and 16th centuries shattered the dreamlike visions of the Middle Ages on the rock of reality, much as Marco Polo's cities whose "buildings have roofs of gold" vanished when the age of mercantilism and trade expeditions arrived.

Yet Renaissance men also had their dreams and visions of utopia. In both the Netherlands and Italy, humanist anthropocentrism did not prevent people from delving into the ultimate truth of the relationship between the human and the divine, the temporal and the transcendental.

Men such as Bosch (1450-1516) who embarked on this path sloughed off the stifling conventionalism of the period and its principle of the sanctity of form while conserving its essence and the requirements of courtly refinement in order to explore the inner depths of Man, the grotesque impulses which motivate him, the anguish which can reduce him to a lawless being seeking truth not through the Classical scholastic routes, but in darkness and confusion. Such artists created worlds which were light years away from the gratifying presence of the divine and susceptible to infernal dangers, worlds in which men and animals alike seem to be caught up in the metamorphoses of human insanity.

The Religious and the Mythological

This fantastic world, at least in the first half of the 15th century, had little room in which to express

itself. The iconography which had been passed down from the early Middle Ages still persisted in Renaissance art, albeit accompanied by an evident intention to secularise, modernise and even cast a critical eye on biblical accounts, particularly when used to comment on the contemporary Church.

While altarpieces and religious murals continued to cater to the tastes and needs of churches and convents, the walls of palaces and country villas not only bore testimony to contemporary historical events and moral allegories, but also to the Classical fervour which gave rise to a new world of images, a world in which Ovid's *Metamorphosis* occupied the place that the Bible and golden legends had occupied in medieval philosophy.

The same neo-Platonic circle which grew around the figure of Lorenzo de' Medici impelled the recre-

ation of the pagan world, with mythological characters being stripped of their original significance and transformed into the protagonists of complex symbolic representations of contemporary thought and life.

It was not only the mythological dream of the quest for a new Arcadia that contributed pagan gods into a world hitherto ruled by the Christian God alone; Roman heroes, Renaissance lords, and celebrities of the day – ranging from *condottieri* to poets – became the demigods of an era, the Renaissance, which had placed man at the centre of Creation.

Art and Reformation
However, Man was not seen in the same way in the culture and art of southern Europe as he was in the north. Nordic man was more inward looking than his southern counterpart; his concept of life was

based more on the individual than on the community, and the emphasis lay more on the search for inner truth than on the visible and ritual.

For these northerners, art was seen as an external means of portraying the inner spiritual life. Since art was a means, there was no attempt to combine form with aesthetic principles; form was used rather as an expression of thoughts and experiences juxtaposed with the flow of existence. And whether the forms were faces, bodies, clothing – with all their intricate folds – landscapes, architecture, or dense compositions intent on avoiding emptiness or the stillness of static objects, they all attested to a world in which Man simultaneously accepted and bemoaned his conflict with his environment and his destiny.

The Reformation did not play a decisive role in the development of this school of art. Lutheran thought had little trust in art or, rather, in images; for the Reformist, images were essentially subjective products of the heart rather than objective visual representations. Neither painting nor sculpture should arouse pleasure in the viewer; they should not appeal to the senses or be a vehicle of gratification. The beauty of painting or sculpture did not reside in the forms themselves, but rather in the meditative response that they prompted and inspired.

But before the Lutheran Reformation revealed the blemishes of the papacy, Dürer's xylographs of *The Apocalypse* (1498) had already opened Pandora's Box, expelling hope along with its other contents. Much the same effect was produced by Cranach's *Crucifixion* (1503, Munich Art Gallery) and, a few years later, Grünewald, whose Isenheim altarpiece (1508-1514) effectively dug away the foundations of human faith by portraying the humanity of a Christ stricken with pain and suffering, a God dying with his hands clasped in supplication, his chest swollen with the contortions of pain, and his body hunched above brutally disfigured feet.

1492

According to the Dutch Baroque essayist Karel van Mander, the artists who depicted these scenes did so independently of Italy, without harking back to Antiquity to kindle their inspirational torch. And this was at the time when Italy dazzled the world with its artistic splendour. But Karel van Mander was well aware that this was by no means true; he knew that Dürer had travelled to Italy in 1494 and then again in 1506; he knew, moreover, that Dürer was an admirer of the Pollaiuolo brothers, of Lorenzo di Credi, Mantegna, Jacopo de' Barbari; that he was fulsome in his praise of the greatest of all the Vene-

tian painters, Giovanni Bellini; that he went to Bologna to study with Luca Pacioli and that he possibly even encountered Leonardo da Vinci in Milan.

There is no doubt that Italy was indeed dazzling the world with its artistic splendour at the time of Durer's visits. The Italy of the late 15th and early 16th centuries had reached the end of a long trail of artistic reflection and exploration and attained a peak of creative energy which caused forms that flowed both with and in spite of current philosophy.

Around 1492, Italy witnessed the decline of the art of the early Renaissance, a period which represented the balance between naturalistic vision and a return to the tenets of the Classical world. The rationalisation of reality so typical of this period began to seem less viable in the light of the social, cultural and artistic changes that were occurring in the closing decades of the 15th century.

The Florentine school underwent a major upheaval when *The Adoration of the Magi* (1482) by Flemish painter Hugo van der Goes, commissioned by the Medicis representative in Bruges, Tommaso Portinari, appeared in Florence. This was not the first impact of its kind. Flemish art abounded in 15th century Italy; important collections were amassed, among them that of Alfonso V of Aragon in the Castel Nuovo in Naples; Flemish painters, including one of the most illustrious, Rogier van der Weyden, worked in Italy. Meanwhile, Italian painters, such as Antonello da Messina, disseminated both in the south and in Venice a style of art forged in Naples impregnated with Flemish, Spanish and Provençal influences. But until that time, the Flemish school – which many wealthy patrons of the arts considered to be even more modern than the Italian art of the time (hence the presence of painters such as Justus of Ghent and Pedro Berruguete in the Urbino court contemporaneously with Piero della Francesca) – had not affected the artistic fabric of the fount of the Renaissance, Florence, or one of its greatest artists: Leonardo da Vinci.

The work of another Florentine, Sandro Botticelli, mirrored the social changes occurring during those years. In 1478, with *The Primavera* (Uffizi Gallery, Florence), Botticelli expressed the neo-Platonic tendencies of the Medici court. A few years later, in his *The Birth of Venus* (1487, Uffizi Gallery, Florence), Platonic melancholy seemed to take possession of his paintbrushes, transforming a pagan theme charged with complex symbolism into something approaching a *Sacra Conversationes*. After the decline of the Medici court, Botticelli went on to condemn his age, adopting a tone of virulent spirituality in works such as *The Calumny of Apelles* (1495, Uffizi Gallery, Florence) and *Mystic Nativity*

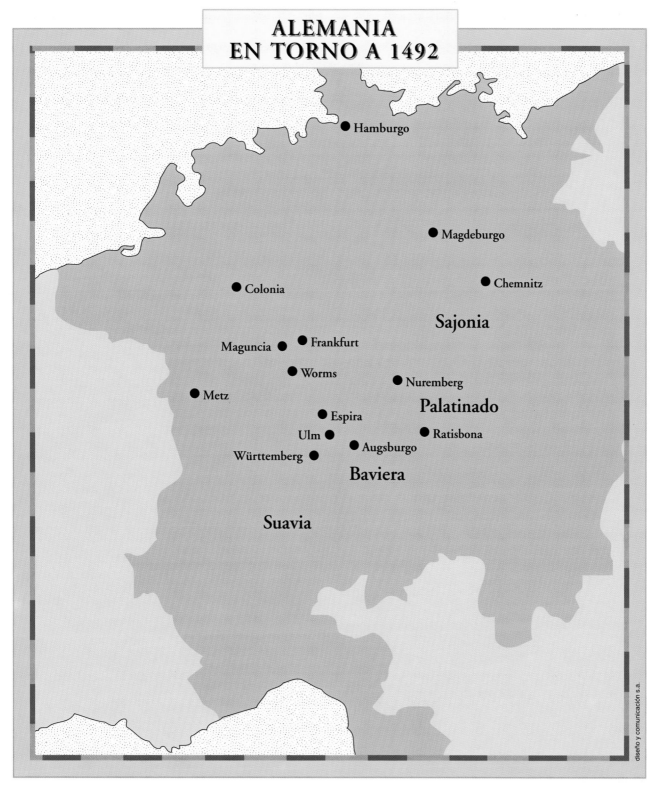

ALEMANIA
EN TORNO A 1492

Hamburgo

Magdeburgo

Colonia

Chemnitz

Sajonia

Maguncia Frankfurt

Worms

Metz

Nuremberg

Palatinado

Espira

Ulm Ratisbona

Augsburgo

Württemberg

Baviera

Suavia

31

diseño y comunicación s.a.

(1501, National Gallery, London) Botticelli thus expressed his rejection, albeit archaically, of the ideals of a world which he did not understand, a world which discovered the great classical models (*The Belvedere Apollo*, 1470; *Laocon*, 1506), and in which an empirico-scientific approach to nature became refined by a more intense relationship between art and science. It was a world in which a mere imitation of nature was rejected in favour of achieving expression for the creative imagination and freedom within a regulated structure; a world in which the Idea re-emerged as a creative alternative, pushing the natural model aside.

But the new cultural climate that this world implied was generated not by Florence but by Milan, city of the Sforza family, Dukes of Milan, and particularly of Ludovico Sforza, known as The Moor, a great patron of innovative artists. The city was alive with the fresh new visions of Bramante (1478) and Leonardo da Vinci (1482). Leonardo's *The Last Supper* (1495-1498), painted in the refectory of Santa Maria delle Grazie Monastery and Bramante's architectural trompe-l'oeil in Santa Maria presso San Satiro were landmarks in this new artistic panorama which, after the decline of the Sforzas (1498), transferred to the papal courts of Julius II (1503-1513) and Leo X (1513-1521), where it extended profound roots.

With Bramantes *Tempietto* of San Pietro in Montorio (1503), Rome was endowed with the most perfect monument to Classical mathematical harmony, and the city became the hub of a school of art whose influence extended well beyond the local to take on national and even European proportions. In the late 15th and early 16th centuries, Rome became a centre of artistic force the like of which had never been seen before. In 1506, the building of the new St. Peters cathedral was begun: it was to be a testing ground for various experiments, by the likes of Bramante, Peruzzi, G. da Sangallo and Raphael. The Vatican enterprise forged ahead, acquiring outstanding contributions from Michelangelo (1505, commission for the tomb of Julius II; 1508-1512, decoration of the Sistine Chapel ceiling) and Raphael (1508, the start of the papal chambers project), along with others by artists from other Italian cities (Sodoma, L. Lotto, Bramantino, Perugino) and even from abroad, such as Spains Alonso Berruguete and Pedro Machuca, and Guillaume de Marcillat from France.

The two-way interchange between Milan and Rome resulted in some artists (Cesare da Sesto, Pedro Fernandez) extending their style as far as Naples. But this axis was clearly not the only area in which Italy manifested the change of direction that art was taking around 1492.

In Venice, the tradition of Giovanni Bellini, the work of Antonello da Messina and Leonardo's brief sojourn (1500), combined with the philosophical tradition of the Paduan school, also gave rise to a maniera nuova which Vasari described as painting only with the colors themselves without drawing on the paper beforehand. It was Giorgione – whom Baldassare Castiglione brought together with the major painters such as Leonardo, Mantegna, Raphael and Michelangelo – who triggered the decisive shift that occurred in Venetian painting at the beginning of the 16th century. The shift left its mark even on the later work of the ageing Giovanni Bellini, but above all on younger artists such as Titian, Palma il Vecchio and Sebastiano del Piombo.

The intellectual and creative activity of the high Renaissance blossomed around 1492, with a first generation of artists who had been born around the middle of the century (Bramante, 1444; Leonardo, 1452), and a second generation born twenty-five or thirty years later (Michelangelo, 1475; Giorgione, 1478; Raphael, 1483). It was to die symbolically in 1527, the year of the Sack of Rome, the death of Machiavelli, and so on. By that time, most of its major figures had already died (Giorgione, 1510; Bramante, 1514; Leonardo, 1519; Raphael, 1520). Others, such as Michelangelo, went on to participate in an era in which the modern came to be valued above the Classical. Such survivors experienced a crisis in the course of which the values of Western Christianity began to show their fragility when faced with religious reform and the epidemics which were again ravaging Europe (never in the history of Christendom have we witnessed such a spectacle of desolation and ruin, wrote ambassadors from England who visited Venice between 1518-1519). The most definitive challenge, however, came in the form of the crystallisation of the modern concept of the world, in which man no longer saw himself as the centre of the universe, was no longer God-like in being the guardian of reason, and no longer dominated Nature.

Art reflected the confusion of a world in which the Ptolomeic mentality had been ousted by the Copernican one. Artists born in the last decades of the 15th century and the first years of the 16th (Andrea del Sarto, 1486; Beccafumi, 1486; Titian, 1487; Correggio, 1489; Giulio Romano, 1492; Pontormo, 1494; Rosso Fiorentino, 1495; Bronzino, 1503; Parmigianino, 1504) submerged themselves in Mannerism, an artistic approach whose model was no longer sought in reality and its rational organisation but rather in its own past. At the very moment in which man lost faith in history, art began to quote itself, transforming and modifying itself from within.

The spirit of the waning Golden Age, the age of Classicism whose masters such as Leonardo da Vinci, Bramante, Raphael and Michelangelo actually created models for a new art rather than simply seeking models in Antiquity, had not only taken root in Italy; Europe was sufficiently saturated with the Gothic for echoes of this spirit and Mannerism to spread to regions that, just a few decades earlier, had barely absorbed the early Renaissance.

Although in the late 15th century major, densely decorative Gothic buildings were still being built in various parts of Europe (1484, Wladislau Hall in the Castle of Prague; 1488, Juan Guas Church of San Gregorio in Valladolid; 1496, Gil de Silos Carthusian Monastery of Miraflores in Burgos; 1499-1500, Diego Boytacs Hieronymite Convent in Belem; 1502, Henry VII Chapel in Westminster Abbey), the turn of the century, and even slightly before (1488, the Diamond Palace in Moscow) witnessed the spread of Renaissance architecture throughout Europe; Michel Colombe's tomb for François II and Marguerite de Foix (1501, Tours) could be seen as a symbol of this expansion, whose finest examples include the François I wing of Blois Castle (1515); the Mausoleum of the Catholic Monarchs, by Domenico Fancelli, in Granada's Royal Chapel (1517); and Chambord Castle (1519). It could perhaps be said to have reached its peak with Pedro Machucas' Palace for Charles V in Granada's Alhambra (1526-1550).

In the first half of the 16th century, both Classicism and the first signs of Mannerism spread throughout Europe. Some years earlier, in 1492, Jaume Huguet (one of the 15th century painters who made the realism of the Flemish school so integral an ingredient of the art of the time) died in Barcelona, on the Mediterranean coast. Also in 1492, in Lisbon, on the Atlantic, Nuno Gonçalves, painter to the Portuguese court, drew his last breath.

Again in 1492, on Friday, October 12, Piero della Francesca died in the small town of Sansepolcro, and with him the early Renaissance which, despite barely having extended beyond the bounds of Italy, contained within it all the seeds which were to engender the modern age. If only for those events alone, 1492 could never be considered a year just like any other.

A Look at the Muslim World in 1492

Purificación Marinetto Sánchez
Museo Nacional de Arte Hispanomusulmán, Granada

34 A look at the Muslim world in 1492 reveals considerable cultural diversity among the various areas in which Islam exerted an influence. Each of these regions reflected not only echoes of earlier cultures, but also the influence of its particular geographical and environmental setting. Although we are dealing here with independent dynasties in different geographical areas, in some cases thousands of miles apart – such as India and the Iberian Peninsula, whose different cultural legacies played a part in the way these cultures developed – all of these were united by a common religion, and by an often common channel of communication, this being the Mediterranean.

These different cultures were not, however, all at the same stage of evolution, or of political, artistic and cultural stability. In some cases a process of decline was about to debouch in an upheaval, while others were in a phase of conquest or at the pinnacle of their splendour.

Since the compass of Islam was vast and its features myriad, it would be impossible to make a detailed analysis here of all facets of all the cultures concerned. For our purposes, therefore, we shall concentrate on a few of these which will provide an impression of the general state of this culture.

We begin with the Iberian Peninsula, which generated two events that radically changed the course of the history of Muslim dominion and, by way of the Atlantic Ocean, opened the gateway to a New World and the interchange on many levels that this implied.

The Catholic Monarchs entered Granada on January 2, 1492, definitively ousting Muslim power from the Iberian Peninsula after a struggle for Reconquest which had lasted centuries.

The continuous succession of emirs in the course of the 15th century reflects the history of Granada during that period. Though it encompassed the reigns of twelve sovereigns, the period actually witnessed twenty enthronements. With the exception of *Yusuf III* and his son *Muhammad VIII*, who both came to power legitimately, the rest emerged through more or less violent means, with fathers being slain by their sons, and sons by fathers for lack of loyalty. Such a case occurred during the reign of Spain's last emir, *Muhammad XI* (known as Boab-

dil) who rose up against his father, *Ali* (Muley Hacen), possibly spurred on by his mother, Fatima, who was wildly jealous of *Ali*'s second wife (Isabel de Solis). The climate of intrigue and suspicion reached such a pitch that the sovereign had his son, prince *Yusuf,* killed. Moreover, these dynastic upheavals were accompanied by the influences and intrigues of the most prominent families of the kingdom, the Benegas and the Abencerrajes.

As if this internal state of affairs were not enough, Granada was obliged to shore up its defences and fight for its independence as a Muslim power in the Iberian Peninsula, by then otherwise totally in Christian hands.

The centuries-old struggle for conquest and reconquest which had resulted in permanent mild, though occasionally intensified, friction, changed at a stroke on the marriage of Isabella I of Castile and Ferdinand V of Aragon. International politics were very important to Ferdinand the Catholic, but he could accomplish nothing without the help of Castile. For Isabella I, reconquest was the first priority and in exchange for assisting her husband in his enterprise, she insisted on the Taking of Granada as a symbol of the furtherance and triumph of Christendom.

Because of its geographical isolation, Granada's Nasride dynasty had often had to resort to calling on its neighbours and fellow Muslims on the other side of the Mediterranean for help. On the one hand, there were the *Marinides*, with whom the Nasrides had maintained fluctuating relations over the course of the years, depending on their need to defend themselves, and later to attack, as their stake in the Peninsula increased.

Another ally which hindered the Catholic Monarchs in their reconquest campaign were the *Burjite* Mamluks of Egypt. However, despite being constantly called upon by the Nasrides, this alliance never became effective, amounting to a mere threat of attack on the Holy Land when Ferdinand the Catholic asked the Pope for permission to sell wheat to Egypt, which saved from famine the Syrian region, which incited the struggle between the Mamluks and the Ottoman Turks: a third potential enemy.

In the end, the Nasrides' geographical isolation,

combined with internal battles and the coercive tactics of the Catholic Monarchs reduced the last Nasride emir, *Muhammad XI*, known as Boabdil, to capitulate with the Christian rulers. This spelled the effective collapse of a cultural and artistic legacy which was nevertheless to persist for many years, in the period known as the Moresque or *Mudéjar*.

In the course of the 15th century, these internal events combined with harassment from outside slowly eroded the boundaries of the Nasride emirate. As a result, Muslims fleeing the Christian reconquest flocked to Granada for refuge, increasing its population and making it necessary to expand the city walls at various times. By the end of the 15th century, Granada was a typically Arabic city of narrow, winding streets, with just one area, the *Alcaicería* (*al-qaysariyya*), rectilinearly designed. There were three large mosques, one for each of the three nuclei: the Alhambra (*madinat al-Hamra'*) which constituted a palatine city, the Albaicín (*rabad al-Bayyazin*), and the city of Granada (*madinat Garnata*). There were also numerous smaller areas which formed around the university, the corn exchanges, and the various trade and craft sectors, and although there were no large open spaces, the whole area was dotted with green surfaces and domestic gardens.

The influence of this last Hispano-Muslim phase did not, however, end with the defeat of the Muslims, but continued in the subsequent *Mudéjar* period in Granada and beyond, leaving a splendid artistic and cultural legacy.

By the 15th century, the architecture of Granada was already in a period of decline, although still redolent of the golden age of Nasride art. Little architecture of note was produced in this period, with the exception of the Tower of the Infanta in the Alhambra, which still features stucco decoration and whose belvedere turrets are reminiscent of that of Dos Hermanas. Also noteworthy of mention is the *Dar al-Hurra* Palace in the Albaicín – once the residence of Fatima, wife of Muley Hacen and mother of Boabdil – which was built in the mid-15th century. There were also interesting remains of important houses, such as the Casa de los Infantes, with its magnificent stucco arch adorned with the Nasride shield as the centrepiece of its decorative

surround, and intricate ornamentation of palm leaves and geometric motifs in the three lattice screens above. It is currently housed in the Museo Nacional de Arte Hispanomusulmán (Granada).

Although the 15th century was by no means a period of splendour in Granada, artistic activity flourished around the Court and the high dignitaries who lived in the palatine *madinat*. Apart from its architecture, the creative output of this period is evident in many surviving examples, characterised by their wide variety of techniques and materials. Indeed, the Christian court's enthusiasm for the richness of Hispano-Muslim decorative art did much to maintain its production after the Reconquest, gradually adapting to the customs and culture of its new clients.

The structure of the palace residences of this period adhered to the traditional scheme, organised around a rectangular courtyard and featuring arcades along the narrower façades. Although the designs and execution of stucco work in different degrees of relief no longer displayed the inventiveness and mastery of earlier periods, it nevertheless remained a significant art form, given that its techniques continued evolving in Moorish buildings throughout the 16th century.

The elaborate decorative panels featuring geometric, heraldic, and epigraphic motifs at their centre and a field of palms occupying the entire space became simpler during the Christian period, with one central motif (such as a knot flower) and the remaining space left smooth providing the most widespread technique.

Meanwhile, there were many different studios in which the artists of the court and the *madinat* worked. Among the work produced in these workshops was parquetry, which followed in the Hispano-Muslim tradition, exemplified in magnificent pieces dating from the period such as a cupboard door in the Palacio de los Infantes and in saddlery decorated, using the same inlay technique, with leather embossed with designs of palm leaves and the Nasride escutcheon. These workshops continued to thrive during the 16th century, and the craft is still traditional in Granada to the present day.

Both architectural and decorative ceramics also continued to flourish during the *Mudéjar* period.

Diaper, or repeated geometrical designs carried over into the early 16th century, from which period magnificent examples survive. Among them are pavings from the Hospital Real, now exhibited in the Museo Nacional de Arte Hispanomusulmán, and the exquisitely designed paving of the corridors and floor surround which frame the central fountain in the Sala de las Camas of the Comares Baths, both of which replicate earlier schemes.

In the early 15th century a more naturalistic decorative style emerged, featuring entire large-leaved trees and tiles with figurative motifs used on floors and other, larger ones framing doorways, as in the Queen's Dressing-room (catalogue) and the famous Fortuny tiles with their epigraphic border alluding to the emir *Yusuf III* (1408-1417). Another example depicting fantastic birds and animals alongside the Nasride escutcheon now forms part of the collection of Madrid's Museo Arqueológico Nacional. These magnificent examples notwithstanding, geometric motifs continued in frequent use as decoration for arris tiles and those made using the *cuerda seca* technique of applying colours and keeping them separate. These continued to be produced throughout the 16th century, and in greater quantities due to the ease and speed of casting the tiles from a mould and being able to compose a complete motif with four tiles.

Domestic ceramics continued to be produced in the Alhambra itself for the use of the emir and the court, in much the same way that Málaga continued to produce commercial ceramics, marking pieces on the base with their place of origin, as shown by numerous finds in excavations in Fustad, Syria and Constantinople. The production of highly-valued luxury ceramics, with a characteristic colour scheme of blue and gold on a white background, continued to maintain a high level of quality and also continued to evolve decoratively and be produced during the 16th century and up to the present day. As in tiles, ceramics also adopted a more naturalistic style of ornamentation in the early 15th century, featuring large trees of life with vine leaves, similar to the stucco work of Toledo. The decorative forms typical of the 14th century also became simpler during this period. In the mid-14th century, Málaga's production of Nasride luxury ceramics was dealt a severe blow by the Aragonese navy, which imposed an export tax and transferred the shipping of merchandise to Christian vessels. This made the products more expensive, and resulted in Nasride craftsmen moving to Manises which, under the protection of the Boils, served as an easier point of export. Little by little, this *Mudéjar* style of ceramics gradually diverged from the Nasride, developing its own characteristic regional style which came to occupy its own prestigious corner of the market.

During the 16th century, the Alhambra – by then the Christian Royal Palace – underwent restoration during the reign of Emperor Charles I. Sevillian ceramicists, the Tenorios and Robles, were employed for the project, and the workshops they set up in the Alhambra continued to operate into the 17th century. The *Mudéjars* not only copied Nasride tiles, such as those in the panel which survives in the centre of the Comares Hall, but also produced pieces that were characteristic of Sevillian arris tiles. Examples of this latter type can still be seen in the Monastery on La Cartuja Island, site of this exhibition, and in the thematically vivid pieces in the Casa de Pilatos.

Woodwork was still used in ceilings as before, both flat and pitched and with cross-piece and batten techniques used to create geometric decorative effects. Famous examples of this remain from the Nasride period, such as the ceiling of the Comares Hall, the symbolism of whose geometric ornamentation is explained by the accompanying epigraphy. Later on, the loop-shaped designs known as *mocárabe* came to be used in three-dimensional geometric decorative ceilings. In surviving examples of 15th century architecture, both decorative styles are present, although by that time the consummate artistry of the 14th century had been lost. Woodwork continued to be used in architecture to great decorative effect, and it was much in demand for the ceilings of churches and the houses of the well-to-do. The primary decorative system continued to be geometric, with myriad variations on loop and knot motifs. Collaboration between Christian and Muslim artists is very evident in some ceilings of this period, as in that of the transept of the Convento de la Merced (Granada), now in the Museo Nacional de Arte Hispanomusulmán. Crafted in the 1530s, its main decorative theme consists of small egg-and-tongue vaults and *mocárabe* knots forming a dome above a frieze carved with plateresque ornamentation and pendentives bearing the Mercedarian escutcheons.

Carpentry workshops adhered to traditional techniques, of which we would probably know little were it not for Diego López de Arenas, himself a carpenter, whose treatise written in 1618 gives a detailed description of the technique and decoration used in this type of ceiling.

In addition to ceramic pieces, luxury table-ware was complemented by glass items including goblets, tumblers and lids, generally very delicate and finely-wrought and following in the tradition of oriental pieces.

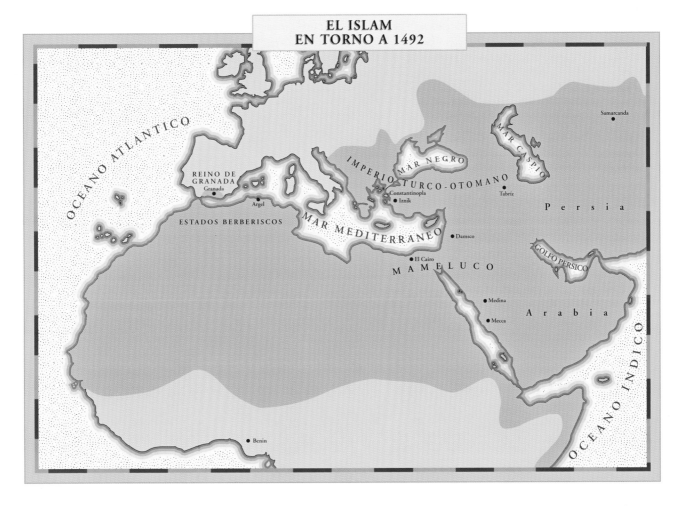

Evidence remains of the lavish carpets and fabrics which complemented the furnishings and lined the walls and floors of winter retreats, as well as of the rich luxury silken fabrics used for clothing, equally appreciated by both the Nasride and Christian courts, and objects of both gifts and trade. In the 15th century, the decorative style of vivid silk colours alternating with Cypriot gold thread was replaced by yellow silk on a predominantly red background, with ribbon decoration including plant motifs, epigraphy, and even revealing Chinese and Mamluk influences, with lotus leaves appearing alongside Nasride shields and crowned lions. After the Reconquest of Granada, textile manufacturing continued to thrive in the same workshops into the 16th century, although styles changed, adopting Gothic motifs from Christian textiles.

Relations between the Nasrides and their neighbours on the other side of the Mediterranean fluctuated, as seen earlier. However, in addition to the fact that Granada had now been reconquered by the Catholic Monarchs, *Marinide* supremacy in Morocco gave way from 1472-1555 to the *Wattasid* dynasty. These monarchs accepted the emigrants from Granada so that characteristic features of the Nasride decorative system were maintained. Morocco

was something of a hub which absorbed and irradiated influence between the eastern and western Mediterranean. Further input was provided by the arrival of waves of immigrants generated by the shift of power in the Muslim area of the Iberian Peninsula. Neighbourhoods where they settled, as in Fez, became known centres of artistic production and trade.

Meanwhile, further east along the Mediterranean, another ally of the Nasrides, the *Burjite* Mamluks, were also going through difficult times. These came to a head in 1517 when the Ottoman Turks, who were still in a phase of conquest, entered and seized Cairo.

The *Burjite* regime imposed heavy financial pressure on the population, but trade agreements and a strategic location on the trade routes between Egypt and Syria and the Mediterranean kept them flourishing in valuable products such as Chinese porcelain, Indian cotton, ivory, and so on. This commercial situation was subsequently truncated by the change in trade routes resulting from Vasco de Gama's rounding the Cape of Good Hope under the Portuguese flag in 1498, thus establishing a direct maritime route while attacking Muslim boats encountered in his path.

The importance of trade with the Far East and the

search for a maritime route were also the motive behind the expedition to seek a Western route to the East Indies, which resulted in the discovery of a new continent. The incentive of returning with a ship laden with valuable spices made hazarding unknown danger a worthwhile venture.

Egypt went into a period of decline almost paralleling that of the Nasrides, allying itself with the Ottomans in its struggle to keep the *Timuride* enemy at bay. The onset of this decline could perhaps be attributed to the Black Death epidemic of 1348, which enfeebled the population and marked the start of a period of famine and commercial crisis. All this, combined with the ill-advised foreign policies of *Qansuh II al-Guri*, brought about a falling out with Selim I, sultan of Constantinople. A declaration of war and a subsequent confrontation ensued, culminating in the Turks' defeating and crushing the Mamluks at Aleppo (1516), due primarily to the advantage afforded them by modernised artillery using gunpowder, not yet accepted by the Mamluks. The following year, the Mamluks defended the gates of Cairo in vain. The city fell, the sultan was summarily executed, and it became an Ottoman state.

Thus, the dynasty which had begun as a force of slaves or *mamluk* bought by the *Ayyubides* from Turkey and Central Asia, and which had flourished thanks to their manifest bravery and organisational and leadership abilities, and had gone on to establish Egypt as a major power – indeed the only one that could check the *Timurides'* zeal for conquest – went into irreversible decline. It became absorbed into the expanding Turkish Empire, which went on to impose a new regime in the Muslim area.

Notwithstanding a state of affairs which was hardly conducive to art and construction, several important monuments remain from the Mamluk period, reflecting the high standards that Egypt had maintained throughout the centuries. Particularly noteworthy in these buildings is the quality of the architecture, sense of proportion and aesthetics.

Indeed, spectacular complexes of buildings were constructed during the entire Mamluk period, of which perhaps the most remarkable were the last ones built by the sultans *Qa'it Bay* and *al-Guri*.

During the Circassian period, architecture retained the tendencies of the previous period, with emphasis laid on façades of hewn stone, with trefoiled arches, and ornamentation contained within a decorative frame, or *alfiz*, of geometric motifs in marble of different colours. Also notable are the magnificent morticed lintels which, in decorative terms, coexist successfully with the line of the undulating crenellations which trim the edges of the

buildings. The main body of the walls is characterised by horizontal bands of alternately yellow and dark red stone.

The tall, monumental entranceways are decorated with stalactite-like decorative elements known as *muqarnas*. Professor Künhel suggests that this decorative technique possibly originated in the Konya region of Turkey. It had been in use since the time of the *Saljuquide* of Asia Minor and had spread to the Iberian Peninsula via Egypt during the Nasride period. The decoration of the entranceway to Granada's Corral de Carbón, or *fundaq al-yadid*, dates from this period, and makes interesting use of the *mocárabe* technique in the approach to the square-headed doorway.

Other typical features are the high minarets which accentuated the slender elegance of this style of architecture, and very high domes, the stone of whose outer surfaces are engraved with geometric motifs.

Interiors were somewhat smaller than those of the previous phase, maintaining the cruciform structure of four *eyvans* or vaulted halls around a central courtyard, in some cases closed in, thus limiting space. An important feature introduced at this time was the *hypostyle* hall, in which the ceiling is supported by a series of columns in the *eyvan* on the *kiblah* side.

Floors, base friezes (*zócalos*) and fountains in marble of various colours attest to the richness of the materials used in the ornamentation of this time.

Epigraphy was also an important decorative motif, used in long friezes of cursive characters along the walls.

During the sultanate of *Qa'it Bay,* which lasted some twenty-nine years (1468-1496), architecture flourished. Sound proportions, rich ornamentation and delicate craftsmanship characterise the period. Predominance was given to military architecture, such as the fortress of *Qa'it Bay* in Aleppo and the Fort of Rosetta. However, there was also considerable interest in civil and public works, such as houses, *wikalas* (inns), and *sabils* (fountains), as well as magnificent examples of religious architecture such as the mosque which bears the sultan's name. During both this period and the sultanate of *al-Guri*, the maintenance and restoration of buildings erected by their predecessors were significant features.

Sultan *al-Malik al-Asraf Qansuh al-Guri* deserves particular mention for his contribution to both architecture and Mamluk history. Starting off as a *mamluk* (slave) and virtually the property of *Qa'it Bay*, al-Guri remained in the latter's service until he was set free. Thereafter, he ascended the official ranks, achieving the highest state office during the time of *al-Malik al-Asraf Ganbalat*. In 1501, he acceded to the throne, reigning until he died in the Battle of Aleppo against *Selim I*, which effectively precipitated the inevitable downfall of the Mamluks.

Al-Guri's singular passion for architecture, in which his emirs followed suit, was matched by his building activity. Among the many buildings which date from his time, perhaps the most remarkable is the one which bears his name, constructed between 1503-1504 and one of the most important examples of *Burjite* Mamluk architecture. *Al-Guri* readily financed its decoration, motivated by the desire to surpass the buildings of the time of *Qa'it Bay*. In what is an outstanding building in itself, some of the most noteworthy features are the craftsmanship displayed in the different-coloured marble decorating the *mihrab* (or prayer niche); its wooden *minbar* with segments of intricately carved ivory; and the *dikka* supported by two wooden corbels with a balustrade which is divided into panels inlaid with ivory and ebony and with other sections of carved wood.

Mamluk decorative arts of this period maintained their earlier high quality and tradition. There are notable examples in this exhibition, such as the magnificent metalwork of the fretted bronze pendant lamps with oil vessels situated at various levels, used for illuminating mosques. Examples of the woodwork of the period are provided by the splendid religious furnishings which survive in the interior of certain mosques. Meanwhile, carpets, which had emerged as an art form in the 15th century, continued to be produced into the early part of the 16th century, when Turkish influence prevailed. Their decoration combined geometric forms – octagons, stars, squares, triangles – with plant motifs such as small leaves, shrubs and cypresses, using very characteristic colours: cherry red, pale green and sky blue.

Timur-Lang (literally 'lame iron') was the Arabic name of the historic figure known in the West as Tamburlaine. Believing himself to be the descendant of *Tchingtz Kagan* (*Gengis Khan*), he set out to reestablish the great empire, carrying out conquest campaigns which were as bloody as those of his purported ancestor. Beginning with Persia in 1380, where the princes offered vassalage, he subsequently entered Iraq, and made his way towards Armenia. Attacked by *Toqtamis* in the Caucasus, he pursued him to Yelec, some 360 kilometres from Moscow, leaving a trail sown with the horrors of war. Extending his frontiers as far as India when he was already over sixty years old, he sent his grand-

son *Pir Muhammad* to Lahore, and the sovereign of Delhi was overthrown in 1398.

The irregular conduct of his son *Miran Sah* triggered attacks by *yala'ir Ahmad* who had by now re-occupied Baghdad. *Timur-Lang* arrived on the scene, and Ahmad fled, seeking the protection of the Ottoman sultan Bayezid. This resulted in confrontation between Ottomans and Timurides. *Timur Lang* attacked the fortified town of *Siwas* on the Turkish border, and seized *Malatya*, also devastating Bursa and sacking Smyrna.

With the intention of stopping possible Mamluk attacks, *Timur-Lang* entered Syria and seized Aleppo, whereupon Damascus surrendered, an act which did not prevent the occupying troops from sacking it anyway. He then made his way towards Baghdad, taking it by storm in 1401.

At the age of seventy, *Timur-Lang* launched a campaign to conquer China. He fell ill during the attempt and died in 1405.

The capital of the Timuride Empire was Samarkand, a city renowned for the beauty of its palaces and gardens. Ruiz González de Clavijo visited it as an envoy of Enrique III of Castile, and wrote a splendid (extant) description of the empire and its capital. Like Baghdad and Tabriz before it, Samarkand became a centre and stopover for merchants much like the Silk Route. Though he spread terror wherever he went, *Timur-Lang* was nevertheless quick to take advantage of the artists and industries of these regions, using them to embellish and enhance his capital. He was also an enthusiastic chess-player, so much so that he named one of his sons *Sah Ruj* ('checkmate'), a position he was about to achieve when he was told of his birth.

Timur-Lang chose his grandson *Pir Muhammad* as his heir, but since the latter was away at the time of his death, the army proclaimed another grandson, *Halil,* as emperor. Four years later, by which time *Pir Muhammad* had been assassinated, a period of relative tranquillity set in. During this time, *Timur-Lang's* son, *Sah Ruj,* considered a pacific and generous man of poetic, artistic and scholarly leanings, enjoyed a phase of prosperity. Upon his death in 1447, a rapid process of decline began. He was succeeded by his brother *Ulug Beg*, who was fifty-four years old when he came to power. He is known to have been a man of letters, an artist and above all an accomplished astronomer. He was assassinated by his son two years after his ascent to power, and the son himself lasted in power only around six months.

The state was then divided into small principalities. Prince *Husayn Bayqara* presided in Herat, ruling from 1469 to 1506, during which time he attempted to unify the empire by seizing other territories. He assembled artists, poets, mystics, philosophers, and historians around Herat, thus making it an important centre of culture. Upon his death, the *Kara Koyunlu* sacked Herat, bringing about the downfall of the Timurides.

The architecture produced under the Timurides shows a continuation of *Il-Khamid* principles, fundamentally particular proportions and a tendency towards verticality. This was above all an imperialistic art favouring monumental buildings, and exploiting interior spaces to the full, a feature particularly evident in the second half of the 15th century. Monumental decorated entranceways were an emphasised element, along with soaring, bulbous cupolas raised on tall drums. These cupolas served no interior purpose, nor were they a functional link, thus making it necessary to construct other much lower ones within. The cupolas rested on squinches in the zone of structural transition, but even so, given its high centre of gravity, this was a very dangerous form of construction in an area subject to earthquakes. Consequently, another system was tried, using intersecting arches joined by ribs, which helped reduce the weight to be borne and lowered the centre of gravity. An example of this approach can be seen in Samarkand's *Ysrat Jana*, whose construction was begun in 1464.

The grandeur of the building was further emphasised by the use of colour and designs. Exteriors were clad with tiles featuring geometric schemes, splendid compositions of cufic and cursive writing in thuluth characters, and plant motifs on tiles of varying sizes. However, this decorative system was replaced around the mid-15th century by the *cuerda seca* technique using turquoise, cobalt and lapis lazuli blues in combination with green, purple and yellow. This decorative style is found in several compositions from the Ottoman Turkish period, due to Persian influence, and also from the Nasride period, during which it flourished, albeit developing independently.

The application of ceramics as an outer cladding makes clever use of highlighting and emphasis techniques.

Architectural ornamentation was complemented in the interior by the use of decorative stucco work.

The characteristic ground plan for mosques of this period featured a central courtyard with four *eyvans*, tall majestic ornamented doorways and minarets.

During the reigns of *Timur-Lang*'s grandsons, an important school of miniaturists that was patronised by the court emerged. Among its patrons were the sultan *Iskandar*, *Ulug Beg*'s son, who ruled Farsistan

from its capital, Siraz, until 1414; his cousin and successor *Ibrahim*, and subsequently Ibrahim's successor, his brother *Baysunkur*, who assembled the best artists around the library of Herat. In later years *Husayn Bayqara* continued this tradition of artistic patronage, along with his vizier, the distinguished poet *Mir Ali Sir Nawa'i*. Among their protégés were *Bihzad*, Persia's most important painter, the poet *Jami* and the historian *Jwandamir*.

The materials used during this time were of unsurpassed quality: paper was prepared with the utmost care; pigments used pure colours, gold, silver, lapis lazuli, malachite...

The Persian miniature emerged at a moment in history when religious and social circumstances were such that painters seldom had the opportunity to express themselves in a form other than the limited space of a manuscript page. The illumination of these manuscripts was closely allied to the art of the calligraphist. Moreover, the Islamic world had always favoured the representation of traditional scenes, constantly repeated. The miniaturist was not concerned with perspective, nor with the dimensions of the components of his picture; the artist depicted an imaginary world in which love scenes or battles took place against the setting of a spring morning or an autumn twilight.

In the school of sultan *Baykara*, Chinese influence is discernible in certain fixed rules of composition, a high eye level and the use of planes of trees and flowers drawn in detail according to traditional representational methods. The drawings do not attempt to imitate the natural world, but everything is depicted as full of life, with pre-determined formulae for representing nature.

Bihzad, the most prodigious Timuride painter, worked in the court of *Husayn Baykara*. His work is memorable for the evocative qualities of its characters, who exhibit feelings of sorrow, isolation, contemplation and retirement, and for its fine draughtsmanship, vivid use of colour, and representation of perspective through the use of light and shade. After the downfall of the Timurides, *Bihzad* went on to work with the Mughal emperor of India while living in the Safarid court of *Sah Tahmasp*. Upon returning to India in 1550, he took with him two Persian painters, *Abd al-Samad* and *Mir Sayd Ali*, thus spreading the Timuride miniaturist influence.

The Ottomans took their name from the first sultan of Turkey, Osman, or *Utman*, who was pushed westwards by Mongolian invasions, forming, around 1299, the kernel of the future Turkish empire.

In the 15th century, during the reign of *Muham-*

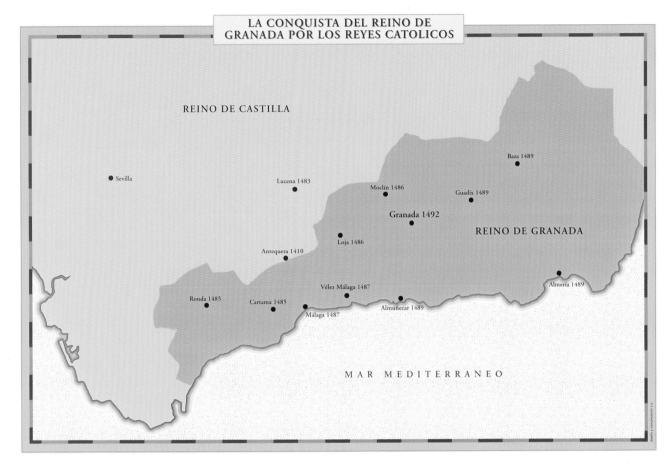

REINO DE CASTILLA

Baza 1489

Sevilla

Lucena 1483

Moclín 1486

Guadix 1489

Granada 1492

REINO DE GRANADA

Loja 1486

Antequera 1410

Vélez Málaga 1487

Almería 1489

Ronda 1485   Cartama 1485

Málaga 1487   Almuñecar 1489

MAR   MEDITERRANEO

mad or Mehmed II, known as *Fatih*, The Conqueror, the vassal states began to unify within the empire, starting off with, among other events, the Byzantines and the conquest of Constantinople. The *Rum-ili-Hisas* fort was built along the narrowest stretch of the Bosporus Strait, with the intention of blocking possible escapes by sea. The artillery was prepared and the siege of Constantinople was begun, involving the amazing maneouvre of transporting boats by land to the other side of the Golden Horn and then positioning themselves in the middle, thus facilitating the assault on the city and its easy seizure on 29 May 1453. Quickly transforming the church of Hagia Sofia into a mosque, the Ottomans made Constantinople their capital and one of the most important cities in the Muslim world at the time.

Muhammad II died in 1481 upon setting out on a military expedition to Asia. Although considered a fierce and cruel man in battle, he combined these characteristics with an appreciation for the arts. He not only founded numerous libraries in his capital – by then called Istanbul – from which important manuscripts remain, but also encouraged scientific studies, took active interest in literature and, keeping abreast of the advances being made in Christian countries, attracted artists to his court. After signing a peace treaty with Venice in 1469, the city provided him with the accomplished portrait painter Gentile

Bellini, author of the portrait housed today in London's National Gallery.

The golden age of the Ottoman Empire occurred during the half century or so occupied by the reigns of *Selim I,* The Grim, and his son *Sulayman I,* The Magnificent.

Selim I was in his forties when he found himself in competition with his brother Ahmed over the succession to their father, *Bayazit II* (1512). Selim emerged the victor. His first concern were relations with Persia, where *Sah Ismail* ruled over an empire comparable to that of the Ottomans in size and might.

Selim seized Tabriz, obtaining a significant booty in the process and availing himself of the magnificent artists' studios for his court. In 1516, after the confrontation in Aleppo that cost the Mamluk sultan *Qansuh* his life, the Ottomans entered Damascus, thus bringing about a change of allegiance for the *sharifs* of Mecca and placing the Ottomans in the position of self-appointed protectors of the two holy cities of Mecca and Medina.

Selim I ruled for eight years, and died in 1520. He was succeeded by his son *Sulayman I al-Qanuni,* also known as The Lawgiver. Although considered a pacific man, *Sulayman's* military campaigns were memorable. Seizing Belgrade in 1521, he went on to conquer Rhodes the following year; after the battle of *Mohacs*, he took over Hungary and even managed to seize Vienna, albeit just for a few weeks. He capitalised on the power wielded by Barbarossa in Algiers, naming him chief admiral of the Ottoman fleet in Istanbul and considering him a trustworthy advisor. At his suggestion, they joined forces in 1534 with François I of France to fight the Spanish in Tunis. They successfully took the city, although it was later reconquered by Charles V. *Sulayman I* occupied Tabriz in Persia, and entered Baghdad, annexing Iraq.

This enterprising military approach made the Ottoman Empire the most important in the Muslim world; *Sulayman's* conquests and his contacts with Europe made his court a magnet for the finest Muslim artists.

The earliest mosques of the Ottoman period follow in the *Saljuquide* tradition, featuring a single arcaded or non-arcaded cupola supported by squinches recalling the type used in Konya. A later model is reminiscent of the architecture of the *madrasahs* (institutes of higher learning), also Seljuq, which feature one axial *eyvan* and two lateral ones. This idea originated with the introduction of meeting rooms and other small rooms for the use of pilgrims.

Upon conquering Constantinople, *Muhammad II* set out to aggrandise his capital. Artists eager to collaborate in the process flocked to the city, and their contributions and courtly recognition of artistic skill raised their social status. Meanwhile, Byzantine architecture was much admired, particularly the church of Hagia Sophia, and this served as a spur to even greater achievement.

The oldest building of the period is the Mosque of Mehmet, or *Fatih Cami*, albeit restored after the earthquake of 1766. Designed in 1459 by Sinan (not the great Ottoman architect, but a namesake, also known as Atik the Elder), its construction lasted from 1463 to 1470.

This mosque forms part of a complex containing six *madrasahs*, a Koranic school, a library, a hospital, an inn, a kitchen, a caravansaray, and the mausoleum of the sultan and his wife, all within the same walled enclosure. Large complexes such as this provided the focus for religious, educational and social gatherings, and were important hubs of activity in the city.

The interior of the former oratory featured a semi-cupola above the *mihrab*, three cupolas on each side and one central cupola supported by columns and two other large "elephant's feet." The oratory gives on its north side onto the courtyard by way of a square-headed doorway within a high arch framed by a protruding *alfiz* and with a *muqarna*-decorated vault.

A series of *riwaqs,* or galleries, surrounds the courtyard, suppported by old columns, each of the twenty-two sections roofed by cupolas. At the head of each arch giving onto the courtyard are square windows featuring a tympanum decorated with epigraphy. In some cases, the decoration is in *cuerda seca* tiles in blue, yellow, green and white, possibly early products of Iznik.

Shortly after 1473, an example of civil architecture – the *Cinili Kiosk* – was erected within the *Topkapi Saray* complex, with constructive and decorative features showing Central Asian influence.

The exterior features a portico supported by pillars, whose original wood, a product of Iranian influence, has since been replaced by stone. The walls contain panels of tiles decorated with geometric motifs and inscriptions recalling those of Tabriz, and possibly produced in the early workshops of Iznik under the influence of refugees from Bursa and Edirne.

The interior ground plan is cruciform, with four halls between the arms and another opposite the entrance. Professor Goodwin points out that this layout is reminiscent of *Fatihpur Sikri*. There, the symbology featured in the throne of Akbar, the zodiacal references in epigraphy and the paradise metaphor links up with that of the wooden ceiling of the Hall of Comares in the Alhambra, which dates from the Nasride period.

In Istanbul, an example of a mosque built during the reign of *Bayazid II* encapsulates earlier architectural experience in Edirne, Amasya and Tokat. Here the oratory is built of stone, rather than brick, which had been used until then. It features a central cupola and two semi-cupolas at either end, producing a longitudinal effect, with a granite column in the middle between the four large pillars supporting the cupolas.

The square courtyard resembles the oratory, with galleries of five arches around it forming independent sections which are capped by cupolas raised on drums, with the exception of the central ones. The ornamentation of the doors is prominent and the gallery displays two levels of windows.

In the late 15th century and early 16th century, ceramics became an extremely important decorative element in the Ottoman area, a tradition which was to be sustained by magnificent work during subsequent centuries. In both architectural ceramics in the form of tiled panels and in domestic ceramics, the Iznik style played an important role in the decorative arts of this period.

After the conquest of Constantinople by *Muhammad II*, artists were drawn there both by the work generated by the embellishment and by the esteem in which artists were held there and the rise in social status that this implied.

Iznik ceramic production went through a period of development which Professor Lane divides into three phases. Doctor Raby divides it into four, corresponding to the different sultans of the period and their respective decorative schools. However, both classifications reflect a clear decorative and chronological evolution.

The objects which coincide with the period under consideration here represent the earliest Iznik phase, in the style known as *Abraham of Kutahya*, the name which appears in the inventories of the *Topkapi Saray* from 1495 to 1505.

These early pieces show the Chinese-influenced 15th century Timuride style known as Hatayid, which coincides with China's Tathay style. Another decorative style, known as Rumi or Roman, an echo of the Saljuquiae, is also seen, featuring ornamental plant motifs, with vine stems and leaves recalling classical motifs.

The pieces produced by Abraham of Kutahya use the *Baba Nakkas* style of illumination in blue and white, and also incorporate Rumi and Hatayid decorative forms such as arabesques, plant motifs and, occasionally, epigraphy. The decoration is influenced both by Chinese forms and, directly, by Ottoman metallic pieces.

The decoration is finely executed, and features decorative medallions and bands accentuated with dark lines which create the chiaroscuro effect of three-dimensional forms. The ornamentation of stalks and palm leaves organised around a central point recalls not only the ornamentation of metallic reliefs but also the decorative forms used by illuminators of the Koran. There are also examples of the decoration organised in such a way that certain areas are left plain.

It is known that during the sultanate of *Selim*, a significant number of ceramicists from Tabriz were drawn to Constantinople shortly after its conquest.

This explains not only the Persian influence in some of the ceramics of the time, but also the re-introduction of the *cuerda seca* technique of tile decoration.

The enthusiasm for Chinese decorative forms intensified around 1520, when many imitations of porcelain models were made.

Apart from the workshops of potters and illuminators which thrived around the court of the Topkapi Saray, there were other studios, such as one which produced magnificent metalwork which bears the seal of the Palace arsenal. Iron pieces were decorated with epigraphy and with the same plant motifs that one sees in the ceramics and miniatures of the time, beautifully crafted in silver, which stands out against the dark background, and adapted to the contours of moulded forms.

Another notable product of the Turkish period, whose influence would spread to other countries and gain great admiration in Europe, was that of carpets and textiles. So important a cultural contribution were they that appear in the paintings of Hans Holbein and Lorenzo Lotto, and different types of carpet became identified with the names of these painters.

The 'Holbein' carpet, with its colour scheme of red, blue, yellow, green, white and black, featured predominantly geometric decorative motifs, while the 'Lotto' type used more plant motifs. Made in Usak, in western Anatolia, the Holbein type exerted considerable decorative influence, discernible even in Spanish carpets of the time.

Similarly, the silk textiles manufactured in Bursa were highly regarded by the court, and demand soon led to their being exported to Europe. The same occurred with wool, velvet, and brocade fabrics, produced in the central part of the Empire: Aleppo, Amasya, Kaffa in the Crimea, and Chios. They were extremely decorative, featuring plant motifs in careful geometric arrangements, and reflecting the fashion in furnishings and clothing at the court of each respective sultan.

The Far East

Carmen García Ormaechea
Universidad Complutense, Madrid

The cultural and artistic picture presented by the Far East around 1492 was an extremely varied one. A look at the situation of the two giants of the Asian continent – India and China – clearly reveals the main historical paths taken by the countries surrounding them, as the progress and evolution of the latter have nearly always been determined by their relationship with these two. At that time, the Chinese imperial system was reaching its zenith under the Ming dynasty, while in India the Vijayanagar empire was being threatened by Muslim invaders.

The whole of South-east Asia, a region immersed in the influence of these two stable cultures since the beginning of its history, was starting to take on the shape we know today, from the nearest country – Buddhist Sri Lanka – to the remotest – Islamic Indonesia. Between the two, Indochina was suffering the death throes of the highly sophisticated Khmer civilisation of Cambodia and the rise of Thailand, which had until then been under Indochinese rule.

To the north, the countries of the Himalyas were experiencing their first taste of Lamaist reform imposed by the Dge-lugs-pa order (exponents of a form of Buddhism), which is still practised today in traditional Tibetan culture. From the highest mountain range in the world and via the Silk Route – Asia's main international link since its establishment by the Chinese Han dynasty in the second century B.C. – interchange occurred with the civilisation which dominated the Far East in 1492: China.

At around the same time, the Yi or Choson dynasty in Korea, spurred on by a strong upsurge of nationalism, began to dislocate itself from the Chinese sphere of influence and establish, among other innovations, a new system of writing. This should be considered in the light of the fact that the great unifying achievement of ancient Chinese culture had been the introduction of writing, by means of which not only could all the Chinese people communicate among themselves – impossible in their respective spoken languages – but also with the Koreans and the Japanese.

For Japan, the late 15th century was living through a period of absolute feudalism under the Muromachi shogun (a line of Hereditary military dictators), who maintained the emperor in a purely symbolic role which was not cast off until the 19th century.

The fabric of the Far East in 1492, therefore, was composed of many rich cultures and independent countries, the great majority of which have continued to consolidate their position right up to the present day.

The Western tendency to label all these countries arbitrarily with the blanket term "Far East" is an age-old trap laid by our own ignorance. It compounds an error inherited historically from the generally subjective and exaggerated descriptions brought back to the West by European travellers.

Since time immemorial the "Far" East has acted as a catalyst for western thinking and mentality. It has sparked off missionary ideals, trading ventures, colonial projects and various utopian notions. But it also played a leading role in the discovery of America. Its coveted products, such as silks, spices and porcelains and the commercial monopoly wielded over them by Islamic intermediaries was what motivated European navigators to open up new communication routes which provided direct contact with "The Indies".

India

The situation in India at the time was lamentably poor and disunited for the destructive Muslim conquest of the north of the Hindustan peninsula, or more precisely of the Indo-Gangetic plain (the area east of the river Indus and west of the Ganges). The Muslim conquerors, mainly Ghurids and Ghaznavids from the high valleys which today are part of Afghanistan, had been gradually establishing independent sultanates since the 13th century. Their artistic output is of little interest as the quality of the materials used was poor and the architectural structures – whether palaces, mosques or mausoleums – were all built in a fortified style.

Nevertheless, some sultanates among the subjugated Indian minorities did produce major works of art. One example is the complex of Jaina temples at Ranakpur, built in costly, dazzling white marble.

Some Hindu principalities were geographically close together and were therefore more influential and had learned to coexist with their conquerors. Among these were Mewar, Malwa and Bundi, whose artistic workshops concentrated exclusively on miniatures illustrating Krishnaist sacred texts, vividly colourful and full of symbolic imagery. A little further south on the Deccan plain there were other focuses of cultural activity, where the Hindu and Persian-Islamic traditions combined. Between 1490 and 1512, these produced sumptuous painting miniature illustrating courtly life, the most important schools being those of Golkonda, Bijapur and Bidar.

The most undiluted Indian culture, namely the Hindu or Rajput, was to be found in southern India, where the impact of the Muslim invasion had been less profound. From 1336 to 1565, the whole of this southern tip of the peninsula was capably governed by one of the most important and cultured dynasties in the history of India – the Vijayanagar or "Victory" dynasty. The Vijayanagar princes established their capital, also called Vijayanagar (present-day Hampi), on the banks of the River Krishna in the fertile Tungabhadra river valley (now in Karnataka state). It became a nucleus for trade; its floating population was larger than its indigenous one, which numbered around 500,000, and a vital hub for the dissemination of the Hindu culture.

Foreign visitors to this capital, such as the Italian traveller Conti and Barbosa from Portugal, wrote that it was as big as Rome and surrounded by seven walls which contained within them crops, gardens and palaces "with ceilings and walls clad in gold and encrusted jewels". They also praised the aqueducts which brought drinking water to the city. The court maintained many scientists, philosophers and artists, and it was a constant scene of concerts and other types of entertainment. Vijayanagar was the main refuge for the many Hindu intellectuals who fled northern India, which was then nearly entirely occupied by the independent sultanates.

The Vijayanagar dynasty had created a relatively well-equipped army of one million men to protect the capital from the Islamic invader. The army was divided into infantry, cavalry, an elephant division and artillery which kept constant guard over the borders from the many bastions and fortresses built for this purpose in strategic locations.

Despite this military objective, agriculture was also fostered and reservoirs and channels to carry water were constructed. Trade benefitted similarly from an extensive network of roads which facilitated contact with the Arabs, Persians and Portuguese on the western Malabar coast, as well as with navigators from South-east Asia on the Coromandel coast.

Besides building up the capital, the Vijayanagar sponsored the restoration of all of the sanctuary-cities in southern India, endowing them with superb *mandapas* (Hindu prayer halls) designed as forests of columns, each of whose skilfully carved monolithic supports is a work of art in itself. This was a period when sculpture began to adorn all architectural surfaces, softening sharp edges and emerging, too, in the form of *gopuras*, the high look-out towers set into the surrounding walls of the sanctuary-cities which still act as beacons and landmarks among the palm groves of the south.

Religious imagery from the Vijayanagar temples, besides providing us with a comprehensive iconography of Hinduism, rightly occupies pride of place in any worthwhile collection of Indian art today, not only for the technical skills displayed, still evident in bronze or stone pieces, but also for the elegance of sculptural expression. All the Hindu gods are portrayed in this way and were worshipped with particular reverence; Vishnu and Shiva figure with equal importance, and Vijayanagar art as a whole is characterised by a rich renaissance eclecticism.

Meanwhile, the eternal mosaic of cultures which constitutes India also included primitive tribes of Dravidian and even Austro-Asiatic origins, which still survive today in small isolated groups. The tribes with the strongest artistic tradition were the Kond (Orissa), Nagaland (Arunachal Pradesh), Gond (Madhya Pradesh) and Chamba (Himachal Pradesh). Their output is fascinating, both ethnologically and artistically, and particularly attractive to modern Western eyes. Unfortunately, the period during which their works were produced does not coincide with the chronological parameters of this exhibition, and is therefore not represented here.

From 1526 and until 1857, the Mughal Empire, the Timurids of India, wielded control over the arts. Though no works have survived from before 1556, the style of the subsequent period displays the most perfect balance between the Hindu and Islamic ever achieved in Indian art.

South-east Asia

The history of Sri Lanka (formerly Ceylon) is that of an Indian cultural colony which has shown unsurprising, albeit very sporadic, attempts of independence and nationalism. Its historical and cultural dependence dates back to the introduction and subsequent flourishing on the island of Buddhism from India in the third century B.C. Present-day Sri Lanka is a Buddhist country which still lives by the *Udana*, "the Word of Buddha", and has sustained the ancient tradition of early Buddhism which is the creative inspiration of Sinhalese art.

There is little to be said about Sri Lanka around 1492 since only in the city of Kotte (a few kilometres from the capital, Colombo) there was a brief and insignificant period of cultural splendour during the reign of Parakramabahu VI (1412-1467). After this time, from 1505 to 1948, Ceylon was under European colonial rule and it took many more years, until 1972, for it to emerge as the present day republic of Sri Lanka.

Modern Indonesia is an enormous archipelago formed by Sumatra, Kalimantan (Borneo), Java, Bali, Sulawesi (Celebes), the small Sonda islands, the Moluccas and Irian Jaya (the western part of New Guinea). Java and Bali produced some interesting art, all of it influenced by Islam. The Islamic invaders arrived in Sumatra and Java in the course of the 13th century and the Muslim invaders had taken permanent possession of the whole archipelago by the end of the 15th century. Since that time the population has stoutly resisted attempts to convert it to Christianity and the imposition of a Dutch administration which once kept the Netherlands supplied with exotic products from its colonial base of Batavia (now Jakarta), on Java. Today, Indonesia is the country with the largest number of Muslims in the whole world.

Authentically Indonesian art forms from the period under consideration can be found in the eastern part of Java (Majapahit) and on the small neighbouring island of Bali. They amount to a few examples of batik (a traditional cotton fabric-dyeing technique, which uses wax to create coloured designs) and miniatures illustrating the ancient Hindu epic poems, the *Mahabharata* and the *Ramayana*. In some exceptional cases, there are larger format versions of these illustrations, either on ceramic or stone, decorating temple walls. The characters are portrayed according to the stereotypes established in the sacred manuals of iconography, and they also appear in the form of puppets in the *wayang*, the traditional shadow theatre. The most spectacular and fully expressive Indonesian art form is the *gamelan*, an orchestra of percussion instruments.

As its name implies, the peninsula of Indochina straddles the two great giants of Asia. It is made up of two vast natural regions, the western and eastern, which are divided geographically by high mountains and mighty rivers. Although in the glorious moments of its past heyday (from the 10th to the 13th centuries), under the Cambodian empire of the Khmer dynasty, the two regions were politically and culturally united, they were almost always differentiated by their greater absorption of either Indian (in the cases of the region which is now Myanma – formerly Burma – Cambodia, and Malaysia) or Chinese (in present-day Laos, North Vietnam and South Vietnam) influence.

Despite the natural physical distance between them and the artificial political differences which divided them, the Himalayan countries maintained their unity thanks to Buddhism. Theirs was a later form of Buddhism (Mahayana), full of local animistic traditions and esoteric tantric rituals, which evolved into the modern Lamaism. Its spiritual leader, the Dalai Lama, or "Ocean of Virtue", wielded not only religious and cultural power but also political and economic power. The nerve centre of this huge religious nation was the Potala, the Dalai Lama's palace in Lhasa, the capital of Tibet. This fact justifies the use of the term "Tibetan style" to describe all sorts of cultural output generated in whatever region of the Himalayas. The only exception is the Nepalese style, which is far more heavily influenced by the Indian.

In the early 15th century, Tibet was under the influence of the religious reformer and saintly scholar Tsong-kha-pa. He was the founder of the Dgelugs-pa order, also known as the "Yellow Hats", who tried to purify the earlier, debased form of Lamaism. This was the period of the palace-monasteries, classically exemplified by the Potala, and it also saw new revised translations of the sacred texts and corresponding illustrative miniatures.

Particularly important examples of the art of this period are the tankas or *thang-kas*, large meditative scroll paintings on cloth, the best of which were produced by the Guge school. Typically, they display a sensual approach to form and use vivid colours, taking their inspiration from Indian and Nepalese painting. There are also countless ritual artefacts in gold and silver (Vajra, Phurbu, Prajña, Lingam) and diverse types of statues in various metals, in the later period adorned with turquoises and other semiprecious stones in the manner of the great religious images in stone and polychrome wood.

The 15th and 16th centuries also saw the artistic peak of the Kathmandu valley in Nepal (a kingdom divided into three independent but linked principalities), with their capitals in Kathmandu, Patan

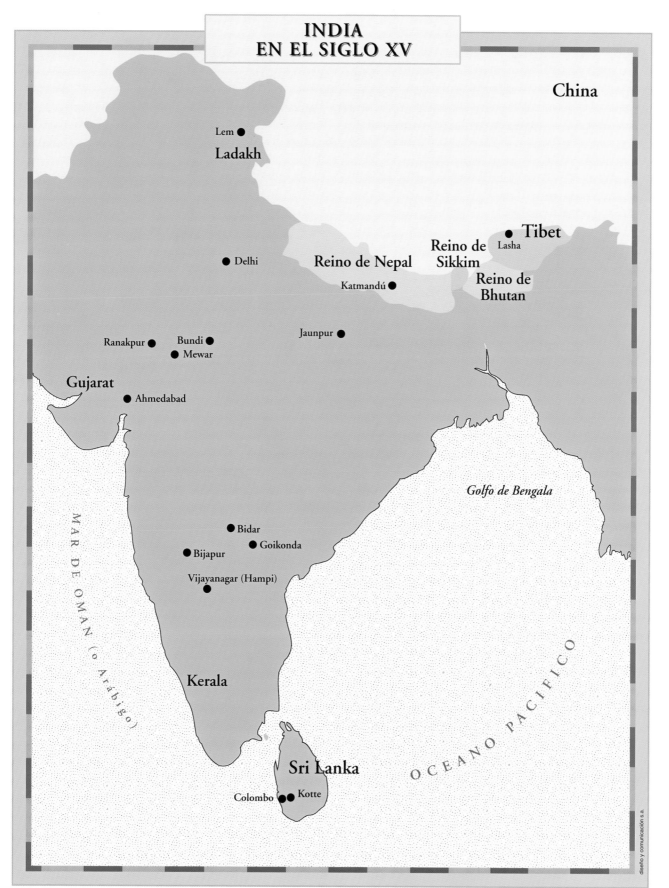

**INDIA
EN EL SIGLO XV**

China

Lem ●
Ladakh

Tibet
Lasha ●

Reino de
Sikkim

● Delhi

Reino de Nepal

Reino de
Bhutan

Katmandú ●

Ranakpur ●   Bundi ●   Jaunpur ●
            ● Mewar

Gujarat

● Ahmedabad

Golfo de Bengala

MAR DE OMAN (o Arábigo)

● Bidar
        ● Goikonda
● Bijapur

Vijayanagar (Hampi)
●

Kerala

OCEANO PACIFICO

Sri Lanka

Colombo ●● Kotte

diseño y comunicación s.a.

and Bhatgaon, ruled by three princes of the Malla dynasty.

After its decline from former glory, the only noteworthy art anywhere in Indochina around 1492 was in the Sukhothai, U thong and Ayutthya styles of Thailand. Although at the time Thai art was still only a pale reflection of Cambodia's earlier Khmer style to which it gave a Chinese interpretation (the Thai people originated in Yünnan, a southwestern province of China), these three schools worked with all the vigour of original creative impulse fuelled, furthermore, by deep Buddhist fervour. In Thai art collections around the world, the Buddhist statues stand out for their stylised delicacy of form and excellent craftmanship in stone, bronze, and ormolu. The ceramic ware is also memorable for its great delicacy, though in the main it lacks originality because of the obvious influence of Chinese porcelain.

The Himalayas

The remote and barely accessible valleys of the highest mountain range in the world, with their sometimes paradisiacal microclimates, have always provided refuge for the people of the region. Geographical factors have shaped the conservative and ritual nature of their culture which places such value on the metaphysical that even today it serves as a spiritual reserve for the rest of the world. In earlier times, the art of Himalayan kingdoms was produced in the natural regions of Ladkah, Nepal, Tibet, Sikkim and Bhutan. Today only two – Nepal and Bhutan – are still independent, Tibet having been occupied by China since 1959, and Ladakh and Sikkim having voluntarily incorporated themselves into India after its independence from Britain in 1947.

However, little remains of the cultural heritage of those kingdoms. The perishable materials (brick and wood) used and the fratricidal conflicts which occurred are the reasons why so few works of art from that period have survived. Some historic buildings are still standing, but they have been much restored.

Continual restoration is a factor relevant to all the countries in the Himalayas, mainly due to the continued existence of ancestral rites which require geomantically consecrated temples and ancient images of proven magical effectiveness. These factors make it extremely difficult for specialists to date any work of art from this region with any degree of confidence.

China

Leaving behind the Silk Route, which in 1492 was in the hands of the Khanatos, Turco-Mongol converts to Islam, we enter the Celestial Empire, the China of the Ming dynasty (1368-1644) whose written symbols (the sun and the moon together), meaning light and brightness, appropriately express the brilliance of its culture.

The 15th century saw the reign of the following emperors: Yung-lo (1403-1424), Hsüan-te (1426-1435), Cheng-t'ung (1436-1449), Ching-t'ai (1450-1456), T'ien-shun (1457-1464), Ch'eng-hua (1465-1487) and Hung-chih (1488-1505). The first two of these were periods of splendour. Yung-lo had the Imperial Palace built in Peking (Beijing, or the "Northern Capital") whence the court had moved from Nanking (the "Southern Capital"), formerly the revolutionary capital of the Ming while the Chinese forces successfully expelled the Mongols, descendants of Kublai Khan, who, represented by the Yüan dynasty, had tyrannised the Chinese nation for a century.

The Imperial Palace, built between 1406 and 1420, was a project on a vast scale. Its 9,000 pavilions extend over an area of 720,000 m² which was levelled and reinforced before building began. As well as being magnificent, its structural network was also functional, with longitudinal avenues providing ready access and large open spaces centred around courtyards around which palace life revolved. Its orientation facing directly north earned it the poetic title the "Purple City", while its impregnable walled section gave rise to the other name, the "Forbidden City", by which it is sometimes known.

The palace is divided into two main parts: reached from the south entrance gates, the first, or public, section of the palace was used for royal audiences, important royal occasions and major events over which the emperor presided. The second, or private, section was used for the administration and the culture and everyday life of the "Sons of Heaven" and their families. The most interesting architectural feature is the T'ai Ho Tien (Hall of Supreme Harmony) which gives onto the first patio and which served as the Throne Room. The rhythmic straight lines and curves of its roofs, the purity of the materials, and the splendid colour combination of white marble, red lacquered wood and yellow glazed ceramic of which this impressive 35 m high pavilion are constructed, are an impressive artistic feat.

The reign of Hsüan-te, the next emperor in the dynasty, produced the best works of art of the Ming period, and gave its name to some of the finest genres, such as "Hsüan-te porcelain" and "Hsüan-te lacquer". However, a period of decadence was to follow – although this is a relative concept within the context of the Ming dynasty –, artistic recovery

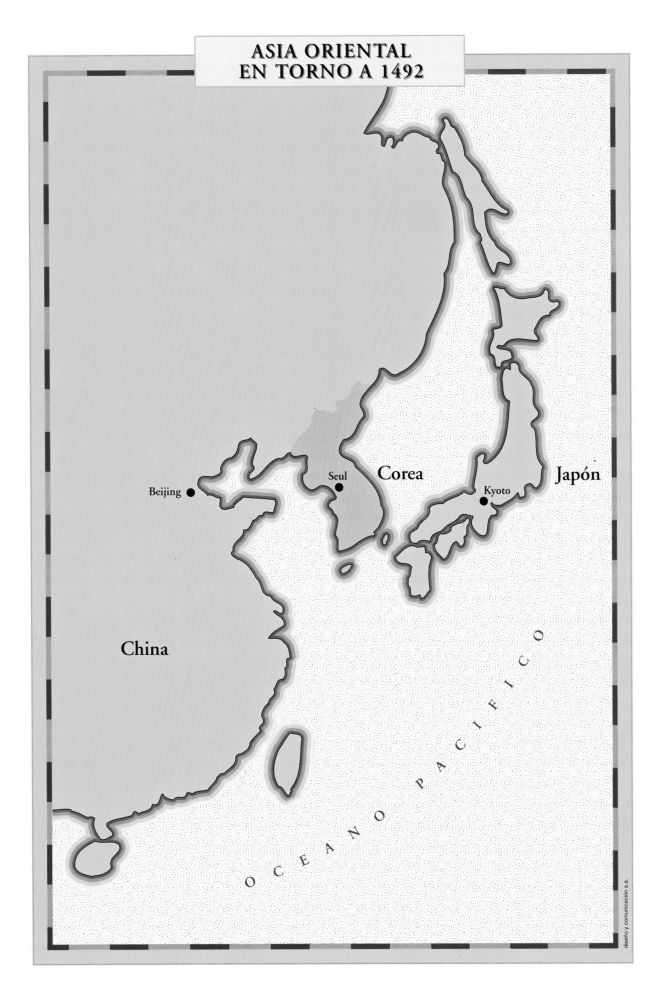

ASIA ORIENTAL EN TORNO A 1492

Beijing

China

Seul

Corea

Kyoto

Japón

OCEANO PACIFICO

diseño y comunicación s.a.

then reaching another high point in the early 16th century during the reigns of Cheng-te (1506-1521) and Chia-ching (1522-1526). Despite ups and downs, the entire duration of the Ming empire – almost three centuries – was an unrepeatably fruitful period in Chinese art.

This stable and original culture astonished the Western world of the Modern Age. Chinese scholars of the time were learned compilers and treatise writers who revelled in Confucian rationalism to a degree which made them, if anything, excessively encyclopaedic in their approach.

Interestingly, the most significant artistic movements of the time emerged not in academic circles but rather in the schools created by Taoist intellectuals and enlightened poets who had voluntarily withdrawn from society to live in harmony and constant union with nature and the Tao philosophy. This is seen clearly in painting, at its finest under the Ming dynasty in the landscapes of the Che School (individual artists working in Chekiang Province) and the Wu School (artists working together in the city of Wumen).

The landscape, an integral part of the Taoist concept of a universal order, provided the inspiration for the most important pictorial genre in what the Chinese call "the art of the brush" as a way of stressing the concept of painting, poetry and calligraphy as one artistic whole. Brush-wielding painters-poets-calligraphers all follow the same aesthetic principles and use the same techniques. Chinese art history does not analyse or study them separately since they are all in pursuit of the same goal, namely capturing the spirit of their subject matter and generating an aesthetic experience which will enrich the poetic spirit of the spectator.

The high cultural standards of the Ming era are evident in all forms of artistic expression. New styles and approaches were sought with a view to achieving both technical perfection and the aesthetic dimension. In porcelain, new decorative polychrome wares came to the fore (two colours, three colours, five colours and contrasting colours), though the blue and white and the monochrome wares are – justly – equally well known. Among the latter, the imperial yellow and the copper reds are particularly noteworthy.

The cloisonné enamel ware created in the workshops of the Imperial Palace was so perfect that historians of Chinese art tend to omit mentioning the fact that this precious metalcraft is actually Persian in origin, albeit a close relation of Chinese porcelain enamelling. However, since Chinese creative genius and craftsmanship overtook the quality of imported examples in the 15th century, cloisonné

work has remained unchallenged as Pekin's most important craft to this day.

Various types of lacquerwork also achieved uniformly high standards. Lacquerwork can be carved, gilded, inlaid with metals, jade and mother-of-pearl. Lacquer's unique sheen, sleekness of surface and the harmonious use of red and black are essential ingredients of this art form, while its impermeability, lightness and tactile appeal make it a very useful material.

Extracting the expressive quality of particular materials is a typical feature of Chinese art, and it is seen at its best in work with jade, fine wood, rhinoceros horn, ivory, fabrics and tapestries, and in screens and other items of furniture. This is a field in which Chinese artists excelled, achieving a clever aesthetic balance between simplicity of form, purity of material and decorative purpose.

Korea

Korean culture of the period around 1492 must be dealt with separately. Although Korea had always been within the Chinese sphere of influence, at this time it was producing its own novelties in the artistic field during a period when a surge of nationalistic feeling led to the creation of a new form of writing.

The Choson, or Yi dynasty as it is sometimes known, reigned in Korea from 1392 to 1910 although its heyday did not last beyond the 16th century in consequence of the Japanese invasion which, in two successive waves, devastated the south of the peninsula in 1592 and 1597.

Despite the nationalism which prevailed during the 15th century, Korean culture became enriched with a new enthusiasm for the Chinese-Confucianism, which led to advances in printing, astronomy, mathematics, music and agriculture.

The most important period for art began in the mid-15th century when Korean scholars became enthusiastic collectors of the works of the ancient Chinese masters. Paradoxically, nationalism made the Koreans more appreciative of what was not Korean. Although temporarily the respective political directions they had taken tended to separate the two countries, the traditional education of Korean scholars, like the Chinese, was based on Confucianism.

Painting from the Choson period is a faithful reflection of the contemporary history of Korea. It continues to reflect the country's cultural links and similarities with China, based both on an identical socio-economic system and comparable administrative institutions. Many notable paintings emerged from this unique cultural environment, among them works attributed to An Kyon and Kang Hui-an, the

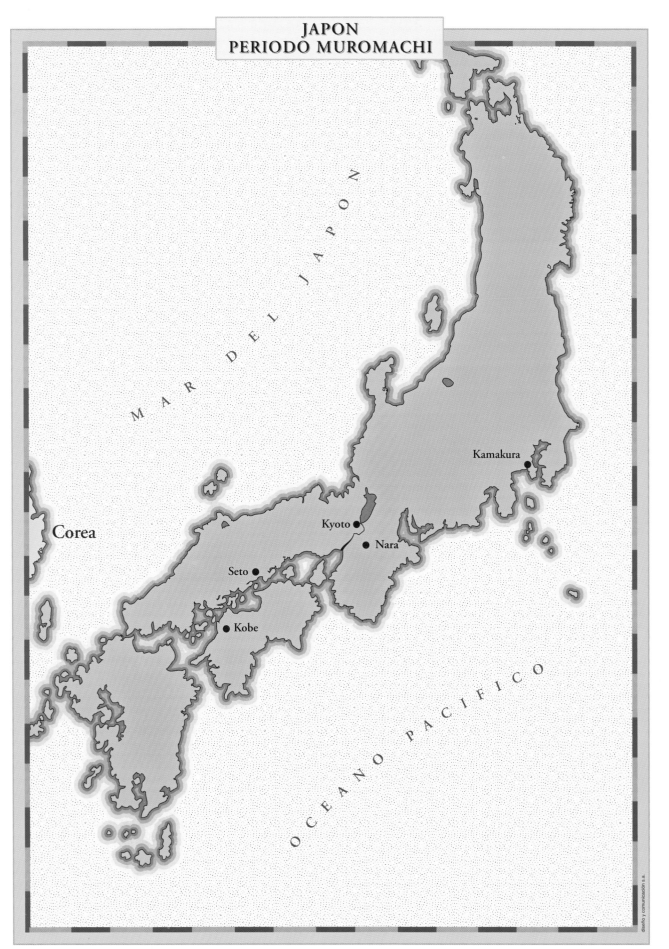

JAPON
PERIODO MUROMACHI

MAR DEL JAPON

Corea

Kamakura

Kyoto
Nara

Seto

Kobe

OCEANO PACIFICO

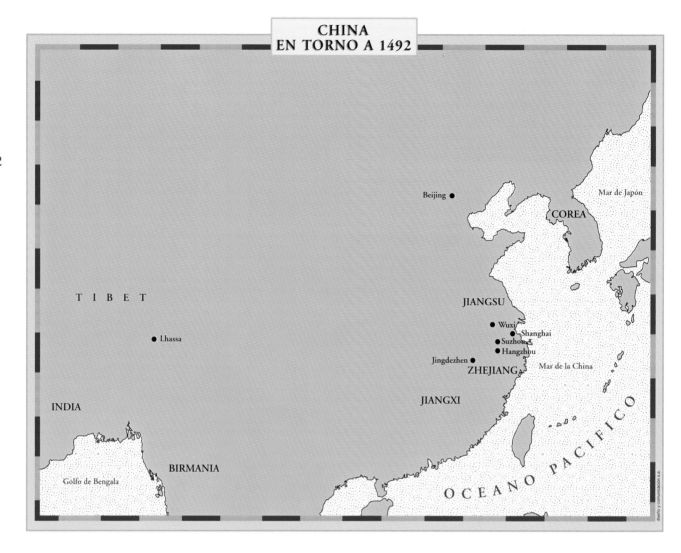

Beijing ●

Mar de Japón

COREA

T I B E T

JIANGSU

● Lhassa

● Wuxi
● Shanghai
● Suzhou
● Hangzhou

Jingdezhen ●

Mar de la China

ZHEJIANG

INDIA

JIANGXI

BIRMANIA

Golfo de Bengala

O C E A N O   P A C I F I C O

52

most famous artists at the Choson court. In their landscape paintings, the treatment of nature and its elements is more realistic; though the symbolic concept of the fantastic landscape is still in evidence, their work is based on natural models. In other words, their landscapes are familiar and beloved Korean landscapes rather than remote unfamiliar Chinese ones.

This same tendency is discernible in the Korean Punch'ong, or "Green Dust", slip-decorated celadon pottery. Its inspiration in Chinese celadon porcelain is clear, yet the use of whitish marbling to break the monotony of the monochrome aqueous greenish glaze is completely original. Similarly, white porcelains, which may also have been inspired by Chinese porcelain ware, are sometimes combined with incised linear designs or brush strokes of cobalt blue glaze under the crystalline coating.

Japan

Around 1492, fully-fledged feudalism still held sway in the Japanese archipelago. Since the 12th century, the emperor had been relegated to a merely sym-bolic role which would not recover its former status until the 19th century. Power was now divided among a few feudal lords known as *daimyos*, who set up a military dictatorship, or *bakufu* led by the shogun.

During the period under consideration, and over a wider spectrum from 1333 to 1573, the Ashikaga family had established its *bakufu* in Muromachi (now part of Kyoto). During its history, its reign was marred by constant feudal conflicts among the *daimyos*. This chivalric world of the warlord or samurai which then existed in Japan, with its love of pomp and luxury in all aspects of life, was well balanced by the austerity of Zen. Zen, or "meditation", is a Buddhist sect which, though actually Indian in origin, had also assimilated Taoist elements as it spread through China. It extended throughout Japan in the 12th century, its own concepts being adapted to the traditional Japanese or Shintoist way of life. From that time on, Zen Buddhism became more and more consolidated in Japanese society, eventually becoming the majority religion, which it still is today.

The triumph of Zen and its philosophy during the Muromachi period was essentially due to the charismatic personality of two of its monks. They were Zeami (or Seami, 1363-1443) and Sen-no Rikyu (1520-1590). Both played an extremely important role from an artistic point of view, since they developed the tea ceremony and landscape gardening into fine arts. They were also responsible for developing and disseminating one of the basic principles of the Zen ethos –*shibumi*. This was literally the love of the essential, the simple, the rough or unfinished. By cultivating the quest for inner qualities, *shibumi* created an aesthetic code appreciative of "ugliness" in an attempt to express the maximum through a minimum of elements.

The *Cha-no-yu*, or tea ceremony (more correctly translated as the "tea road"), was one of the main occupations of the ruling military class. During the Muromachi period, this ceremony became more than just a social ritual and began to take on aspects of an aesthetic-religious experience before finally evolving into the main vehicle for artistic expression which influenced a wide variety of fields such as architecture, gardening, painting, calligraphy, ceramics, lacquerwork... and invested a whole series of vessels with significance which transcended their simple usefulness and made them vehicles for meditation.

The aesthetic aim of landscape gardening is to condense the wider world into limits which impose a human scale. If this fact is considered in the light of the Japanese concept of the house as just the habitable part of the garden, a bridge towards nature, the importance of gardening and its parallel arts like *ikebana* (flower arranging) and *bonsai* (miniature gardening) becomes clear.

Zen produced the meditation garden par excellence. These gardens' surprising, and apparently contradictory, austere vitality based on stones and rocks symbolising universal balance permits contact with the spirit of nature laid bare, and eliminates any other elements which might distract from the solitude and emptiness which are part of Zen.

Apart from the two artistic worlds entered through the tea ceremony and landscape gardening, the Muromachi period also saw a pinnacle of achievement in painting, both through the Zen school and the decorative Kano school. Both produced works and artists of world renown.

Sculpture was still a spectacular art form at this period, although already in decline from an earlier period of splendour. Now its main characteristic was sensationalism derived from an exaggerated dynamism expressed through contorted musculature and disturbing glass eyes. The masks worn in the No theatre were vividly expressive. This theatre form emerged during the Muromachi period as an extremely stylised and intellectualised musical drama, which provided the opportunity for other forms of artistic expression, such as the magnificent kimonos and masks worn by the actors.

The Ashikaga family, which successfully controlled the belligerent *daimyos*, centralised all art and politics in Muromachi (Kyoto), turning the capital into a stage on which the most powerful Japanese families played out their lives in an atmosphere of luxury and exclusivity. The residential palaces built to the taste of this new nobility successfully combine the austere Japanese tradition with the Chinese decorative elements. The original Muromachi style thus produced is well exemplified in the Golden Pavilion and the Silver Pavilion, the latter being built in 1489.

America in 1492

José Alcina Franch
Universidad Complutense, Madrid

The year 1492, the centre of so much attention in recent years in relation to its quincentenary and now being commemorated as the date of the Discovery of America or of the Meeting of Two Worlds, serves as a useful watershed from which to contemplate what went before and what came after – pre- and post-Columbian – as two radically different cultural eras.

Had the first Europeans who arrived in the Americas in the late 15th century had access to the knowledge which archaeologists and historians have since compiled, they would have seen an apparently chaotic, and certainly heterogeneous, ethnic map. Even so, some perspicacious contemporary observers, such as Fray Bartolomé de Las Casas (a dominican missionary to the Americas), were aware of the reality of the situation and, furthermore, attempted to explain it much the same way as we shall do here, albeit in broader terms than the better-informed modern commentator.

One of Fray Bartolomé's most explicit commentaries on the Discovery of the Americas occurs in his *Controversia* (the celebrated controversy on the rights of the american indian with an influential opponent) against Juan Ginés de Sepúlveda, Las Casas writes:

"...there are three kinds of savage. The first, to interpret the word liberally, are those peoples whose opinions and customs are strange, but who have the judgement and capacity for organisation to govern themselves. The second are those whose language is not suited to expression through written characters or letters, as was once the case of the English... The third kind of savage are those who, because of their depraved customs, rudimentary skills and brutish tendencies, are like *wild* animals who live in the countryside with neither towns nor houses, organisation, laws, rites or treaties." (Casas, 1985, pp. 194-195).

The three types of society to which Las Casas alludes were universally applicable, but he had based his (clearly evolutionary) picture on his own experiences in various regions of America: Hispaniola, in the Antilles; the Pariá coast of Venezuela and also in Nicaragua, Guatemala and Mexico. In all these places he had been in contact with groups of natives who fitted into one or another of the ca-

tegories defined by Elman R. Service (1962) as *states*, *chiefdoms* or *tribes*. The only direct experience Las Casas lacked was with hunter-gatherers organised into *bands*.

Although hitherto there have not been many attempts to present a map of the New World based on its political organisation as schematised by Service, there have been some by Sanders and Price (1968) and, more recently, by myself (Alcina, 1987), on the basis of the information provided by Julian H. Steward (1946-50). The differences between the two maps are questions of detail, but in any event there is a lack of detailed maps both of North America and Latin America, and it will be no doubt some time before many questions concerning the definitive classification of many ethnic groups are clarified. In some cases, we are still uncertain whether they belong to the tribal group, the chiefdoms, or whether they are domains rather than states as such.

If we consider a general map of indigenous America in 1492 in the light of the concepts mentioned above, the most salient phenomenon is the existence of two huge nuclei which genuinely qualify for the category of *states*, and are genuine *civilisations*. They are located in Meso-America and in the Andean region. Both are expansionist militarist states – the Mexica or Aztec, and the Inca – which, by different means, had absorbed a large number of ethnic groups, most of which were developing in the direction of a state-like degree of organisation. Some could be called *kingdoms*, while many others were *chiefdoms* or *domains* of varying degrees of social complexity. This is precisely why the study of these empires or large states is so complicated: there are two different levels or aspects to be considered – that of the state itself, and that of the local domains.

States

Both states presented similarities which can hardly be explained by contact or the phenomenon of diffusion. However, neither can they be explained as a consequence of independent evolution. Clearly, this whole area of study cries out for more comparative work along the lines of that carried out by Geoffrey W. Conrad and Arthur A. Demarest (1984).

When the Spaniards arrived at what is now the

coast of Veracruz, the spies and informers of Montezuma II reported the fact immediately to the court in Tenochtitlan. Other mysterious omens and portents had warned the cogitative Mexican sovereign and head of the Triple Alliance that something extraordinary was about to happen. The fact that the Spaniards were fair-skinned and long-bearded, dressed in shining armour and accompanied by ferocious animals served only to confirm the oft-heralded notion of the return of the priest-god King Quetzalcoatl. After humiliation at the hands of Tezcatlipoca sorcerers, he had fled over the sea to the east, declaring that he would return some day to reconquer his former kingdom of Tollan. The moment had clearly arrived, and Hernán Cortés was Quetzalcoatl, or at least his ambassador or emissary announcing the immediate return of the former deity.

What Cortés found in Mexico-Tenochtitlan was actually the result of an already ancient cultural tradition dating back possibly as far as the Olmecs, but certainly derived from the Teotihuacan. It had culminated with the arrival of a sequence of barbarian tribes from the north and northwest of Meso-America such as the *Acolhua* from Texcoco, the *Tepanecs* from Azcapotzalco, the *Chichimecs* from Tenayuca, the *Tlahuics* from Cuernavaca, and finally the *Mexicas*, who founded their city, Tenochtitlan, on an island on Lake Texcoco some time between 1324 and 1370. The Mexicas were destined to rule over not only their fellow tribes in the Valley of Mexico, but also over a wide variety of kingdoms spread throughout present-day Mexico. Through a succession of alliances and wars, the Aztecs had managed to establish what is known as the Triple Alliance with the neighbouring city-states of Texcoco and Tlacopan, and over which Montezuma II was effectively the sole ruler at the time of the Spaniards' arrival. The title "Emperor" which Spanish chroniclers attributed to Montezuma was not, therefore, as inappropriate as one might think, given that the series of wars of conquest fought by the Aztecs/ Mexicas had indeed achieved an empire, economically sustained by means of a complex tribute system, and kept cohesive by a regime which made effective use of terror as a psychological weapon. Prisoners were sacrificed

on the altars of their temples, wars were fought on the slightest pretext (such as the 'Flower War' with the nearby kingdom of Tlaxcala) simply to amass personal prestige and prisoners for sacrifice. But this approach was not only the key to keeping the empire together; it also explains why it fell so rapidly thanks to the readiness to cooperate with the invaders of the peoples subjugated by the Aztecs (Alcina, 1989-a).

The apparent brutality of the Aztec Empire viewed from the perspective of its bellicosity and bloody sacrifices should also be considered within a context of profound spirituality and artistic, literary and intellectual refinement. Such was the atmosphere in virtually all the cities and courts of the central Basin of Mexico, and particularly in the area of Texcoco, where several of the Aztec rulers, among them *Netzahualcoyotl*, were not only excellent administrators, warriors and politicians but also great poets (León-Portilla, 1967).

In fact, Aztec/Mexica culture cannot be understood at all unless we examine the context of religion, mythology and ritual, and these within a complex concept of time. To understand its *Weltanschauung*, one has also to grasp the profound duality implied in the concepts of life and death, heavens and underworlds, in addition to a sense of time and space in relation to the four or five world directions; the notion of paradises or mythical places from which people come or to which they go – *Tamoanchan, Tlalocan, Mictlan* – and an intense and deep rooted yet ambiguous *polytheism* in which countless deities metamorphosed into many and differently named versions according to the role they were required to fulfil. Theirs was an enormously complex world, whose own priests were in constant debate as they sought coherence. However, it was impossible to establish concepts which would embrace the entire Aztec Empire since recognition had to be accorded to local traditions, to cultural borrowings and to the ingredients of an historical amalgam formed over many centuries of tradition.

In order to narrate this complex world of religious ideas, the priests and elders used symbolic languages which were given visual expression in the form of glyphs. While tending towards phoneticism, these never evolved into an alphabet, yet were used to compose complicated *codices* which were used for reading the future, naming new-born babies, setting dates for religious festivals, mapping the kingdoms, recording the history of rulers and peoples, and recording taxes paid by subjugated nations.

Artists, sculptors and potters were all able to use this language to signify the fundamental concepts of religion and to express the ideology of the empire in such a way that the people, either consciously or unconsciously, were indoctrinated or educated in the fundamental principles of their religion: the solar disc, as featured in the *Aztec Calendar*, the "monster of the earth" such as *Tlaltecuhtli* or *Coatlicue*, the "plumed serpent"; the "celestial group" or the paired eagle and jaguar, were symbols which, along with others representing water, smoke, fire, death, and so on, provided artists with the means to express in their sculptures or reliefs, on whatever scale, the whole religious philosophy which imbued the intellectual life of Aztec Tenochtitlan (Pasztory, 1983).

None of this makes sense unless one relates it to the measurement of time by the double – solar and ritual – calendar, which together determined longer periods of time such as the 'century' or *xiuhmolpilli*, lasting 52 years. The *tonalpohualli*, or ritual calendar year of 260 days, combined with the *xiuhpohualli*, or 365-day year, only coincided once every 52 years, at which time all fires were doused so that they could be relit as part of the *New Fire* ceremony.

The other great territorial empire that the Spaniards encountered was that of the Incas. It was located in the cold high plains of the Andean mountain range, but stretched westwards as far as the Pacific Ocean and eastwards as far as the hot valleys formed by the tributaries of the River Amazon. The empire embraced the area inhabited by the *Pastos* indians in south Colombia and the territory of the *Mapuches* in present-day Chile. It was unquestionably one of the largest territorial empires of antiquity. Barely a century elapsed between the enthronement of Pachacutec as head of the Inca Empire and the overthrow of Atahuallpa in Cajamarca by Pizarro's tiny expeditionary force. But that century had seen many military campaigns carried out by an impressive army of tens of thousands of men led by highly experienced generals and under the supreme command of emprerors as celebrated as Pachacutec, Topa Inca Yupanqui, and Huayna Capac. These military campaigns had incorporated dozens of formerly independent cultural and political entities into the Inca Empire, which was by that time a highly sophisticated organisation whose internal mechanisms were both original in conception and efficient in application.

The Inca culture represented the culmination of a long process which had begun at least as early as the *Chavín* culture and had reached maturity with the Tiahuanaco and Pucará cultures and the Wari Empire. In this sense, the Inca Empire contained the very essence of Andean civilisation, despite the fact that, as a tribal group, the Incas were relative newcomers to a stage on which many other peoples had achieved thereto unrivalled status. The similarity to the situation of the Aztecs or Mexicas of central Mexico is obvious. However, one fundamental difference is the fact that the Aztec Empire was based on an alliance or federation, while the Inca was, and always had been, monarchic in nature.

The most original feature of the Inca culture lay in its economic structure, which distinguished between two levels of society. These were, "on the one hand the members of the rural communities or *ayllus*, united by kinship and whose relationships were governed by the principle of *reciprocity*; and on the other the State, which absorbed the contributions owed it by its subjects, and in turn made them beneficiaries of the fruits of their labour by means of *redistribution*" (Wachtel, 1973). Reciprocity and redistribution, then, were the two fundamental layers of the complex economic organisation which functioned in the Andes during the Inca epoch. Blas Valera labels the system of reciprocity the "law of brotherhood", according to which "all the inhabitants of a community *helped one another with the ploughing and sowing and harvesting of crops (...) without any kind of payment.*" This is why, in contrast with the other great empires of ancient times, the Inca Empire levied taxes not in material goods but in labour, in exchange for which communities and individuals were provided with necessary goods at the appropriate time by the State.

Another highly original feature of the Inca economic system was what Murra calls the *vertical control of a maximum number of ecological levels*. This system was based on the ecological structure of the Andes, which contains many ecosystems very different among themselves although geographically close to each other. This meant that the inhabitants of certain areas had access to many different products. The *Yacha* or *Chupaychu*, for example, were within three days' walk uphill of salt mines and pastures, and three or four days' walk downhill of woodland and coca and cotton fields. Thus, regardless of land ownership, the population had a wide range of agricultural alternatives at its disposal (Murra, 1975).

The complex organisation of the Inca State was based on an extensive bureaucracy, which in turn relied on a rapid and efficient information network.

AREAS CULTURALES
DE LA AMERICA PRECOLOMBINA

Artico

Noroeste

Aridamérica

Oasis-américa

Mesoamérica

Caribe

A. Intermedia

A. Amazónica

A. Andina

OCEANO ATLANTICO

OCEANO PACIFICO

diseño y comunicación s.a.

This explains why the Incas' road system was one of the most perfect created by the ancient civilisations. Hyslop has recorded a total of 23,139 kilometres of roads, but suggests that the original network could well have totalled as much as 40,000 kilometres. Sited along this road system were hundreds of *tambos*, buildings used to store raw materials and manufactured goods which were used in times of emergency throughout the territory of the *Tawantinsuyu*.

Meanwhile, the *chasqui* system catered for the transportation of messages and small packages at high speeds in many directions. The *chasquis*, or messengers, and other government officials were adept at using the *quipu* system for recording information about population groups, armies, llama herds, and even stories and legends. The *quipus* consisted of cords with knots held at various intervals and woven of different coloured threads. Essentially, they were mnemonic devices which served to record all sorts of information, including dates and even stories, poems, legends and decrees. So essential a piece of equipment was it, that the Inca Empire is sometimes said to have been governed by the *quipu*.

Unlike the Meso-American civilisation, the Incas used the *decimal system*, both for statistical accounting and for the organisation of the army, and even for the division and classification of the population. At the same time, the calendar system, divided into 12 periods or *quillca,* was closer to the European system than the complicated mechanism of the Meso-American calendars.

Just as Aztecs/Mexica art is among the most beautiful and complex to be found in Pre-Columbian America, that of the Incas was very modest and simple. Genres such as monumental sculpture, reliefs and mural painting are absent throughout the culture. Smaller sculptures in stone or metal, and ceramics high in quality but very simple in decoration are its only noteworthy contributions to the plastic arts. Only the *keros*, semi-cylindrical receptacles carved in wood, provide any exception insofar as they feature painted scenes. Most of these, however, were produced during the colonial period.

Counterbalancing these deficiencies, the Incas paid great attention to architecture and engineering. Relatively small and unimportant sites, such as *Chichero*, which housed the imperial *panaca* of the Topa Inca Yupanqui, contain dozens of palaces and lesser buildings, as well as countless worked rocks and many kilometres of walled agricultural terracing. The craftsmanship is as skilled as that found in the buildings of Cuzco, capital of the empire (Gas-

parini-Margolies, 1977). It is hardly surprising, therefore, that the buildings of the metropolis, such as the main temple or *Coricancha*, the Palace of Pachacutec, the *Acllahuasi*, and the *Sacsahuaman* fortress, are outstandingly beautiful. However, there were hundreds of cities the length and breadth of the *Tawantinsuyu*, the following being among the most important: Pisac, Kenko, Tambomachay, Chinchero, Ollantaytambo, Raqchi, Vilcashuaman, Machu Pichu, Tambo Colorado, Pachacamac, Mixco Viejo, Tomebamba and Ingapirca.

As stated above, there were a large number of smaller states or city-states, kingdoms and fiefdoms within these two great empires, which had been integrated to a greater or lesser degree. This was the case, for example, of the *Mixtec* kingdoms within the Aztec Empire, or the *Cañari* fiefdoms in the Inca Empire. But beyond the frontiers of these two great empires there were still political units which would qualify for the description of small states or *kingdoms* which had remained independent. The *Kingdom of Tlaxcala* was one exceptional example, given its alternately warlike and peaceful relationship, maintained through the institution of the 'Flower War' with its powerful neighbour, the Triple Alliance or *Aztec Empire*. However, the Maya kingdoms in Guatemala, the *Quiches* and the *Cakchiqueles* were all relatively small socio-political entities which functioned quite independently of the Aztec and Inca empires, though their relationship with other groups constituting what are generally called chiefdoms was probably very tense and aggressive.

Chiefdoms, Domains and Fiefdoms
These types of political formations have for the most part disappeared in other parts of the world, since they belong to the stage of history which precedes the formation of states. These early states, with most of which we are familiar through their archaeological remains, in effect wiped out all trace of their chiefdom-type precursors. As Hermann Trimborn established many years ago, the case of Latin America is fortunately different. The Spanish discoverers and conquerors arrived while these chiefdoms were still functioning at this pre-state stage, and their accounts provide us with ethno-historic information which is precise and closely-observed, albeit biassed.

The chieftainships, domains, or fiefdoms that the Europeans encountered during their first contact with various regions of the continent were distributed irregularly, though there was a certain concentration around the Caribbean, both in Central America and the Antilles, in the northern part of

South America and the northern Andean area – Julian H. Steward gives it the overall label of Circum-caribbean. Contacts outside this area worthy of mention occurred with the chiefdoms of the south-eastern United States and of the northwest coast, as well as with some groups along the Amazon and on the Mojos plains.

While accepting that the political and socio-cultural system of the chiefdoms represents what might be called a phase of social evolution, it is still useful to apply typological analysis to the internal evolution of the political system in question. Julian H. Steward distinguishes two types, which he calls *theocratic* and *militarist*. Robert Carneiro refers to three levels – *minimal, typical,* and *maximal* – categories which could be increased to four or five, which would suggest tribal societies well on the way to becoming states in the full sense of the term (Alcina, 1984). I personally opt for four typological categories: *chiefdom I*: gatherer-fishers with storage deposits and stable settlements; *chiefdom II*: crop grower-fisher-gatherers without storage facilities; *chiefdom III*: crop grower-fishers, cultivating bitter yucca and with storage deposits; and *chiefdom IV*: cereal growers with storage deposits. The following examples illustrate these four levels or types of fiefdoms.

The most typical example of the *chiefdom I* model is provided by the Indians of the northwest (Alcina, 1989). Based on a non-agricultural economy, theirs was a hierarchical society in which political power, although very weak, was exercised particularly by the *Tais* as a result of the prestige achieved in *festivals* such as the *Potlatch*. The economic basis of these chiefdoms was provided fundamentally by salmon fishing, but also by sea and land hunting and gathering, particularly of seafood, which combined with the fact that these goods were partially or totally preserved inclined these groups towards fixed settlements. Accumulated goods readily become private property, and as a next step stored items become "currency", exchangeable for non-foodstuffs, particularly luxury goods. In any event, these types of chiefdoms had little future, insofar as they displayed no tendency towards increasing accumulations of goods or *wealth*, while in parallel other aspects of these societies developed in a similarly unsophisticated way.

The *chiefdom II* model evolved in *tribes* with a mainly horticulturally-based economy, albeit importantly supplemented by gathering and fishing. In a certain sense this model corresponds to Carneiro's "minimal" chiefdoms, which represent a transitional stage between the tribal state and chiefdom proper. The most characteristic examples are

found in the Pacific societies, such as the *Kiriwina*, but there are also cases in America, such as the *Cayapas* in Ecuador, or probably the earliest types of chiefdoms to emerge among the *Tainos* of the Antilles.

In this type of chiefdom, the social structure is remarkably similar to that observed in tribes in which a chief has power in certain circumstances (generally bellicose) over the chiefs of other related lineages settled in neighbouring communities. In these cases the tribal chief has a big house, different from those occupied by the other members of the group, and even bigger and better than those of the other related chiefs in nearby villages, as was the case of the Cayapas of the coastal lowlands of Ecuador (Palop, 1986). The political relationships among these models of chiefdom, in which kinship continued to be the predominant structural element, indicate to what degree they have advanced from the tribal model. Vegetable growing provides the basis of their economy: the *yam* in the Pacific, and the *sweet yucca, sweet potato* and the *maguey* in the case of the Americas. These types of crop could only be stored for short periods, and this made redistribution difficult. Although from the demographic point of view the *Tainos*, as encountered by the Spaniards, do not belong to this model, they must have been very similar in their earlier stages, given that many of their cultural characteristics are closer to tribal models than other cases. One example is the "cohoba ritual", or the use of hallucinogens to stimulate artistic expression, which is found more within the circle of Amazonian cultures than in the Circum-caribbean area (Alcina, 1981 and 1983).

Chiefdom III belongs to an intermediary stage of the evolutionary process, the equivalent of a *typical* chiefdom (Carneiro, 1981, 47). It is an alternative to the model just described, although evolved to a more advanced level. The fundamental difference between this and the previous model lies in the fact that some societies developed techniques for preserving some fundamental foodstuffs. *Bitter yucca* is a useful example since its cultivation was widespread throughout America. Some peoples in the tropical area of South America, Central America and the Caribbean use bitter yucca for food. As is well known, this plant's prussic acid content makes it useless as a foodstuff unless subjected to a long and complicated process to eliminate its poisons. The process generates two equally useful products: the pulp, which can be turned into flour or made into *cazabe* cakes, which keep indefinitely; and yucca juice which, used in its pure state, is still poisonous, but when diluted with other products is useful for preserving meat, for example. In addition to these two methods of preserving foodstuffs, there was also the smoking process for fish products. In conjunction, these techniques allow for an economic pattern which must have been very common throughout the regions of America mentioned above. These preserving techniques make it possible to establish a storage system which could serve as a basis for *redistribution*, a fundamental factor in the economic system of chiefdoms.

In the geographical area under consideration, a considerable number of chiefdoms has been detected to date. In general, the piece of archaeological evidence most indicative of this level of development is the *grater*, and this tool has been found among the relics of many pre-Hispanic cultures. But there are also many other data of an ethno-historic kind which prove that this type of chiefdom was very common at the time of the Spaniards' arrival. From this point of view, the most characteristic example is probably the Taino chiefdom of the Antilles.

The final level in the evolution of chiefdoms is *chiefdom IV*, the equivalent of Carneiro's *maximal* level. It is characterised, in the terms relevant to this study, by the use of cereals, mainly maize, which made it possible to preserve and accumulate in storage deposits large quantities of foodstuff, above and beyond the day to day needs of the community. The piece of archaeological evidence indicative of this level of development is the *hand mill*, which replaced the *grater*.

There is also widespread ethno-historic evidence of this type of chiefdom. Many of the chiefdoms of the northern Andean region corresponded to this model, notably (because both ethno-historic and archaeological evidence of them has survived) the *Cañaris* (Alcina, 1978 and 1986).

Some commentators believe that the chiefdoms did not develop a sufficiently sophisticated *market system*. However, in some areas there is enough evidence, both archaeological and ethno-historical, to suggest that such markets did exist and that they functioned at local, regional, and even international level. This was the case of settlements around Quito in the central highlands of Ecuador, and of the Cañaris or Paltas of the Loja region, who held *tianguis* (though it is not known whether they were held on regular days). The same is true of the Ecuadorean coast, where the markets of Ciscala, La Tolita and Atacames were regional or international. In many other areas, too, the emergence of the market seems to mark the threshold of a new type of economy in which, while retaining the systems of reciprocity and redistribution, interchange begins to become crucial (Alcina, 1990 ms).

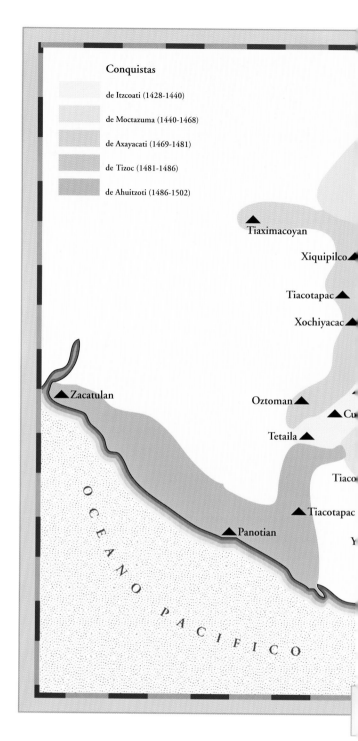

Bands and Tribes

In 1492, beyond the areas occupied by *states* and by *fiefdoms* dealt with above, the whole of North and South America was occupied by ethnic groups which can be categorised as *bands* or *tribes*, that is to say *egalitarian societies*. For the purposes of this study, the definition of an egalitarian society suggested by Service (1962) and Fried (1975) can be applied. The differences between a *band* and a *tribe* are, more than anything, demographic and economic, and have little to do with the social and

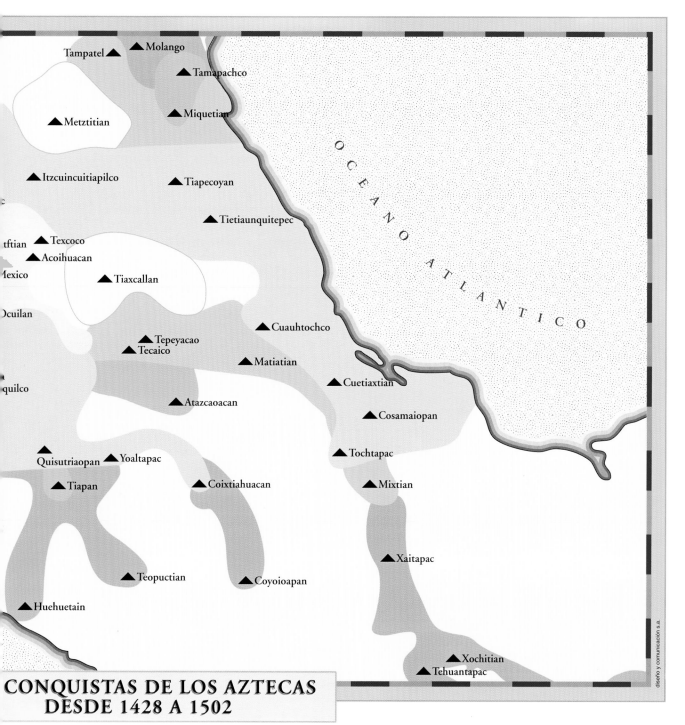

CONQUISTAS DE LOS AZTECAS DESDE 1428 A 1502

political aspects of these population units. Considered sequentially, the first type of society to be described is that of bands of hunter-gatherer-fishers of the period which archaeologists call the Paleolithic. Tribes, on the other hand, were groups which developed an economy based fundamentally on agriculture during the Neolithic or Formative period. In any event, the fundamental fact to be examined is the lack of hierarchical classification or positions of *status* of the people within their society.

From the economic point of view, these societies evolved patterns of integration mainly governed by reciprocity. Productive units were always of a family nature – either conjugal or extended – which meant that all the individuals within the group carried out the same activities according to their age and sex. This in no way affected the system of reciprocity, though productive capacity was relevant to prestige.

This being a subsistence economy, the two activities (hunting and gathering, and in some cases fishing) were divided up between men and youths, and women and children. Social organisation, meanwhile, was patrilineal, patrilocal and exogamous. The fact of where one lived was more important than lineage, so that patrilocality reinforced the cohesion of the hunter group, while exogamy extended the kinship network.

The territory occupied by egalitarian societies – bands and tribes – in North America around 1492 was fundamentally one complete territory in which various cultural areas can be distinguished: the Arctic; the Sub-Arctic area; the Altiplano and California; the Great Basin; and the Plains and Prairies and the East.

The *Arctic*, despite its vast size, was occupied by a single ethnic group, the *Eskimos* or *Inuit* (man). This culture covered a region which extends from 50º to 82º latitude north, which specialists traditionally subdivide into three zones: the West (Siberia, Alaska, and the Pacific coast); the Centre (the area of the Cobre and Caribu Eskimos); and the East (the east and west coast of Greenland and Labrador). At the time under consideration, the Eskimo cultures were in their final evolutionary periods or stages: the Kachemak III culture in south-east Alaska; the Late Prehistoric period in the Bering Strait; the Tikerak culture in north Alaska; the eastern Thule culture in the Canadian Arctic, and the Inugsuk culture in Greenland.

The Eskimos represent one of the best adaptations by human groups to a geographical environment, in their case apparently hostile. They lived in very small groups during the winter and slightly larger ones in summer, living in their hemispherical igloos in winter and in animal-hide tents in summer. Their economy was based on hunting seal, walrus and whale along the coasts, and reindeer and bear in the interior. For sea transport, they created highly original craft such as the individual *kayak* canoe and the collective *umiak*, and for overland travel they used sleighs pulled over the ice by dogs.

Eskimos throughout the Arctic made exhaustive use of the by-products of the animals which they hunted: skins for clothing, tents and boats; bones for the structure of dwellings, boats and sleighs; oil for lighting and heating; ivory for knives and awls; tendons for bonding structures, and so on. Despite the apparent poverty of the environment, the Eskimos produced works of art which were sometimes amazingly vivid and characterful, particularly in ivory, bone and wood (Adanez, 1991).

The *sub-Arctic area* is composed basically of two large linguistic families: the *Athabascan* and the *Algonkian*. Together they occupied the Canadian woods region, and the fact of sharing an ecological unit was reflected in certain cultural similarities. The activities of the Athabascans affected their Eskimo and Algonkian neighbours profoundly. Originally from the interior of Alaska, they spread to the Peace River and Lake Athabasca "forcing on the one hand the forebears of the Algonkians, who had established themselves around Lake Winnipeg, to retreat eastwards, and on the other, the forebears of the Eskimos to move north. This pressure continued to the east and was the reason for the Algonkians, who had hitherto lived in the interior of the continent, to also occupy the coast." (Krickberg, 1946).

The Athabascans who, along with a number of other groups, constituted the *Ma-Dené* linguistic stock, were the most widespread group in North America, extending from Mexico up to the Arctic Ocean and from the Pacific across to Hudson Bay. The Algonkians occupied an equally large area, from Labrador to North Carolina, and from the Atlantic to the Pacific. Some of the most easterly groups were the first *redskins* encountered by Europeans. Like the Athabascans, they had exerted pressure on the Eskimos, and the Algonkians and Eskimos were ousted by farmers from further south, particularly the Iroquois who, by the time Cartier travelled through the area in 1535, had already occupied the entire basin around Lakes Eyrie and Ontario and the banks of the Saint Lawrence River.

The sub-Arctic peoples, like the Eskimos, were perfectly adapted to their natural environment of pine forests and the Canadian cold. Fishing with nets and lines in the region's many rivers and lakes, and the use of snowshoes to aid hunting in the woods were perhaps the most basic elements of survival for these people during the long winters. Their political organisation was at the level of bands or macro-bands and, under certain conditions, of tribes. One noteworthy feature of the Algonkians was the gathering of wild rice from the western lakeside wetlands, although in all other respects their economy was similar to that of the other sub-Arctic peoples.

The areas designated as the *Altiplano* and *California* constituted a mosaic of small ethnic groups. Something of its complexity is revealed by the existence of 117 different languages, registered by Bancroft and subsequently grouped into 21 families by A.L. Kroeber. Today, they can be divided into two main *stocks*: *Hoka* and *Penuti*. For thousands of years, this group of bands had maintained a subsistence economy based on hunting, fishing and gathering, particularly of holm acorns, although they also ate chestnuts, pine kernels, berries, seeds, roots and tubers. Despite this economic system, however, evidence has recently been found of social hierarchy or stratification which in some ways

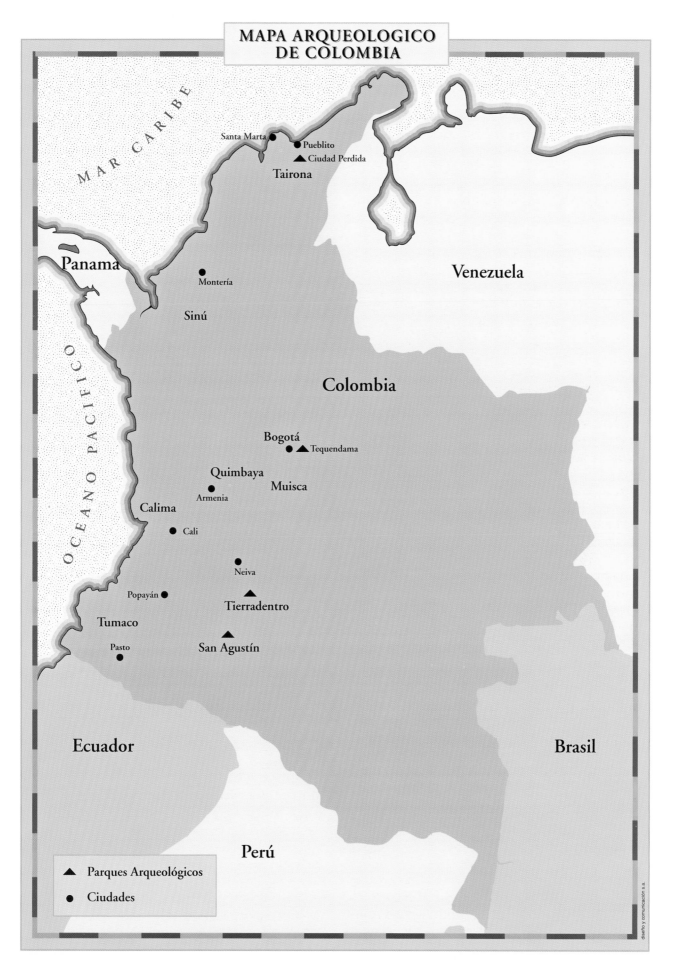

MAPA ARQUEOLOGICO
DE COLOMBIA

MAR CARIBE

Santa Marta
Pueblito
Ciudad Perdida
Tairona

Panama

OCEANO PACIFICO

Montería
Sinú

Colombia

Venezuela

Bogotá
Tequendama

Quimbaya
Armenia
Muisca

Calima
Cali

Neiva

Popayán
Tierradentro

Tumaco
Pasto
San Agustín

Ecuador

Brasil

Perú

▲ Parques Arqueológicos
● Ciudades

diseño y comunicación s.a.

makes them more similar to the chiefdoms of the North-west.

The *area of the Great Basin*, in the western plateau of the United States, is where the *Shoshoni* peoples lived. They had adapted to a mainly arid environment, and had evolved an economy based mainly on gathering and hunting, and occasionally fishing.

The large area of the *Plains and Prairies* was dominated principally by the *Sioux, Caddo* and *Kiowa* who, irregularly distributed, occupied an area stretching from the Mississippi River to the Rocky Mountains and from Saskatchewan to the Arkansas River. They have come to be considered the archetypal *redskin* Indian of the Far West. Before the arrival of Coronado in 1541, these Indians lived by an economy which was fundamentally agricultural, though they also hunted. However, only from the 16th century onward, and particularly during the 17th century, by which time they had acquired horses and guns from the white colonisers, did these Indians become true hunters and achieve the fame later to be popularised by 'Cowboy and Indian' films.

The final area, the *Eastern* United States, was occupied by the *Iroquois* in the north, and in the south, the *Natchez, Caddo, Illinois, Shawnee, Cherokee* and the *Creek*. In the Late Woodland period, the cultural tradition of the Iroquois was based fundamentally on the cultivation of maize, beans, pumpkin and tobacco, complemented by gathering and hunting with bow and arrow. The *long house* dwelling was typical, housing several families. Several of these houses together constituted a clan, and eight clans constituted a tribal unit. Not until much later, in the 17th century, was the great confederation of the Five Nations formed, made up of the Cayuga, Mohawk, Oneida, Onondaga and Seneca.

Turning to the ethnic groups of hunter-fisher-gatherers and crop growers of South America, situated at the level of *bands* and *tribes*, mention should first be made of the Orinoco-Amazon, or tropical rain forest area. The number and variety of peoples makes any overall assessment virtually impossible. The Amazon has been classified into seven subareas, which cover the many ethnic groups of which some still survive to this day. One suspects that in 1492 there were many more, and that some of them, like the *Omaguas* and the *Manaos*, would have reached the chiefdom level of socio-cultural development.

The innumerable ethnic groups concentrated in this vast region can be approached in different ways. Some commentators have opted for an historical approach. From this viewpoint, the oldest and most *primitive* layer of the population would be constituted by peoples sited in different places: the *Sirno* of northeastern Bolivia; the *Mura* from the areas between the River Nadeira and the lower reaches of the River Purus; the *Macun* from the area between the Rivers Negro and Yapurá; the *Shiriana*, from the area between the Rivers Blanco and Orinoco, and a series of peoples belonging to the *Ge* group, among whom are the *Nambicuará*. The second layer of population would be concentrated along the slopes of the Andes and include two main groups – the *Tucano* in the north and the *Pano* in the south – and some other independent tribal groups such as the *Otomaco, Piaroa, Guahibo, Uitoto, Jíyaro, Chiquito*, and others. The most recent population layer would be made up of three main linguistic groups widely distributed throughout the area: the *Tupí*, the *Arawak* and the *Carib*.

From the linguistic viewpoint, five main stocks can be distinguished: the *Arawak, Carib, Tupi-Guaraní, Tucano* and *Pa*. But other groups speaking different languages, notably the *Ge* group, dwelt in the Brazilian highlands; southwest of the Rivers Amazon and Madeira (*Amuesha, Moseten* and others), and near the Rivers Orinoco and Negro (*Timote, Jirajara, Guarauno, Otomaco, Sáliva, Puinave, Guamo, Guajiro*) (Pericot, 1961). Although it is difficult to comment on this large mosaic of tribal groups in general terms, it can be said that in 1492 they were at various stages of socio-cultural development. Although the majority of these groups were crop growers, particularly of cassava – both sweet and bitter – there were also a number of relatively unimportant gatherer-hunter-fisher groups and others – principally the Omagua and Moxo – which were probably at the *chiefdom* stage.

In the region known today as the Southern Cone, the ethnic map was also quite complicated. A first area to look at would be that which includes a large part of the Gran Chaco, the Paraná River basins, parts of the Andes and of present day Uruguay and Paraguay, north of the River Plate. The mountainous area in northwestern Argentina, from the snow-capped Aray to the Lerma Valley in Salta Province almost as far as Mendoza was inhabited by the *Diaguita*.

In Antofagasta Province, on the northern Chilean coast, lived the *Atacama* or *Atacameños*. The *Omaguaca* were focused on the Humahuaca brushland, but were spread throughout Jujuy Province and the Tilcará Valley to Salta Province and the present day border between Bolivia and Argentina. The *Allentiac*, or *Huarpes*, occupied the area around the Huanacache lakes in Mendoza Province; the *Sanavirón* stayed to the southeast of the Diaguita, in the Salinas

Grandes region of Cordoba; the *Comechingon* lived in the Cordoba mountain range. The *Guaicurú* was the most important family in the area, extending the length of the Paraguay and the lower Paraná.

To the south of these groups lived a number of peoples which inhabited the southern Andes, the Argentine Pampas, Patagonia and Tierra del Fuego. The most important of these ethnic groups were the *Araucanos*. Another important indigenous group in this area were the *Puelche*, who occupied a large part of the Pampas, from the Andes to the Atlantic, and a thousand or so kilometres extending from the Cordoba-River Plate line to the River Negro. South of the Rivers Negro and Limay, the territory is arid, dry and seared by freezing winds. This is Patagonia, which was inhabited by the *Tehuelches*, or *Patagones*, as Magellan called them. Today the *Ona* and the *Selkman* are categorised within this group.

This picture of what the American Continent was probably like in 1492 when the arrival of the Europeans brought into contact two worlds – the Old and the New – hitherto separated by two mighty oceans and many thousands of years of independent life is little more than a rough sketch. Its aim is to give some idea of how heterogeneous its many ethnic groups and cultures were, and of how inappropriate it is for modern scholarship to try to simplify and impose patterns on them.

Catalogue

Notes on the Catalogue

Catalogue Sequence

The catalogue for *Art and Culture around 1492* faithfully follows the exhibition's conceptual and spacial development. The notes on the exhibited works are thus included in the catalogue in the same order as in the exhibition areas.

However, as the order is not linear, other criteria had to be used for presenting the information, based on an ideal visit to the exhibition: the visitor's progress is followed from entry to exit starting with the central areas – where these exist – followed by the areas on the left and then those on the right and clockwise in those cases where the exhibition space demands it. The catalogue will thus give the reader a good idea of the concept of the exhibition, except for the fact that one of the principles upon which it is based is that of grouping together small numbers of works, each with a particular significance of its own, which for logical reasons will not be apparent from the catalogue.

Art and Culture around 1492 is centred around four major themes: *The Meeting of Two Worlds, Man and Society, Images of the Divine* and *Man the Creator*, preceded by an introduction, *Cultures around 1492* which is in turn followed by a colophon: *The Beginnings of a New World*. The catalogue is also divided into these sections, with the subdivisions in each theme indicated in the short note which introduces them.

Similarly, the relationship of the works to the various cultures which the exhibition focuses on, European, Islamic, Far Eastern or Oriental, American, African and Byzantine, is represented by six images of human faces, each of them symbolising one of the cultures mentioned.

African culture

Asiatic culture

Byzantine culture

European culture

American culture

Islamic culture

Catalogue Explanatory Notes

Each of the works in the catalogue is presented with three types of information: a graphic illustration, a technical note and an analytical note.

Despite the differences between the cultures and the objects presented, the aim has been to unify the technical notes and, where possible, to give the same type of notes and equivalent concepts for each and every one of the works.

In this respect, it should be pointed out that in the dimensions, the first figure refers to height, the second to length and the third to width or depth.

The bibliography section does not, of course, include those works which are unnamed or those works which are not treated specifically in the scientific notes.

The analytical notes respect the criteria of the various authors who were involved in writing them and therefore some contributions contain new interpretations or slight variations with respect to the scientific analyses published to date.

The Transcriptions

In the case of Latin alphabets, the traditional method of transcription has been followed, introducing supplementary letters or diacritical marks in those languages which require them.

For those languages which do not use the Latin alphabet, the following criteria have been followed: with Arabic, the criteria of the Spanish school of arabists – whose official organ is the magazine *Al-Andalus* – have been followed; as to Chinese, the PINYIN system (phonetic transcription) has been used, which the government of the People's Republic of China adopted on 1 January 1979 as the only official system for transcribing from the Chinese to the Latin alphabet; Sanskrit transcriptions have been used for Indian languages and, finally, the Hepburn system has been used for the transcriptions of Japanese.

Writers

Nimat M. Abu Bakr
Museum of Islamic Art, Cairo

Myrtali Acheimastou-Potamianou
Director of the Byzantine Museum, Athens

V.K. Agili
Head of the Documentation Department, National Museum, Lagos

Naseem Akhtar
National Museum, New Delhi

José Alcina Franch
Professor of History of America, Universidad Complutense, Madrid

James W. Allan
Curator of the Ashmolean Museum of Art & Archaeology, Oxford

Yehya M. Al-Shayb
Museum of Islamic Art, Cairo

Masaaki Arakawa
Idemitsu Museum, Tokyo

Farouk S. Asker
Museum of Islamic Art, Cairo

Shashi Astana
National Museum, New Delhi

Ch. Baltoyanni

Isidro G. Bango
Professor of History of Art, Universidad Autónoma, Madrid

Luciano Bellosi
Professor of History of Art, Università di Siena

Carla Bernardini
Museo Civico Medievale, Bologna

Marthe Bernus-Taylor
Curator of the Musée du Louvre, Paris

Marie-Thérèse Bobot
Curator of the Musée Cernuschi, Paris

Ferdinando Bologna
Professor of History of Art, Università di Roma II

Elena Bonatti
Palazzo Schifanoia, Ferrara

Klaus Brisch
Freie Universität, Berlin

José Rogelio Buendía
Professor of History of Art, Universidad Autónoma, Madrid

Paz Cabello
Director of the Museo de América, Madrid

Claudia Caldari Giovannelli
Galleria Nazionale delle Marche, Urbino

John Carswell
Director of the Islamic Section of Sotheby's, London

Isabel Cervera
Ph.D. in History of Art, Universidad Complutense, Madrid

Maria Grazia Ciardi Dupré
Galleria Nazionale delle Marche, Urbino

Andrés Ciudad
Universidad Complutense, Madrid

Milo Cleveland Beach
Arthur Sackler Collection, Washington

Elena Corradini
Galleria e Museo Estense, Modena

Egidio Cossa
Museo Nazionale Preistorico Etnografico Luigi Pigorini, Rome

José Manuel Cruz Valdovinos
Professor of History of Art, Universidad Complutense, Madrid

Álvaro Cháves Mendoza
Head of the Department of Anthropology, Universidad Javeriana, Bogotá

Pedro Dias
Professor of History of Art, Universidad de Coimbra

Matías Díaz Padrón
Curator of Flemish Painting, Museo del Prado, Madrid

Armand Duchâteau
Museum für Völkerkunde, Vienna

Volkmar Enderlein
Museum für Islamische Kunst, Berlin

Fang Bongehas
National Museum, Shanghai

Antonio Fernández Puertas
Professor of History of Muslim Art, Director on leave of the Museo Nacional de Arte Hispanomusulmán, Granada

Isabel Flores Escobosa

Kield V. Folsach
Director of the David Collection, Copenhagen

Lucia Fornari Schianchi
Galleria Nazionale, Parma

Maria Teresa Franco Fiorio
Civica Pinacoteca del Castello Sforzesco, Milan

Mercedes Garberi
Civica Pinacoteca del Castello Sforzesco, Milan

María Queiroz Ribeiro
Calouste Gulbenkian Fundação, Lisbon

Giovanni Romano
Professor of History of Art, Università di Torino

Van A. Romans
The Paul and Ruth Tishman Collection, Los Angeles

Trinidad Sánchez Pacheco
Director of the Museo de Cerámica, Barcelona

I.K. Sarma
Archaeological Survey of India, New Delhi

Shan Guolin
National Museum, Shanghai

Siham Al-Mahdi
Museum of Islamic Art, Cairo

Álvaro Soler del Campo
Real Armería, Palacio Real, Madrid

Gudrun Sporbeck
Schnütgen-Museum, Cologne

Claudio Strinati
Galleria Nazionale d'Arte Antica, Rome

Joan Sureda i Pons
Professor of History of Art, Universidad de Barcelona

Eva Szmodis-Eszláry
Szépmüvészeti Múzeum, Budapest

Noriko Takahashi
Masaki Museum of Art, Osaka

Chiara Toschi Cavaliere
Palazzo Schifanoia, Ferrara

Enrique Valdivieso
Professor of History of Art, Universidad de Sevilla

Isabel Valverde
Ph.D. in History of Art, Freie Universität Berlin

Consuelo Varela
Researcher at the C.S.I.C. Escuela de Estudios Hispano-Americanos, Seville

Irene Ventura Folli
Biblioteca dell'Università di Bologna
Museo Aldrovandiano, Bologna

Anna Maria Visser Travagli
Director of the Palazzo Schifanoia, Ferrara

Anton von Euw
Schnütgen-Museum, Cologne

Almut von Gladiss
Museum für Islamische Kunst, Berlin

Muhammed Isa Waley
The British Library, London

Rachel Ward
Curator of the Department of Oriental Antiquities, British Museum, London

Johannes Willers
Director of the Germanischen Nationalmuseum, Nuremberg

Yang Chengbin
Imperial Palace Museum, Bejing

Muhammad Yusuf
Instituto Valencia de Don Juan, Madrid

Hildur Zea S.
Instituto Colombiano de Antropología, Bogotá

Zhang Rong
Imperial Palace Museum, Peking

Zhang Wei
National Museum, Shanghai

Zhong Yinlan
National Museum, Shanghai

Zhou Lili
National Museum, Shanghai

Zhu Shuyi
National Museum, Shanghai

Cultures around 1492

The old refectory of the Carthusian monastery
of Santa María de las Cuevas houses the first
four works in the exhibition, works which stand
as symbols of four of the main cultural areas
represented: European, Islamic, Oriental and
American. The pieces selected are
complemented by two others which serve, in
some way, to accentuate the Islamic influences
found throughout the architecture of the
refectory itself, especially in the late *Mudéjar*
roof. In this refectory, arts from the past and
from various cultural worlds begin to coexist
and maintain a dialogue through
the eyes of the present.

1
Italy

Andrea di Francesco
di Cione, known as
"Il Verrocchio" (Florence,
1435-Venice, 1488)
Portrait of Scipio,
approx. 1470-1480
Bas-relief, marble,
68 x 39 x 9 cm
Inscriptions: P. SCIPIONI
Paris, Musée du Louvre,
R.F. 1347
Bibliography: CHASTEL 1954

The Renaissance aimed to unite the reason of the present to what was believed to be the truth of the past. It wanted to change man into a new god, another god, into the earthly god who, according to Leonardo da Vinci, deserved "statues, images and honours." The heroes of History were the mirror in which the *virtuosi* of the present, the *uomini famosi* those who were praised by poets and immortalised in stone or painted by creative geniuses, could see themselves. Captains and other powerful men of the 15th century sought their models in the ancient world: Alexander the Great, Julius Caesar, Scipio, accumulating within themselves the virtues of these "superior talents." The human race was indebted to these men, who had to be honoured because, according to Ficino, "The only way that men have to imitate divine learning is to venerate themselves as gods."

Scipio was one of these legendary heroes to be most esteemed by the humanists. Scipio, that is to say Publius Cornelius Scipio, known as the African (235-183 B.C.), was not only admired for his victories in Hispania and Africa against the Carthaginian troops but also for his chivalric gestures, as narrated by Petrarch in his epic poem *Africa.* He was especially admired for being the image of Perfect Man, having successfully combined an active life with one of contemplation. This assertion is made by Cicero in one of the passages of the *Republic,* the *Somnium Scipionis,* which refers to Scipio's appearing to his grandson in dreams in which he talks about the heavenly mansion into which honourable men such as he were admitted.

Macrobio, the Roman mythologer, took this dream from Cicero and through this, mainly during the Renaissance when Scipio became a model for Universal Man, patrons of the arts and letters abounded, as did the concept of the invincible warrior. This model of the ideal man was the one which "Renaissance princes" had to follow and it had its antithesis in the negative image of the fearsome Hannibal, to whom all kind of evils were attributed.

The theme which A. Chastel calls "Captains in Confrontation," which presents contrasted figures such as Scipio and Hannibal, Alexander the Great and Dario, Mars and Neptune, etc., aroused the interest of Renaissance artists and Vasari, in his *Vite* points to Verrocchio as a good painter of such imaginary portraits: "He modelled two half-relief profile heads in bronze: that of Alexander the Great and that of Dario, both of them made according to a whim and differentiated by their crests, their armour and other details." Both were [...] sent as a gift to Mathias Corvino, King of Hungary, by Lorenzo the Magnificent.

The marble in the Louvre is an example of the period in which the "Captains in Confrontation" theme was at the height of its popularity during the last quarter of the 15th century, as much in the medium of marble relief as in those of bronze, terracotta, drawing and engraving. The second of the pair to which this Scipio belongs could not have been very different to the *Head of a Warrior* which was done by Leonardo da Vinci (Verrocchio's most distinguished disciple) and which is to be found today in the British Museum in London.

The head in the Louvre shows a young, thoughtful Scipio, who appears to be reflecting on the choice of a path to Good or Evil. It shows a young man with a "charming, fair appearance," such as was described by Vasari in his comments on some miniatures preserved in Venice, yet at the same time a strong, brave man adorned with all the attributes of military power. It is the definitive image of the new Renaissance knight, who combines Christian ideals with those of the classical world.
(*Joan Sureda i Pons*)

2
Turkey-Persia

Aqqoyunlu period
Helmet, late 15th century
Armour, steel with inlaid
work in silver, 32 cm;
diameter 25 cm
Inscriptions: Glory be to our
Lord, the acclaimed Sultan,
the powerful Khagan, the
chief that places the chain
around the neck (of nations)
Berlin, Museum für
Islamische Kunst, I.3623
Exhibitions: Darmstadt-
Düsseldorf-Munich, 1965
Bibliography: SARRE 1906,
n. 345; KUHNEL 1925, p. 167

Turban-shaped or large bulbous helmets were made both
in Iran and in Turkey at the
end of the 15th century and
the beginning of the 16th. Production probably began under
the reign of Aqqoyunlu. The
Aqqoyunlu federation was established throughout the
upper Euphrates and Tigris
area and during the period of
Uzun Hazan's rule its authority
was extended to Armenia,
Georgia and Iran. In 1469 the
capital was transferred from
Diyarbakyr to Tabriz.

The helmet on display was
probably made for sultan
Aqqoyunlu Uzun Hasan or for
his son Ya'qub. The inscription "Glory be to our Lord, the
acclaimed Sultan, the powerful Khagan, the chief that
places the chain around the
neck (of nations)" appears on
the edge, with eulogies in
Arabic to an anonymous
sovereign. The secondary inscription, which is seen in the
foreground, contains an association of desires.

The helmets which can be attributed to production under
Aqqoyunlu are characterised
by a central fluted section, a
conical rosette and a base with
a series of hooks from which
protection for the nape of the
neck was hung. Both the
hooks and the protecting
piece have been lost from this
helmet. The intricate central
design is damascened with
large silver flowers and leaves.
The elegant dynamism of the

lines and the exaggerated proportions can be compared
with the artwork in the
Aqqoyunlu book; sultan
Ya'qub in particular was
known as a great patron of the
arts and his taste for luxurious
pieces is evident in the profusion with which silver is used.
The splendour of Aqqoyunlu's
court in Tabriz was frequently
commented on by visiting
Venetian envoys and mer-
chants.

It is still not clear whether

these helmets were made in
Tabriz itself or in other towns,
such as Erzerum, which
served as military bases. Many
of the helmets and other
pieces of armour connected
with this one were captured
by the Ottomans close to Erzi-
can in 1473, or were later confiscated as booty by the Safa-
vidas, who crushed the
Aqqoyunlu dynasty in 1502
and established themselves in
Tabriz.

(*Almut von Gladiss*)

3
India

Kerala
Rama, 15th century
Bronze sculpture,
24 x 18.1 x 14.1 cm
New Delhi, National
Museum, 74.74

A large number of metal images of the god Rama and his brother Lakshmana and consort Sita have been found in the south of India. While large images were placed in temples, smaller ones were worshipped on domestic altars. In this small but graceful image, Rama is shown in a standing position, in the *samabhanga* posture under an elaborate arch. The image rests on a round pedestal fixed to a square base. Rama's right hand rests on arrows vertically positioned in such a way that they touch the pedestal, while his left hand supports an arch, these two elements being Rama's main attributes. Because of his royal state,

Rama is represented as profusely bejewelled, with *kirita-mukuta* necklace, *channavira* bracelets and *udarandha* bangles. The arch framing the figure has been decorated with threaded jewels, loops and flames and is resting on two pillars set at either side of Rama's image. In the centre is a rose and there are two *makarmukhas* on the lower part. Rama is one of the most popular incarnations of Vishnu. In his human form Rama, son of Dashratha, is the hero of the *Ramayana* a famous Indian epic poem telling of his life, virtuousness and heroism. (*Sashi Astana*)

4
Columbia

Caldas, Quindío and
Riseralda Department
Quimbaya culture
Anthropomorphic figure
(reredos)
Ceramic shaped by rolls,
cut, stamped and perforated,
32 x 25 x 10 cm
Bogotá, Museo Arqueológico
Casa del Marqués de San
Jorge, Q-11990

Prehispanic potters in the Quimbaya region of Columbia left a collection of vessels and figures as their cultural testimony. These are still without appropriate archaeological classification, principally owing to the fact that this region is one of those most affected by the destructive work of grave robbery and clandestine excavation. As a result of this, pieces that are recovered reach archaeologists far from their primitive cultural environment.
Quimbaya, an archaeological

region situated on the west slopes of Columbia's Cordillera Central, has brought important quantities of ceramic objects to museums and collections, diverse in shape, size, decoration and colour and undoubtedly originating from a variety of villages in different areas. We know that, when General Jorge Robledo conquered the region towards 1540, he found an indigenous group settled there named Quimbaya, expert craftsmen in pottery but also in textiles, whose use of refined techniques and sober but elegant style gave rise to their being described as "Masters of Gold."
The Quimbayas had only been settled in the region for a short time and the archaeologist Gerardo Reichel-Dolmatoff believes this indigenous group to have arrived from the north, from the coastal plains of Sinú, having been forced into exile by political or economic circum-

stances. This implies that goods made of baked clay, although grouped under the Quimbaya name, have no formal or stylistic unity with work actually from the region. For the moment, we have only one single date for this area: the year 980.
Originating from the valley area of the River Quindío and its surrounding areas where large cemeteries in which very rich offerings have been found, is a highly varied pottery in terms of both shape and style, with an excellent finish, hand-modelled, baked in the open air and with many depictions of anthropomorphic and zoomorphic figures. These consist of one group of simple recipients for domestic use and another of richly ornamented vessels and figures: drinking cups, globe-shaped pots, earthenware bowls, glasses and amphoras. The variety in the way these pieces were painted for decoration is noteworthy, some being of a

single colour, some of two colours and some multicoloured and treated with positive and negative colour techniques. Some of them have shiny surfaces, and different textures and designs were achieved through the application of wax or vegetable elements on the surface to define areas, followed by a second or third coat of the colouring substance. The largest range of colours, as many as five on a single piece, has been found in the Quimbaya region, in Quindío.
The piece in question is an anthropomorphic figure, doubtless an altarpiece. The figure is seated in a frontal position with the legs bent and the hands joined. The body is flat, with a flat rectangular head in which the eyes are formed by incisive lines, and the nose is protruding with a circular nose-ring. The mouth is a thin incisive line, and the ligaments on the cylindrically shaped arms are decorated with geo-

metric shapes. The figure, which is curiously shaped, does not reflect a natural realism but a very particular way of representing the human form. The lower part of the torso is leaning against the floor with the legs projected forwards from the waist, giving the sensation that the figure is seated, although there is no sign of a seat. The piece is of a reddish-brown colour, it is solid and there are six holes in the forehead, two in the chest and one in the navel. Necklaces, feathers, pectoral crosses and genital covers were placed in these orifices. The majority of such pottery comes from funeral tombs, which were well-shaped with a lateral chamber and with a maximum depth of 16 metres. The most typical form of burial was one in which the corpse was laid in the floor, adorned with objects such as nose rings, earrings, pectoral crosses, bracelets and necklaces and was surrounded by pieces of pottery, receptacles and ceremonial figures such as the one in question. This statue may possibly be a representation of the dead person or a magic charm.
(*Álvaro Cháves Mendoza*)

5
Turkey

Ottoman period
Cup with stem, approx 1510
Glazed pottery, 22 cm;
diameter 42 cm
Lisbon, Museu Calouste
Gulbenkian, 211
Bibliography: LISBON 1963;
ATASOY-RABY 1989

The pottery of Iznik, in Turkey, enjoyed a period of great vitality from the end of the 14th century, thanks to the patronage of the Ottoman court which ensured orders for high quality pieces.

This production is characterised by the persistence of decorative Islamic grammar, while at the same time showing innovative influences from Chinese blue and white porcelain (Ming Dynasty) which are reflected in both the shape and the decoration.

One of the most noteworthy creations of Iznak pottery is this spectacularly large drinking cup, whose quality of workmanship and careful decoration are characteristic of a prestigious item. It was destined for a wealthy client, to be used in ritual ablutions and very few similar pieces exist, although another is in possession of the Calouste Gulbenkian. Its singularity is owed to its shape, proportions and decoration in tones of blue and white; we have no knowledge of the existence of any such item after the year 1550.

The pastes used in the making of this type of pottery contain a high level of silicon. White is used as a base for the decoration, painted over a shiny alkaline glaze and conferring on the clay the appearance of china. The *rumi hatayl* decoration, the use of medium blue to highlight dark blue, the alternating of discreet decoration with that on a white background all characterise the production of blue and white pottery between 1510-1520.

On this cup the motifs in vogue during this period are combined in a very original manner. The outside shows a hatayl decoration; festoons of flowers styled in the Chinese manner on a white background. The inside has a central medallion decorated with knots and groups in the *tchi* form. Following a cruciform pattern six four-lobed medallions unfold, two in a radial arrangement and divided with *rumi* decoration.

The *rumi* motifs, with arabesques on a white background that fill the medallions, appear more discreetly in the spaces in between. This is an item of rare sophistication and elegance, where decoration in blue and white is explored to its full potential.
(*Maria Queiroz Ribeiro*)

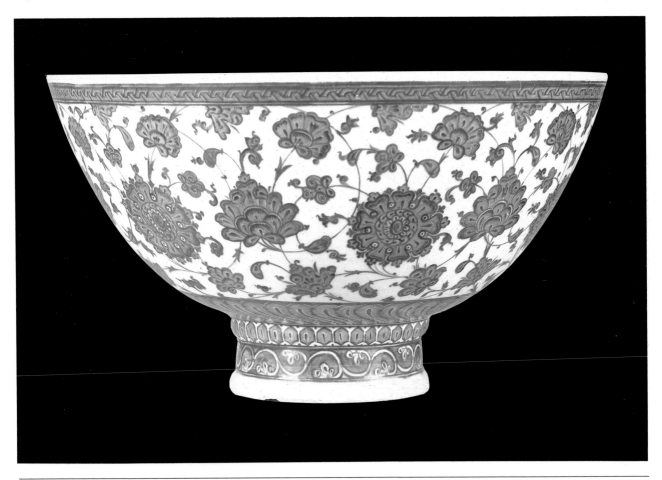

6
India

Military tent, generally known as *Charles V's tent*, 1542-1545
Cotton, taffeta, 4.65 m; diameter 6 m; hangings 2.35 m
From a provincial town under Portuguese rule in Muslim India
Madrid, Museo del Ejército, 40.651

The tent has round shape. The first step to pitch it consists in erecting the central wooden awning, which can be either a single piece or joined to others to gain more height and space. When the awning has been put up, the upper conical element made of weatherproof material is placed on the top of it. The ornamental stud or *yamur* is then placed this, acting as a decorative finial and a means of securing the crown to the awning, preventing the former from being displaced by the wind and leaving no hole through which rain may enter. This is the reason why the cone of the crown is hollow. Two flaps with jagged borders hang from the perimeter of the crown whilst the hooks for the ropes and their wooden bolts hang between them. Ten ropes are linked to the circular perimeter of the crown, and they brace it once they are fixed to the ground with stakes. When the crown has been braced, the hangings are attached, falling to the ground from the hooks and bolts between the flaps. Thus, one flap falls within the tent, concealing the join, and the other is outside to keep out the water which drains from the crown and acts as a windbreak for the interior.

The hangings were sometimes separate, but in most cases they were sewn to each other, except in the entrance where two would open, being attached to two different posts. An alternative was for the entrance to be formed by a single hanging which would be rolled up like a blind (zillu) supported by posts. At the back there was another entrance diametrically opposite this one (which bore the coats of arms) normally remained closed. The floor was covered by a thin carpet or, in hot weather, a tightly-woven mat. The tent was made of taffeta cotton, with satin used in just a few places in order to give a shine; this points to the fact that it was conceived to be used in a hot country such as India, whilst its decoration reveals that it was made in a well-developed provincial town. Silk, and silk and gold embroidery was used in contemporary Iran and Turkey to produce richly decorated tents. The appliqué technique, which was very popular in Spain and Portugal at the end of the 15th century and in the 16th century was used in the embroidering.

The hexagonal awning is now painted in a coarse fashion with themes of vegetal origin. At present we do not know the size of the hangings or whether only one piece of material was used or whether various pieces were joined together and decorated. After restoration it will be possible to see where the hangings are sewn from the vertical fringes which separate the decorative themes repeated in each of them. On the lower skirting band there are twenty rectangular hangings separated by vertical borders; above, there are two continuous vertical bands in the form of a frieze. The higher one is wider and the interior flap, which falls from the perimeter of the crown and decorates it, is attached to it. Above the flap there is a smooth pink band, a second wide band, and, for each rectangular hanging, a tapering rectangle (this shape being due to the conical form of the crown ending with a hollow). The colours of the rectangles are alternately dark blue and pink, and they are separated by bands. At the top, around the hollow, there is a circular motif with blue triangular motifs against it. This is how ornamental motifs are distributed. The horizontal fringe of the skirting band displays a continuous series of rhombic motifs with their sides broken by sprays; the motif is repeated in a concentric pattern in each rhomboid on a white background with alternating blues and reds. All of the hangings have a pear-shaped motif with a triangular base within a seven-lobed pointed arch with a serrated hanging spring motif, and four circles, two in the nets of the arch, and the others at the level of the triangular base. The areas between the above-mentioned motifs are completely filled with spiral shoots and their counterspirals ending in palms or flowers with various petals. The interior of the bulbous motif of the pear-shaped motif contains crisscross rhombic motifs or rhomboids combined with hexagons, with or without floral shoots, or an alternating succession of two geometrical bulbous motifs.

Twenty motifs are repeated on the crown (one for every pear-shaped theme), composed of a pointed pineapple ending in a shoot under a very pointed lobed arch with the crux supporting a bulbous form. The same vegetal and floral motifs appear in all of the blue rectangles, and the same occurs in the pink ones, a sense of *horror vacui* and highly modern design being seen in the pineapples, as in the hangings. The exterior decoration of the crown displays the lower pointed pineapple as the base of another smaller and more flattened one, with a vegetal or floral motif the space outside them. The original ornamental stud or *yamur* was not the double-headed imperial eagle to be seen today. This tent is the only one of its kind to have come down to us in a good state of preservation. The colour of the material on the outside is somewhat faded due to exposure to the light. The pear-shaped motifs of the transverse diameter of the circle of the tent are decorated with a ship to the left of the entrance, a caravel to the right, and with another caravel on the exterior hanging on this side. We owe the identification of these vessels to Guadalupe Chocano, chief researcher at the Naval Museum in Madrid. In the pear-shaped motif of the ship (an ocean-going cargo ship of the type used in the voyages of exploration and discovery in the 16th century and replaced by the galleon in the 17th century) we see the sea with red and blue fish with open gills and an eel. On the ship two armed men are confronting four Indian elephants (a similar elephant can be seen on a fragment of dyed cotton, probably from Gujarat, dated as 15th century, found in Fustat, Egypt, and now kept at the Victoria and Albert Museum, T.254-1958). Pairs of sailors appear at the ends of the yard arms of the three masts. There are blue and red fish in the sea beneath the caravel. The body of the caravel displays five spiral motifs, a different helm, and four masts with yard arms for the sails.

It was not known that the hangings of the main entrance, with a roller-blind form, had the same coat of arms embroidered on them twice on the outside. This dates the tent and reveals for whom it was made. Faustino Menéndez-Pidal de Navascués identified them immediately and kindly sent us this information. The Portuguese arms belong to Martim Afonso de Sousa, the fifth of that name, the grandson of Pedro de Sousa, the first lord of Prado. The arms depict four quarterings on a blue field, two in diagonal with the five smaller shields arranged in the form of the cross of Portugal, whilst in the other two there are rampant lions with long sharp claws, with a six-petalled flower appearing in each corner. When the coats of arms

of the blind were visible the tent was closed and the lord had retired or was resting. The shields are surrounded by a lobed arch with an extrados in a blue background and a vegetal theme reminiscent of the thorny Acanthus of late 15th century Gothic. The heraldic motif was copied from another piece of material or furniture by the Indian embroiderers, which explains this resemblance to the Portuguese Gothic.

Martim Afonso de Sousa, played an important historical role in the service of João III of Portugal in Brazil and India, where he strengthened Portuguese hegemony by supporting Badur, the sultan of Cambala, against the invading Moguls and playing a decisive role in their defeat, after which the sultan allowed him to build the fortress of Dio in 1535. Appointed admiral, he returned to India as governor of the colonial territory from 1542 to 1545 (Zuguete, *Tratado de todos os vice-reis e governadores de India*, [Lisbon 1962], pp. 96-101; de Simas Alves de Azevedo, "As armes dos Sousas, ditos de Prado", *XV International Congress of the Sciences of Genealogy and Heraldry*, publication of the Instituto Salazar y Castro, c.s.i.c., [Madrid 1982], pp. 521-531; *Enciclopedia Universal Ilustrada*, Epasa Calpe, vol. LVII, [Madrid 1927], pp. 704-705). The heraldic shields reveal the identity of the tent's owner and the caravel on the outside his rank of admiral. The presence of two ships on the inside would have served as a graphic aid or map on constant display as he talked with the officers under his command, planning expeditions and the fitting out of ships, etc. This tent came to the Museo del Ejército in Madrid on 22 February 1844 from Toledo and this is the first time it has left the museum since then. As we have mentioned, it is the only known example dating from the period of the independent sultanates of India at the beginning of the Mogul empire, and its origin, history and symbolic iconographic value have been revealed by expert interpretation.

(*Antonio Fernández Puertas* and *Cristina Partearroyo*)

The Meeting of Two Worlds

At the same time as the superb gothic cathedral in the centre of Seville was being built, on the outskirts of the same city the nave of the church in the monastery of Santa María de las Cuevas was also being constructed (1410-1419). A century later, in 1507, the gothic style was still being used in the construction of the buildings around the Santa Ana Chapel. In this chapel, "on the eleventh of April in the year of our lord Jesus Christ fifteen hundred and nine," the mortal remains of Christopher Columbus were deposited.

Both in the church and the chapel, *Art and Culture around 1492* pays homage to the great admiral, to the Hispanic kingdoms who ventured forth on the high seas in search of new routes and new lands, to the faith which guided them and to the American cultures of that New World which were as old as the world of the so-called discoverers. Between them India, that mysterious land which they hoped to reach by sea and which was recalled in 1521 by the Carthusian monk Juan Padilla in *The Triumphs of the Twelve Apostles*.

"The two divisions are *intra* with extra
Which make two Indias large and wide,
With fertile lands, pleasant and agreeable
As the painting of the world shows
One lying to the left
The other lying to the right,
Which the sea revealed to us."

Portugal
Convent of Jesus at Setúbal

Founded just over five hundred years ago, the Convent of Jesus is not only one of the most significant major works of Portuguese art in the Age of Discovery, but is also a testament to renewed spirituality and monastic power, which became gradually more stable throughout the humanist Europe of the pre-Reformation. Coming into being around the year 1492, a mythical date without equal in Iberian consciousness (the end of the Reconquest of Spain and a decisive stage in the expansionist process), the history of the Convent's founding and the early decades of its existence, which this exhibition hopes to evoke, enabled links to be detected between the Iberian peoples, within the universalist perspective characterising them in the heroic age in which they lived, with the emergence of the modern era, and attempts to expand the limits of the possible.

Thinking about the impossible was what started off Justa Rodriguez Pereira, founder of the Convent. Apart from the strong support she was given by the court of the king and queen of Portugal, this strongwilled woman did not possess great titles or a fortune which would enable her to begin the difficult task of founding a Convent destined to receive, into an entirely cloistered life, ladies of the nobility who chose to embrace the rigorous discipline of the Order of St. Clare, which was as yet unpractised in any monastic institution. Lover of the Carmelite D. Fraile João de São Lourenço, Bishop of Ceuta and member of the Order's provincial guard, Justa Rodriquez Pereira was on close terms with the parents of queen D. Leonor, wife of D. João II and of king D. Manuel I. The children resulting from her union with the bishop (D. João Manuel and D. Nuno Ma-

nuel) were legitimised and later played prominent roles at the court. After the death of D. João Manuel (a poet of some merit who maintained correspondence with the famous Italian humanist Cataldo Siculo) and during the years 1499 and 1500 when negotiations for the marriage of the Infanta Doña María, daughter of Ferdinand and Isabella of Spain, to king D. Manuel of Portugal were drawing to a close in Castille, Justa Rodriguez Pereira obtained papal authorization for the burial of her offspring in a funereal chapel which had been built beneath the altar of the Church of Jesus. After receiving considerable support for the purchase of the land on which she intended building the Convent of Jesus, she achieved the necessary permission for its construction (from the pope in 1489 and from D. João II in 1490). The first stone was laid on August 17th, 1490, during a ceremony recorded in a testimonial letter written by Sor Leonor de São João, the Convent's first chronicler, between 1630 and 1644. Inserted into the *Essay on the Ancient and Curious Founding of the Convent of Jesus in the Town of Setúbal* was the licence from pope Innocence VII "to make the Convent in the form desired, with all the workshops, church, choir, bell tower, garden, orchard, both inside and outside the order for the confessor, chaplains and servants." This was a starting point for the building programme which Justa Rodriguez Pereira had requested from His Holiness the pope and which Boitaca, the great master architect of the Manueline era, made into a reality. One year on from the laying of the first stone king D. João II, as the Convent's patron, attended the lying of the foundation stone on the premises of the future church. It so happened, however, that he was not satisfied with the scanty dimensions of the foun-

dations and gave the order for new ones to be dug. As a result of this the ceremony for the laying of the first stone was held again in 1491, during which the king, the master builder and the founder measured the length and breadth of the cloisters themselves.

Work progressed quickly and alms were collected on the Island of Madeira, the great centre of sugar production (1492-1494) for the financing and speedy conclusion of the building. When D. João died in October 1495 his successor D. Manuel became the Convent's second patron. This was to the redoubled satisfaction of the founder, who attached herself to the court to be able to obtain the money necessary for the Convent to be finished quickly and more efficiently. The king was more than responsive to this and gave orders for the whole church, and not only the main chapel, to be domed. This was finished during his lifetime, thanks chiefly to his donations.

In 1496, to signal the finishing of the church and the start of Convent life with seven nuns brought from Gandía (Valencia) by Justa Rodriguez Pereira and seven novices, D. Manuel offered to contribute the bells (one large one with inscriptions and the date and one small one) which are preserved today in the museum. Two years later, at Justa's request, the king made a payment to the master builder Boitaca for the work carried out on the Convent. In 1500 work was still in progress only on the convent wing.

If the ceremonies for the laying of the first stone had been presided over by the Bishop of Ceuta and Tangiers, both of them in Africa and both conquered by the Portuguese in the 15th century, the first confessor was Friar Henrique de Coimbra. Friar Henrique de Coimbra had followed Pedro Alraz Cabral's fleet and in 1500 gave the laying of the first stone in the

recently discovered Brazil. Later, while Bishop of Ceuta, he gave the order for the building of the Church of the Magdalena in Oliven'a, in whose naves the architectural lessons learnt from the Church at Setúbal are highly evident. From the period in which work was carried out at the end of the 15th century and the beginning of the following century the entire Church has been preserved, with a monumental headpiece which rises above the body of the naves, in the facade of which is the main door; the cloisters, with their beautiful arcade with its pink semi-precious stone from the neighbouring Arrábida mountain range and covered with Valencian tiles, and which were served by water taken from the 14th century aqueduct at Setúbal; the galilee of the west wing facing the Convent wall and the overall structure of the monastery. In the middle of the 15th century repairs were carried out on the antechoir and a communicating staircase was built between the two floors of the building. On the occasion of Felipe II of Spain's visit a new chapterhouse and sacristy were offered to the convent to replace the outbuildings destroyed by fire some time before. The author of the new chapterhouse and sacristy was the master architect of the Renaissance Antonio Rodriguez, who practised in the Setúbal region in the latter part of the 15th century and who was an outstanding figure in the artistic panorama of the age. The chapterhouse (the only outbuilding from its day to survive) is a magnificent building in pure classical style, the glazed ornamental tiles covering the floor and walls constituting a dynamic element amid the asceticism of the building, which is not denied by the curious painting (rigorously contemporary) on the ceiling and reredos. The 17th and 18th centuries brought few improvements to the

building, least of all to the decoration. The Convent was closed in 1888 and was then ceded to the Holy House of Mercy at Setúbal for the installation of its hospital. When vacated in 1959 the Convent was adapted for the establishment there of the Setúbal Museum, which opened its doors to the public in 1961. Important work for the restoration of the church was carried out between 1940 and 1946.

The Church and the Convent of Jesus constitute one of the starting points of the renewal of the Portuguese artistic panorama, known by historians as "Manuelino". The Church of Jesus is considered to be the first attempt in Portugal to build a church with unitary isotope space (homogeneously lit), a planimetric and spacial solution also introduced by Renaissance aesthetics. Several innovations within the manueline architectural framework were first seen in the Convent of Jesus, such as the preference for perfectly round or careening arches over pointed arches and the systematic use of domes

set on low arches and networks of ribs.

The introduction of the system of lintels, permitting the base of corbel ribs to be isolated in the walls (making possible the autonomy of the roofs with respect to the elevation), appears to have had one of its first airings in the Church of Jesus. It is still worth pointing out the generalised dissemination of certain motifs in monumental Manueline sculpture which would become very popular, such as the "torsade" (which characterised the columns in the nave, the triumphal arch and the bases of the domes in the main chapel), and the use of semispheres that appear in the main chapel's large window, in the nave capitals and the washroom arcades and in the capitals of the north wing, found in excavations carried out at the end of the 1960s.

The elegant columns in the naves, executed in the lovely ornamental stone of Arrábida (also chosen for the main door, the main windows, the arches and the domes) consist of three bulls which run into

one another, forming a single column in a curious and pleasing artistic representation of the Holy Trinity.

Making the most of the two-coloured effect produced by the pink ornamental stone and the ribs on the roof of the Main Chapel Boitaca produced a complex dome divided into two areas corresponding to the rectangular section and the apse, where curved ribs in the "torsada" style were used for the first time in Portugal. The main door of the Church of Jesus, using Arrábida's beautiful but fragile stone initially anticipated an iconographic plan combining eighteen images, which were probably never made, with the letters of the Greek alphabet A (an allusion to the mystery of Creation), and Y, the latter repeated twelve times on the interior arch. This may be interpreted as an allusion to the twelve Apostles or to the twelve nuns for whom the Convent was initially planned. For this hypothesis to be confirmed the main door would have to be dated before 1497, the date on

which D. Manuel obtained the Pope's permission to increase the number of nuns to thirty-three.

Denouncing the late Gothic accentuated fondness for decorative formulas (above all the lintel), the large window in the main chapel opens almost at the full height of the south elevation of the headpiece, reinforcing the idea of unitary space and homogenous lighting in the church's interior.

A pioneering building in its day, the Convent of Jesus at Setúbal, for the sources of finance it mobilised and the importance of the personalities connected with its founding and early years, occupies an unparalleled place in the politico-cultural scene of the period of the great voyages of discovery.

(*Fernando Antonio Baptista Pereira*)

7
Portugal

Corner stone from the Church of the Convent of Jesus at Setúbal, 1491
Architectural piece, calcerous stone,
22.2 x 23.4 cm
Inscriptions: Y
Setúbal, Museu de Setúbal-Convento de Jesús, 1886
Exhibitions: Setúbal, 1990
Bibliography: TAVARES DA SILVA-PEREIRA 1989

When narrating the second ceremony for the laying of the Convent's foundation stone in her *Essay on the Ancient and Curious Founding of the Convent of Jesus in the Town of Setúbal* written between 1630 and 1644, the Convent's first chronicler Sor Leonor de São João describes "a white stone of two palms' breadth, carefully fashioned and holy, with a cross and the name of Jesus written on it." This ceremony took place on August 22nd,

1491 (the first having been held on the 17th of August in the previous year) and the stone was placed in the foundations by the bishop of Tangiers, D. Diego Ortiz in the presence of king D. João II and the master builder in charge of the work, Boitaca, at the end of the first Mass held on the land on which the Church of Jesus would be built. The repetition of the ceremony was due to the fact that the foundations begun in 1490 appeared to the king to be too small when he visited the works a year later, so he gave orders for new ones to be dug. The stone laid during the first ceremony by the bishop of Ceuta, D. Giusto Baldini, was simply engraved "with the sign of the Cross." During restoration works carried out on the Church of Jesus from 1940 to 1946 a piece of stone displaying a sculpted Gothic Y was found. From its dimensions (around a palm's breadth), or because of the inscription alluding to the name of Jesus (which in the

15th century could be symbolized by the letters JHS) it appears be the other half of the foundation stone referred to by the chronicler, with the piece on which the Cross is sculpted missing. (*Fernando Antonio Baptista Pereira*)

8
Portugal

Bell, 1496
Cast bronze, 63.3 cm; diameter 58.5 cm
From the Convent of Jesus at Setúbal
Inscriptions: EMMANVEL PRIMVS REX PVRTVGALIE ET ALGVARBIORVM CITRA AT VLTRA MARE IN AFRICA ET DOMINVS GUINEE/1496
Setúbal, Museu de Setúbal-Convento de Jesús, 411/T 24
Exhibitions: Setúbal, 1969; Setúbal, 1990
Bibliography: BORBA 1976-1977, n. 2-3; p. 447; PEREIRA 1990, p. 39

In the year 1496, when the Church of the Convent of Jesus was almost finished, king Manuel I offered the religious community two bells. It is believed that this offer was made to symbolise the completion of the church and the Convent's occupation by seven nuns from Gandía, who were brought over personally

by the Convent's founder, Justa Rodriguez Pereira.
The main bell is exhibited here and displays the title of king Manuel I of Portugal, predating the discovery of the maritime route to the East Indies. The Convent's first chronicler, Sor Leonor de São João, in her *Essay on the Ancient and Curious Founding of the Convent of Jesus*, says that the two bells were located in the church tower, the small one being rung only at certain hours and the large to attract the attention of the people of the city on the occasion of religious ceremonies and also to calm storms (chapter XXIX).
The second bell, which is the smaller, carries designs of flowers, fowl and ophidian together with the letters IHS on one side, and MARIA on the other side. The inscription around the mouth, which is now only partly legible, SERVIR: ADEU.....AR. ESTE, has been identified as SERVIR: ADEU: DO-

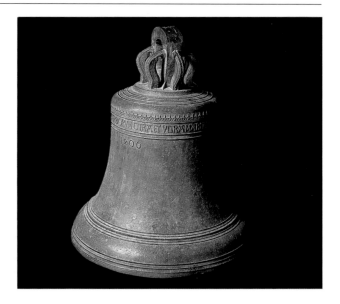

BRAR: ESTE (Serve God, ringing this bell).
The engineer João Botelho Moniz Borba, founder of the Setúbal Museum, believes that the small bell can be compared with that to be found in the Church of St. Mary at Sintra, whose inscriptions and motifs are similar although of

different dimensions. It has to be assumed, then, that both bells originated from the same workshop.
(*Fernando Antonio Baptista Pereira*)

9
Portugal

Fragment of stained glass,
1539
Stained glass,
22.9 x 13.6 x 0.3 cm
Coming from the large
window in the main chapel
of the Church of the
Convent of Jesus at Setúbal
Setúbal, Museu de
Setúbal-Convento de Jesús,
511
Exhibitions: Lisbon 1989;
Setúbal 1990
Bibliography: Borba 1975,
n. 1, p. 227 and n. 15;
Barros da Silva 1983; Pereira
1990, p. 43

This fragment formed part of
the stained glass in the large
window in the main chapel of
the Church of Jesus. It carries
the date 1539, this being the
year in which it was either
made or placed in the window. This is, therefore, one of
the pieces of stained glass
used in the Church after the
earthquake in 1531.
The glass would have been
paid for by João III and produced by Antonio Taca I. Active between 1529 and 1543,
Antonio Taca was the stepson
of the Flemish glassmaker
"Mestre João", who held the
post of master glassmaker at
Batalla Monastery. He would
later take his father's place,
and the family monopolised
this work until 1608. According to Antonio's contract he
would only work to attend to
the necessities of buildings
under royal patronage and
was thus employed on Alco-
baça Monastery and the
Church of Montemor-o-Novo,
on the Alentejo and anywhere
else determined by the king.
Taking into account the Renaissance nature of this piece
of glass and the royal protection of the Convent of Jesus
Gozava, it is not difficult to accept that this piece is from the
Church of Jesus, or that it belongs to one of Antonio Taca's
works, made under the pa-
tronage of D. João III.
(*Fernando Antonio Baptista
Pereira*)

10
Spain

Seville
Quimera, early 16th century
Glazed arris tile,
14 x 14 x 2.6 cm
Originating from the
Convent of Jesus at Setúbal
Setúbal, Museu de
Setúbal-Convento de Jesús,
531/Az 20
Bibliography: Meco 1985;
Pereira 1990, pp. 116-118;
Santos Simòes 1990

Throughout its five centuries of history the Convent of Jesus has accumulated various types of tile floor coverings, concluding a whole history of this sector of artistry in Portugal at the turn of the 15th and 17th centuries. Some of the most noteworthy are still to be found on the walls and floor surfaces for which they were originally conceived.

The most famous collection is, without doubt, that covering the walls of the false crypt over the main altar, the resting place of D. João Manuel and his brother D. Nuno Manuel, sons of the Convent's founder. Usually to be found in Lisbon's National Tile Museum, they were withdrawn not long ago for restoring and so that the walls on which they were placed could be sealed and reinforced and they will not be replaced until the restoration work is completed. This is an exceptional collection of Mudejar and Gothic patterns from around 1505, dominated by the arris technique and enriched by the well-known funereal epigraph (now mutilated) MEMENTO HOMO QUIA PULVIS EST ET IN PULVEREM REVERTERIS and by the Manuels' coat of arms. During the restoration work bird designs and that of a hare were discovered on the underside of the tiles, undoubtedly the work of apprentices and identical with those employed in the decoration of pottery by craftsmen in Seville.

The remains of the washroom floor in the Convent cloister are definitely from an slightly earlier date. Discovered dur-

ing excavations carried out at the beginning of the 1970s, these are Valencian "encadenal" tiles – knots and cables in blue on a white background – which formed an eight-pointed star whose contours were delineated in green and white clay, with the central octagon raised on two levels and defining the fountain. This is the most important group of Valencian tile work of its period still in place in Portugal, all of which leads to the belief that it was probably brought by Justa Rodriguez Pereira from her visit to Valencia (Gandía) to collect the Convent's founding nuns in 1496.

During the excavations refered to above, many fragments of a Mudejar pattern were discovered in the rubble of various halls in the Convent, these having been pro-

duced using the Sevillian and arris techniques and decorated with the geometric motifs of the Gothic pre-Renaissance period. From among these the rare "chimera" motif should be mentioned, made in Seville using the arris technique and displayed in the exhibition.
(*Fernando Antonio Baptista Pereira*)

11
Portugal

Processional Cross,
late 15th century
Rock crystal and silver gilt
silver, 53 x 20 cm
From the Cofradía de
Anunciada (Setúbal)
Setúbal, Museu de
Setúbal-Convento de Jesús,
360/0.20
Exhibitions: Setúbal, 1960;
Setúbal 1969; Antwerp 1991;
Setúbal, 1991
Bibliography: TAVARES DA
SILVA-PEREIRA 1989, p. 43;
PEREIRA 1990, p. 106

Processional Cross case,
late 15th century
Leather, 54.5 x 33 x 6.5 cm
Originates from the Cofradía
de Anunciada (Setúbal)
Inscriptions: SENHORA VIRGEM
SANTA MARIA LEBRATE DO TEU
DEVOTO NUNO GONCALVES
Setúbal, Museu de
Setúbal-Convento de Jesús.
420/0. 20-A
Exhibitions: Setúbal, 1990;
Gante, 1991
Bibliography: COUTO 1961,
n. 13. pp. 15-23; PEREIRA
1990, p. 106

Outstanding among the Setúbal Museum's rich collection
of jewellery is this beautiful
processional cross, which
originates from the Cofradía of
the Santa Casa de la Misericordia (Guild of the Holy
House of Mercy).
The cross is made from rock
crystal and silver gilt and dates
from the last quarter of the
15th century, coming to light
as a result of the pillaging of
the ancient Cofradía de la Anunciada, from which Justa Rodriguez Pereira bought the
land on which to build the
Convent of Jesus.
The cross is characterised by its
fine engraved decoration and
by the carved knot, from which
the motif of a rose (symbolizing
the Virgin) projects, and by the
two-coloured figure of Christ
crucified which complements
the crystalline transparency of
the rocky material, defining its
shape, slightly heightened by
silver gilt, and which is dec-

orated with geometric motifs .
The cross's typology dates back
to the 14th century and it is one
of the most important pieces of
jewellery of its day.
The case, made of leather and
wood, is of the same shape as
the cross which was offered in
it and on the inside there is an
inscription alluding to its donation. The pious donor
mentioned in the inscription,
Nuno Gonçalves, must have

been a chancellor at the court
of king João II who, as we
know, spent a great deal of
time in Setúbal.
The case consists of two boxes,
one inside the other, both made
of pieces of highly stiffened
leather sewn together. The
inner box contains a wooden
cross which was restored recently.
*(Fernando Antonio Baptista
Pereira)*

12
Germany

Simonius Grynaeus
Collinitium (Beringen,
Suabia, 1493-Basel, 1541)
Novus Orbis, 1532
Printed book, paper bound
in leather,
32.5 x 23 x 4.9 cm
Setúbal, Museu de
Setúbal-Convento de Jesús,
681 (García Pérez Library)
Bibliography: PEREIRA 1990

The Protestant theologian and German philologist Simonius Grynaeus was born in Beringen in 1493. He studied in Ptortzheim and Vienna and taught Greek in various cities of the empire before settling in Basilea in 1541. An enthusiast of the Reformation he was a friend of Melanchton, Luther and Calvin, although on equally good personal terms with humanists who did not adhere to Protestantism, such as Erasmus and Thomas More. He shared a taste for classics with the latter and the translation and editing of works by Plutarch, Aristotle, Plato and Ptolomy can be credited to him, as well as tributes to the disciplines of history and medicine. He was equally interested in the geographical discoveries of his times, compiling accounts of the journeys of Marco Polo, Cadamosto, Columbus, Vespucci and Pinzón among others in his *Novus Orbis*. This work, published in Basilea and Paris in 1532 and reprinted in 1535, 1537 and 1555, is considered to be the one of the first general histories of the voyages of discovery. The letter from king D. Manuel I to pope Leo XIII, dated Lisbon, June 8th 1513, which told of the conquests of Goa and Malaca in the East by armies commanded by Alfonso de Albuquerque is also transcribed in the volume.

The text of *Novus Orbis* starts with the introduction and verification, written by Sebastián Münster, of a strange engraved map signed by Orontius F. Delph and dated July 1531. Entitled *Nova et Integra*

Universi Orbus Descritio the map is in the shape of a flattened heart (*Ex centris proportione gemina cordis humanis formula in plano coextensam*) which represents the world as it was then known by geographers and hydrographers (*Juxta recentium Geographorum ac Hidrographorum mentem*). On the design on the globe Asia appears linked with North America and the latter is very incorrectly represented indeed. In fact, the designation "America" is drawn over South America and the area covered by this continent, the most recent discovery of another part of the world, is shown as being smaller than that of Antarctica. Other inaccuracies in the representation of the world are to be found, justifiably, in the Far East, far less recognisable to Europeans than other parts of the world at this time. On the other hand, it is clear that the designer has used Portuguese maps in the part referring to determined areas of Brazil, the West coast of Africa and the Orient, in which names given by the Portuguese to places appear in contrast to the Latin place names derived from early and later medieval descriptions or from versions of accounts of journeys used by compilers and map-makers.

This copy of the first edition which is on display belonged to the Portuguese delegate and doctor of Spanish origin, Domingo García Pérez, who bequeathed his priceless library to the Holy House of Mercy in Setúbal; it was then incorporated into the Convent of Jesus Museum in 1961.
(*Fernando Antonio Baptista Pereira*)

13
Flanders

Andrea Vesalius (Brussels, 1514-isle of Zante, 1564)
De Humani Corporis Fabrica, 16th century edition (1604?) of the 1543 *princeps*
Printed book, paper bound in leather,
30.5 x 23 x 4.9 cm
Setúbal, Museu de Setúbal-Convento de Jesús, 1404 (García Pérez Library)
Bibliography: GARRINSON 1926; PANOFSKY 1955; PREMUDA 1957; SINGER 1957; PEREIRA 1990

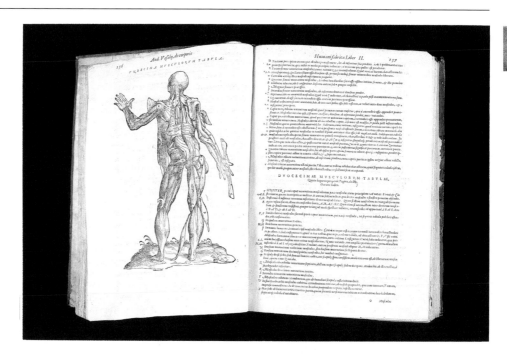

This is a copy of the fourth edition of the celebrated *Anatomia,* written by Andrea Vesalius (1514-1564), doctor to Carlos V and Felipe II of Spain. First published in Basilea in 1543, the work, whose original title was *De Humani Corporis Fabrica libri septem,* revolutionised the study of anatomy and opened a new chapter in the artistic study of the same. In that same year Copernicus' *De Revolutionibus Coelestis* was published in Nuremburg, which in its turn broke new ground in the field of astronomy.

Vesalius' *Fabrica* follows Galen's descriptive-anatomical system, with the division of physiology into three groups of systems: structural, corresponding to the skeleton (Book I), and to the ligaments and muscles (Book II); connectors, dealing with the veins and arteries (Book III), the nerves (Book IV), the impulses, referring to the nutritional organs, and procreation (Book V), the organs of the "vital facility", the heart and its neighbours (Book VI), and the organs of the "animal facility", the brain and senses (Book VII). The teaching of anatomy pioneered by this brilliant doctor was based on "free" knowledge or on discoveries made by the followers of the Galen tradition, using the dissection of human corps, direct observation and experimentation on live animals as basic methods by which to correct previous errors. In 1537 Vesalius became Professor of Anatomy in Venice at the invitation of the Venetian Senate, followed by similar posts in other cities such as Pisa, Bolonia and Basilea.

Vesalius' work was the first to show anatomical illustration in its prime, clearly surpassing the tradition immediately prior to its publication, which was represented in works by Mondino de' Liucci, Pietro d'Albano, Berengario de Carpi and G.B. Canano. The illustrations in the latter's work were drawn by Girolamo da Carpi, once a disciple of Dosso Dossi, and initiated Vesalius' interest in having first class artistic collaboration on his own work. This attitude vouches for a change of mentality in the process of the acquisition of knowledge: according to what was written in the preface to his work Vesalius wanted students of anatomy to learn through direct contact with the human body but he trusted implicitly in the power of the image as a decisive contribution to learning. "Do not the images before our eyes conjure up the object in a more exact way than the most explicit speech?" concluded the illustrious doctor, thus putting at the service of scientific discourse (as a visual artificial memory) the graphic tools perfected in the workshops of the Renaissance.

Vesalius' *Anatomia* contains more than three hundred engravings in wood credited to artists of great talent. Today we do not question the fact that one of the authors was the Dutch artist, resident in Venice, Jan Stefan von Kalkar, designer of the six *Tabulae Anatomicae* which Vesalius had published in the city of the Doges in 1538. Certain studies suggested the hypothesis that the great painter Titian, who produced wood engravings between 1508 and 1568 may have participated in the task, but the scanty evidence accumulated indicates that the group of artists working with Kalkar under Vesalius' supervision were Venetians. Under whoever's authority the exceptional engravings in the *Anatomia* were produced, Vesalian iconography sought to dramatise the structures and functions of the human body, not only as an aesthetic symbol but also in a pedagogic sense, and it was this which provided the basis for his fame.

The Venetian edition has a different cover to that of the first. The anatomical theatre full of students, before whom Vesalius is portrayed displaying a corpse and a skeleton, which occupied the whole cover of the Basilean edition is substituted here by an architectural structure in whose niches images alluding to various anatomical themes can be seen, with the central niche filled by a scene in which the figure of the celebrated doctor is seen teaching a small assembly of sages about a corpse; beneath this there is a table of medical and surgical instruments. The garlands and wreaths of flowers that habitually graced this type of mannerist cover have been replaced by anatomical elements.

The copy on display belongs, like the work of S. Grynaeus, to the illustrious doctor, delegate and bibliophile Domingo García Pérez, who bequeathed his priceless library to the Holy House of Mercy, Setúbal, after which it was installed in the Convent of Jesus and then became part of the museum established there after 1961.

(*Fernando Antonio Baptista Pereira*)

14
Portugal

Quentin Metsys (Louvain, 1466-Antwerp, 1530)
An Angel Appears to Saint Clare, Saint Agnes and Saint Colette, between 1497 and 1507
From the high choir in the Church of Jesus at Setúbal.
painting, Oil on oak panel
Setúbal, Museu de Setúbal-Convento de Jesús, 1/PR 1
Exhibitions: Antwerp, 1960; Setúbal 1960; Setúbal, 1969; Lisbon, 1983; Setúbal, 1990
Bibliography: REIS SANTOS 1958, II, n. 12; COUTO 1961, I, n. 163; MARKL-PEREIRA 1986; PEREIRA 1990

The theme of this beautiful painting, which Luis Reis Santos attributes to the painter Quentin Metsys, appears to have been highly appreciated in more than one of the convents of the Order of Saint Clare. The nuns of the Convent at Setúbal, to whom queen Leonor presented the painting in 1517 or 1518, asked for it to be reproduced so it could be hung in the reredos of the high altar. The nuns of the Monastery of the Madre de Deus in Lisbon then received a replica of the picture from the same generous donor, this one probably done by a disciple of Metsys, Eduardo el Portugués, which is now in the Museum of Art in the Portuguese capital. The scene is portrayed with typical serenity in the painting which was executed in Louvain's reredos period, and the soft chromatism which would characterise production immediately afterwards is evident. The Archangel Gabriel crowns the virtues of the three principal figures of the Order of Saint Clare, who are seen coming out of the convent with their respective attributes: Saint Agnes' abbess's staff, the stick with which Saint Clare raised the siege of Assisi and the book of Rules reformed by Saint Colette. These ideas, which nuns of the Order had to have present in their lives, became very

popular at that time. The building represented in the painting, through whose half-open door the curious multicoloured statue of St. Bartholomew is visible is, according to Reis Santos, characteristic of Louvain architecture.

Quentin Metsys was born in Louvain in 1465 and died in Antwerp in 1530. He was certainly Antwerp's best painter, the Bruges school at that time declining in favour of that of Antwerp. He received his training in Louvain, probably at the hands of Dirck Bouts, but from 1491 he was to be found in Antwerp registered in the Association of Saint Luke. The paintings which can be attributed with certainty to Metsys' Louvain period of activity reveal not only Memling's touch but the opening of the painter to Italian influences, especially that of Da Vinci, who was then unknown to Flemish painters. Between 1507 and 1509 he executed and signed the monumental triptych of the *Life of St. Anne,* now in the Museum of Art in Brussels, in which the contradiction between the staticism of the religious figure and Italian narrative appear definitively resolved, thanks to the adoption of humanist time – space. From the stylistic point of view the work is characterised by the use of light, delicately graduated chromatism and by marked novelties in the structure of the compositions from diagonals and the abandonment of the "Gothic" treatment of the clothes. Between 1508 and 1511 Metsys produced his second great triptych, now in Antwerp Museum, whose central panel is dedicated to the *Resignation in the Tomb,* while those on either side show the life and martyrdom of Saint John the Baptist and St. John the Evangelist. In this painting Metsys achieves a masterly synthesis of the contributions of the great fourteenth century Flemish painters and Renaissance classicism.

In the same period he would produce *The Rejoicing of the Virgin* for the Monastery of the

Madre de Deus in Lisbon, today dispersed throughout various museums in the world, in which the landscape in the background reveals his connection with "Patenier", with whom he would later produce the celebrated panel *The Temptation of Saint Anthony,* now in the Museo del Prado in Madrid. The social and artistic prestige enjoyed by Metsys in Antwerp attracted other painters to the city, from both northern and southern Europe, who were interested in getting to know his work and then became his disciples, like Eduardo el Portugués. The artist also played a very important role as a catalyst in the definition of the paths towards the artistic evolution of Flemish painting, then besieged by the Italianising taste of the Romanists.

(*Fernando Antonio Baptista Pereira*)

15
Portugal

*The Great Altarpiece
from the Church
of the Convent of Jesus*

Setúbal did not have its own studio workshops in the first half of the 16th century and was not able to deal with such an important royal commission, for which reason, at the beginning of the third decade of the 16th century, the royal protectors of the monastery of Jesus, the building of which had been completed, as we have seen, round about 1505, turned to the studios of Lisbon. It is in this context that the fourteen remarkable, large oil paintings on oak wood have to be understood; these make up the great altarpiece of the great chapel and are unanimously considered to be one of the major works of the Portugese Renaissance. The Renaissance painting produced in the studios of Lisbon was centered around certain well-known artists who have been identified in the course of this century: in the first generation we find the Flemish painter Francisco Henriques (who died prematurely in 1518) and the anonymous masters of 1515 (Jorge Afonso, according to most authors), de Laurinhâ (probably responsible for the introduction of the Renaissance aesthetic into the Lisbon school) and de Santa Auta (already influenced by some mannerist innovations) in the second generation, we find Gregorio Lopes, Jorge Lea, Cristovão de Figueiredo and García Fernandes, painters who often worked together as a "parcería" (company). Regarding the first generation, the body of work ascribed to the Master of 1515 (Jorge Afonso) shows great technical purity in its execution, a balanced composition, brilliant colouring, refinement in the transposition of the costume and decoration, anatomic correctness, and at the same time, a marked connection with the Flemish iconographical models. We are dealing with a painting whose

origins lie in a cosmopolitan centre distinguished by the splendour of a court which had converted it into a stage whereupon it could display its power, both civil and religious. It is also a painting sensitive to the values of the Nordic Renaissance (in its presentation of landscapes, in its spatial perspective) not that it ignores the achievements of Italian art (with its humanist space-time concentration, its human scale, in the serene, clear and quiet atmosphere in which the themes are laid out) and which, even more, knows how to blend these contributions into a synthesis which could well be considered, as the Portuguese historian Adriano Gusmão has pointed out, as "one of the roots of the family tree of old Portuguese painting."

The old altarpiece of the Church of Jesus in Setúbal was made, presumably, between 1519 and 1530. It was the result of a commission from queen Doña Leonor, widow of Don João II and sister of Don Manuel I, as is shown by the painting *An Angel appears to Saint Clare, Saint Agnes and Saint Colette*, in which the well known emblem of the queen is clearly visible at each side of the escutcheon with their coats of arms which end at the church portico, which can be seen at the back, to the left. The altarpiece, apparently, was completed after the queen's death (1525), but under a different patron (probably the duke of Coimbra, Don Jorge, bastard son of Don João II, if the presence of a scallop in the tympanum of the portico that can be seen in the middleground of the *Annunciation* is an allusion to the intervention of the Master of the Order of Santiago). On the other hand, the *An Angel appears to Saint Clare, Saint Agnes and Saint Colette* is almost a replica of that painting by the Flemish school ascribed by Luis Reis Santos to Quentin Metsys (1466-1530), which had come to the monastery (with other Northern works of art donated by Doña

Leonor, who in her turn had received them from her cousin Maximiliano de Austria) around 1517-1519, which is the latest possible date, as far as we know, for the execution of the altarpiece. It is possible that under the direction of Jorge Afonso, court painter of D. Manuel I and João III, the three principal masters of the following generation who had worked together more than once, in partnership (Cristovão de Figueiredo, Gregório Lopes and Garcia Fernandes) had a hand in its execution. This altarpiece – twin of the altarpiece of the monastery of la Madre de Dios, in Lisbon (completed around 1515), due to its commission, to its various formal and iconographical solutions and even to certain, historical vicissitudes (like for example, the significance of some censored overpainting, visible in the canvases of both altarpieces and done during the Philipian period) represents the highest point of Jorge Afonso's studio. The court painter of D. Manuel I and his successor D. III, Jorge Afonso was the head of a prestigious studio whose activity extends from 1504 until around 1540, the year in which he died. Excluding participations, and bearing in mind the positions occupied, the rewards he received and the commissions of which we have knowledge, we can ascribe to Jorge Afonso a significant body of work in which the aforementioned altarpieces of la Madre de Dios and Setúbal are to be found despite the lack, even today, of sufficient information to correctly identify all his work. The reconstruction of the altarpiece of the Church of Jesus is very simple, as long as the adopted iconographical meaning is considered as a narrative, that is as a base for the creation of self-contained episodes that follow the rules of humanistic time/space, making it possible to read three "stories"; the series of the *Passion of Christ* in the upper row, in the centre, the *Calvary*; immediately below, the series of the *Infancy of Jesus* or of the *Joys of the Virgin*, in the centre the *Assumption* (a canvas of similar dimensions to the *Calvary*), and finally, the series of the *Saintly Franciscans*, which leaves a space for the tabernacle in the centre. Taking into account the iconographical programme and the dimensions of the altarpiece, it is possible to speculate about its recomposition in the great chapel of the Church of Jesus, taking as an example the only large Portuguese altarpiece of the period which survived in its original setting – that of the cathedral of Funchal. To adapt it better to the structure of the apse, the vertical courses would have to form an angle of 140 with the three central courses (as they do in the Funchal). The unit was covered by a sort of overhang as well as by beautiful frames in the gothic-emmanueline style, with Renaissance motifs already present. It was kept like this until the beginning of the 18th century, when it was dismantled and the paintings scattered over the walls of the naves of the church. In this exhibition it is presented, for the first time since this date, in its original composition. In reality, only the series of the *Passion* presents a perfect narrative sequence: that of the *Road to Calvary, the Descent* and the *Resurrection*. If the *Christ and Veronica* follows current Northern models, accessible through engravings (or even at first hand, through the painting of the German school to be found in the Convent of Jesus: the altarpiece of the Passion of the Cologne school, now in the National Museum of Ancient Art, in Lisbon); however, the subject of the composition *Crucifixion of Christ* could have been suggested by an engraving of the *Legend and Passions of the Holy Martyrs*, published in Lisbon in 1518. In these two paintings the representation of the faces of the warders and the executioners of Christ is reminiscent of the physiognomic deformation of a Metsys. In the *Calvary*, the dual construction of the composition underlines the profound dramatic nature of the scene. During the reign of Felipe I of Portugal (II of Cas-

tilla), this painting was subjected to an important reworking of the group around the Virgin, who has fainted in the arms of the armed apostle, placing the Mother of God, tearful but erect, between one of the holy women, and having the figure of Saint John cover up the representation of Jerusalem in the background. The censorship carried out (identified by a chronicler of the convent as the "reform of the altarpieces" ordered during the reign of the first Castilian monarchs to govern Portugal) seem to have adapted the subject of the picture to the dictates of the Counter-reformation, which preferred a visual interpretation that followed Scripture more closely: *Stabat Mater, dolorosa, juxta crucem lacrimosa*. After laboratory studies, the overpainting was removed in 1939, thus revealing the painting in its original condition. In the canvases *Descent* and *Resurrection* several details enabled indications of heterodox deviations with respect to the dogmas of Christianity to be detected a few years ago, which the variability of the textual and iconographical sources of the period justified in part. In the first example, the gesture of Saint John when he turns his nose away before the dead body of Christ, which shows signs of decomposition (representation of the macabre was one of the most frequent subjects at the end of the Middle Ages and of the Renaissance), in the second panel the representation of the body of Christ is continued, ethereal as it rises in front of his closed tomb; both examples carry echoes of the Docetist heresy, which considered the body of Christ to have been on loan and, as such, perishable. It is still curious that such details (scarcely visible, given the considerable height at which they were to be found in the great chapel of the church) had escaped the censor – a reformer who, as we have seen, at the height of the Philipian period, ordered the repainting of the

motif of the Virgin fainting on Calvary (as was the case with one of the canvases of the altarpiece of the Mother of God). The *Infancy of Jesus* and *Life of the Virgin* series similarly present a narrative sequence for the *Nativity, Annunciation,* and *Presentation of the Child in the Temple* cycles, broken only by the *Assumption*, making the latter a more explicit celebration of the Virgin's *mysterious joys*. On the other hand, this is the one which shows the most similarity to the panels on the same themes from the altarpiece of the Mother of God; the analogy between the architectural styles, the backgrounds (Renaissance in the two panels of the *Annunciation*, emmanueline in the *Presentation of the Child in the Temple* or in *Saint Francis delivering the Statutes* from the Mother of God); the interest in including everyday objects (the jewels in the canvases of the *Adoration of the Magi*, the little oven in the Nativity or the egg basket in the *Adoration of the Shepherds* from the Lisbon altarpiece; the rush mats of the two *Annunciation* panels), the treatment of costumes and face masks (especially in the two canvases of the *Assumption*, both very similar to each other). The differences to be found tend to enrich the formal repertoire (the device of the *Drap d'honneur*, a greater naturalness in the representation of landscape, an adoption of architectural backgrounds which show greater and greater Renaissance tendencies without rejecting a gothic-emmanueline influence in certain backgrounds in the Franciscan series) which created a stylistic revolution, so mature and homogenous does the "style" of the studio where the two altarpieces were made appear to us. In the *Adoration of the Magi* the group of the pages (one of the most pronouncedly Italian of the subjects of the altarpiece, full of Raphaelesque suggestions in the poses, and of a Giorgionesque feeling of colour) represent the three areas of the Old World

through a curious device of a dialogue between two Europeans, a black man, and a Hindu. The main interest of the Franciscan series does not lie so much in the novelty of its thematic autonomy – already present through other models in the altarpiece of San Francisco de Evora, around 1503-1508 – as in the way in which it combined certain imported iconographical models (the representation of Saint Anthony, the appearance of the angel before the Holy Clarissas or the Stigmatisation of Saint Francis of Assisi) with the sensitivity of the Portuguese of the time to the movement, expression and vibration of colour, as well as a conscious rigorousness when dealing with such a typically Portuguese subject as *The Holy Martyrs of Morocco*. As there is no narrative sequence to give a natural order to the canvases, this series, composed of paintings slightly inferior to the lesser of the other two series, causes compositional problems with the distribution of the paintings and with the organization of the four vertical lines which flank the central axis. Whereas the panels of the *Apparition of the Angel before the Holy Clarissas* and of the *Stigmatisation of Saint Francis of Assisi*, were joined at the centre, as their compositional structure required, the representation of the *Holy Martyrs of Morocco* and of the *Saint Buenaventura, Saint Anthony* and *Saint Bernard of Siena* trio, would form the sides of the *Resurrection* and *Presentation in the Temple* and of the *Road to Calvary* and of the *Annunciation*, given the iconographical relations which can be established between each of these themes. The altarpiece of the church of the Monastery of Jesus, in Setúbal, is an almost limitless source of formal iconological and sociological readings, and thus shows itself to be a first class example of the art that was being created in Portugal at the time of the Discoveries.

(Fernando Antonio Baptista Pereira)

15A
Portugal

Jorge Afonso's studio
(approx. 1508-1540)
*Saint Buenaventura, Saint
Anthony and Saint Bernard
of Siena*, approx. 1520-1530
Oil painting on oakwood
panel, 178.5 x 110 cm
Panel from the great
altarpiece from the Church
of the Convent of Jesús
de Setúbal
Setúbal, Museo de
Setúbal-Convento de Jesús,
13/PR. 13
Exhibitions: Lisbon, 1940;
Setúbal, 1960; Setúbal 1969;
Lisbon and Abrantes, 1971;
Setúbal, 1990
Bibliography: Couto 1938,
IV; Reis Santos 1943, pp.
147-155; Viera Santos 1955;
Reis Santos 1960; Reis Santos
1966; Barbosa-Pereira 1984,
n. 2; Pereira 1985, I, pp.
29-38; Markl-Pereira 1986,
IV; Pereira 1989; Pereira 1990

The beginning of the altarpiece's lower edge evokes

these three saints and is decisive in establishing a parallel
with sacred history, illustrated
in the upper rows, and the
glorification of the Franciscan
order, to which the convent belonged. Saint Buenaventura,
the great theologian of the
Franciscans, is shown here
holding a staff, wrapped in a
monumental raincape, which is
treated as if it were a reredos in
its own right, with a succession
of Christ figures, of the Virgin
with the Christ Child, with Jesus
and the saints in the centre, and
the Portuguese Saint Anthony,
the great preacher of divine
love, depicted according to the
iconographical traidtion of
Northern Europe; finally, Saint
Bernard of Siena, with the three
plans that he renounced for
love of humility at his feet,
points at the heavens, where
the name of Jesus appears (JHS),
he being the main instigator of
devotion to Jesus, a devotion to
which the convent is dedicated.
(*Fernando Antonio Baptista
Pereira*)

15B
Portugal

Jorge Afonso's studio
(approx. 1508-1540)
*Apparition of an Angel
before Saint Claire, Saint
Ines and Saint Coleta*,
approx. 1520-1530
Oil painting on oakwood
panel, 153 x 93.5 cm
Panel from the great
altarpiece of the Church
of the Convent of Jesús
de Setúbal
Setúbal, Museu de
Setúbal-Convento de Jesús,
12/PR 12
Exhibitions: Lisbon, 1940;
Setúbal, 1960; Antwerp,
1960; Setúbal, 1969; Lisbon
and Abrantes, 1971; Lisbon,
1983; Setúbal, 1990;
Amberes, 1991
Bibliography: Couto 1938,
IV; Reis Santos 1943, pp.
147-155; Vieira Santos 1955;
Reis Santos 1960; Reis Santos
1966; Barbosa-Pereira 1984,
n. 2; Pereira 1985, I, pp.
29-38; Markl-Pereira 1986,

VI; Pereira 1989; Pereira 1990

This panel is an almost exect
replica of the painting ascribed to Metsys which may
also be seen in this exhibition.
It was probably ordered by
the nuns of the Convent of
Jesus of the Portuguese
painters who made the altarpiece. In it the Portuguese
masters followed the iconographical style of the Flemish
master but introduced some
innovations as regards the
representation of gesture, colour range, and the disguised
symbolism (of the painted
flower or of the lizard which
"spies on" the virtuous saints).
On the left, above the portico
of the gothic-emmanueline
church to be seen at the back,
a little shield with the queen's
coat-of-arms can be made out,
flanked by symbolic shrimp
nets, which indicate who was
responsible for the original
commissioning of the altarpiece. (*Fernando Antonio
Baptista Pereira*)

15C
Portugal

Jorge Afonso's studio
(approx. 1508-1540)
Stigmatisation of Saint Francis of Assisi,
approx, 1520-1530
Oil painting on oakwood panel, 177 x 109 cm
Panel from the great altarpiece of the Church of the Convent of Jesús de Setúbal
Setúbal, Museu de Setúbal-Convento de Jesús, 14/PR 14
Exhibitions: Lisbon, 1940; Setúbal, 1960; Setúbal, 1969; Lisbon and Abrantes, 1971; Setúbal, 1990.
Bibliography: Couto 1938, IV; Reis Santos 1943, pp. 147-155; Vieira Santos 1955; Reis Santos 1966; Barbosa-Pereira 1984, n. 2; Pereira 1985, I, pp. 29-38; Markl-Pereira 1986, VI; Pereira 1989; Pereira 1990

The scene represents the mountain where Saint Francis, kneeling in front of an open book, receives the stigmas with which Jesus Christ rewarded his dedication and preaching of God's word. In the foreground, below, various botanical species are represented with great exactness, which reminds one of the scientific interest revealed by the paintings of Durero. Behind Saint Francis, Friar Léon, asleep, appears to be unaffected by the mystery, as does the Franciscan community visible in the background, next to the coenobium, represented by a late gothic architectural style which already has the simple and delicate forms and layout of the convent of Jesus.
(*Fernando Antonio Baptista Pereira*)

15D
Portugal

Jorge Afonso's studio
(approx. 1508-1540)
The Holy Martyrs of Morocco, approx. 1520-1530
Oil painting on oakwood panel, 180 x 110 cm
Panel from the great altarpiece of the Church of the Convent of Jesús de Setúbal
Setúbal, Museu de Setúbal-Convento de Jesús, 15/PR 15
Exhibitions: Lisbon, 1940; Setúbal, 1960; Setúbal, 1969; Lisbon and Abrantes, 1971; Setúbal, 1990
Bibliography: Couto 1938, IV; Reis Santos 1943, pp. 147-155; Vieira Santos 1955; Reis Santos 1960; Reis Santos 1966; Barbosa-Pereira 1984, n. 2; Pereira 1985, I, pp. 29-38; Markl-Pereira 1986, VI; Pereira 1989; Pereira 1990

This subject could not be left out of an altarpiece made for a Franciscan convent whose history was so closely linked to the discoveries and which had been financed by the Madeira sugar company. The monastery had Friar Henrique de Coimbra as its head confessor; the latter gave the first mass in Brasil, in the course of the expedition led by Pedro Alvares Cabral, and was later ordained as the Bishop of Ceuta. The picture of *The Martyrs of Morocco* tried to strengthen the idea that it was necessary to fight the enemies of the Christian faith and of the conversion of the people, to the bitter end. In the composition the gesture of sacrifice of the five Franciscan friars is framed within a symbolic triangle marked out by their executioners. Among the figures represented, the Miramolim stands out, as he grasps a scepter and prepares to strike, a gesture imitated by the Moor opposite.
(*Fernando Antonio Baptista Pereira*)

15E
Portugal

Jorge Afonso's studio
(approx. 1508-1540)
Annunciation,
approx. 1520-1530
Oil painting on oakwood
panel, 196 x 109 cm
Panel from the great
altarpiece of the Church
of the Convent of Jesús de
Setúbal
Setúbal, Museu de
Setúbal-Convento de Jesús,
2/PR 2
Exhibitions: Lisbon, 1940;
Setúbal, 1960; Setúbal, 1969;
Lisbon and Abrantes, 1971;
Lisbon, 1983; Setúbal, 1990
Bibliography: Couto 1938,
IV; Reis Santos 1943,
pp. 147-155; Vieira Santos
1955; Reis Santos 1960; Reis
Santos 1966; Barbosa-Pereira
1984, n. 2; Pereira 1985, I,
pp. 29-38; Markl-Pereira
1986, VI; Pereira 1989;
Pereira 1990

The angel, sent by God, surprises the Virgin in a private place, which the painters have depicted as a contemporary palatial interior: the "chamber", with a canopy bed and an arch below the window; the "antechamber", a transitional space furnished only with the *Drap d'honneur* which frames the Mother of God symbolically; and finally the "triplechamber" in the foreground, in which the Virgin reads next to a little bench, on a imported from the Congo. The architecture shown reflects the cross between the emmanueline and Renaissance styles which was popular at the time this painting was made.
(*Fernando Antonio Baptista Pereira*)

15F
Portugal

Jorge Afonso's studio
(approx. 1508-1540)
Nativity, approx. 1520-1530
Oil painting oil on oakwood
panel, 196.5 x 108 cm
Panel from the great
altarpiece of the Church
of the Convent of Jesús
de Setúbal
Setúbal, Museu de
Setúbal-Convento de Jesús,
3/PR 3
Exhibitions: Lisbon, 1940;
Setúbal, 1960; Setúbal, 1969;
Lisbon and Abrantes, 1971;
Setúbal, 1990
Bibliography: Couto 1938,
IV; Reis Santos 1943, pp.
147-155; Vieira Santos 1955;
Reis Santos 1960; Reis Santos
1966; Barbosa-Pereira 1984,
n. 2; Pereira 1985, I, pp.
29-38; Markl-Pereira 1986,
VI; Pereira 1989; Pereira 1990

In a setting of ruined architecture with emmanueline and Renaissance influences, the scene represents the Holy Family and the angels adoring the Christ Child in the Nativity. In the foreground, a little oven, a bowl and a spoon remind us of the everyday objects of the 16th century, whereas in the background the painter has depicted the traditional animals: the ox and the mule. In the background, a gentle landscape illuminated by the morning light, an angel announces the birth of the Christ Child to the shepherds. It is curious to notice that, a few years earlier, on the altarpiece of the church of the Mother of God of Lisbon (also present in the exhibition), Jorge Alfonso's studio introduced, for the first time in Portuguese painting, the episode of the Adoration of the Shepherds, which he did not want to deal with here so as not to make demands on the iconographical norms of the time.
(*Fernando Antonio Baptista Pereira*)

15G
Portugal

Jorge Afonso's studio (approx. 1508-1540)
Adoration of the Magi, approx. 1520-1530
Oil painting on oakwood panel, 195.5 x 109 cm
Panel from the great altarpiece of the Church of the Convent of Jesús de Setúbal
Setúbal, Museu de Setúbal-Convento de Jesús, 4/PR 4
Exhibitions: Lisbon, 1940; Setúbal, 1960; Setúbal, 1969; Lisbon and Abrantes, 1971; Lisboa, 1983; Setúbal, 1990
Bibliography: Couto 1938, IV; Reis Santos 1943, pp. 147-155; Vieira Santos 1955; Reis Santos 1960; Reis Santos 1966; Barbosa-Pereira 1984, n. 2; Pereira 1985, I, pp. 29-38; Markl-Pereira 1986, VI; Pereira 1989; Pereira 1990

Part of the *Joys of the Virgin* series, this panel once more reveals his studio's taste for showing off the courtly fashions of its time, a clear sign of the cosmopolitan atmosphere in which it functioned. It is obvious in the representation of the three Magi, who symbolize the three Ages of Man – youth, maturity and old age – where the painters seize their chance to divert themselves with some depictions of sacred jewellery. The group formed by the Magis's pages to the right of the composition, is where Italian influences are most obvious, in the Raphealesque poses and a Giorgonesque feeling of colour. At the same time the painting becomes a window onto the world, alluding to different parts of the world, through figures who are adoring the Christ Child.
(*Fernando Antonio Baptista Pereira*)

15H
Portugal

Jorge Afonso's studio (approx. 1508-1540)
Presentation of Jesus in the Temple, approx. 1520-1530
Oil painting on oakwood panel, 194.5 x 109 cm
Panel from the great altarpiece of the Church of the Convent of Jesús de Setúbal
Setúbal, Museu de Setúbal-Convento de Jesús, 5/PR 5
Exhibitions: Lisbon, 1940; Setúbal, 1960; Setúbal, 1969; Lisbon and Abrantes, 1971; Setúbal, 1990
Bibliography: Couto 1938, IV; Reis Santos 1943, pp. 147-155; Vieira Santos 1955; Reis Santos 1960; Reis Santos 1966; Barbosa-Pereira 1984, n. 2; Pereira 1985, I, pp. 29-38; Markl-Pereira 1986, VI; Pereira 1989; Pereira 1990

This panel is a beautiful illustration of the episode described by Saint Luke (II:22-35). The scene shows obvious emmanueline influences (the window of the great chapel could have been inspired by the church of Jesus itself). In the foreground, Simon takes the Christ Child's arms as he says the *Nunc dimittis* which foretells his Passion; the Virgin next to Saint Joseph, who accepts the offering demanded by the Hebrew tradition, is shown weeping as she is in the Calvary; in the background, above the altar, two angels form the wedding arch, which the Christ Child came to renew, and which is represented as an arch of Gothic jewellery.
(*Fernando Antonio Baptista Pereira*)

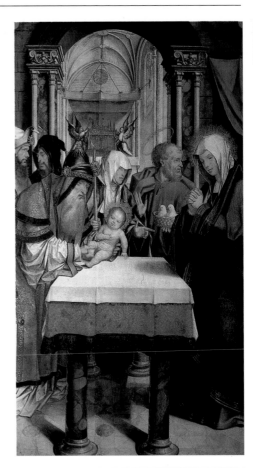

15I
Portugal

Jorge Afonso's studio
(approx. 1508-1540)
Christ and Veronica,
approx. 1520-1530
Oil painting on oakwood
panel, 196 x 110 cm
Panel from the great
altarpiece of the Church
of the Convent of Jesús
de Setúbal
Setúbal, Museu de
Setúbal-Convento de Jesús,
8/PR 8
Exhibitions: Sevilla, 1929;
Lisbon, 1940; Setúbal, 1960;
Setúbal, 1969; Lisbon and
Abrantes, 1971; Setúbal,
1990
Bibliography: Couto 1938,
IV; Reis Santos 1943,
pp. 147-155; Vieira Santos
1955; Reis Santos 1960; Reis
Santos 1966; Barbosa-Pereira
1984, n. 2; Pereira 1985, I,
pp. 29-38; Markl-Pereira
1986, VI; Pereira 1989;
Pereira 1990

The Passion series begins on

this altarpiece with the walk
along the road to Calvary,
where Christ meets Veronica.
Inspired by an engraving of
Martin Schongauer, in this
composition, the painter syn-
thesised various aspects of this
episode: Simon the Cyrenian,
painted in portrait-fashion
(was a patron being invoked?)
helps Christ during his short
rest by cleaning his face with
the cloth that is handed over
by Veronica, who is dressed in
the fashion of the court.
(*Fernando Antonio Baptista
Pereira*)

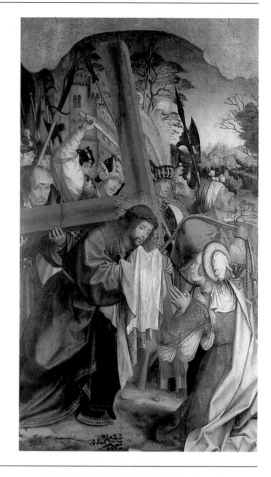

15J
Portugal

Jorge Afonso's studio
(approx. 1508-1540)
Christ nailed on the Cross,
approx. 1520-1530
Oil painting on oakwood
panel, 195 x 109 cm
Panel from the great
altarpiece of the Church
of the Convent of Jesús
de Setúbal
Setúbal, Museu de
Setúbal-Convento de Jesús,
9/PR 9
Exhibitions: Lisbon, 1940;
Setúbal, 1960; Setúbal, 1969;
Lisbon and Abrantes, 1971;
Setúbal, 1990
Bibliography: Couto 1938,
Reis Santos 1943, pp.
147-155; Vieira Santos 1955;
Reis Santos 1960; Reis Santos
1966; Barbosa Perreira 1984,
n. 2; Pereira 1985, I., p.
29-38; Markl-Pereira 1986, VI
Pereira 1989; Pereira 1990

The composition is dominated
by the beautiful fore-
shortening of the naked body

of Christ, whose suffering,
made obvious by the stigmas
which mark his body, is in
contrast with the serenity of
his face. It is underlined by the
deformed physiognomies of
the executioners and by the
blood which runs down from
the cross and soaks the very
land as well as by the arms
traced in the sky. This theme,
which originated in Northern
Europe, may have been in-
spired by an engraving in the
*Legend and Passions of the
Holy Martyrs,* published in Lisbon in 1518, and lies behind
one of the most important
paintings on this altarpiece.
(*Fernando Antonio Baptista
Pereira*)

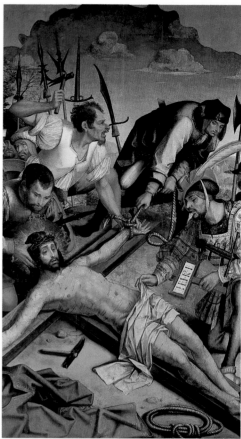

15K
Portugal

Jorge Afonso's studio
(approx. 1508-1540)
Deposition,
approx. 1520-1530
Oil painting on oakwood
panel, 196.5 x 109 cm
Panel from the great
altarpiece of the Church
of the Convent of Jesús
de Setúbal
Setúbal, Museu de
Setúbal-Convento de Jesús,
10/PR 10
Exhibitions: Lisbon, 1940;
Setúbal, 1960; Setúbal, 1969;
Lisbon and Abrantes, 1971;
Setúbal, 1990
Bibliography: Couto 1938,
IV; Reis Santos 1943,
pp. 147-155; Vieira Santos
1955; Reis Santos 1960; Reis
Santos 1966; Barbosa Pereira
1984, n. 2; Pereira 1985, I,
pp. 29-38; Markl-Pereira
1986, VI; Pereira 1989;
Pereira 1990

Next to the foot of the de-
cidedly upright cross, and in
the background Joseph of
Arithmea and Nicodemus
holding the body of Christ are
shown. Christ's face shows
evident signs of decomposition – a taste for the macabre
was common at the end of the
Middle Age – which accounts
for the gestures made by Saint
John and the holy women.
(*Fernando Antonio Baptista
Pereira*)

103

15L
Portugal

Jorge Afonso's studio
(approx. 1508-1540)
Resurrection,
approx. 1520-1530
Oil painting on oakwood
panel, 194.5 x 109 cm
Panel from the great
altarpiece of the Church
of the Convent of Jesús
de Setúbal
Setúbal, Museu de
Setúbal-Convento de Jesús,
11/PR 11
Exhibitions: Lisbon, 1940;
Setúbal, 1960; Setúbal, 1969;
Lisbon and Abrantes, 1971;
Setúbal, 1990
Bibliography: Couto 1938,
IV; Reis Santos 1943,
pp. 147-155; Vieira Santos
1955; Reis Santos 1960; Reis
Santos 1966; Barbosa-Pereira
1984, n. 2; Pereira 1985, I,
pp. 29-38; Markl-Pereira
1986, VI; Pereira 1989;
Pereira 1990

The figure of Christ rises up in
front of the closed burial
mound. His body is outlined
by the morning light. Far
away, in front of a depiction
of Jerusalem, similar to the
painting of Calvary on the
same altarpiece, the Angel
predicts the Resurrection to
the holy women. In the reading of the sequences that this
panel establishes, with that of
the *Deposition* in which Saint
John holds his nose in front of
the dead body of Christ,
which shows obvious signs of
decomposition, one recog-
nized, a few years ago, echoes
of the Docetist heresy, which
considered the body of Christ
to be a man's body and therefore perishable.
(*Fernando Antonio Baptista
Pereira*)

15M
Portugal

Jorge Afonso's studio
(approx. 1508-1540)
Assumption of the Virgin,
approx. 1520-1530
Oil painting on oakwood
panel, 255 x 156 cm
Panel from the great
altarpiece of the Church
of the Convent of Jesús
de Setúbal
Setúbal, Museu de
Setúbal-Convento de Jesús,
6/PR 6
Exhibitions: Lisbon, 1940;
Setúbal, 1960; Setúbal, 1969;
Lisbon and Abrantes, 1971;
Setúbal, 1990
Bibliography: Couto 1938,
IV; Reis Santos 1943,
pp. 147-155; Vieira Santos
1955; Reis Santos 1960; Reis
Santos 1966; Barbosa-Pereira
1984, n. 2; Pereira 1985, I,
pp. 29-38; Markl-Pereira
1986, VI; Pereira 1989;
Pereira 1990

The subject represented on
this panel is one of the Fran-

ciscan's basic iconographical
motifs. The scene takes place
in a golden yellow setting
which envelops the Virgin as
she ascends towards the Eternal Father. She is surrounded
by a group of angels playing
the wind instruments in use at
that time. In the lower part of
the painting an excellent gallery of portraits is shown.
These are considered to be a
fine example of the outstanding quality of Portuguese
painting in the first half of the
16th century.
(*Fernando Antonio Baptista
Pereira*)

104

15N
Portugal

Jorge Afonso's studio
(approx. 1508-1540)
Calvary, approx. 1520-1530
Oil painting on oakwood
panel, 255 x 155 cm
Panel from the great
altarpiece of the Church
of the Convent of Jesús de
Setúbal
Setúbal, Museu de
Setúbal-Convento de Jesús,
7/PR 7
Exhibitions: Lisbon, 1940;
Londres, 1955; Setúbal, 1960;
Setúbal, 1969; Lisbon and
Abrantes, 1971;
Setúbal, 1990
Bibliography: Couto 1938,
IV; Reis Santos 1943,
pp. 147-155; Vieira Santos
1955; Reis Santos 1960; Reis
Santos 1966; Barbosa-Pereira
1984, n. 2; Pereira 1985, I,
pp. 29-38; Markl-Pereira
1986, VI; Pereira 1989;
Pereira 1990

This panel, a true masterpiece
of Portuguese Renaissance

painting, was placed in the
upper frame of the greater altarpiece, which alluded to the
Passion of Christ. In the Lisbon
studio where this composition
was executed, they must have
known the various formal solutions popularizised by the
engravings of Albrecht Dürer.
The *lansqueret* on the right (a
motif which was reproduced
to an obsessive extent in the
Portuguese painting and
sculpture of the period); Magdalen embracing the cross and
the Virgin fainting in the arms
of Saint John. But the Portuguese painters knew how to
explore the variety of feelings
and attitudes caused by the
cruxifixion of Christ; on the
one hand, the arrogance and
cynical impassiveness of the
courtly figures and on the
other hand, the suppressed
sadness of the holy women
and Saint John.
(*Fernando Antonio Baptista
Pereira*)

16
Colombia

Magdalena Department
Tairon culture
Anthropomorphic vase
Modeled, incised, excised
and printed pottery,
11.5 x 11 x 8.5 cm
From the Atlantic Coast
Department
Bogotá, Museo Arqueológico
Casa del Marqués
de San Jorge, Ta. 9765

A small anthropomorphic recipient, with a cylindrical body, the frontal part of which shows a masculine figure, seated on a chair. His arms have the form of a two-headed serpent, the heads of which emerge on each side. The figure has certain monkey-like characteristics, such as the bulging shape of his jaw, and is adorned with a chestpiece, belt and a complex headdress consisting of six serpent heads. The facial decoration, which is dotted, shows a circular adornment on the forehead, and he is sticking his tongue out. His sex is clearly depicted, the hands and feet have been turned into serpent heads, decorated with incisive linear and triangular designs.

Pieces similar to this have been found at sites in the Sierra Nevada of Santa Maria, an immense mountainous massif in northern Colombia, with an excellent climate that allowed its ancient inhabitants to take full advantage of the most varied agricultural resources. Although this Sierra Nevada was inhabited by several different communities, the name "Tairon culture" is now used to identify all of them, along with their different material achievements, which according to the most recent research were developed between 1000 and 1500. This culture populated the full length of the Sierra Nevada, thanks to an extraordinary piece of urban stonework, which has no parallel in prehistoric Colombia and to a complex system of man-made

terraces which followed the curves of the mountainous terrain. An infrastructure of this magnitude must have come about through strong and efficient socio-political organisation, based on the rule of different categories of landlords. The Tairon infrastructure must have been similar to that of the Mayans: cultural unity based mainly on religion but without any political unification. The Tairons were a people of brave and warlike soldiers, organised according to a military hierarchy in which the most conspicuous warriors, known as *manicatos*, had considerable prestige, comparable to that of the priests or *naomas*, figures who had a great deal of influence and power over the landlords.

As far as pottery is concerned, the hundreds of pieces which have been preserved are evidence of intense production of baked clay and a specialesed pottery tradition, for both domestic and cerimonial use. The latter are objects for funerals, depictions of dignatories, priests and warriors, as well as personifications of the gods. For the latter, the indigenous population used animals whose characteristics were admired or feared, symbolically; such as jaguars, for their fierceness, or serpents, for their deadly power, and all manner of amphibians, emblems of fertility, earth and water.

Another way of representing the gods was as fantastic beings with features that combined human and animal elements. This is the case of the figure in question, as it shows a person in whom the repetition of the Ophidian theme, symbol of life and fertility, is integrated into the figure of a sitting man.

This theme represents a mythical being, made into the shape of a recipient, where the offerings were placed, in an attempt to obtain favours or to avoid calamity.

(Álvaro Cháves Mendoza)

17
Antilles

Tayan culture
Guayo, 15th century
Carving, volcanic rock,
47 x 26 cm
Santo Domingo, Museo
del Hombre Dominicano

106

It has an elliptic and shortened shape, and its functional part, which has two lateral flaps to operate the piece, is surrounded by a thick edge.

In general, the Tayan *guayos* are cut from volcanic rock and its porous surface is used to grate some food products such as yucca (*Manihot esculenta Cratnz*) and guava (*Zamia debilis L.f.*) which is probably where the word *guayo* comes from. Once grated, the pulp of this edible tubercle was squeezed in a *cibucn* or woven tube, thus obtaining a flour which was later toasted in a *buren* or clay plate, to make a dry pancake known as a *casabe*. This pancake was the staple diet of the Tayan people, and it was later adopted by Spanish conquistadors and African slaves, and was called "conquest bread."

The Tayans also manufactured wood graters with tiny stones or small sections of incrusted flint. Moreover, there are indications that in the coastal villages pieces of naturally shaped coral were used for the same purposes, as simple *guayos* or graters.

(*Manuel Antonio García Arévalo*)

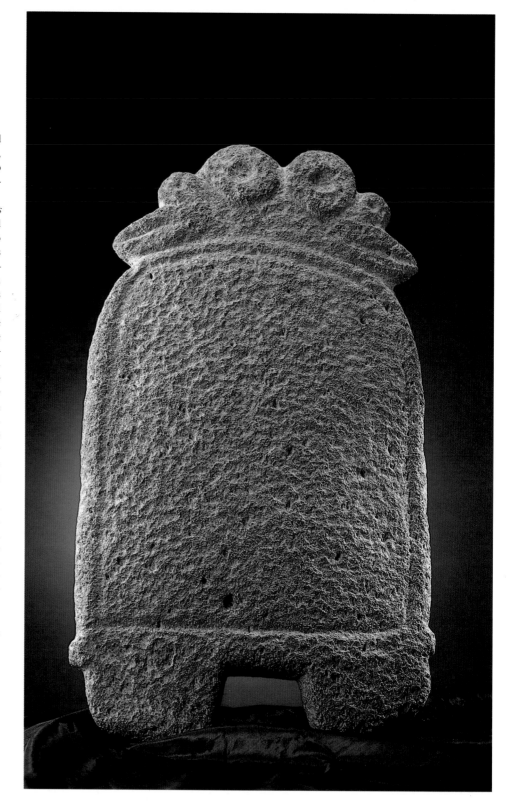

18
Antilles

Tayan culture
Trigonolite, 15th century
Carving, marble rock,
15 x 27 cm
Santo Domingo, Museo
Regional Arqueológico
de Altos de Chavín

A *cemí* or three-pointed idol which shows a serpent with a prominent head, whose body – decorated with fine incisions which simulate the scaly skin of such reptiles – twists itself around a female breast. Its back part consists of a depiction of two human legs, bent, which give a feeling of movement to the object. The ocular and oral cavities, as well as the upper part of the head, are done in bas-relief, so that decorative motifs in the shape of small laminas or discoidal plates of either gold or shell might be added, to accentuate the facial expression. The *humanoid* legs of the idol, are marked at the height of the calves by a pattern of crisscross incisions reminiscent of the woven decorative bands worn by the Tayans; whereas the gluteals have two hollows carved in the middle, where ornamental inlays would have been placed. Its fine surface and exquisite finish complement the natural beauty of the marble used to make it.

Three-pointed idols, known by archeologists as "trigonolites" or "tricuspid icons" are very common in Tayan culture and are found in abundance in the Higüey territory, in the eastern part of the island of Santo Domingo, as well as on Borinqen Island and in Puerto Rico. Christopher Columbus wrote of these idols: "Most of the chiefs have three stones, which they and their villages hold in great veneration. They say that one of them is good for the cereals and beans which have been sown; that another helps women to give birth painlessly; and that the third is to get water and sun when they need them."
Friar Ramón Pané describes

them in more detail in his *Relación acerca de las antigedades de los Indios*: "The stone idols are made in different ways. Ther are some which have three points, and they believe that these give birth to yucca." As can be seen from the descriptions given by these chroniclers, the tricuspid icons were gods who were linked to fertility rites for the *conucos* (plantations or agricultural estates) and to assist human reproduction. And so some writers consider that the upper cone-shaped protuberance to be found on these idols, the tip of which is in the form of a nipple, suggest a representation of female breasts, the organ of lactation and thus of care and reproduction of children.

This extraordinary Tayan idol, an exceptional example of the level of skill to be found in Tayan carved artefacts, has great expressive qualities, whith overtones of genesis, and birth, formed as it is by a harmonious combination of three clearly symbolic elements: a bulging female

breast, a large-headed serpent, and the stylisation of two bent human legs. This anthropozoomorphic combination is not unusual in Tayan art, in which bimorphism, or the mixing of human elements with mythical animals – such as the frog, the owl and the bat – is fairly common. They believed that snakes would come to the assistance of the *behique* or Tayan medecine man if he had failed to cure an illness and was being beaten to within an inch of his life by the dead man's family. "And at night," wrote friar Ramón Pané, "they say that many different types of serpent appear, white, black and green, which lick the face and body of the aforementioned doctor who had been left for dead, as we have said. He rests in this manner for two or three days, and while he is like this, they say that the bones of the arms and legs rejoin and fuse, and that he rises and walks a little and returns home. And those who see him question him saying: Were you not dead? But he replies

that the gods, in the form of snakes, assisted him."
In the light of these mythological accounts, this three-pointed idol is clearly not only a deity who ensured the nourishment and reproduction of the Tayan people, but is also the divine do-gooder who, in the form of a mythical serpent, came to the help of the unfortunate *behiques*.
(*Manuel Antonio García Arévalo*)

19
Peru

Department of Cuzco
Inca culture
Ceremonial Knife (tumi),
second half of the 15th
century-first half of the 16th
century
Melted and forged bronze
with copper and silver inlay,
16.8 x 17.3 cm
Madrid, Museo de América,
7360
Exhibitions: Paris, 1933;
Madrid, 1935; Cáceres,
1984-1985; Vienna 1986;
Budapest, Cologne, 1987;
Alicante, 1988 - Murcia,
Cadiz, 1989
Bibliography: PARIS 1933,
n. 355; MADRID 1935, plate
LXXXVI-II;
TRIMBORN-FERNANDEZ VEGA
1935, n. 500; CUESTA DOMINGO
1980, p. 379; CUESTA
DOMINGO-ROVIRA LLORÉNS 1982,
p. 226; CÁCERES 1984-1985,
fig. 299; VIENNA 1986, p. 310;
MARTINEZ 1988, p. 128; ROVIRA
LLORENS 1990, pp. 395-396

Crescent-shaped ceremonial
knife with cylindrical handle
ending in a llama head. The
handle carries a decoration
consisting of inlaid feline
figures, llamas, serpents and
butterflies laid out in four horizontal rows.
This is a typical Inca knife of
the type used for sacrifices,
whose half-moon shaped
blade allowed the skin to be
cut and separated. The llama
head indicates that it was used
in the sacrifices of these animals, which usually took place
during various festivities, at
which it was a common practice to extract and examine
their entrails in order to pre-

dict the future; the meat
would then be shared for consumption at the feasts which
accompanied the rites. The
decorative motifs on the
handle are common and their
symbolism is probably linked
to some rite or myth in which
the knife played a part: the
jaguar symbolised the power
of the ancestors and of the
Inca, the fertile energy of the
earth; the snake, power and
immortality; the llama, a domestic animal, had no special
significance apart from its use
as a sacrificial victim; the butterfly appears occasionally in
the Inca world as an element
in mythical scenes.
Although its shape is typical of
this type of knife, this one
shows a carefully worked precision in the lines and manufacture of its blade as well ass
excellent workmanship in the
carving of the llama head, all
of which make it exceptionally important from an aesthetic point of view. The min-
utely detailed decoration of
the handle, of somewhat imperfect workmanship perhaps
due to the difficulties of the
inlay technique used, under-
scores the quality of the piece.
The use of silver and copper
or bronze is a device which
allows colour to be introduced
while still working with metal.
If we bear in mind that iron
was unknown and that bronze
was a recent alloy whose use
had spread over this period,
the working of three metals to
make this knife implies a wish
to combine beauty with modernity.
(*Paz Cabello*)

108

20
Peru

Department of Cuzco
Inca culture
Vessel, second half of 15th
century-first half of 16th
century
Pottery, 36 cm; maximum
diameter 22 cm
Madrid, Museo de América,
8493
Exhibitions: Paris, 1933;
Madrid, 1935; Santillana
del Mar, 1982-Zamora, 1983;
Alicante, 1988-Murcia, Cadiz,
1989.
Bibliography: PARIS 1933,
n. 124; MADRID 1935, n. 70;
CUESTA DOMINGO 1980,
p. 373; SANTILLANA DEL MAR
1982-ZAMORA 1983, p. 33,
n. 39; ALICANTE 1988, p. 83

Vessel with a spherical body
and conic base, with a long
stretched neck, two bow-
shaped lateral handles and a
zoomorphic appendage at the
start of the neck. Painted red,
black and white on an orange
background, it is decorated by
a central stripe of vertical lines
and, on both sides, schematic
depictions of fern leaves.
These vessels were normally
used to distribute the *chicha*
among those taking part in
any given ritual, and they represent Inca pottery in its most
characteristic form.
Inca pottery is, generally
speaking, rather fine, well finished and of harmonious proportions; that notwithstanding,
it cannot be compared to the
aesthetic quality of Mochica or
Nazco earthenware. Although
on occasion a piece will be
found which is adorned with
reliefs of animal heads, they
are usually just painted in
black and white on a red
background. The colours are
circumscribed by geometrical
drawings (squares, rhom-
boids, triangles, frets, etc.) laid
out in horizontal lines and repeated endlessly.
Their cultural influence over
the ethnic groups under their
political control was very
weak.
Very common in the outskirts
of the Imperial capital, this

pottery is extremely scarce in
the Imperial provinces. It only
appears in the settlements of
the regional cities occupied by
state functionaries, in the
ayllus consisting of *mitimaes*
of Cuzcan origin and, on occasion, in the buildings inhabited by the *curacas* who
belonged to the provincial nobility.
(*Félix Jiménez*)

21
Peru

Inca culture
Ceremonial cup (kero),
end of 15th century-first half
of 16th century
Polychromated wood,
17 cm; diameter
of the mouth 13.5 cm
Madrid, Museo de América,
7515
Biliography: CUESTA DOMINGO
1980, pp. 229, 343;
MARTINEZ-CABELLO 1988, p. 56;
CABELLO CARRO 1989, p. 89;
CABELLO CARRO 1991, pp. 470
on

Cylindrical cup, with a somewhat concave profile, with decoration laid out in horizontal bands. On the first band there are two birds in profile, separated by four schematic flowers, face on, on the second are different interwoven schematic motifs, and on the third, two inclined friezes whose hooks interlace like links in a chain; this is a *pawsa* sign, a fertility symbol. After an empty band there is the final one, with *k'antu* flowers, also known as floripond (*Cantua buixifolia*), in profile; this is a plant with certain hallucinogenic qualities and which is associated with Inca royalty.

The layout of the decoration in horizontal stripes, and with the main motif both wider and on the upper stripe, is typical of these ceremonial cups. In this case the decoration is simple, schematic and without figures. It belongs to a group of seven keros of decreasing size, found in a sepulchre which Charles III had in the Palace of Buen Retiro in Madrid, from where it was transferred to the Royal Cabinet of Natural History, in 1775, as is stated in an inventory of objects transferred from the king to the Cabinet.

It is highly probable that it formed part of the material excavated in 1765, in the course of the first anonymous digs carried out in Peru, and sent back by the viceroy in the same year, as is confirmed by a receipt chit for a series of antiques. It must have come from a tomb located in Tantalluc hill, near Cajamarca, known as *Huaca de Tantalluc*, whose stratified ridge, with dates indicated, was drawn a few years later by the bishop of Trujillo, Baltasar Jaime Martínez Compañón, in the ninth volume of the *Natural History in Drawings* of his diocesis.

That this cup was found, with others similar to it and a few others with complex decorations, in a native tomb of the type used before the Conquest, seems to indicate that wooden keros with polychromatic decoration are not a product that belongs to the period after contact had been made with the Spanish, as has been indicated – only those which have no figurative decoration or colour are usually dated as being prior to Spanish contact rather they must have been of purely native origin, later continuing, during the colonisation, with the same themes and the traditions which had originated earlier.

(*Paz Cabello*)

22
Mexico

Mexican culture
Vessel (Chalchiuthtlicue)
Polychromatic pottery,
moulded and modeled,
48 cm, maximum diameter
31.5 cm, minimum diameter
27.6 cm
Found in Offering
Chamber III of the Great
Temple of Tenochtitlan
Mexico City, Museo
del Temple Mayor, 10-220338
Bibliographia: Matos
Moctezuma 1988

This vessel, whose workmanship is typical of Cholula pottery, was discovered in one of the richest offering chambers of the Great Temple at Tenochtitlan. Beside it, other urns were found which contained over three hundred necklace beads cut in green stone. Without a doubt, the collection belonged to an offering made to the god Tlaloc of the Great Temple, as is clear from the repeated images of this god in the decoration on the pottery, as well as the fact that the subject represented on the vessel is Chalchiuthtlicue, wife, sister or mother of Tlaloc.

Chalchiuhtlicue's image has been modelled and painted on one side of the vessel. Her head takes up the neck of the vessel, while the body is shown on the belly. The divinity's headdress, which has certain things in common with those architectonic sculptures showing the same iconography, is of feathers and roses, that surround the triangle-shaped abstract face. In this image of the goddess, another similar image is displayed on her belly, and on her breast is a symbol for the four paths of the universe and the currents of water.
(*José Alcina Franch*)

23
Colombia

Departments of
Cundinamarca and Boyaca
Muiscan culture
Antropomorphic recipient
(earthenware jug),
approx. 1200
Modeled, incised and
polychromatic pottery,
33 cm, diameter 23 cm
Bogotá, Museo Arqueológico
Casa del Marqués
de San Jorge, M-10709

This piece stands as a fine example of the pottery production of the Muiscans, who inhabited the high plateau and the surrounding area of Colombia's Cordillero Oriental at the time of the Spanish Conquest. The earthenware jugs, like other articles made from baked clay, were modelled by hand, the curve of the vessel's body being made by rolling it in leather straps. The anthropomorphic figure in relief which adorns the vessel's body was shaped by fingers and by features cut into it with nails or with small pieces of cane. The whole piece was covered with a "engobe" or bath of chestnut coloured muddy water, and once dry, mineral colourings were applied and the geometrical design that surrounds the neck was drawn, in red on a cream background; as for the figure, the head, chest and arms stand out, the headdress decorated in dark red and the face with lines reminiscent of a beard. The vessel was baked in an oxidising atmosphere, in the open air; it is not known if the pre-hispanic potters of Colombia used ovens.

The vessels, characterised by a spherical body, a flat handle and high neck, are decorated with animal figures, usually lizards or frogs, or by human figures, as well as by painted designs. Together with painted cups and bowls, with double vessels and with hollow anthropomorphic figures that were used when making

the offerings, these are the main exponents of ceremonial pottery, which ceased to be manufactured after the Colonisation.

One of the specific functions of this vessel is to be found described in the reports made by the chroniclers of the Conquest, such as friar Pedro Simón, who writes about their ceremonial use as offerings and as part of the burial objects: "They were buried in a vault, which had been made for this purpose, and were wrapped in fine blankets and had many corn cobs placed around them, along with "chicha" bowls and their weapons". Chichas were fermented drinks made principally from corn. The chronicler quoted above tells us about the vessels designed to be used to receive the offering in the temples, which he describes as follows: " In the common temples they had two kinds of stocks in which the offerings were placed, one

being the figure of a man made of clay, without feet, completely hollow, the top of the head open so as to receive the offerings, which were made of gold in the form of various animals." The second type of offering vessels "was a vessel like an earthenware jug buried in the floor of the temple, with only its mouth visible....where they also placed the offerings."

In the formal structure of the Muiscan earthenware jug, the following variations have been discovered: those whose body is composed of a lower semi-spherical part and a tronco-conic upper part; those which have a handle that connects the mouth to the shoulder of the vessel, and those whose bodies are in the shape of a horizontal cylinder with a neck which sticks out of the middle and which has two side handles or a rear handle. As far as decoration is concerned, they may be painted, or modelled, or may combine

both techniques, but when this is the case it always affects the upper part of the vessel, the neck and the handle; some earthenware jugs only have a superficial "engobe" and were not decorated with reliefs or with coloured patterns.

The piece in question shows a dignatory, painted and moulded on its neck, a chieftain, priest or person of importance; this is indicated by his central, striking position, his headdress in the form of a round cap, his necklace, his facepaint, and the face-on posture characteristic of someone who is facing an auditorium or receiving homage.

The function of pottery was ceremonial in the case of those pieces which are most delicately modelled, most profusely decorated, and those which are clearly the work of the most skilful potters, in which their labour, imagination, and variations developed over the course of time, their manual dexterity

and their expertise are combined. Naturally we should make some mention, as an underlying reason for what has been explained above, of the profound religious spirit that moved these indigenous peoples, which inspired them when they made their pottery. Among their numerous deities we can find Nencatacoa, god of the craftsmen, of the drunkards, of the weavers, the painters and potters, a companion of the celebrations when he appeared to the natives wearing his fox tail, inspiring manual work and the manufacture of sacred vessels, of the offering cups and the earthenware jugs used for rendering homage to supernatural beings.

(*Álvaro Cháves Mendoza*)

24

Guatemala

Mayan culture, late postclassical
Zoomorphic mask, 1250-1500
Pottery, 14 x 13.6 cm
Found in Alta Verapaz, Guatemala, Museo Nacional de Arqueología y Etnología, 5805

This clay object would appear to be a breastplate, given its dimensions and shape; the artist has not tried to make it conform to the trajectory of a definite motif, but has respected the traditional breastplate shape. The orifices located around the edge of the piece are functional. Another less likely possibility is that it is a small waist mask. Representations of such objects are common on sculptures to the south of the Mayan area, dating from the late preclassical and continuing right through the classical period.

Inside the piece the gullet of a lizard has been modelled in

one stroke, in such a way that it respects the symmetry of the axis, this being an element typical of the decorative traditions of the Pacific coastal strip and of the central and southern plateaus of Guatemala from the beginning of our era. The toothed decoration of the gullet stresses this detail. The eyes have been made from deep cuts, executed with less care than the mouth, which has been traced with great precision. The special way in which the latter has been executed, and the toothed decoration, are more in line with the ornamental tradition of the protoclassical and classical periods that with later cultural forms. From this open gullet a small figure modelled in clay sticks out, its arms open, a clear reference to the concept of the "transport" of a divine entity and his contact with the real world.

This concept has obvious Mesoamerican antecedents, dating from the early preclassical

period, and was often used by the ruling classes and the artists of this complex cultural region to explain the links and communications between the inhabitants of the natural world and the supernatural universe. Acts of political legitimation and communication

with ancestors are expressed in this manner, a form of expression which would culminate in the monumental art of the Mayan lowlands.
(*Andrés Ciudad*)

25
Mexico

Mexican culture
Eagle head
Sculpture, polychromated
stone, 9 x 25 x 11 cm
From offering 78 of the
Proyecto Templo Mayor
Mexico City, Museo del
Templo Mayor, 10-220043
Bibliography: Matos
Moctezuma 1988[a]; Matos
Moctezuma 1988[b]

This eagle head, cut from stone
and polychromated with
various colours, was found in
one of the richest offerings in
which a stone tortoise was also
found, in the Red Temple to the
south of Mexico's Great
Temple, Tenochtitlan.
The offerings constitute some
of the most important evidence
available regarding Mexican
ceremonies.
They are at the pyramid corners, or on the way through the
entry staircases, or where the
two parallel staircases separate,
or in the intermediary zones
between the two sides of the
pyramid. They are in the form
of chambers, baskets, or boxes,
they contain a wide, rich variety
of artistic pieces, the remains of
sacrified animals, sumptuary
objects etc. which has meant
that the artistic pieces have
been saved together, something never achieved on any
other site.
The piece in question has some
special characteristics: the
crown with a bow on the head,
and the tufts.
The eagle clearly has direct
connotations with the sun, war
and Huitzilopochtli. As an emblem of the order of the Knights
the eagle is as common as a
symbol on the helmets of certain warriors; as the ascending
eagle is related to the sun, or
Tonatiuh, and appears thus in
the Huehuetl of Malinalco and,
inasmuch as the eagle-warriors
take part in the festival of Tla-
caxipehualizuli and the gladia-
torial sacrifice, it is constantly
present in the Cuauhxicallis.
(*José Alcina Franch*)

26
Mexico

Mexican culture, late
postclassical period
Ligature (xiuhmolpilli),
1325-1521
Stone, 46 cm; diameter
23 cm
From Puebla state
Mexico City, Museo
Nacional de Antropología,
10-46492

The sculpted pieces known as
xiuhmolpilli are ligatures for
rods that represent the 52 year
cycle which results from the
combination of the sacred
yearly cycle of 260 days or *tonalpohualli* and the yearly
solar cycle of 365 days and
which is usually considered to
be equivalent to the Aztec
century. Some of these
xiuhmolpilli carry calendar
dates which may correspond
to the years 1403, 1455, or
1507, dates which mark the
end of the 52 year cycles before the Conquest.
As indicated by some depictions of the New Fire (Fuego
Nuevo) in several codices, and
by the discovery of at least
three skull altars in the holy
chamber of Tenochtitlan, the
bundles of cane or wooden
sticks which represent the 52
year cycles symbolically were
buried at the end of each cycle
at the New Fire ceremony in
one of these skull altars,
which had probably been
constructed to celebrate this
type of burial.
The xiuhmolpilli in question
are especially interesting due
to the fact that they may possibly be Aztec artefacts which
were reused in the colonial
period and decorated with
flowers, and are, therefore,
further data to help us understand the period of encounter
between the indigenous world
and the western world in the
centre of Mexico.
(*José Alcina Franch*)

27
Colombia

Cauca complex, late middle period
Quimbaya culture
Holder of offerings,
12th-16th centuries
Roll polychromated pottery,
18.9 x 11.8 x 9.5 cm
From Montenegro, Quindio Department, Colombia
Bogotá, Museo Nacional, Instituto Colombiano de Antropología, 44-VI-4728
Bibliography: Rojas de Perdomo 1979; Salgado 1986

114

The pre-hispanic Quimbaya tribe settled in the region which is now composed of the Caldas, Quindio, Riseralda and Valle Medio departments of the Cauca river, from the 11th to the 16th centuries. Its communities lived in hamlets of small houses, around which their farmland was laid out, land that was farmed using the terrace system.

They mainly grew corn, kidney beans, fruits, potato and yucca on the region's different thermic levels.

This tribe was remarkably developed both sociologically and politically, in contrast to its social standing, and had specialised groups of people for activities as diverse as agriculture, mining, goldwork, pottery, etc.

The Quimbayas practiced the rite of cranial deformation, as well as that of arms and legs. They applied paint to their bodies and faces, and adorned themselves with numerous objects such as necklaces, diadems, breastplates, earrings, nose-rings, etc.

They were especially skilled in making magnificent and highly realistic artefacts of gold and tumbaga (an alloy of gold and copper), manufactured with varied and sophisticated techniques such as soldering, embossing, laminating, hammering, lost wax basing, and giltwork.

Especially interesting are the octopods, the anthropomorphic, zoomorphic and phytomorphic figures, the quills and

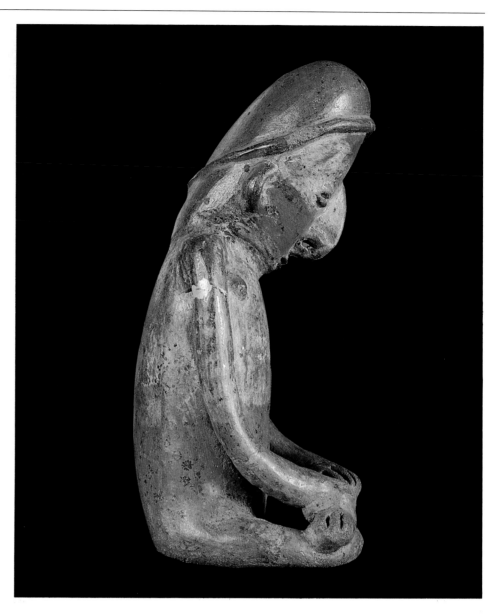

other bodily adornments. These artefacts have excited the interest of numerous scavengers, both past and present, who have raided the indigenous Quimbaya tombs, and by doing so have destroyed much valuable archeological information.

This tribe is also known for its magnificent pottery tradition, of which this piece is fine example. The decorative methods used on it include negative painting, especially black on red, and tricolours. This and other pieces form an important part of the funeral trappings of the chieftains, shamans and so-called "people of standing."
(*Hildur Zea S.*)

28
India

Gujarat
Jaina mandala with Ganesa and Devi Ambika,
approx. 1500
Painted miniature, 60 x 58 cm
New Dehli, National Museum, 79210

The illustration shows the great central platform on which Tirthankara is seated in the *dhyana* position. The four corners of the miniature are occupied by the gods Mahavira and Ganesa and the goddesses Vindhuadevi and Ambika. The painting has been done on silk, in bright colours: orange, red, green, yellow, blue and gold.

The inside circle is divided into eight hexagons of different colours, which are subdivided in their turn into eight rows above which various Jaina mantras have been written. The latter show how one may control one's destiny by acquiring and practising faith, knowledge and seemly behaviour.

(*Daljit Kahare*)

29
Spain

Original document from the Catholic Monarchs

Cantillana, 24th of February of 1502.
Letter of grace from the Catholic Monarchs to the monks of the Carthusian monastery of the Caves of Seville, confirming them in their possession of certain houses and shops in the city of Seville, which used to belong to various Jews and converts and which were confiscated by the tribunal of the Inquisition; drawn up for the receiver of the Inquisition, Juan Gutiérrez Egas, who desisted from all judicial actions against the monastery as a result.

"Don Fernando and Doña Isabel, King and Queen of Castile, León, Aragón, Sicily, Granada, Toledo, Valencia, Galicia, Mallorca, Seville, Cerdeña, Cordoba, Corsica, Murcia, of the Algarve, Jaén, Algeciras, of Gibraltar and of the Canary Islands, Count and Countess of Barcelona and Lords of Vizcaya and Molina, Duke and Duchess of Athens and of Neopatria, Counts of Rousillon and Cerdagne, Marquises of Oristn and Gociano, by the grace of God, do here declare to the Prior and monks of Saint Mary of the Caves, which is outside and close to the city of Seville that it has come into their hearing that, while owning and posessing quietly and pacifically certain houses in this city of Seville which were the property of Alonzo Gonzalez of Seville, that are in the district of Saint bartholomew, and other houses which were the property of Benito de Torralua, and two shops, which are in the neigbourhood of the rag-and-bone men, and other houses which were the property of Diego Gonzalez Canpouerde, in the aforementioned district of Saint Bartholomew and others which were the property of Miguel Marroquí, say that Juan Gutiérrez Egas, our receiver of goods confiscated and passed to our Exchequer for the crime of heresy in the said city and its archbishopric, has brought an action against you with regard to the aforementioned houses which were the property of Alonzo Gonzalez of Seville and Juan de Sevilla Tapón and Benito de Torralua, and to the aforementioned shops, and that you fear that he will furthermore bring similar actions with regard to the aforementioned houses of Diego Gonzalez Canpouerde and Miguel Marroquí, saying that they belong to our Exchequer, because the people who held them before were condemned for the aforementioned crime for which reason you the said Prior and monks and monastery would have had to have suffered grave damages because in the aforementioned houses you had to pay a certain quantity in tribute, and you begged us and asked us that we grant you a pardon and made a gift of any right or due which belonged to us or may belong to us in any way from the aforementioned houses and shops, for which said rights our receiver has brought the aforementioned actions against you, and for the further rights for which you fear he will bring further actions against you, depending on our mercy. And we, respecting your aforementioned pleas and for the devotion in which we hold the house and monastery of Saint Mary of the Caves, from whom, our receiver informs us, we are owed from the aforementioned houses and shops for which he has brought and will bring actions against you, a quantity of approximately two hundred thousand maravedís, from the tributes owed by the said monastery for the said houses, we look favourably upon you, and for the present we grant a full perfect and irrevocable pardon for now and for ever more to you, the said

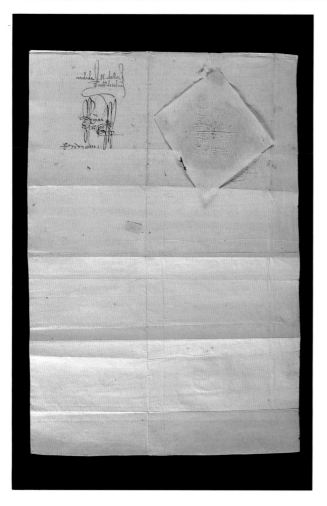

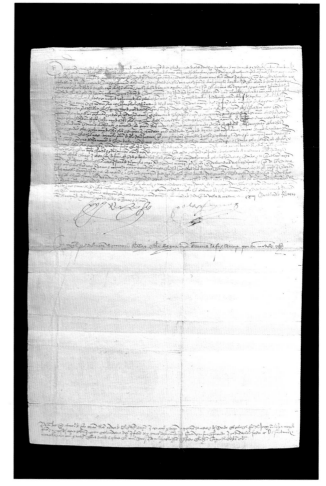

Prior and monks and monastery, from any right and due which belongs and may belong to us in any way for the said houses and shops for which the said receiver has brought and will bring said actions against you, fixed in the said quantity of two hundred thousand mrs., which shall be yours, which you may give and exchange and barter with and do with as you wish and which for your own good you have as your own property, freely and without restriction, and aquired by just and right decree. We order our said receiver Juan Gutiérrez Egas that after with this our letter he will be required to desist from the said actions which he has brought against you for the said houses and shops, and that from here on he may not bring any further action whatsoever for the said houses which were the property of Diego Gonzalez Canpouerde and Miguel Marroquí, because our mercy and grace is to make a gift of them to you along with any right or due which is and may be owed to us from the said houses which has been said to be fixed at two hundred thousand maravedís, and we order to those who are of our council who have to do with the affairs of the Holy Inquisition and to our assistant and to any other of our judicial representatives in the said city of Seville that they do uphold and respect this said letter of grace which we do hereby draw up for you, and against the letter and spirit of which they may not do, act or consent anything at any time and in any way, and that none of them shall do thus in any way, under pain of losing our grace and of paying ten thousand maravedís, to our Exchequer. And moreover we order to the man who will show this letter to you that he summon you to appear in our court wherever it may be, the first fifteen days following our summons, and we order thus to any public scribe who may be summoned for this, that he sign his signature at such time to the document shown, so that we know how our order is being carried out. Written on the island of Cantillana on the xxiiij of February, year of the birth of our lord Jesus Christ one thousand five hundred and two. I the King. I the Queen. I Miguel Perez de Almazan, secretary of our King and Queen who made him write this by order." (*Consuelo Varela*, transcribed by *Juan Gil*)

30
Spain

Manises
Plate from the "string" series, last quarter of the 15th century or early 16th century
Glass pottery; ceramic turned by means of "strings" and small spikes or nail heads, background of stanniferous glass with gilt decoration, diameter 45.8 cm
Madrid, Instituto Valencia de Don Juan, 334
Bibliography: González Martí 1944; Ainaud de Lasarte 1952; Llubiá Munné 1967; Martínez Caviró 1983; Martínez Caviró 1991.

The technique for gilding pottery, which started early in Al-Andalus, with Abbasi production as a model, in the late Middle Ages and afterwards was known as "malica work," because the main Andalusian potteries were in Nasrid Malaga. Valencian gilt pottery, which was born in the potteries of Al-Andalus and was known in Paterna from the early 13th century onward would achieve unusual splendour in Manises from the 14th century on, as shown by the large quantity exported. From then on Manises production developed as far as its ornamentation was concerned.

The earliest decoration, in which cobalt oxide alternated with gilt, shows a preference for Muslim motifs – wings, *atauríques, lacerías*. But from the last quarter of the 15th century on the decorative patterns of the backgrounds of the pieces changed, with preference for small motifs which were repeated constantly, done only in gilt. Among these the "solfa" is important, a motif which probably comes from ivy and ilex leaves, though which degenerated with time. Also the "thistle flower" motif, open and in bud, was frequent. Both patterns can be seen on this piece. At the turn of the 15th and 16th centuries, the shapes of the plates also

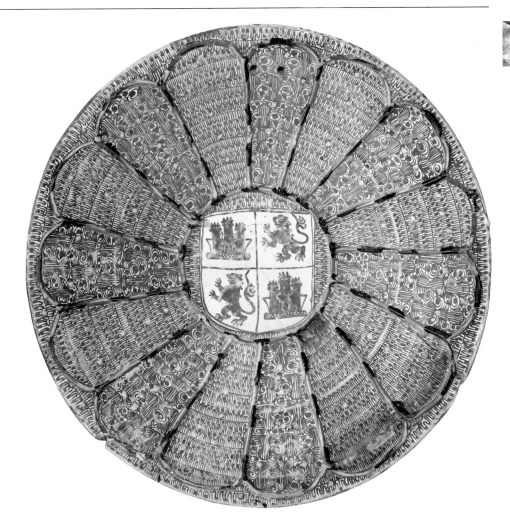

changed, largely due to the influence of metal pieces. That is when segmented forms appeared, often made in a mould, as a striking central figure, or small relief motifs, such as the strings and the nailheads, like small spikes.

Using the strings mentioned, a subdivision into segments has been obtained, which latter are full of the small motifs also mentioned above.

The centre, on the other hand, is decorated with a quartered coat-of-arms of castles and lions. As in the Moorish series, which this plate belongs to, as in those of the Mudejars in earlier centuries, heraldic themes wer given undeniable preference. In this case the coat-of-arms shows that not only the monarchs of the crown of Aragon, but also the Castilians, were clients of the Manises potteries.

(*Balbina Martinez Caviró*)

31
Italy

Florentine school
Shield with the stigmas of pope Leo X, 1513-1521
Stone, 126 x 67 cm
Florence, Museo Bardini, 85/26

Giovanni de' Medici (Florence, 1475-Rome, 1521) who arrived at the papacy with the name of Leo X (1513-1521), symbolized the troubled "Golden Age" of the Vatican's temporal power. Son of the great Lorenzo the Magnificent, who died in 1492, he was named pope without having been either bishop or priest. After the bilious and tempestuous period of Julius II, Rome became the capital of the Renaissance and a festive, orgyloving, diplomatic, wasteful man sat on the papal throne, who was at the same time, however, a great patron of literature, art, and science.

A continuer of the Lateran Council, Leo X had to face the serious problem of church reform, and even though he may have wanted to reach a compromise with Luther, he had to confirm his death sentence (*Exsurge domine*, 1520). Among the artists he took under his wing, were, notably, Raphael and Michelangelo. The first, whom he distinguished by making him responsible for managing the Arts, was given the commission, among others, of continuing the building of Saint Peter in the Vatican, and of decorating the lodges; to Michelangelo fell the task of designing the Medici family tombs in the new sacristy of the church itself, as well as the façade of San Lorenzo in Florence, which was never built.

(*Joan Sureda i Pons*)

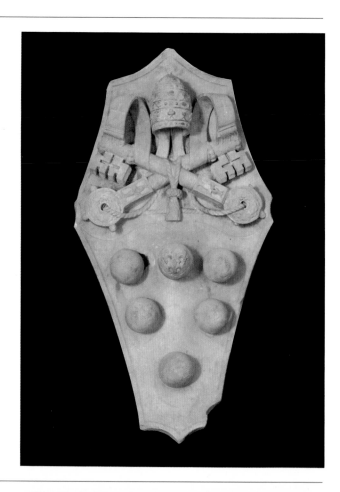

32
Spain

Manises
Plate, 1513-1521
Ceramic, mayolic, 6.3 cm; diameter 47.2 cm
Bologne, Museo Civico, 2789
Bibliography: González Martí 1944, fig. 907; Ainaud de Lasarte 1952, pp. 94-97; Martínez Caviró 1983

Upright, centred by a decoration of stylised flowers, appears the Medicean stigma with the tiara and keys, which is doubtless an allusion to pope Leo X, and the inscription GLO (to the left) VIS (to the right). This inscription corresponds to Giuliano di Lorenzo de' Medici's tetrastic, which can be understood by reading it from left to right SI VOL, an expression which ends with GE LA FORTUNA, as can be seen from the *Sentenziose Imprese* (Lyon, 1561) of Paolo Giovio.

(*R.E.*)

33
Netherlands/Spain

Juan de Flandes (approx.
1465, documented in Spain
from 1496 onwards-
Palencia, 1519)
*Christ and the Canaanite
woman*, between 1496
and 1503
Painting, oil on panel,
21 x 15.6 cm
Originally part of a triptych
(polyptych and oratory),
included in the inventory
of the property of queen
Isabella the Catholic in
Toro (1505), part of which
was purchased by Margaret
of Austria, from whom it
was passed on to Charles V
Madrid, Palacio Real,
Tranvía de Carlos III,
10002022
Exhibitions: Madrid, 1986
Bibliography: Justi 1887,
pp. 157-169; Bertaux 1991,
pp. 895-896; Sánchez Cantón
1930-1931, pp. 97-152;
Sánchez Cantón 1950,
pp. 151 on; Bermejo 1962,
pp. 10-17; Reynaud 1967,
XVII, 6, pp. 345-352;
Reales Sitios 1969, VI;
Trizna 1976; Coo-Reynaud
1979, pp. 125-144;
Vandevivere- Bermejo 1986;
Ishikawa- Garrido 1987,
n. 94; Bermejo- Portus 1988;
Marías 1989, pp. 151-160

34
Netherlands/Spain

Juan de Flandes (approx.
1465, documented in Spain
from 1496 onwards-
Palencia, 1519)
The Raising of Lazarus,
between 1496 and 1504
Oil painting on panel,
21 x 15.6 cm
Inscriptions: on the tablet,
LASARA
Originally from an altarpiece
(polyptych and oratory)
from the collection of queen
Isabella the Catholic,
part of which was
purchased by Margaret of
Austria, from whom it
passed on to Emperor
Charles V
Madrid, Palacio Real,

Tranvía de Carlos III,
10002019
Bibliography: Sánchez
Cantón 1930-1931, VI and
VII; Sánchez Cantón 1950;
Begemann 1952, XXV;
Bermejo 1962, Reales Sitios
1969, VI; Ishikawa-Garrido
1987, n. 94; Bermejo-Portus
1988

Michel Zittow and Juan de
Flandes worked on paintings
for the oratory of Isabella the
Catholic approximately be-

tween the years 1496 and
1503. In February 1505, three
months after the queen's
death, fortyseven small panels
were inventoried in the Castle
of Toro. These, together with
other possessions, had been
used to pay off debts and
pious bequests by means of
successive sales. Thirtytwo of
these small paintings were
purchased by Margaret of Austria. Later on, twenty were
passed on to Charles V and,
with the exception of five

which had disappeared before
1850, these have all been kept
in an excellent condition in
the Palacio Real in Madrid.
Their frames are in the style of
the eighteen century. The remaining fourteen, coming
from the original collection,
are kept in museums and collections of western Europe.
Although her collection included Spanish and Italian
works of unquestionable
quality, Isabella of Castile had
a predilection for Flemish

painting. She owned works by Rogier Van der Weyden, Hugo van der Goes, Dirk Bouts, and Memling, some of which are still part of the treasure of the Royal Chapel in Granada. She not only bought works from abroad, but even had painters, educated in Flanders, work for her. Outstanding among these were Michel Zittow and Juan de Flandes. The former was born in the then Hanseatic port town, Reval, now Tallinn (Estonia). He perfected his style and technique in Bruges, between 1484 and 1491. Nevertheless, certain Germanic elements in his work, as can be observed, came from the art of the Hanseatic towns. When the conquest of Granada was over, he began to serve the queen of Castile and stayed almost until her death in 1504. In the documents pertaining to the palace he is quoted as Master Michel and Melchor the German (Trizna, 1976; Liebmann 1977; Marías 1989). For the work of portrait painter he received a grant of 50,000 maravedís, a considerable amount, compared to payments to other artists.

In Castile, a painter, called Juan de Flandes or Juan Flamenco, is mentioned in documents. His apprenticeship as a miniaturist had probably taken place between Bruges and Ghent, in contact with the workshops of Memling and Van der Goes. He must have been called Juan Astsat, since he signed the back of the *Raising of Lazarus* with this name although this had earlier been read as Astrat. A new interpretation, with the help of Moya Valgañón, forces us to this conclusion. He possibly worked as a miniaturist and, in 1496, was hired by queen Isabella to work on the Saint John the Baptist altarpiece for the Miraflores Carthusian monastery. This was finished not earlier than 1499. In the meantime, he painted portraits: Isabella of Castile, Madrid (Palacio del Pardo), Joan the Mad (Thyssen Collection), while Zittow represented

other personalities.

Before the start of the new century, the two painters began, as already mentioned, their meticulous work on the Isabeline oratory. When his protectress died, Juan de Flandes looked for new patrons among the old members of her court. Thus, Salamanca University ordered an altarpiece for their chapel (1505-1507); Juan Rodríguez de Fonseca, who had been ambassador in Flanders, entrusted him,

in 1507, with the panels of an altarpiece for the Palencia cathedral, in which town he worked in 1519. Zittow, upon Isabella's death, left for England, Denmark and Flanders, and from Flanders accompanied Charles V during his journey to Spain. He finally returned to his native town where he died in 1525.

After the unification of the Peninsula had been consolidated, Isabella of Castile had a pious-artistic desire to possess

a rich portable oratory. During her travels, everyday mass could thus be officiated and, at the same time, the oratory would stimulate her piousness and please her fine sensibility. It has been possible to observe that she had two artists at her disposal, who were qualified to carry out this arduous enterprise, for both Michel Zittow and Juan de Flandes cultivated a similar style and were trained and skilful miniaturists. The Master of Reval had worked for the Bishop of Granada, painting small panels with religious scenes. A possibility exists that he was the one who started the work on the portable oratory, four or five years after the conquest of Granada, and that Juan de Flandes joined him after finishing the altarpiece for the Carthusian monastery. As explained below, the oratory must have been finished before the queen's death.

We are assuming that the so called *polyptych* of Isabella the Catholic was probably a portable altarpiece-cabinet. As proved by existing examples and documents, this was quite common in the royal houses, from the Middle Ages up to the 18th century. The inventory made in Toro on 25th February, 1504 by Juan Velzquez, mentions it as "a *cabinet* with all these small panels, all alike," and in folio n. 20 there is a marginal specification: "Valuation of altarpieces. They are in a cabinet" (Sánchez Cantón, 1930, p 99, n. 1). A precise reading reveals that the quoted panels were not simply kept in one of the cupboards or cabinets of the castle, but that they formed part of an altarpiece-cabinet or portable oratory.

This was possibly made of two parts: a kind of polyptych on top and a chest-altar beneath, in which liturgical utensils and ornaments were kept. As was usual, the small panels must have been detachable in order that they could be preserved during transport which, in those times, used to be rather difficult.

With regard to size, taking into consideration the frames, the height of this unique polyptych would be approximately one and a half metres. Placed on the superior part would have been three panels of height 21 cm: *The Coronation of the Virgin*, *The Ascension* and *The Assumption*. The latter two are documented as Zittows work and the former is painted by the same hand. Be-

neath, the central piece there would be five rows of four panels placed horizontally and two rows of six panels on each wing. The total amounts to the forty seven panels mentioned in the documentation. According to their stylistic affinity and their divergences from the work known as being Juan de Flandes', the following should also be attributed to Zittow: *Jesus Stilling the Storm*, *The Last Supper*, *Jesus Arrested*, *Jesus Before Pilate*, *The Coronation with the Crown of Thorns*, and probably *Christ's Apparition to the Virgin*. Sánchez Cantón was the first to observe that some of the panels differed from those by Juan de Flandes although he was not able to ascribe them to Zittow. As Reynaud pointed out (1979, pp. 139-40, n. 17), this was due to the famous historian's deficient reading of the text, written in Old French, of the inventory of Margaret of Austria. In his opinion, only two of the panels were by Master Michel. Neither did the French scholar risk his opinion as to attribution though she indicated that in the paintings by the painter from Reval "a desire is dominant, to construct the space on the basis of profoundly articulated groups composed of an inseparable unit, stressed by the sense of atmospheric unity giving subtle diffusion to the bodies." Marías shrewdly observes that "a special manner of focusing the scenes almost *da sotto in su*, with an extremely low point of view and an equally low horizon" exists in the work of Zittow (Reynaud, 1979, pp. 153-54). Consequently, the figures are usually silhouetted against the space. What one can also perceive in Zittow's work is a marked expressionism, due to his early training, which was Germanic. This appears in his compositions and figures, as well as in the paint, more clotted and sparkling, one could even describe it as effervescent, than his companion's

mottled and subtly refined brush-strokes. The episode of the *Canaanite woman* is narrated in the Gospel according to St Matthew (XV, 21-28): ... Jesus withdrew to the region of Tyre and Sidon. A Canaanite woman /.../crying out /.../: "My daughter is suffering terribly from demon!possession." /.../ The woman came and knelt before him: "Lord, help me!" she said./.../ Then Jesus answered: "Woman, you have great faith!" There are very few representations of this scene dating from the Gothic and the Renaissance periods. The work is, however, characteristic of Juan de Flandes. The scene is set in a bucolic bay, in which Christ's figure is solemnly outlined. He is wearing his characteristic blue tunic. The elegant Canaanite appears in front of him, trembling and quivering on her knees. As in his other compositions, the Apostles form a beautiful, but impersonal, chromatic whole.

The Raising of Lazarus is a more complex composition than the previous one and this led Sánchez Cantón to the conclusion that it was not by Juan de Flandes. Following other scholars we believe, however, that this is a development of his style and we even consider his work to be the most beautiful in this piece. Although the composition is apparently motley, it is precise and clear. Two diagonals, one formed by Christ and Saint Peter, and the other by Lazarus' sister, Martha, and a bearded man, lead one's attention to the nude body of Lazarus in the centre. The well-known theme is taken from the Gospel according to Saint John (XI, 38-45). Suggestions have been made that the figure of Martha might correspond to one of the Catholic Monarchs' daughters. The architecture emphasizes the symbolic value of the scene: its decrepitude coincides with that of his masterpiece painted for St Lazarus' Church in

Palencia, now kept in El Pardo. The church we see here is being restored. Together with the *The Raising of Lazarus*, it may signify the remodelling of the ancient Temple of Solomon. Juan de Flandes again did not limit himself to mere narration, but rather went deeply into the mysteries of faith. Proud of his work, he signed it on the back: "Juan Astsat."
(*José Rogelio Buendia*)

Man and Society

After leaving behind the historic area of the
Carthusian monastery of Santa María de las
Cuevas and imagining what it must have been
like before 1841 when it was turned into a
ceramic workshop, the visitor to *Art and
Culture around 1492*, on penetrating the
reconstructed space of the monastic cloisters,
descends into the vanities, fears, anxieties and
sentiments of man five hundred years ago.
That is what becomes clear through the
various sections of the theme "Man and
society." In the first works (n. 35-77; 86-88),
the longing to overcome the temporary nature
of the human being is clear in the instruments
of war and the vanity of the images of power.
But the world did not change only through
the affirmation of power but also through the
irradiation of thought (works n. 78-85).
Nevertheless, neither by the force of weapons
nor of the mind did man manage to stop
feeling, to overcome his astonishment in the
presence of life and his fear in the presence
of death (works n. 89-130). Life and death
succeed one another in an endless circle that
passes from youth to old age, that takes
refuge in reflection and in suicide, in which
the joy of music coexists with the pain of
illness, in which the fear of living in the
beyond turns the daily existence into a ritual
of death. Still, within the diverse cultures, man
sought to give a sense of immediacy to the
forms of daily existence (works n. 131-166),
forms which had to be useful as well as
beautiful.

35A
Germany

Valentin Siebenbürger
(Nuremberg, 1510-1564)
Suit of armour, approx. 1535
Beaten steel, polished and
refined, with rivets for the
leather straps,
103 x 82 x 75 cm
Nuremberg, Germanisches
Nationalmuseum, W 1307
Exhibitions: New York-
Nuremberg, 1986
Bibliography: ESSENWEIN
1887-1889, pp. 216-222;
THOMAS-GAMBER 1976,
pp. 133-176; WILLERS 1978,
pp. 833-859; NEW YORK-
NUREMBERG, 1986, p. 456

35B
Germany

Valentin Siebenbürger
(Nuremberg, 1510-1564)
Shield, approx. 1500
Beaten steel, polished, with
rivets for the leather straps,
36 x 36 x 2 cm
Nuremberg, Germanisches
Nationalmuseum, W 1313
Exhibitions: New York-
Nuremberg, 1986
Bibliography: ESSENWEIN
1887-1889, pp. 216-222;
THOMAS-GAMBER 1976,
pp. 133-176; WILLERS 1978,
pp. 833-59: NEW YORK-
NUREMBERG 1986, p. 456

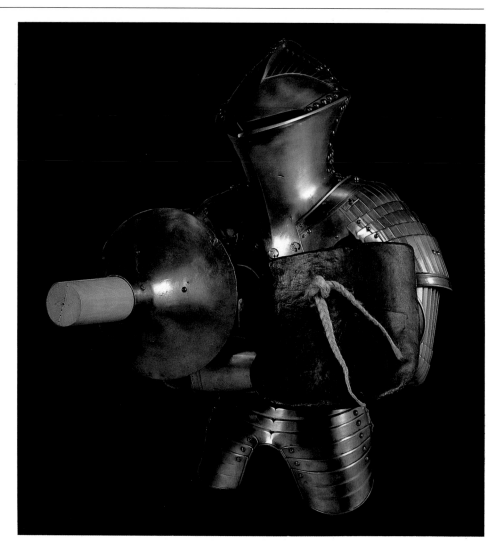

The corrugated tilting helmet is fastened to the breastplate by means of several screws, and to the backplate with concealed nuts. A rest to hold the lance is fastened to the bevelled breastplate. A tassel with pompoms is screwed to the lower part in order to shield the muscles. The corrugated cuirass ends in a habergeon ·protecting the pelvis in case of a fall. The pauldrons fall over to the back and are screwed into the straps on the shoulders, thus joining the breastplate with the backplate. Traditionally, only the left brassard was furnished with a rather heavy tournament gauntlet. The right hand was protected by the hilt of the lance. The armpits were covered too, but only one of the pieces has been preserved. The coat of arms is on the breastplate. The principal elements have the insignia of the master armourer of Nuremberg, Valentin Siebenbürger (born in 1510, given the title of Master in 1531 and died in 1564) and the town inspection marks.

According to the 16th century inventory, the Nuremberg arsenal possessed eight tilting armours and four suits of armour for the German route (the Rhine). In 1800, during the French threat to the town, an Austrian official illegally sold these to the military contractor, Dietrich, and moved them to Feistritz, to his Castle of Wechsel in Austria. Prince Sulkowski inherited seven of the tilting armours, which were, in 1889, acquired by the Germanisches Nationalmuseum. The museum also possesses the four hunting armours. With the exception of the Vienna collection, this is the biggest set of ancient tilting armours in the world. Dietrich did not purchase the eighth armour, so it is highly possible that this is the one now kept in the Higgins Armory of Worcester, Massachusetts (cat. n. 271).

In the time of the Roman Empire only noblemen were allowed to participate in tournaments. Since ordinary citizens were excluded, the Nuremberg patricians, like those of many other towns, decided to organize their own jousts. In Nuremberg, these encounters were called "The Bachelor Jousts" (*Gesellenstechen*). The first took place in 1446 and greatly irritated the aristocracy, since they considered it an offence against their ancient privileges. Nevertheless, even several princes later took part in the Bachelor Jousts of Nuremberg. The interest for this sport declined during the 16th century, the last tournament being celebrated in 1561.

At the beginning, tilting armours were private property. Towards the end of the 15th century, however, the Town Council purchased a number of suits to be rented out later to participants in the Bachelor Joust. This purchase apparently had certain connections with the sumptuary laws prohibiting displays of luxury, due to which patricians were not able to spend great amounts of money on armour. Armours were to be used for the purpose of sport only. Thus the families paid only for the colour decorations, the panache, the arrays of the horses.

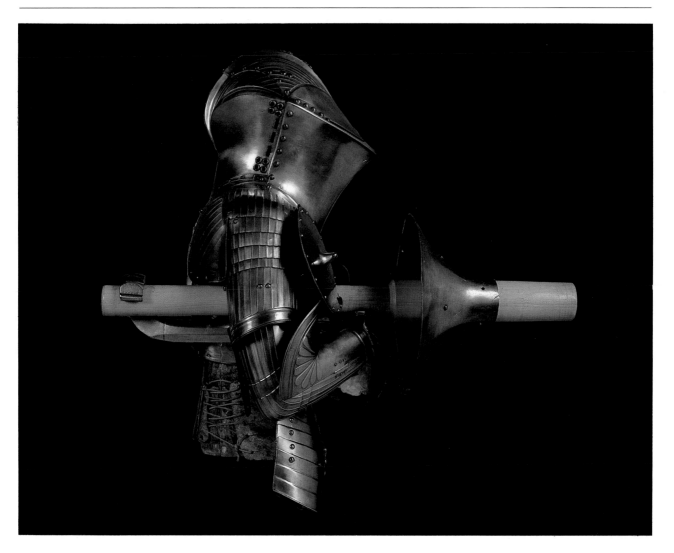

The joust was a special type of tournament. The opponents fought on horse-back, in the open-air, on sandy ground and with no separation line. The adversary was floored using a pointed lance, twelve feet (3.7 m) long and weighing 33 pounds (15 kg). Although the weight of the armour was considerable, the combatants were often badly wounded and accidental deaths were frequent. Owing to the weight of the armour, the rivals had to mount their horses by means of a kind of small ladder. To a certain extent, the armour was simply sports equipment and had no use in war. The tilts were a well received interruption of everyday life and became a high-ranking social event. Each of them was to be remembered in future.

Five of the seven armours in the Germanisches National-museum date back to 1480-1490. In 1535 Valentin Siebenbürger made new pauldrons and brassards either for these or as spare parts. Two of the last pauldrons from the end of the 15th century are kept in the Germanisches National-museum. When the oldest suits of armour were modernised, Siebenbürger seems to have ordered three completely new ones. The tilting armour of the Higgins Armory seems to be one of these three. (*Johannes Willers*)

36
Turkey

Turkish Ottoman period
or Osmanli
Alí ibn Qa lu Med
Helmet, between H 848-850
(1444-1446) and H 855-856
(1451-1481)
Steel, engraved decoration
and background in *cufti
cari* technique or gold
granulation, 49 cm,
diameter 23 cm
Madrid, Instituto Valencia
de Don Juan, 3101
Bibliography: Batuta 1904;
Lane-Poole 1925; Barthold
1928; Combe-Sauveget-Wiet
1931; Mayer 1933; Al Maqrizi
1942; Zaki 1961; Kühnel
1963; Al Basha 1965;
Ettinhausen 1966;
Papadopoulo 1977; Al Basha
1978; Paris 1991

On the helmet, to the left of
the nose protector, there is an
inscription engraved in tugri
script, which is of Turkish
origin. According to this, the
author was Alí ibn Qa lu Med.
Next to it there is a coat of
arms, probably of the royal
workshop, which is repeated
on the back of the gorget or
neck protector. The coat of
arms is designed as a half
moon with two bars.
The inscription on the nose
protector is written in nasji
script and its small size is not
very elegant. The remaining
inscriptions that appear on the
helmet, however, are written
in zulzi and are bigger and
much more elegant. Both the
nasji and the zulzi scripts are
of Arabic, not Turkish origin.
The suggested chronology,
between 1444 and 1481 is due
to the presence, in the inscription on the nose protector, of
the name Mehmed II al Fatih
(the Conqueror), who con-
quered Constantinople in
1453. According to the noble
title, it has been suggested that
the helmet be dated immediately after the conquest.
One of the adjectives accompanying the name of this sultan, is *jaqan*, a noble title
meaning *the chief of the
chiefs*. The word *jaqan* is an

arabised version of the Turkoman word *qagan*, meaning
king in the Turkoman usage
from the 6th and 7th centuries
onwards. The origin of this
word lies in *qan al gan*. The
denomination of *jaqan* was
given to some Turkish Muslim
sultans, and later also to certain *jans* of Turkistan. It was
also used by the Mongoles in
order to designate the supreme political hierarchy,
whereas the sound *jan* was
reserved for lower rank chiefs.
The expression *jaqan* spread
through other countries, as a

consequence of the Mongo-
lian and Turkish dominion. In
Egypt, it was used by the
Mameluke sultan Qa'it Bay.
The decorative technique *cufti
cari*, later than niello, is of Persian origin although it was
later known in Turkish workshops. The granulation was
achieved by means of a chisel
and the use of very fine sheets
of gold.
(*Muhammad Yusuf*)

37
Turkey

Helmet, 16th century
Metal, 41 cm, diameter 21 cm
Istanbul, Topkapi Saray
Museum, 1/2591

The helmet exhibited follows
the line of helmets in the European and Ottoman taste although, in contrast to these, it
is not made of rich metals,
neither is it decorated with
precious stones, diamonds or
a plume of feathers on its top.

On the helmet, made of gilded
metal, there are rivets at the
rim of the skull, serving to join
the ring, fastened to the skull,
with the rest of the helmet.
The design of the piece is
stylized. It is made of tiny metal straps which appear at the
ring, fitted at the edge of the
skull. They become progressively smaller as they rise upwards, joined at their sides,
and culminate in a small metal
sphere.
(*R.E.*)

38
Italy

Lombard school
Helmet, first quarter of the
16th century
Metal, 24 x 19 x 27 cm
Florence, Museo Bardini, 502
Bibliography: Boccia 1984,
p. 28

This piece of armour to cover
the head, is a helmet from the
beginning of the 16th century,
made in the workshops of
Milan. Originally, this helmet,
which now appears to cover
the head only, would also
have protected the face. It is
therefore an example of the so
called *a la veneciana* type,
with austere decoration, but
stylized vegetal motifs, typical
of the Lombard armouries of
that time.
(*R.E.*)

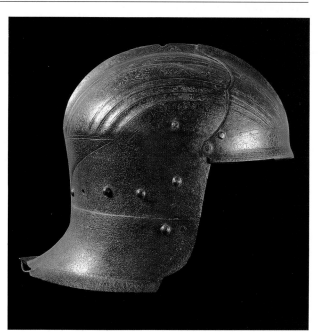

39
Turkey

Sword, approx. 1550
Metal, 93.5 cm; long of the
sheath 87.8 cm
Istanbul, Topkapi Saray
Museum, 1/294
Bibliography: ROGERS-WARD
1990

A curved sword, with golden
damascene decoration at the
end of the blade. The remains
of a decorative inscription on
the blade are illegible.
The handle shows the cross
with golden relief damascene
decoration with undulating
Chinese clouds with snakelike stems and palm leaves in
a painstaking tracing in very
fine black, and connected to
the decorative examples of
Iznik ceramic. The faceted
handle is covered with black
leather with a metal fish with
scales in damascene work.
The end of the handle is also
faceted with a round finish
and ornamented in damas-
cene with a band of botanical

motifs with palm leaves at the
base and different motifs on
each side that are very fine
and intricately worked.
The sheath is lined with black
leather with damascene fer-
rule and lockets, with a motif
of Chinese clouds.
There is also the figure of a
fish, which, as Professor
Rogers indicates, may be the
symbol or emblem of an as yet
unknown person.
(*Purificación Marinetto Sánchez*)

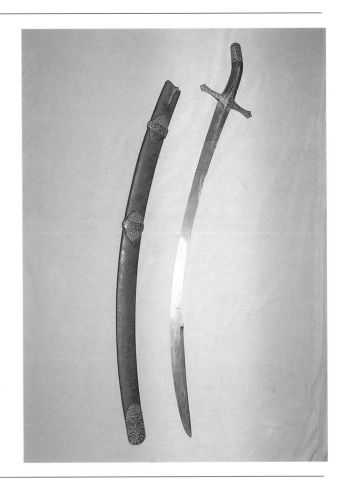

40
China

Ming dynasty (1368-1644)
Dragons in the clouds,
15th century
A gold plaque with
decorative bands, gold
with inlaid precious
and semi-precious stones,
14.5 x 18 cm
London, British Museum,
London, OA 1949.12-13.1

This rectangular plaque is
made of solid gold and is decorated with two dragons and
a flaming pearl among clouds
worked in relief with chased
detail. The whole is joined by
openwork scrolls formed by
piercing the metal. In the
centre of the clouds and in a
double row around the border
of the plaque are semi-
precious stones in settings
formed by upright enclosures.
The plaques are pierced
around the edge for attach-
ment to official or ceremonial
robes. This dragon plaque can
be seen as a very high quality

version of the embroidered
rank badges adopted in the
Ming dynasty and in wide-
spread use in the Qing dynasty (1644-1911). Civil and
military officials were differentiated in rank by the different
animals and birds em-
broidered on their rank
badges. This plaque is one of
a pair that probably came
from an Imperial tomb.
(*J.R. Knox*)

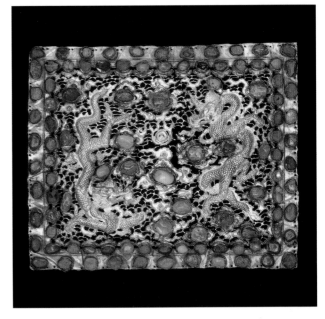

41
China

Ming dynasty (1368-1644)
Plate (bread), 1488-1505
Porcelain, 4.7 cm;
diameter 26.3 cm
Inscriptions: the seal
of the kingdom of emperor
Hongzhi (1488-1505)
London, Percival David
Foundation of Chinese Art,
A.773.
Bibliography:
Lion-Goldschmidt 1957;
Medley 1976, 1978

"Imperial" yellow was the favourite colour of emperor Hongzhi. It was given this name when, centuries later, it was chosen as the protocol colour. Most of this type of Ming pieces carry the usual imperial mark, "da Ming HongZhi Nian Zhi" (made in the rule of Hongzhi of the great Ming Dynasty), painted on the base in cobalt blue, under covering and within a double circle.
"Er Cai" are two Chinese char-

acters meaning "two colours," and are used to describe pieces that only use two colours for decoration. One colour serves as a base, covering large areas and is usually applied by immersing the piece in a bath of varnish. The other is a linear design making the decorative motifs, widely spaced but without losing the harmony of the structure. The most frequent combinations in Ming porcelain are yellow and blue, yellow and purple, yellow and green, yellow and red and green and red.
This "Er Cai" piece owes its yellow colour to antimony oxide, and the blue to cobalt oxide. They need to be fired at different temperatures, so all these pieces have been fired at least twice. The porcelain paste is often fired first. In this case, the unfired porcelain was decorated with the linear design in cobalt blue to be fired at high temperature. Then the monochrome layer of antimony yellow was care-

129

fully applied and the piece was fired again, after which it attained its full glory.
The decorative motifs refer to the Summer: on the inside of the plate, a spray of flowers within a double circle decorates the base, and the sides show lotus flowers, wild apple, pomegranates and a bunch of grapes; on the outside, gardenias.
(*Carmen García Ormaechea*)

42
Indonesia

Eastern Java
Scene from a narrative relief, approx. 15th century
Tuff, relief sculpture
23 x 16.5 x 9 cm
London, Victoria and Albert Museum, IS 12-1989
Bibliography: Boisselier 1990

The 14th and 15th centuries were a period of unprecedented prosperity and wealth in Eastern Java. Power was centred around the court of the Majapahit kingdom (1293 to about 1520), whose capital was in the vicinity of the modern town of Trowulen, on the Brantas river, inland from Surabaya. Although essentially an agrarian state with its prosperity based on rice production, Majapahit came increasingly to generate its wealth from the control of the Java Sea trade through which the rich spice trade of eastern Indonesia had to pass. The rulers of Majapahit built

numerous temples throughout the region, utilising both local stone and fired brick, sometimes dressed in a locally quarried chalk-like limestone known as tuff.
All were decorated with flamboyant designs, usually figurative reliefs, often in a series of registers providing elaborate illustrations to well-known religious texts.
In addition to religious structures the royal household of Majapahit built extensive palace complexes, both at the capital and at regional centres. It is evident from the excavated remains that such structures were richly decorated, in both modelled terracotta and carved brick and tuff. The subject matter of this relief has not been identified and it is unclear if it was carved for a religious or secular building. Its charm lies in its delicate detailing of scenes of everyday life: approaching a stream a woman holds the folds of her skirt (sarong), while servants carrying baskets wade

through the water; the landscape elements are stylised into flamboyant foliage. The frieze above and below is decorated with alternating flower and "eye" motifs. The stylisation of the human figures, and particularly the frontal treatment of the figures with the heads in three-quarter profile, is a convention preserved to this day in the shadow puppets (wayang kulit) of Java and Bali.
(*John Guy*)

43
China

Ming dynasty (1368-1644)
Zhu Yongming (1440-1526)
Poem in italic calligraphy
(kuangcao), 1523
Calligraphy, ink on paper,
horizontal roll,
655.6 x 24.6 cm
Inscriptions: written by
Yongming on the 25th day
of the 4th month
of the second year of the
reign of Jiajing
Seals: Zeng Ketian, Lu
Tunan, Tang Yongqian, Bi
Qiufan, Jiaqing and
Xuantong Beijing, Imperial
Palace Museum

130

A native of Changzhou (now
Suzhou in Jiangsu Province),
Zhu Yongming, also known as
Zhu Xizhe, lived from 1440 to
1526. He often called himself
Zhishau or Zhizhisheng because he was born with an
extra finger on one hand. He
passed the provincial examination in 1492 and became

magistrate of Xingning County
in Guangdong Province. He
was then appointed assistant
prefectural magistrate of Yingtian (now Nanjing) but before
long he gave up the post and
returned to his native town
because of illness. He was an
excellent poet and calli-
grapher. He learned calligraphy from his maternal
grandmother when he was
young. Later he studied Wang
Xizhi, Wang Xianzhu, Zhang
Xu, Huai Su, Li Yong, Su
Dongpo, Huang Tingjian, Mi
Fei and Zhao Mengfu, all great
masters of past ages. He was
an expert in all the major
styles of calligraphy regular,
"running" and "grass" and developed a unique style of his
own by bringing together the
strong points of each. He was
considered, along with Wen
Zhengming and Wang Chong,
one of the three great calligraphers of the much hon-
oured Wu school of scholar
artists.

The manuscript poems of *Zhu
Yongming* contain three
poems, entitled *The Terrace of
the Song of the Great Wind,
Ascent to the Li Bai Restaurant – in Lieu of a Letter to Mr.
Shi of Huzhou* and *Ready to
Return Home*. The poems
were written in the "grass"
style, containing 405 characters in 94 lines. They were
composed when the author
meditated on an ancient event
at a historic site, or felt home-
sick at his official post away
from home or called to mind
his old acquaintances. The
poems can be found in his
work *The Huaixintang Collection of Essays and Poems*.
"The restaurant, to the south
of the Tianjin bridge was built
by Dong Zaoqi in memory of
the great poet, Li Bai. Li and
his poet friend He Zhizhang
have now departed but their
beautiful poems never fail to
move my heart. Dusty and
windy, the imperial capital is
not an attractive place to live,

and so I decided to return to
the south where I could enjoy
the beauty of the autumn
among the ruins of the Gusu
palace in my home town. My
ship was in Jiyang where I
bought a jug of wine to forget
my yearnings. Whilst I was
going up to the restaurant to
offer a libation to the great
poet, in my mind I saw him
smile while his friend stayed
silent. Outside the laments
drifted under the bridge and
the sun set, little by little, behind the floating clouds." "In
lieu of a letter to Mr. Shi of
Huzhou I wrote these lines to
him wishing we could share
peace and the pleasure of
fishing together in the river
next to Xisai hill or Heron Island. One summer day, I went
to visit Wang Xu at his house.
Then Yun Zhuang joined us.
After several glasses of wine
Yun showed me several fans
and invited me to write on
them. I agreed because I had
good quality brushes and ink

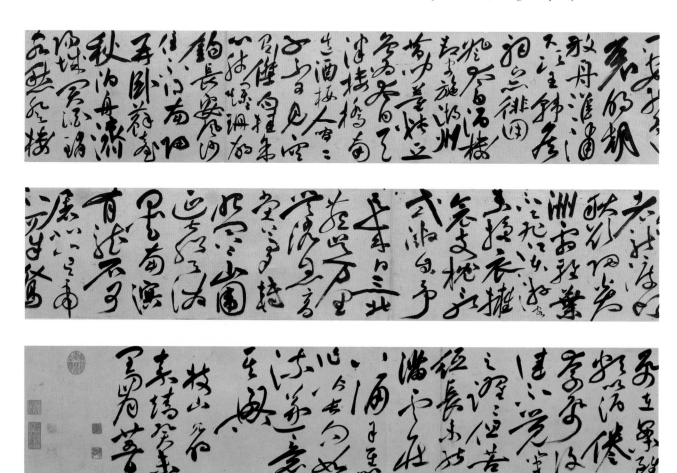

available. Then Yun unrolled a piece of paper on the table to take advantage of my calligraphy. Although I felt tired after drinking, I could not resist the temptation offered by such high quality paper. To fill them, they asked me to write some of my poems, helped by Yu's dictation."

The Terrace of the Song of the Great Wind

"I left the imperial capital without a single glance backwards. When I was crossing the Mang and Dang mountains I climbed up to the terrace where Lord Pei sang the song of the great wind. All the brave soldiers were prepared to die for him because he knew how to choose the right person for the necessary task. At last he found an empire with modest arms and impassive, he sang the Song of the Great Wind. Han Xin, Peng Yue, Ying Bu and Lu Wan died, one after another, at the hands of perverse court-

iers, without fulfilling their aspirations. Nearly two thousand years have passed, but who does not bemoan their death? When my ship reaches the shores of Huai tomorrow I shall probably walk through the riverside temples of Xiang Yu and Han Xui."

The characters are well formed and spaced. The strokes are vigorous and graceful with movement in every stroke and a dynamic structural equilibrium. The many variations in the shapes and structures all combine to form a balanced whole. Two seals, one bearing the words "The Seal of Zhu Yongming" and the other the words Xi Zhe appear after the work. The scroll also bears inscriptions made by Zeng Keqian, Lu Tunan and Tan Yongqian and the seals of Tan Yongqian, Bi Qiufan and the Qing Dynasty emperors Jiaqing (1796-1820) and Xuan Tong (1909-1911). This indicates that the

scroll passed through private hands before entering the imperial collection under the Qing emperors.
(*Yang Chengbin*)

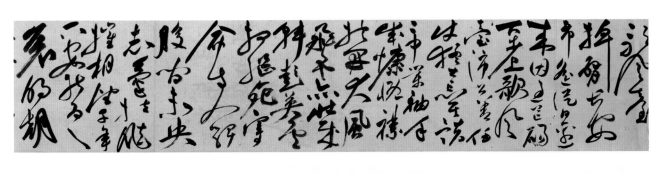

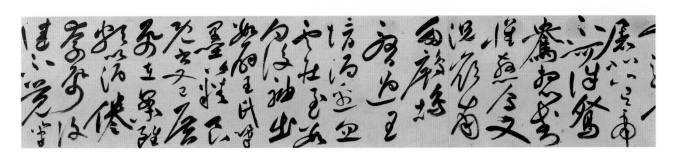

44
Italy

Lorenzo da Mugiano (active in Milan at the beginning of 16th century)
Louis XII, king of France, 1508
Sculpture, marble
70.4 x 38 cm
Inscriptions: MEDIOLANENSIS LAURENCIUS DE MUGIANO OPUS FECIT 1508
Paris, Musée du Louvre, M. R. 1596
Exhibition: Paris, 1968
Bibliography: GUILHERMY 1852, XII, pp. 90-91; VITRY 1900, pp. 150-151; CHIROL 1952, p. 173, cat. 60, fig. 24; WEISS 1953 XVI, pp. 1-12, 351; PARIS 1968, n. 268; BEAULIEU 1978, pp. 166-167

This statue of the French king Louis XII dressed in the "Roman style" has had a chequered history. It was sent, together with two other statues, from Milan to the castle of Georges d'Amboise on February 25, 1509. It was installed in the Grand Maison, first in the patio, then in a gallery. After many mishaps the piece, now without the head and right arm, entered the Musée des Monuments Fra????nais, where it was restored by Beauvallet, who made new parts to replace those that were missing, including the legs. The sculpture then went to the Versailles Museum and then to the Louvre (1850), where the added parts were removed.

Although mutilated, the torso is an extremely beautiful example of ancient influence in the Lombard artistic environment where Lorenzo da Mugiano trained. He was one of the few sculptors of the *cantiere* of the duomo of Milan whose works have survived. For this commemorative statue Lorenzo da Mugiano performed an extremely painstaking task as can be seen in the decorated breastplate of the French king, the folds of the sash and the

sleeves of the shirt, as well as in the collar of the order of Saint Michael that rests upon his shoulders.

The right hand is lost, and the left hand rests upon a map of Italy (ITALIA) in which the main cities are symbolised by their most important monuments; the duomo of Milan, the Colosseum of Rome, the baptistry of Florence, etc.
(*Joan Sureda i Pons*)

45
Mexico

Mexican culture, late postclassical
Box of the warriors, 1321-1521
Stone, 44.5 x 73 x 65 cm
From Mexico City
Mexico City, Museo Nacional de Antropología, 10-46626

This is one of the largest stone boxes known in all Aztec art. Its sides are decorated with scenes of warriors, a theme that is relatively frequent in Mexican iconography, as in this culture military activity was one of the main motifs. These usually adopt the form of processions of warriors, as in the Stone of the Warriors, or the frieze in the Great Temple, but sometimes they are they are pairs of warriors – generally one victorious and one defeated – as in the Tizoc stone or the Cuauhxicalli of Moctezuma I.

This piece shows pairs of opposed warriors, wielding clubs or *macuahuitl,* swords with obsidian blades, or shields. In general terms, it can be said that the style of these reliefs is closer to Toltec art than to the monuments of the Aztec empire's periods of greatest splendour; the arms are not very differentiated, the heads are large, the design is deeply hollowed out, etc. This leads us to believe that it is a very early work, maybe from the first third of the fifteenth century, or perhaps before this. Looking at the proportions of the human figures represented, they are closer to the proportions used in codices, which also tends to confirm the antiquity of the piece.
(*José Alcina Franch*)

46
Iran

Gilan
Battle between Kay Khusraw and the King of Makran, 1493-1494
Miniature painting, watercolour on paper
From the *Shah-nama* by Firdausi
Copenhagen, The David Collection, 22/1979
Exhibitions: Humlebaek, 1987
Bibliography: REVY 1987, 27, n. 3, cat. n. 216; FOLSACH 1990, n. 23

The *Shah-nama* (*The Book of the Kings*), written by Abu'l Qasim Firdausi around 1000, is unquestionably the greatest Persian epic. In some 60,000 verses Firdausi relates the history of Iran from the first mythical kings to the end of the Sasanian dynasty. One of the poem's central themes are the endless disputes and wars between the Persians and their neighbours in which their skills, courage and nobility, as well as their deceits, are depicted, though scenes of requited and unrequited love, among others of a domestic nature, are also described.

The painting depicts the battle between the armies of the Persian king-hero Kay Khusraw and the king of Makran, who had refused to supply the Persian army with provisions. The king dies in the battle and the Persian hero Tus is about to cut off his head. The noble Kay Khusraw stops him, saying that a prince should be given an honorable funeral even though he be an enemy. Many illustrated manuscripts from the *Shah-nama* have been preserved since the end of the 15th century and beginning of the 16th century. This miniature painting is from the two volume copy made by Salik b. Sa'id in 1493-1494 for the sultan Ali Mirza, the ruler of Gilan, to the south of the Caspian sea. Its style has been described as "royal Turkman" as opposed to "commercial Turkman," but although it is a fine manuscript it lacks the elegance that characterises royal commissions. A typical feature of the paintings in this version of the *Shah-nama* is the bold use of colour and the preference for representing human figures with relatively big heads which is why the manuscript is often referred to as the "Big-Head" *Shah-nama*.
(*Kield V. Folsach*)

47

Iran

Gilan
Salik b. Sa'id
*Battle between Kay Khusraw
and Afrasiyab*, 1493-1494
Painting, opaque
watercolour, ink and gold
on paper, 23.4 x 20.6 cm
Washington D.C., Arthur M.
Sackler Gallery, Smithsonian
Institute, S 1986.175
Exhibitions: Washington
D.C., 1988-1989

134

This miniature painting is from
a copy of the *Shah-nama*
often referred to as the "Big-
Head" *Shah-nama*, which is
divided into two volumes. The
first volume, in the Turk ve
Islam Eserleri Muzesi, Istanbul,
contains 202 paintings, while
the second, in the Istanbul
University Library, has 109
paintings. Although the exact
number of dispersed folios
from the manuscript is not
known, they all appear to
come from the first volume of
the manuscript. Their removal
must have occurred before
1929, when a scholar noted
that the manuscript had been
stolen from the Monastery of
the Dancing Dervishes in Ga-
lata. While there has been a
certain amount of confusion
over the proper reading of the
manuscript's date and the
source of its striking paintings,
it is now accepted that they
were produced for sultan Ali
Mirza of Gilan (1478-1504).
The paintings in the manuscript can be divided into two
groups. Some are executed in
a manner closely related to
miniatures from Turkmanistan
such as those found in the
Makhzan al-asrar of Haydar
copied for sultan Ya'qub in
1478. Others (such as the
*Battle between Kay Khusraw
and Afrasiyab*) reflect a striking departure from the conventions of 15th century painting; they are composed of
large figures with big heads
(from which the manuscript
derives its sobriquet) set in unusually dramatic postures.
In the confrontation depicted
here, Kay Khusraw, having

just slain the warrior Shida, is
attacked by three more of
Afrasiyab's men. The Iranian
king quickly dispatches the
first of the Turanians, then
turns towards the second but
is unable to wound him with
his spear. Impressed by his
strength and courage, Kay
Khusraw draws his sword and

cuts him in half. This so
frightens the third of the Afrasiyab's warriors that he flees
the field of battle, causing the
rest of the Turanian forces to
retreat.
(*Milo Cleveland Beach*)

48
Iran

Tabriz, Shiraz
Iskandar and the seven wise men, 1500-1510
Miniature painting, tempera on paper, 30 x 18 cm
From the *Iskandar-nama*, the fifth book of the *Khamsa* of Nizami
Copenhagen, The David Collection, 43/1981
Exhibitions: Humlebaek, 1987
Bibliography: Revy 1987, 27, n. 3, cat. 218

The *Iskandar-nama* (*The Romance of Alexander*) is the fifth book of the famous *Khamsa* written by the Persian poet Nizami in the last quarter of the 12th century.

The conqueror Iskandar, or Alexander the Great, was the natural enemy of Iran and the ancient Persian chroniclers represented him as such. This attitude underwent a gradual change until he was depicted, in the Koran Dhu'l-Karnayn (Alexander), as an example of a just ruler. In Iran, Firdausi was the first to praise Iskander in his *Shah-nama* (*The Book of the Kings*). He describes him as courageous, prudent and wise, and to make him more acceptable to the Persians he says he was the son of Shah Darab (Darius II) and a Greek princess and hence the legitimate heir to the Persian throne after the death of his stepbrother Dara (Darius III). Nizami was the first to portray Alexander in a positive light, stressing his noble character and philosophical wisdom. The scene depicted in the painting shows Iskandar surrounded by Greek philosophers such as Aristotle, Socrates and Plato.

Around the year 1400 Timur (Tamerlane) and his family ruled virtually the whole of the Islamic east. From the middle of the 15th century, however, the west was lost to Turkman confederations from Inland Anatolia but soon they were to conquer Azerbaijan and western Iran. Although the Turkman court and art

were not as refined as the Tamerlanes, schools specialising in miniature paintinngs were established around Tabriz and Shiraz. Shiraz became the centre of a great output of miniature paintings, considered to be executed in the "commercial" Turkman style as opposed to the prestigious royal commissions. The paintings, like this one from a dispersed *Khamsa* manuscript, are fairly conventional but often display a certain characteristic appeal.
(*Kield V. Folsach*)

49
Persia

Herat, Khurasan
School of Kamal al-Din
Bihzad
*Workmen constructing
the castle of Khavarnaq,*
(1494-1495)

Miniature painting, gouache,
gold and black ink
on paper, 24.3 x 17 cm
From Nizami's poem Haft
Paykar (Seven portraits,
or Seven beauties)
in the Kahmsa (or Five
Poems) of Nizami
From The Moghul Imperial
Library, London, The British
Library, 6801, folio 154 verso
Exhibitions: London, 1967;
London, 1971; Washington
D.C.-Los Angeles, 1989
Bibliography of the
miniature: MARTIN-ARNOLD
1926; STCHOUKINE, 1950, 27,
pp. 301-313; STCHOUKINE,
1954, pl. 69-71, 83-88; GRAY
1961, pp. 120-123; ROBINSON
1967, p. 51; TITLEY 1977,
p. 141; LUKENS-SWIETOCHOWSKI
1979, pp. 206, 209; TITLEY
1983, pp. 72, 76-77;
LENTZ-LOWRY 1989,
pp. 287-291, 296-297, 299,
357-358
Bibliography of the text:
LONDON 1924; RITTER 1927;
ISTANBUL 1934; NIZAMI 1934;
PAGLIARO BAUSANI 1960; NEW
YORK 1975; OXFORD 1978

The painting depicts the construction of the castle of Khavarnaq for Nu'man, a king of
Yemen. In Nizami's poem, the
young Persian prince Bahram,
later to become the Sansanian
emperor Bahram Gür, is sent
to this citadel, "whose towers
touched the moon." Raised
among Arabs in the pure atmosphere of the countryside,
Bahram was educated in the
arts and sciences and the accomplishments of chivalry and
warfare.
Haft Paykar (Seven portraits,
or Seven beauties), tells of the
Bahram Gür and his seven
wives, princesses from various
regions around the world. On
each day of the week, Bahram
visits one of his consorts, who
tells him a story. (The source

– via Schiller – of the plot of
Puccini's opera *Turandot* is to
be found in the tale of Turan-
dukt, the Russian princess).
Each of the seven stories has
a different mood and associ-
ations, and illustrates a particular aspect of human destiny. However, *Haft Paykar* is
no mere collection of tales: it
is a conceptually integrated
work of genius. In Rudolph
Gelpke's words, Nizami "creates an artistic image of the all-
embracing cosmic order with
its intricate symbolic system,
which we encounter in so
many cultures and civilizations." One might add that the
poem also portrays both an
ideal picture of kingship and
a subtle image of the inward
nature of the human soul.
This painting of the construction of Khavarnaq exemplifies
the tendency towards greater
visual *realism* – by the standards of Islamic art – found in
Herat painting of the later 15th
century. Novel, for Persia, is
the concern to portray character through facial features and
with the details of implements
and materials. But the form
and disposition of the ladder
against the building show "realism" to be subordinated to
compositional and other
priorities. Elegance and technical virtuosity are evident in
the draughtmanship as well as
in the highly refined sense of
design and colour characteristic of the Persian miniature.
In addition, there may well be
a symbolic value in the scene
depicted here. Just as the
cosmos is made up of com-
plementary elements, so the
process of building depends
upon the orderly deployment
of qualified workmen and of
materials. Royal patrons ex-
pected to see the harmony
and order – real or claimed –
of their domains reflected in
their architecture and court
art. The impeccable composition of the painting is perhaps
intended to reflect the good
order and control of the process of construction and
hence, by implication, of the
patron's domain in general.

In the year H 900 (1494-1495),
when this exquisite manu-
script was completed, literature and the arts were
flourishing under the patronage of Mir sultan Husayn and
his circle. The city of Herat
was the focus of a high culture
as vital and sophistocated as
any to be found in Europe at
the time.
(*Muhammed Isa Waley*)

50
India

Mandú
Preparation of sweets for Ghiyas al-Din Sultan of Mandú, approx. 1495-1505
Miniature painting; opaque watercolour paintings and gold, and black and red ink on paper;
folio 31 x 21.5 cm;
text and picture panel: 29.5 x 15 cm; miniature: 18 x 15 cm
196 folios; 10 lines of bold Nashji script in black ink, with headings in red, within text panels ruled in gold, black and blue;
50 miniatures in the sultanate style of Mandú
London, The British Library, 10. 149 (Ethé 2775), folio 6 verso
Exhibitions: London, 1982, n. 41; Boston, 1985, n. 2; New York, 1985, n. 78
Bibliography: ETHÉ 1903, n. 2775; SKELTON 1958, pp. 44-50; KHANDALAVALA-CHANDRA 1969, pp. 58-63; LOSTY 1982, pp. 40-42, 66-68

Illustration from the *Ni'matnama* (*Book of Recipes*), book begun for the sultan Ghiyas al-Din of Mandú (1469-1500), and completed in the reign of his son Nasir al-Din Khalgi (1500-1510). This is the only copy, and is probably a holograph.

This miniature is from a book of recipes for preparing meat dishes, sweets, perfumes and aphrodisiacs, written for Sultan Ghiyas al-Din of Mandú (reg. 1469-1500). Mandú was the capital of Malwa, a fertile plateau in Central India, which became independent of the Sultans of Delhi in the 15th century. It was ruled by a dynasty of Turkish origin from Central Asia. On succeeding to the throne, Ghiyas al-Din announced that he was handing over the cares of state to his ministers and that henceforth his life was to be devoted entirely to pleasure. In pursuit of this principle, he recruited an army of 10,000 Abyssinian slave-girls to protect him. This

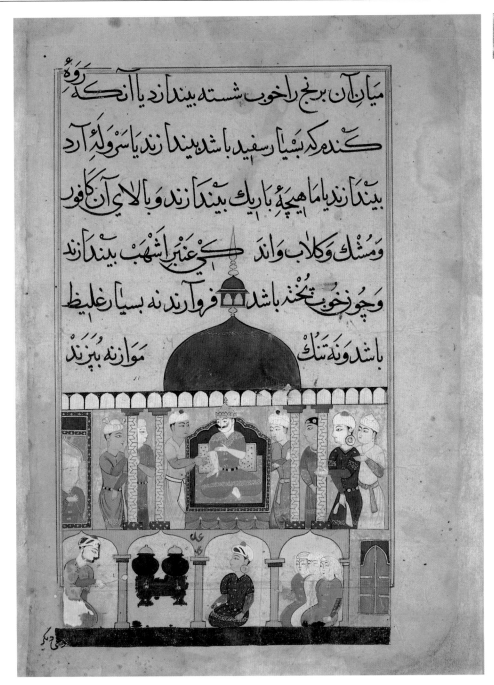

book of epicurean delights was begun for him, but was not finished until the reign of his son. Many of the attendants in the miniatures are the Sultan's women, dressed in male costume but wearing large earrings and gold rings round their necks.

In this miniature the sultan Ghiyas al-Din is seated on a throne in his palace conversing with his attendants (mostly male) on either side. One of the female attendants has a white handkerchief, a tradi-

tional symbol of royalty in medieval India. Above is a great blue dome, which like many of the domes in this manuscript seems, in a cosmological symbolism, to represent the blue vault of heaven. A door-keeper with a slender staff of office looks on from the left. Beneath, at a lower level in the palace kitchens, *sarüla* (sweets made of flour, sugar, ghee, poppyseeds, dates and almonds, which are then cooked in milk) is being prepared in two pots; the

cook looks thoughtfully at his ladle, while the assembled women (one of them a royal attendant in male attire) wait expectantly.
(*Jerry Patrick Losty*)

51
India

Mandú
Preparation of a meat broth for Ghiyas al-Din sultan of Mandú, approx. 1495-1505
Miniature, opaque watercolour pigments and gold, and black and red ink on paper; folio 31 x 21.5 cm; text and picture panel 23 x 15 cm; miniature 14 x 15 cm
It contains 196 folios; 10 lines of bold Nasij script in black ink, with headings in red, within text panels ruled in gold, black, and blue; 50 miniatures in the sultanate style of Mandú
London, The British Library, 10. 149 (Ethé 2775), folio 18 recto
Exhibitions: London, 1982, n. 41; Boston, 1985, n. 2; New York, 1985, n. 78
Bibliography: ETHÉ 1903, n. 2775; SKELTON 1958, pp. 44-50; KHANDALAVALA-CHANDRA 1969, pp. 58-63; LOSTY 1982, pp. 40-42, 66-68

From the same manuscript as the illustration *Preparation of Sweets for Ghiyas al-Din Sultan of Mandu*. Sultan Ghiyas al-Din is seated on a throne in a pavilion in his garden, surrounded by attendants, while outside two cooks prepare a *yakhni* or meat broth. A female attendant brings the finished food in a blue-and-white dish (Chinese porcelains were highly prized in medieval India) covered with a gold lid while another hands a cup to the sultan. A Chinese cloud floats above in a golden sky. Indian and Persian elements are blended here, as they are throughout the manuscript. The throne, costumes (apart from the earrings), and landscape are of 15th century Persian origin, from the Turkman school of painting in Shiraz; the endless panorama of the horizon, the faces in full profile, and the architectural details are Indian. Medieval India's Muslim rulers imported illustrated manuscripts, calligraphers, and painters from the Iranian world into India to prepare for their own libraries the prized illustrated manuscripts which were a significant feature of Persian culture. Shiraz was the most common source of both artists and manuscripts. Few artists, however, could be induced to leave Persia or to remain long in India; consequently the Indian artists, whose painting traditions were quite different, had to learn what they could as quickly as possible and soon reverted to painting in an Indian manner. Thus the so-called "sultanate" manuscripts (those produced for the Indian Muslim rulers before the Mughal dynasty) are thus rich mixtures of Persian and Indian styles.

(*Jerry Patrick Losty*)

Boabdil's clothing

When the emir Boabdil was taken prisoner, his captors were given his rich, ornate weapons and clothing as booty and in 1892, on the 400th anniversary of the taking of Granada, the heirs handed these articles over to the Museo del Ejército in Madrid. Of the arms that were seized a splendid sword and a magnificent Nasrid court rapier, which in my opinion were ceremonial court arms rather than battle arms, have been preserved. The sword perhaps dates from the end of the 14th or the beginning of the 15th century while the rapier, judging from the palms that adorn its hilt and sheath, dates from the reign of Yusuf I (1333-1354), and was partly restored in the 15th century due to wear. If either weapon had been needed for use in battle, however, they would have been as effective as any.

The clothing taken from the prisoner included a long, wide cloth of linen for the turban; a magnificent *malluta* or *marlota* of red velvet (the colour of the Nasrid dynasty, the Banu Ahmar) made in the Gothic textile mills of the Christian kingdoms of the peninsula; a pair of *ajfaf* (singular: *juff*) or very thin knee-length leather boots and a pair of *rawahi* (singular: *rihiyya*) or leather shoes. Perhaps these were the garments that were taken from the prisoner: the rich footwear to prevent him from escaping, the splendid *malluta* coat, the sovereign's distinctive fine white linen of the *imama* and, of course, the magnificent court arms from the Nasrid armory. The clothes were new, practically worn for the first time by Boabdil, since the footwear is spotless, show no signs of wear, have no creases, or evidence of the form of his feet and legs. The same is true of the immaculate *malluta* and the linen of the *imama*. It seems that the Nasrid emir was "dressed for the occasion," for his first battle as

sovereign. The clothes were probably made after he had succeeded to the throne, as the *malluta* is worn when it is cold as is typical of spring in Granada or eastern Andalusia. This would explain why he was armed with the best sword and rapier from the Nasrid armory of his forefathers and not his overthrown father, Abu l-Hasan, to symbolize his being the legitimate Nasrid emir. If the horse was captured as well, neither the saddle, trappings, or reins have been preserved, perhaps because they were used for two or three generations given their splendour and practicality. The *rawahi* and at least one of the weapons would have been carried in the saddle since it would have been very uncomfortable to carry them in the bandoleer across his shoulder from Granada to Lucena due to both their weight and the horse's movement. Perhaps a page carried at least one of the weapons, but we do not know for sure. This question has yet to be resolved. Let us begin by describing the clothing.
(*Antonio Fernández Puertas*)

52
Spain

Al-Andalus, Nasrid period
Malluta or *marlota of Boabdil "El Chico"*
Crióson velvet embroidered with gold thread,
90 x 40 cm; length of sleeves, 50 cm
Madrid, Museo del Ejército, 24.702

Bibliography: FALKE 1922; BERNIS 1956; BAER 1967; ROMERO 1975; GONZÁLEZ MENA 1976; SHEPHERD 1978; BERNIS 1979; DODDS 1992; HERRERO 1992; PARTEARROYO 1992

53
Spain

Al-Andalus, Nasrid period
Imama or *turban of Boabdil "El Chico"*
Linen, 312 x 60 cm
Madrid, Museo del Ejército, 24.702-1

Bibliography: FALKE 1922;
BERNIS 1956; BAER 1967;
GARCÍA GÓMEZ 1970; ROMERO
1975; GONZÁLEZ MENA 1976;
SHEPHERD 1978; BERNIS 1979;
DODDS 1992; HERRERO 1992;
PARTEARROYO 1992

140

54
Spain

Al-Andalus, Nasrid period
Ajfaf or *boots of Boabdil*
"El Chico"
Leather, 63 x 18.5 cm; right
foot 25 cm; left foot 24 cm;
rear opening to allow the
leg to bend 7.3 cm
Madrid, Museo del Ejército,
24.702-3
Bibliography: FALKE 1922;
BERNIS 1956; BAER 1967;
ROMERO 1975; GONZÁLEZ MENA
1976; SHEPHERD 1978; BERNIS
1979; DODDS 1992; HERRERO
1992; PARTEARROYO 1992

55
Spain

Al-Andalus, Nasrid period
Ribiyyas of Boabdil
"El Chico"
Leather; right foot 25.5 cm;
left foot 24.5 cm; width
8.5 cm; height of heel
9.5 cm; uppers 12.5 cm
Madrid, Museo del Ejército
24.702-2
Bibliography: FALKE 1922;
BERNIS 1956; BAER 1967;
ROMERO 1975; GONZÁLEZ MENA
1976; SHEPHERD 1978; BERNIS
1979; DODDS 1992; HERRERO
1992; PARTEARROYO 1992

This *malluta* or *marlota*,
which belonged to the Nasrid
emir Boabdil, is a typical
example of this Spanish-Mos-
lem garment. It is a magnificent red garment, red being
the Nasrid dynasty colour,
which was probably made
after he succeeded to the
throne, and designed for the
cold years of 1482-1483. It is
made of Gothic Christian velvet and the pieces left over
after cutting the cloth for its
length and width were used
for the sleeves and for the
areas under the armpits. Per-

haps this was done for lack of
more velvet due to the economic crisis, the civil war between father and son and
against the Christians, and the
need to finish it quickly.
These remnants were attached
to areas that would not normally be seen. The garment
was worn over the other
clothes and close-fitting across
the shoulders, some 40 cm
wide, and was 96 cm long.
Knives were inserted in both
sides so the rest remained
loose-fitting. Its bell-shaped
skirt reaches to the knees and
it is completely open at the
front from its loose low neck
and is fastened from the waist
downwards by only three
pleats. The wide rectangular-
shaped sleeves are 50 cm in
length and the ends are open
and cut on the bias from the
outside to the inside. The front
parts have a slightly slanted
slot on each side to put the
hands in, but they are not
pockets. Judging from the
width of the shoulders, the
length of the sleeves, and the
size of his feet Boabdil must
have been between 1.60 and
1.65 metres tall and of fairly
slight build.
The malluta in the 15th cen-
tury. The term *marlota*, which
appears in documents from
the beginning of the 15th century, apparently referred to
different garments, like the *al-*
yubba or *aljuba*, with different tailoring. They could be
ankle or knee-length. Its name
comes from the Greek gar-
ment meaning "the Egyptian
Copts will be transformed."
Prince Radzivil described the
costumes worn by the Egyptian Mamelukes as "marlotas,"
which had very wide sleeves.
During the 15th century, a letter to Alfonso V of Aragon
from the Granada *Diwan al-*
Insa, or chancellery, under
Muhammad VIII, dated May
1418, listed the magnificent
presents that the Nasrid sovereign had sent him. These included a *yubba* with golden
trimmings, a silk *yallabiya*, a
durra, a *burnus*, two head-
dresses with silk embroidery,

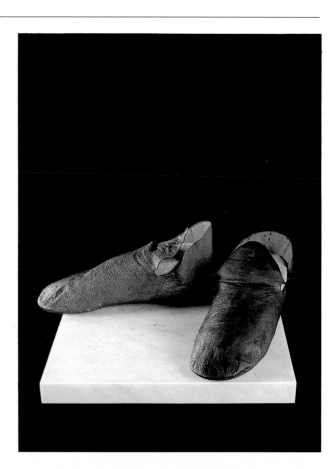

and a *yalläbiya marlota* with gold embroidery. The monarch's inventory of goods written in 1424 also mentioned Moorish garments.

The count of Plasencia's inventory of goods, made up in 1456, also mentions three *marlotas*. The *Arab-Granada Documents* mentions the sale of a *marlota* on 25 December 1483 and another sold to a woman on 7 December 1492, eleven months after the taking of Granada. So it was worn equally by Nasrid women and men.

In 1485, in Castile, queen Isabella I ordered a brocade *marlota* to be made for prince Ahmad, Boabdil's oldest son and heir, who was being held hostage in the court as part of the agreement signed to free Boabdil in 1483. When she found out about his interest in Christianity, she regretted ordering his return from Moclín Castle to his father, Boabdil, after the taking of Granada in January 1492. The *marlota* also appears in the wardrobe inventory of Infante Juan, the son of the Catholic Monarchs, in 1486, and appears several times in the accounts of Isabella I's treasurer, and once in king Ferdinand V's accounts. Pedro Mártir, in the account he gave to the Catholic Monarchs in 1486 of his ambassadorship to Mameluke Egypt, said that, as far as the Egyptians' clothes were concerned, "there is little difference between their coats and what your people of Granada call *aliubbas* and the Spanish call *marlotas*. Their length varied with some reaching to the ankles, like those worn by Don Rodrigo Ponce of Leon, marquis of Cádiz, before he was buried."

Fray Pedro of Alcala translates *malluta* as "the hooded habit of a monk," pointing out that in the Iberian peninsula it was also called *yubba* or *aljuba*. It also appears with this meaning in *A Thousand and One Nights*. The Spanish ballads mention it frequently. It should be borne in mind that in the 15th and 16th centuries there were probably at least two garments with the same name. R. Dozy thinks that Muslems wore the *malluta* under the *capellar*, or hooded cloak that is shorter than the *burnus*, while R. Richard defines the *marlota* as "a relatively short, closed garment with sleeves, that probably had a hood," which for Rachel Arié means that it was fairly similar to the present *yellaba*, which in turn might have been what was called the *yallabiya* in the last quarter of the 15th century.

Carmen Bernis thinks that the *marlota* was a winter costume, thicker and heavier than the summer *quezote*, and on studying its pattern says: "The book by Juan of Alcega, one of the most curious Spanish books about tailoring, published in 1850, explains the patterns used to make a *marlota*. A short bell-shaped garment is obtained from these patterns formed by placing a knife on both sides, with sleeves and without a hood." Boabdil's *marlota*, which we have studied here, is like this as are the *marlotas* represented in some of the fifty four wooden panels in the Toledo low choir stall by Rodrigo Alemán between 1489 and 1494, at the time of the war of Granada. The same is true of those depicted in paintings like the one worn by the kings in Bartolomé de Caznedas' *Adoration of the Magi* in the Royal chapel or chancery in Granada Cathedral.

(*Antonio Fernández Puertas*)

The imama or turban of Boabdil "El Chico". This is a smooth and very thin band of taffeta linen. Being transparent it is folded in half, lengthwise, to give it greater consistency. The warp is twisted using Z torsion and has threads arranged lengthwise. The weft also has the same threads twisted with Z torsion, although they are thinner than the warp. Before the ends are reached there are two thick alternate patches of linen weft. The ends are finished and adorned with braid that is made with the linen warp, with golden and red silk wefts, and gold braid threads in alternating diagonal patterns which resemble an ear of wheat and form geometrical shapes. The braid edging has three strips of red silk that simulates a delicate form of a golden ear of wheat. The tassels are formed by interlacing the linen thread of the warp with the red and golden silk of the weft and the gold braid threads, producing threads of different thickness. The turban is mentioned constantly in the *Court Annals* of Al-Hakan II, as part of the caliph's presents (García Gómez, 1970, p. 49), and due to its delicate and transparent nature it was doubled in two or three parts, like the *imama* of Hixam II (Partearroyo, 1992, pp. 225-226). It appears at the end of the caliphate in the gold and silk caliph embroidery, known as the shroud of Saint Lazarus of Autun (France), in the figure of a falconer with the word "al-Muzaffar" (the victorious) engraved on the belt, and refers to Abd al-Malik, the son of Almanzor, for whom it was made between 1007 and 1008. It would originally have been an embroidered mantle. Falconers with *imama* or turbans with conical caps are also depicted in this embroidery (Baer, 1967, p. 43, fig. 4, 5, and 6). It also appears in the figure of a drinker, during the *Taifa* epoch in the 11th century, in one of the circular medallions of the *Játiva* font (Baer, 1970-71, pp. 142-166; Dodds, 1992, p. 261, fig. 49). In the 12th century it appears in the Almoravid tapestry called the "lion strangler" (Partearroyo, 1992, 320). In the 13th century it is depicted many times, beginning with the manuscript of Hadiz Bayad wa Riyad, where the figures wearing turbans resemble his contemporaries depicted in the tapestry of Bishop Gurb of Barcelona (Shepherd, 1978, 111-134).

(*Cristina Partearroyo*)

The ajfaf or boots of Boabdil "El Chico". These are probably made with very thin cowhide and have no lining. They are made with two pieces, one for the sole and the tongue, the other for the rest of the boot. The seam is hidden by the decoration, made with linen thread, between the decorated part and the leg of the boot. Atypically, it has no sole. The colour of the hide appears to be natural and is not in very good condition as the tears on the back necessitated restoration.

(*Cristina Partearroyo*)

The rihiyyas or shoes of Boabdil "El Chico". These are probably made of goatskin, originally dyed dark red. Each shoe is made of two pieces, one for the sole and the other for the rest of the shoe. They are sewn with linen thread and there is no adornment, only a striking design. There are some pleats which could possibly be mistaken for the seams. Although they do not appear to have been worn very much, they are not in very good condition; they carry stains of unknown origin and are slightly deformed due to their poor preservation.

(*Cristina Partearroyo*)

56
Turkey

Kaftan, 16th century
Cotton, silk, 138 cm
Istanbul, Topkapi Saray
Museum, 13/46
Exhibitions: London, 1990
Bibliography: ROGERS-WARD
1990

This kaftan has been attributed to Selim I (1512-20), although the decorative style is more reminiscent of the end of the 16th century.

It conserves its yellow lining with cotton quilt finish. The outside part of the kaftan has a shiny brocade finish with a red background design of trapezoid forms set against each other that give the fabric different degrees of brilliance. There is a design of gold thread with a twisting floral stem that links up to another, enfolding some canes. The stem is green and is adorned with small, red-and-white lotus flowers and carnations which enrich the design.

The kaftan has short sleeves with a curve trimmed at the front to enable the arms to move more freely. It is taken in at the waist, has a checkered neck and a striking skirt. It opens at the front and overlaps. It still preserves its lined buttons which fasten to small loops that go from the waist to neck, with fifteen parallel cords which adorn the front of the kaftan.

(*Purificación Marinetto Sánchez*)

57
Turkey

Kaftan, 16th century
Cotton, silk, 138 cm
Istanbul, Topkapi Saray
Museum, 13/985
Bibliography: ROGERS 1986,
p. 209, fig. 98, p. 155, fig.
53; ROGERS-WARD 1990

Trousers formed by some straight parts fasten in way to form the model. The background is white with blue circles which have three white circles within; these little while circles are adorned with blue circles.

The pattern of circles disposed in a piramidal form always returns in many times and on different materials like, for exemple, on the caftan of Topkapi Saray, 13/93, 13/92, or on some piece of furniture, like the throne which lies in this palace, 2/2879, decorated with incrustations and dated 1560. Another caftan kept in Topkapi Saray, 13/522, and associated with Ahmed II (1691-

1693) presents the same pattern which, in a more simplified form, is also typical of the second style of Iznik in ceramics.

(*Purificación Marinetto Sánchez*)

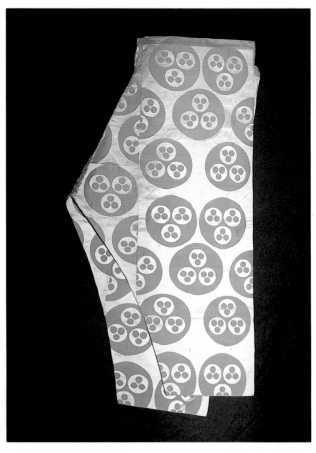

58
Turkey

Cushion, end of 16th century
Cotton, 106 x 102 cm
Istanbul, Topkapi Saray
Museum, 31/15
Bibliography: ROGERS 1986

This cushion made of white fabric is decorated with peonies in red framed by palms forming four motifs directed from the corners to the centre where another similar motif appears. The remaining areas contain small pomegranates and carnations. The decoration is related to 16th century motifs in the ceramics of the third Iznik style, with limitations of the technique and materials used indicating the relationship between architectonic ceramics and the domestic decorative elements. Its decoration points to Gevher Sultan, who died in 1574. (*Purificación Marinetto Sánchez*)

59
Turkey

Cover, 16th century
Embroidered fabric,
120 x 115 cm
Istanbul, Topkapi Saray
Museum, 31/67

The delicately embroidered surface of this rectangular cover is decorated with a floral design. The edges are marked by a border which takes up the same floral thames as the centre, where four stylised flowers mark the central medallion, composed of two circles repeating the same scheme. The ornamentation is characteristic of Turko-Ottoman cloths as seen in covers for chests, bed covers, nd even those done on other materials, such as ceramics. (*R.E.*)

60
Italy

Bonifacio de' Pitati, also called Bonifacio Veronese (Verona, approx. 1487-Venice, 1553)
The Eternal Father and Saint Mark's Square, after 1540, date of the construction of the *Loggetta del Sansovino*
Oil on canvas, 188 x 132 cm
Central panel
of *Annunciation and the Eternal Father*, at present dispersed
From the Magistrato della Camera degli Imprestiti
Venice, Gallerie dell'Accademia, 998
Bibliography: Moschini Marconi 1962, n. 73, p. 46; Nepi Sciré-Valcanover 1985, n. 213, p. 151

Venice, "the Serene," has been depicted in forms that vary from pure description to pure fantasy in ways that reflect human sentiments rather than visual perception. At the height of the Renaissance, artists like Gentile Bellini and Vittore Carpaccio transformed Venice into an object to be handled with loving care, while in 1500 Jacabo de Barbari depicted it from a birdseye view, creating a complex topographical vision that was unique at that time.

In the 16th century any biblical scene was a good excuse to use Venice as the ideal background or as a symbolic presence, either with its people or just with its architecture. One of the outstanding artists that used it this way was Bonifacio de' Pitati, also called Bonifacio Veronese due to his place of birth. He was influenced by the great Venetian paintings, whether those by Giorgione, Titian, or Palma il Vecchio, without underestimating the potential attraction that the Raphaelesque world held for him. Bonifacio de' Pitati managed to build up a well-organized workshop whose main work was the decoration of the Palazzo dei Camerlenghi, built between 1525 and 1528, during the dogeship of Andrea Gritti. Bonifacio de' Pitati painted a beautiful triptych of the *Annunciation* for one of the palace rooms (the seat of the Magistrato della Camera degli Imprestiti). The left panel features an archangel, on the right is the Virgin and, in the centre, God the Father and the dove of the Spirit rising from a stormy sky above Saint Mark's Square. In 1808 the triptych was dispersed, and between 1816 and 1919 the centre panel remained in Vienna, returning to Venice with the other panels in 1919. In the triptych Bonifacio succeeded in transforming an "intimist" scene that had become grandiloquent into a contemporary Venetian painting and he repeated its compositional structure a few years later in his *Annunciation* of the Uffizi, in an allegory of Venice.

The columned foreground with which Bonifacio de' Pitati, from the Loggia Clock, introduces Venice is almost scenographic. Saint Mark's Basilica, hiding the Ducal Palace from view, appears on the left together with a common shop in the foreground. On the right stands the *campanile* and at its base the *Loggetta del Sansovino* (1538-1540). The gaze of the people who stroll across the square is lost among the two granite columns of the *piazzetta* that were brought to Venice from the East in the 12th century. One of them is crowned with a lion, the symbol of Saint Mark and the other with the image of Saint Theodore. Ruggero Maschio has described the scene as illustrating the pact of protection of the Eternal with the Roman and Christian Republic of Venice, the latter being seen as the new Jerusalem.

It is true that Bonifacio de' Pitati portrays a Venice threatened by dark storm clouds that even manage to cover the top of the *campanile*, the city's greatest symbol of pride, but one might also say, that as well as painting the stormy sky in a symbolic sense, he was depicting the storm that struck Venice on 29 June 1548. During this storm lightning seriously damaged the *campanile*.

(*Joan Sureda i Pons*)

144

61
Italy

Vincenzo Catena (Venice, approx. 1480-1531), also attributed to Giovan Antonio de Sacchis, also called "il Pordenone" (Pordenone, approx. 1484- Ferrara, 1539)
Portrait of the Doge Andrea Gritti, 1532-1538
Oil painting on canvas, 97.2 x 79.4 cm
London, National Gallery, 5751
Bibliography: Fiocco 1939, p. 69; Robertson 1954, p. 69; Gould 1975, pp. 53-54 (see preceding bibliography)

The terms *post* and *ante quem*, from the portrait's chronology, refer to Gritti's election in 1532 and death in 1538. Nothing of the portrait's history is known until 1855, when Otto Mündler saw it in the Venetian palace of the Contarini del Zaffo, described as a portrait of the doge Agostino Barbarigo and attributed to Titian. Its attribution to Titian was maintained in the following decades when it was owned by Gilbert Elliot and then John Ruskin (before 2 September 1864), and later by Arthur Severn, Langton Douglas, and Otto Gutenkunet whose widow, in 1947, donated it to the National Gallery (Gould, 1975).
During this period, however, some scholars (Wilde, Tietze) had expressed doubts about Titian's authorship and G. Fiocco suggested that it had been painted by "il Pordenone" around 1536, though with little immediate response. G. Robertson, on the other hand, suggested that Catena and most scholars endorsed this view.
Although there are justifiable grounds for believing that it is not a painting by Titian, there is no doubt that there is a certain relation, albeit collateral, between the portrait and a painting signed by Titian: the votive painting depicting Andrea Gritti venerating the Virgin that was painted in 1531 for the College room in the Ducal Palace which was destroyed by fire in 1531. It is preserved in a xylograph reproduction wherein the face of Andrea Gritti has been replaced by that of the doge Leonardo Dona (Von Hadeln, *Über Zeichnungen der früheren Zeit Tixians,* in "Previssichen Jahrbuch," XXXIV, 1913, pp. 234-238; Murando-Rosand, *Tiziano e la xilografia veneziana del Rinascimento,* Vicenza 1976, pp. 135-136). Jacopo Tintoretto resorted to this when he was commissioned to repaint the lost painting by Titian and, needing another pictorial source in order to capture Gritti's features more accurately, used the painting that is now hanging in the National Gallery. The argument remains whether he obtained the workshop copy, that is in the Fitzwilliam Museum in Cambridge, or used the original as his model. But Jacopo Tintoretto's choice of source is not, in our opinion, sufficient proof. We do not believe he could have favoured a portrait that was not officially approved. The portrait of Gritti in London – that stresses the superior dignity of the doge more than features of his personality – suggests a portrait that is designed to exalt the glory of the virtues of the Serene Republic rather than the qualities of the man and patrician. To exalt the public rather than the private, the doge rather than the man.
This suggests that it is unlikely that it was painted by Catena, not known to have had dealings with the political class after the succession of Gritti, who, in addition, also favoured Titian until the death of Vicenzo. Furthermore, the peculiarities of its style reflect – as Fiocco points out – the hand of Pordenone more than that of Catena. In this respect, it is important to point out the situation in 1536. Pordenone was close to Gritti, and after relations with Titian started to deteriorate, he was commissioned to work in the Ducal Palace (Puppi, *Iconography of Andrea Gritti,* in Tafuri, revised by, *Renovatio Urbis. Venezia nell'età di Andrea Gritti,* Rome 1984, pp. 216-237; 221-222).
(*Lionello Puppi*)

146

62
Italy

Andrea Della Robbia
(Florence, 1435-1528)
Medallion with the
Portuguese royal arms,
end of the 15th, beginning
of the 16th century
Glazed ceramic, diameter
with frame: 107 cm
From the Madre de Deus
Church in Lisbon
Lisbon, Museu Nacional de
Arte Antiga, 678
Exhibitions: Washington
1991, n. 25
Bibliography: BELEM
1750-1755; MOLINIER 1886,
p. 115; POPE-HENNESSY 1980[a]

One of the most beautiful panels in the Museu Nacional de Arte Antiga is the one which, as part of a series, depicts the arrival of the relics of Saint Auta, one of the eleven thousand virgins that accompanied Santa Ursula, to the Madre de Deus church in Lisbon.

The altarpiece was commissioned by queen mother Leonor (1458-1525) and it portrays a real event that occurred on 4 September 1515 when emperor Maximilian I handed over the saint's relics to Leonor. The panel depicts the emmanueline facade of the beautiful church and the glazed ceramic medallion executed in the style of the Florentine workshop of the Della Robbia. It also symbolizes the presence of Italian art in Portugal.

Three years earlier, on 12 March 1514, king D. Manuel arrived in Rome to see pope Leon X. His arrival with great pageantry, magnificent presents, and exotic animals demonstrated Portugal's ecumenicalism.

Portugal and Italy had close contacts during the Renaissance, and, especially during the reigns of D. João II and Manuel I, Italian humanists such as Stefano da Napoli and Cataldo Parisio Sículo were very influential in Portugal. Similarly, Portuguese humanists such as João Teixeira formed part of the Florentine

Neoplatonic circles. It is therefore not surprising that Italian art, despite a closer relation to Flemish art, was greatly valued in Portugal or by the Portuguese governing class as the cardinal of Portugal's tomb in San Miniato al Monte in Florence shows. It is one of Antonio Rossellino's finest works and is in the same funeral chapel where Luca Della Robbia worked.

It is not certain that queen mother Leonor commissioned the sculptures and reliefs from the Della Robbia workshop because of king Manuel's stay in Rome. But judging from their style, we do know that the sculptures and reliefs, the most important ones being in the Museu Nacional de Arte Antiga in Lisbon, must have been executed by Andrea Della Robbia during the first years of the 16th century and certainly before 1517, when

one of them appears in the aforementioned panel of Saint Auta. If Leonor commissioned them when the monastery had already been founded, in 1508, it would mean they were made between 1508 and 1517, although it is possible that they were among the goods that the queen mother donated to the monastery.

The medallion with the coat of arms and the emblems granted by D. João II, as well as his cufflink with a pelican on it, also a symbol of royalty, are a typical example of the art that made the Della Robbia so famous: a garland of fruit that encloses a space wherein white figures, in this case angels, carrying the Portuguese royal arms are outlined against a blue background.

(*Joan Sureda i Pons*)

63
Italy

Gerolamo Mazzola Bedoli
(Viadana, approx.
1500-Parma, 1569)
*Parma embracing
Alessandro Farnese*, approx.
1555-1558
Oil painting on canvas,
163 x 132 cm
From the Farnesian
Collection in the Palazzo del
Giardino in Parma
Parma, Galleria Nazionale,
1470
Exhibitions: Ferrara, 1985;
Bologna, 1986; Tokyo, 1990
Bibliography: CAMPORI 1870,
p. 236; RICCI 1896,
pp. 163-164; DE RINALDIS
1927, pp. 16-17; QUINTAVALLE
1943, pp. 59-89; QUINTAVALLE
1948; WÜRTENBERGER 1962,
pp. 194-197;
GHIDIGLIA-QUINTAVALLE 1965,
p. 25; POPHAN 1967,
pp. 109-110; DEL VECCHIO
1972, fig. XI; MATTIOLI 1972,
p. 221; MILSTEIN 1978, p. 239;
FORNARI SCHIANCHI 1983, p.
108; FORNARI SCHIANCHI 1986,
p. 66

This is the first portrait of duke
Alessandro Farnese (1545-
1592). Apart from the other
known portraits, eight medals,
consisting of twenty paintings,
there are an uncertain quantity
of engravings and two famous
equestrian statues, which in
one way or another exalt his
many ventures as well as his
magnificence and fame.
Many of them are mentioned
by F. Kelly in a reconstruction
of the iconography of the
duke included in L. van der
Esse's *Alessandro Farnese,
prince de Parma. Governeur
des Pays Bas* (Brussels 1933-
1937). Other studies have also
been made that try to clarify
the sometimes confusing array
of portraits of the third duke
of Parma and Piacenza, one of
the most emblematic members
of the Farnese family, and one
of the most most widely portrayed figures in European culture (Winne, in *Aurea Parma*,
1966 pp. 151-153; Id., in
Aurea Parma, 1968, pp. 31-
34; Riccomini, *Ordine e vag-

*hezza, la scultura in Emilia
nell' età barocca*, Bologna
1972, pp. 44-45; Ceschi Lava-
getto, *I bronzi di Piacenza,
rilievi e figure di F. Mochi dai
monumenti equestri farne-
siani*, Bologna 1986, pp. 7-23;
Bertini, in *F.M.R*, 74, 1989, pp.
81-96; C. Riebesell, *Die Sammlung des Kardinal Alessandro
Farnese*, Hamburg 1989, fig.
88).
In addition to the works already described or referred to,
we should also mention the
marble half-bust of Alessandro, on a pedestal of the same
period, that is in the Prefecture
Palace in Parma, and two
beautiful full portraits, presently in a private collection in
New York. One of the painting
depicts Alessandro in court
dress and wearing a beautiful
cape, like the one in the painting in the National Gallery in
Dublin, or the fresco by Tad-
deo Zuccari da Caprarola. In
the other, one can admire the
solemn background of three
rooms also depicted in painting n. 1080 in the Galleria Nazionale in Parma.
The two elegant and refined
portraits are almost certainly
the work of Antonio Moro,
from whom A. Sánchez Coello
may have derived his small
paintings.
Bedoli's painting, executed
between 1555 and 1558, depicting the young Farnese,
around twelve years old, is the
first portrait of this future head
of state who was later to
become a great military leader.
The portrait is described in
great detail by Vasari in the
biographical appendix on Parmigianino in his *Vite*. He mentions the work of Bedoli who
produced vast series of frescoes, complex and im-
pressive altarpieces, and fine
interpretations of human
figures and personalities.
Vasari writes that Bedoli "has
painted a portrait for Margaret
of Austria, the duchess of
Parma, of her son prince
Alessandro armed with a
sword above a globe in which
Parma is depicted armed and
kneeling before him." The

portrait is described in similar
terms in the Garden Palace Inventory of 1680.
Bedoli's portrait for the Parma
court is full of symbolism, virtually foreseeing Alessandro's
glorious political career. The
young Alessandro is seated
upon a globe and a female figure, symbolizing Parma, approaches him in a delicate embrace with admiration and
devotion. He is dressed in re-
splendent armour holding a
sceptre while Parma, with a
slight manneristic movement
of the hand, announces to the
world the glory of his future
accomplishments.
Although it is not a large portrait, almost intimate in its
choice of gestures, it does not
lack the elegant composition
that is typical of official portraits.
It is a work of great formal
elegance in which the transparent sheen of the silk and of
Parma's hair – who appears in
clear profile – interlace with
the city's symbols (the bul-
lock, the Farnese sons' coat of
arms, and the yellow cross

with its blue edge) and the
glitter of Alessandro's steel armour. Alessandro's posture is
exquisitely unnatural, following the canons of manneristic
portrait painting, and his bent
legs and red footwear are the
only sharp chromatic note in
a dark homogeneous tonality
which is scarcely touched by
any ray of light.
(*Lucia Fornari Schianchi*)

64 and 66
Italy

Francesco di Giorgio Martini (Siena, 1439-1502) (design); Ambrogio Barocci and assistants ? (execution)
Bastion known as Arab Machine (64), *Siege chariot* (66), between 1474 and 1480
Bas-reliefs, travertine rocks with polychrome,
84 x 69 cm
From the *art of war* frieze on the central facade (called *ad ali*) of the Urbino Ducal Palace
Urbino, Galleria Nazionale delle Marche, 772, 810
Bibliography: Bernini-Pezzini 1985 (see preceding bibliography)

Until 1786 seventy-two stone *formelles* were placed on the support of the settling that stretches across the central facade of the Ducal Palace in Urbino, representing machines, structures, and symbols of war.
Classical historiographic sources have provided us with important information that helps us understand this unique frieze from the Montefeltro residence. Luca Pacioli, in his treatise *De divina proporcione*, completed in 1497, says that the frieze was commissioned by Federico and that the themes were taken from Roberto Valturio's treatise *De re militari*. In 1587 Bernardino Baldi affirmed that it was Francesco di Giorgio who had suggested the theme for the *formelles*, and Ambrogio Barocci of Milan who transformed Martini's drawings into stone (*Description of the Urbino Ducal Palace*, Venice 1590).
Despite these authoritative sources, many doubts have arisen throughout the centuries as to the function and significance of the frieze which G. Bernini, in a recent study, has attempted to clarify. By returning to literary sources, it has been possible to restore to the sculptures in "the art of war" their original symbolic meaning. This theme

150

had already appeared on the magnificent portals of the duchess' apartments. But by placing the *formelle* on the palace exterior – that was at an advanced stage of construction – Federico intended to enrich his residence and publicly exalt his military virtues.
The obvious analogies between the decorative elements of the arcades and the *formelle* show that they were conceived as a whole with the idea of exalting military ventures, thanks to which, Federico, "the captain of good

fortune," had risen to become duke, a position that was held in great esteem by the Italian nobles of the *Quattrocento*.
The honours bestowed upon the nobleman of Urbino by king Edward IV of England (the order of the Chivalry) and by Ferdinand of Aragon, king of Naples (the order of the Stoat) in 1474 – the same year as his investiture as duke – appear in a *formella*, which gives us a clear idea that the frieze was executed at the same time as the masonry work continued.

Francesco di Giorgio Martini, born in Siena, was commissioned by Federico di Montefeltro to continue the work by Laurana, and lived in Urbino from 1476 onwards. During his youth, he studied painting and sculpture, and the influence of his city's figurative tradition was evident in both. But frequent contact with the Florentine workshops of Filippo Lippi, Pollaiolo, and Verrocchio, together with the advice he gained from meetings with the Sienese miniaturists – Liberale da Verona and Girolamo da Cremona – working for pope Pius II Piccolomini, enhanced his figurative style and refined his palette.

When he arrived in Urbino, he came into contact with the learned environment of the Feltrescan court where the figurative arts, mathematics, the natural sciences, as well as military technique and strategy, were discussed. He worked for duke Federico for over a decade, supervising the works under construction in the palace as well as undertaking civil and military engineering projects where his modern and original genius stood out. He designed several fortifications, aqueducts, and war machines, wrote treatises on architecture and artillery, and developed a formidable theoretical and practical experience in the "art of war" while working for the duke, whose contemporaries considered to be one of the greatest military leaders of the Renaissance.

In Urbino he completed the treatise *De instrumentis bellicis et de aliis machinis*, which he dedicated to duke Federico and which is now in the ducal library together with his treatise *De architectura*. In this latter treatise there are numerous drawings whose themes bear a striking resemblance to those of the *formelle*. Other inspiring pictoral sources of such bas-reliefs have already been described in the aforementioned work by Valturio (1462) and in the *Códice* by Mariano di Jacopo, also called "il Taccola", a contemporary of Francesco di Giorgio who probably influenced his cultural development.

It is likely that the task of translating the "art of war" drawings into stone was commissioned to a team of sculptors and stonemasons, although their names are still unknown due to its poor condition.

The gradual deterioration of its surface led to the decision to remove the stone frieze from the palace facade and

created, as has already been mentioned, confusion over its iconographic significance. It is only until recently that the frieze has been given a new and rational location inside the museum of the Galleria Nazionale delle Marche. Although it lacks the suggestive context of the facade and cornices, its symbolic importance can still be felt today, due either to the genius of the man who designed such perfect civil and military machines and instruments or to the greatness of the man who,

transforming war into an art, exalted, for himself and his contemporaries, the impressive Ducal Palace in Urbino.

(*Maria Giannatiempo de López*)

65
Italy

Francesco di Giorgio Martini
(Siena, 1439-1502) (design)
*Portrait of Federico di
Montefeltro*, approx. 1485
Bas-relief,
marble 47 x 38.5 cm
Inscriptions: on the base,
DIVVS. FE. VRBINAT. DVX.
Pesaro, Musei Civici, 87/4142
Exhibitions: Tokyo 1990
Bibliography: VENTURI 1908,
p. 1044, n. 713; VENTURI
1914, p. 439 n.1; VENTURI
1925, pp. 197-228; SERRA
1934, p. 150; POLIDORI 1956,
p. 27; SANGIORGI 1982, p. 82,
pl. XXXII; GIARDINI 1990,
pp. 165-166

In 1450 Federico lost his right
eye and since then he only
allowed himself to be portrayed in left profile. This bust
clearly expresses the prince's
dominant nature and reminds
us of the beautiful realist portrait painted by Piero della
Francesca between 1465 and
1466, which now hangs in the
Uffizi museum.

The portrait's unrelenting realism captures all the strength of
Federico's character. No defect
is corrected or modified. His
nose is not shortened and the
wart, the deep line round his
eye, the sagging mouth are all
present. This magnificent
work is so real that, despite
the distance in time, we are
able to sense the great personality of Federico di Montefeltro.

The duke, born in 1422, looks
some sixty-years old, from
which we can infer that this
marble bas-relief was probably executed between 1480
and 1485.

The inscription below, DIVUS.
FE. URBINAT. DUX. closely resembles the many engraved
inscriptions to be found in the
Urbino Ducal Palace.

Many portraits of Federico
were made during his lifetime,
many of which he himself
commissioned, making it easier to place the work of
Francesco di Giorgio Martini
in the decade mentioned earlier. It has been attributed to

many artists and resembles the
work of Francesco Laurana,
Justo de Gante and Paolo de
Ragusa. The most convincing
evidence in support of Francesco di Giorgio's authorship is
the copy in the Bargello, in
Florence.
(*Claudio Giardini*)

67
Peru

Cuzco Department
Inca culture
Ceremonial receptacle
(kero), end of the 15th, first
half of the 16th century
Polychromatic and
lacquered wood, 21 cm;
diameter of rim: 17 cm
Madrid, Museo de
América,7521
Exhibitions: Paris, 1933;
Madrid, 1935; Alicante, 1988;
Murcia, Cadiz, 1989
Bibliography: Paris 1933,
n. 19; Madrid 1935, pl. XLII
sup.; Cuesta Domingo 1980,
p. 339; Trimborn-Fernández
Vega 1935, n. 19; Martinez
1988, p. 148

The Andian name for this
ceremonial receptacle with
truncated conical form is kero.
A prominent band across its
lower half divides the decoration into two unequal sections,
and each section in turn is also
divided into two parts. In the
lower section there is a field
with three rows of *ñucchu*
(*Salvia oppositiflora*) flowers
and another with a plant from
which two bunches of *chin-
chircuma* flowers (*Mutisia
acuminata*) hang.
In the upper section there is a
central design with two scenes
of differing size. The main
one, which is descriptive and
realist, depicts a battle. In the
centre is what appears to be
an outline of a fortress,
flanked, below, by two large
spears whose poles are
adorned with feathers and
above, by two panoplies
formed by two rectangular
Inca shields, crowned with
semi-spherical Inca helmets
and two spears adorned with
feathers. This would seem to
indicate an Inca fortified town.
Above this are four warriors
running, one blowing a shell
– an instrument associated
with war – and preceded by
three armed warriors with
similar helmets, shields, and
spears. They are attacking another warrior whose head is
adorned with feathers and carries onlya abow. Behind him

is an unarmed warrior. Below
these warriors, to one side of
the fortress, there is another
Inca warrior striking a fallen
enemy next to two trees with
birds. To the other side another, or perhaps the same,
Inca warrior with feathers on
his head leads two enemy
warriors who are tied, while a
long-tailed bird carries a bag
where the stone missiles or
coca leaves were kept. The
scene clearly depicts a battle
between the Incas and an-
other tribe, probably from the
jungle, judging by the landscape and the feathered head-
dresses. Scenes like this of
battles between the Incas and
other tribes are common, although this one is particularly
rich in descriptive detail.
The other scene, in contrast, is
full of symbolism and shows
a rainbow that comes from the
mouths of two jaguars. Under
this is a warrior who is approaching two women. The
first is holding a *k'antu* flower
in her hand and the other is
carrying two *keros*, or ceremonial receptacles, like the
one described here. Above the
rainbow and the warrior is a
sun, and next to it, three
women wearing the typical female shawl. One is holding
and playing a small drum and
is helped by another who, like
the third woman, holds her
hand to her mouth apparently
to demonstrate that they are
playing some flute-like instrument. The rainbow sym-
bolizes the sky held by two
jaguars that represent the
world. The sun, which is the
most important Inca deity, appears above the warrior and
seems to symbolize the Inca,
its son.
The rainbow, sun, and jaguars
give this section a sacred
quality. The two women who
offer the *k'antu* flower –
which possesses halluci-
nogenic powers and is associated with royalty – and the
ceremonial receptacles,
together with the three figures
linked by acoustic instruments, represent a ceremony
that must be connected to the

battle scene below, perhaps
either of preparations for it or
of victory.
The decoration's division into
two parts, one above and one
below, and its further subdivision into left and right reflects
the Inca's four-fold conception
of the cosmos, which also sustained that the world and men
were similarly divided; the
section above the band dominates the one below and those
on the right dominate those
on the left.
(*Paz Cabello*)

68
Italy

Ferrara school
Fragment of commemorative plate, third quarter
of the 16th century
Glazed graphite ceramic,
terracotta worked with
gubia, 4.5 cm; maximum
diameter 30 cm; diameter
of base 12.8 cm
From excavations in Palazzo
Pendaglia, Ferrara, in 1912
Ferrara, Museo Schifanoia,
OA, 177
Exhibitions: Modena, 1971;
Ferrara, 1972; Ferrara,
1989-1990
Bibliography: MODENA 1971,
n. 80; FERRARA 1972; FERRARA
1989

The plate's edge is decorated
and has a rim which slants towards the concave bowl and
a wide round base. The outside is engraved and vitrified
while the inside is made of
painted graphite and shows
traces of the tripod used for
the kiln. The rim has a bou-
quet of mulberry leaves that
spread across the bottom
which is twisted with closely-
knit grooves.

On the receptacle there is a
young married couple that can
be seen over a reed fence and
flanked by two luxuriant trees.
The top of one of the trees can
just be seen. The dotted background is enriched with
flower petals.

The mulberry tree, the fence,
and the luxuriant trees are
motifs used in Ferrarian
graphite pottery and sym-
bolize wisdom, faith, and virtue.

The portraits are on different
levels and are seen in left
profile, following the idealized
classical Roman tradition of
portrait painting that was recovered by the Renaissance.

The young man is wearing a
hat worn by the aristocracy
and his hair covers his ears
and shirt collar that can be
seen from under his gold embroidered costume.

It is a typical Ferrarian portrait
and bears a striking resemblance to Cosmè Tura's port-

rait that hangs in the Metropolitan Museum in New York.
The young woman's hair is arranged in the form of horns or
a chair, a style which originated in Burgundy and became
fashionable among Italian aristocracy – especially in the
Esten court – in the second
half of the 16th century. This
hair style can also be seen in
the frescoes by Schifanoia, in
the Borso's *Bible* and in *cas-
soni*'s wedding portraits executed in Ferrara.

The composition, the clothing,
and the use of antomiry yellow, which simulates the
young man's golden hair and
costume, show that these
were official portraits representing a wedding ceremony.
They can thus be grouped
with the medal portraits that
were so popular in the Esten
court and with the geneologi-
cal miniature portraits that
were enclosed by a circle, as
in pottery, with which there
are clear formal and stylistic
similarities.

The stylization of the elements
over the background com-
bined with the high quality of
the portraits indicate the hand
of a great artist.

The clear features, highlighted
by the shading that sharply
delimits the outline give body
to the faces, lighten the
cheeks, and bring the figures
to life. The young couple are
shrewdly depicted with subtle
strokes and finishing that ani-
mate the lips and eyes. The
drawings in the stained glass
windows of the San Giovanni
in Monte church in Bologna,
executed by Francesco del
Cossa about 1467, show, albeit
in a different context, the
same graphic sensitivity.

This confirms, as we know
from the sources, that great artists also produced cartoons or
models for the applied arts
and pottery, and that during
the last decades of the 15th
century they were deeply involved in figurative art and the
cultural climate that made Ferrara such a great centre of Renaissance art.

(*Anna Maria Visser Travagli*)

69
Italy

Petrecino da Firenze
(attributed to both Pietro
de' Neri Razzanti, Florence
1425-1480, and Petrecino
da Firenze, documented as
being in the service of
Borso d'Este in 1457 and
1458)
Portrait of Borso d'Este, 1460
Medal, smelted bronze.
diameter 9.1 cm
Inscriptions: recto, BORSIVS.
DVX. MVTINE. Z. RGII. MARCHIO.
ESTENSIS. RODIGII COMES; verso,
OPVS PETRECINI DEFLORETIA
MCCCCLX
Ferrara, Museo Schifanoia,
51139
Bibliography: KRIS 1929,
p. 35; HILL 1930, p. 26,
n. 96; POLLARD 1984, p. 83,
n. 27; JOHNSON-MARTINI 1986,
p. 88, n. 389-390

Only three medals, dated
1460, by the Florentine Petrecino are known, but it is not
certain that the portrait was by
Petrecino. Hill considers Petrecino to be the painter of card
games who was in the service
of Borso d'Este, and rejects
Kris' claim that it is the work
of the engraver Pietro de' Neri
Razzanti.
In the medal the duke is depicted wearing a magnificent
costume and a tall red cloth
cap with a gem on it. On his
chest is a prominent, splendid
jewel.
The portrait resembles those
of the smelted medals that
Antonio Marescotti and Lixig-
nolo executed for Borso and
those on the gold ducats that
Borso, one of the first to do so
in the Renaissance, ordered to
be smelted showing his portrait. The facial features are
typical examples of court portraits and comparable to those
of the painting by Baldassare
d'Este in Milan (Castello Sforzesco) and the miniature of
the *Genealogia Estense* (Modena, Biblioteca Estense).
They also bear a striking resemblance to the portrait of
the duke in the Mesi room frescoes of the Palazzo Schifanoia in Ferrara, the splendid

palace that Borso chose to
exalt his image and his government.
In the inscription the Estenian
marquis appears with the title
of duke of Modena and Reg-
gio, and count of Rovigo, bestowed upon him by emperor
Federico III in 1452. In 1471
Pope Paul II made him duke
of Ferrara.
The "accomplishments" motif
also appears on the back of
the Borso medals. In this one,
the hollow font in the centre
represents "the baptism," one
of the duke's favourite motifs,
and symbolizes purification,
complementing the extensive
charitable works carried out
by Borso in the impoverished
valleys of Ferrara.
This theme also appears in the
magnificent miniatures in the
Borso codices, in the fresco in
the "room of accomplish-
ments," and the stuccos in the
"room of virtues" in Palazzo
Schifanoia.
(*Maria Teresa Gulinelli*)

70
Italy

Sperandio Savelli (Mantua, before 1431-Venice, 1504)
Bust of Ercole I d'Este, 1475
Marble sculpture,
58 x 38 x 16 cm
From the Barco portal, Ferrara
Ferrara, Palazzina di Marfisa d'Este
Exhibitions: Ferrara, 1933; London, 1984
Bibliography: FERRARA 1933; VARESE 1980, p. 36; LONDON 1984, n. 72, p. 121

In 1889 the art historian Adolfo Venturi published a document from the Modena State Archives which mentions the payment made to Sperandio Savelli for his two marble busts of duke Ercole I (1471-1505) that were to adorn the the main portal of the Barco, his hunting residence to the north of the city. In 1933 Nico Barbantini discovered one of these busts, while the other is now in Musée du Louvre in Paris.

The bust had a stone tablet, now in the lapidary of the Casa Romei in Ferrara, which contained the following verses in Latin: MCCCCLXXV. QUAE SPATIOSA HOSPES MIRARIS CLAUSTRA FERRARUM / HERCULIS HAEC MAGNI SUNT MONUMENTA DUCIS / POST OBITAS REGNI CURAS URBISQUE LABORES / VENATU ET PLACIDIS HIC VACAT AUCUPIIS. The text says that the Barco was a residence used for "pleasure" and hunting where the duke could relax after the hard task of governing the state, and from city life.

The portrait in full, right profile, that was to be placed on the wall, is not engraved on the back and there are gaps that were probably meant for a circular, inscribed medallion. It would have blended in with the building, like the portrait of Borso d'Este, Ercole's predecessor, that appeared in March in the Schifanoia frescoes where it can be seen in the top half of the portal of an elegant Renaissance building.

Ercole I is wearing an aristocratic hat. His fringe and long shoulder-length hair is typical of that period. The cuirass alludes to hunting as a noble sport and bloodless simulation of war. The bust follows the classical heroic portrait tradition that can be seen in paintings, miniatures, pottery, and, above all, medals.

Savelli's experience as a medal portrait artist is evident in the clear outlines, the knowledgeable use of the spatial planes – despite its small size – the careful, almost calligraphic, execution of the hair and in the cuirass. This minute attention to detail does not impair the modelling of the face or the volume of the bust.

The bust is thus a work of great quality and is among the finest that were produced in Ferrara.

(*Anna Maria Visser Travagli*)

71
Italy

Antonio di Puccio Pisano, known as "Pisanello" (Pisa, approx. 1395-approx. 1455)
Portrait of Lionello d'Este, 1441-1444
Medallion, cast bronze, diameter: 6.8 cm
Inscriptions: recto, between two circles: LEONELLVS MARCHIO. ESTENSIS. D. FERRARIE. REGII7. MVUTINE; verso, between two circles: PISANVS PICTOR FECIT
Ferrara, Museo Schifanoia, 51183.
Bibliography: HILL 1930, p. 9, n. 28; PANVINI ROSATI 1968, p. 20, n. 10; JOHNSON-MARTINI 1986, p. 93, n. 410; TRENTI ANTONELLI 1991, pp. 25-35

Antonio di Puccio Pisano is known as the creator of the portrait medallion, in the modern sense of the word. This was a new medium of expression, born within the atmosphere of Humanism. It had connections with their previous knowledge of the imperial Roman coin, although it possesses its own distinct characteristics.

It is characterized by its commemorative markings and inscriptions, by the fact that it wasn't legal tender, and was minted not only for princes and nobility, but for wealthy individuals as well.

The Lords of the Paduan courts of the fifteenth century used the medallion as a means of exalting their personal virtues, an affirmation of their ostentatious political power, and as propaganda for their own principles of government. We are certain that it was in Ferrara that Pisanello cast his first medallion, dedicated to Juan VIII Paleologo, on occasion of the Council of the Two Churches of 1438. The master's style of medal production is consistent throughout this celebrated series bearing the effigy of Lionello, to which this example belongs. He was, without a doubt, connected to the Estense court.

As a new mode of expression, the portrait medallion immediately rose to the height of fashion in Ferrara, as well as in other courts of north-central Italy, and many important craftsmen dedicated themselves to this new art. Among others, Matteo dei Pasti, who worked principally in Rimini, in the service of Sigismondo Malatesta, and Sperandio Savelli, one of the most productive medalists of his day, who was active in Ferrara, Bologna, and Venice.

The magnificent bust on the front side of the piece shows the Marquis wearing an abundant head of hair, and draped in richly decorated cloth. Legend has it that Pisanello was considered to be a *pictor* (a picture painter), but this effigy reveals his great skill at portraiture. The finely delineated lines of the face, are strongly reminiscent of a tablet in the Accademia Carrara in Bergamo, which bears a portrait in profile, and has been attributed to the artist.

The reverse side bears the symbolic blindfolded lynx, the same theme which is to be found on two other medallions carrying Lionello's face, one signed by Amadio of Milan, the other by one Nicolaus, whose identity is still disputed. The meaning of the motto *quae vides ne vide*, constitutes the foundation for the significance of Lionello's political code. According to legend, the lynx was capable of seeing through walls, and was thus a symbol of vision. The lynx might represent the sagacity of the man of government, who with no apparent knowledge, was well capable of discerning the truth of his political situation.

This explanation seems to be corroborated by the presence of a blindfolded lynx in the portrait of Francesco d'Este, attributed to Rogier Van der Weyden (Metropolitan Museum, New York), which bears the motto *voir tour.*

The message may be interpreted within the general context of the medallions created

by Pisanello for Lionello d'Este, alluded to by other symbols of difficult or controversial meaning, such as a candle nailed to the floor, a cup with anchors, a head with three faces, etc. In this symbology of multiple and complex allusions, strong political meanings are apparent, conditioned by the prince's regard for a guarantee of peace, security, and prosperity.
(*Maria Teresa Gulinelli*)

Ferrara school
Magister Gratianus (monk, documented at various times throughout the 12th century), Nicola Jensen (editor, active in Venice from 1470) and miniature-painters of the Ferrara school
Decretum Gratiani (Concordia discordantium canonum), 1474
Incunabular folios of bound parchment (in one volume), with a leather binding, printed in moveable type with red and brown ink, miniature illustrations in the margins, in the vignettes, and in the beginning of each *causae*, 43.2 x 29.2 cm
Originating from the monastic library of the convent of San Giorgio fuori le Mura, from the Olivetan monks of Ferrara
Ferrara, Museo Schifanoia, OA 1350
Exhibitions: Modena, 1925; Rome, 1953; Modena, 1954; Ferrara, 1981; Ferrara, 1988; Ferrara, 1991
Bibliography: Venturi 1900; Varese 1983, XII, n. 1-2, pp. 18-31; Mariani Canova 1988

The printed editions of Graziano's repertory, perhaps due to the spread of juridical sources, promoted by the Studio of Padua, or to the fervor of the Venetian editorial houses' production in the 1570s, were genuine masterpieces of the art of printing, which was still at the experimental stage. The example from the Museo Schifanoia shows its excellence, above all, through the nobleness of its miniature illustrations, whose characteristics reflect the masterly examples of Cosmè Tura, Francesco del Cossa, and Ercole de Roberti, tempered at the same time by a strong Pierfrancescan influence. Above all, there is a marked influence from Ercole; he was taken as a model in many of these miniatures in

158

the *Decretum*, as well as in some of the splendid codexes adorned with miniatures from the convent of San Cristobal. All of these are inspired, in particular, by the polyptych artist Griffoni, and by the ruined altar of San Lazzaro.
The destiny of this precious work ties the incunabular to the Estense duchy, in whose precinct the Roverella family, represented in the shield of the first miniate page, received prestigious commissions, especially ecclesiastical ones. In spite of the fact that the great majority of artists who worked on the *Decretum* of Ferrara remained anonymous, the indisputable homogeneity of the miniatures reveals a tendency toward a unified style; this has resulted in a tendency to restrict the narration of historical actions toward that which is strictly decorative. The first page is austerely adorned with miniatures, and the initial subordinate letters of the vignettes

are crowded within the margins of the page. The floral motifs proffer examples which are almost identical to other contemporary incunabula of Lorenzo Canozi. It is worth noting that here, reproduced in miniature, are the exquisitely worked volutes which crown the Canozi choirs, often similar to the folio backgrounds of the *Decretum*, a sensibility one also notes within the architectonic perspectives of wooden marquetry.
The miniate scenes show images of the thirty-six juridical cases indicated in the medieval text, at times presenting the circumstance in question, at other times the case or dispute in the presence of the corresponding ecclesiastical authority.
As an introduction to the series of miniature episodes, the Pope is depicted receiving the work of Graziano at the Papal court. The most com-

monly accepted interpretation of this scene distinguishes the hands of that "superior master," from those responsible for these keenest of illustrations, which served as a guide for many other artists. The remaining episodes are distinguished by the attention and intensity with which the gestures, the landscape, and the sober backgrounds of interior architecture have been treated. Among the artists who have intervened we find the so-called "granular miniaturist," characterised by his treatment of the hairstyle; the "miniaturist of the round, shining heads," and the "miniaturist of solitude," thus named because of the solitude within which the figures are isolated. Stranger and subtler still, in his depictions of postures and characters is the one known as the "affectionate master," for his meticulous treatment of ornamentation and details.
(*Elena Bonatti*)

73
Egypt

Mamluk period
Sword, early 16th century
Gilded forged steel, 95 cm
Inscriptions: on the blade,
dedicated to the Mamluk
sultan Tumanbay I, in Nasji
script
Cairo, Museum of Islamic
Art, 5267

This steel sword of the *Qlig*
type was crafted for the Mamluk sultan Tumanbay I in
1501. The safeguard is of
gilded silver. The curved hilt is
made of horn. The curved
blade is delicately gilded on
one side, with an italic inscription which reads "The sultan,
The Royal, al-Malik al-Adil
Abu al Nasar Tumanbay, sultan of Islam and all Muslims,
father of the poor and the
miserable, killer of the ido-
laters and polytheists, reviver
of justice among all, may God
prolong his kingdom and may
his victory be glorified." The
Qlig swords were of Turkish
origin and were the most revered weapon of the Mam-
luks. They were originally
decorated with gold inscriptions showing the name and
titles of the sultans, praising
their works. Sometimes the inscriptions included Koranic
verses which referred to victorious battles. During the
Mamluk period, the post of
the Silahdar, or sword bearer,
was the highest in the state.
The scabbard of this sword is
of stamped leather and dates
from the Ottoman period,
somewhat later. The sultan
Tumanbay I reigned for three
months in 1501 A.D. He was
killed by the Mamluk emirs
and was succeeded on the
throne by the sultan Qansuh
al-Ghory, who reigned from
1501-1516.
(*Siham al-Mahdi*)

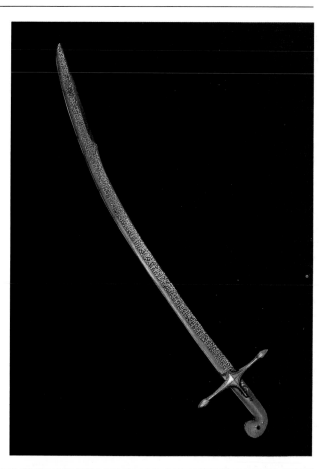

74
Spain

Al-Andalus, Nasrid period
Genet sword, 15th century
Niello brass, steel, gold, silver,
openwork, 95 cm
Inscriptions on the blade
referring to the attributes of
the divinity
Madrid, Museo Arqueológico
Nacional, 51056
Exhibitions: Madrid, 1893
Bibliography: FERNANDEZ and
GONZALEZ 1875, pp. 398-400;
MADRID 1893, pl. XCIX-C;
FERRANDIS TORRES 1943, fig. 11,
pp. 154-155; TORRES BALBAS
1949, IV, pl. 258, p. 233;
GARCÍA FUENTES 1969, pp.
15-16, 23

There are very few pieces of
preserved Andalusian wea-
ponry. Among those which
stand out is a group of Nasrid
swords known as *jinetas* (*jennets*), preserved because of
their great value. Their importance lies in the formal originality of the hilts, unparalleled
among contemporary wea-
ponry, and by the techniques
and materials used, illustrating
the vitality of Nasrid production, which was dedicated to
the manufacture of luxurious
weapons. Until its donation to
the Museo Arqueológico Na-
cionl in 1968, the jennet was
found in San Marcelo de León,
in the hands of the patron
saint's effigy.
The hilt is composed of a thick
round grip with circles embossed on both sides; a grip of
two pieces which widen at the
centre; a hilt-guard composed
of nine hollow pieces, with an
upper profile of five sections;
an escutcheon of three sections,
one of which was lost after
1892, and hooked arms decorated with circles in openwork. The decoration, which
has been retouched on occasion, is based on the development of a network of interlocking circles, combined with
bands carrying inscriptions of
praise for the divinity. These
are laid out longitudinally on all
the pieces, following the ar-

rangement of the axes marked by the circles, or transversally on the grip, evoking the virules present on other jennets. The intermediate spaces are decorated with stylized caudices on the pommel and the grip, or with palmettes on the hilt-guard, all of this nielloed, (that is, inlaid with an alloyed metal), like the previous objects. Golden Damascene diagonals form the background of the design. The blade, probably the original, is double-edged, with a shallow groove in the center running one-third of the length. Above the groove are two four-pointed stars, possibly lotuses, bounded by three concentric circles on either side. The intermediate space contains fifteen crescents, with a small triangle in the center. The hilt-guard corresponds to a model characterized by an undulating profile, an absence of animal heads in its maximum curvature, and openwork on the exterior of the arms, the same as the jennets in the Real Armería,

(cat. num G. 28) of the descendents of Campotejar, and of the Museo del Ejército, (inv. 24920). Together with this last piece, the jennet from the Museo Arqueológico Nacional constitutes a variant within the group. Both swords share the same overall concept of design, inscriptions, and the arrangement of bands modelled on the principal motifs. This trait suggests that the adornments of the scabbard, lost at an unknown period, continue the development of the pattern, as the inconclusive circles of the arms of the hilt-guard seem to indicate. The absence of enamels or ivory work is a distinctive trait of the decoration, which is based on the use of nielloed brass. All this indicates the existence of swords that, without ceasing to be objects of luxury, are closer to being a common armament, accounting for the absence of the typically sumptuous techniques or materials that characterize the other jennets. (*Álvaro Soler del Campo*)

75
Spain

Al-Andalus, Nasrid period
Sword of All-altar, major of Loja, 15th century
Marble and iron with golden veneer
Length of blade, 81 cm;
total length, 98.5 cm
Inscriptions:
"The perpetual Empire";
"The everlasting Glory"
Madrid, Museo del Ejército, 24.904

The hilt of this sword is composed of a spherical pommel, elongated in the style of a conical button, with the hilt demonstrating the tripartite design which is characteristic of other jennet swords. Two smooth sections suggest virules and border the decorative work which develops into successive bands above strips bearing inscriptions, braids of eternity, and Moorish plaster work that define the background. The curved hilt guard has an undulating

profile around the top, with the maximum curvature depicting elephant heads. From these, the arms of the hilt-guard run parallel to the blade, in the manner of a tongue ending at the head of a curved serpent. Openwork pieces adorn the weapon's exterior. The decoration of the pommel and the hilt-guard stand out due to the predominance of the Damascened goldwork, but they have only been partially conserved. The pommel combines plaster work and geometric motifs. The boundaries of the hilt-guard are marked off by a band that encircles the upper profile and a five-part escutcheon. The interior design contains a network of bows over plaster work. The point of the double-edged blade has been lost. A groove runs along one-third of its length, with a mark of two concentric circles composed of points, not solid lines.
(*Álvaro Soler del Campo*)

76
Spain

Al-Andalus
Sword of the cardinal-infante d. Fernando
Jennet sword of iron, steel, and bronze; chiselled, burin engraving, with *cloisonné* enamel, 109 x 10.2 cm
Hilt: late 15th century; blade: 16th century
Origin attributed to the estate of the cardinal-infante Don Fernando
Inscriptions: on the hilt: "No hay divinidad sino Dios; Mahoma es el enviado de Dios" (There is no divinity but God; Mohammed is the envoy of God), according to Valencia de Don Juan
Madrid, Patrimonio Nacional, Real Armería, 10000033, cat. G-28/1 (hilt); 10000035, cat. M-29 (blade)
Bibliography: Valencia de Don Juan 1898; Ferrandis Torres 1943, pp. 142-166

The hilt of this sword has a rounded pommel, embossed with rosettes on the centre of both faces, and crowned with a button of the same basic rounded shape. The area of the rosettes is bordered by crenelated tooling and bands of red and green enamel, partially missing, separated by shallow molding. In the interior of both faces, over the background of green enamel appear each of the two seals of Solomon in green, red, black, and white *cloisonné* enamel. The arrangement of the palette varies on each side. The tripartite grip with virules, originally golden, is decorated with buring engraved lotus flowers, bordering chiselled plaster work in the centre.
The hilt-guard belongs to a model which enables it to be placed, typologically, within a group formed by the jennet swords of the Museo Arqueológico Nacional (Inv. 51056), the so-called sword of Boabdil in the Museo del Ejército (Inv. 24920), and one from the col-

lection of the descendents of Campotejar. All of these are characterized by undulating profiles, the absence of the heads of animals on their maximum curvatures, and perforated decorations on the outside of the arms. The jennet sword of the Real Armería Armory must be considered a variation, since this last trait has been substituted for a ship in the centre of the arms, terminating on the outside in the form of a palmette. It also differs from the group in that it has a pointed shield as opposed to the three-sided or five-sided models.
The area is decorated by plaster work of different make on each face with evidence of green enamel traces within the lines, which originally stood out above the golden base. On the front side a rosette reproduces the decoration of the perimeter of the pommel's rosettes, giving way, in this case, to four red enamelled lotus flowers above a quadrific motif of white enamel. On the reverse side, the cartel bears the profession of faith on green enamel bordered by a red enamelled band.
The high regard for jennet swords in the Christian world, which eventually spread beyond the Nasrid area, can be documented from the 14th century on.
According to the inventory of the Real Armería of 1594-1652 (fol. 177v) this sword was found among the objects belonging to the cardinal-infante D. Fernando of Austria (1609-1641), brother of Phillip IV, and following his death came to form part of the collection in 1643.
"A short, wide sword with its decoration of gilded antique copper, the blade is of gilded ricasso with two shields of arms on one side and on the other a coin from the dukes of Brabant and Lumberg": the blade described here in the inventory is kept in the Real Armería, but was replaced by the original in 1908.
(*Álvaro Soler del Campo*)

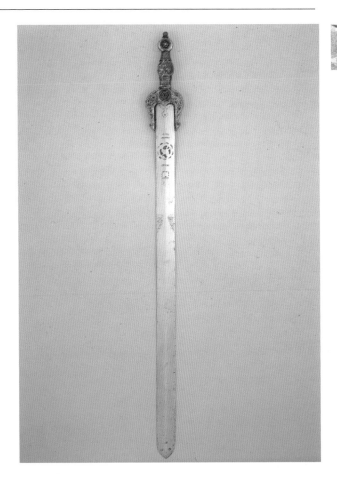

77
Spain

Al-Andalus, Nasrid period
Dagger and sheath with knife, late 15th approx.
Ear-shaped dagger, inlaid with ivory, wood, steel, gold, silver, leather and silk, engraved with nitric acid, with gilding, filigree and *cloisonné* enamel
Length of dagger: 35.3 cm; scabbard, 25.2 cm
Madrid, Patrimonio Nacional, Real Armería, 10000012 to 10000014, cat. G-361
Exhibitions: Cordoba 1953; Granada 1992
Bibliography: FERNANDEZ and GONZALEZ 1875, pp. 389-400; RODRÍGUEZ LORENTE 1963; XXXVI, pp. 119-130

Nasrid steel weapons, as they are preserved today, stand out not only for the richness of their decorations, but also, in a special way, for the originality of their form. Together with the jennet swords, the so-called *dagas de orejas* (ear-shaped daggers), a name that came from the peculiar form of their pommels, constitute an identifiable production whose success spread beyond the cultural and chronological limits of the Nasrid kingdom. This dagger from the Real Armería is one of the most significant examples of the symbolism and richness of decoration associated with the figure of Mehmet XII Boabdil, who was apparently the owner of a set of weapons which, after the battle of Lucena, was ceded by the Catholic monarchs to Don Diego Fernández of Cordoba. His descendents preserved a large part of this set, which has been deposited, between 1906 and 1927, in the Museo del Ejército and in the Real Armería, thanks to the bequests of the widow marchioness of Viana and her son. The hilt is formed by exterior pieces of ivory, symmetrically carved giving way to a design with a pommel composed of two conical pieces, a grip which widens at the centre,

and a biconcave guard. Both pieces are set over fine wood laminas, each with a bronze base, equally contoured to the shape of the hilt, and tapering to a curve, like the base of the guard. Five bronze pins or rivets fasten the handle together, spaced between the centre of the pommel, the ends of the grip, and the ricasso, thus avoiding the points of greatest fragility. This scheme of construction is not exclusive to the ear-shaped daggers of the Nasrid period, as it was also employed in the making of a hilt which is preserved in the Museo del Ejército (Inv. 24903). As is the case with the latter, the design is based on a dichromatic ivory device worked around a black background, but here includes drawings of flowers, pineapples, palmettes, bows, water spouts, and "braids of eternity."
The blade is single-edged, except at the point where it forms a rhomboidal section with a discoidal spike in the upper part to balance the

curves, the ears of the pommel, and the tripartite grip similar to that of the jennet swords. The spike of this partially gilded blade was engraved using an awl or metal punch, but the majority of the designs, the lotus flowers, the palmettes, and the inscriptions to the divine were engraved using nitric acid, a technique that was not employed with other known Nasrid weapons. Nevertheless, the engraving shows a masterly execution unusual to contemporary Western armament. Fortunately, the scabbard has been preserved along with the dagger; it is the only known piece of its type. The existence of a second compartment, intended to house a small, partially gilded knife, meant that this scabbard was made in two parts, thus the adaptation of the chape and the ring piece at the opening, both of silver worked in filigree. The ring piece shows a central medallion and relief on either side. The first indicates its royal origin through the presence of

the Nasrid shield, conserving the remains of the green enamel which is lost from most of the piece. On the ring piece, which is finished in the head of a lion, there is a circular medallion and another hexagon, which have possibly lost their enamelling. The leather shows circular medallions on the front and back, and a reticule on both sides, all showing signs of having been gilded. The scabbard is bound by a cord made of silver threads, and red and yellow silk, from which crimson tassels decorated with reticulated silver dangle in an elegant mark of distinction.
(*Álvaro Soler del Campo*)

78
Flanders

Quentin Metsys (Leuven, 1466-Antwerp, 1530)
Portrait of Erasmus of Rotterdam, approx. 1517
Oil painting on wood, transferred to
cloth, 59 x 46.5 cm
Rome, Galleria Nazionale d'Arte Antica, Palazzo Barberini, 1529
Exhibitions: Rome, 1966; Rotterdam, 1969; Brussels, 1977; London, 1978
Bibliography: DI CARPEGNA 1969, n. 69, 49, fig. 106 (see previous bibliography)

The portrait of Erasmus at the Galleria Nazionale in Rome offers the scholar an opportunity which goes beyond the limits of painting and all its aesthetic compromises; its external history testifies to the reasons for its execution and the essence of the friendship, culture, and dignity of an age which was inclined towards the grandeur of the spirit and dignity of man. It speaks of a painter, Quentin Metsys, and three humanists who helped to forge modernity in different ways: Erasmus of Rotterdam, Thomas More, and Aegidius. All were united in their ideals and all contributed to the publishing of *Utopia*. The portrait forms part of a diptych which complements the portrait of Pierre Gillis (Aegidius) of Longfares Castle.

It was shortly after the publication of *Utopia*, in 1517, when Erasmus, invited to the house of Aegidius, had the idea of commissioning Quentin Metsys to do both their portraits, to send to Thomas More. In a letter of 30 May 1517 he writes: "Pierre Gillis and I are having our portraits painted on the same tablet: we will send it to you soon as a gift." Thomas More answered on 16 July: "You would not believe with what impatience I await the canvas which will furnish me with your portrait and that of our Pierre." The painter's slowness was noticeable, as a letter which Erasmus

wrote to Aegidius testified: "Urge Quentin to hurry and finish the work, and when he has it done, I will myself make haste to come and agree with you as to the most comfortable and secure manner of sending it to England, and at the same time we will settle our debt with Quentin." It was finished on the 9th of September, as it was then that Erasmus announced the shipment to More. On the 6th of October he expressed his delight in a letter to Pierre Gillis, with a note to Erasmus and a beautiful poem alluding to the portraits, in which he addresses the efforts of Metsys, making note of the diptcyh: "I, Thomas More, declare to Erasmus and Aegidius, such great friends as were Castor and Pollux in ancient times, and lament being separated from them by this distance, being as I am united to them by love, as intimately as I am united to myself." And, referring to the painter: "Oh Quentin who makes anew an ancient art, artist who does not bow down before the great Apelles, that due to the delightful harmony of your palette, you know how to breathe life into the inert drawing."

In the painting at the Galleria Nazionale of Rome, the philosopher Erasmus is absorbed in his thoughts, while Aegidius is shown as more eloquent and vivacious. In his gesture and expression, observes De Bosque, the light accentuates the warmly toned countenances on a plain dark background, with off-handedly arranged book shelves, in Erasmus' portrait, the features of whom are easily recognizable: pointed nose, prominent chin, and slight smile, a mixture of irony and piety. With equal excellence the painter accentuates the hands on the manuscript. The differences in dimension are due to the possible damage to some centimeters of the Erasmus tablet, which was quite poorly transferred to the cloth; that which

remains luminous and rich in colour is confined to the interior, thanks to the original white priming.

As More has written, Erasmus translated the letter of Saint Paul to the Romans, proving without a doubt that the portrait in Rome is the same one and should dispel the confusion of various 19th century authors, who associate this work with Holbein's version, in which the most similar book deals with the labors of Hercules. It was Quentin Metsys who painted this portrait of Erasmus, where the philosopher is absorbed in thought in an atmosphere impregnated with the symbols and values of intellect, austerity, and elegance, incorporating examples of meridional culture admired equally by the philosopher and the painter, the latter absorbing it completely from the former. Metsys was the first to use that simple, pure language that Erasmus wanted for art, in a portrait which is opposed to the confusion and abusive,

decorative splendor of the dying flammiferousness so popular at the time.

The portrait in the Galleria Nazionale in Rome was the property of Thomas More in 1517, recorded as part of the Stroganoff collection before his donation, reappearing in the 19th century, and is attributed to Holbein. Two anonymous copies are known to exist: one in Hampton Court, with the inscription "Hieronimous," on the fore-edge of one of the books on the shelf, and one in the Royal Museum of Fine Arts in Amsterdam, of poor quality and without background detail. (*Matías Díaz Padrón*)

79
Japan

Muromachi period
(1333-1573)
Joki
Portrait of Kakinomoto no Hitomaro
Painting, ink on paper,
82.1 x 32.8 cm
Osaka, Masaki Museum of Art

164

Kakinomoto no Hitomari was one of the authors of the *Manyoshu*, the oldest surviving anthology of Japanese poetry. The figure of Hitomaro, known after his death by the name of Kasei, was highly venerated by later poets. The *tokonoma*, a hall where poets gathered, used to be adorned with a portrait of Hitomaro, which was to a certain extent an indispensable part of the gatherings where the poets would write and recite their verses. This portrait of Hitomaro was done by Joki, an artist whose activity developed around the middle of the Mu-romachi period. Owing to his relationship with the artist and monk Banri Shukyu, from the Mino region, Hitomaro is associated with the Sesshu circle.
(*Noriko Takahashi*)

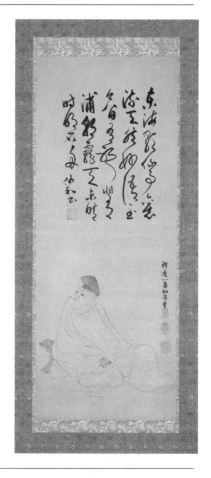

80
Japan

Muromachi period
(1333-1573)
Sekkyakushi
Kanzan and Juttoku
Painting, ink on paper,
107 x 31.7 cm
Inscriptions: Ryotasu Kiego
(1514)
Osaka, Masaki Museum of Art

Kanzan and Juttoku, legendary characters in Zen Buddhism, have been a frequent theme in the paintings done in monochromatic ink after the Chinese style. Known for their eccentric conduct, they lived in the temple of Kokusei-ji (Kuo quing si) on the mountain of Tendai (Tianti-shan) during the T'ang dynasty.
In this painting the pair has been represented together on a rocky crag, the somber landscape of mount Tendai in the background. Kanzan and Juttoku are dressed in simple clothes, their faces reflecting the enigmatic smile characteristic of the Zen sages. The author knew how to capture the special feel of these characters, reflecting the joy and spiritual fullness of life.
Sekkyakushi, a painter of the early part of the Muromachi period, was both monk and artist, and carried out his activities in the temple of Tofukuji.
(*Noriko Takahashi*)

81
China

Ming dynasty (1368-1644)
Wu Wei(1459-1508)
*Brief Rest in the Shade
of a Pine Tree*
Painting, ink on silk, vertical
scroll, 166.8 x 48.5 cm
Seal: Xiao Xian
Shanghai, National Museum,
31767

Wu Wei, also named Shi Ying,
Lu Fu, Ci Wong, and Xiao
Xian, was a native of Jiangxia,
(present day Wuchang), in the
Hubei Province. He went to
Nanjing at very joung age, and
became successful there. He
started to work in the imperial
palace during the reign of
Chenghua (1465-1487), was
given an official position at the
beginning of the Hongzhi
reign, and was awarded the
seal of "Number One Painter."
The restrictions of life at court
ran counter to the young
painter's unruly personality,
and so he left Beijing for good
and travelled south. Wu Wei
was skilled at depicting mountains and waters, people, and
at thick and fine line drawing
in the traditional ink and
brush style. His early mountain and water paintings followed the style of Dao Jin,
while his later works combined the traditions of Ma
Yuan and Xia Gui. The
painter's own style is characterized by bold, unrestrained
strokes.

This work depicts three
farmers taking a rest under a
pine tree after lunch. The old
man, still holding his hoe,
points with his left hand to the
other side of the river and
bends down to speak to his
fellow farmer who is tighte-
ning his straw sandals. A basket containing bowls and
chopsticks rests on the
ground. A third farmer, young
and barefooted, takes a nap
on a nearby rock, tired from
carrying their lunch to the
fields from home. The old
farmer's short clothes, made of
coarse material, like his wea-
thered face, offer an image of
honesty and simplicity. The

pine tree, situated in the
centre, inclines its twisted
boughs, while the plum tree
with its tender shoots, and the
new grass upon the hill create
a charming, peaceful scene.
The shades and textures of the
rock in the lower part of the
picture are expressed through
forceful strokes, while the distant mountains are given a
light treatment, creating a
foggy image of surreal emptiness.
(*Zhong Yinlan*)

82
Flanders

Hieronymus Bosch
(s'Hertogenbosch, approx.
1450-1516)
*The Extraction of the Stone
of Madness*, approx. 1490
Oil painting on wood panel,
48 x 35 cm
Madrid, Museo del Prado,
2056

The scene takes place around
a night watchman placed
within a landscape. A patient
is seated and is being operated
on by a surgeon wearing a
funnel-like hat, under the attentive gaze of the other two
characters. There is an inscription on the panel in Gothic lettering, in which one can read:
*Meester synt die Keye ras /
Myne name is Lubbert Das*
(Master, treat me right away /
My name is Lubbert Das). The
theme, a frequent one in 16th
century painting from the
Netherlands, popularly alludes
to the vanity of the medical
profession, and has had many
other diverse interpretations
throughout history. The panel
has been dated around 1490,
and four copies with variations are known to be in existence.
A painting similar to this was
found in the dining room of
Don Phillip of Burgundy,
bishop of Utrecht in 1524. The
painting, together with five
others by Bosch, was acquired
in 1570 for Phillip II by the
heirs of Don Phillip of Gue-
vara, and has since remained
in Spanish royal collections.
In 1794 it appeared in the
archduke's inventory of the
villa, and from there on to the
Prado.
(*Museo del Prado*)

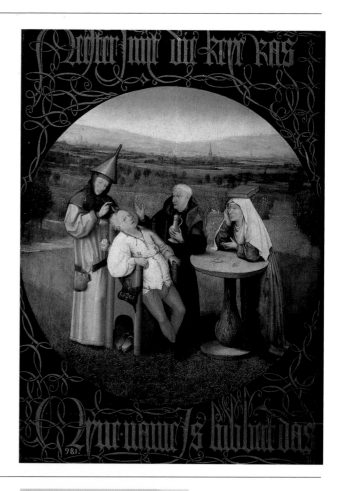

83
China

Ming dynasty (1368-1644)
Wu school
Wen Zhengming (1470-1559)
Springtime in the Forest
Painting, ink and colours on
silk, vertical scroll, 170 x
65.7 cm
Seals: Chun Sheng Gao Shu
Lu Cheng Wei, Guo Yu Han,
Cuan Bai Quan Xue Fei,
Zuo Jin Ru Zhi Zhan Ri Luo
Shanghai, National Museum,
4979

Wen Zhengming, also known
as Bi, Zheng Zhong and Heng
Shan, was born into a family
of public officials in Changzhou (today Suzhou), in the
province of Jiangsu. During
his infancy, he received a fine
education which helped him
to develop a humane and artistic personality. His pictorial
apprenticeship began with his
initiation into the works of
Shen Zhou and was com-
pleted with studies of the classics. *Springtime in the Forest*
is a scene full of colour. It
shows two scholars seated on
a stone floor before a country
house. In the distance, the
shadowed forest shows the
beauty of the springtime
forests. From the high peaks,
sketched in light green ink,
cascades of water brighten the
countryside, in a highly colourful scene.
(*Zhong Yinlan*)

84
China

Ming dynasty (1368-1644)
Wu school
Tang Yin (1470-1524)
Landscapes of Guan Shan,
1506
Painting, ink and colour
on paper, horizontal scroll,
277 x 78 cm
Inscriptions: "Painted by
Tang Yin of Wuxian on the
fourth day of the month
of summer of the first year
of the reign of Zhengde"
Seals: Tang Bohu, Xiang
Zijing, Cai Weigong
Beijing, Museum of the
Imperial Palace

Tang Yin (1470-1524) was
born in Wuxian, in the province of Jiangsu. He called himself the "withdrawn scholar of
Liuru," but was named Bohu
or Ziwei after his death. His
apprenticeship begun at an
early age with studies in
poetry, painting, and calligraphy, and surpassed himself
in the provincial exam in
Yingtian (present day Nanjing), in 1489.
His master in painting was
Zhou Chen, who introduced
him to the techniques of Li
Tang and Lui Songnian,
painters of the Song dynasty.
Tang Yin created his own
exemplary style when painting people, birds, and flowers.
In proclamating of his own
global view of his work he
carved his seal with the following inscription: "The Wil-
dest Genius of the South." As
for his contributions to the development of Chinese painting, he is considered to be one
of the four most influential
painters in the Wu school. His
written works include the exceptional *Collection of Essays
and Poems of a Withdrawn
Scholar of Liuru*.
Landscapes of Guan Shan is
one of the most representative
works of Tang Yin. In the
foreground, nestled among
tall, old trees is a city gate. The
mountaintops are partially
concealed by the clouds and
the woods on the mountain
slopes are shrouded in a thin

veil of mist. Down along the
hill are fantastic rocks and
bamboo groves, which add to
the desolate feeling of the
mountain scene. A traveller
with a bundle on his shoulder
treks toward the city gate. The
composition is balanced and
the brushwork elegant. In the
upper right hand corner appears the author's inscription
which identifies his work,
together with two seals in red,
on which are engraved "Tang
Bohu," and "The No. 1 provincial graduate from Nanjing."
The date corresponds to 1506,
when the artist was 36.
The painting also carries a
poem by Wu Yi: "Travels
among mountains are beset
with hardships./ Even wild
geese are unable to reach the
gate of fame and wealth./ The
mountain scene is indeed
desolate,/ but it becomes all
the more so under Tang's
paint brush." The poem is accompanied by Wu Yi's seal
with characters cut in intaglio,
and six other seals, belonging
to Xiang Zijing and Cai Weigong.

(*Yang Chengbing*)

Alessandro Bonvicino, known as "il Moretto" (Brescia, approx. 1490-1554)
Portrait of Gerolamo Savonarola, 1524
Inscriptions: IUSTUS UT PALMA FLOREBIT
Oil painting on canvas, 73.5 x 65 cm
Verona, Museo di Castelvecchio, 287
Exhibitions: London, 1930; Verona, 1947
Bibliography: BERNASCONI 1865, p. 32, n. 185; DA PONTE 1898, p. 86; SGULMERO 1899, pp. 45-46; TRECCA 1912, pg. 130; BOMBOSI 1943, pg. 114, n. 187; FIOCCO 1948, p. 334; BOSELLI 1954, p. 52; MARINELLI 1979, p. 14; BEGNI REDONA 1988[a], pp. 182-184; BEGNI REDONA 1988[b], pp. 72-73; MARINELLI 1991, p. 61

The painting came to the museum in 1852 with the collection of Giulio Pompei. Strangely, despite the clearly decipherable signature, it was catalogued as anonymous. Whilst stylistic analysis has led the experts to agree that the painting is of Venetian origin and from the Giorgionesque school (Fiocco 1948, p. 334; Boselli 1954, p. 52; Marinelli 1979, p. 401), bigger problems have arisen over the identity of the character depicted and the interpretation of the inscription on the cartouche, which is unfortunately very faded.

It was suggested in the nineteenth century that the hooded friar could be Gerolamo Savonarola (Da Ponte 1898); this intriguing hypothesis was adopted by subsequent critics, although it has never been proved with complete certainty.

The recent restoration has provided no new evidence; the paleographic reading of the cartouche proposed by Giulio Sancassani (Marinelli 1979, p. 38) is no less arduous and obscure than before. Savonarola had preached a sermon on the twenty-four ancients of the Apocalypse in Brescia during Advent of 1489, announcing that a scourge would descend on the city. But such predictions were commonly made by contemporary preachers, who frequently prophesied calamity. The figure of this friar gained a very different status after his death, being connected with the promise of reform in the Church, which was so necessary and still so far off.

It is for this reason that this painting by Moretto, who we know to have been sincerely religious and connected with reformers such as the bishop Mattia Ugoni and sister Angela Merici (Guazzoni 1981), must undoubtedly be a genuine homage to the visionary friar, who is depicted with the martyr's palm. Since the painter could not have met him, he must have represented him with the attributes of some clergyman from Brescia who shared the same ideals; perhaps the Augustine Inocencio Casari (Guerrini 1986, p. 14), who commissioned Moretto to do paintings for the Church of Saint John the Evangelist on several occasions.

(*Giovanni Peretti*)

86
France

Pierre Bontemps
(approx. 1504-1568)
Bust of Guillaume Froelich,
approx. 1562
Marble sculpure,
54 x 59 x 35 cm
Paris, Musée du Louvre,
L.P. 475
Bibliography: Brice 1713,
II, p. 457; Sauval 1724, 1,
p. 448; Guiffrey 1880-1881,
VIII, p. 280; Vitry 1922, I,
pp. 13-19; Vitry 1934, p. 28;
Beaulieu 1953, p. 88;
Beaulieu 1978, p. 47

Guillaume Froelich was born in
1492, in Zurich. In 1520 he
joined a Swiss regiment serving
the king of France, and died in
1562. This bust comes from his
funerary monument in the
monastery of the *cordeliers* in
Paris. It is a good example of
the art of Pierre Bontemps, a
sculptor who worked in Fontainebleau and whose works
display a good assimilation of
the Italian Mannerism imported
by Primaticcio.
However, this work provides
an example of the way Bontemps (to whom the bust may
be attributed despite the lack
of documentary evidence) appears to return to the Classicism highly characteristic of
the French Renaissance, and
even French Baroque, in his
portraits. Although the bust is
all that is left of the monument, the abundant written
evidence and exact descriptions situate it as a good
example of the funerary architecture and sculpture of the
time.
The *L'Inventaire des peintures
et sculptures du convent des
Cordeliers de Paris* (1790) says:
"Un mausolée en pierre for-
mant une niche ronde, dans la-
quelle est une buste de guerrier
sculpté en marbre blanc, porté
par un socle de marbre noir;
au-dessous sont ses armes en
marbre blanc. De chaque coté
du buste est une femme voilée
éteignant le flambeau de la vie,
sculptés (*sic*) dans la pierre; il
est orné de consoles et de trois
plaques en marbre noir in-

scristés (*sic*) et par divers mar-
bres de rapports." In *Histoire et
recherches des antiquités de la
ville de Paris* (1724), Sauval
refers to the bust as follows: "Le
tombeau ... de Guillaume Froelich, seigneur allemand, est fort
remarquable par un buste de
marbre que l'on croit être un
des bons morceaux de Paris; le
front en est bien plissé; les sour-
cils bien froncés, les yeux sont
accompagnés de beaucoup de
gravité; la barbe fort longue
fouillée et recherchée plus déli-
catement et plus profondément
sur le marbre qu'on ne pourrait
faire sur le bois, marque bien
cet air et ce port majestueux qui
ne se rencontre que dans les
personnes extraordinaries."
(*Joan Sureda i Pons*)

87
Greece

Byzantium
Six Saints, early 16th century
Painting on panel,
99 x 52 cm
Athens, Byzantine Museum
Bibliography: SOTIRIOU 1924,
pp. 100-101; SOTIRIOU 1931,
p. 74; CHATZIDAKIS 1969,
p. 42; SKROBUCHA 1961,
pp. 87-88; CHATSIDAKIS 1970

The six Saints form two registers. In the upper one we see the figures of Saint George, Saint Demetrius and Saint Pantaleon, and in the lower one Saint Theodore, Saint Tirana, and Saint Anthony. Saint Demetrius is the only one to be represented frontally, with his two companions leaning towards him.

His figure is also more noticeable, possibly because the work is dedicated to him. He is wearing a luxurious garment, a cuirass and pearl necklace, and is holding a shield bearing a "horror mask," all in gold leaf, like the rest of the composition. The image stands out thanks to the perfection with which the craftsman burnished the gold, which demonstrates the skill and quality of the workshop where this piece was made.

The extraordinary height, slenderness, and clothing of the characters relate them, iconographically speaking, to the typical representations of warrior saints. This is possibly due to the existence of prototypes that may have been used throughout the 15th and 16th centuries. Despite this, certain stylistic features date the piece to the early 16th century, a product of a Hellenistic workshop in the post-Byzantine period.

Its relationship with the circle of the Castoria workshop is patent if we compare its figures with those that appear in Greek monuments, such as that of Kato Lapsista, of certain "Anarguirous Saints" of Serbia, or the murals of the Romanian churches of the so-called "Greek painter" period.
(*Ch. Baltoyanni*)

88

Burma

Pegu, the daughters of Mara
late 15th century
Stoneware, 48 x 35 cm
London, Victoria & Albert
Museum, 173-1875
Bibliography: GUY 1990;
STADTNER 1991 pp. 39-52

It is not known when glazed ceramics were first produced in Burma, but by the pagan period (11th-13th centuries) glazed bricks and tiles were a regular feature of temple architecture.

King Dhammaceti (r. 1472-1492) was a devout Buddhist and initiated the building of temples in Burma and restored the temple of Mahabodhi in Bodhgaya, eastern India. His devotion extended to the building of a complex of temples which replicated the sacred Buddhist temple complex at Bodhgaya.

These temples, which appear to have been laid out in a scheme which copied the ar-

rangement at Bodhgaya, had at their centre the Shwegugyi temple, built in 1476, which appears to have been a replica of the Mahabodhi temple itself. The site is situated at the village of Payathonzu, 4.8 km south of Pegu. In the niches of the enclosure walls, glazed relief tiles were installed, illustrating the monstrous army of Mara (The Evil One) sent to disrupt the Buddha's meditations on the eve of his Enlightenment. At the nearby Ajapalla shrine were tiles representing the beautiful daughters of Mara, sent to distract and tempt the meditating Buddha.

The tile displayed would appear to be from this series, although a similar series was photographed in the ruins of the Kyaikpun temple in 1893. The tile depicts two daughters of Mara represented as graceful dancers, attired in what we may assume was the costume of court dancers of this period in Burma.

(*John Guy*)

171

89

Colombia

Cundiboya Plateau
Muisca culture
Votive figure of a jaguar
Gold cast in lost-wax,
3.1 x 7.1 cm
From Pasca, Cundinamarca
Bogotá, Museo del Oro,
28513
Exhibitions: Washington, 1991

In Muisca society, gold had a supplicatory function intimately linked with religion. Most of the objects found on the plateau are popular offerings known as *tunjos*.
When collections of votive objects are discovered, they normally include between five and thirty cast figurines. They were usually deposited in a ceramic vessel, placed under flat stone slabs in open spaces not associated with living places or burial sites, in caves, or in areas of outstanding natural beauty. Most of them have an elongated or triangular form suitable for being

fixed in the ground or placed in elongated ceramic vessels. The offerings were made through the priest, the mediator between those making an offering and the gods. Careful observation of the *tunjos* and other frequently occurring representations leads us to posit a specific language, specific conventions to request a miracle or to give thanks for one. Warriors, masculine figures clearly identified by their attire, women with instruments for coca or with children, miniatures, condors, snakes and jaguars, and scenes from political and social life all represent distinct forms of offering.
The votive function of these objects meant that copper was allowed to be clearly shown. Immediately after being produced, the thin layer of gold common to other traditions was deposited. Most of these pieces are flat, without a nucleus. They were cast in lost-wax in individual moulds,

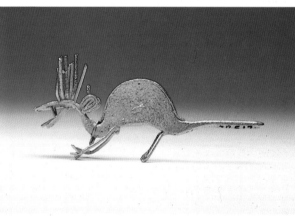

with the same figure sometimes serially reproduced. This mode of production undoubtedly arose to meet popular demand. The figure which occupies our attention here is a votive object in the form of a jaguar, the yellow cat whose power elevated it to the level of the sun, and hence of gold. It is the golden animal par excellence.
The Muisca jaguars are not particularly aggressive. Sometimes their whiskers are exag-

gerated, giving them the appearance of dragons, especially when their tails formed part of the tunnel through which the smelted metal was poured in.
(*Clemencia Plazas*)

90
Colombia

Sierra Nevada de Santa Marta
Tairon culture
Pectoral, 1000-1500
Gilded tombac cast in
lost-wax, 9.1 x 6.6 cm
Bogotá, Museo del Oro, 14525
Exhibitions: USSR, 1988;
Finland, 1988; Israel, 1988;
Greece, 1988

The culture of the Tairons, former inhabitants of the Sierra
Nevada de Santa Marta in the
north of Colombia, dates from
the early part of the modern
era. During its formative stage
around the 6th and 7th centuries, metal work represented
by objects with a mixture of features was produced: some display the influence of traditional
metalwork from the south, and
others display themes which
were to become common in
classic Tairon metalwork.
These reveal a very advanced
technology and it is possible
they were influenced by more
developed cultures before

gradually developing their own
culture with its own force and
coherence. The classical era of
this culture, located on the
coast and the northern slopes
of the Sierra Nevada, is
reckoned to be between the
10th century and the Spanish
conquest, when dense popula-
tions were concentrated in
numerous towns. Today we
know of more than 200 settlements dispersed from the lowlands to a height of 2,000
metres. This is the age of classical Tairona gold and silver
work, which has its own distinct character within the panorama of pre-Hispanic metallurgy in Colombia. The object
in question is a golden pendant
in the form of a bird of prey.
According to Ijka mythology,
birds with human forms
brought the seeds of all the
plants important to mankind.
The hummingbird brought
coca, the eagle brought cassava, and other birds the
brought trees and flowers.
(*Clemencia Plazas*)

91
Colombia

Sierra Nevada de Santa Marta
Tairon culture
Pendant, 1000-1500
Gilded tombac cast in
lost-wax, 4 x 3.7 cm
From Minca, Santa Marta,
Department of Magdalena
Bogotá, Museo del Oro,
16013
Exhibitions: USSR, 1988;
Finland, 1988; Israel, 1988;
Greece, 1988

This pendant represents a bat-
man, it's features formed by
gold adornments. Amongst
these are the diadem with
raised protuberances representing the tragus of the ears,
the double tubular nose ring
reminiscent of a bat's nose,
and the sub-labial decoration
which exaggerates the lower
jaw. The head of a snake with
a forked tongue appears on
the belt which supports the figure.
Despite its varied decoration,
Tairona gold and silver work

reveals great homogeneity in
technique, subject, and its extremely ornate style. The Taironas used the lost-wax technique for casting. Each mould
was very original and had a
perfect finish. These objects,
including diadems, necklaces,
nose rings and rings, were
made to be used, which is
why they show signs of wear.
The usual iconography consists of frogs and toads,
snakes, birds of prey, and cats,
which frequently combine to
form complex hybrids: bat-
men, jaguar-men, bird-men,
etc. These representations express the close relationship
between society and nature in
the myths which live on
amongst the Ijkas and Koguis,
native communities with a
population of 10,000 who still
live in the Sierra Nevada de
Santa Marta. This iconography
expressed a system of beliefs,
a vision of the world which
justified the function of these
products of the goldsmith's art
in society. The highly ornate

designs of Tairon artefacts are
thus in accord with their emblematic function. This great
mixture of representations of
human figures with animal attributes helped to identify social groups which were related, through ancestral myth,
to certain animals.
(*Clemencia Plazas*)

92
Colombia

Cundiboya Plateau
Muisca culture
Ceremonial necklace,
600-1500
Stone and gold cast in
lost-wax with the aid of
stone moulds, each bead
3.8 x 1.4 cm
From the Carmen area,
Cundinamarca
Bogotá, Museo del Oro, 8232

The Muiscas, the last pre-Hispanic inhabitants of this plateau in central Colombia produced hundreds of gold and
copper casts which have been
dated, through the use of
carbon-14, as being from the
7th century onwards.
This ceremonial necklace has
21 anthropomorphic beads
cast in lost-wax with the aid of
stone moulds. This technique
facilitated mass production,
and popular use of the necklaces and offerings led to the
widespread development of
this technique.
This people's need for communication led to the creation
of new languages, sometimes
tacit, as in the decorations,
and sometimes immediate and
explicit, as in the case of
tunjos or popular offerings.
Examined together, they reveal an original aesthetic formula. Their large heads contrasting the small minuteness
of their limbs and other objects, the difference in size between figures within the same
scenes, and the exaggeration
of some characteristics go beyond the merely descriptive,
communicating the deeper
and more spiritual function in-
herent in the character of the
offering. Although these representations appear naive or
strangely proportioned, they
nonetheless achieve their objective effectively.
(*Clemencia Plazas*)

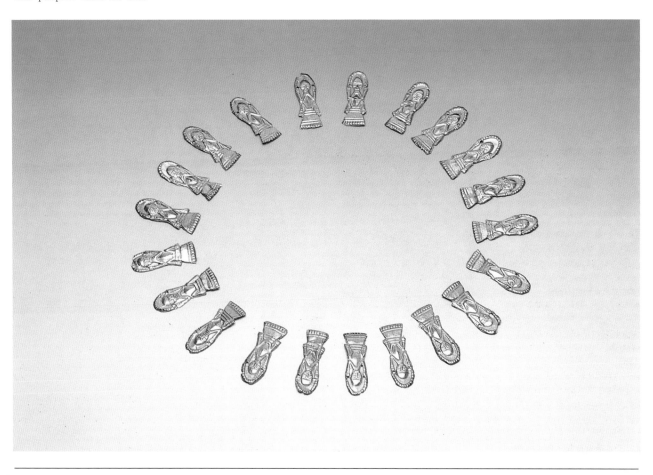

93
Colombia

Finland
Quimbaya culture
Male figure
Gold, lost-wax cast,
21.5 x 9.2 cm
Madrid, Museo de América,
17457
Exhibitions: Madrid, 1982;
Madrid-Seville-Cadiz-
Santillana del Mar-Barcelona,
1985; Vienna, 1986;
Budapest, Cologne, 1987
Bibliography: MADRID 1892;
GOROSTIZAGA 1896; ÁLVAREZ
OSSORIO1925, p. 200, pl.
CLVII, CLVIII; PÉREZ DE
BARRADAS 1966; CUESTA
DOMINGO-ROVIRA LLORENS 1982,
p. 91; MADRID 1985, p. 80;
VIENNA 1986, pp. 28, 260

This hollow masculine figure standing upright bears an orifice in the head allowing it to be used as a recipient. It is unclothed and wears the same adornments as the "chieftain" figure from the same find: a hat or head-dress, a series of earrings which go all the way around the outer ear, a nose ring, a necklace, coiled round several times, and bracelets on the wrists, beneath the knees, and on the ankles. It has a bundle consisting of four volutes in each hand.

It belongs to the so-called Treasure of the Quimbayas, which consists of six complete human figures, this being one of the four male ones. Two of the female and one of the male figures are seated on stools, a posture which indicates their social position; the rest of the male figures, including this one, are standing, but we do not know the significance of this posture within the group. The figure is symmetrical in form and volume, with a marked left-right axiality.

Although it is a rounded figure, it is clearly supposed to be seen from the front, as the volumes are gradually leveled out so that the front view is brought out more than the profile; this is due to the fact

that the figure is conceived on two juxtaposed planes, the frontal and the rear.

A hieratic attitude is also to be observed, along with an absence of movement, despite the way the figure extends its arms forward.

(*Paz Cabello*)

94
Colombia

Finland
Quimbaya culture
Vessel
Gold cast in lost-wax,
225 x 15.7 cm
Madrid, Museo de América
17451
Exhibitions: Madrid, 1892;
Cáceres, 1984-1985; Madrid,
Seville, Cadiz, Santillana
del Mar, Barcelona, 1985;
Vienna, 1986-Budapest,
Cologne, 1987
Bibliography: MADRID 1892;
GOROSTIZAGA 1896;
ÁLVAREZ-OSSORIO 1925, p. 200;
PÉREZ 1966; CUESTA
DOMINGO-ROVIRA LLORENS
1982, p. 90; CÁCERES 1984-85,
fig. 106; MADRID 1985,
p. 126; VIENNA 1986, pp. 25,
259

A recipient known as a canteen because of its form, although it could be better described as a gourd. It has a rectangular body with two lateral lobes and a long neck which widens at the mouth and is closed with a stopper. In a hollow between the lobes, there are two standing female figures with their hands on their bellies. These figures, like the rest of those in the Treasure of the Quimbayas to which the piece belongs, are unclothed, wearing nothing but a few adornments. Like all the hollow pieces in this collection, it bears small light incisions in various places. These barely visible circles are the marks left by cannulas which allowed the gas to escape at the time the piece was cast in lost-wax. These circular orifices remained, and were later covered over.
It is probable that this vessel was used for storing the lime which would be added to the coca leaf which was chewed in order to increase the power of its active ingredients. In different regions of Colombia, the Indians still use narrow-necked gourds to store lime, which they retrieve by dipping in a stick wet with saliva.

The Treasure of the Quimbayas to which this piece belongs, was discovered in 1892 in two adjacent tomb pits. It was exhibited by Colombia in the 1892 exhibition of American history in Madrid, after which it was presented to the Spanish people. It comprises 130 gilded pieces, mostly jewelry such as needles, necklaces, and earrings, but also includes helmets and gourds, some with human figures, two musical instruments, a pot in the form of a human head, and six figures which constitute due to technical quality, beauty, and because they represent a completely preserved funeral set, perhaps the best and most beautiful example of native American goldsmithery. (*Paz Cabello*)

95
Colombia

Finland
Quimbaya culture
Seated female chieftain
Gold cast in lost-wax,
29.5 x 12 cm
Madrid, Museo de América,
17456
Exhibitions: Madrid, 1892;
Cáceres, 1984-1985; Madrid,
Seville-Cadiz-Santillana del
Mar-Barcelona, 1985; Vienna,
1986; Budapest, Cologne, 1987
Bibliography: MADRID 1892;
GOROSTIZAGA 1896; ÁLVAREZ
1925, p. 200, pl. CLVII;
PÉREZ-DE BARRADAS 1966; CUESTA
DOMINGO-ROVIRA LLORENS 1982,
p. 87; CÁCERES 1984-1985,
fig. 98; MADRID 1985, p. 77;
VIENNA 1986, pp. 28, 260

This female figure seated on a
long piece of wood, smooth in
front and somewhat cylindrical behind, is completely hollow and bears a hole in the
head which would allow it to
be used as a receptacle. The
figure is unclothed, wearing
only adornments: a hat or
headdress, a series of earrings
around the outer ear, a nose
ring, a necklace coiled several
times, and bracelets on the
wrists, below the knees, and
on the ankles. In each hand
she carries a bundle com-
posed of four volutes which
end, beneath the fist, in two
rings for hanging a piece of
decoration, perhaps made of
feathers or cloth, or some
other organic material which
has not survived.

It belongs to the Treasure of
the Quimbayas, in which there
are six complete human
figures, two of them female. It
has the same conventional
features as the rest, but is
identified as female by the
sexual organs. The idealized
realism of the figure involves
a disproportionately enlarged
head, shoulders, and thorax –
the most characteristic elements of the human figure –
and a seated posture, with
smaller legs, characteristic of
important persons. The face,
which is also of an idealized
beauty, has closed eyes, like

the rest of the gilded Quimbaya figures; it also has an expression of its own, perhaps
conferred by its slight smile.
However, it is not a portrait,
since these were not produced
in pre-Hispanic America, but
an expression of convention,
as is the treatment of the body.
(*Paz Cabello*)

96
Peru

Department of Cuzco
Inca culture
Ceremonial vase (kero),
end of 15th century-first half
of 16th century
Lacquered polychrome
wood, 21.5 cm; diameter
of mouth, 15 cm
Madrid, Museo de América,
7504
Exhibitions: Paris, 1933;
Madrid, 1935; Huelva, 1981;
Vienna, 1986-Budapest,
Cologne, 1987; Alicante,
1988-Murcia, Cadiz, 1989
Bibliography: PARIS 1933,
n. 9; MADRID 1935, pl. L;
TRIMBORN-FERNANDEZ VEGA
1935, p. 39; CUESTA DOMINGO
1980, p. 297, 344; CABELLO
CARRO 1981, p. 38; VIENNA
1986, p. 380 and n. 4.98;
ALICANTE 1988, p. 152

Ceremonial vase in the form
of a human head schemati-
cally worked to conserve the
truncated conical form of this
type of recipient. The character's face is painted with four
rectangles in the contrasting
colours of red and ochre, and
the forehead is framed by a
decorative band with a frieze
of birds, whilst the neck is
covered by a pattern of rhombuses filled with dots. The rear
of the vase has a decorative
surface, and a pronounced
wide rectangular band con-
figures the hair providing the
main scene, framed by two
more decorative bands, a
lower one representing the
character's neck and a higher
one which goes all the way
round the mouth of the vase
which also serves as the character's forehead.

In the main scene, we see a
person of high rank who is
bigger than the other characters despite his seated posture.
He holds a rectangular Inca
shield, with an axe and the
blade of a lance adorned with
feathers appearing over its
top. A female character appears opposite him carrying a
large *maywa* (*Stenomesson
variegatum*) flower. Two
standing masculine figures

hold parasols over the heads
of these characters and close
the composition. In the spaces
between the central characters
there are two ñucchu (*Salvia
oppositiflora*) flowers; a bird,
which is somewhat faded, appears over the head of the servant of the main character,
whilst a flower, similar to the
one she is carrying, appears
over the head of the woman's
servant. The motif of the Inca
warrior, probably the Inca
lord, and the noblewoman,
probably the Coya, or wife of
the Inca, appear frequently on
these coloured wooden vases
made by the Incas. They are
the earthly representatives of
the sun and moon, the gov-
ernors of the heavens, symbolizing the generating principle
of the masculine and fe-
minine, and possessors of the
power of reproduction of
everything in this world. In the
lower decorative band appear
a dog and a jaguar, one on
each side of a schematized
chonta tree (genus *Iriatea* or
Euterpe); at the ends there are
other schematized trees, one
of which is almost completely
faded, whilst ñucchu flowers
fill the spaces. The birds decorating the frontal band close
the composition.

This vase combines the tradition of the sculpted anthropomorphic vase, which occurred
frequently in pre-Incan cultures in Peru and to a lesser
extent amongst the Incas, with
the tradition of the smooth
vase with decorative scenes
painted on it, producing an
unusual mixture. The result is
a vase with two faces, one
sculpted and the other with
painted scenes. Both faces follow the laws of axial symmetry, with the nose acting as
the line of symmetry for the
sculpted anthropomorphic
face, whilst the shield, the
symbol of power, and the
chonta tree – the tree of life –
fulfil this function on the
smooth, pictorial side. The
duality of the two faced vase,
each one divided into two
symmetrical parts, is related to
the principle of duality in Inca

thought: the world, space, and
society divide into two parts –
left and right, or up and down;
each part also has the possibility of being divided in two
which means that the duality
can be multiplied into four
parts. This vase has four parts
due to the divisions of the
sculptured and painted parts –
the painted face divides into
two parts with inverted facial
features, and the scene into
two parts, one with the Inca
and one with the Coya.
(*Paz Cabello*)

97
Mexico

Mixtec culture
Tláloc or Quetzalcoatl,
1400-1500
Wood, stone, coral,
and shells, 33 cm
Copenhagen, National-
museet, ODlh 41

178

Three specialities may be distinguished in the postclassical
art of central Mexico: gold and
silver work, featherwork, and
turquoise mosaics. It seems
that all three were the specialities of Mixtec craftsmen
who, either in their home
towns or in the city of Tenochtitlan, created these adornments for the dominant social
class of the *pipiltin*, the
nobles, the warriors, and even
the sovereigns (*tlatoani*) of
the Triple Alliance.

This anthropomorphic mosaic
pendant, which is kept in the
Nationalmuseet of Denmark,
is undoubtedly one of the
most beautiful masterpieces of
Mixtec art in Mexico. It comprises a piece of wood representing a human face with a
grand headdress, covered in a
mosaic of turquoise and
shells. Although not in perfect
condition, it is still extremely
beautiful.

Most of the few mosaic works
known to us came to Europe
in the years immediately after
the conquest, and many were
undoubtedly gifts from Hernán Cortés and other Spanish
captains to the Emperor
Charles V, who in turn gave
these "oddities" to his many
relatives amongst European
royalty. It is therefore no surprise that the majority of these
works are now in European
museums, principally the
Museo Luigi Pigorini of Rome,
the British Museum in London, and the Nationalmuseet
of Denmark. Turquoise stands
out amongst the stones used
in these mosaics, its sky-blue
colour undoubtedly being of
symbolic value. Blue was the
colour of water and therefore
of the divine couple Tláloc
and Chalchiuhtlicue, but it
was also the colour of the day-

time sky and therefore of the
gods who ruled it during the
day, Tonatiuh and Huitzili-
pochtli. Turquoise was also in
itself the symbol of precious-
ness, along with jade, and its
glyph or emblem frequently
appears on sculptures, apparently as a qualifying adjective.
(*José Alcina Franch*)

98
Italy

Leonardo da Vinci (Vinci 1452-Cloux, Amboise, 1519)
Head of a girl known as "The dishwelled",
approx. 1508
Painting on panel,
27 x 21 cm
Parma, Galleria Nazionale, 362
Exhibitions: Naples, 1983; Bologna, 1985
Bibliography: Martini 1872, p. 85; Pigorini 1887, p. 38; Ricci 1896, p. 34; Venturi 1924, pp. 56-57; Suida 1929; Milan 1939, p. 167; Quintavalle 1939[a], pp. 273-280; Quintavalle 1939[b], p. 265; Bottari 1942, p. 38; Quintavalle 1948, p. 55; Pedretti 1953, pp. 5-8; Ghidiglia Quintavalle 1965, fig. XI; Ottino Dalla Chiesa 1967, p. 96; Fornari Schianchi 1983; Pedretti 1983, pp. 115-116; Riccomini 1985, pp. 141-142

The first reference to this work in the inventory of the Callani collection identifying it as a small Leonardo da Vinci ("Un piccolo Leonardo da Vinci, rarissima cosa da trovarsi ai dì nostri"), was confirmed in 1875 by Martini and again in 1887 by Pigorini. The beauty of its execution and its authorship were subsequently commented on, but Ricci, in his catalogue of 1896, points out that it came from the studio of the academic painter Callani and raises the possibility of a late forgery, although he presents no evidence for this.

The painting was effectively rediscovered in 1924 by Adolfo Venturi, who ventured to identify it with number 343 in the inventory of the Gonzaga collection, drawn up for the sale of 1627: "a painting depicting the head of a woman with ruffled hair, the work of Leonardo da Vinci, L.180." The work would have been alongside the *studiolo* and the *grotta* of Isabella d'Este, who had asked Leonardo during his stay in Mantua in 1500 to do a painting to place in her "divine studio," for which Perugino, Mantegna and Francesco del Cossa, and later Correggio, also worked. It seems that this painting was mentioned again in 1531, when Ippolito Calandra proposed to hang "a painting with the head of a woman with ruffled hair [...] by Leonardo" in the bedroom of Margherita Paleologa, the wife of Federico Gonzaga.

Since Venturi's rediscovery, critics have confirmed the painting's authorship with growing conviction, emphasizing the rhythms of the vibrant chiaroscuro, the thoughtful gentleness that highlights the lightly sketched feminine features, framed in fine, masterly lines which are short and brief, lively and intertwined. They frame the "imperceptible tremor of a smile," without adornment, in a balance of soft lights and darks broken by the rough surface of the panel.

It was on the basis of such considerations that Pedretti re-examined the dating of the picture in a recent book. He definitively accepted its authenticity and recognized in it the mysterious, sublime force of communication only found in masterpieces, estimating the year of its execution as 1508. This falls within the later period of Leonardo's work, when he took inspiration from the works of his youth to analyze matter and recompose the processes of mechanical transformation.

The style and technique appear to refer to the cartoon of *Saint Anne, the Virgin, the Baby Jesus and John the Baptist*, or the second version of the *Virgin of the Rocks* at the National Gallery in London. This would rule out the 1490 dating proposed by Ottino dalla Chiesa and would pose a problematic relationship with the *Virgins* that Leonardo was painting around 1508 for the king of France, the cause

of great excitement amongst his French protectors. Unfortunately, we only know these works through descriptions. Riccomini recently considered it as a unique piece of work, an exception to the tradition of painting of the age for being both "highly finished yet incomplete." On the one hand, it appears to be a curious preparatory study on a panel and on the other, the most autonomous and complete of Leonardo's works.
(*Lucia Fornari Schianchi*)

99
Nigeria

Igbo Laja, Owo
Yoruba culture
Head, 15th century
Terracotta, 17.4 cm
Lagos, National Museum,
73.2.7
Exhibitions: North America-Canada-Europe, 1980-1985;
Lagos, 1985; Japan, 1989;
New York 1989-1991
Bibliography: Eyo 1974; Eyo 1976, VI, pp. 37-58; Eyo 1977; Eyo-Willet 1980; Japan 1989; New York 1989-1991

Owo is a Yoruba city-state almost halfway between Ife and Benin, and its art reveals connections with both cultures. This terracotta head is sensitive and naturalistic in its modelling and displays Ife characteristics. These include the parallel grooves all over the face, the way the lower eyelid is superimposed on the upper, and the parallel with the edge of the upper lip, the marked commissures of the mouth,

and the raised edge of the lips. The eyebrows are more prominent than is usual in Ife terracottas. In contrast with Ife sculptures, this one does not wear a crown, but a large flat cap decorated with almost vertical lines. The sculpture has the calm, serene stare of most of the bronze and terracotta faces.

Its mid-15th century dating conveniently supports the thesis that the Owo terracotta tradition may represent a continuation of classical Ife art, arising after the end of the classical period of the Ife terracottas and bronzes.

In Owo, the Benin and Ife styles are found in the same cultural context, which suggests that Owo could be a bridge between the art of Ife and the art of Benin. The features of the Owo terracottas range from the grooved heads of the Ife style to the works which reveal ethnic characteristics typical of Benin.
(*V. K. Agili*)

100
Italy

Neroccio di Bartolomeo
de' Landi known as
Neroccio de' Landi (Siena,
1447-1500)
*Portrait of a Young
Woman*, approx. 1490
Painting on panel,
46.5 x 30.5 cm
Washington, National Gallery
of Art, 643
Inscriptions: in the lower
left-hand triangle, A.P; in the
right-hand one, NER; on the
panel: QVANTVM HOMINI FAS. EST
MIRA ASSEQVAR ARTE. / NIL AGO:
MORTALIS EMVLOR ARTE DEOS
Bibliography: EDGELL 1932,
pp. 249, 291; POPE-HENNESSY
1947, pp. 22-23; BRANDI
1949, pp. 271 on; CARLI
1955, p. 270; COOR 1961,
p. 57 and *passim*; BERENSON
1968, n. 1, p. 293; RUSK
SHAPLEY 1979, n. 634 (with
relevant bibliography);
CHRISTIANSEN-KANTER-BRANDON
STREHLKE 1988 (exhibition
catalogue with relevant
bibliography)

This is one of the most distinguished works produced by Neroccio de' Landi, and of Sienese painting in general, at the end of the 15th century, when portrait painting was practised very little. In fact, this is the only portrait in the catalogue of the known works of this artist, also distinguished sculptor, who was very important in the Siena of his time. Neroccio di Bartolomeo de' Landi belonged to the noble Sienese family of the Landi del Poggio. He probably did his apprenticeship as an artist in the workshop of Vecchietta, and certainly within the sphere of the latter's influence. Setting off on his own in 1468, he worked in association with Francesco di Giorgio until 1475, after which he worked independently.

Within the Sienese school of the *Quattrocento*, in which Renaissance ideas, coming mainly from Florence, were altered through the persistence of a taste for the great Sienese masters of the previous century (Duccio, Simone Martini, and the Lorenzetti), the work of Neroccio de' Landi stands out for its marked accent of conservatism, its soft, precious cadence in line and volume, its clear colours and its decorative refinement, with solutions which reveal a taste for the Gothic, everything that Bernard Berenson summed up in his rather excessive words of praise: "Simone Martini reborn."

This painting is definitely a portrait, depicting a beautiful young woman richly attired in the style of the late 15th century (stylistic analysis dates the painting at around 1490), with a wide décolletage trimmed with pearls, as is her headdress, whilst she wears three pearl necklaces, two with jewels hanging from them. The identity of this woman is unknown. The inscriptions in the triangles have been tentatively interpreted as the initials of "Alessandra Piccolomini," a member of one of the most distinguished families in Siena, although there is little evidence for this, and the abbreviation of "Neroccio"; it is even possible that these inscriptions were added at a later date. It has also been suggested that because the face of the young woman is very similar to one we see in other portraits by this artist at around the same time, that she might be Neroccio's future wife, known to have married him in 1493. This hypothesis would not be easy to verify. What does seem beyond doubt is that, as Coor pointed out in his 1961 monograph on Neroccio, her loose hair identifies her as being unmarried, since it was the custom for married women to tie their hair in a bun. Coor also discovered that the decorative motif of two eagles' heads pecking a golden ball that is repeated on the frame (which is the original) come from the arms of the Baldisinis, a noble house of Siena. The painting might therefore have been for them.

The Latin inscription on the panel, in which the artist declares himself incapable of emulating the divine creation of nature, repeats a commonplace of Renaissance art theory. From the compositional point of view, the panel also function as a parapet which emphasizes the separation between the simulated world of the portrait, created by painting, and the real world occupied by the spectator. This device, which was used frequently in 16th century painting, was introduced in Flanders (already appearing in Jan van Eyck) and later spread to Italy by Antonello de Messina, where it was in general use by Neroccio's time. Direct or indirect Flemish influence can also be seen in the way the artist has not used his habitual abstract gilded background, replacing it with a landscape with trees and a river, a city, distant mountains, and a sky with clouds. Against this natural background we see a image of the beautiful young woman painted in Neroccio's unmistakable style, in the delicacy of the facial expression, the sharpness in delineation, the smooth ivory skin, the beautiful blonde hair, which is almost compact in texture but reveals small details, all of which goes to make up one of the most fascinating works by this master.
(*José Milicua*)

QVANTVM HOMINI FAS EST MIRA LICET ASSEQVAR ARTE
NIL AGO MORTALIS EMVLOR ARTE DEOS

101
Italy

Andrea di Francesco di Cione, known as "il Verrocchio" (Florence, 1435-Venice, 1488)
Head of Saint Jerome,
approx. 1465-1470
Tempera on paper fixed to panel, 49 x 46 cm
Florence, Galleria Palatina del Palazzo Pitti,
Palat. 1912, 370
Exhibitions: Florence, 1990
Bibliography: Florence 1990, p. 180, n. 12

It is difficult to explain why this head is painted on paper in such an unusual manner. The picture must have been the same size originally, if one allows for the way it has been cut slightly by the panel's edges. It has deteriorated considerably in the area beneath the neck, whilst the rest, especially the face, has been conserved quite well; in contrast, the ear has been repainted.

This head of Saint Jerome has such a magnificent quality that one commentator even wondered if it could be the work of the young Leonardo da Vinci (G. Passavant 1959, p. 133). The head stands out against the black background like the moon on a dark night. We cannot be sure, however, that the black background is the original one, or that this "space odyssey" effect was intended by the painter.

It is obvious that we are examining a face emaciated by age, lit by a cruel silvery light which highlights the subtle wrinkles, emphasizing the ravages of time on the flesh. Each of the fine hairs with their silken shine is clearly depicted. Even the hairs of the eyebrows are represented with an unprecedented meticulousness. This leads us to think that Saint Jerome was conceived from the first as an independent work to be looked at from very close quarters. But despite the meticulous detail, the head retains a magnificent unity and

is powerfully framed by the foreshortening of the volumes; the light embraces everything, giving surprising effects in the area behind the neck. It is therefore a masterpiece, and has been accorded its rightful place in the history of Florentine painting of the second part of the *Quattrocento*.

The original attribution to Pollaiolo does not stand up to the evidence. I believe that anyone who knows the works of the young Verrocchio – the *Madonna with Child Giving Blessings*, in Berlin; *Raphael and Tobias*, in London; the *Crucifixion*, in Argiano; the *Madonna with Child and Two Angels*, in London – would find it difficult to attribute this work to him. The head of Saint Jerome also contains two undoubtable references to the fresco of Saint Domenico in Pistoia and the head of the same saint in the *Crucifixion* in Argiano. The chiaroscuro, which is more subtle and velvety than that of

the work at Argiano, would seem to indicate that this work was a slightly later one, produced at a date closer to the *Madonna with Child and Two Angels* at the National Gallery in London. Despite the difference in subject, Saint Jerome resembles the angel on the left-hand side in the foreshortening of the head and the subtle locks of hair, which fall ornately over the head, reflecting the light. The delicate flesh of Saint Jerome also has a softness and transparency comparable with that of the proud *Madonna* in London.

The great luminosity and the firmness of the foreshortening enables us to see how greatly the drawing still partakes, during the middle of the 6th decade of the quattrocento, in the ideas of the 15th century. (*Luciano Bellosi*)

102
Sierra Leone

Sherbro-Portuguese or Temne-Portuguese culture
Head (Mahen Yafe),
before 1550
Carving in soapstone,
20.3 cm
Los Angeles, The Paul and Ruth Tishman Collection of African Art, Walt Disney Co.
Bibliography: Vogel 1981, p. 64

Like the well-known stone figures (*nomoli*) of the Sherbero, this head (*mahen yafe*) dates from the time when the Sape kingdoms still occupied a large part of the Mende territory. The Sape ruled over the Sherbro, the Temne, and other linguistic groups on the west coast at the time the Portuguese arrived in the 15th century. But in 1550 they came under pressure from the Mende, who came from the south, and had to abandon most of their lands in what is

now Sierra Leone. Like the stone figures, these heads were found buried in the ground by the Mende and other peoples, sometimes as far south as the diamond mines. The original purpose of the figures and the heads remains obscure, and the descendents of these artists in the coastal areas were unable to provide relevant information. Some of these stone heads seem to belong to the Sherbro, but others, such as the head in question, could be a product of Temne culture. (*Van A. Romans*)

103
China

Ming dynasty
*March of the Guard
of Honour*, between 1453
and 1493
Glazed polychrome
earthenware
Shanghai, National Museum,
4829-4894

186

A set of seventy-six ceremonial figures and objects representing a funeral cortege, composed of people, horses of transport. The warriors on horseback lead the procession and are followed by civil servants, servants on foot, slaves, and sedan chairs and four bearers with their spare carriages. These figures are accompanied by women and two sedan chairs.

The figures form part of the burial trappings of a high-ranking civil servant whose position is shown by the sedan chair. The jade seals and belts of the civil servants indicate that he probably belonged to the civilian branch. This work can be dated to the fourth year of the Emperor Jingtai reign (1453) when it was established in the sumptuary and transport codes that civil servants above the third grade could use sedan chairs. The norms established in the seventh year of the reign of Hongzhi (1493) allowed civil servants and army officers to use sedan chairs with four bearers. From this we may deduce that this set of ceremonial figures could not have been produced later. The quality and faithfulness of the representation of funeral customs in this set together with other historical and artistic evidence provide a good record of funeral rituals for high-ranking civil servants under the Ming dynasty.

(*Fang Bongehas*)

104
Greece/Crete

Miguel Damascenus
Saint Anthony, 16th century
Painting on board,
86.5 x 67 cm
Athens, Byzantine Museum
Bibliography: SOTIRIOU 1924,
p. 30; SOTIRIOU 1931, p. 35;
XIGOPOULOS 1957, p. 140;
CHATZIDAKIS 1964, p. 43;
SKROBUCHA 1961, pp. 123-124

An image of the torso of a
saint holding an open book,
Ilitario, revealing the words:
BEING BENEVOLENT I PROPITIATE THE
EARTHLY SCHEMES OF THE DEVIL. He
is wearing a reddish-brown
cloak and a blue-grey hood,
with the artist's signature appearing in the folds of the
cloak.
Iconographically, the painting
follows the typology of the
saints of the Cuger fresco in
Yugoslavia and the icons from
Corfu. Undoubtedly, the
model would have been a full-
length standing image from
the end of the 14th century or
the beginning of the 15th, but
was later turned into an image
of the upper body. This sort
of representation is characteristic of the Cretan workshops,
as can be seen in the Byzantine Museum's icon T-176
from Messina, Italy. The *ilitario* is one of the most characteristic motifs of this period,
appearing in an icon at the
Benakis Museum, the central
theme of which is "the Virgin
and the obedient angels,"
which has been dated to the
15th century and comes from
the circle of Andrés Ritso's
workshop. The same motif
and iconography are found in
image 129 at the Greek Institute in Venice, which is also
dated 15th century. The saint
is always represented with the
book in the left hand, although in the Venice Institute
this hand is hidden by the
cloak.
As we have said, this figure is
also used in the painting of
icons, where we see the frontal image of Saint Anthony
with his left hand resting on
the book. This is how he ap-

pears in the icon by the Cretan
Theophanis in 1535, in the former chapel of the Lavra monastery on Mount Athos.
This figure was possibly reduced to an upper torso by
Miguel Damascenus. It is distinguished from traditional
paintings by the way the left
hand shows a slight move-
ment, an almost Renaissance
touch, which demonstrates
the late date at which it was
produced.
In a technical sense, this icon
constitutes a valuable example
of the early work of the great
Cretan painter in the 16th cen-

tury, and can be dated to the
time that he painted the
prophet Elias for the Stauroni-
kita monastery on Mount
Athos.
(*Ch. Baltoyanni*)

105
France

Provence school
Saint Dionysius at Prayer,
approx. 1505-1510
Oil painting on panel,
49 x 35 cm
Inscriptions: on the
parchment hanging from the
lower shelf: MAGNUM MISTERYUM
ET MIRABILIS SACRAMENTUM; on
the paper next to the
shelves: DIVUS DIONYSIUS
PARISIORUM EPISCOPUS THEOLOGUS
ARIOPAGITA
Amsterdam, Rijksmuseum,
A3116 (deposited in the
Mauritshaus in the Hague)
Exhibitions: London, 1932;
London, 1949
Bibliography: LONDON 1932,
n. 90, fig. 105; LONDON 1949,
n. 275, fig. 174; LACLOTTE-
THIEBAUT 1983,
p. 273, n. 103

Sixty years after the first exhibition of this panel there is
no need to challenge its date
– around 1510 – or its attribution to the School of Avignon.
The diverse origins of the
painters who worked in
Provence at this time serve as
an explanation of the northern
traits (such as the folds of the
sleeves of the surplice), the
elements of local culture (the
sharpness of the portrait, the
realism of the badly trimmed
beard), and the references to
a famous work (the books and
objects on the shelves in the
background are similar to the
still lifes above the Prophets at
the sides of the altarpiece of
the *Annunciation* painted in
1453 for Aix cathedral).
The character in the painting,
who is tonsured and dressed
as a prelate, has been identified as Saint Dionysius the
Aeropagite, a Greek philosopher converted to Chris-
tianity in the first century, although the preferred explanation is that he is Saint Dionysius (Saint Denis), the bishop
of Paris beheaded in the 3rd
century.
However, the inscription on
the piece of paper in the
painting mixes their bio-
graphies: DIVUS DIONYSIUS PARISIO-

RUM EPISCOPUS THEOLOGUS ARIO-
PAGITA. This confusion is not
surprising, since from the 9th
century onwards the two
saints were often confused.
This confusion was inspired
by the monks of Saint Denis
and spread via the *Golden
Legend* and miracle plays, appearing in paintings dedicated
to the saint.
The introduction of the cult of
this saint to the south of
France was undoubtedly due
to his attributed power of cur-

ing headaches, rabies, and sy-
philis. This is revealed by the
paintings in eastern Provence
(the cycle of the Saint Erige
chapel in Auron, 1451; the
panel at Luceram, approx.
1480) and western Provence
(contracts requested in Rognes
1472, in Aix in 1514, and in
Châteaurenard in 1532).
Because of its smallness, it is
possible that this panel was
commissioned for a private
chapel.
(*Marie-Claude Léonelli*)

Melozzo degli Ambrosi, known as Melozzo da Forlì (Forlì, 1438-1494)
Angel Playing a Lute, approx. 1481-1493
Fresco, 117 x 93.5 x 7 cm
From the apse of the Basilica dei Santissimi Apostoli in Rome
Vatican City, Vatican Museums, 40269.14.10
Exhibitions: Japan, 1989
Bibliography: TAJA 1750, pp. 360-361; PISTOLESI 1829, II, pp. 176-177; VASARI-MILANESI 1878, III, pp. 52, 64; RICCI 1911, p. 11; VENTURI 1913, VII, 2, pp. 24-37; TULLI 1932, III, pp. 5-6; SALMI 1938, XVI, pp. 4-8; SCHIAVO 1977, I, pp. 89-110; NEW YORK 1982; MANCINELLI 1983, pp. 148-150, n. 76; IV, pp. 111-122; CLARK 1989, pp. 61-72; AGOSTI 1990, p. 193, n. 49

Melozzo da Forlì is one of the most important figures of the late 15th century Renaissance, especially in central Italy, to which he brought both the abstract intellectualism he had learnt from Piero della Francesca in Urbino and the realism he had seen in the painting of Justo de Gante and Pedro Berruguete.

In Rome he entered the intellectual circles of the Papal court, as can be seen in the fresco he painted in 1477, *Sixtus IV Naming Platina,* prefect of the Vatican Library, an official recognition of humanistic scholarship by the church. There is controversy over the dating of the work he did for the Basilica dei Santissimi Apostoli, also in Rome, which marks the peak of his artistic career. Some commentators, such as E. Zocca (*La basilica dei Santissimi Apostoli in Roma,* Rome 1959) have given an early date (1477), drawing on a description of the basilica by F. Albertini in 1510 in his *Opusculum de mirabilibus novae et veteris urbis Romae*. At the other end of the scale, P. Toesca ("Melozzo da Forlì" in *Nuova*

Antologia, 8th series, XVI, May-June 1938, p. 316) opts for a later date (1489). The most plausible dating is perhaps 1481-1483, the period during which Melozzo was not working on the Sistine Chapel.

Like many other important works, this fresco later suffered serious damage, and in 1702 it was already (according to a commentary by Francesco Fontana quoted by Zocca 1959, p. 40) in a "stato di poca considerazione." Things became worse with the reconstruction of the basilica under Clement XI (1702-1711), which would have destroyed the frescos had it not been for the efforts of Sebastiano Resta and Agostino Taja who saved their remains. Fourteen fragments were preserved in the Vatican Museums (four heads of the Apostles, eight angels with musical instruments, and two groups of cherubim) whilst the *Christ blessing* was kept in the Quirinal Palace (certain studies, such as the recent one by Nicholas Clark, still mention the fragment which the Prado considered to be by Melozzo until 1991, it had been commented on during the preparations for the Cambó Collection exhibition that it was not). The fragmentation of the fresco makes the old commentaries priceless; these include Taja's (in the *Descrizione del Palazzo Apostolico Vaticano,* Rome 1750), and especially Vasari's (from the life of Benozzo Gozzoli in his *Vite*): "Melozzo was an attentive student of fine art and paid special attention to foreshortening ... His talent can be seen in the *Ascension of the Lord*, in the middle of a choir of angels who are leading him to heaven. The foreshortening in the figure of Christ is done so well that He appears to cleave the vault in two, and the same may be said of the angels who fly through the air in various positions. The same occurs with the apostles, who are on the ground, foreshortened in different attitudes

189

with such perfection that it was greatly praised at the time and still is by other artists who have learnt much from the work of this artist. He practiced perspective, as we can see from the buildings painted in this work, which was commissioned by cardinal Riario, the nephew of pope Sixtus IV, who rewarded him splendidly." Vasari describes the decoration correctly, but errs in the identity of the patron, who was not cardinal Piero Riario, deceased in 1474, but Giuliano della Rovere, who became pope under the name of Julius II and who was Michelangelo's patron at the time.

A reconstruction of the apse of the Santissimi Apostoli with these fragments was attempted in 1938. It is a praiseworthy effort that gives us an idea of the importance of these frescos which are considered, as far as certain aspects go, to be the forerunners of the work of Michelangelo in the Sistine Chapel, of Raffaello in the Chigi Chapel in Santa Maria del Popolo, and

other domes and vaults which open onto infinite heavens.

In the figures of the Santissimi Apostoli apse, the art of Melozzo da Forlì acquired a noble grandeur; his figures exemplify an almost rhetorical style of painting which both intensifies the visions in perspective and delights in the lyrical rapture of the angels embellished with blond curls, whose faces are perhaps the most idyllic and sensual of the entire Renaissance.

(*Joan Sureda i Pons*)

107
Italy

Domenico di Tommaso
Bigordi, known
as "Ghirlandaio"
(Florence 1449-1494)
Saint Jerome in His Study,
approx. 1470-1480
185 x 120 cm
Florence, Church of
Ognissanti
Exhibitions: Kyoto Setagaya
Nagoya, 1991
Bibliography: Frulli 1987, II,
p. 636 (with previous
bibliography)

"And in the Church of Ognissanti in Florence, working in competition with Sandro Botticelli, he painted a fresco of Saint Jerome surrounded by various instruments and books, which is now next to the door leading to the choir. When the monks found it necessary to move the choir from its previous position, this painting, along with the one by Sandro Botticelli, was fastened with irons and transported to the centre of the church without any damage at all, this at the time that these Lives is being printed for the second time." These words by Giorgio Vasari come from his biography Ghirlandaio in the second edition of the *Vite*, published in 1568 after several years of preparation. In the same work this information is confirmed in more detail in the life of Botticelli: "In Ognissanti (he) painted a fresco of Saint Augustine for the Vespucci (their arms can in fact be seen in the fresco) in the transept leading to the door of the choir, attempting to surpass all his fellow painters, especially Domenico Ghirlandaio, who had painted a Saint Jerome on the opposite wall. He worked with great determination, and the resulting work was highly praised [...] As mentioned in the life of Ghirlandaio, this painting was safely moved from its place in 1564." (Vasari, *Le Vite*, R. Bottarini and P. Barrocchi edition, III-1, Florence 1971, pp. 479-489 and 512-513 respectively).

A little earlier in the 16th century, shortly before the first edition of the *Vite* (1550), the Anonimo Magliabechiano had stated: "Domenico del Ghirlandaio [...] painted a fresco on the pillar of the choir in the Church of Ognissanti, working in competition with Sandro Botticelli, who was painting a Saint Augustine opposite him at the same time" (*L'Anonimo Magliabechiano*, A. Ficarra edition, Naples 1968, p. 115). Although largely ignored by modern critics, and usually mentioned only in connection with Botticelli's painting, this fresco represents a high point in Ghirlandaio's first decade as a painter. According to Vasari, Ghirlandaio did his apprenticeship with Baldovinetti, completing it in the workshop of Verrocchio alongside Perugino and the young Leonardo da Vinci. By then, he had already produced important work in the Church of Ognissanti with the fresco of the *Virgin of Mercy* and the *Pietà*, painted at the top and bottom of the altar in the chapel of the Vespucci family around 1472. It was evidently the same illustrious Florentine family that commissioned the *Saint Jerome*, which is closely related (at least in an iconographic sense) with the *Saint Augustine* (which depicted the vision he had at the moment of Saint Jerome's death, having written him a letter on his beatific vision of souls in paradise). With the special daylight effect which produces heavy shadows, the *Saint Jerome* is an example of the new direction taken in this master's work, following both the model of the great Flemish painters and the tradition of Domenico Veneziano, which he had learned from Alessio Baldovinetti. Vasari's commentary on the meticulousness to be seen in the "infinity of scholarly instruments and books" is a first indication of this Flemish influence, whilst studies carried out in the first half of the present century, in particular those of Panofsky

(*Early Netherlandish Painting*), have led to the conclusion that Ghirlandaio's *Saint Jerome* and Botticelli's *Saint Augustine* were "patterned after an Eyckian *Saint Jerome* then owned by the Medici" and that "the adoring shepherds in Ghirlandaio's *Nativity* of 1485 were inspired by Hugo van der Goes' *Portinari Altarpiece*, which had reached Florence just three or four years before" (Panofsky 1953 and 1958).

Panofsky must also be recognized for acknowledging this problem in the two editions of his book on the earlier Flemish painters, and the essay on the letter to Saint Jerome which comes between them, allowing others (Hall 1968) to draw more definitive conclusions. The thesis that Ghirlandaio's *Saint Jerome* may have been modelled on a painting by van Eyck was based on the fact reported by Eugene Müntz in *Les collections des Medicis au XVe siècle* (Paris 1888, p. 78) that in 1492 the Medici's possessed an oil painting, which was stored with special care, depicting *Saint Jerome Studying*, with a small bookcase in perspective containing various books with a lion at his feet, by the master Jan of Bruges. However, it cannot be established when the van Eyck arrived in Florence, and this single reference is not enough to corroborate its character. In 1936 a Flemish painting on this theme with the characteristic style of van Eyck entered the collection of the Institute of Art of Detroit. The fact it was dated 1442, a year after van Eyck's death, led to its initially being attributed to Petrus Christus rather than van Eyck. However, there were still writers who connected the Detroit painting with the one described in 1492; Panofsky pronounced his favour of this connection, basing his thesis on the idea that the work was started by van Eyck and finished by Christus, and on the visual evidence for this being

the model for Ghirlandaio's *Saint Jerome* and Botticelli's *Saint Augustine* in the Ognissanti (Panofsky 1953, 1954, and 1958, with a commentary on the bibliography). After a careful cleaning, it was established that the date of 1442 was incorrect, and the outstanding quality of the painting led to the decision of restoring its authorship to van Eyck (Hall 1968, pp. 3 on). This confirmed Panofsky's twin thesis: 1) The *Saint Jerome* of Detroit was identified with the one by van Eyck possessed by the Medicis in Florence; 2) Ghirlandaio's *Saint Jerome* (and, to a lesser extent, the *Saint Augustine* by Botticelli) was undoubtedly derived from the Detroit painting. It must, therefore, have been in Florence long before 1492, and served as a model for Ghirlandaio's earliest Flemish influences, which were combined with the specifically Florentine composition of light, inherited from the tradition which passed from Domenico Veneziano to Baldovinetti and Verrocchio's circle, which included Leonardo da Vinci.

(*Ferdinando Bologna*)

108
Flanders

Jan Sanders van Hemessen
(Hemixem, Antwerp,
approx. 1504-Haarlem,
approx. 1575)
Saint Jerome,
signed and dated JOES DE
HEMESSEN PINXIT 1531
Oil painting on panel,
109 x 148 cm
Lisbon, Museu Nacional
de Arte Antiga, 1651
Exhibitions: Brussels, 1963;
Lisbon, 1983; Lisbon, 1985
Bibliography: MARLIER 1954,
pp. 206-209; BOLETINS, III,
n. 1, 1955; OBRAS PRIMAS 1965

Saint Jerome is one of the
saints who appears the most
frequently in Western art. He
was venerated as a Doctor of
the Church (stella doctorum)
and depicted as such in the
early Middle Ages (as in the
inner part of the Boethius diptych, n. 604, Museo de Brescia), although in later centuries the hagiographies emphasized more attractive aspects of his rich biography, especially his period of
penitence in the Syrian desert.
There arose an iconography
based on his epistles, which
were to be found in most medieval monasteries, as well as
the *Golden Legend* and the
Hieronymianus by Giovanni
d'Andrea (1342), in which
Saint Jerome was depicted as
an old man half naked and
clothed in leaves mortifying
his flesh in the desert, usually
accompanied by his cardinal's
hat, a rude cross, a skull, and
the lion. This closely follows
the description of the ascetic
life to be found in his *Letter to
Eustaquia* (Ep. 22:7): "In that
immense sun-baked solitude
which offers horrible sanctuary to monks [...] I felt alone,
because I was brimming over
with bitterness. My limbs bris-
tled and [...] the colour of my
dirty skin had become as an
Ethiop's [...] My face was pale
from fasting [...] and my flesh
had died before I was myself
dead [...] beyond all help, I
threw myself at the feet of
Jesus, watering them with my

tears and tamed my repugnant
flesh with fasts which lasted
weeks [...] If I came across a
deep valley, rugged moun-
tains or crevices in the rocks,
I made them my place of
prayer, the dungeon of my
wretched flesh." However, the
Renaissance discovered in
Saint Jerome the man of letters
who had dedicated his youth
to the study of the classics and
had assembled a large library,
as the saint himself reported in
his *Letter to Florentinus* (Ep
5:2). The Saint Jerome who recalled that Solomon had recommended the study of philosophy and that Saint Paul
had quoted from the poems of
Epimedies, Menandrus, and
Aratus; the Saint Jerome who
translated the Bible and was
accused of working for the
benefit of Jewish learning
rather than the Church; and
the Saint Jerome who dreamt
that God accused him of being
a Ciceronian rather than a
Christian (Ep 22:30) was the
one that the humanists, with
Erasmus first and foremost
amongst them, took as their
model, and who artists, beginning with Tommaso da
Modena in 1352 (in San Nicolò
in Treviso), solemnly represented in his study. In his
Saint Jerome in his Study (ap-

prox. 1470; National Gallery,
London) Antonello da
Messina, perhaps following
the models of van Eyck or Co-
lantonio, depicted a Saint
Jerome invested with absolute
authority, still including the
traditional elements of the crucifix, cardinal's hat, and lion,
but substituted the skull with
the peacock, symbol of the
immortality of the soul. However, it was a Dürer's engraving of 1514 that established
the definitive iconography of
Saint Jerome in his study,
characterizing the saint not as
an ineffable doctor of the
church but as a true and dedicated lover of knowledge. But
just a few years later, in 1521,
with his *Saint Jerome* (Museu
Nacional de Arte Antiga, Lisbon), Dürer depicted the saint
reflecting on death, visibly indicating the skull on his desk
with the index finger of his left
hand. *Saint Jerome's Vision of
the Last Judgement* by Marinus
Claeszon van Reymerswaele
(Museo del Prado) is related to
this work. An inscription dates
it as 1521, although it could be
a little later. The relationship
between the two works is studied in depth by Friedländer
in *Die altniederländische
Malerei*, XII, 1935. In the
Flemish painting, the eschato-

logical theme is made patent
with the presence of a miniature of the Apocalypse on
the saint's lectern. Such considerations, which were typical of German and Flemish
art, can be seen in this work
by Hemessen, a painter who
did his apprenticeship in the
studio of Hendrick van Kleve
(1519) and who set himself up
as an independent artist in
1524. The Mannerism of the
Antwerp school can be seen
in this as in most of his paintings, although the clear Italian
influence, which is combined
with a naturalism full of daring, dramatic gestures, would
seem to indicate that he
visited Italy around 1530, a
year before this painting was
produced. Without abandon-
ing Dürer and Marinus Claeszon van Reymerswaele, He-
messen returns to the typology of the penitent saint, although he also depicts him as
a man of passion. The religious theme appears to be se-
cularized, and we see more
concern for anatomy and
movement than for intellectual
satisfaction in the body of
Saint Jerome.
(*Joan Sureda i Pons*)

109
Italy

Marco Palmezzano,
(Forlì 1459-1539)
Saint Jerome,
signed work, 1503
Oil painting on panel,
86.5 x 62 cm
Rome, Galleria Nazionale
d'Arte Antica, Palazzo
Barberini, 1293
Bibliography: Venturi 1981;
Di Carpegna 1965, pp. 47-48;

Until the appearance of C. Grigioni's 1956 monograph (*Marco Palmezzano*, Faenza 1956), Marco Palmezzano was an enigmatic figure who was usually mentioned for the work he did with Melozzo de Forlì on the walls of the Feo chapel in the church of San Biagio in Forlì. Melozzo's influence can be seen in his work, but his development as a painter, sometimes considered somewhat lacking in evolution, relegated him to second rank in the history of the passage from the *Quattrocento* to the *Cinquecento*. Later exhibitions (1957) and studies (Mazza, Viroli) revealed the great master that he really was, proof of which can be seen in works such as the *Annunciation* in the Civic Art Gallery of Forlì or the *Virgin with Child between Saint Michael the Archangel and James the Younger* in the Art Gallery of Faenza. However, not enough attention has been paid to either the influence of Bellini and the generally Venetian character of some of his works, or the possible influence of Antonello da Messina. The *Saint Jerome* in the Galleria Nazionale d'Arte Antica of Rome provides an example of them. The saint is depicted with the elements normally associated with him (the books, the lion, the stone, the crucifix) in a detailed landscape where the rocks become true pieces of architecture shaped by a light which is very Venetian, although it does not attain the subtlety of a Bellini.
The painting does not conceal

the eclecticism which guided the artist's brush, and we see both images which are "all reason and intellect," and therefore geometrical (e.g., the books in the background on the shelf at the bottom of the rock), and others which, whilst not escaping such concepts, approach the world of naturalism and detail (e.g., the treatment of the roots of the tree trunk on which the saintly hermit is sitting). In his study entitled *La Galleria Nazionale in Roma, Quadri e sculture*

(1896), Venturi transcribed the inscription on the double scroll in the foreground next to the left foot of the saint: *Marcus Palmezanus Pictor forliviensis faciebat MCCCCCIII*. As Viroli indicates on page 18 of his *Pittura del Cinquecento a Forlì* (1991), this date (1503) situates the painting at the time of important political changes in Forlì (the advent of Cesare Borgia and the fall of Caterina Sforza) and Palmezzano's "golden period."
(*Joan Sureda i Pons*)

110
Germany/Netherlands

Utrecht school
Saint Kunera,
approx. 1480-1490
Carving in oak,
64 x 22 x 19 cm
From Cleves cathedral
Cologne, Diocesan Museum

According to legend, Kunera of Rhenen (in Utrecht) was the companion of Saint Ursula and of royal blood. The wife of her master strangled her out of jealousy. Her murder is represented here, as in a painting of the saint in Kalkar, by the veil knotted around her neck. The slender, gracious figure is formed with well-defined lines of movement which go in all directions, developing freely and flowing into each other, giving an overall impression of great vivacity. The head leans to the left, thereby breaking the vertical line. One leg is set forward, its line being continued by a slight inclination of the torso. This dramatic displacement of the figure's axis gives special intensity to the saint's gaze towards an open book that she is holding at waist level. The bending of the right arm interrupts the composition. The hand catches hold of the folds of the shawl which fall from her shoulders to combine with those of her dress in a harmonious common structure. A diadem decorated with strings of pearls crowns her head.

The authorship of this magnificent carving is still not clear. H. P. Hilger noted certain stylistic similarities with four figures of saints with approximately the same format from the Franciscan church at Cleves (*Saint Gertrude of Nivelles, Saint Veronica, Saint Catherine and Saint Margaret*) which, in his opinion, are to be attributed to the master Arnt who worked in Kalkar and Zwolle. These images, considered to be the remains of a late medieval altarpiece, were associated with *Saint Kunera* by H. Meurer, who believed that they belonged to

the same set, although he was aware of discrepancies in their execution. According to him, *Saint Kunera* and *Saint Veronica* are by Arnt, and believes that the style of Kersten Woyers can be detected in the others. Woyers could have worked on the altarpiece under Arnt's direction or may have finished the figures upon the death of the latter. The problem of the origin and relationship of these figures has still not been solved. The attribution of *Saint Veronica* to Arnt seems beyond doubt, but the same cannot be said about *Saint Kunera*. It could be the work of another artist who,

unlike Arnt, attempted to avoid all constraints in his sculpting. He was probably a wood carver who took his inspiration from Dutch religious imagery, drawing on older models such as the work of Jean Delemer and Niclaus Gerhaert of Leyden, and certain anonymous artists of the early and mid-15th century. The idea that the creator of *Saint Kunera* worked in the lower Rhineland seems questionable in light of the work's closeness to the Utrecht style. This can be clearly seen, despite certain conceptual differences, if this carving is compared with the works of

Adriaen van Wesel, in particular, *Saint Ines* (in the Rijksmuseum of Amsterdam) *Saint Paul* (private collection), or the two saints in the church of Saint Aldegunda of Emmerich. (*Harmut Krohm*)

111
Germany

Master of Elsloo
Saint Michael,
approx. 1490-1500
Wood, 114 x 42 x 30 cm
From Lövernich in Erkelenz
Cologne, Schnügen
Museum, A 214

The saint is represented as a knight in armour who has conquered the dragon lying at at his feet. The curly hair which falls to his shoulders gives him a very youthful appearance. In his right hand he holds a sword of which there is nothing left but the handle; in his left hand he holds a shield to protect himself from the devil. His cloak, which is spread wide and falls in a profusion of folds, hangs from two cords around his shoulders. His posture is firm and, leaning slightly forwards, places his foot on the front paw of the devil who, as he retreats, attempts to catch hold of the saint's left leg with a

claw. This has always been considered to be a statue of Saint Michael since he was commonly represented as a young knight from the early Middle Ages onwards.

The cross on his cuirass also identifies him as Saint Michael and provides a stylistic relationship with the contemporary works of Israhel van Meckenems.

These images have often been used as a model and were faithfully copied, an example of this being the image of Saint Michael, produced in the studio of Tilman van Der Burch, for Saint Andrew's Church in Cologne.

This sculpture is from Lövenich in Erkelenz, a region which had close artistic ties with the Meuse Valley, and especially with Lüttich. The most recent study attributes this work to the Master of Elsloo. Comparison with the documented works of this master and analysis of the carving and treatment of details (such

195

as the decorative detail of the hair) enable us to classify it as one of his early works.
(*Gudrun Sporbeck*)

---

112 and 113
Italy

Sebastiano Luciani known as Sebastiano del Piombo (Venice, approx. 1485-Rome, 1547)
Saint Sinibald and Saint Louis of Toulouse,
before 1511
Oil on canvas, 295 x 137 cm
Inner doors of organ
From the church of Saint Bartholomew of Venice
Venice, Galleria dell'Accademia (deposit)
Exhibitions: Sydney, 1988
Bibliography: SCANELLI 1657, p. 235; BOSCHINI 1660, pp. 396-397; BOSCHINI 1674, p. 109; ZANETTI 1771, I, p. 278; NARDINI 1778, pp. XL-XLI; MOSCHINI 1815, I, pp. 560-565; CROWE-CAVALCASELLE 1876, VI, p. 371; PROPPING 1892, pp. 16-17; BERENSON 1899, p. 121; BENKARD 1907, pp. 20-25; BERNARDINI 1908; D'ACHIARDI 1908, pp. 33-36; JUSTI 1908, (1926, 1936), I,

p. 230; pp. 12-13; WICKHOFF 1908, p. 29; VENTURI 1913, pp. 154-155; VENTURI 1915, VII, p. 773; 1928, IX, pp. 74-77; 1932, IX, p. 18; GOMBOSI 1933, XXXVI; WILDER 1933, p. 116; PALLUCCHINI 1935, pp. 41-42; BERENSON 1936, p. 449; RICHTER 1937, pp. 241-242; PALLUCCHINI 1941, pp. 448-456; DUSSLER 1942, p. 23 and 141, pl. 4 and 5; PALLUCCHINI 1944, pl. 6 a and b, p. 154; GOULD 1969; WILDER 1974 (1988), pp. 197-113, fig. 81 on p. 108, fig. 82 on p. 109, fig. 83 on p. 110; VON ERFA 1976; LUCCO 1980, p. 93, cat. 10 and 11

It must be pointed out, as it has been on many occasions in the past, that the antas or organ doors painted by Sebastiano del Piombo for the Church of Saint Bartholomew of Venice were not well received by early critics. They were first mentioned by F. Sca-

nelli of Forlì in *Il Microcosmo della pittura* (1657; Milan 1966, G. Giubbini edition) and three years later with more precision by M. Boschini in his *Carta del navegar pittoresco* (1660; Rome 1966, A. Pallucchini edition). In 1771 we learn that the organ had definitely been taken apart, although the images of Saint Sinibald and Saint Louis of Toulouse remained within the church. A short time later (1788), the discovery of a document revealed that the antas had been commissioned by Alvise Ricci, the vicar of Saint Bartholomew's between 1507 and 1509, and confirmed Sebastiano del Piombo as their author: "Confici etiam mandavit Frati Sebastiano a Piumo propia impensa Quator Tabulas eximias nostru temporibus instauratas."

The antas were tampered with and restored several times, both before and after this date, making several writers (Crowe-Cavalcaselle, Benkard, Wick-

hoff, Richter, and Fiocco) unsure of their authorship. This problem was resolved in 1940 after a conscientious restoration returned them to their original state. Since then, there has been no doubt that they are one of the masterpieces of the young Sebastiano del Piombo. Perhaps the most complex point in the study of these beautiful canvases is the relationship between Giorgione and Sebastiano del Piombo and, in particular, the influence that the mural on the Fondaco dei Tedeschi could have had on del Piombo's monumental figures. Whilst avoiding judgements, which are hard to substantiate due to the scarce remains of the paintings by the master of Castelfranco on the facade of the Fondaco, we can nonetheless affirm from examination of the remaining fragments and Zanetti's engravings of them that Sebastiano del Piombo's work in Venice must have been influenced by the nearby and almost contempor-

ary murals by Giorgione. If the grandeur of *Saint Sinibald* and *Saint Louis*, whose sculptural effigies rise like pieces of marble in a deep niche, are reminiscent of anything it is of such figures as the *compagno della calza* of the Fondaco dei Tedeschi. But the relationship of the human figure with architecture, is not the only thing that reveals the meeting of the masters; it could be said that the treatment of the light which models the volume in a dense and pronounced manner in Sebastiano del Piombo's saints, cannot be understood without reference to Giorgione's understanding of space, even though the two masters have different concepts of painting. Whereas Giorgione's brush strokes are soft and caress the forms they construct, they become nervous in Sebastiano del Piombo, who forgets the apparel in order to turn light into something material.

(*Joan Sureda i Pons*)

114
Italy

Francesco Morone
(Verona 1471-1529)
Saint Francis Stigmatised,
1510
Oil painting on canvas,
84.5 x 56.5 cm
Verona, Museo
di Castelvecchio, 348
Exhibitions: Verona, 1947
Bibliography: Bernardini
1902, pp. 1379-1380; Trecca
1912, pp. 43-44; Venturi, VII,
1915, p. 782; Avena 1947,
p. 61; Pallucchini 1947[b],
p. 236; Del Bravo 1962,
pp. 14-15; Cuppini 1981,
pp. 438-439; Vavra 1982,
p. 544; Zeri 1988; Marinelli
1991, p. 43

Although of unknown origin, there have never been any doubts as to its authorship and it has always been considered to be one of the masterpieces of Francesco Morone.

The only problem is determining to which point it belongs in the career of this painter, whose style apparently underwent no development.

The formal abstraction of the figures, influenced by Antonello da Messina, are highly synthetic, as if carved in wood, and the influence of Mantegna in the rugged, stratified depiction of nature suggests, an early dating around 1510.

The recent cleaning of the painting has revealed its splendid colours, with refined strokes of tempera which would have been appropriate for a painting on panel. Reflectography has revealed the meticulous sketching of the saint's robes.

Vasari's seductive description, which defined Morone as quite religious and an expert painter, is confirmed by his membership with the severe Confraternities of Saints Syro and Libera, the Holy Body of Christ, and also by extensive, well-documented relationships with the Olivetans of Santa Maria in Organo and the Franciscans of San Bernardino.

The painter wished to be laid to

rest in the latter church dressed in a friar's habit.

This painting follows the traditional iconography of Saint Francis developed by Giotto (in Assisi and the panel in the Louvre), with a very similar example to be seen in the painting of Antoniazzo Romano, dated 1488.

(*Giovanni Peretti*)

115
France

Josse Lieferinxe (a painter from Heinaut in Cambrai who practised in Marseilles and Aix-en-Provence from 1493 and 1505, and who had died by 1508)
Pilgrims at the Tomb of Saint Sebastian,
1497-1499
Oil painting on panel,
82 x 55 cm
Rome, Galleria Nazionale d'Arte Antica, Palazzo Barberini, 1590
Bibliography: BRIGANTI 1938; STERLING 1945; RING 1949; MARTÍN-MERY 1952; LACLOTTE-THIEBAUT 1983, p. 260

The most notable of the painters working in Provence at the end of the 15th century is undoubtedly the artist to whom we owe the series of paintings illustrating scenes from the *Legend of Saint Sebastian*, which are now dispersed between Philadelphia, Baltimore, Saint Petersburg, and Rome. Another series of panels from an altarpiece dedicated to the Virgin (Avignon, Brussels, Musée du Louvre) and a large *Calvary* (Musée du Louvre) can also be attributed to the Saint Sebastian Master.
Ch. Sterling suggests that the scenes from the *Legend of Saint Sebastian* formed part of the lost altarpiece which the painters Josse Lieferinxe and Bernardino Sismondi were commissioned to do on 11 July 1497.
Josse Lieferinxe, a native of Heinaut, is known to us from various documents relating to other commissions for paintinngs (now lost) in Marseilles and Aix-en-Provence between 1493 and 1505. He died between 1505 and 1508. The formal identification of Josse Lieferinxe with the Saint Sebastian Master remains a hypothesis. However, the historical information we have about Lieferinxe coincides with the results of a stylistic examination of the Saint Sebastian Master: a basically Flemish training (Lieferinxe was from Heinaut) close connections with Piedmontese culture (his partner, Sismodi, was from Venasca in the diocese of Turin and his heir, the painter Hans Clemer, was from Saluces) but above all, a deep assimilation of the great style of the Avignon school following the model that the Master of the Annunciation of Aix, Barthélémy d'Eyck, and Enguerrand Quarton had established in the middle of the century. This style survived until the end of the century, as is shown by the work of the first-class artist responsible for *The Prophets* of the Louvre, identified by Ch. Sterling as Jean Changenet, the most famous painter in Avignon. Lieferinxe married his daughter and may have studied under him.
The geometrical monumentality of the Saint Sebastian Master (i.e., Lieferinxe), the way in which light constantly defines the volumes, and the moderate naturalism fit well into this tradition. In addition to the in his style with the art of Piedmont, and especially with Martino Spanzotti, we must include his relationship with Lombard culture, particularly with Bramante, and a certain kinship with Spanish painters such as the Master of Light of Palencia, hypothetically identified by Ch. Sterling with the Castilian Juan de Nalda, a disciple of Changenet in Avignon, or even with John of Burgundy. He also came into direct or indirect contact with the work of Antonello da Messina. Therefore, thanks to him, a kind of internationalism, and receptiveness to the most modern Mediterranean currents continued to be a feature of the Avignon school at the end of his career.
First attributed to the German school, and then to a Hispano-Neapolitan master, this work was restored to the Provence school by R. Longhi (quoted by G. Briganti) and compared, by Ch. Sterling, with a series of scenes from the *Life of Saint Sebastian* that were all from the same polyptych. These were the following paintings: *Saint Sebastian Destroys the Idols* (Philadelphia Museum of Art, the John G. Johnson Collection); *Saint Sebastian before Diocletian and Maximilian* (Saint Petersburg, Hermitage Museum); *Saint Sebastian Cured by Saint Irene* (Philadelphia); *Flagellation of Saint Sebastian* (Philadelphia); *Saint Sebastian Intervenes During the Plague of Rome* (Baltimore, Walters Art Gallery); *The Pilgrims before the Tomb of the Saint* (Rome, Galleria Nazionale d'Arte Antica).
The first four panels undoubtedly constitute the left-hand side of the altarpiece, and the other three, along with one which is missing, from the right-hand side. According to Ch. Sterling, these eight panels could be the ones mentioned in the contract by which the priors of a fraternity devoted to Saint Sebastian commissioned the altarpiece for the chapel of the saint in the former church of Notre-Dame des Acoules in Marseilles. The centre of the altarpiece was to depict *Saint Sebastian with Saint Antonio and Saint Roch*. The painters in question were Josse Lieferinxe and Bernardino de Sismodi.
The date of the contract is 11 July 1497. We know that Sismodi died and that Lieferinxe finished the painting by himself in January 1499. Some historians have thought that the nuances of style in the Saint Petersburg fragments could be explained by the fact it was executed by the two artists together. However, we believe that one painter is basically responsible for the entire work, the same painter who produced the panels of the *Altarpiece of the Virgin*, the *Calvary* of the Louvre and the *Pietà* (Antwerp, Royal Museum of Fine Arts). These were undoubtedly later than the Saint Sebastian altarpiece, produced between 1500 and 1505.

The scene depicted in the panel in Rome evokes the piety of the faithful, the sick, and the pilgrims who come to venerate the tomb and shrine of the saint in the reliquary of honour to the right of the statue of Christ. This panel, like the one now in Baltimore, emphasizes the role of Saint Sebastian as a protector, like Saint Roch and Saint Anthony, against the plague in an age when epidemics were frequent.
The composition, with its strong construction and the simplification of the volumes clearly outlined by a lighting which accentuates the chiaroscuros, falls clearly within the tradition of the Avignon school. The compassion, somewhat rough in its nobility, with which human wretchedness is described recalls the rustic cordiality of Spanzotti. Another link with the figurative culture of northern Italy is the perspective in the architecture of the church, modelled on Bramante, and also used in certain scenes of the *Altarpiece of the Life of the Virgin*.
(Michel Laclotte)

116
Italy

Michelangelo Buonarroti
(Caprese, 1475-Rome, 1564)
The Two Cleopatras,
before 1533
Pencil sketch on paper,
23.4 x 18.2 cm
Florence, Casa Buonarroti, 2F
Bibliography: Dussler 1959;
Barocchi 1962; Barocchi
1964[a]; Barocchi 1964[b]; Berti
1965; Hartt 1971; Tolnay
1975; Tolnay 1975-1980;
Berti 1985

In his account on the life of Properzia de' Rossi, Giorgio Vasari mentions that in 1562 Tommaso Cavalieri presented duke Cosimo de' Medici with a drawing of Cleopatra by the "divine Michelangelo." It is generally, if not unanimously, considered that this Cleopatra (from the Casa Buonarroti in Florence) is the same as the one mentioned by Vasari, which also supposes that it formed part of the group given by Michelangelo to Cavalieri in 1533.

This work of exceptional quality is imbued with a deep melancholy that is not without pathos, portraying the beautiful face of the queen of Egypt with a snake coiled around her neck and about to bite her breast. It thus narrates the suicide of Cleopatra after the defeat of her troops and those of Mark Anthony at the battle of Actium. The dramatic likeness of Cleopatra in this drawing perfectly expresses Michelangelesque pathos and the sorrowful character of the artist who throughout his mature years sought desperately for the emotional satisfaction that he never found with either his beloved Vittoria Colonna or the person he gave this drawing to, Tommaso Cavalieri.

A recent restoration in 1988 by Sergio Boni and Benedetta Ballico discovered another face of Cleopatra on the reverse side, also undoubtedly by Michelangelo. Whilst Paolo Barocchi and Giovanni Agosti believe that it is a preparatory study for the Cleopatra on the other side, Michael Hirst believes the opposite. Whatever the case may be, as Barocchi points out, the melancholy of the finished Cleopatra becomes a dramatic and almost grotesque expression in this sketch, its relationship with the *maniera antica* being accentuated. The face of Cleopatra seems to be a mask rather than a study of the woman herself (it bears a clear relationship to Guiliano de' Medici in the New Sacristy of San Lorenzo in Florence) and turns the almost sweet Cleopatra on the other side, who stares away from the snake which is about to kill her, into a real being.
(*Enrique Valdivieso*)

117
Italy

Michelangelo Buonarroti
(Caprese, 1475-Rome, 1564)
Study for the Head of Leda,
approx. 1530
Sanguine on paper
35.5 x 18.9 cm
Florence, Casa Buonarroti, 7F
Bibliography: DUSSLER 1959;
BAROCCHI 1962; BAROCCHI
1964[a]; BAROCCHI 1964[b]; BERTI
1965; HARTT 1971; TOLNAY
1975; TOLNAY 1975-1980;
BERTI 1985

According to Vasari, Michelangelo painted a picture of *Leda and the Swan* during the siege of Florence in 1530. Although it was destroyed in an outburst of moralism in France in the 17th century, its characteristics are known to us through various copies, the best of which is in the National Gallery in London, which classifies it as anonymous, although it has sometimes been attributed to Rosso Fiorentino.

The drawing, which only captures the head of the female character, displays an exceptional quality and reflects a profound study of feeling. Viewed in isolation, it transmits none of the erotic sensation to be seen in copies of the overall composition, where Leda is sexually embraced by Zeus in the form of a swan.

Michelangelo's inspiration for the lost painting seems to have come from a Graeco-Roman relief now in the British Museum in London, and the artist seems to have studied the details of the physical relationship between Zeus and Leda deeply and thoroughly. However, in his expression of feeling and in the vitality with which he infuses the bodies Michelangelo seems to have gone beyond the classical model, which he simply used as the starting point for this exceptional creation.

(*Enrique Valdivieso*)

118
Italy

Gianfrancesco Caroto
(Verona, approx. 1480-1555)
Sophonisba, after 1507
Oil painting on canvas,
94 x 66 cm
Verona, Museo
di Castelvecchio, 341

Bibliography: TRECCA 1912,
p. 32; FIOCCO 1913, p. 130;
FIOCCO 1915, II, pp. 15-75;
VENTURI 1928, p. 888; DEL
BRAVO 1964, p. 13; FRANCO
FIORIO 1971, p. 103; MARINELLI
1983, p. 78; FRANCO FIORIO
1987, p. 24; MARINELLI 1991,
p. 60

As Fiocco and Franco Fiorio have demonstrated, *Sophonisba* is a formal variation on a theme of da Vinci's inspired by a *Magdalen* by Giampetrino in Isola Bella. It can therefore be dated after Gianfrancesco Caroto's stay in Milan around 1507, and subsequently adapted the techniques he had learnt there within a Venetian context.

But even for a painter who paid as much attention to the female figure as Caroto, *Sophonisba* represents a unique work of timeless classicism within such elements as the attentive gaze towards heaven, the clothes clinging to the body, the naked breast, and the *Savonarola* chair, which contribute to an atmosphere of rarified classicism that seems to foreshadow the age of Reni or, indeed, of neoclassicism.

In addition to the Lombard elements, the painting also appears to reveal the influence of Francesco Francia.

The few profane objects that remain from the figurative culture of Verona at the beginning of the *Cinquecento*, which was still saturated in humanistic literature, represent scenes from history or classical mythology, narrative sequences on chests containing few figures, usually heroines from the classics, examples of virtue like *Lucretia*, or *Sophonisba*.

X-ray examinations after cleaning have revealed interesting corrections, such as the arm rest of the chair; the hair, which was initially tied back and later made loose; and the hand, originally holding but the material and now releasing it with open fingers. The two latter modifications demonstrate the intention of accentuating the poignant languor rather than the narration of the episode.

The composition is executed diagonally and the strokes of the original blockage appear to demonstrate that it was never reduced, except perhaps just a little bit in one corner or another. The subject has been treated by Sallust: Sophonisba, queen of Numidia, poisons herself before being repudiated by the husband, Masinisa, accorded with Romans, against his father-in-law Sifax.

(*Sergio Marinelli*)

119
Italy

Venetian master, following the model of Tullio Lombardo (Venice, 1455-1532)
Female bust, early 16th century
Rock crystal on gilded plate, 9.5 x 7 cm (bust); 11 x 7.5 cm (plate)
Budapest, Szépmüvészeti Múzeum, 79.2
Exhibitions: Budapest, 1981; London, 1983
Bibliography: BUDAPEST 1981, pp. 97-104; LONDON 1983, n. 11

This crystal relief representing an idealiZed female head is an important carving from the beginning of the *Cinquecento*. During the first half of the 16th century, it was mounted on a silver-plated plaque. The eyes are characteristic of of this period and are almost closed. The nose is straight, with a classical profile, and the closed mouth has an ex-pression of suffering. The hair-style is Roman, with a parting in the middle and rhythmical waves of hair. It is believed that the relief was modelled on Tullio Lombardo's wax model because of its close re-semblance to the works of this artist. Since we know of no works in crystal by Lombardo, this bust may be the work of some important crystal carver of the Renaissance. Antique gems, especially those from the time of Augustus, were highly esteemed by the patri-cian collectors of Venice dur-ing this period. The cutting of these gems was one of the most highly-reputed and widely practized arts in the ar-tistic circles of Venice. They were influenced by the works of Mantegna and the bronze casters of Padua, as well as by the classical forms of Maderno and Tullio Lombardo.
(*Eva Szmodis-Eszláry*)

120
China

Ming Dynasty (1368-1644)
Bao Tiancheng
Goblet in the form of a raft, 16th century
Carved rhinoceros horn, 9.7 x 25.5 x 9.9 cm
Inscriptions: Tianchen
Shanghai, National Museum, 15214

The rhinoceros horn has been traditionally used in China not only in the field of medicine but also as a material for art. When used for this purpose it was coloured black or yellow, giving it a texture similar to bamboo veins. Its artistic value, which was often greater than that of bamboo or wood, was due to its aged appear-ance and its semitransparent surface.
Carvings in rhinoceros horn were very popular during the Ming (1368-1644) and Qing (1644-1911) dynasties, and particularly during the reigns of the emperors Jiajing (1522-1566) and Wanli (1573-1619). Goblets in varying shapes, bowls, and small ornaments were produced. This goblet was made between 1522 and 1644 and is one of the few for which the artist's name is known. Bao Tiancheng chose the form of a boat, carving an old man with long whiskers comfortably seated inside it. On the lower part the artist has represented waves in order to give the sensation that it is floating. The theme comes from the book *Registers of Strange Things*, which in-cludes the story of a man who decides to sail in search of the Milky Way. On his journey he meets a female character with whom he falls in love and begins an adventure which ends with their separation.
(*Zhang Wei*)

121
**Germany/Eastern
Switzerland**

Memento mori in the form
of a sarcophagus, 1520
Inlaid ivory, 12 x 42 x 15 cm
Cologne, Schnütgen
Museum, Ludwig Donation

204

Six columns with embossed
figures are raised on a base
decorated with the delicacy of
a cut diamond. These are
placed in each corner and in
the middle of the two longer
sides of the tomb. In the
spaces between the columns,
six supports in the form of a
baluster bear the upper part of
the tomb and the hinged
cover, the interior decoration
of which is the same as that
on the base, as is the exterior
decoration of the two rows in
the corners of the supports of
the upper part.

A body is lying on top of the
tomb and is being devoured
by worms and insects. The
sarcophagus is typical of the
sepulchral monuments of
France and Burgundy of the
early 16th century, and most
resembles the tomb of Jacques
de Alain, who died in 1527 in
Saint-Martin-de-Lux. This has
been destroyed, but was composed of eight columns with
figures leaning against them,
one of which has been
preserved in the Louvre,
which supported the platform
carrying the prone figure. The
six figures which surround this
Memento mori, are not
mourning, but are in pairs and
represent the contrast between the spiritual and terre-
strial worlds, as depicted in
the 15th century *Dance of
Death* from Paris. One can see
the pope, the emperor, a pa-
triarch, a sultan, a monk (with
a phylactery which reads:
morir nous faut, we have to
die) and a gentleman (with the
inscription: *quant dieu pla*,
when God pleases), repre-
senting humanity before
death. This thematic motif is
parallel to the images which
appear in a fresco (1458), in
Saint Maurice d'Annecy and in
a funeral tapestry (dated be-

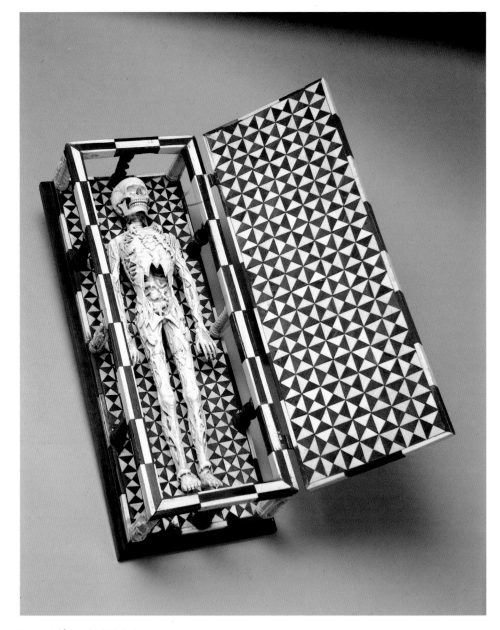

tween 1460 and 1475) belonging to the Order of Saint John
of Jerusalem in Wartburg,
western Switzerland. In both
works, dignitaries of the temporal and spiritual worlds ac-
compained by ladies can be
seen, gathered around a tomb
with a corpse. The style of the
reliefs and the delicate inlaid
work on the columns can be
compared to the choir stalls of
Lausanne cathedral, and those
of the parish church at Es-
taver-le-Lac, in Savoy, dated
1515 and 1525, respectively.
(*Anton von Euw*)

122
Italy

Attributed to Marco Bigio (sienese painter from the first half of the 16th century) and to Giovanni Antonio Bazzi, known as "il Sodoma" (Vercelli, 1447-Siena, 1549)
The Three Fates, first half of the 16th century
Oil painting on canvas, 200 x 212 cm
Inscriptions: on the coins in the bottom part are some names, such as "Lucrecia, Alfonso, and Cesare"
Rome, Galleria Nazionale d'Arte Antica, Palazzo Barberini, 2350
Bibliography: SRICCHIA SANTORO 1988, pp. 138-139, fig. 84 (see preceding bibliography)

The painting, acquired by the then Minister of Culture F. Bottai in 1933 at an antique market in Assisi, comes from the estate of the count Pieri family in Siena. It was described in detail by Romagnoli (before 1835, vol. VI, fol. 905-913): "Outstanding among the works painted by three well known geniuses of the Siena school and attributed to Bigio and to Tozzo; such is the beautiful painting in the possession of count Pieri, *The Three Fates*, described, by Della Valle in folio 301. This huge canvas is full of allegorical figures. The main figures are the three Fates, intent on the labours attributed to them by the poets. They are nude, well designed and superbly coloured. At their feet, two idle Cupids, in a loving embrace, can be seen playing with some medals, on which one can read the names of great men.
There is a figure representing a river, surrounded by aquatic plants, swans, and unknown monstruous animals. Time is represented by an old man, and Death by a wandering skeleton. Many other objects are painted on this canvas, but they are so thoughtfully positioned that they cause no con-

fusion. Romagnoli, following the research of Della Valle, also cites other works by the same artist, including a Venus, in the house of Ciani, which has recently been identified in a work sold in an antique market in Rome. This is the work that is most closely related to the painter of the picture in the Galleria Nazionale, along with the *Apollo and Daphne* from the Chigi Seracini collection. A detailed examination of the recently restored painting using x-ray techniques, leads to the same conclusions arrived at by traditional sources; that is to say, there were two artists involved in the work, one of them less gifted than the other.
F. Hayum had already removed the painting from Sodoma's catalogue, attributing it to a disciple whose work is similar to the painter of the frescoes and altarpiece in the Nativity Chapel of San Francesco in Subiaco, paintings

which were not only earlier but were the work of a different hand than that which did the painting in the Galleria Nazionale. Nolfo di Carpegna (1953), who attributes the work to Sodoma, comparing it to the Castello Sforzesco school of painting, such as the *Archangel Michael* and the *Sacrifice of Isaac* from the cathedral of Pisa, suggests 1530-1540 as an approximate dating, pointing to the artist's activity in Siena in 1541.
(*Claudio Strinati*)

123
Italy/France

Giovanni Battista di Jacopo, known as "il Rosso Fiorentino" (Florence, 1495-Fontainebleau, 1540)
The Tomb of Alberto Pio of Savoy, Count of Carpi, 1535
Bronze sculpture,
56 x 167 x 65.4 cm
Paris, Musée du Louvre,
M.R. 1680 and 15092
Exhibitions: Paris,
1972 - 1973
Bibliography: Corrozet 1585, p. 85; Brice 1684 II, p. 457; Sauval 1724, I, p. 448; Dezallier D'Argenville 1749, p. 332; Piganiol de la Force 1765, VII, pp. 14-17; Thiery 1787, II, p. 367; Lenoir 1796-1810, III, p. 52, fig. 99; Courajod 1878-1887, I, p. 20, 187; Dimier 1900, p. 123; Raunie 1899, III, pp. 284-285; Venturi 1904, VII, pp. 469-477; Roy 1921, pp. 33-47; Roy 1929, pp. 138-147; Kusenberg s.f.

(1931), p. 131; Hollande 1936, 73, pp. 11-13; Carrol 1966, p. 79; Blunt 1970, note 32, p. 252; Thirion 1971, p. 47, n. 13; Paris 1972-1973, n. 552; Raggio 1974, p. 75, n. 23

Alberto Pio of Savoy, count of Carpi, belonged to a noble family of Modena, which, as a result of services rendered, had been linked to the dukedom of Savoy from 1450 onwards. Alberto Pio served the French king, Francis I, who named him ambassador to popes Leo X, Adrian V and Clement VII. After the conflicts with the imperial troops of Charles V in 1527, the count of Carpi had to go into exile in France, where he died of the plague shortly afterwards. The count was paid extraordinary homage after his death, and it seems that it was the king himself who contracted Rosso Fiorentino, for a large sum of money, to construct the sepulchral monument for his Italian captain. Although the relevant documents are indisputable, some researchers doubt that Rosso Fiorentino was really responsible for this work. M. Roy, however, along with other authors, using old descriptions and a drawing of the sculpture preserved in the British Museum (n. 48 of the Kusemberg catalogue), supports this hypothesis.

The monument was dismantled during the French Revolution and nowadays only the upper part of the burial mound survives. There was a commemorative inscription which, according to C. Corrozet's transcription, ran as follows: ALBERTO PIO DE SABAUDIA / CARPENSIUM PRINCIPI / FRANCISI REGIS FORTUNAM SECUTO / QUEM PRUDENTIA CLARISSIMUM REDDIDIT / DOCTRINA FECIT IMMORTALEM / ET UNA PIETAS COELO INSERUIT / HERIDES MOESTISSIMI POSUERE ANNO DOMINI / M.D. XXXVL. The figure of Alberto Pio of Savoy corresponds to the Renaissance ideal of the universal man: on the one hand, he dresses in Roman style armour, like an ancient hero, and on the other, he is seen half lying on his bed in a meditative pose, with an open book in his left hand and more volumes at his feet, thus representing the union of the active and contemplative life.

(Joan Sureda i Pons)

124
Portugal

Coimbra school
*Sepulchre of D. João
de Alburquerque,*
approx. 1495-1496
Limestone sculpture
(from the Ança region),
157 x 230 x 172 cm
From the old convent
of Santo Domingo de
Aveiro, now Sé de Aveiro
Aveiro, Museo del Convento
de Jesús 270/B
Bibliography: FERREIRA NEVES
1938, IV; FERREIRA NEVES
1946, XII; CHAVES DE ALMEIDA
1947, XIII; NOGUEIRA
GONCALVES 1959, pp. 123-125

This is a large burial mound
made from soft limestone
which came from the Ança or
Potunhos quarries near Coimbra. It was made in the last
few years of the 16th century,
commissioned by one of the
descendants of D. João de Alburquerque, who, on 20 August 1477, signed a contract
with the monks of Santo Domingo de Aveiro, for the establishment of a chapel for
masses and the construction
of a mausoleum.
D. João de Alburquerque died
sometime between June 1483
and the middle of the following year. Two of his sons, Pero
and Lopo de Alburquerque,
who partecipated in the con-
spiracy against D. João II, died
in 1484; the former, also
known as "Admiral of the
Kingdom," was executed. It is
therefore extremely unlikely
that anyone would have been
able to build a monument to
D. João de Alburquerque during the reign of D. João II,
when the subject's descendants had fallen into disgrace, a
theory supported by the style
of the sepulchre.
It was probably the third son,
Henrique de Alburquerque,
who initiated the work following the death, in 1495, of D.
João II and the subsequent re-
habilitation of the nobles and
exiled families. As he himself
died in 1498, the starting date
of the work must have been
in 1495 or 1496.

That there existed first temporary mausoleum, is confirmed
by the words of friar Luke of
Santa Caterina who continued
the *Historia de Santo Domingo,* which had been started
by friar Luis de Sousa.
D. João de Alburquerque belonged to the illustrious house
of the *Cunha,* gentlemen of
Tabúa, and from his father he
inherited lordship over
Angeja, Pinheiro de Loure,
and the Assequins. The name
Alburquerque was used later,
and written on the burial ark
he is said to be the great
grandson of D. João Afonso,
who built the Alburquerque
castle and who was a direct
descendant from the Castilian
kings.
D. João de Alburquerque took
part in the overseas expeditions to the Canary Islands and
Tangiers, where he covered
himself in glory. This burial
mound was transferred from
the old convent of Santo
Domingo to the Museum of
Aveiro in 1945.
This work, which approaches
the art of Diogo Pires Sr., is
part of the development of

Coimbran sculpture, whose
workshops dominated the
Portuguese stylistic scene from
the middle of the 15th century
onwards and were respon-
sible for three quarters of the
national production.
The great ark presently rest on
three huge lions, the present
time, the fourth having been
lost. The coats of arms of D.
João and his wife Helena, held
by two adult angels, are
prominently displayed. The
prone figure of the knight is
rigid and there is a lion lying
at his feet. His armour is typical of the end of the 15th century and is similar to that of
other contemporary prone
figures produced in Coimbran
workshops. The head, which
is bare, is intended as a portrait, but the artist was not sufficiently skillful, and so it falls
short of the desired result.
The decoration of the ark's
wall is outstanding. Children
are playing with leaves, a
clearly naturalist tendency,
heralding the last phase of the
peninsular Gothic style.
The presence of "savages"
holding the shield of Helena

must also be mentioned. It is
possible that this is a reflection
of a taste for the exotic, which
was currently in fashion, as
well as an allusion to the
deeds of D. João de Alburquerque in the Canaries and
North Africa. A long text,
carved in Gothic characters, a
common practice at that time,
identifies the knight, praises
his lineage and deeds, and
names the high offices he held
at the court.
(*Pedro Dias*)

125
Italy

Andrea Briosco, known
as "il Riccio" (Padua,
approx. 1470-1532)
Death, 1516-1521
Bronze sculpture 37 x 49 cm
From San Fermo
Maggiore, Verona
Paris, Musée du Louvre,
OA 90995
Bibliography: LONDON 1983,
pp. 372-373; see preceding
bibliography

This bas-relief was made for
the sepulchral monument
erected in the church of San
Fermo Maggiore in Verona, in
honour of the famous professors of medicine, and friends
of Leonardo da Vinci, Girolamo della Torre, and his son
Marco Antonio.
It is inspired by Virgil's *Aeneid*
and narrates the life of the deceased, and the journey of his
soul in the beyond. The soul
appears as a winged child
carrying a book.
Through the eight bas-reliefs,

which make up the series, Riccio reflects upon the philosophical and literary preoccupa-
tions of the scholarly world
and of the professors of the
University of Padua, which he
visited frequently.
A prolific creator of figures belonging to myth and fable, Riccio opted for a classicism inspired by ancient models,
combined with the realism
and poetry of northern Italian
artists.
(*Amaury Lefébure*)

208

126
Persia. Mazandaran

Safavide period
Galal
Sepulchral tympanum, dated
26 Rabi II 915 H
(13th August, 1509)
Polychrome woodcarving,
76.5 x 133 cm
Berlin, Museum für
Islamische Kunst, I.1990.1
Exhibitions: Cairo, 1935
Bibliography: WIET 1935,
n. B 12,41; WIET 26, n. 31;
MAYER 1958

Donation made by Bibi Saadat
for the sanctuary of Sheikin
Shihab ad-Din Kunaiba.
The wooden lunette originally
formed part of the ogee arch
at the entrance to a Shiite
sanctuary. Isolated from its
architectural environment, the
original context can only be
deduced from the two inscriptions in *nasji*, profusely covering the entire surface. The
main inscription, composed of
five lines, in the centre of the
panel is a historical text, com-

memorating the donation of a
door for the mausoleum of the
wise Sheikin Shihab ad-Din
Kunaiba by the pious lady
Bibi Saadat, daughter of Baba
Muhammad, son of Bahman,
on the 26th of the month of
Rabi II of the year H 915 of
the Muslim era (13 August
1509). On the far left of the
last line, the words: "This was
written by Jafl, the slave," appears after the artist's signature. Both stylistically and for
its protocol, this inscription is
very similar to those on a
series of woodcarvings from
the Mazandaran region, at the
south of the Caspian Sea
which date from the same
time. In this mountainous
zone, characterized by large
areas of forestland, a school of
wood-carvers was established
in the 15th century. Early in
the 16th century these wood-
carvers created the wooden
decorations for various sanctuaries and mausoleums and
Shihab-Din Kunaiba's lost
building could possibly be

one of these. In fact, the lady's
family tree even records family
relations with the local Badis-
panid dynasty of Mazandaran,
two sovereigns designated
with the name of Bahman.
The frieze framing it is indisputably related to religion and
politics. Quoting the names of
the twelve Shiite imams, the
text confirms that the traditional bastion of Shiite Islam
lay to the north of Iran. It was
from the regions bordering the
Caspian Sea, where the future
Shah Ismail (1501-1524) man-

aged to reestablish Shiite supremacy. From there, this religious leader and statesman
organized the military conquest of Iran, which resulted
in the creation of the Safavide
Empire, and constituted a
serious threat for the orthodox
caliphate of Baghdad by chal-
langing the supremacy of the
neighbouring Ottoman Em-
pire.
(*Michael Meinecke*)

127
Iran or Central Asia

*Fragment of a funerary
stele*, second half
of the 15th century
Basalt, sculpted,
and engraved decoration
on the front and two sides
of the stele, 38 x 58 cm
From the collection
of D. Stephanie de Neufville,
1957
Arabic inscription, Koran
CXX,7
Paris, Musée du Louvre,
MAO 342
Exhibitions: Paris, 1971;
Paris, 1977; Washington
D.C.-Los Angeles, 1989
Bibliography: VON ERFA 1946,
pp 184-190; GOLOMBECK 1969,
n. 15

About a quarter of the width
of the stele is missing due to
an oblique fracture. It is completely covered with intricate
sculpted and engraved or-
namentation, raised by sharp
and profuse carving. In the
centre of the composition,

defined by a continuous triple
border, there is a large inscription inset in an oblong medallion which is rounded at the
ends. The text is written in
two lines: "Sovereignty belongs to God, let him be
praised / because He knows
the secret, although it is hidden" (Koran, CXX,7).
The last word of this quotation
is on the top line and the last
letter, as is often found in
Timurid inscriptions, is
stretched horizontally in a dis-
proportionate manner and
separates the two parts of the
text by means of a line.
The large rectangular frame
which surrounds the inset
with the epigraph, the wide
border which surrounds this,
and the two narrower ones
which embellish two sides of
the stele, are covered in highly
stylized vegetal decoration:
small palm trees, palms leng-
thened, meeting, and giving
rise to new shapes which curl
in much the same way as
Chinese decorative clouds,

209

leaves and open flowers,
sometimes viewed from the
front, and sometimes in
profile.
The elegant delineation, accompanied by strong rigo-
rously vertical lines, the carving technique, the decorative
elements and the rounded
contours are characteristic of
the magnificent Timurid era.
These are also found on the

ceramics that adorn the walls
of religious buildings, particularly in places where wood
was used, such as the en-
graved wooden door of the
Mazar of Shams al-Dil Kulali in
Shahr-l Sabz in Uzbekistan.
(*Marthe Bernus-Taylor*)

128
Colombia

Middle Magdalena cultures
Sepulchral urn lid,
12th-16th centuries
Coiled and incised pottery,
24.5 x 26 cm
Bogotá, Museo Nacional,
Instituto Colombiano de
Antropología, 88-V-8
Bibliography: ROJAS DE
PERDOMO 1979; LÓPEZ 1991

The archaeological area located around the central region of the Magdalena River
(Colombia), encompasses the
areas of the south of Tamal-
ameque (César), Simití (Bolí-
var), Barrancabermeja (Sant-
ander), Puerto Boyacá
(Boyacá), and the valleys of
the rivers Guarinó and La Miel
(Caldas).
Its ancient inhabitants practiced secondary burials (individual and group) in ovoid
urns. These had zoomorphic
figures as handles and lids and
on the top, a characteristically
stylized anthropomorphic fi-

gure (masculine or feminine)
seated on a stool. The hands
of the figure are usually resting on its knees or holding a
bowl. Animal figures, particularly birds, are usually also
present. The colours applied
to the urns vary from various
shades of grey to light brown.
The lids also have numerous
linear and dotted incisions,
and in some cases, a decoration of small white limestone
spangles.
Sixty-three sepulchral urns
were found in Puerto Boyacá,
in a tomb with two side chambers. In addition, sixty-three
vessels of different types and
funeral gifts, were also found.
A mixture of adult, child, and
animal bones, reduced to
ashes, were found in some
urns. Around the 16th century
the archeological region of
Middle Magdalena was in-
habited by numerous Caribbean tribes (Pantágoras, Ca-
rares, Opones, Calimas,
Muzos). However, very little
archaeological research has

been carried out in the area,
preventing us from fully understanding these peoples'
way of life.
(*Hildur Zea S.*)

129
Italy

Raffaello Sanzio (Urbino,
1483-Rome, 1520)
*Eusebius Raising Three Men
from the Dead*, 1502-1503
Oil painting on panel,
26 x 44 cm

210

Forms part of the altar
of *Crucifixion*, painted
for the Gavari Chapel in San
Domenico, Città di Castello
Lisbon, Museu Nacional
de Arte Antiga, 568
Exhibitions: Paris, 1935;
Vila Viçosa, 1986
Bibliography: PASSAVANT
1839-1858, II, p. 9;
GROWE-CAVALCASELLE
1884-1891, I, p. 97;
MARGHERINI 1897, p. 235;
ROSENBERG 1908, pp. 220-221,
fig. on pp. 10-12; ORTOLANI
1945, pp. 18-19, 75; FISCHEL
1948, I, p. 358; GAMBA 1949,
p. XLVII; CAMESASCA 1958,
fig. 10-15; DE VECCHI 1968,
cat. 23 p. 89

Raffaello, one of the great geniuses of the Renaissance, one of the greatest exponents of European art around 1492, studied his trade in Urbino, under his father, Giovanni Santi, and achieved the title of Master in Città di Castello (around 1500) where he painted his first important paintings. Here, the influence of Perugino, as well as other less significant influences, such as Melozzo de Forlì and Signorelli, is obvious. In fact Vasari wrote, in his *Vite,* that the altarpiece that he painted for the Gavari Chapel in San Domenico "with a Crucifix.... if his name were not on it, none would believe it to be the work of Raphael, but rather that of Perugino." Raffaello received the commission for this *Crucifixion* from Domenico Gavari in 1503; anyone visiting the Gavari Chapel in San Domenico in Città di Castello nowadays, will find an architectural setting (a barrel vault, which rests on columns by means of an entablature) and within it, a copy of the *Crucifixion* that Raffaello painted in 1503, the original of which is to be found in the National Gallery in London.

Underneath the copy, there are three empty compartments, which must have been the original settings for the panels of the predella. It is known that these, together with the central panel, have passed through several hands. The central panel, at least, was in the Fesch collection in 1818; from there it went to the Canino collection, and later to Ludwig Mond (hence the name *Mond Crucifixion*). It arrived at the National Gallery in 1924.

The panel from the Museu Nacional de Arte Antiga, in Lisbon, was seen in Rome in 1845, by J. H. Passavant, who attributes it to Perugino in his *Raffaello di Urbino e il padre suo Giovanni Santi* (Florence 1882-91). From there it went to the Husson da Camara collection, and from there to king Ferdinand II, who donated it to the museum.

Cavalcaseile thought it was the work of Raffaello, and Rosenberg and Gronau associated it with another panel of the same size, which was then in the Cook collection in Richmond, but is now in the North Carolina Museum of Art in Raleigh. Both panels have also often been considered to be the side panels of a *Climb to Calvary* (previously in Lord Winter's collection and since 1913, in the National Gallery). Although *Calvary* is cited as the central panel of the predella of the Colonna altarpiece (Metropolitan Museum of New York), it is not incorrect to think that it may well correspond to the altarpiece of Città di Castello. The difficult question is the iconography of the panel in question. There are no doubts about the other half of the pair, as it shows a miracle by Saint Jerome, who appears as a cardinal among the clouds. However, the *Raising of the Three Men from the Dead,* on the Lisbon panel has been interpreted equally as a miracle by Saint Eusebius and as a miracle by Saint Jerome. Both versions are partly correct. In fact, Raffaello painted a scene which many other artists also painted at that time, as for example Francesco Bianchi Ferrari, in 1505, on the altarpiece of the Basilica di San Pietro of Modena, perhaps because of the interest evinced by the polyglot saint in Renaissance times (it should not be forgotten that in 1494 *De vita et actibus sancti Hieronymi presbitery et gestis eiusdem* was published in Venice). In reference to Raffaello's miracle of Saint Eusebius of Cremona, the Pseudo-Cyril says (PL 22: 290-92): *Largitor gratiarum deus, qui pro*

defensione fidei per beatum Hieronimum tres simul mortuos suscitasti nostros et ommes in vera fide defunctos a delictorum quae lugent laqueis et latebris liberatos tuae lucis facias esse consortes. That is to say, that Saint Eusebius of Cremona, to the surprise of the noblemen who were present, resuscitated three dead people, using the robe of Saint Jerome, which he passed over their bodies.
(*Joan Sureda i Pons*)

130
Italy

Michelangelo Buonarroti
(Caprese, 1475-Rome 1564)
The Virgin and Child,
approx. 1520-1525
Drawing, black crayon
and red chalk on paper,
54.1 x 39.6 cm
Florence, Casa Buonarroti,
71F
Bibliography: Dussler 1959;
Barocchi 1962; Barocchi
1964ᵃ; Barocchi 1964ᵇ; Berti
1965; Hartt 1971; Tolnay
1975; Tolnay 1975-80; Berti
1985

This splendid drawing has
been the object of a certain
amount of controversy in the
last few years, as the experts
are not unanimous in attributing this drawing to Michelangelo. Some claim that it
may have been drawn by an
anonymous follower of the
artist. It has also been suggested that it may be the work
of Giuliano di Piero di Simone, known as Bugiardini, a
Florentine artist who was active in the first half of the 16th
century and who was a friend
and imitator of Michelangelo.
However, the conception of
the figures in the drawing,
their emotive expressiveness
and the similarity of the drawing to the *Madonna Medici* in
the New Sacristy of San
Lorenzo, make it feasible to
suggest that this is an original
Michelangelo dated around
1520-1525.
There is a feeling of spiritual
transcendence in the figure of
the Virgin in this drawing,
present with the same intensity in sculptures on this theme
by the same artist, like the
Bruges Madonna. This feeling
seems to be determined by the
revelation that the Virgin is experiencing at that moment, the
future passion and death of
her son reflected in her intense dramatic expression, as
opposed to the industrious attitude of the Child, who is
looking for his mother's breast
in order to feed.
(*Enrique Valdivieso*)

131
Spain

Seville
Plate, first half
of the 16th century
Barcelona, Museu
de Cerámica, 5366

This plate is part of a series, most of which is to be found either in the Instituto Valencia de D. Juan, of Madrid, or in the Museu de Ceràmica in Barcelona.

In Seville, towards the end of the 15th century, there was a return to the technique of *cuerda seca*, a term coined by D. José Gestoso in his book *Historia de los barros vidriados sevillanos*. The technique consists of drawing an outline with manganese mixed with a greasy substance (which disappears in the kiln) that marks out the different parts of the decoration, after the first firing and before the second. In this way, the glazes of different colours do not mingle but remain smooth and bright. In the piece presented here however, the green overlaps the line that delineates it.

This is almost certainly due to the fact that a higher temperature is needed to fire copper oxide than other pigments, especially cobalt oxide.

The *cuerda seca* technique was used by the Arabs from the 9th century onwards. A small jug from Susa (Mesopotamia), currently in the Louvre, is the first piece to be attributed to this date.

In Spain they are found in Medina Azahara, in their fully developed form, from the 11th century onwards, during the rule of the *ta'ifah*. The finds at Badajoz, and the pieces from Cordova (Museo Arqueológico) can be attributed to the 11th century, while those from the Alcazaba of Malaga and those of Palma de Mallorca (in the Museu de Ceràmica in Barcelona) are considered to be somewhat later.

The *cuerda seca* technique was used intermittently. In the 15th century it was used in the

decoration of the spandrils of the Puerta del Vino in the Alhambra, carried out during the time of Mohammed V.

From the 16th century to the present day, only pieces of crockery using this technique have been found in Toledo and Seville, cities steeped in Islamic traditions, and outside Spain, in Syria, Anatolia, and Iran.

The *cuerda seca* was often applied to the ceramics used in architecture. In Toledo, the top of an arch in San Juan de la Penitencia has survived, and in Seville there still exist numerous houses and palaces with ceramic panels, e.g. the Casa de las Conchas, Casa de Pilatos, and the Casa de los Pinelo. Although already made at the time of the Renaissance, this plate shows, both in its decoration and the techniques used, a continuation of the Mudejar style.

The plate has an open shape,

with its edge curving slightly towards the reverse side. In its centre there is a concavity and a bevel, a shape often found in 12th century Persian plates. The decoration has that sense of fullness and balance that are characteristic of Arabic art. It has a floral pattern, with the leaves converging towards the centre, producing a kaleidoscopic effect.

The alternating colours break the monotony of the pattern and the white lines add a dynamic rhythm to the piece. The white colour is repeated in the palmettes in the centres of the leaves.

This dynamism is accentuated by the differences between the live spaces which converge towards the centre and the spaces used for "filling," which are honey coloured triangular shapes found between the leaves.

The centres of these spaces

are decorated with degenerations of palmettes, adopted by the Arabs, but with much earlier origins in the history of decoration.

(*Trinidad Sánchez Pacheco*)

132
Spain

Al-Andalus, Mudejar period
Vase, 15th-16th century
81 cm; diameter 65 cm
Granada, Museo Nacional
de Arte Hispanomusulmán,
n. 3,670

Examples of the classical stamped decorative tradition are found in the Spanish-Muslim world from the earliest times. However, its technical and decorative characteristics, where stamps were applied to fresh clay as it came off the wheel, required a certain thickness of clay and, therefore, could only be used on larger pieces. Important examples from the Almohad era have been preserved. They are large stamped earthenware jars with high quality patterns in horizontal bands, used to decorate functional pieces, such as water containers, illustrated by the system of bases on which they are placed, which channel any possible exudations or spillage through the spout.

The remains of this type of piece, found in Seville, Cordova, Toledo, and Granada, show a certain constancy and only small differences; characteristic evolutionary decorative and typological variants. There are, however, important similarities and connections between them. From its decoration we know that this piece can be traced to the workshops of Seville and Cordova.

In Granada, during the Nasrid era, the vases of the Alhambra, were highly influential as far as their type and proportions were concerned, giving rise to important stamped pieces of very similar proportions in the well-known white, blue, and gold glazes. Later, this tradition would reach the other above mentioned schools. In Granada it would continue, but in smaller pieces with a more evolved shape, as in the case of this piece, which has an exaggerated pear-shaped form, with a rather tall trun-

cated, conical neck, and strong lateral handles. The decoration is limited to the upper part of the belly with a small moulding on its surface. The green glaze on some of the borders is similar to the pieces from Cordova and even has a similar presentation, although the clay is different, coinciding with exhibits 7933 and 6737 of the Museo Arqueológico of Cordova. In the case of the pieces from this series, the first has a border of stems criss-crossed with small palmettes; the second has a border of Kufic characters with small flowers repeating

the slogan *al-mulk*, the third is similar to the first, but is glazed; the fourth, also with Kufic characters, crosses from one side to another and includes floral elements in the writing. Lastly, on the neck, the glazed border, repeating the *al-mulk* theme, appears on one side and on the other; the first border is repeated. The five borders are separated by smaller ribbed ones and finally reach the base of the neck which ends in a saw-tooth cresting reminiscent of the terraced crenellations which appear, for example, in the Gazelle vase.

The handles originate in the upper half of the belly and do not rejoin the neck, as is found with some of the vases from the Alhambra. The neck is a conical trunk and finishes in a plain upper border with a vertical wall.
(*Purificación Marinetto Sánchez*)

133
Spain

Al-Andalus, Nasrid period
Bowl, 15th century
Pottery, shaped on wheel,
tin-bearing glaze
and handpainted decoration,
12.6 cm; diameter 33 cm
Possibly from Alhambra
Granada, Museo Nacional
de Arte Hispanomusulmán,
132

Ceramic bowl for household use, made of orange-coloured clay, with an open rim and dish. The inside is glazed in green, while the outside is left unglazed, so that the clay is visible. This is usually the case with this type of pottery, which has no glaze on the outside, with the occasional exception of small drops left on the rim.

Unfortunately, the border has been lost. It would complete the form of the bowl and, particularly, the decoration around the figures in the central part, drawn with manganese. Two people are shown, making a toast with their glasses. The glasses are similar to the conical glasses preserved from a Nasrid dowry. Another figure is holding a rope on which a round water bottle with handles is hanging. Somebody else holds a large bottle with a rather narrow neck.

The figures wear drapes, similar to the so called "striped" or "creased" drapes, typical of Manises pottery. These are said to have been in fashion in the first part of the 15th century. Professor Arié has shown us how Christian influence affected Muslim clothing and how, according to "an eyewitness, the learned al-Basti tells us that Muhammad al-Galib Billah, when he entered Granada in 1258, rode his horse through the town, dressed in a striped petticoat (*saya*) made of cloth (*walf*), such as Castilian peasants were wearing." The drapes have tighter sleeves than those of the figure in Manises pottery. They are plain, with stripes on the part

covering the body, while the skirts are gathered by means of belts or coiled ribbons in the Muslim fashion (*tikka*).

The faces are either in profile or half-turned away from the spectator. The features are also shown in a rather schematic way, using straight lines. Although the hairstyle, with a parting, and covering the ears, was common, the heads of the figures in this case seem to be covered with a big *imama*.

Carved in the centre is a winding line, from which sprout curled-up double palm leaves. One of the leaves starts from the carved line itself and ends in a palmette with five petals.

It is similar to those presented in other contemporary ceramic pieces, also in white-and-blue, and related to the palmettes in Paterna art. From the 14th century onwards, the Nasrid potters from Malaga began to move toward the east. Ever since, these relations have continued, and there exist parallel ornamental themes common to both the Nasrid pottery produced on Muslim territory and that produced on Christian territory. The Alhambra themes, such as the palm leaf or the 14th century profiled leaf, which were influenced by Christian decoration through painters com-

missioned for the palace, as in the case of the Hall of the Monarchs, and in the imitations of their figures in floorings, as in the Queen's Tower, are also found in the Alhambra. Here is another example of pottery related to that of Paterna and Manises, a type of genuinely Nasrid design, but without the monotony and abstraction typical of the Paterna area.

(*Purificación Marinetto Sánchez*)

134
Turkey

Iznik
Ottoman period
Washbasin, beginning
of 16th century
Glazed ceramic,
15.5 cm; diameter 29 cm
Berlin, Museum für
Islamische Kunst, I.4227
Exhibitions: Celle, 1947
Bibliography: Museum
Catalogue n. 558

This deep basin on a high
stand, in the form of a pedestal, characteristic of early
Iznik pottery in the second
half of the 16th century, is
decorated with increasingly
complicated and vivid de-
signs.
This basin shows the brilliant
work of the Iznik potters from
the beginning of the century,
when they were influenced by
the designs which appeared in
the official documents called
firmans. The central pattern –
four floral palmettes, sprout-
ing from an elaborate
arabesque lacework and forming a six-pointed star enclosing a rose-window design –
draws inspiration from enamelled silver articles manufactured in the Balkans and exported to the central Ottoman
regions. The outside of the
basin, decorated with huge
flowers, was inspired by
Chinese models. The first
Chinese articles reached the
Ottoman Empire around 1430
and the influence of the Ming
blue-and-white pottery of the
14th and 15th centuries is easily perceived in the tiles in the
Murad III mosque in Edirne.
This was constructed during
the Edirne phase of the Ottoman Empire, before the fall of
Constantinople in 1453. Other
examples of this type of basin
were manufactured with
stylized motifs of scrolls of
clouds in the centre, and,
there are even more elaborate
and fanciful ones in existence
that almost have the quality of
diadems and tiaras.
(*John Carswell*)

135
Turkey

Plate, 1575-1580
Ceramic, 5.5 cm; diameter
28.2 cm
Istanbul, Archaeological
Museum
Bibliography: LANE 1971;
ATASOY-RABY 1989

Ceramic plate from Iznik in
the third Iznik style according
to Professor Lane: an even
border with a Ming Rock of
Ages pattern and naturalistic
floral motifs in the centre.
Each flower has a symbolic
meaning, such as the resemblance to the grace of "Allah,"
in the case of the tulip.
In the centre of the plate there
is a bunch of flowers. These
emerge from the bottom central part and open into a fan
with very fine turquoise stems.
The flowers are arranged symmetrically around a central
axis. Various types of flowers
are represented: daisies, tulips,
and carnations, and these occupy, in a very simple manner,
the whole dish of the plate.
The colours used are blue and
red. On the border, which is
even, there is Ming Rock of
Ages patterned with decoration typical of ceramic plates
between 1575 and 1580.
(*Purificación Marinetto Sánchez*)

136
Turkey

Iznik
Plate, 1575-1580
Ceramic, 4.4 cm; diameter
30.4 cm
Istanbul, Archaeological
Museum

Ceramic plate in the third
Iznik style, according to professor Lane. The central design is a floral motif, emerging
from the bottom central part
with thin leaves and fine stems
from which sprout leaves,
buds, peonies, and tulips, as
well as an undulating *saz* leaf.
The central motif is very elegantly painted in blue, green,
and red. The even border carries the Ming Rock of Ages
pattern.
(*Purificación Marinetto Sánchez*)

137
Iran or Central Asia

Seal ring, approx. 1450-1500
Gold jewellery, jade
mounted on gold, 3.5 cm,
diameter: 2.5 cm
New York, Metropolitan
Museum of Art, Rogers
Fund, 1912.12.224.6
Inscriptions: Arabic prayer in
the seal: "Invoke Ali, the
revealer of miracles. He will
be your comfort in
misfortune. All worries and
all sadness will be over in
your company, Ali, Ali, Ali";
around the Persian encasing:
"Oh, my Lord! Instead of
writing Thy name, I
pronounce the following
sentence: 'Oh, my soul! Let
your conversation be as
wise as Solomon. My world
and heaven are in this
ring'"; and in the cone:
"Mahoma."

The ring is made of gold,
which was melted and
mounted with a light green
jade seal. The ornamental top

pieces of the ring have the
form of dragon heads. Al-
though these are more delicate and smaller in size, they
are similar to those on a series
of jugs made of metal and jade
and other vessels from the
second half of the 16th century (Lentz-Lowry 1989, cat.
n. 110: copper jug dated H
886 in the Muslim calendar
[1461-1462 AD]; illustration
p. 206, cat. n. 57: copper jug
dated H 871 in the Muslim
calendar [1467 AD]; other
vessels with tops in the form
of dragon heads can be found
in the cat. n. 120-122. Also a
jade vessel dedicated to Ulugh
Beg, sovereign of Samarkand,
dated 1449, fig. 46). The lower
part of the setting, supported
by dragon heads, is in the
shape of an inverted incomplete cone. It is decorated with
roses, a geometric lacework
and intertwined vines full of
perforated leaves and shoots.
On the truncated part of the
cone is an engraved Kufic inscription saying "Mahoma."

On the outer part of the rim of the ring – on the dragons' back – is an engraving, which has partially disappeared. This is a volute in the form of a leaf with a rhombus in its centre. The Timurids were the first Islamic dynasty to be associated with the art of jade engraving, a taste which would continue until the first part of the following Sassanidae dynasty period. Royal workshops probably existed in both the important Timurid capitals, Herat, and Samarkand, a short step from North India, where the Mongolian descendants of the Timurids were continuing the tradition of collecting and decorating precious objects made of jade.

While it has been suggested that the ring dates from the beginning of the Safavide period, due to the form of the prayer to Alí (Komaroff, p. 14), its attribution to the Timurid period has raised strong protests. "With the growing interest in mysticism and the disappearance of the differences between Shiite and Sunni Islam during the second half of the 15th century, numerous references to Ali and other Shiite martyrs appear in the epigraphy of the Timurids as an example of their dynastic approach to religion." (Lentz-Lowry, cat. 142, p. 358).

The Sassanian dynasty raised the Shiite sect of Islam to the category of a state religion. According to Shiites, the line of succession to the caliphate must have corresponded to the family of Mahoma, i.e. to his cousin and son-in-law, Ali, and his descendants. The Timurids, however, belonged to the orthodox sect of the Sunni who believed in an elected caliph. The owner of the ring was clearly piously inclined to mysticism.

(*Marie Lukens-Swietochowski*)

138
Antilles

Taino culture
Ceremonial seat (duho),
15th century
Carving, lignum vitae
(Guayacum), 22.4 x 39.5 cm
Santo Domingo, Fundación
García Arévalo

Anthropomorphic ceremonial seat, with four legs. The feet of the front legs contribute to the predominantly figurative presentation of the piece, whereas the back feet are simple supports. In the front, a spheroid stands out, symbolizing the male sex. The pattern on the back of this bench consists of incised schematic motifs with a large central circle set in a framework of crossed stylized arms, showing the palms of the hands. The *duhos*, or ceremonial seats, were used by chiefs and other important tribal personalities while they were officiating at the *cohoba* rituals, as well as when presiding over ball games and other festivities celebrated in the *batey* or central square of the indigenous West Indian villages. These shiny benches, carved from hard wood, were highly praised by the chroniclers of the Indies, among them Pedro Mártir de Anglería, Las Casas, and Oviedo. The Taino *duhos*, together with the grand *cemiés* (Taino gods) of the *cohoba*, are considered to be exceptional examples of primitive art the world over.

(*Manuel Antonio García Arévalo*)

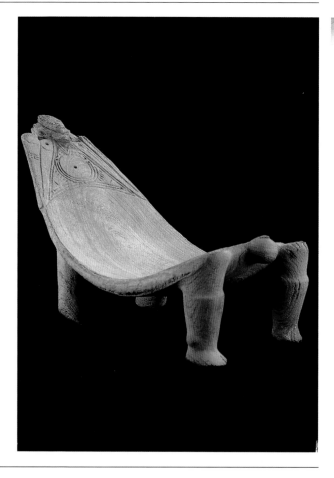

139
Spain

Al-Andalus, Nasrid period
Mule-chair, 16th century
Marquetry, 100 x 67 x 53 cm
Madrid, Museo Arqueológico
Nacional, 62044
Exhibition: Toledo, 1958
Bibliography: Torres Balbás
1935, pp. 438-442; Ferrandis
Torres 1940, pp: 495-467;
Torres Balbás 1949, p. 406,
fig. 479; Toledo 1958,
n. 974; Fritz Volbach and
Lafontaine-Desoque 1968,
p. 200 pl. 89 and p. 169 pl.
12; Pavón Maldonado 1973,
pp. 330-333; Sourdel-Thomine
and Spuler 1973; Castillejo
and Otros 1984, p. 217,
fig. 111; Drown-Kelch-Van
Thiel 1991, p. 75 pl. 17, 18,
p. 304 pl. 56, p. 217, fig. 111

This piece was possibly restored after the 3 March 1967, according to the M.A.N. stamp where the number of the photographic negative (7978) is specified and "not restored" is written by hand. Added during this restoration was the leather back, which it did not have either in the 1949 or 1958 exhibitions. (L.Torres Balbas, 1949; Toledo, 1958). Its state of preservation is not exceptional, given that the decorated leather seat does not appear to be original either and that the marquetry has largely been lost in the arched legs and is chipped in other places. The supports which are inclined towards the interior and which join the front legs to the back legs look like a modern restoration, and end with embossed, protuberant legs which rest on the floor.

It is based on the type of folding chair used by ancient sovereigns or campaigning generals, which when closed was easy to transport along with the military gear, with legs which could be crossed back and held in place with a crosspiece. This type of chair with a cushion was adopted by the consuls and magistrates of the Roman and Byzantine empires, as can be seen in the ivory diptychs; (plate of the consular diptych of Clementinus, consul in Con-

stantinople in the year 513 (Liverpool Museum), ivory consular diptych plate of Flavius Anastasius, also consul in Constantinople in the year 517 (Victoria and Albert Museum, n. 368-1871, London) and of Paris in the same year, (Bibliotèque Nationale, Medals Room n. 40; cfr. Fritz Volbach and Lafontaine-Desoque, 1968); the inferior artistic quality of the consul Rufus Granadius Probus Orestes, ivory made in Rome in the year 530 (Victoria and Albert Museum n. 139-1866), copying that of Clementinus. The consul appears seated on an ivory aedile chair the legs of which normally show the head and legs of a lion, and become thicker at the point where they curve to reinforce the edge of the joint so that the weight of the person seated does not break it. On the seat, there is an embroidered cushion to make it more comfortable for the person seated, whose feet would normally be rested on the footstool. This type of chair sometimes comes with arms, and later on a back will also be added. From its origin, this type of chair has been conceived to be used by people in positions of power. It first appeared around the year 900 in the mosaic of the narthex of Saint Sofia in Constantinople, where the emperor Leon VI is prostrate, adoring the figure of Christ, seated on a folding chair made up of arms, back and cushion and situated on a platform. The throne of temporal power has been converted into the throne of divine majesty. It is possible that thereafter, with the spread of the Byzantine empire, its use was extended throughout the Christian and Muslim areas of the Mediterranean, still appearing in Gothic painting as a folding chair (Fritz Volbach and Lafontaine-Desoque, 1968). The type described earlier with a lion's head on a leg of the same animal appears throughout this whole period as a symbol of the divine or royal seat. This can be seen, for example, in the seat of the *Virgin and Child* in the al-

tarpiece on the front of the Margarito de Arezzo, in use between 1260 and 1270 (National Gallery, n. 564-1837, London). Marquetry originated in the Near East, copying onto wooden furniture the mosaical adornments of Byzantine metal, stone and ivory furniture found in churches and palaces. "Marquetry", from the Arab *tarsi* (inlay), is made using a previously drawn out geometric design, cutting the small, sometimes minute, pieces of silver, ivory, bone – either natural or dyed light green or brown – and fine woods (ebony, aloe, sandal, fruit tree, lemon tree, jakam, etc.) all of which are cut into long narrow strips in the shape required by the drawing - squares, triangles, trapeziums, rhombuses etc.. At first (in the 12th century) in little blocks and later (in the 14th century) in extremely fine sheets which are applied to the wood with glue. Previously, the surface to be decorated was measured and the geometric design drawn by means of drilling. Thereafter, the marquetry artist matches the drawing onto the surface to be decorated. (Torres Balbas, 1935; Ferrandis Torres, 1940).

Marquetry appears in Al-Andalus under the Almoravids (12th Century), and in the *minbar*, made in Cordoba and preserved in the Kutubiyya mosque in Marrakesh (Morocco), from the epoch of the emir Cali ibn Tasfin (approx. 1120-1130). For the moment, nothing is known from earlier periods (Sourdel-Thomine and Spuler, 1973; Terrasse, pp. 285-286, plates 230, 231).

In Museo Nacional de Arte Hispanomusulmán in the Alhambra, a folding chair (registration n. 3,113, incorporated in the museum on 17-5-1957) is preserved. It was acquired for the museum by don Manuel Gomez-Moreno from don Juan Rodríguez Mora. It was appropriately restored in 1989; before being acquired, the leather back had been restored. It must have been used as the sovereign Mohammed V's throne

(Kursi, sirir) since it displays on its embossed back the coat of arms of the Nasrid dynasty, and on each side a wading bird walking towards the centre with its neck and head turned behind. This animal theme together with the type of palm attached to the stems, date the piece as from the same time as the Riyad (Garden) palace, now known as The Lions. The marquetry work is based on a figure of eight motif made up of eight 22.5° points inside an octagon which is repeated and adjusted to the front and sides of the legs, to the thick circular wooden hinge, curved wooden sides of the chair which extend out into the arms and completely covered with marquetry. The wood is without decoration in the main part and the upper part of the inside of the legs, under the original leather seat which has now been lost, with only the outside strips remaining, held in place with thick nails. The curve of the legs has wooden polygonal reinforcements at the turn. A lot of the marquetry work on the crossbeams and legs has been lost due to wear. In the lower parts of the folding chair, where the marquetry has fallen off, the circular repeat pattern can be seen drawn in ink, following the previously worked out geometric design.

There are also various folding chairs still in existence which date from the *Mudéjar* period, held in official, ecclesiastical and private collections in Spain, although a few are also in overseas collections.

The folding chair from Burgos in the National Archeological Museum, was without doubt made in Granada in the first half of the 16th century. It displays the typical low frame which serves as a counterweight and reinforcement for the curved legs. These have an arc-shaped curved segment, with polygonal joints to make it stronger, and from that point on the wood becomes thicker until it meets the circular hinge. The folding mechanism of the curved beams of the legs and

seat is situated in the circular front of the hinge. Although one can sit on the leather of the curved seat it is more comfortable to use a cushion, since the curve of the leather yields and within a short time one's legs are completely together so that they must be crossed to alleviate the pressure of one leg against the other, which does not happen if a cushion is used, maintaining the legs separate and allowing ease of movement. This is also advisable due to the height of the arms, which have a circular form at the front to allow free use of the hands, while the arm curves up at the elbows to connect it with the back, which is made of leather or of velvet from the Renaissance period. If a cushion is used, the arms and the back of the folding chair support the back allowing the forearms and hands to be rested, while a footstool may be used if the seat restricts movement of the legs, and thereby isolate them from cold or dampness. The use of the cushion is shown in the consular diptychs, the Constantinople mosaic and in paintings.

The angular sides of the legs, frame, seat and arms, reveal a finely polished profile, and the interior of each frontal or lateral surface – except the lower internal parts of the legs and the rear side of the back of the chair – reveal a decoration of marquetry forming a rhombic pattern, based on a system of equilateral triangles. The rhombuses consist of white pieces of bone, filled with fine wood, with other white rhombuses at the centre. In the "joints" of the legs, and in the thicker parts as well as in the curved wood of the seat, there are diagonal inlays within the square, triangular or polygonal areas.

The circular frame shows a composition of a figure of eight with an eight-pointed star in the centre with 90˚ vertices, slanted so that its highest point is not on a vertical axis. The vertices of the star are elongated so that they cross,

forming a second star with 45˚ angles, the spaces between them being filled with knots with three bows which are formed by ribbons which overlap the points of the 45˚ angles. The centre of the star includes a series of eight-pointed stars decreasing in size until they reach the tiny central wooden piece. The interior surfaces of the arms are of polished wood and have three separate marquetry motifs in the form of stars; the exterior surfaces only have a circular motif. The cylindrical grip at the end of each of the arms is enriched with a circular marquetry motif. A characteristic of the *Mudéjar* chairs is that of using smooth, polished wood on numerous areas of the chair and not only the lower part of the legs and back.

Folding chairs were used by royalty and the ecclesiastical hierarchy, and they have been preserved for this reason in cathedrals and convents for the use of high prelates, abbots and canons. One need only think of the Capitular room of the cathedral in Toledo at the time of Cardinal Cisneros. Some Moorish chairs are also preserved in the Santa Cruz museum. This tradition is not exclusively Hispanic, as is illustrated by the portrait of Thomas Cranmer, archbishop of Henry VIII, painted by Gerlach Plicke and dated 1546 (London, National Portrait Gallery, n. Ro 535). Here the archbishop is seated on a folding chair with a red velvet Moorish cushion. A good part of its wooden frame visible, revealing the marquetry adorning the front curve of the seat and arm, with the repeated motif of an eight-pointed star of 22.5˚. This geometric motif differs from the two on the side of the folding chair: one with a cylindrical pommel on a pattern of squares and one with the arm on a triangular frame with a similar pattern of inlays to the one from Burgos. From the rear part of the arm upwards,

the wood remains exposed. Both the frame and the arms of the chair show the smooth, polished wood, the Moorish folding chair and the lack of marquetry as is represented in the paintings of the 16th and 17th centuries up to the Rembrandt school. Moorish folding chairs stopped being manufactured in the 17th century (Castillejo et al, 1984; Drownkelch and Van Thiel, 1991).

It is worth pointing out that the Moorish romantic movement from the middle to the end of the 19th century revived the making of folding chairs in Granada, distinguishing themselves by the hinge mechanism, their treatment of leather or fabrics and, most importantly at first sight, by being completely covered with inlays, including the interior part of the frame which supports the legs. They also display the same repeated geometric motif of an eight-pointed star inside an octagon. All this dates them from the second half of the 19th century. The Granada workshop where they were made still exists today. Of this series, I know three: one in a private collection in Avila; the second in the Metropolitan Museum of Art; the third on the international market. The first and the third have similar embossed leather on the seat and back, with an italic inscription from the Qalahurra of Mohammed VII in the Alhambra which has serious linguistic and spelling mistakes, even more so since it misses out the essential part of the sovereign's name, and even misses out the last letter of his title, sultan. The translation is given here, with what was omitted placed between brackets: "Glory to our lord the Sulta(n) Abu CAdb (Allah) al-MustaCin bi-llah. May god protect you." The one from Avila was described as a Nasrid folding chair belonging to Mohammed VII (Pavon Maldonaldo, 1973). It is impossible to imagine a Nasrid folding chair with such faults; the Moors neither made them, nor would

they have attempted to falsify. That these two folding chairs have identical mistakes in the inscriptions; the fact that they are decorated with few if any differences between them; the embossed leather dyed red during its processing – a technical innovation of the 19th century –, and the rigid geometry, totally lacking that creative Muslim or Moorish rythmic quality, is proof enough of their origins. The folding chair in the Metropolitan Museum of Art has the seat and back upholstered in velvet and is referred to as 16th Century Moorish. (Otto Kurz "Folding chairs and Koran Stands", *Islamic art in the Metropolitan Museum of Art*, ed. by R. Ettinghausen, New York 1972, pp. 304-306, fig.10, donated by William H. Riggs, 27.225.1). However, the marquetry motif is the same as that of the two folding chairs mentioned earlier and covers the entire inner surfaces of the legs, unlike other known Nasrid and Moorish folding chairs. For this reason, I consider all three as "sisters" from the Granada workshop. They are the product of a period when "revivals" appeared and enjoyed a certain popularity: the second romantic period. The folding chair belonging to the count of *Las Almenas*, referred to by J. Ferrandis Torres, I know only from the plate. However, it has a leather seat and back which date from this century, and from the dark photo it is impossible to distinguish whether it has marquetry on the back legs, thereby making it impossible for me to pass judgement on it. (Fernandis Torres 1940, 464, pl. 21). Copies are still being made to this day, such as those made by Granada City Council for the opening of Spanish kings at the Alhambra in the days of the Ahga Khan, 22-26 April, 1986.

It is helpful to avoid making dating errors and to make a clear distinction between the Nasrid and *Mujédar* periods and the 19th century romantic school.

(*Antonio Fernández Puertas*)

140
Greece/Crete

Abraham's Hospitality,
15th century
Panel painting, 72 x 57 cm
Athens, Byzantine Museum
Exhibitions: Florence, 1986;
London, 1987; Baltimore,
Miami, Fort Worth,
Cleveland, Detroit,
Richmond, 1988-1990
Bibliography: Sotiriou 1931,
p. 74; Chatzidakis 1961, n. 3;
Charalambous Mouriki
1962-1963, p. 870;
Chatzidakis 1969, p. 45;
Aa.Vv. 1986, n. 88,
pp. 138-140

The scene is taken from Genesis (18: 1-15), describing the supper Abraham offered to three angels near the "great trees of Mambré." The three angels are seated around a square table, full of dishes and food. Also present are Abraham and Sara, and the scene is completed by two tall, straight buildings at the sides and two luxuriant trees, bending in towards the centre. All this is arranged in a closed, vertical composition around the figure of the central angel. The frequent appearance of this scene from the Old Testament in the Byzantine and post-Byzantine periods is explained by the fact that it symbolizes the Holy Trinity.

The iconography of *Abraham's Hospitality* was established as early as the beginning of the Christian Era. But the iconographical type shown on this panel from the Byzantine Museum, was probably formulated in Constantinople, during the Early Christian period, as can be deduced from a number of examples in manuscripts, miniatures, icons, and wall paintings. The predominant aesthetic preferences of the capital's refined circles of artists and patrons at that time, had to do with the rebirth of the ancient world. This can be observed in this icon in a number of details: classical proportions, elegant postures and the refined faces of the angels. Abraham's pa-

triarchal appearance also follows the iconographical models of the Ancient World. It is shown also in numerous details, such as the carafe on the table, covered with an upturned glass which can be seen in a wall painting from Herculanum, the mask of a lion on the facade of the building on the right, with foliage bursting from its mouth, made in grisaille enamel, and the red drapery on the roof. The monumental size of the figures and the small-scale size of the architecture and the trees situated in the background, the return to a plainer conception of space, and the inexpressive forms of the bodies and drapery, are some of the features which have led to this icon being dated after 1453, although various dates have been attributed: the 15th century, the first half of the

16th century, connecting it to the early creations of the Cretan School (Chatzidakis 1961, n. 3, with a colour illustration; Charalambous-Mouriki 1962-1963 pp. 87 on), or more precisely still to one Cretan work (Chatzidakis 1969, p. 45). Nevertheless, that this icon is a work of the Cretan School, may become questionable after the publication of the relevant documents by Catapán in the archives of Venice, and the discovery that painting materials, attributed to this school, were unknown at that time. The result is that the suggested dates regarding the majority of the icons of this circle have to be changed for later ones, in some cases as much as a century. Taking into consideration the latest discoveries, one could suggest that the icon with *Abraham's Hospitality* be dated in the

second half of the 15th century. It's precise relation to the Cretan school is also in doubt, at least until the research into the wall paintings dated into the 15th century is completed. Specially important among these is the decoration in Pantanassa in Mistra (1428). There exists a strong stylistic and iconographic similarity between the icon from the Byzantine Museum and two other icons with the same theme, kept in the Hermitage Museum, and the Narbonne Museum, respectively. These were probably painted earlier, though still sometime in the 15th century. This iconographical model has frequently been repeated in later paintings, the majority of which are icons.
(*Myrtali Acheimastou-Potamianou*)

141
China

Ming dynasty (1368-1644)
Box, 1547
Carved lacquer,
16 x 17.5 x 14 cm
Beijing, Imperial Palace
Museum

Lacquer is one of the most traditional materials in Chinese art. Neolithic remains exist dating as far back as seven thousand years ago. Since then, it has developed and has been applied to different types of objects with multifarious uses. With the Ming and Ch'ing dynasties (1644-1911), lacquer reached its maximum splendour as an exponent of a complex and rich craft tradition. Carving is one of the most typical of the techniques applied to lacquer. Although its origins stretch back to the T'ang dynasty (618-907), we know of no surviving carved lacquer objects dating from before the song dynasty (960-1279). Carved lacquer is categorized according to col-

our: red, green, yellow, and black. Usually the base is of wood, on which as many lacquer coatings are applied as are needed to achieve the desired thickness. Once it is cold and compact, this coating is carved in order to obtain the desired design. The rectangular box is divided into two parts. The pattern is geometric at the edges, combined with floral ornamentation: a plum tree in blossom and, in the background, a Taihu rock with a bird on top. Close to this scene, there is a blossoming camellia. The sides of the box are decorated with a pattern of diamonds, and in the middle of each there is a small flower. The decoration of the rim repeats the pattern of the two front parts, that is to say, blossoming plum trees and camellias.

From the technical point of view, the carving is cut deeper than in the lacquer articles from the beginning of the Ming dynasty.
(*Zhang Rong*)

142
Japan

Muromachi period
(1333-1573)
Box, 15 century
Lacquer, 31 x 20.3 cm
Tokyo, Idemitsu Museum

The piece is of the so-called "Negoro" type and is made of lacquer. The surface of the recipient has a base of black lacquer, over which a layer of crimson lacquer has been applied. The name Negoro comes from the temple of the same name in the Kishu region (Wakayama prefecture). With time, this name has become generalized and is now applied to all lacquer articles of this type, regardless of the region in which they were made.

This box, characterized by its unusual silhouette, shaped according to Chinese taste, is called a "medicine box," even though it is not known exactly what purpose these boxes were meant to serve.
(*Masaaki Arakawa*)

143
Japan

Muromachi period
(1333-1573)
Bottle, 14th century
Lacquer, 30.3 cm; diameter
of the body 21.7 cm;
diameter of the base 14 cm
Osaka, The Masaki Museum
of Art

The bottle is decorated in red
on a black background and
was used to serve sake or
other drinks during private
ceremonies and meetings. The
lacquer base is black, whereas
the pattern is crimson. According
to researchers, the red lacquer
drawing technique was
first used in the Heian period
(794-1185), although no object
from that time is known. During
the Kamakura and Muromachi
periods, this type of
bottle was very popular and
was therefore produced in
considerable quantities.
(*Noriko Takahashi*)

144
Japan

Muromachi period
(1333-1573)
Box, 16th century
Lacquer,
27.2 x 18.6 x 21.8 cm
Osaka, The Masaki Museum
of Art

The box was used to keep a
complete set of materials
needed for incense burning.
On the front is a door with a
lock. Inside, there are six small
drawers. A metal handle on
top, in the form of a plum tree
blossom, completes its decoration.
The pattern of arabesques, *karakusamon*, is applied on a
black background, using the
maki-e technique.
(*Saishi Namiki*)

145
Sierra Leone

Sapi-Portuguese culture
Salt cellar, approx. 1490-1530
Carving, ivory, 33 cm
Copenhagen,
Nationalmuseet, ODlh 41

224

The art of the Yoruba people, settled on the coast of the Gulf of Guinea – Benin, Nigeria – has been chronologically categorized by recent research, into the first phase or "First Period," from about 1350 to 1550. This is followed by a "Middle Period" leading up to the 18th century, and a "Late Period" in the 19th century. Between 1472 and 1484, the Portuguese established their contacts with Benin and began trading actively. Portugal intended to Christianize the African kingdoms of this coast, from Benin to Congo, and the Portuguese merchants showed their interest in the people's skillful ivory carving. This was manifested in a series of works done for them by African artists from the 16th to the 17th centuries.

As a result of the relationship with the Portuguese, the Kingdom of Benin became an important centre of sculptors working with ivory and bronze smelters. The artistic achievements of Benin can also be explained by the high degree of civilization it had reached, a consequence of its abundant population and of the kingdom's urban structure. In the above mentioned "First Period," this art was at its best. Extraordinary works have remained, corresponding to the Kingdom of Benin, constituted in the 12th century by the Yoruba people of the Nigerian coast. From this period, a number of boxes and chalices carved in ivory, skillfully decorated with themes inspired by Christianity, have been preserved. The same people also made salt cellars, spoons, and forks with richly decorated handles, and other wonderful objects. These pieces all followed European examples. This salt cellar seems to be-

long to the "First Period" of Afro-Portuguese art. It is made of ivory, was created by Yoruba carvers from Benin, and has an African base with European motifs. Among the ornamental motifs are a sphynx in movement, a kind of sirene, and African animals – small crocodiles – also in movement and climbing the walls of the cellar. These carvings are of great value. The present salt cellar forms part of a group of

analogous objects which seems to indicate that they are all the work of the same artist or team of artists and demonstrates the existence of a powerful "school" of African sculptors at that time in this country.

(*José U. Martínez Carreras*)

146
Sierra Leone

Sapi-Portuguese culture
Salt cellar, approx. 1490-1530
Carving, ivory, 24 cm;
diameter of the base 9.8 cm
Bologna, Museo Civico
Medievale, 694
Exhibitions: New York, 1988
Bibliography: BASSANI 1985,
n. 49, pp. 79-80; BASSANI
1986, n. 9, pp. 46-56;
BASSANI-FAGG 1988, pp. 61-81,
fig. 43, pp. 69, 72-75, 225

According to an old reference
from the end of the last century, this salt cellar can be
identified with almost complete certainty as the "old
ivory chalice with its lid and
figures," recorded in 1685 in
the collection of marquis Ferdinando Cospi. According to
Ezio Bassani's research (1985-
1986-1988), it is an example of
exceptional formal perfection
and, as far as its typology is
concerned, probably belongs
to the non utilitarian objects
recorded in the localized area
of production in Sierra Leone,
where the Sapi tribes (who
preceded the Bullom in this
zone) were dedicated to the
production of ivory objects,
spoons, forks, hunting trum-
pets, and dagger hilts commissioned by the Portuguese between the end of the 15th and
the first decades of the 16th
century.
The formal prototypes may
come from local figurative
tradition, the basically typical
stone-carved, spherical human
figures, such as are found in
European figurative sources.
Some scholars, like Bassani,
have stressed that the qualities
of this salt cellar are an
example of the successful synthesis of elements of European origin with indigenous
culture. A drawing by Albrecht
Altdorfer and two engravings
by Albrecht Dürer (1505-1507)
and Hans Baldung Grien
(1506-1510), respectively,
have been particularly cited as
possible sources of iconographical inspiration for the
female figure on the he-goat,
whilst the base, in particular,

has a relation to the formal
prototypes of the Italian Renaissance. However the significance of the female figures
sculpted in the base and lid remains obscure. It seems to be
linked with a magic-erotic ritual or a scene of witchcraft,
and possibly refers to the European environment.
The example from Bologna
and a series of other similar
pieces have the plain decoration with vegetal motifs in

common, while the trilobate
form of the support, the division of the cup into segments
and the laying out of pearls in
lines are common to almost all
the known examples of this
type of article.
(*Carla Bernardini*)

147
Nigeria

Bini-Portuguese culture
Salt cellar, first half
of 16th century
Carving, ivory,
19.2 x 8 x 7.2 cm
Antwerp, Etnografisch
Museum, A.E. 74.25.1.-3/3
Exhibitions: Antwerp (Musea
Danken), 1975, n. 29;
Antwerp, 1975, n. 2;
Antwerp, 1976; Brussels,
1977, n. 184; Lisbon, 1983,
n. 31
Bibliography: Fagg 1959;
Bassani-Fagg 1988;
Herreman-Holsbeke-Van
Alphen 1991

When the Portuguese navigators established their commercial colonies along the West
and Central African coast in
the 15th century, they entered
into contact with the local
kingdoms. The city-state of
Benin, now situated in Nigeria, was one of the most flourishing cities of the time. A
great number of artists, belonging to the *igbesamwan*
corporation, worked at the
king's court (*oba*). Their brass
statues, cast in the lost-wax
method, were especially distinguished, as were their
carved ivory works of art and
objects for everyday use.
These two materials were,
above all, reserved for the
king. The skill of these artisans
impressed the Portuguese and
and so it was that commercial
exchanges followed. The ivory
articles made by Bini artists,
following the European
model, since this was the continent where they were to be
sold, were highly appreciated
export goods.

The decorative Bini salt cellars, which are not part of the
traditional culture of that
country, are composed of
three superimposed elements.
The topmost part is a lid of the
central recipient, and this sits
on top of the lower part. Only
three complete sets have been
preserved, one of them being
the present salt cellar.

The ornament, in relief, shows
European soldiers with winding drapery, on foot or on
horse-back. They are all in
profile and are not facing forwards, as is usually the rule in
African art. The decoration is
very important, since it serves
to date the pieces. A gun, for
instance, held by a cavalry-
man, is of the type that was
used in Europe in about 1520-
1530 allowing the work to be
dated to the first half of the
16th century. In addition to
this decoration, which could
be called European, there is
another: abstract patterns,
taken from the elements that
decorated Bini baskets.

With regard to its form and
iconography, one could put
forward the following hypothesis. A European customer
showed the Bini sculptor certain designs which served as
models for the main motifs,
whereas the traditional repertoire of the artist served as a
source for the decoration of
the rest of the surfaces.

All this leads to the conclusion
that the work was done following the criteria of an artist
of Portuguese origin. He
would live in the trading posts
of the Benin region, making
designs and initiating the artisans working in ivory in certain European methods,
thereby completely changing
their own artistic language.
When he died or left, this production lost its raison d'être.
According to Bassani and
Fagg, the fifteen preserved
pieces come from the same
workshop and can be at-
tributed to nine artists. The
same authors attribute this salt
cellar to the so called 6th artist.
If this is correct, it would be
the only complete work by
this artist that has reached our
time.

(*Frank Herreman*)

148
Sierra Leone

Sapi-Portuguese culture
Salt cellar, last quarter
of the 15th century-first
quarter of the 16th century
Carving, ivory, 29 x 12.7 cm
Modena, Galleria Estense,
2433
Exhibitions: Ferrara, 1989;
New York-Houston, 1989
Bibliography: BASSANI-FAGG
1988, pp. 69-69, fig. 46;
pp. 127, 130-131, fig. 166
and n. 28, pp. 229; FERRARA
1989, pp. 369

In the Afro-Portuguese ivory
production identified by Fagg,
three chronologically and geographically different groups
appear: Sierra Leone, the
Kingdom of Benin, and the
mouth of the river Congo.
Ivory production from Sierra
Leone has been attributed to
the Sapi people, although they
were not the first to produce
engraved and sculpted ivory
for Europe. The Sapi-Por-
tuguese production, however,
is the only evidence of this
ancient contact between Europeans and Africans.
The term *salt cellar* was first
applied to objects of this type,
composed of a base supporting a recipient by Sir Wollas-
ton France in 1860-1890. They
do not carry any direct references to European art, but are
similar to African products.
This salt cellar, which has an
extraordinary structural design,
has six supports joining the
conical base with the recipient,
which is in the form of a flattened sphere, giving the entire
object a slightly irregular shape.
This recipient is divided into
two parts: container and lid. Its
special structure makes it comparable to another salt cellar,
kept in the Pitt Rivera Museum
of Oxford University (Inv. No
1884.88.73). The decorative
motifs on the supports of our
example consist of quite deep
cross lines, in which are alternated images of typical African
animals: two crocodiles and
two serpents. Six parrots act as
counterpoints to the base.
The recipient is decorated

with geometrical patterns:
wide bands composed of
strings of pearls in vertical
rows, alternating with plain
fields. In the centre of these
fields on the recipient itself
there are concentric circles of
pearls, and in those of the lid,
little roses. These motifs are
usual in many Sapi-Por-
tuguese salt cellars.
On top of the lid there was
probably a seated human figure. This is suggested by the
preserved remaining legs and
back part of a three-legged
seat. Fundamental characteristics can be observed: attention
to the human figure, and a
preference for pure geometrical form and decoration that
complements the form of the
objects rather than hiding it.
Their relatively low price resulted in European orders for
ivory objects from African
sculptors: in 1504-1505 a salt
cellar cost less than a ruffled
linen shirt. The entire lower
part of this piece is made from
a single tusk, from which a
considerable quantity of material has been cut. The conical base is hollow and its walls
extremely subtle.
The object probably formed
part of the collection of curiosities and marvels which the
duke, Alfonso II d'Este, in
common with other princes
and sovereigns, e.g. the
Medici in Florence, the prince
Elect of Saxony in Dresden, or
archduke Ferdinand of Tyrol
in Ambras, possessed in his
castle in Ferrara in the second
half of the *Cinquecento*.
The importance of the object
increased, due to the fact that
it was a salt cellar, an object
considered as fundamental
during the *Quattrocento* and
Cinquecento. Salt was taken
not only as a seasoning, but
also due to a religious and ascetic belief that it had astrin-
gent and purifying qualities
for the organism.
(*Elena Corradini*)

149
Sierra Leone

Sapi-Portuguese culture
Salt cellar, approx. 1490-1530
Carving, ivory, 34.5 cm;
diameter base 11 cm
Vienna, Museum für
Völkerkunde, 63.468
Exhibitions: Brussels, 1987;
Linz, 1988; New York, 1988
Bibliography: Bassani-Fagg
1988

During the Renaissance period, objects traditionally considered as articles for everyday use, began to form part of great art collections, such as that of archduke Ferdinand of Tyrol in Ambras (Tyrol, Austria).

On numerous occasions, objects of this type were a product of various cultural influences. They combine iconographical and stylistic elements of two or more cultures (in this case, the European, the African, and to a certain extent the Hindu).

This salt cellar reflects the influence of goblets with lids, usually made of precious metal, which were used in Europe during the 15th and 16th centuries. "Metal goblets with lids and a spiral-gallooned decoration are frequently described in the art of the 15th and 16th centuries as recipients containing the gifts of the three Magi to the infant Christ" (Bassani). While it is possible that they found their models in European painting, the adornment with human and animal figures on this Afro-Portuguese salt cellar is clearly of African origin.

These ivory pieces were made by artists from the Sapi people, the predecessors of the present-day Bullom, Temne, and other peoples of Sierra Leone.

In 1596, this salt cellar was mentioned in the inventories of the Castle of Ambras (Tyrol) as a "Turkish recipient," since Africans were not considered capable of such refined work. What can be distinguished as

a typically African feature on this salt cellar is the human figure on the upper part of the lid, the principal decorative element, whereas the European influence can be observed in the non figurative decoration, that is to say, in the gallooned designs and the decoration in the form of a spiral with dotted lines, profusely used in this case.
(*Armand Duchâteau*)

150
Japan

Muromachi period
(1333-1573)
Teacup, end of the 15th
century-beginning of the
16th century
Mino ceramic, 6.5`x 12.3 cm
Inscriptions: Shishi
Tokyo, Idemitsu Museum

Cup used for drinking *matcha*, a kind of powdered tea, used during the tea ceremony. The characteristic feature of *Tenmoku*-type teacups is their brown or black colour. They were introduced in Japan by a Buddhist monk who it is supposed first saw them in the Zen monastery situated on the Tenmokusan mountain, called *Tianmu shan* in Chinese, in the province of Zhejiang. As the diameter of the base of the cup is rather small, it was served on a saucer in order to make it more stable. The production of *Tenmoku*-type cups, like that of much pottery that followed continental

models, began in the kilns of Seto towards the end of the Kamakura period. This corresponds to the period when the habit of taking tea in Zen temples reached the height of its popularity. This piece is distinguished by the characteristic purity of its profiles and the peculiar shade of colour achieved by means of glazing. The body of the cup rises diagonally, so its base remains defined by its horizontal cut. Although the cup is catalogued as *Tenmoku*, it is of a more yellowish colour and therefore it is also known as *O-Tenmoku*, Tenmoku yellow.
(*Masaaki Arakawa*)

151
Japan

Muromachi period
(1333-1573)
Ko-Seto
Bottle, 15th century
Ceramic, 25.5 x 17 cm
Tokyo, Idemitsu Museum

The seto kilns, located in the Aichi and Gaifu prefectures in the centre of Japan, started to produce ceramic bottles at some time in the 13th century. The bottles, first made during the Kamakuru period (1185-1333) emulated the Chinese pottery of the Southern Song dynasty, and continued to be produced in large numbers throughout the Muromachi period. These bottles were used as containers for sake, although they were sometimes also used as funeral urns in which the ashes of the dead were kept. The thick neck and the solid body combine to make the bottle's form highly stable, a characteristic of the Muromachi period.
(*Masaki Arakawa*)

152
Japan

Muromachi period
(1333-1573)
Ko-Seto
Cuenco, 15th or 16th century
Ceramic, 9.5 x 8 cm
Tokyo, Idemitsu Museum

Most of the recipients, cups, and other articles related to the consumption of tea are highly valued for their artistic value. Both the tea ceremony and the recipients necessary to perform it are of Chinese origin, and were first made during the Song and Yang dynasties. In Japan, they were first made in the kilns at Seto towards the end of the Kamakura period and they continued to be made throughout the Muromachi period.
This kind of small pottery article was intended to be aesthetically pleasing and moreover to reflect the sensitivity of the Chinese originals, called *karamono*.
This was the name given to the products imported from China, because *kara* is the Japanese reading of the Chinese character Tang.
(*Masaaki Arakawa*)

153
Japan

Muromachi period
(1333-1573)
Tanba style
Vessel, 15th century
Ceramic, 39.7 x 16.5 cm
Inscription: KEN
Tokyo, Suntory Museum

A vessel, or short-necked pitcher with three small handles on the upper part. Between the handles, there is an engraved motif reminiscent of the roots of a tree, and an inscription with the Chinese character *ken*. This item belonged to a family in Wakayama prefecture, and it was used for the storage of tea.
(*Suntory Museum*)

154
Venice

Gentile Bellini's Circle
The Audience of the Ambassadors in Damascus
approx. 1488-1499
Oil painting on canvas
175 x 201 cm
From the royal collection of
Louis XIV
Paris, Musée du Louvre
Départmrnt des Peintures
Bibliography: SALVAGET
1945-1946; PALLUCCHINI 1966,
pp. 49-51; RABY 1982,
pp. 56-60, n. 51, p. 63, n. 86

In 1660, M. Boschini attributed this painting to Gentile Bellini. It represents the Ottoman Turk Grand Vizier giving an audience to the Venetian knight-commander in Istanbul at the court of Mehmet II, some time after September 1479 (*The Charter of Navigation*, Venice 1660, pp. 31-32). It was later considered representative of an audience given by the sultan himself to the Venetian ambassador, until

1895, when Ch. Shefer correctly described it as a scene from the Mamluk territories due to of the styles of clothing and architecture. In his opinion, it was Cairo in the times of the sultan Qansuh, seen receiving a Venetian emissary in the citadel. He suggested the emissary was Domenico Treviano, the procurator of San Marco, that a meeting took place in 1512 which ruled out the possibility that Gentile Bellini, who died in 1507, could have painted it. A detailed account of the interview is not consistent with the scene represented in the painting (*Note sur un tableau du Louvre naguère atribué a Gentile Bellini*, in "Gazette des Beaux-Arts" XIV, 1895, 201). It was Jean Sauvaget, a great expert on Muslim art in Syria and on the city of Damascus, who stated in 1945 that the picture was a view of Damascus with astounding detail, although he pointed out that the details of the composition are rather

forced, creatively combining the sites occupied by buildings and altering their positions (*Une ancienne représentation de Damas au Musée du Louvre*, in "Bulletin d'Etudes Orientales" XI Beyruth, 1945-1946, pp. 5-12 edition by Institut Français, Damascus).
This painting was the first to be known in Europe that dealt with the life and architecture of the Muslim Middle East and had great influence among Venetian painting circles. It has been attributed to several of them, but there is no conclusive proof.
The painting. The pictorial composition shows two clearly defined planes; the background consists of buildings and landscape, and the foreground shows three scenes from the life of the city. The scenes are represented together but they are not related to each other.
The distant background is Mount Qasiyun (Casius), to the north of Damascus with a

blue sky, white clouds above, and is illuminated by the afternoon sun or the sunset (Elisseéff, *Damashk*, en *E.I.*, 2nd ed., Leiden, 1965, p. 278). Covering part of the background is the great eighth century Omeya mosque, seen from its south wall, or *gibla*, showing on the left or to the west of the painting, the polygonal minaret of Qa'it Bay (1468-1496). This minaret was finished in 1488, so the date of the painting must be after this. The various levels have balconies from which the muezzin summoned the faithful to prayer, and the lantern with its bulging covering crowned by the metallic *Ayamur* with the crescent moon, or *hilal*. The fact that the mosque is illuminated from a beam scaffolding, mainly during the nights of the month of Ramadan, makes me think that the minaret had already been in use for some time when it was depicted in this work. The central nave which divides the oratory can be seen through the windows of the claristory, with its finish of moulded fronting with a side niche and circular windows with lattice shutters on each side. The roof shows the sloped lead sheeting covering it, under the double row of windows in the supporting wall covered with another *yemur*. This dome and supporting wall do not correspond to the ones now on the mosque, which were rebuilt in 1904-1910. On the right and on a more distant plane we can see the more or less central minaret of the patio's north *riweq*, or gallery. The eastern minaret can be seen to the right of the house in the foreground. This minaret's cubic base with double windows has lasted until today, although the upper part was remodelled during the Ottoman period.

The house in the foreground is typically Syrian, and many like it can still be seen in Damascus today. The upper floor has two flying balconies, one larger than the other, with railing and wicker shutters or "mullioned" windows, known as *masrabiyye* in the East and *simese* in al-Andalus and North Africa. From these the women could observe without being seen, unless they opened the shutters or sat on the terraces, as in the painting. In both places, their heads and most of their faces are covered in the style of headdress known as *tartur* (Mayer, *Mamluk Costume, A Survey*, Geneva 1952, p. 71, pl. XI-2). Among the patio gardens with orange and lemon trees of the other houses, we can see a domed building finished in open flower work with a *yamur*, similar to the one mentioned above. In the main, cubic structure we can see windows with wicker blinds. Next to it, on the right, we can see a square-shaped room covered with a vault with the *madwas* or skylight of the *hammam* at the bazaar of the corn sellers, *suq al-Buziriyye*, to the south of the great mosque. So far, the topographical accuracy of the image is relatively correct, as the *hammam* is actually further to the left than the painter's representation of it. This work appears to have been painted from inside the Venetian *fundug* (corn exchange), located at the centre of Damascus' medieval bazaar.

This set of buildings ends in an adobe wall with a semicircular arch, and three circles with a poorly executed Mamluk emblem of the cupbearer, common among the Mamluk emirs and sultans, and the same as sultan Qa'it Bay's. It consists of the lower part of a circle with a small white cup on a black background, an intermediate strip with a cup in which an enamelled inkwell was painted, with a "horn" on each side. This "horn" in fact represents the trousers of the nobility (*sarawil alfutuwwa*). In the upper red segment of the emblem a rhombus represents the cloth of the servant responsible for serving drinks (Raby, *Venice, Dürer, and the Oriental Mode, The Hans Huth Memorial Studies.* I, London, 1982, pp. 43, 53). In this case, the emblem has been painted with some errors, such as the joining of the *sarawil* (the trousers or "horns" at the base of the cup); although it coincides with that of the sultan then reigning in Cairo, the emblem was in such common use among the Mamluks that it is difficult to use it to date the painting from the time of this sultan's rule, as opposed to earlier.

The adobe wall ends in a right angle and connects with the great *bab-iwan* of the palace of the *na'ib* or Governor of Damascus. This construction shows a pointed arch using the *ablad* technique, a combination of two different coloured marble blocks, in this case black and white with a pointed keystone. Among the pendentives, we can see a lower pair of decorated golden circuits with an inscription in red characters; the other pair of circles, nearer to the keystone, are also heraldic and above them is a rectangular band with lobulate ends containing golden characters on a pale blue background. The great arch of the *bab-iwan* is covered by eaves supported by curved wooden bases painted in blue, red, black, and white. The upper part of the entrance is a flat terrace facing west with semicircular windows that allow

231

slanted sunlight to enter and illuminate the wall at the bottom of the *bab-iwan* where, on the right, we can see the faint glow from the landscape reflected from the outside *basura* (Cresswell, Bab, in "E.I.", 2, I Leiden 1960, 831).

The *bab-iwan* is built on a platform of five steps on the extreme right of which there is a *mastaba* (a seat normally made of stone or marble). The guard might either be guarding in a sitting position or standing in military fashion. On the right of the *bab-iwan* we can see an adobe wall with battlements and decorated with three emblematic circles behind which there is a lush garden of orange trees, lemon trees, cypresses, and a palm tree. Amongst them is a low straight building and, on the right, there is a polygonal minaret with two balconies for the muezzin; around the bulbous pediment there is a wooden structure to hang lamps which is thought to be an invention of the painter to counterbalance the minarets of the great Omeya Mosque (Raby, p. 58).

I consider that the composition by the painter is clearly creative, combining the view of Damascus from the Venetian corn exchange or *fundug*, with a view of the *bab-iwan*, the facade of the palace of the *na'ib*, or governor of Damascus, enabling the scenes with people in the foreground of the picture to be joined together. From right to left, there are three clearly differentiated scenes of life in Damascus. The first shows Damascus as a commercial city and stopping point on the routes travelled with caravans of camels. Perhaps this is the part closest to the *fundug* showing two camels, one seated and the other standing, harnes and with their rider, while a person wearing city clothes appears to be welcoming them. The scene is watched by a child with a tall headdress that covers his head and is leading a leashed mon-

key that is walking on all fours. Behind them and to the right, there are three bearded men wearing *imama* headdress and talking to each other. In the background there is a horseman on a short horse, dressed in white with a high headdress covering his entire head. In front of the horse and the group there are several soldiers, a child with a lance, and another, their page, in silhouette. Both are wearing *rihiyyas* on their feet, and on their heads they wear *zamis* or caps. These red caps wrapped in veil were originally typical of the lower classes, but an edict of the sultan in 841/1438 restricted their use to the military Mamluks (Mayer, *Mamluk Costume*, 24, 32 notes 3., 42, pl. XI-2; Raby, *Venice*, 41, 43, fig. 29). Behind the page, there is a black-skinned man carrying a weight on his shoulder. The different groups, such as the three men talking, the soldiers, the horseman, etc., are urban scenes showing life in the streets.

Next, more or less in the centre of the painting's right-hand section, is the main scene of the picture. This is the reception given by the *na'ib* of Damascus to a European ambassador, possibly Venetian, and his retinue of five people. The ambassador is dressed in a red tunic and cloak, while the others are wearing black or grey clothes, and they are all wearing black caps. The *na'ib* is sitting within an *arika*, a large wooden dais with carpets on the floor and cushions behind his back. The structure is portable as is shown by the visible feet. The audiences given to ambassadors and subjects at the palace gates is an ancient custom that goes back to the times of the Egyptian Pharaohs, the Persian Sassanids, etc., and persisted in the modern era, both in the Middle East and Al-Andalus (Deny, *Bab-Cali*, in "E.I.", C, I, Leiden 1960, 836; Fernández Puertas, *The Facade of the Palace of*

Comares. Location, Function, and Origins, Granada, 1980, pp. 150, 281, Patronato de la Alhambra). This custom of appearing before the people *mutul* survives to this very day, and as in the case of the pope, for example. When the audience had finished, the dais was taken down and stored in the palace. The *na'ib* is wearing a different headdress from which a series of "horns" spread out; this is called the *al tajfifa al-kabirs*, but was popularly known as the *al nac-ura*, the Persian Wheel, due to its similarity to this wheel and its ruffs (Mayer, *Mamluk Costume*, 30 note 6). This headdress was white, as were the clothing of the *na'ib* and the two privy counsellors seated on the dais in the middle ground, who were perhaps two *gadies*. Between the ambassador's group and the dais there is a person with his back to us, perhaps the chamberlain or *rasm*, responsible for introducing those received, or perhaps a dragoman, or translator. On the platform of the *bab-iwan* and to the right of the dais or *arika*, there are several compact groups of soldiers and functionaries, facing forwards, while talking and looking at each other. Most of them wear a tall, large headdress, the *tagiya* adopted by the Circassian Mamluk military class, which consists of a base that is narrower than the top, and could be red, or have the lower part green and the upper one black (Mayer, *Mamluk Costume*, 31, note 10, pl. I.; Raby, 1982, p. 40). In the foreground of the reception scene there are a pair of deer, one male and one female, suggesting to me that the painter directly observed the reception scene from within the palace, and at a distance from a precinct within its public area in which there were stray animals, going from the *bab-iwan* to another area of the palace. Thus, the painter has tried to give a complete scene representing life in Damascus

on a single canvas, and therefore brings together buildings and human scenes that, in fact, corresponded to different locations. Confusion has been caused when people have studied the painting without bearing this in mind. This painting caused a great impact in the Venetian school headed by Giovanni and Gentile Bellini and influenced the scenes of the life of Saint Mark painted by Gentile and Giovanni Mansueti for Saint Mark's School. Gentile painted the *Arrest of Saint Mark* in 1499 for the Crociferi Church and many details have been adopted from this painting. This makes the latest possible date 1499 (Raby 1982, p. 63). It may be supposed that the painting arrived in Venice in the second half of the 1490s, as there is no trace of its graphic influence in the work of Dürer after his visit in 1494-95. Recently, it has been suggested that the artist might have been Benedetto Diana (Raby, 1982, p. 63) who lived temporarily in the Venetian corn exchange in Damascus, but his style and characteristics are different from those of this work.

(*Antonio Fernández Puertas*)

155
Asia Minor

Ottoman period
Carpet, 16th century
Wool, 230 x 155 cm
Budapest, Museum
of Applied Arts, 14785
Exhibition: Budapest, 1924;
Budapest, 1962; Budapest,
1974; Hungary, 1975;
Hungary, 1982; Budapest,
1986; Prague, 1986
Bibliography: Jajczai-Kanyo
s.f. fig. 22; Budapest 1962,
n. 2, fig. 1; Budapest 1974,
n. 1, fig. 1; Hungary 1975,
fig. 2; Budapest 1977, p. 64,
fig. X; Budapest 1979 p. 310,
fig. 2; Hungary, 1982; Vorr
1983, p. 40, pl. 54, fig. 63;
Budapest 1986, n. 3; Prague
1986, Gantzhorn 1991,
p. 412, fig. 548

This carpet belongs to one of
the best known types of early
Ottoman carpets, also known
as Holbein carpets. They are
based on the geometric designs that were used in the
15th and 16th centuries in Asia
Minor, probably in the areas
around Ushak or Bergamer or,
according to more recent research, in the area of Smyrna
(Izmir). This type of carpet is
called a Holbein carpet due to
a painting by Hans Holbein
the Younger (1497-1543)
showing a carpet of this type.
The portrait is of the merchant
Georg Gisze (1530, Berlin
Staatliche Museen). Experts
make a distinction between
Holbein carpets with small designs and Holbein carpets
with large designs on the basis
of the layout of the motifs in
the design. This carpet has a
large design.

The background colour of the
carpet is dark green and in
each of the two rows, there
are three braided insets with
arabesque crosses of the "four
lotus" type. Each of these is alternately red, yellow, white,
and dark brown. In the space
between the insets there are
octagonal rosettes, in plaits,
smaller in size than the insets.
The rosettes show a certain resemblance to the tribal emblems of the Ottoman peoples

of central Asia (the *gul* design), and they are also called
Holbein-gul. The space between the crosses is decorated
with small eight-pointed stars.
The main trimming, in white,
on the hem is decorated with
a continuous strip of dia-
mond-shaped stars, with the
traditional elements of this design but in a new combination. The two sides of the
main trimming are adorned
with a narrow streamer, and

the two narrower hems are
finished in broad red trimmings of woven fabric.
(*Emeze Pasztor*)

156
Egypt

Mamluk period
Carpet, end of 15th century
Textile, wool, knotted
filaments, asymmetric knots,
210 x 132 cm
Berlin, Museum für
Islamische Kunst, 82.704
Bibliography: ENDEMANN
1940, p. 66 n. 66, n. 22;
ERDEMANN 1966, p. 94;
SPUHULER 1987, n. 63

Carpets of this pattern and size were produced in Cairo during the last decades of Mamluk rule and up to the middle of the 16th century, even after the conquest of Egypt by the Ottoman sultan Selim I in 1517. The inner field of this carpet is dominated by an eight-pointed star surrounded by concentric octagonal forms. Above and below the centre are cross-bars separated by palm trees and pairs of cypresses. Rosettes alternating with elongated cartouches form the border decoration.

The pattern consists of different ornamental forms like arabesques, umbrella-leaved shrubs, small rosettes against a cherry-red ground. The small-sized ornaments evidently contrast with the pictorial representation of the palm trees and cypresses. The use of trees introduces the garden motif into the carpet's decoration. This can be related to the idea of the Garden of Paradise, represented many times in 16th century Persian carpets.
The way the border decoration is laid out on this carpet establishes a definite connection between its designers and those of contemporary Egyptian book drawings.
(*Volkmar Enderlein*)

157
Spain/Alcaraz

Carpet, 15th or 16th century
Warp, fine ivory coloured
wool, made up of one
strand with two torsion
threads in the Z dimension
and spun in the S dimension
Weft; fine ivory coloured
wool made of three strands
with a single torsion thread
in the Z dimension, used
together in multiple weft
after each row of knots
215 x 125 cm
Madrid, Museo Nacional
de Artes Decorativas, 3.207

The frame consists of two edging strips separated by wide braiding. The internal edging shows Moorish influence, with forms similar to that of a scorpion in shades of green and white on a black background. The external edging is a simplification of the inscriptions on the carpets in the "Admiral" series. In this case, they have been reduced to compartments containing red and yellow

trees, with red and green branches on a blue background. On the longer sides the compartments show, in the upper angles, very small figures of animals confronting each other. In the lower angles there are geometrical designs. The background is decorated with large tooth-edged leaves that are full of little dark blue points, with clusters of yellow, green, and white, within a hexagonal network of interlaced green threads. These carpets were very common to judge from frequent references to them in the documents of the end of the 15th and the first third of the 16th century. They were referred to as "brocade work" or "embossed work" due to their similarity to Gothic brocades and velvet. They are also referred to as "linkwork," which was, no doubt, very similar. Other examples of this type can be seen in the Victoria and Albert Museum, London; the Brooklyn Museum of New York; or the Textile Museum of

Washington. The design of the carpets is similar to the ceramic tiles made in Seville at the end of the 15th century and the first third of the 16th century.
(*Cristina Partearroyo*)

158
Spain

Mudejar period
Mosaic panel of enamelled tiles, 15th or 16th century
Glazed ceramic, 38 x 30 cm
Possibly from the Alhambra
Granada, Museo Nacional de Arte Hispanomusulmán, 4610

This stretch was mounted with original Nazari pieces in the 1940s. It forms a geometrical, Muslim layout, with Moorish elements, but without paying much attention to the disposition of the light honey-coloured pieces and the dark brown ones. The white curved trays that form the same triangular figure as the concave-convex sides, are missing from the piece. In the centre of the figures there are six-pointed stars, forming a swastika with six curved arms between every six figures. This piece was mounted by the plasterer José Molina Trujillo under the supervision of the then director of the Museum J. Bermúdez Pareja, who considered it appropriate to leave the scar of the plasterwork visible amongst the pieces, in order to soften this contrast between the light and dark brown pieces. In the Nasrid period, the layout of these triangular compositions was either performed in a *sebca*, whose colour layout was exceptional, or in oblique rows at 60°. This system was to continue under the Moors in the 16th century. At the base of the north-west alcove of the "Patio de los Arrayanes" gallery in the Alhambra, two different systems can be seen. The Nasrid system is used on the north side, and is based on *sebcas* made up of black rhombic schemes on a background of white pieces, with each scheme containing four triangular pieces with curved sides, which were either honey-coloured, blue, or green, with a white hexagonal centre and with identical white shapes of violet, green, or honey-coloured stars in the centre.

The Moorish restoration of the patios to the south and east of the alcove simplified the system of oblique rows inclined at 60°, alternating the colours from row to row, and separating them by white lines. (Brisch, in Sourdel and Spuler, *Die Kunst des Islam,* Propyläen Kunstgeschichte, 4, Berlin 1973, p. 320, pl, 285).
The apparent simplicity of the design comes from traditional and empirical knowledge of an extremely old proportional system, formulated by Pythagoras. According to him, it was based on the number three, but when the craftsmen built this design they generally tended to use the system handed from master to apprentice, of a 30°, 60°, and 90° set square.
To draw up the design, it was necessary to perform fourteen steps. The draughtsman drew the primary network of equilateral triangles, each one of which represented one of the tiles in the piece. Then, with the help of the set square, they drew parallel lines from the vertices of the network of triangles from left to right, then right to left. Thus they obtained a secondary hexagonal network, at a proportion of 1:3 with respect to the previous diagram. Once this had been done, the craftsman drew parallel lines intermediate to the lines slanted at 30°, in steps 3 and 4, and then parallel vertical lines intermediate to those of the primary network of triangles in steps 1 and 2. This formed a third proportional network of smaller triangles, so that the position of the triangles in the original network contain three sides of another three equilateral triangles that have been proportionally reduced. There is also a third hexagonal network that is exactly half the size of that obtained by step 4.
Then they took each vertex of the network of primary triangles, in step 1, as the centre of a smaller hexagon. The centres of the bends of the pieces are located in the vertexes of these hexagons. In

4610

235

order to draw these bends they used as a radius the measure corresponding to half the diagonal length of the hexagon in the third network. This radius is equal to the side of the small triangles and, at the same time, to the side-length of the hexagon. The arched or bent sections are drawn first as convex then as concave, coinciding at their start and finish with the parallel lines established in step 1. Then the same process was carried out on the oblique sides of the equilateral network from right to left, then left to right. After the drawing lines were removed we have the plan that appears in the bayt al-barid (*frigidarium*) of the hammam of the Comares Palace in the Alhambra. To obtain this pattern with the six-pointed star, the basic pattern is used once again. From the centre of each triangle in the smaller network a line was drawn, perpendicular to the midpoint of three of the sides of the hexagon. Based on the three midpoints, which are where the concave-convex sides have been cut, equilat-

eral triangles were drawn, which when turned, form the six-pointed star. The layout of this stretch of wall only shows rows of triangular figures lobed with stars.

(*Antonio Fernández Puertas*)

159
Spain

Al-Andalus, Nasrid period
Tile, 16th century
Ceramic with tin-based
enamel with decoration in
manganese green, blue, and
gold, 26.5 x 37.5 cm
From the "Queen's Boudoir"
in the Alhambra
Granada, Museo Nacional
de Arte Hispanomusulmán
164-2041 and 162
Bibliography: GÓMEZ MORENO
1904, pp. 259-270;
FOTHINGHAM WILSON 1951

236

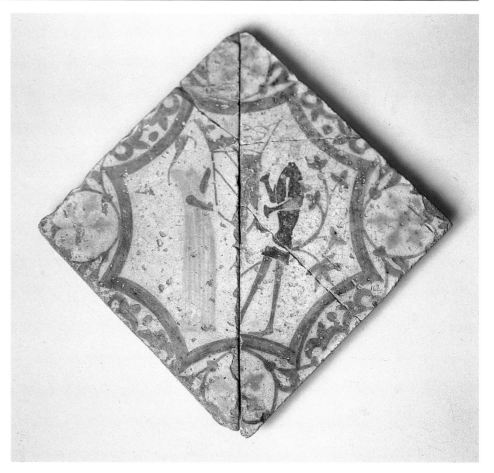

The tower of Abül-Yuyüs is
built on top of the fortified
path in the Alhambra enclosure. It suffered extensive
changes in the Nasrid period;
then it was completely
changed and remodelled from
1528 to 1533 when it was
made into the personal living
quarters of the Empress Isabel,
the wife of Carlos V, which is
where its Christian name, the
Queen's Boudoir, comes from.
The writing on the cross piece
states that this tower was the
work of Emir Abül-Yuyüs Nasr
(1309-1314). He was de-
throned by his nephew Ismael
I, the son of his sister Fatima,
and died in exile in Guadix in
1322. With his death, the direct male line of the Nasrid dynasty disappeared, and the Is-
mailiyya Nasrid dynasty continued through the female line.
The first reformation was carried out by Yüsuf I, the son of
Ismael I, who partially
changed the plasterwork in
the room, where his name,
Abül-Hayyäy, now appears.
These changes occurred when
he realized that the name of
his uncle, the legitimate Emir
Abül-Yuyüs Nasr, appeared on
the four parts of the frieze, the
cross piece with Damascene
work, and in each tablet of the
two rectangular corbels with
lobed extensions, in the repeated inscription: "May there
be divine help and protection
and victory for our Lord Abül-
Yuyüs, Prince of the Muslims,
may he be glorified and
helped by God." Yüsuf I ordered the name of his uncle

to be suppressed by lowering
the level of the wood, carving
his name in its place. His
name, Abül-Hayyäy, which
has the same number of characters in Arabic, was written in
improvised characters with a
background of interweaving
flowers that was totally out of
keeping with the original, and
was badly planned and ex-
ecuted.
His son Muhammad V built
the Riyäd (garden) Palace,
(now known as the Palace of
the Lions), and he also carried
out important renovations on
the buildings, beginning with
the entrance facade, on the
threshold of which appeared
the ornamental theme of the
clenched fist with the thumb
stretching out supporting a
cluster of flowers. This theme
also appears in the Room of
the Two Sisters, whose architectural style was called *Qub-
bah Mayor* by Ibn Zamrak in
his *Diwan*. They also appear
in the arch of the access to the
Qubba's enclosed balcony.

In the arch that frames the facade, we can see the name of
Muhammad V, al-Gani Billah,
so the changes must have
taken place after he took this
honorific title in 1367, after the
campaigns of Jaén, Ubeda,
and the siege of Baeza. This
modification was responsible
for the current access stairway,
with its polychrome geometric
plaster skirting, and for the
room's flooring.
This type of flooring has been
found in the ruins of the Alijares Palace, and this would
date it, albeit indirectly, as
coming from the period of
Muhammad V.
The existing remains of the
flooring are a few square
pieces and several triangular
ones from the edges of the
room, less trodden than those
in the centre of the room.
They have ornamental themes
that were painted before they
were fired, so that the triangles
could then be made into pairs
joining them by the hypote-
nuses of the right angled

triangles, to form a square
with sides of 27.6 cm. Access
to the light shaft in the interior
of this tower is from the south
east corner, and the layout of
the floor was slanted.
It followed the diagonal of the
rectangular light shaft so that
the first thing that people saw
on entering was the flooring's
figurative themes, the right
way up.
The flooring shows a pre-Is-
lamic layout, an octagonally
limited series that is, curved
because the sides of its octagons show compass-based circular segments, forming cir-
cumferences in the secondary
circles which give the
measurements of the arcs of
the circle. On the four other
side there are oval spaces. The
pieces have a white back-
ground; the octagons are
painted in a very pale, cop-
pery green, the flowers in cobalt blue, and the images and
heraldic motifs in this same
colour, as well as pale green
and violet (manganese oxide).

The faces, hands, feet, and other elements of clothing, the animals, and some heraldic motifs were in gold, now removed by damp and wear. It has left an imprint that can be seen by the use of chemical and photographic techniques. This golden decoration was also used to ornament the areas with floral design. This tower was restored in 1928-1929 and one tile was left in the northeast corner, the rest being stored at the National Museum of Hispano-Muslim Art, except for two tiles in the Don Juan Institute of Valencia. The floral decoration which runs through the circles and oval spaces shows looped stems, double palms with a heart, and flowers with six petals, each beginning in the centre. In my opinion, the result is innovative, whereas for others it is simply Gothic or Mudejar.

Within the octagons, there are other images and designs: a youth and a maiden, or two squires, carrying shields with a transverse band in the foreground and completed with a crown; a youth and a maiden face-to-face; a square tile with a rider falling from his horse (now lost, but there is a watercolour sketch); a square tile with winged Gothic dragons; squires similar to the ones above; a tile (now lost) with two swans face-to-face with interchanging colours; two goats confronting each other with a floral background of leafy shrubs and low trees. There must have been many more themes to judge from the numerous fragments that still exist.

All the golden decorative work on these pieces has disappeared. To judge by the clothing of the persons depicted, I think we should date these tiles as contemporary to the painted arches in the Room of the Kings, that is to say, 1380-1390, or shortly afterwards. This was at the beginning of the international Gothic period, as this art became much more complex from the 1390s onwards. Until the 1380s Christian knights used long, loose robes in their social life, and short robes for hunting and duels, which made it possible for them to wear armour. Short clothing was introduced as a novelty in the last third of the 14th century. It emphasized the virile characteristics of the male body and became common in everyday civilian life. The feminine clothing also confirms the date.

I believe that, once the *Riyad* Palace was finished, Muhammad V started the remodelling of the tower with its lantern room; it is a charming pavilion for the soveriegn's private enjoyment. It is open to the countryside, which is close to, but isolated from the palace, and there is a stairwell in the fortified-wall lane leading to an underground passage permitting departure or escape to the side of the hill near the River Darro, to the Northwest. It is a place that is a delight to the senses. The plasterwork of a high frieze was later reformed by his grandson Muhammad VII (1392-1408), and this would be the latest possible date for the flooring. Once under Christian rule, the Renaissance changes mentioned previously took place (1528-1533).

(*Antonio Fernández Puertas*)

160
Spain

Al-Andalus, Mudejar period
Covered panel, 16th century
Wood, 352 x 178 x 10.5 cm
Granada, Museo Nacional
de Arte Hispanomusulmán
7.360-1

This is part of the covering for the former Church of San Gil, which was demolished during the revolution of 1869 in order to build houses on the left side of the Plaza Nueva in Granada. According to Manuel Gómez-Moreno, it was built between 1543 and 1563 by Francisco Hernández de Móstoles, but the roofing was done by the master Miguel between 1543 and 1549 for the church of Santiago (Saint James). "The base was octagonal, with racemes of loop-shaped ornaments in the pendentives, corpulent ones in the central ceiling panel, and two series of inclined, wide friezes in the Roman style." When the building was demolished, the panel was deposited in the Provincial Archaeological Museum and later transferred to the National Museum of Hispano-Muslim Art.

On the basis of the surviving remains and the description made by Gómez-Moreno, it would seem to have the same form and decoration as the octagonal roofing in the cross vault of the Merced Convent, which has now also been installed in the National Museum of Hispano-Muslim Art. The panel on show forms part of the octagonal roofing with interlocking decoration with knots of ten and twenty. Four of the panels that formed the roofing have been preserved and in them we can see half of the twenty-pointed wheel opening with conglomerate and hexagonal tiles, surrounded by ten-pointed wheels formed by the star, the *sino*, the conglomerate and blunt trays, and ten lights to round it off. Knotwork decora-

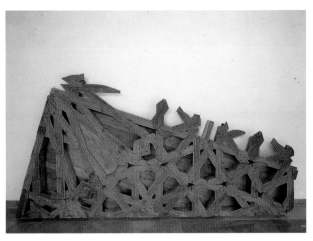

tion formed by the scrolls o *halibas* show carved marking gauges in which there are no traces of any colour they might have had.

The geometric spaces (hexagonals and sinos) are crossed by rafters and are covered in panelling that shows traces of the original polychromy, which served to disguise the structure of the roofing.

(*Purificación Marinetto Sánchez*)

161
Damascus

Mamluk period
Votive lamp, 1488-1496
Brass plate, 60 cm;
diameter 44 cm
Inscriptions on the bulbous
cover, "Glory to our Lord
the sultan, the king, the
warrior, defender of the
frontiers, sultan of Islam and
the Muslims, destroyer of
the infidels and polytheists,
bringer of justice to the
world, companion to the
Knight Commander of the
faithful, king of the two
continents and the two seas,
servant of the two noble
sanctuaries, the Sovereign
Al-Malik Al-Ashraf
Abu'l-Nasr Qa'it Bay, may
his victory be glorious."
Cairo, Museum of Islamic
Art, 4081
Bibliography: Wiet 1932,
pl. XVIII

The lamp consists of a base
sheet with orifices for glass
containers, a bulbous cover
with openwork decoration,
three oval units, and a hemispherical finish with a hook for
hanging it. Its origins go back
to the polycandelon of the Byzantine world; this supported
a flat bronze disc on which the
glass lamps were placed. It is
not known when this more
highly ornamented Islamic
style arose, although the first
known examples date from
the middle of the 14th century.
The style is still popular in the
Middle East.

In the inscriptions, the sultan
is compared symbolically with
the sun, and his subjects to the
sun's rays. None of the pieces
belonging to sultan Qa'it Bay
displayed in this exhibition are
adorned with inlays of
precious metal. This is surprising when one compares it to
the sumptuous inlaid Mamluk
plates from previous centuries,
and even more so if we consider that the candleholder exhibited was for the tomb of
the Prophet in Medina. At the
end of the 14th century and at
the beginning of the 15th century the Mamluk empire suf-

fered an economic crisis from
which it had barely recovered
when it was conquered by the
Ottomans in 1517. The lack of
inlays is thus probably a direct
reflection of the scarcity of
precious metal available to the
Mamluk state at this time.
(*James W. Allan*)

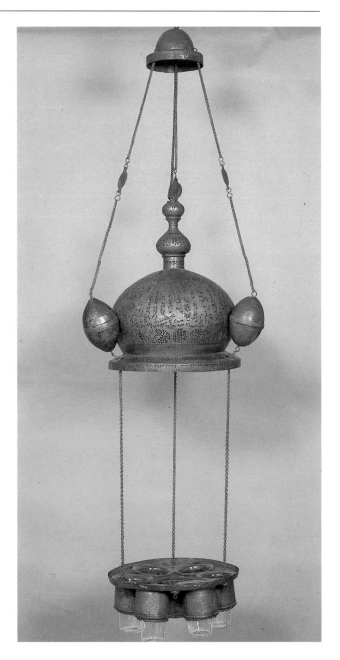

162
Cairo

Votive lamp, posterior
to 1474
Brass sheet, 130 cm;
diameter 45 cm
From the Asalbey mosque in
Madinat al-Fayyum
Inscription on the pyramidal
part, "Glory to our Lord the
sultan, the wise king, the
defender of our frontiers,
conqueror with the help of
God, sultan of Islam and the
Muslims, destroyer of the
infidels and polytheists,
bringer of justice to the
world, father to the poor
and indigent, associate of
the prince of the Faithful,
pilgrim to the Sacred House
of God, al- Malik al-Ashraf
Abu'l Nasr Qa'it Bay, may
his victory be glorious."
Cairo, Museum of Islamic
Art, 384
Bibliography: WIET 1932,
pl. XVII; LONDON 1976, n. 227

This lamp and its pair in the
same museum come from the
mosque of Asalbey (the wife
of Qa'it Bay) in Madinat al-
Fayyum where they were discovered in 905h/1499, three
years after the death of sultan
Qa'it Bay. It is not known for
which mosques they were
made, and it is possible that
they formed part of a royal
consignment that was never
delivered. They were later
used by his widow to decorate
her residence. The inscriptions
with interwoven *hastae*
(posts) with the name of the
ruling sultan, are typical of
metalwork in Damascus at this
time. The roundels, or be-
zants, have extensions in the
form of a palm leaf on each
of the six sides and are reminiscent of 15th century designs for metal door coverings,
and the designs stamped on
leather book covers at this
time.
The main inscription around
the pyramid provides us with
more detail than does Qa'it
Bay's candleholder about the
royal titles to which Qa'it Bay
aspired. Sultan Qa'it Bay completed a pilgrimage to Mecca

in 1474, so the lamp can not
be from before this date.
This lamp has a sheet at the
base into which glass lamps
(containing oil and a wick)
fitted, as in ancient poly-
candles. The Ottomans also
adopted the pyramidal form,
and an interesting example of
this is the silver lamp dating
from the end of the 15th century that is in the Museum of
Turkish and Islamic Art in Istanbul. A similar conical form
was used in Spain, as is shown
by the magnificent fretwork
chandelier with the name of
Muhammad III, dated H 705
(1306), now in the National
Archaeological Museum of
Madrid.
The polycandle also formed
the base of the great North African lamps. However, in that
case the usual conical form
with three or four rings of
horizontal lamps, was de-
veloped further, probably with
a view to decorating and re-
using the bells of Christian
churches.
(*James W. Allan*)

163
Spain

Al-Andalus, Mudejar period
Lattice window, 15th
or 16th century
Polychrome wood,
106 x 86 cm
From the Comares Bath, in
the "Sala de las Damas" in
the Alhambra
Granada, Museo Nacional
de Arte Hispanomusulmán,
256
Bibliography: Gómez
Moreno, 1982 p. 98

240

The vaulted part of the *hammam* dates from the times of
sultan Ismahil I (1314-1325),
and was decorated by his son
Yusuf I (1333-1354), as shown
by a six-verse poem on a
marble panel in the arch. Hot
or cold water flowed from the
deposit to the basin east of the
al-bayt al sajún (caldarium).
(Lafuente Alcántara, *Inscripciones árabes de Granada*,
Madrid 1860, 150, 151, n. 160;
Nukl, *Inscripciones árabes de
la Alhambra y del Generalife*,
"Al-Andalus", IV, 1936-1939,
183; García Gómez, *Poemas
árabes en los muros y fuentes
de la Alhambra*, 1985, 109,
110, n. 12). The Damascene
frame, roofed area of the *bayt
al maslaj (apodoterium)* dates
from the times of Yusuf I. This
was where, after the turkish
bath, people rested on the
stone benches or "beds", to
the east and west, while they
calmly chatted, and received
massages and other bodily attentions from their servants.
The *bayt al maslaj* room in
the Comares Palace *hammam*
is a lantern room with the
square central lantern space
supported by marble columns
and pillars, around which
there is a corridor running
from east to west, where the
cubicles to lie down and relax
in are visible. The light in this
gubba was zenithal when it
came through the light shaft,
with its set of high arched
windows – four on each side
– located under the damask
work covering the square
space that extends over the
rooms at the side.

From 1537 to 1542 this room
was consolidated and restored
with Moorish work, as is documented in docket 2-2 in the
Archives of the Alhambra.
At this time, Francisco de las
Maderas remade the flooring
of the square central area, copying the original, and the
other ceramic flooring and
skirting was restored, adding
Renaissance tiles with the imperial symbols as a finishing
touch. Perhaps because he
had to repair the roof of the
light shaft, which was in bad
condition, and because he
considered that not enough
light entered through the medieval light shaft, he decided
to add a new level of lattice
work windows between the
16 semicircular arched windows and the repaired cover-

ing, in order to illuminate the
room better. It is one of these
Moorish lattice work windows
that is on show here.
Why was the *hammam* renovated? Firstly, because it had
deteriorated. Secondly, because the private apartments
of Carlos V and the Empress
Isabel next to the Lindajara
patio were built by Pedro Machuco between 1528 and
1533, and the Nasrid *hammam* was restored in Moorish
style so that it could serve
these apartments.
The twelve lattice work windows that were installed show
a variety of geometric designs
based on interwoven scrolls
within a rectangular framework. The design was based
on the relation between the
side of a square and its diag-

onal. That is to say, on the 1:2
proportion known empirically
and in practice by craftsmen
on the basis of the set square
with this proportion, although
they were unaware that the
theoretical principle had been
formulated by Pythagoras.
Given that the design corresponds to a normal system of
grid squares with another one
superimposed diagonally at
45°, like a figure of eight, the
two listens that go crosswise
to the upper and lower horizontal edges do not reach the
corners of the frame's rectangle. For the same reason,
above and below there are
rectangular triangles (or a rectangle divided along its diagonal) while horizontally, the
squares form the beginning of
the oblique sides. The geome-

tric composition revolves around the central crossing between the listens in crosswork, surrounded by a regular octagonal prism. Maintaining a strict width between the horizontal and vertical sides, there is a second octagon with four horizontal and four vertical sides showing a 90° angle in the corners, and is longer than the four diagonal sides. In each of these points the scrolls are extended to join the octagons that are cut by the framing listens. This second octagon is surrounded by another one with straight sides, alternating between different sizes in groups of four, and without extended listens. These listens are half-scrolls of wooden joinery work, are decorated with tracery, and maintain the interweaving rule of one crossing above followed by one below.

At the base of the grooves of the tracery there are traces of "minium red." The length of the tracery work listens varies with their form and straight length before finishing at an angle forming a joint with another piece. These lattice work windows did not have glass inlaid in their grooving, as the listens show no trace of this. Between the tracery work frame and the listens with their interwoven design, there is a relief moulding.

We can see these lattice work windows in engravings and plates from the first half of the 19th century. It was this particular window that is shown by Lewis in his engraving of the *hammam* in 1834 (*Sketches and Drawings of the Alhambra,* London 1933-34) and it also figures in the sections on the *hammam* in the book by Owen Jones and Jules Goury *(Plans, Elevations, Sections and Details of the Alhambra,* London 1842) In 1827, these windows were dismounted and stored in the storehouse of the Alhambra, until they entered the Museo Nacional de Arte Hispanomu-

solmán, with the accession number 256-259; five of them are on display to the public. Rafael Contreras restored the *bayt al maslaj* between 1848 and 1856 (Contreras, *L'Alcazar et la grande Mosquêe d'Occident,* 4th ed., Madrid 1889, p. 285; Gallego y Burín, *La Alhambra,* Granada 1963, pp. 96, 97).

(*Antonio Fernández Puertas*)

164
Spain

Al-Andalus, Nasrid period
Door, 15th century
Wooden gates,
163 x 104 x 65 cm
From a house in calle de la Tiña, Granada
Granada, Museo Nacional de Arte Hispanomusulmán
n. 2.764, 2.765

The upper part of outdoor wooden gates decorated with geometrical themes and Damascene work on both sides, each featuring a different theme. The size of this gate indicates that it was for sealing an arched entrance, opening into the main rooms of the house through a portico in front of the central patio. These gates open on the outside around a longitudinal axis that fits onto a hinge pole, normally marble, and onto the upper part of poles projecting from the wall. These were made of wood, or wood and marble. According to all the

information on this subject, and in accordance with all the examples known, there are certain consistent elements in this type of double door, which, in the case of these examples and the ones preserved in the room of the Two Sisters and the Abencerrajes, also have a small, independent wicker gate that allows people to pass when the main gates are closed.

These doors belonged to number 34 calle de la Tiña in the Albaicín quarter of Granada, and were the property of Antonio Moreno Moreno who donated them to the museum, which they entered on September 28, 1951. Their external position, exposed to changes in temperature, sun, rain, and wood-eating insects,

has meant that they have lost almost all their lower parts. There is still enough decoration left – in the gilt section – to know what the original size was.

The main part of the gate is formed of planking consisting of horizontal boards joined together by long, iron nails, which then join with a wide frame at the same height as the Damascene work decoration that covers the gate on both sides.

The decoration is different on each side, always showing an unpatterned frame with marking gauges in the centre, on the jamb-posts, and at the upper and lower extremities. The rest of the piece is a decorative continuation, with an axis in the centre of each part

of the gate and one in the centre where they join. When the decoration continues into the space of the central jamb-posts it is directly worked, rather than being Damascene work like the rest.

On both sides we can see the remains of a layer of iron about, five centimetres wide running along the top and, according to the traces that can still be seen and their remains on the edge, they may very well have been repeated on the bottom part. It was nailed to the door by fourteen nails with square section bodies, and circular heads five centimetres in diameter, judging by the traces. They served to protect and reinforce the door as well as for decoration, like most other surviving Nasrid

doors, which also show sheet metal with undulating outlines and nails with heads decorated with mouldings. The decoration on both sides consists of different figures of eight formed by trimmed, interlocking listens that leave geometrical spaces that are filled with pieces of wood, joined to the centre of the door by iron nails with T-shaped heads.

On one side, the long axis of the door consisted of a grid of three squares high by two squares wide, formed of rows with eight-pointed stars at 45° in the corners and the centres of each one. They also formed part of another, smaller diagonal grid. The centre of each square has an eight-pointed 45° star, which is 22.5° in the case of the central star, because one of the irradiation stages is suppressed and a larger star or "unit" was carved directly.

Each 45° star is conglomerate and forms another 22.5° star, and in conjunction with the hexagonal tiles, forms another 45° eight-pointed star.

The centre of the diagonal scheme has an eight-pointed 45° star, opening at 27.5° with conglomerate, and is surrounded by alternate hexagonal tiles and smooth pieces to make up the square.

The geometric decoration is complemented by the remains of the original colour, black, in the widest marking gauges. The framing of the geometric pieces also shows remains of red, as does the interior of the conglomerate. Possibly, the surface of each geometric piece was painted, but there are no surviving traces of this. On the other side, the geometric structure is simpler. It is also a network of eight-pointed stars, opening to form another 22.5° star by the conglomerate placed between the corners and, again, radiating hexagons and serrated pieces that close the vertical grid the design is based on. In its corner, there are also eight-pointed 45° stars. From the evidence available, it would seem that the central part is not differentiated, as on the other side of the door.

The decoration also continues along the central jambs, where it is directly carved, and there are also holes left by locks and ironwork dating from after its creation. On this side, the rows that form the geometric grid are quite wide, maintaining the same width over their entire length except for the central star, which is reduced to half its size, maintaining its width in the 22.5° radiant line. Curiously, the knotting rules followed by these scrolls do not follow the normal pattern which is interlacing once above and once below. In fact, when the scrolls cross they are represented as two scrolls that run parallel and interweave, forming square and rhomboid knots.

On this side, there are also remains of the original polychrome, although all that is left are traces of black in the marking gauges.
(*Purificación Marinetto Sánchez*)

165
Iran

Isfahan
Panel of tiles,
approx. 1480-1481
Ceramics, 85.1 x 52.1 cm
From the tomb of Zayn al-Mulk
New York, Brooklyn Museum, 77.196.3
Exhibitions: Los Angeles, 1989
Bibliography:
GOLOMBAK-WILBER 1988, n. 171; LENTZ-LOWRY 1989, n. 144b, p. 257

Aq Qoyunlu was the name of a confederation of Turkish tribes called the *White Sheep* after the totem they carried around with them. The earliest reports of them date from 1378 in the region of Diyabkr in Anatolia. They submitted very early on to the Mongol empire (1370-1405) of Timur and his successors up until 1506. The fall of Constantinople in 1453, in the face of the Ottoman Empire, shook Christianity to its foundations. For this reason the Christian troops, with the support of the pope and the duke of Burgundy, sought the help of the Aq Qoyunlu. Venice collaborated by sending arms. Once the troops were assembled they moved eastwards without any setbacks, although they met opposition from subsequent Timur rulers on several occasions. They occupied Azerbaijan and territories in Iraq, Iran, and the Persian Gulf, choosing Tabriz as their capital. Between 1479 and 1490 they even occupied Isfahan in central Iran.

During the Aq Qoyunlu occupation of Isfahan various buildings were constructed, including the mausoleum where this panel comes from. It is one of a series of decorative elements which were taken out of Persia at the beginning of this century when the mausoleum was already a ruin. They are now to be found distributed among several museums in the West. There is an inscription, now in the Royal Ontario Museum in Toronto, Canada, which informs the ruler, Yaqub (1478-1490) of the master Jafar, who ordered the mausoleum to be built in order to house the tomb of his father Imad, Zayn al-Mulk (885 H /1480-1481).

This panel, like all others from the mausoleum, was made using a technique known in the West as faience. It is made in the same way as Mediterranean mosaics, using vitreous paste, but instead of using glass tiles the fragments are hand-cut into the shapes required, out of tiles glazed in a single colour which are then put together following a predetermined design. The name of the technique comes from the Italian city of Faenza where craftsmen tried to imitate Oriental pottery.

The panel is asymmetrical because it was part of the decoration of one of the doors. The decoration is divided into rectangular blocks, each one imitating the shape of an architectural niche. Each niche is decorated with floral patterns, in some cases with a white surround which stands out against a dark blue background. Stylistically speaking, the panel belongs to the Timur art which evolved during this period, in Iran.
(Klaus Brisch)

166
Spain

Al-Andalus, Mudéjar period
Panel of tiles, 16th century
Glazed ceramics, arris tiles,
105 x 104 cm
Granada, Museo Nacional
de Arte Hispanomusulmán,
7.299

A panel formed by a series of thirty-six tiles composing nine complete arrangements of circles of bows, executed using the arris technique.

The *cuerda seca* technique was developed prior to the arris technique and with very similar decorative results. There are marvellous examples of *cuerda seca* architectural ceramics dating from the reign of Muhammad V, during which the magnificent composition of the *alfiz* from the facade of the Puerta del Vino or Gate of Wine was also done. This technique allows the artist freedom of composition so that he can draw the theme of his choice in the correct decorative space.

The need for rapid production brought in the arris technique; this employs a mould, possibly made of wood, which is used to mark out the lines of the design by pressing down on the still unfired clay and uses the arris to separate the colours wherever necessary. The decorative composition of bows does not usually appear in its entirety on every tile; it is formed by the juxtaposition of four tiles.

This panel is a sample of late fourteenth and early fifteenth century tile production which, while showing Nasrid influences in its decoration, came before the introduction of Renaissance tiles from Seville; use of the latter then spread to the Secano area of the Alhambra, the workshops of the Tenorios, the Robles, and of Gaspar Hernández. Hernández was married to Luisa Tenorio, (who may have been Christian) and was a Moor who had stayed in Granada after the expulsion of the Moors.
(Purificación Marinetto Sánchez)

Images of the Divine

Religion is rooted in the deepest part of both
the human being and his communities. In
every culture man has sought the reason for
his own existence and for that of the visible
world, and has believed it to be found in
some transcending absolute, in one or various
gods who dominate the universe or the
powers that govern it. Religion – and, for that
matter, magic –, imply worship, ritual and
myth and, above all, the symbolic presence of
those gods or powers, inhabitants of a
macrocosm conceived in the image of the
microcosm of man. The works in this
field reveal man's experience of religion
around 1492 and on occasions reveal
that the presence of the sacred, through
art, goes beyond geographical distances
and belief systems.

167
Portugal

Attributed to Cristovão de Figuereido (approx. 1480-1490, after 1543)
Christ among the Sages, 16th century
Oil painting on wood, 120.5 x 142.5 cm
From the Convento de la Encarnación of Lisbon, Lisbon, Museu Nacional de Arte Antiga, 1575
Exhibitions: Lisbon, 1940; Lisbon, 1941
Bibliography: LISBON 1938; Aa.Vv. 1951 and 1956; Aa.Vv. 1957

Cristovão de Figueireido is one of the outstanding artists of emmanueline and, above all, Joanine painting. The identification of this piece of work is based on a letter from Gregorio Lourenço to king Dom João III concerning the panels at Santa Cruz de Coimbra and a description of these panels provided by Mendanha (1540); these panels date from approximately 1522-1530. The other sound basis for its identification is the altarpiece by Ferreirim (1533-1534).
Painter to cardinal Dom Alfonso, Cristovão de Figueiredo was probably trained in the workshop of Jorge Alfonso alongside his colleague and collaborator Gregorio Fernández. The panel called *Christ among the Sages* has on occasion been attributed to the collaboration of the two. It is remarkable for its sense of space, the composition consisting of progressive planes which dwindle towards arcades in the background. The confrontation with the large group of sages includes Joseph and the Virgin Mary; the isolation of the Holy Child, seated under a canopy of rich brocade, has its counterpoint in the still life of books in the foreground, a detail which emphasizes the Flemish character of the composition.
(Joan Sureda i Pons)

168
Portugal

Maestro de la Madre de Deus, identified with Jorge Alfonso
(approx. 1470-approx. 1540)
Adoration of the Shepherds, 1515 (according to an inscription on another panel of the same altarpiece)
Oil painting on wood, 165 x 137 cm
From the church of Madre de Deus, Lisbon
Lisbon, Museu Nacional de Arte Antiga, 2096
Exhibitions: Lisbon, 1940; Lisbon, 1958; Lisbon, 1983
Bibliography: CORREIA 1921, LX; GUSMAO 1960; SANTOS 1961, series 2, n. 16-17

Two important groups of paintings come from the church of Madre de Deus in Lisbon. One of these is the group of panels telling the story of Santa Auta, originally located in the sacristy, and the other is the group of panels, including the *Adoration of the Shepherds*, which were located in the high choir of the church. This group of pictures consists of seven panels (*Annunciation, Adoration of the Shepherds, Adoration of the Magi, Appearance of Christ to the Virgin Mary, Ascension, Pentecost and Assumption*) and were originally attributed (José de Figuereido) to Gregorio Lopes who collaborated with his son, Cristóvão Lopes, who became court painter in 1550. Once the panels had been cleaned and restored for a large exhibition of primitive Portuguese painting (Lisbon, 1940) the date 1515 was found written on one of them and Reis Santos, who had allowed the attribution of the painting to lie with Gregorio Lopes for some time, called the unknown painter the "Mestre de Madre de Deus" or the "Mestre de 1515."

The problematic identification of the painter did not rest there; the quality of his work led Martín Soria and Gregorio Kubler, in their *Art and Architecture in Spain and Portugal*, to see in it the hand of the court painter Jorge Alfonso, an attribution which, with reservations, has been maintained until the present day.

The *Adoration of the Shepherds* is one of the most beautiful scenes of the piece, the first one in Portuguese painting to have this iconography in which two worlds are clearly described: the heavenly and the earthly. They share a background consisting of a ruined building whose extremely precise geometry allows us to see a landscape which cannot be interpreted as anything less than metsysian.

In the celestial world four angel musicians play accurately painted instruments, the close detail of their robes compensated for by their magnificently outstretched wings. In the lower part of the panel, apart from the strongly contrasting red and blue of the robes of Joseph and the Virgin Mary, the figure of the Holy Child stands out; he is resting on straw, which has been depicted in painstaking detail, on top of a large, severely cut stone.

The scene, which includes the ox and ass, reaches the peak of realism in the figures of the three shepherds. The one in the foreground is lost in prayer, his crook having fallen onto the curiously paved floor. He has put down his basket of eggs and his shepherd's flute, forming a genuine still life; the second shepherd, who also has a musical instrument, has put down his honey pot and has piously joined his hands in prayer. The last shepherd, bearded and dishevelled, has a natural quality as he presents the Holy Child with his milk churn and bares his head as a sign of respect; this is obviously the adoration of the common people, of men cured and tanned by the sun for a little naked god with a white and unblemished skin.

(Joan Sureda i Pons)

169
Spain/Italy

Pedro Fernández (a painter from Murcia who worked in Lombardy, Naples, and Rome between 1500 and 1518, and is documented as being in Gerona between 1519 and 1521)
The Adoration of the Shepherds, approx. 1508-1509
Oil painting on wood,
110 x 72 cm
Pedrola, Colección de la Duquesa de Villahermosa
Bibliography:
Crowe-Cavalcaselle (1871)
1911-1912; Ferrari 1963,
n. 157, pp. 14-29;
D'Agostino 1972; Navarro
1982, LXVII, n. 14,
pp. 37-68; Navarro 1985,
n. 42, pp. 62-64; Naldi 1986,
n. 42; Giusti-Leone de Castris
1985; Frangi 1991

The origins of this piece are unknown; however, there is a verbal tradition in the Villahermosa family, to whom we are grateful for this information, which indicates that the piece was brought to Spain from Naples by Don Juan de Aragón, Count of Ribagorça. Juan de Aragón was the grandson of Ferdinand the Catholic king and lived in Naples from 4 June 1504 until 8 October 1509 (D'Agostino 1972, vol. 1, pp. 14-18); and so, if we take this information as being accurate the *ante quem* date of the panel is 1509.
The attribution to Pseudo Bramantino-Pedro Fernández was made by Zeri and published by F. Navarro (1982, pp. 50-51). Until that time the piece had gone practically unnoticed, generally assumed to be an Italian work from the early 16th century. In the publication mentioned above, F. Navarro held it to be a work from the Lombardy period of Pseudo Bramantino, and that it was painted prior to 1515. Some elements, such as the modelling of the Virgin's face, which is very Leonardo-like, made Navarro consider the possibility of the collaboration

of another master. However, Navarro (1985, pp. 63) partly rectified this opinion and proposed setting the date earlier, basing it on what was to be Pseudo Bramantino's first stay in Lombardy (approx. 1507). This chronology was upheld by P. Leone de Castris (1985, pp. 7,8) and R. Naldi (1986, pp. 238).
The *Villahermosa Nativity*, as this *Adoration of the Shepherds* is sometimes also known, is a work saturated with Lombard artistic culture and, more specifically, that which took shape around Bramante, Bramantino, and Zenale, without forgetting Leonardo da Vinci.
The artistic development dominating the composition is monumental and classical with an evident predilection for ruins, and is an offshoot of the development of prints such as the famous one by Prevedari taken from a drawing by Bramante (*Interior of Temple with Figures*, 1483). But one should not forget that the concept of architectural surroundings in this panel appears, for example, in paintings from Atri, contentiously attributed to Pedro de Aponte, and also in the work of Francesco Pagano with whom Pseudo Bramantino had obvious links (paintings in the chapter house at Valencia cathedral, 1472-1476). This makes one think of the early training of Pedro Fernández, who studied in Valencia with Francesco Pagano, and which would explain the first artistic steps of one of the great painters of the Spanish Renaissance.
As for the panel itself, apart from pointing out the significant Nordic and specifically Flemish influence (detailed floral decoration – similar to that to be seen in the work of Cesare da Sesto-Candela de San José and also to that adorning Saint Joseph in the altarpiece by Caponapoli) the relationship with Zenale is fundamental.
This can be seen when one

compares the angel musicians in the Villahermosa panel with those on the organ loft doors from the Santa Maria de Brera Church in Milan, which are currently part of the Sormani collection (Lugaro d'Erba). The identity of the person responsible for painting this heavenly choir has been much disputed, since an attribution to Leonardo can be seen written on one of the panels (1780). The attribution to Leonardo was maintained until the 19th century when Cavalcaselle and Crowe (1871, 1912, II, pp. 346-347) attributed the panels to Bramantino. Subsequently, they have been attributed to Butinone, Zenale (Suida), Civerchio (Berenson), etc. until M.L. Ferrari (1963, p. 21) found documentation which confirmed that Zenale had worked on the Santa Maria di Brera Church (1506-1507).

The treatment of some of the musical angels and the triangular composition of the whole are identical in both works, making us think that Pseudo Bramantino was involved in the Sormani panels or at least had direct knowledge of them. This fixes the period Pseudo Bramantino lived in Milan as being around 1506-1507, and makes it possible to make the previously mentioned *ante quem* dating of the Villahermosa panel.
(*Joan Sureda i Pons*)

170
Italy

Giovanni Bellini (Venice, 1430-approx. 1516)
and collaborators
Annunciation, after 1489, date of the completing of the Santa Maria dei Miracoli Church in Venice
Oil painting on canvas, 224 x 106 cm
Organ loft door from the Santa Maria dei Miracoli Church, Venice
Venice, Gallerie dell'Accademia, 959 (cat. 734)
Exhibitions: Leningrad, 1986; Sydney, 1988
Bibliography: MOSCHINI MARCONI 1955 (with preceding bibliography); NEPI SCIRÉ-VALCANOVER 1985; GOFFEN 1989, pp. 279-280

Santa Maria dei Miracoli is a small church built between 1481 and 1489 by Pietro Lombardo and his sons Antonio and Tullio. It has been said that it is more fantastic than real, fruit of the brushes of Bellini and Carpaccio. If the marble facing its exterior has suffered from the passage of time, the grey and pink marble cladding its interior still reflects the scene of the *Annunciation* painted on the organ loft doors. Although the church retains much of its decoration in terms of both sculpture and painting, the organ loft doors must have been one of the most valued treasures, as can be seen on reading the writings of the Venetian painter and art dealer M. Boschini in his book *Le ricche miniere della pittura veneziana* (Venice 1664, an edition added to in the 18th century by A.M. Zanetti). Boschini attributes the doors, on whose inner faces Saint Peter and Saint Paul appear (lost when the whole was dismantled during the Napoleonic invasion), to Pier Maria Pennacchi. The two wings of the door were submitted to the exhibition at the Gallerie dell'Accademia in 1907 as coming from two different places. They have generally been at-

tributed to the workshop of Giovanni Bellini, although several references to Carpaccio have also been made. However, the possibility that the design may be by Giovanni Bellini and the execution of the work by some of his assistants does not solve the problem of the attribution of this beautiful painting, which cannot under any circumstances be considered as coming from a workshop.

It is indisputable that Bellini's art is present in the work, and the treatment of some parts such as the central panel may owe something to some of his relatively early work such as the *Coronation of the Virgin of Pesaro*, a direct parallel; but the canvases also seem to be influenced by Pierfrancesco and even by the Flemish school.

However, the Bellini and Carpaccio of the *Story of Saint Ursula* have nothing to do with the *Dream of Saint Ursula*, despite the compositional similarities, especially in the positioning of the angel (although light is treated in a very different way), and do not explain the considerable intellectual force of the composition or the geometrical construction of spaces and robing. For this we must turn to the artistic climate in Lombardy, to Bramantino and Bramante.

The treatment of the roof vaulting or the angel's robes bear direct reference to this climate, something which several authors have wanted to see in works by Pier Maria Pennacchi such as *Uomini d'arme* of the Onigo tomb in the church of San Nicolò in Treviso. All of the works attributed to Pennacchi, a painter who was born in Treviso in 1464 and who died around 1515 (the prophets of the Santa Maria dei Miracoli Church in Venice, the organ loft doors in the Church of Santa Maria degli Angeli in Murano, the *Lactating Virgin* in the Museo Civico in Bassano, the *Death of the Virgin*

in the Gallerie dell'Accademia, and the *Salvator mundi* in the chapel of the Holy of Holies in Florence cathedral) do not go to make up a homogenous body of work by themselves or with the lost panels from Berlin.

The *Annunciation* from Santa Maria dei Miracoli can be provisionally attributed, as Giovanna Nepi Sciré has shown, to Pier Maria Pennacchi, but this does not account for the high quality of the work unless we make another revision

of the career and catalogue of the works attributed to the painter from Treviso.
(*Joan Sureda i Pons*)

171
Italy

Ludovico Mazzolino
(Ferrara,
approx. 1480-approx. 1530)
Circumcision, approx. 1510
Oil painting on wood,
40 x 29 cm
From Palazzo Pitti
in Florence, in possession
of the Uffizi family in 1796
Florence, Galleria degli
Uffizi, 1890-1355
Bibliography: ZAMBONI 1968
(with preceding
bibliography); ZAMBONI 1978,
pp. 144-145

Ludovico Mazzolino, trained
at the Ercole de Roberti and
Maineri school, shows from
the start an eclectic personality
which brings him close to
northern painting (Dürer),
either directly or via Jacopo de
Barbari and de Lotto, as well
as submerging him in Gior-
gione-like experimentation.
Taking this into account, what
most characterizes him is his
tendency to recall the antique
world in architectural terms,
where forms are dominated
by grisaille reliefs, and the
grandiloquent drama with
which he treats some themes
(versions on the *Massacre of
the Innocents*, Galleria Doria
Pamphili, Uffizi). But in Mazzolino's case the "antique"
loses its classical quality and,
while not being part of the
mannerist break with tradition, it creates, in the same
way as the work of Amico As-
pertini did at this time, a
universe of bizarre forms
which was hardly going to
please the clients of the day.
This may explain the career of
the artist from Ferrara who,
despite his early involvement
with large undertakings, such
as the decoration of the walls
of the new Church of Santa
Maria degli Angeli in Ferrara
(decoration destroyed in 1604)
and that of Lucrezia Borgia's
camerini, became a painter of
small pictures for family cha-
pels as well as painting *studi-
oli* for private palaces.
Precise dating of the *Circumcision* is difficult if it is true

that the "stylistic romanticism"
which Longhi attributed to it
can already be found in a *Circumcision*, dated 1511, which
was part of the Manning collection. This may therefore be
a reference point for the Uffizi
Circumcision.
(*Joan Sureda i Pons*)

Spain

San Benito de Valladolid altarpiece

The most important and complex piece of Alonso Berruguete's work is probably the altarpiece from the high altar of the San Benito Church in Valladolid where Berruguete worked as a tracer, sculptor, painter, and colourist. The work was commissioned in 1527, but its completion was beset with difficulties because Berruguete could not find a valuer to act on his behalf. He finally appointed the painter Julio de Aquilis. Complaints were registered by the valuer appointed by the monastery, Andrés de Nájera, and the case was judged by Felipe Vigarny. The verdict (1533) specified various defects which were to be set right by Alonso Berruguete. One year later, the monastery accepted the altarpiece.

The work took the form of an imposing triptych with slanting lateral wings and a hemispherical central panel (or rather, to be more precise, semi-elliptical), finished with scalloping which, like a canopy, sheltered the altar itself, thus demarcating the sacred area. A profusion of sculptures, reliefs, painted panels, and various decorative motifs (friezes, medallions, pilasters, and balustrades) go to make up a tremendous whole whose rich colour scheme is dominated by blue and gold. Around 1845, much of the altar piece was dismounted and moved from the Benedictine monastery to what was then the Fine Arts Museum, where in 1851 it was exhibited in large pieces, some of it separately. In 1881 parts of it still remained in the church as part of the structure of the altarpiece. The fragments were progressively dismounted and taken to the Museum until 1930, when Constantino Candeira embarked on the reconstruction work, by which time it was a sorry sight. However, the effort was worthwhile and

although there may be some inaccuracies he managed to reassemble several of the sections, identifying the correct positions of the reliefs, sculptures, paintings, and decorative fragments. Using this as a basis, Mariano de Cossio painted a canvas which was intended to represent the original appearance of the whole. It is inevitable that this altarpiece, which Berruguete must have executed with the help of a large workshop, should vary in style and quality, corrections and adjustments, some of which were undoubtedly carried out once the altarpiece was set up, and should contain a tremendous and inventive wealth of decorative elements.
(*Luís Luna Moreno*)

172
Spain

Alonso Berruguete (Paredes de Nava, approx. 1486-Toledo, 1561)
Adoration of the Kings, 1527-1533
Sculptures, carved and coloured wood,
133 x 106 x 40 cm
From the altarpiece of the high altar at the monastery of San Benito de Valladolid
Valladolid, Museo Nacional de Escultura, 271
Exhibitions: Madrid, 1961; Madrid, 1972
Bibliography: Arfe 1585 (ed. 1979), II, fol. 2 v.; Bosarte 1804, p. 156, 359; Llaguno y Amirola 1829, I, p. 11; Martí-Monsó 1901, p. 137; Agapito y Revilla 1910, p. 542; Agapito y Revilla 1913, p. 226; Agapito y Revilla 1920-1929, I, p. 85; Agapito y Revilla 1926, p.81; García Chico 1941, p. 12; Gómez Moreno 1941, p. 159; Candeira Pérez 1945, p. 15; Azcárate 1958, p. 146; Candeira Pérez 1959; Wattenberg 1963, p. 107; Wattenberg 1966, p. 29; Camón Aznar 1967, p. 178; Zaragoza Pascual 1976, p. 222; Martín Gonzalez

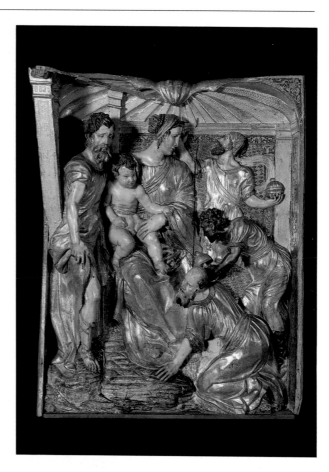

1977, p. 27; Wattenberg 1978, p. 11; Camón Aznar 1980, p. 62; Rodríguez Martínez 1981, p. 231

The relief of the *Adoration of the Kings* was found on the lower part of the altarpiece of the San Benito Church where other themes from the childhood of Jesus also appeared: the relief of the *Circumcision* and panels showing the *Birth* and the *Flight into Egypt*.

This scene is remarkable for Alonso Berruguete's disregard of the rules of true perspective, producing strange spatial contractions typical of the Medieval world. In this way, each character's size bears relation not to the space they occupy in the picture but to the importance they have within the story. This recovery of values which the Renaissance obliterated is not, however, strange to the mannerist aesthetic and thus helps us to define Alonso Berruguete.

Colours help to maintain the ambiguity of the relief. There are some eye-catching elements, such as Joseph's sandals which are painted and not carved, while in some areas the colours "jump out" of the carved forms producing a sense of imprecision and movement, particularly in the area around the three wise men. This contrasts with the distant serenity of the Virgin Mary; her figure, that of a Roman matron, and the remarkable profile of her face both carry a clear reference to the classical world.
(*Luis Luna Moreno*)

173
Italy

Cesare da Sesto (Sesto Calende, Varese, 1477-Milan, 1523)
Virgin with the Holy Child, Saint Isabel, Saint John, and Saint Michael (The Virgin with the scales)
Oil painting on canvas, 95 x 69.5 cm
Paris, Musée du Louvre, 785
Bibliography: Villot 1849, n. 1487; Ricci 1913, n. 1604; Hautecoeur 1926, n. 1604; Berenson 1968, fig. 1502; Bora, 1982, p. 175; Giusti-Leone de Castris 1985, pp. 104-127

From the collection of Louis XIV, this *Virgin with the Scales* appears in a series of catalogues from the Louvre as the work of an anonymous imitator of Leonardo, and Hautecoeur (1926) sees fit to validate the attribution to Cesare da Sesto. Da Sesto trained in Milan, doubtless under the influence of Leonardo, and later went to Rome where he came under the influence of Peruzzi and, as was pointed out by F. Bologna, most probably Rafael too. The *Virgin with the Scales* from the Louvre is probably an example of the phase most strongly influenced by Leonardo in which echoes of versions of the *Virgin of the Rocks* are quite obvious.

Reconstruction of the training period of Cesare da Sesto is, of course, difficult. He was mentioned briefly by P. Summonte in his *Lettera a Marcantonio Michiel* (1526) and also by Vasari in his *Vite*, making experts such as P. Giusti and P. Leone de Castris (1988, pp. 104, 127) doubt the attribution of the work, but they are unable to put forward another alternative. In fact, the work has not been studied in detail and is an extraordinary example of the creative abilities of the followers of Leonardo, skills which Roberto Longhi questioned in his study *Il Costa ritrattista* when referring to Predis and Conti:

"questi macabri imbalsamatori di busti in cera e cute, questi tristi descrittori di beltà rifredde, incapaci, anche una volta sola, di rigalvanizzare i cadaveri che poco prima avevano pure tremato sotto il tocco di Leonardo traumaturgo anatomista." In this case, the judgement of Roberto Longhi has gone unheard in the main exhibitions, studies, and talks on Leonardo; these studies have of course done little more than scratch the surface of the various prob-

lems, including the training of Cesare da Sesto. As for the *Virgin with the Scales* only some additional notes can be made, such as those by Giulio Bora on the occasion of the exhibition entitled "Zenale e Leonardo" (1982). Following indications given by Vasari, which were also taken up by Suida, Bottari, and Campori, he shows the possibility of Bernazzano having collaborated in the treatment of the landscape in the picture.
(*Joan Sureda i Pons*)

Francesco Bonsignori
(Verona,
approx. 1455-Caldiero,
Verona, 1519)
*Virgin with the Holy Child
and Saint Margaret*, end
of the 15th century
Oil painting on canvas,
73 x 56.3 cm
Verona, Museo di
Castelvecchio, 2166
Bibliography; AVENA 1914,
p. 122; AVENA 1949, p. 74;
GARAVAGLIA 1967, p. 120;
MARINELLI 1990, pp. 641-642;
MARINELLI 1991, p. 40

The *Virgin with the Holy
Child and Saint Margaret* has
always been classified as belonging to the Mantegna can-
non, although nobody has
ever directly ascertained this.
The composition does in fact
make use of Mantegna prototypes such as the *Madonna
with Cherubim* from Brera
and some parts of the *Holy
Family* from the Museo di Castelvecchio. The figure, holding
a small cross and a palm frond
and accompanied by the dragon, is indisputably Saint Margaret, and was more fre-
quently painted in Mantua
than in Verona.

On top of the debt to Mantegna this piece also includes
stylistic features corresponding to those of the Veronese
artist Francesco Bonsignori in
the works he produced prior
to his move to Mantua in
around 1490. These are particularly evident in the face
and snakelike hair of the saint,
the general treatment of the
hair and robing, and the rigid
quality reminiscent of wooden
sculpture apparent in other aspects such as the hands; these
all go to strengthen the parallel with the most elegant Man-
tegna-type treatments.

Even the reflectography of the
painting constitutes a design
with fairly clear outlines which
differs from that of the Mantegna *Holy Family* from Castelvecchio; the latter is tenser
and is of great beauty, perhaps
because of the use of silver

point. This hardness also
makes the involvement of
Francesco Bonsignori feasible,
who was still enjoying being
in the lime light as main court
painter at Mantua. Within the
limits of its characterization
and its poor state of conservation, the quality of the painting
is still undeniably and unmis-
takably different from that of
the work of Mantegna's other
close collaborators. It was
painted more or less at the
end of the 15th century.
(*Sergio Marinelli*)

175
Italy

Tommaso Fiamberti
(Campione, documented in
1498-Cesena, approx. 1525)
*Virgin with the Holy Child
and Angels,*
approx. 1495-1498
Stone sculpture, 77 x 57 cm
Urbino, Galleria Nazionale
delle Marche
Exhibitions: Japan
1990-1991, n. 17
Bibliography: SERRA 1930
pp. 48-82; ROTONDI 1948,
p. 136-194; ROTONDI 1950,
p. 474; MAZZINI 1982, p. 273

This *Virgin with the Holy Child*, generally attributed to Tommaso Fiamberti, adheres to a specific iconography which was very popular in the 15th century. It is clearly derived from Tuscan models and has obvious analogies with other works on the same theme by the same artist which are conserved in the church of Saints Stephen and Cecilia in Florence, the Bargello Museum, also in Florence, and the Ducal Palace in Urbino.

There is little information and documented work on this artist – he belonged to a group of sculptors who were part of the *Quattrocento* movement in northern and central Italy whose activity became known prior to 1498.

Based in Romaña, in 1501 he completed a tomb in the Santa Maria dei Servi Church in Forlì as well as the font in the cathedral. In Tuscany he collaborated with other sculptors on the Camaldoli chapel.

One can venture the hypothesis that he worked on the Ducal Palace in Urbino alongside Tuscan artists who had been active in the city for some time previously. He probably assisted in the creation of some of the rooms in the west wing and, particularly, in the execution of some of the angels sculpted onto the cornice in one of the rooms. Previously known as the "Master of the marble Madonna," Fiamberti had an eclectic

training derived from Tuscan models, particularly from the *Madonna* sculpted by Antonio Rossellino in 1477 for the Opera of Florence cathedral (now in the Bargello). The lips, mouths, and noses of Fiamberti's two faces are treated in the same way as that of Rossellino's *Madonna.*

The vigorous plasticity and solidity of form of Rossellino's late work are carried over to Fiamberti's sculpture and there combine with the delicacy, grace, and ingenuous,

childlike sweetness derived from the Mino da Fiesole, but with vastly differing results.

The high relief is executed in a very concise and synthetic fashion, robbing it of any robustness or expressiveness.

The composition, execution, and feline expression of the two characters, almost as if they were in an ironically festive atmosphere; the treatment of the robing draped in the usual way but to a decorative end, are elements which characterize Fiamberti's work.

Despite conventional belief, the high relief in fact does not lack a kind of monumental quality. Fiamberti's effort to follow his models is similar to the way he shows his originality in the defining of an image.

(*Claudia Caldari Giovannelli*)

176
Spain

Pedro Berruguete (Paredes de Nava, approx. 1440-Avila, approx. 1504)
Virgin and Child,
approx. 1475
Oil painting on panel,
65 x 51.5 cm
Madrid, private collection
Exhibitions: Madrid, 1961; Madrid, 1987
Bibliography: Angulo Iñíguez 1943, n. 56, pp.111-115; Angulo Iñíguez 1954, XII, p. 100; Madrid 1961, n. 119; Camón Aznar 1970, XXIV, p. 183; Madrid 1987, pp. 20-21

The theme of the Virgin and Child is not usual in Berruguete's work. There are relatively few versions which can be attributed to him and experts are sure that the one in question, along with those in the Madrid Municipal Museum and the Prado, is one of the most important. This was commented on extensively for the first time by Angulo, who considered the piece to be unusual in the Castilian painter's career.

Although the iconography may appear conventional, it is not at all the case because of the symbolic load of the representation. What would otherwise be a *Lactating Virgin* changes its meaning completely thanks to the symbols and inscriptions accompanying it; the Holy Child, sitting in the lap of the Virgin Mary, abandons the breast of his mother although he sweetly hangs on to her little finger and turns his face towards the two angels who are presenting the implements of the Passion from on high: the lance, the crown of thorns, the cross, and the scourge. The suffering to come is not only patent in this wordless dialogue of looks between the angels and the Holy Child, but is actually emphasized by the entreating *miserere* inscribed on the window ledge: *miserere mei mater dei domine mea*. The forewarning of the Passion is

undeniably stressed by the presence of the psalter – the L (Ll) pointing to the word *miserere* – and the cherries and farmyard stories hung on the wall in the background in symmetry with the angels.

The presence of the gotisant canopy, consisting of beautifully made gold brocade and some secondary elements such as the Virgin's halo, the crystal balls of the throne and the little columns of the throne arms are all details of marked, although not exclusively, Flemish character, and have meant that the essentially Italian quality of the piece has not been fully appreciated.

This is doubtless what Buendía was referring to when he mentioned, in relation to this piece and the corresponding one in the Prado, the series called "*Artes liberales*" which Berruguete painted, with or without collaboration, during his stay in Urbino. In fact, neither the entirety nor the painstaking detail of this *Virgin and Child* can be admired without bearing in mind *La Gramatica* housed in the National Gallery in London.

The positioning on the parapet of the beautifully executed psalter is evidence of a concept of space not far removed from that apparent in the positioning of the helmet in the portrait of *Duke Federico di Montefeltro with his son Guidobaldo* (Ducal Palace, Urbino).

This all leads us to believe that the panel should be considered as having been painted in the early years of the "return home" of Pedro Berruguete. It should also be thought of in clear relation to the altarpiece at Paredes de Nava which Lafuente Ferrari also believed to date from around 1483, that is to say shortly after the painter's return from Italy.
(*Joan Sureda i Pons*)

177
Spain

Pedro Berruguete, (Paredes de Nava, approx. 1440-Avila, approx. 1504)
The Appearance of the Virgin to a Dominican community, approx. 1499
Oil on wood, 130 x 86 cm
Madrid, Museo del Prado, 615

The Virgin, surrounded by angel musicians, appears and blesses the community. To the left, four characters appear through a door and in the cloisters to the right a demon is beating a friar. The panel, along with its accompanying panels numbers 609 and 610 in the Prado catalogue, formed part of the altarpiece dedicated to Santo Domingo de Guzman in the Church of Santo Tomás in Avila. It came to the Prado from the Museo de la Trinidad which had been founded using funds from repayments. It was numbered 1670 in the inventory of the Museo de la Trinidad.
(*Museo del Prado*)

178
Greece

The Catalan Virgin,
mid-15th century
Fresco painting,
117 x 157 cm
From a demolished church in Athens
Athens, Byzantine Museum

A semi-circular fresco. In the centre of the composition is the Virgin, seated on a red bolster on a low throne against a violet background with grey and white floral decoration. She is holding Christ in her arms and is gently touching the legs of the Holy Child with her fingertips. The Virgin is positioned frontally with an upright torso and is looking straight ahead. Christ, holding a parchment in his left hand and making a blessing with his right, lifts his head and looks at his Mother. In two of the four trees positioned symmetrically on either side of the group are heraldic coats of arms flanked by the

initials of the owners in Gothic script; F.A. on the left and L.S. on the right. Below the gently curving line which finishes off the scene there is a series of rhombus-shaped motifs. The form and composition of the fresco, along with the representation of the *Virgin Seated with the Holy Child*, reminds us of examples from the main apses of Byzantine churches. As can be seen from its arched form, the fresco was taken out of the tympanum of the door of the now demolished Athens church. It is said that it was the church of the prophet Elias and lay next to the gate of the Roman *agora* and the church of the Taxlarches. The Virgin is known as *The Catalan Virgin* since it was thought that the coat of arms belonged to the Catalans who were masters of Athens in the 14th century. It is more likely that she represents the *Genoese Virgin*, confirming the old theory of D. Kansbouroglou that the shield on the left is that of

Francesco or Franco Acciaiuoli, duke of Athens from 1451 to 1460, and the shield on the right is that of the Genoese nobleman Lorenzo Spinola, who is said to have died in 1453 during the rule of Franco Acciaiuoli. It is known that a Genoese community with its own church did exist in the commercial centre of Athens, next to the entrance to the market. The coats of arms with initials, the iconography and the style allow us to date this fresco as being from the mid-15th century. The iconography, which is unusual in its wealth of detail, is also found in two icons of the *Virgin Seated Holding the Holy Child* (Vrephokratousa): one from Cyprus and dated from the first half of the 15th century, and the other from a private collection in Greece which dates from around 1500. The delicacy of the Virgin in the fresco, her position and the fineness of the drawing of the face and neck, which are slightly elongated, make it more similar to the Cypriot icon.

The fresco presents us with a unique and attractive synthesis of elements from the Byzantine and late Gothic styles. The Byzantine Virgin appears against a Western background which reminds us of tapestries of the era with their decoration of trees and floral motifs. The grace and spirit of the piece are typical of the late Gothic period, as are the rich fabric of the robes, the soft, modelled contours of the faces, the gaze of the young Virgin and the childlike features of Christ. The Athens fresco was probably commissioned by Lorenzo Spinola for the church of the Genoese community and is probably the only example from this period and style in Athens to have survived. Whether it followed a Byzantine line to attract foreigners or was done by a Greek painter following specific instructions to adapt the Byzantine model to the taste and technique of Western techniques, it is an exemplary piece of Western craftsmanship. Whichever is the case, this combination of Byzantine and late-Gothic pictorial techniques is an example of the "hellenizing" tendencies of the Genoese who settled in Athens and of the influence which Byzantine art had on their art and culture.

(*Myrtali Acheimastou-Potamianou*)

179
Spain

Alonso Berruguete
(Paredes de Nava,
approx. 1488-Toledo 1561)
*The Virgin with the Child
and the Young Saint John,*
approx. 1516

260

Oil painting on wooden
panel, diameter 85 cm
Florence, Palazzo Vecchio
Exhibitions: Florence, 1940;
Florence, 1956; Florence,
1980, Siena, 1990
Bibliography: KUSENBURG
1931, p. 128; LENSI 1934,
p. 45; FLORENCE 1940, p. 148;
BECHERUCCI 1944, p. 27;
BAROCCHI 1950, p. 44-45;
LONGHI 1953, p. 9; BALDINI
1956, p. 115; PROTO PISANI
1980, p. 77; SRICCHIA SANTORO
1990, p. 404-405

In 1926 Carlo Loeser donated
this painting to the Florence
Commune and was then
placed in the Palazzo Vecchio.
In 1931 Kusenburg attributed
it to Rosso, and Becherucci
seconded this opinion in 1944.
In 1953 a daring article by
Longhi brought Alonso Berruguete into the limelight as
author of a certain number of
paintings in Italy. Berruguete's
prestige in Spain came from
his having been a painter in
the service of Carlos V, but his
reputation centred chiefly
around his work as a sculptor.
Allende-Salazar had brought
to light information referring
to his stay in Italy, saying, for
example, that "Berruguete was
Michelangelo's companion in
Rome," and in his argument,
Longhi used Vasari's references, such as a letter from
Michelangelo in 1508. Filippino Lippi had died in 1504
leaving an unfinished painting
in Alonso Berreguete's hands
for completion; this painting
has been placed in the Musée
du Louvre and shows *The
Crowning of the Virgin*; according to Longhi, the angels
on both sides of the Virgin are
Berruguete's work. As a result
of this, more paintings were
attributed to Berruguete,
among them the one studied
here, a *Salome* (Uffizi), and

others. Zeri supported Longhi's line of reasoning, expanding the catalogue of Berruguete's work in Italy.
Professor Angulo showed
some reservations in 1954, but
supported the basic idea of
Berruguete's participation in
the *Crowning* of Louvre. Longhi, however, attached greater
significance to Berruguete's
work, believing him to have
had a fundamental influence
on the new mannerism as well
as on Rosso and Pontormo.
Freedberg also supported
Longhi in his attributions, especially with reference to the
painting studied here, which
was known as *Tondo Loeser*.
He did, however, reduce the
significance of Berruguete's
role, feeling that his work represented the resolution of the
expressionist roots of his
Spanish training rather than
the evolution of a classical
concept (which he did not

know of). Post appreciates Filippino Lippi's influence on
Berruguete and considers that
it is the *Tondo Loeser* that
shows the most links with the
painter in Spain.
The painting is now unanimously accredited to Ber-
ruguete and has been shown
in prestigious exhibitions,
such as those dedicated to
Pontormo and the art of the
Medici period. Although rec-
ognizing that this painting, as
well as that of Salome, are
"very precise and brilliant"
examples of early mannerism,
Paolucci estimates that Berruguete's stay in Italy was too
brief for him to have been
able to influence the direction
of its art to any greater extent.
The composition of this painting is influenced by a work of
Raffaello's, the *Madonna in
the Chair* (1514-1515), which
determines the date *post
quem*: 1516. The stylistic

change is evident, however:
passing from the classicism of
Raphael, based on spherical
structures, to a mannerism
based on vertical ones. It is
also believed that the engraved frame is Berruguete's
work as it is similar to those
of the tondos of St. Jerome
and St. Catherine produced by
the painter for the *Mejorada*
altarpiece (Museo Nacional de
Escultura, Valladolid).
(*Juan José Martín González*)

180
Italy

Florentine school
Story of the Passion
of Christ, first half
of the 16th century
Oil painting on canvas,
95 x 170 cm
Florence, Loeser collection
Exhibitions: Philadelphia,
1989
Bibliography: LOESER 1922;
GAMBA 1934, pp. 380-386;
LENSI 1934, pp. 12, 31-32;
ZERI 1962, pp. 216-236,
314-326; BACCI 1966, p. 19

This curious canvas is a totally scenographic work which, within a wide panorama centred on Roman architectural ruins, shows scenes from the Passion of Christ. Donating the painting to the city of Florence in his will, Loeser presented it as an "opera tarda di Piero di Cosimo, che deve avere impiegato un aiuto per dare gli ultimo tocchi ai piccoli gruppi a distanza media."
The canvas, while sharing some elements that are proper to Piero di Cosimo, such as the breadth of the landscape, cannot be attributed to him, nor to the Imolan painter Gaspare Sacchi, as was proposed by C. Gamba, an attribution which has been further distorted on occasion, when Gaspare Sacchi has been confused with Piro Francesco Sacchi (following the initial mistake made by A. Lensi in his study of the Loeser donation).
Although based on Italian forms, ranging from Perugino to Sodoma, and possibly associated with some of the Florentine eccentrics studied by F. Zeri, there is no doubt that the painting's composition is closer to northern European art, and especially to Memling's circle. With respect to this, Alte Pinakothek of Munich's *The Seven Joys of Mary* could be cited, although this work was not known in early 16th century Florence, as could the *Passion*, now in the Galleria Sabauda in Turin.
In this case, we can be certain that the work was done in Florence at the time that Vasari, writing about Memling in the first edition of his *Vite* says "the panel at Careggi, near Florence, in the Ilma, house of the Medicis, is by him." In the second edition (1568), he returns to the subject, commenting: "In Florence there is a small painting which is in the hands of the duke, one of Hausse's, in other words, Hans Memling's, representing the Passion of Christ." Apart from this, Warburg indicated that the two donors appearing on either side of the highly complex scene could be Tommaso Portinari and his wife Mari (*Flandrische Kunst und florentinische Renaissance,* 1902).
Finally, the author of this little-known canvas could well be a Florentine artist who moved in the circles of Franciabigio, and Granacci and, more closely still, in that of Bachiacca, especially at the time of the *Legend of the Dead King* (1525-1527, Dresden, Gemäldegalerie).
(*Joan Sureda i Pons*)

181
Italy

Bartolomeo Suardi, known
as "il Bramantino" (Milan,
approx. 1465-1530)
Christ Blessing, last decade
of the 15th century
Oil painting on canvas,
62 x 55 cm
From the Collections of the
dukes of Urbino
Urbino, Galleria Nazionale
delle Marche
Exhibitions: Japan,
1990-1991, n. 16
Bibliography: VENTURI 1914,
VIII, n. 10, pp. 316-319;
BUSCAROLI 1955, pp. 72-74;
MULAZZANI 1969, pp. 82-85;
CIARDI DUPRÉ DAL
POGGETTO-DAL POGGETTO
1983, pp. 184-190

This painting was attributed to
Melozzo da Forlì by Lionello
Venturi in 1914, and this attribution has been maintained
ever since.
Christ Blessing does not, however, offer concrete stylistic
similarities with da Forlì,
whose work in Le Marche region, where he painted the
frescos decorating the Saint
Mark sacristy in the Loreto basilica (Ancona), is known. Because of the subtle but undeniable differences of the work
in question, its association
with Melozzo da Forlì cannot
be maintained. We can,
though, consider it to be the
work of Bramantino, and one
of the masterpieces of the Italian Renaissance's mature
period: "It is difficult to forget
the perfect geometry of the
head, the sweet immobile
face, those transparent eyes in
which the light of the universe
seems to be reflected" (Ciardi
Dupré 1983).
Bartolomeo de Alberto Suardi
was born in Milan around
1465 and died there in 1530.
He was not only a painter, but
an architect and probably a
sculptor and miniaturist as
well. He is known today for
his pictorial work, although
not as well as he deserves to
be, and ought to be con-
sidered as one of the greatest
exponents of the Italian Re-

naissance. The information we
have about his life is full of
gaps, especially until 1503. In
1508 he worked for a year on
the Vatican residences in
Rome and in 1525 he was
named "Court Architect and
Painter" by duke Francesco II
of Milan.
His artistic development is
both unique and important
within the Renaissance. Connected with the world of the
great Lombard artists Butinone
and Zenale, his destiny was
sealed by Bramante's arrival in

Milan in 1477. From Bramante
he learned about a perspective loaded with "squarist" effects. Bramantino seems to
have known other artists in
central Italy, between Florence and Rome, such as Bartolomeo della Gatta himself
and the Florentine Fra'Bartolomeo della Porta.
Bramantino created his particular classicism – geometrical, with perspective, luminous, abstract yet human at
the same time.
(Maria Grazia Ciardi Dupré)

182
Bohemia

Master of the Litomerice altarpiece (painter active in Bohemia between the late 15th and early 16th centuries)
Holy Trinity Triptych, approx. 1510
Tempera painting on wooden panel, central panel: 120 x 67.5 cm; lefthand panel: 120 x 29.5 cm; righthand panel: 120 x 29.5 cm
Prague, National Gallery of the Cloister of Saint George, Bohemian Art Collection, NG O 1587-O 1588-0 1489
Exhibitions: Prague, 1935; Prague,1978; Litomerice, 1989

The open altar shows the *Holy Trinity* in the central panel, *God the Father Holding the Cross of the Dead Christ, With the Holy Ghost above them.* On the left, at the foot of the Cross, appears the kneeling figure of the donor. The identity of the donor is unknown, although his attire shows him to be a member of the nobility. On the inside, on the left wing, appears the Virgin Mary with her hands folded in an attitude of prayer. Her robes are covered with dispersed ears, a fairly rare motif in Bohemian art, but one used more often in certain regions of Italy and southern Germany. On the left part is the figure of Saint Barbara with the chalice and the body of Christ. The unusual position of the Virgin Mary is accounted for by the desire to represent iconographically the idea of a peaceful life from beginning to end. Saint Barbara has always been invoked as the patroness of the Good Death and the Virgin Mary of the Blessed Conception. When the altar is closed, the figure of Saint Wenceslas appears on the left wing and that of Saint Sigismund on the right. These two saints are considered to be Bohemia's main patrons, although the second was the emperor

Carlos V's personal patron and did not represent the whole population. For this reason, the iconographic content of the altar is clear proof of an intentional regression to the artistic tradition of the Middle Age.

The triptych is complete, the only part which may have disappeared being the prelada, which is either unknown or has been destroyed.

Taking the works of the "Master of Litomerice" in chronological order, we find the first depictions of *Saint Wenceslas* and *Saint Vitus,* which have been named as the altars of Krivoklat Castle, and are from before 1490. The main work, the Litomerice Altar, is dated shortly after 1500 when the artist returned home from the Danube area and northern Italy. His work as painter to king Vladislav's court was carried out in his first period, which is to say in the early 16th century. The murals on the walls of Saint Wenceslas' Chapel are dated 1509 and during this period he also

undertook important work for people of standing in the church and at court. The date of the *Holy Trinity Triptych* is set at around 1510 for stylistic reasons, this being the final period of his artistic activity, from which works dated as late as 1515 are known.
(*Ladislav Kesner*)

183
Netherlands/Spain

Juan of Flanders
(approx. 1465, documented
in Spain from 1496-Palencia,
1519?)
Baptism of Christ, 1496-1499
Oil painting on wooden
panel, 186.6 x 110.5 cm
From the altarpiece of Saint
John the Baptist in the
Carthusian monastery at
Miraflores (Burgos)
Madrid, Colección Juan
Abelló
Exhibitions: Madrid, 1986
Bibliography: Ponz
1776-1794; Arias de Miranda
1843, carta 3,9, p. 1045;
Ceán Bermúdez 1965, I,
p. 119; Tzeutschler Lurie
1976, LXIII, 5, pp. 117-135;
Madrid 1986, pp. 75-77;
Bermejo-Portus 1988, pp. 93

Juan of Flanders's first documented work is the altarpiece in the Carthusian monastery at Miraflores, which
presided over the lay choir's
Gospel side. In 1788 Ponz
published the news that it was
the work of "Juan Flamenco,"
done between 1496 and 1499,
and that he had received
26,735 mrs. for it, facts which
were confirmed twelve years
later by Ceán Bermúdez. Solo-
món Reinach states that the
napoleonic general D'Armagnac acquired the monastery
and all its belongings in 1809,
taking almost all its paintings
to France a year later; this was
ratified by Arias Miranda in
1843. It is possible, however,
that because of its enormous
size the central panel with its
splendid *Baptism of Christ*,
exhibited here, stayed in Spain
and passed into the Adanero
collection at the end of the last
century. The remaining smaller panels were dispersed during this period.
In the attribution of the Miraflores altarpiece to the Flemish
artist, apart from the evidence
already described, the fact that
the queen resided in Burgos in
1496 should also be taken into
account (Reynaud, 1979,
pp. 134-135). At this time, Gil
de Siloé and Diego de la Cruz

were working on the main altarpiece at Miraflores; while
Juan of Flanders was working
on this altarpiece he was also
in the queen's service and received financial assistance
from her on June 12, 1496. In
a way, therefore, the erection
of the altarpiece is linked to
the Crown, and as the wedding of the Infante D. Juan of
Spain to Margaret of Austria
was held in Burgos around
that time, it is not hard to believe that the work was commemorative. Furthermore, as
Ponz suggested, the painter
must have undertaken other
royal work. It is worth remem-
bering that the Miraflores
monastery was founded by
queen Isabella's father, Juan II,
who planned its conversion
into a royal pantheon. After
1494 the queen had more time
to dedicate to piety and patronage, and one of her
undertakings was to erect the
solemn sepulchre for her ancestors in the same building.
Thanks to Tzeutschler Lurie
and Reynaud we know of the
structure of the primitive altarpiece or triptych, which was
made up of five panels
carrying episodes from the life
of Saint John the Baptist. The
central panel showed the
Baptism of Christ, and on its
left, arranged from bottom to
top, would be the *Birth of
Saint Juan* (Cleveland Museum) and the *Preaching* (?),
which disappeared in the
XVIIIth century when the altarpiece was readapted. On
the opposite side, from top to
bottom, would be the *Decapi-
tation* (Geneva Museum) and
Herod's Revenge (Antwerp,
Mayer van den Bergh Mu-
seum).
Various points of style which
are typical of John of Flanders'
work emerge from the altarpiece, especially in the *Baptism* – monumental static
figures and a meticulously finished production, for
example. Because of this, and
the slowness with which the
work was done, it has also
been attributed to Michel Zittow. The panel of the *Baptism*

of Christ follows, as far as its
composition is concerned, the
most widely used model in
Flemish painting. If the right
hand of Christ is today raised
in a position of blessing, the
left rests over the genitals,
which are themselves covered
by a piece of cloth. The latter
is the result of an addition to
the painting, as Christ's body
originally appeared totally
naked, whereas before the
meticulous restoration to
which the painting was submitted, the hands were
together. Situated in the centre
of the panel, Christ is united
with the Eternal Father
through the Holy Spirit. In
spite of the great size of the
panel the landscape acquires
a miniaturistic character of
Eyckian origins, and the trees,
with their rigid trunks,
together with the river, help to
develop the space. The Jordan
appears as a great river complete with fishing boats, while
in the background, an
idealized Gothic city can be
made out.
This subject would be referred
to later on another panel, now
in the Washington National
Gallery and coming from the
Saint Lazarus altarpiece. From
a typological point of view,
however, the Saint's head
corresponds to that of Saint
Joseph in the *Nativity* in the
city of Palencia, and the sky in
both altarpieces opens in a
similar way. It should be
noted that other panels from
the Miraflores collection have
parallels with models from
queen Isabella of Spain's altarpiece, so *Herod's Revenge*
may be compared to the *Din-
ner at Simeon's House*, apart
from similar internal atmos-
pheres, both works display almost identical clocks, and
without doubt, this latter work
can also be attributed to Juan
of Flanders.
(*José Rogelio Buendia*)

264

184
Italy

Francesco di Giorgio Martini
(Siena, 1439-1502)
The Flagellation,
approx.1480-1485
Bas-relief, bronze,
57 x 40.7 x 3 cm
Perugia, Galleria Nazionale
dell'Umbria, 746
Exhibitions: London,
Amsterdam, Florence,
1961-62; Florence, 1986
Bibliography: VENTURI 1902,
5, pp. 43-44; SCHUBRING 1907,
p. 186; WELLER 1943,
pp. 142, 151, 154, 157, 167,
259, 261, 268, 272, 290;
SALMI 1949, I, pp. 11-55;
MALTESE 1966, pp. 5-6;
MALTESE 1969, n. 4,
pp. 440-446; CARLI 1980,
p. 45; POPE-HENNESSY 1985
(3rd ed.), pp. 307-308; SANTI
1985, pp. 236-238; FLORENCE
1986, pp. 227-229

This work was donated to Perugia's Civic Museums between 1872 and 1875 by the Russian count Demetri Bourtolin and, around 1909 it passed into the hands of what is now the Galleria Nazionale dell'Umbria.
It is not known where the work was originally kept, although the most likely place is a house in Perugia. The sculpture, splendid for the elegant treatment of the material used and for the strong play of light, had been attributed to Verrocchio, to Leonardo da Vinci, to Francesco de Simone and to Bertoldo di Giovanni, before Schubring (1907), followed by other critics, recognized it as the work of Francesco di Giorgio Martini, an artist in whom all the qualities of the Ideal Man of the Italian Renaissance were united, and who achieved very high standards in painting, sculpture, architecture, and engineering. This work was dated by Weller (1943), Maltese (1949), Salmi (1949), Carli (1980), Pope-Hennessy and Santi (1985), as being done during the years spent by the artist in Urbino, that is between 1478 and 1488, and refer to the architectural

scenes inspired by the ideal cities of Francesco Laurana and Piero della Francesca. Del Bravo, on the other hand, placed it around 1490-1495 as it showed clear signs of having been influenced by Leonardo da Vinci, who Francesco di Giorgio Martini met in Milan in 1490.
Fumi, for his part (1986) dated the work in the period between 1480 and 1485 because of evident connections with the decoration on the cover of an old sarcophagus in the

Museo Diocesano in Cortona, where Francesco di Giorgio Martini worked between 1485 and 1495, a factor also mentioned by Salmi in 1949. The sarcophagus had also been studied by Donatello, with whom the Sienese sculptor, as Fumi points out, referred to through his treatment of surfaces and in the pictorial conception of the relief, where he used a Donatellian "lack of finish" to achieve a feeling of elegance and freshness.
(*Vittoria Garibaldi*)

Pietro Vannucci, known as
"il Perugino"
(Città della Pieve,
approx. 1445-Fontignano,
Perugia, 1523)
Dead Christ,
approx. 1479-1496
Tempera painting on
wooden panel,
55 x 57 cm
Crest of the Pala dei
Decemviri
From the Palazzo dei Priori
in Perugia
Perugia, Galleria Nazionale
dell'Umbria, 248
Exhibitions: Perugia, 1945
Bibligraphy: BERENSON 1897,
p. 165; VENTURI 1913, VII, 2,
pp. 538-556, 742; GNOLI
1915, IX, 5, p. 309; BERTINI
CALOSSO 1935, XXVI,
pp. 911-913; PERUGIA 1945;
SCARPELLINI 1984, p. 90

This piece is the crest of the
Pala dei Decemviri ordered for
the Priors' Palace in 1479. The
work was originally in the
hands of Pietro di Galeotto,
but was given to Perugino for
completion and was finished
around 1495. The altarpiece
was taken to pieces in 1797
and the central panel was req-
uisitioned by the French and
placed in the Louvre, where it
remained until 1915 before becoming part of the Vatican Art
Gallery. The crest, on the
other hand, with its original
frame, remained in the chapel
until the 1800s, when it was
moved to the Magistrates'
Chambers. In 1863 it was
placed in the Galleria Nazionale dell'Umbria.
This is one of the most beautiful works from Perugino's
mature period. It was mentioned by Vasari (1568) and
then by all the local writers;
Orsini (1784-1804) attributed it
to Raphael because of its high
quality. This hypothesis was
sustained by Venturi and Ga-
lessi (both in 1913) but only
with reference to the crest, although it was rejected by
other scholars because of Raffaello's youth at that time.
The painting shows Christ

coming out of the tomb showing his wounded hands
(*Christus patiens*), a fairly typical theme in Umbria during
that period. This is one of Perugino's finest creative moments, by now a fully recognized painter after his experiences in the Sistine Chapel.
Although in the years during
which Perugino was active between Rome, Florence, and
Perugia, he developed a new
scheme of spacial composition
in which figures with blurred
outlines are set against atmos-
pheres of light colours, in this
painting the lifeless body of
Christ emerges in mono-
chrome from a very dark
dense space, testimony to the
extraordinary versatility of the
artist.
(*Vittoria Garibaldi*)

186
Spain

Jaume Huguet (Valls, Tarragona, approx. 1415-Barcelona, 1492)
The Archangel Michael, 1456
Tempera painting on wooden panel, 213 x 136 cm
From the Retailers' Guild altarpiece in Saint Michael's Chapel, Church of Santa María del Pi, Barcelona
Barcelona, Museu Nacional d'Art de Catalunya, 37.759

Bibliography: FOLCH I TORRES 1926; ROWLAND 1932, p. 124-131; POST 1938, p. 114-122; GUIDIOL I RICART 1948, pp. 48-53; AINAUD DE LASARTE 1955, pp. 28-30; PADROS 1980, pp. 81-84; GUIDIOL I RICART-ALCOLEA BLANCH 1986, p. 169; AINAUD DE LASARTE 1990, p. 105

This panel, together with the main one containing *The Virgin and Child* and the crest with the *Crucifixion*, forms part of the altarpiece in the Retailers' Guild Chapel in the Church of Santa María del Pi, Barcelona. It was consecrated in 1456. Originally, the altarpiece must have consisted of three parts distributed among three compartments with the central one showing the scenes mentioned above, while those at the sides contained different episodes and miracles from the life of the Saint. Jaume Huguet is one of the artists most representative of the influence of Flemish art in Catalonia and in the cultural milieu of the Mediterranean, however, an influence which shows a clear connection with the Italian world. Flemish art makes itself felt here in the decorativeness of certain treatments, such as the gold and silver work on the crown worn by the Archangel, the brooch of precious stones on the robe, the gold stucco in the background and the rich gold brocade of the vestments. Despite this, the image of the Archangel triumphant over the forces of Evil (the figure of the Devil was completely re-painted in the 18th century and cannot be seen here) is undoubtedly related to that of the Christian knight, in this case, the *Saint George* sculpted by Donatello for the facade of the Orsanmichele in Florence, which had so much influence on later iconography concerning this subject in particular, and also on that of the Archangel Michael.

Without renouncing medieval iconographic elements, such as the eyes covering the wings, Huguet constructed a solid figure in which the hieratic attitude of the image is subtly transcended by the light grace of the body and the visual play created by the conjunction of gold and red with the green of the robe. It is rare that 15th century art from outside Italy reached the harmony of perfection seen in Huguet's *Saint Michael* (only in the work of Melozzo da Forlì is such sensitivity found in the treatment of faces), a majestic figure who emerges from a strict but very well-treated landscape to reach towards the luxurious goldenness of heaven.
(*Joan Sureda i Pons*)

187
France

Antonio de Llonye
(documented in Toulouse
and Barcelona from
1460-died in Piedmont
after 1480)
The Angel and Trinity,
approx. 1465
Tempera painting on
wooden panel transferred to
canvas, 167 x 80 cm
Piece of altar wing
Turin, Museo Civico d'Arte
Antica, 4113-470/D
Exhibitions: Turin, 1939;
Turin, 1977; Turin, 1988
Bibliography: MALLÉ 1963,
p. 125; STERLING 1972, n. 215;
TURIN 1977; MOSSETTI 1985,
pp. 30-33, 40; PASSONI 1986,
p.30; ROMANO 1988,
pp. 22-24; AVRIL 1989, n. 85,
pp. 9-34; ROMANO 1989,
n. 85, pp. 35-44; ROMANO
1991, n. 5

This piece belonged to the
collection of Senator Leone
Fontany and was donated by
his children to Turin's Musei
Civici in 1909. The iconographic composition (related
to the *Thronum Gratiae)* appears unbalanced on the right
because of an earlier reduc-
tion of the paint which must
also have affected, although to
a less significant extent, the
other edges of the original
panel. During its restoration in
1972 the old wooden support
was discarded and the piece
was transferred to an im-
mobile support.
Commenting on the bequest,
Pietro Toesca described the
painting for the first time as "a
delicate and beautifully coloured Trinity, perhaps the
work of a XVth century artist
from Burgundy" (P. Toesca
1909, p. 483). From then on
the hypothesis that this was
not a Piedmontese painting,
but rather, one imported from
France prevailed among critics
for many years, although they
were unable to agree to which
particular French pictorial
school this extraordinary masterpiece should be attributed.
(Motta Claccio 1922, p. 278;
Viale, 1939, p. 67; Gillet 1941,

tav. 63, 1946, p. 21; Ring 1949, p. 228; Sulzberger 1951, pp. 52-54; Bernardi 1954, p. 54; Malle 1956, vol. I, p. 164; Castelnuovo 1960, pp. 42-43; Castelnuovo 1963, tav. 18; Malle 1963, p. 126; Malle 1973, p. 138).

In the search for the anonymous "Master of the Turin Trinity" the picture was linked with murals on the facade of Sant'Orso in Aosta and with the *Stories of Saint Peter* (Viale-Viale Ferrero 1967, p. 60; see also Rossetti Brezzi 1989, pp. 25-26).

Independently of the latter proposal, Charles Sterling examined the problem again and placed the picture in a broader artistic climate, convincingly suggesting that the work belonged to the Piedmontese-Savoyan area (1972, pp. 14-27). The group put together by Sterling (Turin's Trinity, the *Death of the Virgin,* previously in the Balbo Bertone Collection, the *Marriage of the Virgin,* now in Greenville, the *Nativity* in the Mayer van den Berg Museum in Antwerp and two panels from the Kisters Collection, *Saint Anthony* and *Saint John the Baptist*) have been the source of much dispute and their grouping has not always been accepted. Despite this, the group can be considered as a base to which other works may be added, such as the frescos in the abbey and altarpiece in the parish church at La Novalesa in Piedmont, Turin cathedral's *Saint Anne,* the *Beato Amadeo* in San Domenico, three panels with Dominican saints, and St. *Michael,* previously in the Molinari collection, a *Holy Family,* once in the Balbi Bertone collection and later in that of Galli of Carate Brianza, and the *Saint Francis* in Battagliotti de Avigliana (Romano pp. 207-209; Castelfranchi Vegas 1983, p. 259; Mossetti 1985, pp. 73-77; Passoni 1987, p. 40).

The problem now appeared to be centred definitively in the Piedmontese-Savoyard area,

when F. Avril and this author independently proposed placing the picture in the juvenile period of the painter Antonio de Llonye, alias Antonio de Llonhe or Antoine de Lonhy from Toulouse. The artist was known to be in Barcelona during the years 1460-62 where he did a multi-paneled altarpiece (Museu Nacional d'Art de Catalunya), and for the beautiful stained glass on the facade of the Church of Santa María del Mar (Romano 1988, pp. 23-24; Avril 1989, pp. 9-33 especially 18-20; Romano 1989, pp. 34-44; for Antonio de Llonye in Barcelona see Guidiol-Alcolea Blanch 1986, pp. 199-200). Through this identification, the catalogue of the "Master of the Turin Trinity," Antonio de Llonye, can be enriched with other works, important either historically or artistically: six panels showing the Apostles in a Turin collection and numerous miniature manuscripts, among which the magnificent *Saluzzo's Hours,* (London, British Library, ms. A.dd. 27697) are outstanding; two books of *Hours* (New York, Pierpont Morgan Library: ms. 57; Baltimore, Walters Art Gallery, ms. W. 206), a *Gradual* for the Church of San Domenico in Turin (Detroit, Institute of Art, ms. f. 1984), and the *Semita recte ad montem salutis* by Lorenzo Traversagni for Bernard de Rosier, bishop of Toulouse (Paris, Bibliothèque Nationale; ms. lat. 3231). Cluny's illuminated *Book of Hours* (private French collection) is of particular interest as F. Avril considers it the painter's first work, highly influenced by mid-16th century Burgundian painting. Finally, it should be said that the painting was originally placed over the altar of the Trinity in Turin cathedral (Romano 1990, pp. 259-270; further references in Romano 1991, pp. 33-37; Santucci 1992, p. 241).

The figure of Antonio de Llonye, therefore, assumes a vital role in the panorama of cultu-

ral exchanges between Burgundy, southern France, Catalonia, Savoy, and Piedmont, and in his fascinating *Trinity* the value of a documentary link connecting the great stained glass window of Santa María del Mar in Barcelona (1461-1462) and *Saluzzi's Book of Hours* can be appreciated (the latter may have been made for Yolande of France, duchess of Savoy, between 1460 and 1470 during which period as-yet unknown painters such as Nicholas Robert, Hans Witz, and Amadeo Albini were working at the Savoyan court). It would seem appropriate to date this exemplary masterpiece of contact between the Flemish world with that of Burgundy at around 1465 (derivations from Rogier van der Weiden's models are evident), but containing refinements which bear witness to another cultural component which it is difficult to place: the possibility that reciprocal exchanges with Jaume Huguet during his youthful period may have taken place should not be discounted.

Antonio de Llonye shows himself to be a master in the vibrations of twilight, the translucent glow of gems, the change between the brilliance and opaque of white damask, the sudden blooming of a red rose like blood on the pallor of the dead Christ (on the knees, the nipples, and the fingertips). It would be interesting to linger for a while in the poetic apse of cultural relations between Burgundy and the Mediterranean world, highlighting the irrationality of the architecture lacking in classical order, but also the boldness of perspective of the dove in flight. Unable to find words adequate to define the anatomy, neither heroic nor humble, of the body of Christ, sweetly formed through mobile transparent shadows before the onset of rigor mortis, which is manifested in the atrocious torture of the thorns sticking into the forehead.

(*Giovanni Romano*)

Hernando Yáñez de la Almedina (Almedina, La Mancha, approx. 1489-Cuenca? approx. 1536) in collaboration with Hernando de los Llanos (Santa María de los Llanos, Cuenca?-Murcia? approx. 1525)
The Resurrection, at the bottom the *Noli me tangere*, first third of the 16th century
Oil painting on wooden panel, 130.1 x 98.3 cm
Valencia, Museo de Bellas Artes San Pío V, Colección Real Academia de San Carlos, 457
Exhibitions: Toledo, 1958
Bibliography: Anonymous 1877; González Martí 1914-15, IV, n. 2, pp. 397-402; Tramoyers y Blasco 1915, p. 37; Tormo y Monzo 1932, pp. 52-53; Lozoya 1940, 3, pp. 340, 342; Caturla 1942, n. 49, pp. 35-49; Angulo Iñiguez 1954, p. 48; Garín Ortiz de Taranco 1964, p. 16; Camón Aznar 1970, p. 55; Post 1970, pp. 212-213; Rico de Estasen 1973; Garín Ortiz de Taranco 1978, p. 199; Garín Ortiz de Taranco 1978, pp. 123-124, 226, Pl. 26; Garin Llombart 1980, p.27; Prats Rivelles 1983; Company i Climent 1987, p. 48; Guia 1991, p.213, Garín Ortiz de Taranco 1987, 3, pp. 211, 228, 230, 231

Yáñez de la Almedina, "the most exquisite Renaissance painter in Spain," as Elias Torno said in 1915, is one of the main artists to introduce, through Valencia and later Cuenca, the aesthetic formulas of the Renaissance into Spain. Sharing the credit is his friend and companion Fernando de los Llanos and, even today, it is difficult to separate the work of one from that of the other. In effect, the notorious influence of Leonardo on the artist, which was reflected not only in faces and attitudes but in his particular sense of elegance and boldness and the exquisiteness and rigor of his figures, or in the interpretation, as subtle as that of the

master, of feminine beauty, amounts to a certain Giorgionism. This is in sharp contrast to his almost certain collaboration with the "Maestro" in the *Battle of Anghiari* (1505) and was brilliantly defended years ago by M. L. Caturla in an extensive work. A certain "Raphaelism" is also present, in the soft shapes, the consolidation of the end result, and broad, realistic settings. Little is known of his life, although we can be certain that he was born in 1489 in Almedina, a village in La Mancha, and died in 1536 in Cuenca where he had gone in 1531 to undertake a series of commissions on the cathedral. It has been said that he could have been of Moorish origin and, although this has never been confirmed, there is no doubt of his taste for the representation of Islamic canvases and stoles decorated with ancient Arabic characters.

His twelve great panels-doors on the main altar of Valencia cathedral, (contracted by he and his companion Hernando de los Llanos, along with the chapter in 1507) form an important group in the history of 16th century Spanish painting. Valencia Museum's *Resurrection*, which is displayed here, is stylistically linked with the cathedral panels mentioned above and also with another similar work in the Albornoz chapel in Cuenca. The rigorously portrayed anatomy of the ressuscitated figure (although rather short) contrasts strongly with the sleeping warrior and especially with the splendid figure of a soldier facing downstage, and balances the already restful composition. The work unites the painter's essential outstanding characteristics as a brilliant introducer of the ideas and forms of the Renaissance at its height into Spain, making Valencia one of the earliest regions to effect this assimilation, and one which would have such a great influence on the painters in its vicinity.
(*Felipe Vicente Garín Llombart*)

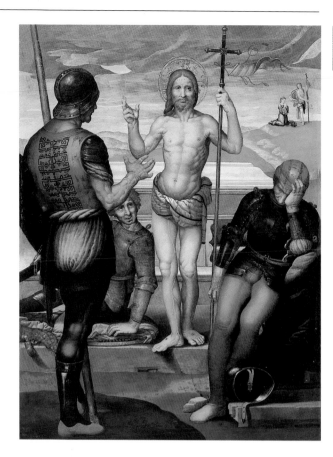

271

189
Spain

Alonso Berruguete (Paredes de Nava,
approx. 1486-Toledo, 1561)
Ecce Homo, approx. 1526
Sculpture, carved
polychromatic wood,
106.5 x 58 x 48 cm
From the Monasterio
de la Mejorada in Olmedo,
Valladolid
Valladolid, Museo Nacional
de Escultura, 728
Exhibitions: Madrid, 1961;
Seville-Granada, 1982;
Palencia, 1991
Bibliography: Pérez
Villanueva 1933-1934, p. 41;
Gómez Moreno 1941, p. 158;
Azcárate 1958, p. 146;
Wattenberg 1966, p. 111;
Camón Aznar 1967, p. 176;
Martín González 1977, p. 27;
García de Wattenberg 1978,
p.13; Camón aznar 1980,
p. 59, Luna Moreno
1982, p. 24

This sculpture, discovered and
publicized in our century
(Pérez Villanueva, 1933-34) as
the work of Alonso Ber-
ruguete, entered the Museo
Nacional de Escultura in Valladolid in 1968. It came from
San Joan de Olmedo (Valladolid) where it was preserved
after the sale of church lands
and goods in the 19th century.
It was originally executed,
however, for the church in the
Monastery of San Jerónimo de
la Mejorada, near Valladolid,
the altarpiece of which was
commissioned from Vasco de
la Zarza and Alonso Ber-
ruguete and is now in the
same museum. It was as-
sumed that this sculpture was
part of the altarpiece and even
that it was the image of the
central niche.
However, Wattenberg (1960)
indicated that *Ecce Homo*
came from the Zuazo Chapel
in the same monastery. In the
inventory drawn up for the
sale of church property the
details are set down as follows: "Zuazo Chapel. Altar
without adornment containing
the effigy of the Ecce-Homo in
bust form. Nothing of merit in

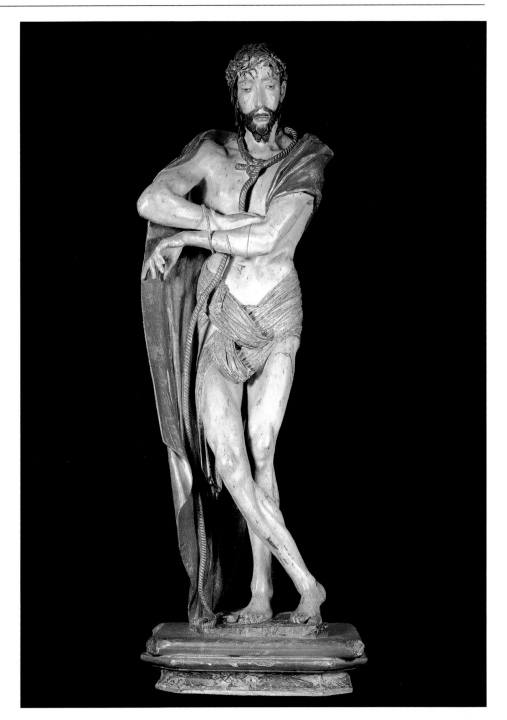

San Juan." On the other hand,
it is known that the monastery's name came from the Virgin and Child.
It is interesting to comment on
the inventory entry ("nothing
of merit"), which clearly
shows the academic posture
prevailing in the Spanish taste
of the day when faced with a
work by Alonso Berruguete,
when the carving was not endorsed by the artist's authorship. That it is Berruguete's

work has never been doubted
since Perez Villanueva's attribution because of the indisputable stylistic evidence.
The date generally accepted
for this work (towards 1526)
appears less certain; it could
have been motivated more by
the chronology of the monastery's altarpiece than by strict
stylistic considerations. Berruguete's unstable, unbalanced and expressive world
finds solid form in the work,

which unfortunately is somewhat impoverished by the
nude's many colours, the result of a repainting. The tactile
qualities of the body have
been disturbed and the
strength of the face has been
lost, leaving it rather rigid and
distant.
(*Luis Luna Moreno*)

Giulio Romano (Rome, approx. 1499-Mantua, 1546), (cartoons); Nicola Karcher (documented since 1517-Mantua, 1562), (execution)
Cupids at Play, approx. 1540
Tapestry, wool, silk, gold, and silver, 350 x 410 cm
Lisbon, Museu Calouste Gulbenkian, 29 C
Exhibitions: Paris, 1878, Mantua, 1989; Vienna, 1989-1990

Bibliography: DARCEL 1878 II, p. 1007; MUNTZ 1879-1884, pp. 61-68; MUNTZ 1882, p. 231; GUIFFREY 1886, p. 230; GRUYER 1897, II p. 478; MUNTZ 1897; BADIN 1909; MIGEON 1909, p. 254; MONZO-TORMO-SÁNCHEZ CANTÓN 1919; GOBEL 1923, II pp. 374-375, 358; PAZZI 1928, pp. 67-69; MIGEON 1929, p. 297; KENDRICH 1930, pp. 216-217; JANNEAU 1947; NEW HAVEN 1958; GATTI GRAZZINI 1958, pp. 114-116; WINGFIELD DIGBY 1959, p. 233; HEINZ 1963, p. 264; VIALE FERRERO 1963, pp. 2I, 54; ENGHIEN 1964; PARIS 1965-1966; GUERREIRO 1966; p. 41; BURDEOS 1968; pp. 2-9, 52; LAUSANNE 1969; GUERREIRO 1970, p. 229; JARRY 1971, pp. 2-9, n. 204; FORTI GRAZZINI 1982, pp. 76-79, 92-93; VIALE FERRERO 1982, pp. 133-134; VIALE FERRERO 1984, pp. 18-19; DEL MARCEL-BROWN 1988, pp. 109-121; DIGBY 1989, p. 233, n. 6

Among the numerous skills attributable to Vasari's "great friend" and praised by him in the *Vite,* is that of painting cartoons for tapestries. "He drew many tapestries for the duke of Ferrera, which were worked in silk and gold by the masters Nicolò and Giovanni Battista Rosso," says Vasari, whose friendship with Romano was, in fact, based purely on correspondance. It was the success of these tapestries, which referred to the power of Ercole II d'Este,

273

which inspired Romano's great patron, Federico II Gonzaga, to commission a series of works exalting the Gonzagas as architects of the new "Golden Age" enjoyed by Mantua under their rule. After the death of Federico II in 1540, cardinal Ercole Gonzaga continued the project.

The representation of an arcadian Mantua, in which play and dance symbolize a state of perfection through beauty and harmony, has its immediate antecedents in Giovanni da Udine's *Giochi di putti,* made for Leo X in 1520. The literary source of the theme of the happiness of the Nymphs' children dancing in a leafy wood can be found in Flavio Filostrato's *Imagenes fabulae.* The Fundación Gulbenkian's tapestry shows a happy moment in which the *putti,* or cupids, dance together, while their intertwined bodies are reflected in the water before the gaze of the Nymph, who draws festive music from her harp. (Shearman, 1972, fig. 18, has pointed out the coincidence of this nymph with

that in Raphael's tapestry *The Stoning of Saint Stephen)* However, the scene, which is presided over by the heraldic emblem of the Gonzagas, is not as happy as it at first appears: the central cupid has been injured by one of the arrows shot from the quiver of one of his companions who is seated in the top of one of the leafy trees.

The accident could be interpreted as part of the game, but there is no doubt that it alludes to a concrete fact. Nello Forti Grazzini (1989, pp. 477) interpreted it as symbolizing the death of Federico II Gonzaga, the first to commission the tapestries.

The group, made up of a total of fifteen pieces, was executed by Giulio Romano between 1539-1545 and was sewn in the workshop which Nicola Karcher had set up in Mantua in 1539, as the documents now in the hands of C. M. Brown and G. Delmarcel appear to show, contradicting the belief held until recently that the tapestries were done in Ferrara where Nicola Kar-

cher and Giovanni Rost had sewn the *Gigantomaquia* dedicated to Ercole d'Este.

Romano's preparatory designs are now divided between Chatsworth, London, Nottingham, Copenhagen, and Vienna. Of the tapestries themselves, apart from those preserved in the Fundación Gulbenkian in Lisbon, the only piece of which there is some knowledge is that in the Poldi Pezzoli Museum in Milan, although versions from Karcher's workshop are to be found in the Victoria and Albert Museum in London and in the collection of the Marquis of Northampton.

Giulio Romano's drawings gave way to other interpretations such as that made by the Brussels manufacturer Wilhelm Pannemaker (approx. 1574), which was bought by Philip II of Spain under the name of *Vines and Naked Children.*
(*Joan Sureda i Pons*)

Alonso Berruguete (Paredes de Nava,
approx. 1486-Toledo, 1561)
Children with Fruit Tree,
1527-1533
Relief, carved polychrome wood, 117 x 48 x 7.5 cm
From the altarpiece of the monastery of San Benito de Valladolid
Valladolid, Museo Nacional de Escultura, 271
Exhibitions: Madrid, 1961

Bibliography: Arfe 1585 (ed. 1979), II, fol. 2v.; Bosarte 1804, p. 156, 359; Llaguno y Amirola 1829, I, p. 11; Marti-Monso 1901, p. 137; Agapito y Revilla 1910, p. 452; Agapito y Revilla 1913, p. 226, Agapito y Revilla 1920-1929, I, p. 85; Agapito y Revilla 1926, p. 81; García Chico 1941, p. 12; Gómez Romero 1941; Candeira Pérez 1959; Wattenberg 1963, p. 107; Wattenberg 1966, p. 29; Camón aznar 1967, p. 1788; Zaragoza 1976, p. 222; Martín González 1977, p. 27; García de Wattenberg 1978, p. 11; Camón 1980, p. 62; Rodríguez Martínez 1981, p. 231

This relief forms part of a series with the same theme that adorned the altarpiece of San Benito, flanking vast pictures with busts of unidentified figures. In principle, they do not seem to have any purpose other than to be decorative, no symbolic content being apparent. The idea for this representation could have come from the Piccolomini altar in Sienna cathedral, the work of various artists, Michelangelo among them. The upper part of the Italian chapel contains reliefs with angels flanking a candelabrum; this positioning is similar to that used by Berruguete in his reliefs, except that his figures are youthful, robed angels. In the Valladolid reliefs children with fruit trees are shown, whose appearance is, if not exactly pagan, certainly profane.

It is interesting to comment on the use of a variety of dark tones on the back leg of one of the children, probably the result of a correction made to the altarpiece to increase the effect of depth.

Interventions of this type, obscuring or highlighting different parts of the altarpiece have been frequent.

(*Luis Luna Moreno*)

192
Spain

Attributed to Xanto Avelli
Plate, 16th century
Earthenware, polychrome,
4.7 cm; base of diameter
11.5; diameter of top 18.5 cm
Barcelona, Museu
de Ceràmica, 50.429

A plate with wings, decorated on the obverse side with a single mythological scene which occupies the whole surface of the piece.

The scene, of the *istoriato* genre, shows Aeneas' flight from the city of Troy accompanied by his father and son Ascanius, divided into two sections. In the first, Aeneas is seen walking on the right, holding a robe with his left hand and followed by his father and son; this scene passes immediately to that of the escape, with Aeneas carrying his father on his shoulders while his son walks ahead showing him the path. They are accompanied by two *amorini*. The city of Troy is in flames behind them, and at the bottom, separated from them by a strip of sea, another city can be seen, probably Rome, Aeneas' future home. The scene is set in a landscape of rocks, sea, and trees, and coloured in greens, browns, yellows, and blues.

In the centre of the plate, towards the top, is a shield containing a helmet over which appears the motto *Tapies dominabitur astris.*

The reverse side of white enamel is decorated with three yellow lines which separate the edge, the end of the wings, and the stand. The inscription *quando Anchisa fugo di Troia* appears in blue enamel.

A number of plates were produced along the same lines, taken from the *Aeneid* and inspired by engravers such as Raimondi and Caraglio. This plate, together with another plate in the British Museum, are examples of this production. The story served as a source of inspiration for many

275

more craftsmen, as shown by the plate by Casteldurante, decorated approx. 1520 by "pseudo-pelliparop" (Rackam, *Catalogue of Italian Maiolica*, Oxford 1989, p. 209, f. 723). (*Trinidad Sánchez Pacheco*)

193
Mexico

Mexica culture, late postclassical
Chac Mool, 1325-1520
Stone sculpture,
64 x 94 x 50 cm
From Mexico City
Mexico D.F., Museo Nacional de Antropología, 10-1078

The *Chac Mool* sculpture is of a similar nature to that of the standard-bearers, in the sense that it has more than one meaning. This is not a god or any kind of divinity, but a sculpture that serves as an architectural complement which represents a range of divinities. It consists of a reclining human figure with the legs bent, holding a vessel (a *cuauhxicalli*, in the examples from Aztec culture), or indicating that he is holding something. There are numerous hypotheses about its meanings and function. According to Lizardi (1944), this is Tláloc; other authors believe it to be Tezcatzincatl (Cuellar 1981), or the god of *pulque* (a fermented drink), already drunk, while to others this is Centeotl the corn god, Xiuhtecuhtli the fire god, Curicaueri (Corona Nuñez), Tlalchitonatiuh or "sun close to Earth" (Gutiérrez Solana), the sacrificial stone of the Tláloc temples (Graulich) etc. These sculptures began to appear in the Tolteca or Maya-tolteca period, as did those of the standard-bearers. In addition to the Tula specimens, there are thirteen in Chichén Itzá and a very large one in Quintana Roo, although they also appear in Central America and Michoacán. Several like this one, which holds a *cuauhxicalli* with one side decorated in pleats and whose face shows characters which identify it with Tláloc, exist in Aztec sculpture.
(*José Alcina Franch*)

194
Germany

Martin Schongauer (?)
(Colmar?,
approx. 1445-Brisach, 1491)
Medallion, 1490-1500
Partially-gilt silver
From the art and curiosities
room of Basilius Amerbach
in Basel
Basel, Historisches Museum,
1978.42
Exhibitions: Karlsruhe, 1970
Bibliography: FRITZ 1965,
p. 55, cat. n. 47;
LANDOLT-ACKERMAN 1991, p. 103

The medallion is comprised of two slightly concave silver discs tied at the edges, forming a small, empty capsule. The *Orchard Prayer* is represented on one face and the *Arrest of Christ* on the other. The piece appears in inventory D (1585/1587) of the Basilius Amerbach Room in Basle, referred to as an *Agnus Dei* belonging to Martin Schön (as Schongauer was called at that time).

The two scenes were inspired, in effect, by two engravings by the engraver and painter Martin Schongauer, around 1475-1480 (Bartsh n. 9 and 10; *The Petit Palais Exposition*, Paris 1991, n. 30 and 31), which are followed almost exactly, with some extension of the sides due to the different shapes – rectangular and circular – of the works. In the *Prayer*, he also changes the positioning of the branches on the left, which deletes an arm and a stick next to the torch, and enlarges the fallen lantern lying on the ground. In the silver piece, the final result is more compact, giving greater value to the engraving's foreground and offering a freer space, with more countryside. It is not known when the work came to form part of Amerbach's collection, although no mention is made of it in the 1578 inventory. Landelt and Ackermann suspect that it may have been obtained among the pieces that he bought throughout that year from the silversmith Hans Jacob II Hoffmann, and they believe that it could also have

belonged to the silversmith Balthasar Angelroth – whose inventory of possessions at the time of his death included many *Agnus Dei*, including a very large one – to whose house (the famous Haus Zum Tanz, the facade of which was painted by Holbein) the silversmith Hans Jacob I Hoffmann went to live, and whose son of the same name subsequently inherited it.

Joan Michael Fritz wonders if, in view of the attribution made to the inventory of Amerbach, Martin Shongauer might at one time have worked in silver and made the piece himself. This, of course, would not have been the first case of a great engraver who worked with silver plate. But other possibilities certainly exist. Gaspar Schongauer, Martin's father, settled in Colmar at some time after 1440. Three of his sons were silversmiths: Jörg, Gaspar the younger, and Paul;

the latter two worked in Colmar but Jörg is recorded as having worked in Strasbourg and Basle, both on the Rhine and equidistant to the north and south from nearby Colmar; according to some authors, Paul was also in Basle between 1489 and 1491. It seems most logical that one of the Shongauer brothers produced the work, but it should not be forgotten that due to the cities proximity to one another, Martin's engravings could easily have reached Basle, and that there were numerous silversmiths in that city, any one of whom might have been the creator of the piece. Both the casting of the work and what to call it have been the subject of argument, hence the difficulty in identifying it. It has generally been referred to as an osculatorium, but we are not sure if this is correct. This is partly because such pieces, to judge from the

extremely rare examples that have come from central Europe frequently made in silver, cannot very often have been made of silver; and also because the typical form of these – a small alterpiece with a handle at the back – bears no relation to a circular medallion. In addition to that, it is difficult to explain the existance of an osculatorium in a private collection in which it is referred to as an *Agnus Dei*. As Landelt and Ackermann clearly explain, the term *Agnus Dei* – which, in its strictest sense, is applied to the small wax medals depicting the Lamb, which were blessed by the pope in great numbers in ceremonies celebrated every seven years and considered the object of great veneration by the faithful – came to be applied, by extension, to medallions and lockets.

(*José Manuel Cruz Valdovinos*)

195
India

Adinatha, 15th century
Bronze sculpture,
27.5 x 18.7 x 10 cm
New Delhi, National
Museum, 47.109/172

The Jaina community in India venerates the Tirthankaras, which represent the supreme being, both in individual and group images. On occasion the twenty-four Tirthankaras appear together in a sculpture referred to technically as *chaturvimsatipatta* or *chovisi*, a term that etymologically means twenty-four. This example represents a *chovisi* with the image of Rishabhnatha, also known as Adinatha, the first Tirthankara Jaina.

According to the tradition preserved in religious texts, Rishabhnatha was the son of King Nabhi and Merudevi; he married Sunanda and Sumangla, and had two sons, King Bahubali and the Jaina Saint Bahubali. After ruling for a long period of time, he renounced the world to dedicate himself to the practice of severe penitence, with the purpose of achieving enlightenment. Rishabhnatha was the first male Jaina saint. He is identified in icons by his long hair which he let grow at the request of the god Indra, or of the Bull of Knowledge, *vrishabha*, since his mother saw a bull in the first of the sixteen good omen dreams she had before his birth.

In this sculpture, Adinatha is depicted seated in the centre flanked by other Tirthankaras. This type of representation suggests to us the idea of a universe filled to the brim with sages in contemplative posture and imbued with the incomparable serenity of enlightenment. Here the Tirthankara is seated on the throne of the lion and submerged in meditation, underneath the *chatra*, or parasol, flanked by two elephants. Two Tirthankaras appear seated on both sides in the mudra *dhyana*, while on the columns of the arc nineteen Tirthankaras, in the same posture, accompany the principal figure.

On the pedestal, Yaksha and Yakshi, semi-divine masculine and feminine beings, sit on each side, flanked by the chauri-bearers. Other motifs are included such as the nine planets, two worshippers, and a human figure on the centre of the pedestal. Situated between the planets, in front of the throne of the lion, is the *dharmachakra*, or sacred wheel, with two deer.
(*Shashi Astana*)

196
Mexico

Mexican culture
Xiuhtecuhtli, god of fire
Sculpture, polished volcanic
rock, with grooves and
incisions, 18.2 x 30.5 x 19.7 cm
From the offerings 88 of the
Principle Temple Project
Museum of the Principal
Temple, 10-25023, Mexico D.F.
Bibliography: Beyer 1955, 8,
pp. 8-42; León-Portilla 1986

This is one of the numerous
examples depicting the god
Xiuhtecuhtli which appears
within the set of Principal
Temple offerings. It is shown
as a squatting anthropomorphic figure with its arms
crossed. Its most significant
anatomical characteristics are
the details of the fingers and
toes, together with the mouth,
whose turned-up corner reveals two protruding teeth.
This individual, as if pertaining
to a *macehualli*, is dressed
only in the typical loincloth or
maxtlatl. On his head he is
wearing a diadem decorated
with four circles, which may
represent a Chalchihuitl. Two
protuberances stand out on
the upper part, while lower
down there is a simple paper
decoration of six ribbons that
fall from the head. The two
square earflaps, with elongated elements hanging from
them, are prominently de-
picted at the sides of the face.
Although some authors have
doubts about the identification
of this work as Xiuhtecuhtli,
many others agree on this interpretation. Xiuhtecuhtli is
the god of fire, thereby related
to Huehueteotl, and, in consequence, is placed at the centre
of the universe, as occurs in
the *Fejervary-Mayer Manuscript*. Xiuhtecuhtli also came
to be something like the patron or protector of the sovereigns and Tlatoanis, over
whose enthronement cere-
mony he presided. According
to Hermann Beyer, "Xiuhtecuhtli was the fierce warrior,
fraternal governer and impar-

279

tial judge all at the same time,"
and in the *Rios Manuscript* he
was referred to as the *advo-
cato della guerra*, while in the
Tonalamatl he is accompanied
by the emblem of atl-achinolli,
the symbol of war.
(*José Alcina Franch*)

197
Italy

Sandro Botticelli
(Florence, 1445-1510)
*Illustrations of The Inferno
from The Divine Comedy by
Dante Alighieri*
Drawing, silverpoint redone
in ink on parchment,
32.7-34 cm x 47-47.4 cm
Vatican City, Biblioteca
Vaticana
Bibliography: Lippmann
1894-1887; Horne 1908;
Venturi 1921; Gamba 1936;
Mesnil 1938; Clark 1976;
Chastel 1982; Dreyer 1984,
pp. III-15; Bashir Hecht 1985,
pp. 1031-1034; Parronchi 1985

If there was a certain reticence
in the Florentine humanist
circles during the first half of the
15th century with regard to the
valuation of the person and the
work of Dante Alighieri, appreciation of the poet evolved
considerably from the middle
of the century, especially with
the proliferation of Neoplatonic philosophy disseminated
by the Marsilio Ficino Academy
which, under the auspices of
the Medicis, was to have such a
fruitful influence in the arts. It
is, then, from within the ranks
of Platonic Humanism that
dominated Florentine intellectual life until 1494 – with
Lorenzo the Magnificent and
Ficino himself at the head – that
Dante's official cult emerged:
his consecration as Florence's
supreme poet and principal exponent of its new humanist
orientation. Dante's assumption of Neoplatonic postulates
culminated in 1481 with the
publication of the much discussed edition of *The Divine
Comedy* supervised by Cristoforo Landino, one of the most
prominent members of the Platonic Academy. It is worth noting that the edition was financed by Lorenzo de Pier-
francesco de' Medici, the second cousin of Magnifico, as
young as he was precocious,
and for whom Sandro Botticelli
had, out of the goodness of his
heart, painted his *Primavera*.

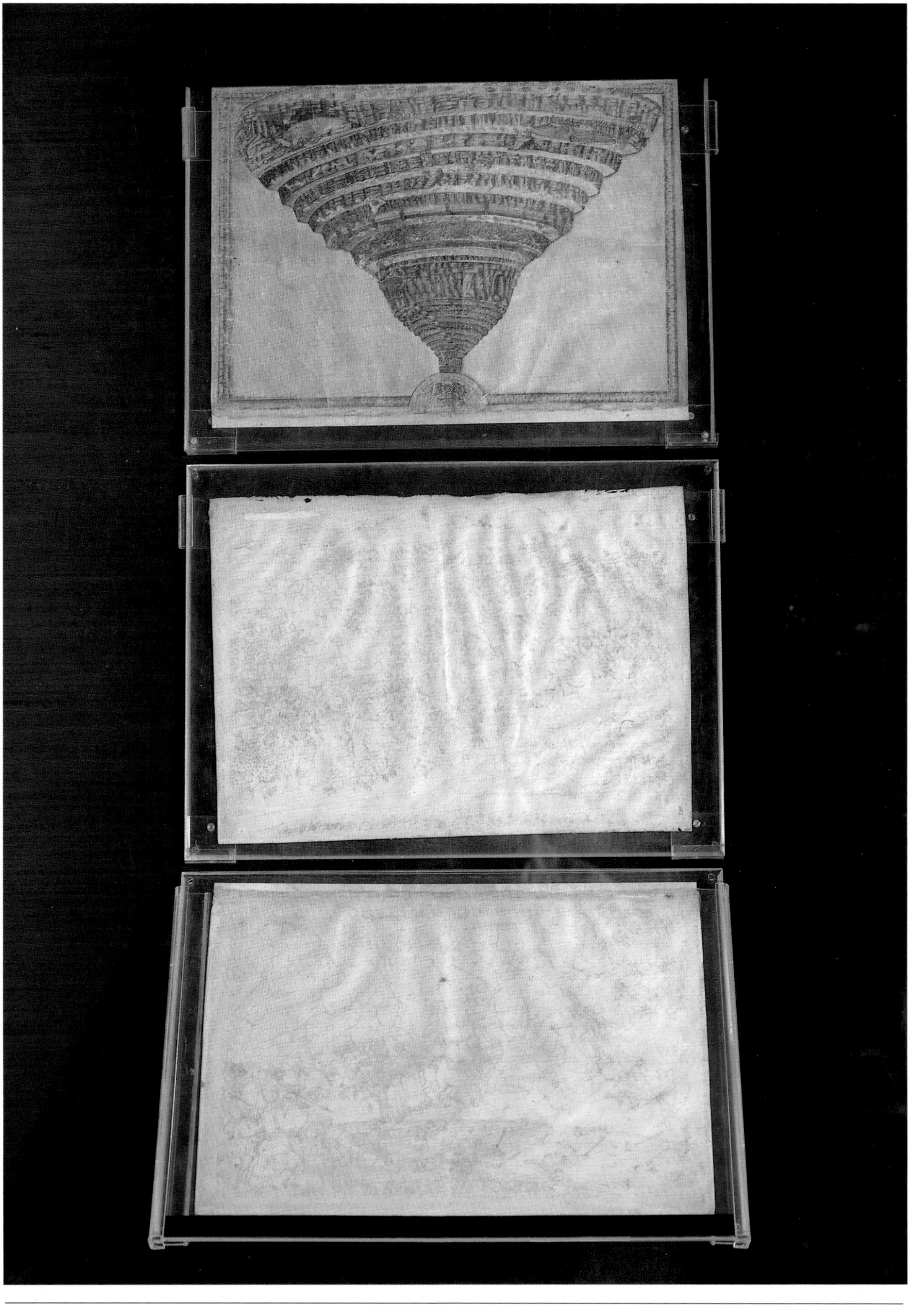

The publication amounted to an event of quite remarkable repercussions, contributing to the spread of Dante's new interpretation of Neoplatonism among humanists, poets and, above all, artists. In his commentary, Landino emphasized how close he found Dante to be to the fundamental thinking in the academic circle. *The Divine Comedy* thus confirmed the theological symbolism of the ancient fable, the Neoplatonic philosophy of love as nexus between the corporeal and the world of the intelligible, but illustrated, above all in the songs of *Paradise*, the fundamental concept of Fisian thought: the ascent to the state of plenitude through the contemplation or direct knowledge of God.

The important role of *The Divine Comedy* in the education of the great teachers of the Renaissance is directly related to its enthusiastic adoption by the Ficino Academy, and it is in this light that the illustrations by Botticelli for the work of Dante should be considered. The history of their gestation is both complex and the subject of some dispute. Botticelli made a series of 19 drawings based on scenes from the *Inferno* for the Landino edition which was engraved by Baccio Baldini, a point confirmed by Giorgio Vasari. An anonymous source from the sixteenth century, the *Magliabechiano Manuscript*, affirms that the artist "painted and illustrated a Dante for Lorenzo di Pierfrancesco de' Medici and considered this work marvellous."

The accepted thesis, until more recent studies identified the illustrations of the *Divine Comedy* as being the work of the young patron, thus constituting a later opus, independent of the 1491 series (Chastel). This source nevertheless opts for considering them as a work carried out for purely personal enjoyment and bases his opinion on the incomplete and experimental character of the set as well as the diverse styles and tecniques displayed in the plates. Botticelli's *Divine Comedy* must therefore have been the fruit of slow and irregular labour which occupied the painter during the late stage of his career, from the beginning of the decade of 1480 to the closing part of the century.

Despite the knowledge that Botticelli must unarguably have had of the old and extensive tradition of illustrations of *The Divine Comedy* – especially in the field of the miniature – his work underlines the limited noteworthiness of his predesessors not only through his general conception of volume or the purity and coherence of his compositions, but also through the intensity with which he manages to translate Dante's text, offering in some of the illustrations of Paradise, the closest possible expression of that beatific vision so dear to Florentine Neoplatonism.

(*Isabel Valverde*)

281

198
India

The Holy Koran,
15th century
Miniature painting,
37.5 x 2.5 cm
New Dehli, National
Museum, 54.29/1,

The Koran, the holy book of Islam, is a collection of the dogmas and principles communicated by the Almighty to the prophet Hazrat Mahoma through the mediation of the archangel Gabriel. Its compilation took twenty-three years of discovering the history, society, and culture of a group of nations with the objective of relating how disobedience of the Almighty led them to perish.

The book, decorated exclusively in gold and lapis lazuli, shows on its title page two stamps of the Mogul emperors Shah Jahan and Aurangzeb. At the beginning of the manuscript, two images are shown of sunlight bursting through

clouds decorated with gold and lapis lazuli, forming a beautiful floral pattern. At the end of the book, five pages are dedicated to liturgical prayers and matters of astrology. The binding is from the period, decorated in gold and with inscriptions from *Ayatal Kursi*, a part of the Koran, in the interior sections of both sides.

(*Naseem Akhtar*)

199
India

Gujarat
Jaina Kalpasutra, 1500
Miniature painting,
11 x 25.5 cm
New Dehli, National
Museum, 78. 288

282

This page belonging to the *Jaina Kalpasutra* represents the history of the monk Jaina Kalaka, who changed the date of the *Paryushana* festival where the *Kalpasutra* was recited. The tradition of presenting the *Kalkacharya-katha* and the *Kalpasutra* in a richly decorated form reached its height in the Gujarat. These manuscripts were painted with local red and ultramarine, giving them great decorative appeal; the use of aureoles or halos is characteristic of the Jaina style. The margins were decorated with little images of elephants, swans, flowers and human figures. The birds and animals were represented in a more naturalistic manner than that of the stylized human figures. The finish is at its most perfect in the faces of the women, who are depicted with prominently aquiline, papal noses.
(*Daljit Khare*)

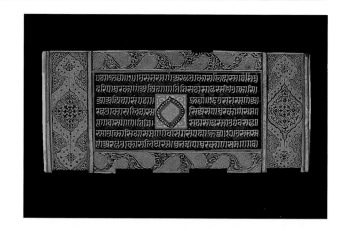

200
India

Amir Khusrau
Khamsa-i-Amir Khusrau,
1496
Miniature painting,
26.5 x 16.5 cm
New Delhi, National Museum,
52.81

Khamsa is an Arab word which means five, hence, the manuscrip is a collection of five poems. Nazami Ganjavi commissioned Amir Khusrau to write this *Khamsa* during the 12th century. The five poems included in the *Khamsa* are: *Makhzanul Assaar, Khasrau Shirin, Laila Majnun, Haft Paikary,* and *Sikandar Nama.* Nizami wrote the *Khamsa* in Persian while Khusrau wrote it in Nastaliq, a local Indian language.
The manuscript was illustrated by a Persian scribe whose name remains unknown. These miniature paintings are in the style of the Shiraz school.
(*Naseem Akhtar*)

201
Poland

Breslau, Silesia
Reliquary Arm, 1499
Cut glass, partially gilt silver,
chiselled and engraved;
remains of opaque enamels,
58 x 14 cm
On the pedestal, shields
of the donor, Joannes
Hermann, pope Alexander
VI and the king of Poland
and Hungary, Latislav II
From the collection
of Maria, wife of emperor
Maximillian II of Austria
Inscriptions: BRA (C) HIUM DIVI
SEBASTIANI MARTIRI / IOHANN (E) S
HERMA (N) I DECRETOR (U) M
DOCTOR CUSTOS ETCANONIC (US)
WRATISSLAVIENSIS DECORAVIT 1499
Madrid, Descalzas Reales,
00610863,
Bibliography: CARILLO 1616

This cylindrical bracket is built
on two bases, one hexagonal,
the upright faces of which are
adorned with fretwork
squares and tracery of four
and three lobes, and another
with undecorated warped
faces. The lower section has
engravings in the form of ogee
arches and on the base, six
angels support Polish shields,
still partially enameled; the
central section consists of
three little pilasters under pro-
tective glass containing a bone
with a phylactery bearing the
name of the saint; the upper
part bears the inscription
quoted in the index; each section is sepatated by little crenellations. The piece culminates in a hand of which the
thumb – which bears a ring
with a blue stone –, the index
finger and the middle finger
are outstretched bearing a
statuette of Saint Sebastian
wearing a cape and carrying
an arrow. The inscription
serves to date the bracket from
1499 at the same time as identifying the donor: doctor Johannes Hermann, a canon of
Bratislava. The shields correspond to pope Alexander VI
Borgia, king Latislav II of Poland and Hungary from Bohemia (1490-1516) and to the
donor (three stars on a blue

background, repeated three
times) and another with six
fleurs de lis on a background
of heraldic red, the person to
whom it corresponds remaining unknown. When Hermann
had the bracket made, he was
canon of Bratislava (Breslau in
German, presently belonging
to Czechoslovakia), a city in
the dukedom of Silesia. During the 15th century, the silversmith's craft flourished in
this city and the names of
about a hundred craftsmen are
known; by around the year
1500 it was already standard
practice to hallmark pieces.
For this reason it would seem
logical that the reliquary
bracket was made in Bratislava. But there exists yet another fact which perhaps offers confirmation: in the city's
cathedral there is another reliquary arm of Saint Stanislav
(Fritz, n. 601) which is almost
completely identical to that of
Saint Sebastian, with only one
insignificant difference worthy
of note; the wings of the
angels who support the
shields curve inwards. One of
these has been identified as
bishop Jodocus von Rosen-
berg (1456-1467), which
means that the work must be
dated a third of a century earlier than the piece in the *Descalzas*. Fritz points out that
among the treasures of Bratislava Cathedral there exists another reliquary arm of Saint
John the Baptist, from 1512,
with the hallmark of Oswald
Rothe, which forms a pair with
that of Saint Stanislav. The
piece in Madrid is undo-
cumented and does not ap-
pear in Fritz' splendid book.
However, it would seem clear
that the one with bishop
Rosenberg served as a model
first for the Hermann and then
for the one made by Rothe.
The book offers a sufficient
number of particular details to
consider it as being from Bratislava. Others from the same
period – such as those in Münster, Essen or the one in Saint
Servaas in Maastricht – coincide in terms of the length of
the arm and the one in Hol-

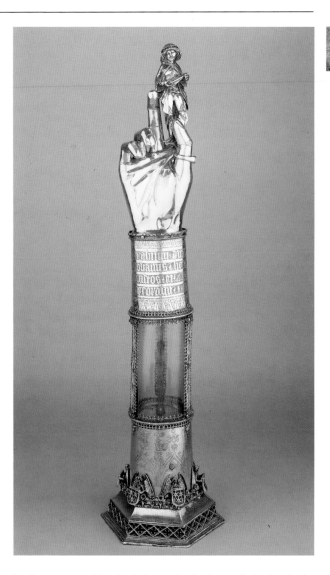

land even coincides both in
the position of the hand and
fingers and in having a hexagonal base, but they also display many differences and are
of different types. The positioning of the papal and royal
shields is not in itself a distinguishing feature. The two
sceptres of cardinal Zbigniew
Olesnicki followed by that of
cardinal Friederich des Jagel-
lonen, dating from around
1495, from the Alexander VI
Museum and, below, that of
the king of Poland together
with that of the donor.
The work is of exceptionally
high quality, with the craftsman constantly seeking variety
in its different parts: two distinct bases, statuettes and engraving in the lower part, glass
in the following section and
the body with the inscription

in the last, culminating in the
hand with the statuette. The
naturalism of the hand has
been particularly carefully executed and the figurine is a
clear example of late gothic
Germanic sculpture.
(*José Manuel Cruz Valdo-
vinos*)

202
Portugal

Osculatorium,
approx. 1520-1530
Engraved silver, 56 x 30 cm
From the convent of Nuestra
Señora de Espineiro de Evora
Lisbon, Museu Nacional de
Arte Antiga, 93
Exhibitions: Lisbon, 1882;
Seville, 1929; Lisbon, 1988,
cat. 11; Luxembourg-Lisbon,
1988, cat. 11
Bibliography: LISBON 1882,
n. 109, p. 15; COUTO 1941,
II, n. 2, p. 9; COUTO 1946,
I, n. 1, pp. 15-23, 57;
COUTO-GONÇALVES 1960,
p. 111; SMITH 1968, p. 265;
OREY 1984, p. 11

This beautiful example of a
mediaeval *osculatorium* from
the first third of the 16th century also serves as a highly
decorative casket. In the central section, supported by a
runner in which two angels
are found holding the Portugese shield crowned with
thorns, there is a richly icono-

graphic engraving of the Virgin and Child: the tree of
thorns is at one and the same
time a reference to the tree of
Joshua, the *Lignum vitae*, the
half-moon and the shell,
which seems to close the
space, inside which two
angels raise the crown of the
mother of the heavens. The
Manuel period baldachin that
the *osculatorium* converts itself into is crowned by the
image of the Almighty
carrying the earthly, crucifying
globe, held up by pillars
which bear the images of
David and Saint Paul on the
right and Saint Peter on the
left. In the niches in mid-air
which open up towards the
sides, the figures of Saint Augustine and Saint Jeronimo.
(*Joan Sureda i Pons*)

203
Portugal

Chalice, first quarter of the
16th century
Gilt silver, engraved
and with uncut amethysts,
garnets and inlaid glass,
36.5 cm; diameter of the base
21 cm
Inscriptions: on the cup,
CALVCUM SALUTARIS ACIPIAN EN
From a convent in the
Coimbra district
Lisbon, Museu Nacional de
Arte Antiga, 815
Exhibitions: Seville, 1929;
Coimbra, 1940, cat. 57;
Lisbon, 1983; Luxembourg-
Lisbon, 1988, cat. 10
Bibliography: VASCONCELOS
1914; COUTO 1927, n. 24, 25,
26, 27; COUTO-GONÇALVES 1960;
SMITH 1968; OREY 1984

During the reign of D. Manuel I
(1495-1521) Portugese gold
and silver work reached the
height of its splendour, not only
in the religious sphere, but also
among the aristocracy of the
period. Indeed, so ostentatious

was their use of it that D. Manuel (1521) and then D. João III
and then after him D. Sebastião
(1560) all had to dictate orders
prohibiting "the use and abuse"
of silks brocaded with precious
stones, silver, gold and enamels. This plenitude reached
what was surely its highest
point in the famous taking into
custody of Bélem, ordered by
the monastery of the Jeronimos
for O. MUITO ALTO. PRICIPE-E. PO-
DEROSO. SEHOR. REI. DO MANUEL, with
gold from Quíloa brought back
by Vasco de Gama after his second voyage to the Indies
(1503). It is within this range of
magnificence, as inventories
and chroniclers from the period
readily bear witness to,
together with the paintinngs which themselves reflect it,
that this chalice from a convent
in Coimbra must have been
made.
Although its architectonic
forms could still be considered
as being rooted in the gothic
world, its decoration is of the
Manuel period and contains

motifs clearly typical of the
Rennaissance such as the
niche-like shells on the base
which hold the prophets and
those on the main body of the
chalice which show episodes
from the Passion of Christ. On

the cup, a very beautiful decoration opens up six recesses in
which, below arches, the
twelve apostles appear two by
two with their respective attributes.
(*Joan Sureda i Pons*)

204
Mexico

Mexica culture,
late postclassical
Head of a Serpent 1325-1521
Sculpture, stone,
72 x 81.5 x 1.14 cm
From Mexico City, forms
part of the decoration of a
ramp on a ritual Aztec
building
Mexico D.F., Museo
Nacional de Antropología
10-46561

The ramps on the stairways of
the Mexica pyramid temples
often finished in serpents'
heads, as this piece, suggesting that the body of the serpent was in fact a long ramp
which descended from the top
step of the stairway to the
floor of the atrium. Evidence
of this has been found at the
Great temple in Tenochtitlán.
The serpents' heads were
usually carved in a realistic
and natural fashion and, although traces of inscriptions
as to the dedication of the

temple exist, the clearest
examples to be seen of these
are at the Great temple to Tláloc which appears to have
rattlesnakes and, at the temple
of Huitzilopochtli, *nauyaca*
snakes.
(*José Alcina Franch*)

205
Mexico

Mexica culture,
late postclassical
Quetzalcóatl, 1325-1521
Sculpture, stone,
99 x 39 x 30 cm
From Mexico City
Mexico D.F., Museo
Nacional de Antropología,
10-392932

The god we know as Quetzalcóatl, or Ehecatl-Quetzalcóatl,
is possibly one of the most
ancient of the Meso-American
deities for there are images
from the Teotihuacan era that
could represent the "Fea-
thered Serpent" and heads and
bodies of serpents decorating
friezes and ramps of the
temple or pyramid to Quetzalcóatl, named as such because
of this, inside the great city of
Teotihuacan. In any event,
Quetzalcóatl as god and priest
– Ce Acatl Topilzin – un-
doubtedly formed part of the
mythical and religious world
of the Toltec civilization.

Varied representations of
Quetzalcóatl in Aztec or Mexica statuary exist in abundance: there are many plumed
serpents, some of them showing an anthropomorphic face
emerging from the mouth of a
serpent, sometimes with other
human features such as arms
or legs. This piece shows the
image of the god in an
elemental ovoid form, in
which a characteristic emblem
of the god can be distin-
guished: a sectioned snail –
the whorl may also represent
the movement of a hurricane.
The emblem is inscribed on
the pectoral.
(*José Alcina Franch*)

206
India

Vijayanagar
Royal Devotee, 16th century
Sculpture, stone,
124 x 46 x 30 cm
Hampi, Vijayanagar
Museum, 607

Sculpture of a male figure, in which the head is missing, in the *samabhanga* posture and the hands in *añjali* or the *namaskara* mudra of adoration. Particularly noteworthy are the *vajñopavita*, lavishly decorated with precious stones, a diamond button at the neck and the *Kankanas* studded with gems on the wrist. The lower *vastra*, cloth which is gathered to a band at the waist and a fabric sash are clearly visible on the left knee.

The attributes of the figure suggest a royal or noble personage as the nuphar on the right ankle indicates a special adornment called *Ganda penderamu* worn by princes during the Vijajanagar period. Placing images of kings, queens, nobles and their families, and even members of their retinue, in the temples was commonplace throughout the period.
(*I.K. Sarma*)

207
India

Vijayanagar
Royal Devotee, 16th century
Sculpture, stone,
98 x 42 x 30 cm
Hampi, Vijayanagar Museum

Female figure with both hands in the *añjali* gesture or *namaskara* mudra of adoration. Richly ornamented with jewels around the neck, *kanthikas*, double bands and bracelets on the arms, the apparel consists of two parts; the jacket fits tightly over the breasts as a further indication of feminine beauty. The diaphanous clothing is held by a fairly wide girdle to the *kati* and the *mekhalas* are loose, studded with diamonds and precious stones. The navel indicates virginity.

The male and female devotee figures together form a pair, either prince and princess or nobles. Representations of this kind were common in temples or palaces during this period in Vijayanagar. (*I.K. Sarma*)

208
Mexico

Mexica culture,
late postclassical
Brazier, 1325-1521
Polychrome ceramic,
98 x 82 cm
From Mexico City
Mexico D.F., Museo
Nacional de Antropología,
10-219953

Although the Aztecs produced
many braziers, very few were
found *in situ* until the excavations at the Great temple of
Tenochtitlán. Usually the large
cylindrical-shaped vessel is
adorned with figures in relief,
as in this case which is polychromed. It shows repre-
sentations of Mictlantecuhtli,
God of the Underworld,
whose face appears stripped
of flesh.
(*José Alcina Franch*)

209
Mexico

Mexica culture,
late postclassical
Musical instrument
(teponaztli), 1325-1521
Wood, 95.5 x 25 x 87 cm
From Malinalco, State
of Mexico
Mexico D.F., Museo
Nacional de Antropología,
10-220924
Bibliography: CASTAÑEDA-
MENDOZA 1933, 8, n. 2,
pp. 287-310, n. 4, pp. 649-
665; NICHOLSON 1983; ESTRADA
1984

One of the most common instruments among the Aztecs was the famous horizontal drum called *teponaztli*. It usually consisted of a hollowed out log cut out in the form of an H at the top, thus leaving two small tongues, and was beaten with a stick (*olmaitl*). "It performed the most delicate and strictest function in the band of musicians, for it was this drum that governed the song and the dance, the two tones it commonly produces gauging the syllables of the song. The metrics and beat of the rhythmically patterned song lyrics were determined by the *teotlamazqui*, whose role was to conduct the hymns" (Estrada, 1984). This instrument can be considered one of the most notable examples in terms of wood carving. It shows a mythical creature that has been compared to a crocodile – *cipactli* or *ahuitzotl* – and the coyote or wolf – *cuetlachtli*, an animal that is now extinct in central Mexico. In conforming to the shape of the piece of wood the paws are curled back as if the creature is swimming. It has curly hair, mostly on the head and the jaws are wide open revealing several inlaid teeth. Although there are certain stylistic factors that might be interpreted as showing European influence, in general it can be termed a magnificent, though late, example of an Aztec teponaztli. It was acquired by the Museo Nacional de Antropología before 1891 and forms a pair with another instrument, also from Malinalco, the *huehuetl*.
(*José Alcina Franch*)

210
Mexico

Mexica culture,
late postclassical
Standard-bearer, 1325-1521
Sculpture, stone,
126 x 43 x 26 cm
From the Valley of Mexico
Mexico D.F., Museo
Nacional de Antropología,
10-222040

The sculptural figure known as a standard-bearer in the nomenclature of Meso-American art is, without a doubt, one of the most typical of its ornamental architecture. It usually consists of a figure, standing or crouching, holding the wooden staff of a flag or standard in his hands. He played a significant role in the rituals and ceremonies performed during feasts periodically celebrated in the temples. These sculptures which started appearing around temples, at least from the Toltec empire onwards, can commonly be found at ceremonial centres of the Mayan-Toltec period on the Yucatán peninsula, especially at the city of Chichén Itzá, at Mexica settlements, naturally enough, and in particular at the Great temple of Tenochtitlán where numerous examples have been discovered.

This one almost certainly represents the figure of a *macehualli*, a village man. He is wearing few adornments and a large *maxtlatl* as his only garment. His principal function was to serve as the standard-bearer.
(*José Alcina Franch*)

211
Peru

Department of Cuzco
Inca culture
Aryballos, second half
of 15th century-first half
of 16th century
Ceramic, 98 x 62 cm
Madrid, Museo de América,
7627
Exhibitions: Paris, 1933;
Madrid, 1935; Vienna, 1986;
Budapest, Cologne, 1987
Bibliography: Paris 1933,
n. 122; Madrid 1935, pl. III;
Trimborn-Fernández Vega
1935; Vienna 1986, p. 380,
n. 3.86

Large vessel in the form of an aryballos. It has two handles at the widest part of its diameter on the slant, a sharply pointed base and a long narrow neck with the wide mouth curling under; two smaller handles hang from this lip. The central body has a wide vertical band patterned with rhombi positioned lengthways and a chequered background. The rest of the vase is tightly patterned with zigzag lines.

The aryballos is the Inca vessel *par excellence* for it has only made its appearance in this culture. It is remarkably common, found in all sizes, from miniatures, perhaps toys or votive objects, to large pieces like this one, in all probability used for storing liquids. A simple and very beautiful jar, functionality has prevailed in its manufacture: the long globular form gives it a greater capacity and the pointed base served as a point of oscillation when the suspended jar was moved. The nodule on the band of rhombi was used for the cord passing over to the handles by which it was hung, either for storage or when transported, for any slight jolt would have made the jar tip and spill its contents; the small handles at the mouth also served for suspension and use.

The most common ornamentation on the aryballos was geometrical. Here, the entire surface of the jar has been meticulously covered in a kind of *horror vacui* that appears in Inca ceramics to enrich the decoration. The motif of rhombi, containing various other engravings, is one of the most typical and appears to have had funereal connotations. The triangles, in this case chequered, produced by engraving rhombi in a rectangle, form another pattern common in Inca decoration where geometrical elements were combined. The zigzag lines are in fact black superimposed triangular friezes that draw additional triangles in the reddish colouring of the jar. The simplicity of lines and volumes, its practicality and the interplay of geometrical forms are as typical in this aryballos as they are of Inca art in general.
(*Paz Cabello*)

212
Guatemala

Mayan culture,
late postclassical
Earrings, 1250-1550
Gold, 5.4 x 5.5 cm
From Gumarcaj, Quiché
Guatemala, Museo Nacional
de Arquelogía y Etnología,
12153

Metal objects in copper, gold or its alloy – tombac – do not appear in the highlands of Guatemala, where Gumarcaj is located, until the beginning of the early post-classical period. Nevertheless, they did exist here and there in the Mayan lowlands throughout late Classical times. The entire Mayan region falls between two metal producing areas: southern Central America, a mainly gold producing zone, and central and northern Mexico where workings were usually silver and bronze. These raw materials were not available in the Mayan lowlands and they had to be im-

ported from both regions, either as ready-made products or, preferably, unworked so that they could be fashioned according to their own artistic customs. This did not happen in the highlands of Guatemala where there were gold and copper deposits that could support a local metal working industry. Thus, during the post-classical period metalwork is common, nearly always associated with the personal belongings of high ranking personages.

The most common objects made in metal were earrings, rings, necklaces, adornments for the hair, nose rings, bells, discs and animal figurines. The techniques used were also very varied, ranging from embossing and relief work, hammering, filigree, lost-wax, etc. In some pieces, a combination of techniques was used, as in this case where the earring is decorated with the face of an individual from whose ears and chin hang two

types of filigree joined to plain, unadorned bells.

Some of these objects have been discovered on the high plateau of Guatemala associated with "Tohil" plumbate, dating therefore from 1000 A.C., although its use did not become widespread until the proto-historic period.

From the functional point of view, metals are clearly associated with funereal offerings, ceremonial rites and personal adornments belonging to high ranking individuals. However, in times immediately before the conquest, other objects with different kinds of use do appear, particularly axes, used for wood carving and war, and bronze pins, albeit few in the archaeological context of the Guatemalan high plateau. (*Andrés Ciudad*)

213
Guatemala

Mayan culture, postclassical
Twin vases
Plumbate ceramics,
11.6 x 18 cm
From Salcajá, Quezaltenango
Guatemala, Museo Nacional
de Arquelogía y Etnología,
6605

These two matching cylindrical vases made in "Tohil" plumbate ceramics have similar modelled and engraved decoration.

The glossy appearance produced by the nascent process of glazing and the introduction of special decorative elements (animal, human and god-like effigies) are the two characteristics underlying the importance of "Tohil" plumbate for the Meso-American area during the early postclassical period. From then onwards this type of ceramic ware started to appear in the principal cities of Meso-America, associated with lofty

occasions such as ceremonial rites, offerings and burials. Given both its wide distribution, trading in this type of ware crossed the majority of the ethnic and cultural borders of Meso-America, and the existence of the very powerful and influential central state of the Toltecs, it was thought that it was the artisans of Tula who made these objects for export. They appear in locations as far apart as Tula itself and Chichén Itzá, to settlements of the great Chichimeca and Panama, which appeared to confirm this idea. However, nowadays it is thought that this ware was made in the same region as the San Juan type, on the border between Chiapas and Guatemala. The appearance of animals, gods and elements from the Toltec culture, such as the eagle warriors, are now considered to result from the demand of the Meso-American elites, who had a taste for all things Toltec and the products of craftsmen who catered for

the needs of the day.
This explanation makes the idea of colonization from Tula more unlikely, although it does not explain the presence of these elements of Toltec culture – as in this case where some god is represented, possibly the rain god Tlaloc – on major sites in Guatemala during the early postclassical period, such as Zaculeu, Tajumulco and Zacualpa.
In this sense there is a close correspondence between what happened with the fine orange-coloured ceramics, another type of internationally traded pottery that travelled along the main routes controlled by the Toltecs, but that was made around the Isla de Sacrificios on the coast of the Gulf of Mexico.
"Tohil" plumbate disappears from archaeological records with the arrival of the Mexica peoples in the highlands of Guatemala towards 1250, which also coincided with the former decadence of Tula and

Chichén Itzá, two of the centres where this type of ceramics was in most demand during early postclassicism.
(*Andrés Ciudad*)

214
Peru

Department of Cuzco
Inca culture
Offerings dish, end of 15th century-first half of 16th century
Polychrome ceramic, 7.4 cm; maximum diameter 15.2 cm
Madrid, Museo de América, 8546
Exhibitions: Paris, 1933; Madrid, 1935, Santillana del Mar, 1982-Zamora, 1983; Alicante, 1988-Murcia, Cádiz, 1989
Bibliography: Paris 1933, n. 200; Madrid 1935 n. 148; Cuesta Domingo 1980, p. 359; Santillana del Mar 1982-Zamora 1983, p. 56, n. 69; Martinez 1988, p. 105

Zoomorphic offerings dish with a handle in the shape of a bird. The ornamentation, painted in black and cream on red shows highly schematic figures of deer radiating out from the centre of the dish to the rim.

These dishes usually take the form of birds, perhaps ducks, swimming. Thus, sometimes the handle forms part of the head and the limbs are represented by two small appendages. In terms of decoration, the dish often imitates the bird's plumage, others have

geometrical motifs or, as in this case, they show schematic forms.
(*Félix Jiménez*)

215
Peru

Inca culture
Vessel (pajcha), end of 15th century-first half of 16th century
Polychromed and lacquered wood with silver inlay,
12 x 40.5 cm
Madrid, Museo de América, 7573
Exhibitions: Paris, 1933; Madrid, 1935, Santillana del Mar, 1982-Zamora, 1983; Alicante, 1988-Murcia, Cádiz, 1989
Bibliography: Paris 1933, n. 124; Madrid 1935 n. 70; Cuesta Domingo 1980, p. 373; Santillana del Mar 1982-Zamora 1983, p. 33, n. 39; Martínez 1988, p. 159

Vessel or *pajcha* for ritual libations. The spheroid body is decorated in polychrome in ochre, red, green, black and brown. It has tiny silver inlays arranged in a band forming parallel jagged lines around the mouth and six sullu-sullu

flowers (*Bomarea uniflora*) painted beneath the band. There are three birds drawn on each side of the vessel spout and there are four crosses and two stars at the top. These wooden vessels, usually found in funereal settings, were used during particular ceremonies for libations of chicha, the sacred drink. The spout was used to pour the liquid from the bowl. The *pajcha* existed in many distinct forms and was one of the

most traditional ritual vessels in the Andean region extending far back in ancient times. The Incas used wood in preference to other materials and popularized the form shown here which spread even to the confines of the Tawantinsuya. (*Félix Jiménez*)

216
Antilles

Taino culture
Joined vases, 15th century
Ceramic, 18 x 20.4 cm
Santo Domingo, Fundación García Arévalo

Joined ceramic vessels consisting of two vases side by side in the shape of female breasts, ornamented with engraved geometrical and exciting abstract patterns.
There is a sepulchral face with empty eye sockets modelled in the centre, recalling the penetrating look of an owl (*Strigidae, sp.*), the mythical bird of the Tainos, that was considered the herald of the lord of Coaybay, that is to say the land of the dead.
The vessel also has two legs flexed in an arc on both sides of the face which adds to the anthropomorphic character of the figure represented.
It has a beak or spout in the shape of a phallus. The bisexual form of this vase effigy

therefore suggests a propitiatory use, related to the Taino rituals of fertility and the reproduction of the human race. (*Manuel Antonio García Arévalo*)

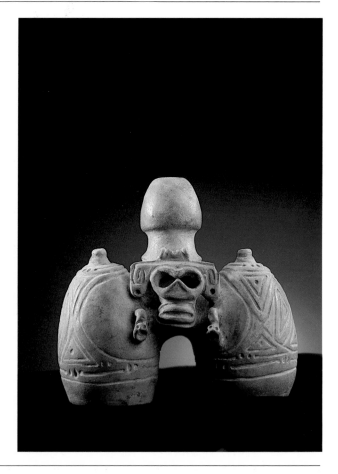

217
Peru

Department of Cuzco
Inca culture
Ritual vase (pagocha),
second half of 15th
century-first half of 16th
century
Stone, 7 x 5 cm
Madrid, Museo de América,
8724
Exhibitions; Paris, 1933;
Madrid, 1935
Bibliography: Paris 1933,
n. 475; Trimborn-Fernández
Vega 1935, n. 340; Cuesta
Domingo 1980, pp. 315, 356

Vessel in the shape of an al-
paca with open mouth used in
propitiatory rituals for the fertility of herds, the animal
propitiated represented by the
image on the vase. The simplicity of its forms is suited to
its role in utilitarian and
household rites. It was buried
after the ceremony during
which small offerings of
feathers and beads along with
other ritual artifacts were

burnt. The form of the animal
is suggested by the vertical
volumes simulating the manner in which the animal's wool
hangs down from its head and
neck. It sought to show both
the splendour of the wool itself and its high economic
value. Black was the most
common colour of stone for
this type of vessel.
Small vessels in the shape of
llamas or alpacas were known
as *illa* and *pagocha* respectively. However, they were
usually referred to by their
generic name conopa, the
name used for all sacred objects used by the extended
families in their rites, small
idols, among which this type
of vessel has been found, as
well as strange objects from
nature.
(*Paz Cabello*)

218
Antilles

Taino culture
Vomitive spatula,
15th century
Carving, manatee bone
(*Trichechus manatus, L.*),
26.3 cm
Santo Domingo, Fundación
García Arévalo

Anthropomorphic spatula employed as a vomitive during
the ceremony of inhalation of
the hallucinogen *cohoba* powder or during the ritual ceremony of invocation of the
cemiés, Taino gods.
The handle is a seated male figure, whose legs are sup-
ported by his hands and
whose member is exhibited in
erection. The man's bulky
head is distinguished by large
eye sockets and a mouth with
a set of protruding teeth giving
the figure an unearthly appearance. A design, similar to
a hair – do is incised on the
top back part of the head. A
cylindrical partition separates

the figure from the blade of
the spatula. The blade or
scoop is slightly concave, on
its front is a triangular design
in relief, and on the back a
symbolic schematic composition of incised lines and bas-
relief zones in which diverse
ornaments could be applied.
(*Manuel Antonio García Arévalo*)

219
Antilles

Taino culture
Ceremonial axe, 15th century
Carving, polished stone,
22 cm
Santo Domingo, Fundación
García Arévalo

Anthropomorphic lithic axe used in the religious and funeral ceremonies of the Taino culture. Its stylised form represents a crouching man. The figure is carved in bas-relief and executed with great perfection. This distinguishes the function of this axe from that of a simple axe used in agriculture or any other work that requires that sort of tool, and gives it the ritual character of an object used by chiefs and heads of the tribe.

These lithic axes were made of very hard stone, the polish was excellent and they were generally inserted in a wooden mallet which serves the function of a handle. The shape of these axes reminds us of flower petals and this is why, in archeology, they are classified as *petaloids*.
(*Manuel Antonio García Arévalo*)

220
Antilles

Taino culture
Mortar, 15th century
Lithic carving, length 24 cm
Santo Domingo, Museo
Arqueológico Regional
de Altos de Chavón

The mortar is in the form of a stylised turtle. A ledge in its centre, executed in high relief, delimits the functional area of the piece, i.e. where the pestle would do its job.

Taino lithic mortars and pestles are generally adorned with beautiful sculpted figurative motifs in human or animal forms. These motifs, as well as the symbolic abstractions in bas-relief, lend these utensils a ceremonial character. Carved with great care, they must have had a ritual function. They were used to pulverize hallucinogenic plants which the Indians inhaled during *cohoba* as well as in the magic-curative practises of the witch doctors.

The chronicler, Friar Ramón Pané, on the instructions of no other than Christopher Columbus, interested himself in the study of the religious beliefs and customs of the natives of the Spanish island. In chapter XVII of his *Relación acerca de las antigüedades de los indios*, describing the practices of the aboriginal medicine men, he says: "They actually extract the juice from the leaf, then they cut the dead man's nails and the hair that fell over his forehead. These they reduce to powder between two stones, mix this with the juice of the above mentioned herb and give it to the dead to drink through his mouth or nose. While doing this, they ask the dead whether the doctor was the cause of his death and if he kept to the diet."
(*Manuel Antonio García Arévalo*)

Taino culture
Vase, 15th century
Pottery, 24 x 15 cm
Santo Domingo, Fundación
García Arévalo

Anthropomorphic effigy vase.
A male figure is seated on a
duho or ceremonial seat. His
crossed arms rest on his
knees. His eyes must have had
incrustations of shells or gold-
leaf thus achieving a more intense expression.

On the back of the piece one
can observe the well defined
ribs and spine, from the top of
which emerges the spout of
the recipient. The body is notably slim, reflecting the suffering of the medicine men or
witch doctors of the Taino
tribes after the long fastings
they maintained during the
celebration of their magic-curative rituals.

On the head of the figure is
an incised pattern illustrating
the cotton bands or ribbons
which the natives used as their
personal decoration, while the
shape of the head shows the
cranial deformation practiced
by Taino people.

Effigy vases are the most
highly perfected form of Taino
pottery. Mythological personalities or animals are represented, which sometimes
achieve great plastic realism
and are therefore given great
symbolic value.
(*Manuel Antonio García Arévalo*)

222
Guatemala

Cakchiquel culture, late postclassical period
Anthrophomorphic pitcher,
1250-1500
Pottery, 28 x 28 cm
From Mixco Viejo,
Chimaltenango
Guatemala, Museo Nacional de Arqueología y Etnología, 6826

Globular high-necked vessels or pitchers, such as the present one, belong to "Chinautla Polícromo" pottery. Like the "Fortaleza Blanco sobre Rojo" vessels, they were frequently used as containers for the ashes of the most revered personalities. This typology was developed by two different ethnic groups with the same culture; these were the so called *pokoman* and *quiché* people, established in the central Altiplano of Guatemala.

The basic form – but not the only one – is the pitcher. This usually has two decorated handles in the zone of maximum diameter. Animal faces appear on them, the most common being that of a jaguar. In general, they are crematory urns, completed by a lid, made of a piece of ceramic or pumice-stone. In many cases, as in the present example, there are three small orifices in the central zone of the vessel. These symbolize the eyes and the mouth of the person whose ashes are contained in the urn.

The characteristic decoration of these vessels is carried out in red and dark brown, or black applied on white or off-white engobe. The motifs are rather conventional and represent various stylised versions of the jaw and eyes of a serpent. Set in vertical bands, these elements are then repeated four or five times. Geometric patterns – grecque, rectangles, triangles and spirals – are less common. They are always associated to the typologies of other pottery, not related to the funeral world, like the three-legged

and semi-spherical bowls.

The principal decorative element of the exceptional example shown in this exhibition is a human figure. The face of the figure occupies the neck of the vessel and its hands are joined on its bosom, which is the belly of the pitcher. This documents the practice, which could have been related to the leading class, of the decorative adornment of the face by means of tattooing with designs. The examples showing the association of the serpent motifs with human figures have been interpreted as the manifestation of military orders, which had a strong tradition in the mexicanized centres of postclassical Indo-America.

(*Andrés Ciudad*)

223
Antilles

Taino culture
Ceremonial ring,
15th century
Carving, hard limestone,
10 cm; diameter 48 cm
Santo Domingo, Museo
del Hombre Dominicano

Lithic ring, oval in form and of rough surface. On one end there is a decoration of four pairs of ornithomorphic heads, possibly pelicans or gannets (*Pelecamus occidentalis*). The series of these birds' heads, looking at one another, is framed in an incised design of thick crossed lines suggesting the pattern of wefts and warps in woven material. Taino lithic rings, common in the islands of Puerto Rico and La Española, are related, like a kind of catapult used by the advanced Indo-American civilizations, in the practise of pelota, a game, in which a rubber ball was used. The rubber was possibly extracted from the copey tree (*Clusia rosea Jacq.*).

The skilful execution and careful finish of these rings, as well as the symbolic motifs on the rim, make it possible that they were emblematic objects denoting the rank or social position of their bearers.
(*Manuel Antonio García Arévalo*)

224
Turkey

Iznik
Ottoman period
Mosque lamp,
turn of the 16th century
Glazed ceramic, 31 cm;
diameter 21 cm
Berlin, Museum für
Islamische Kunst, 00.125
Exhibitions: Düsseldorf,
1967; Istanbul, 1989; Paris,
1990
Bibliography: LANE 1957,
p. 247; ATIL 1980, p. 257;
ATASOY-RABY 1989, p. 94

The lamp dates from the reign of sultan Bayaceto II (1481-1512). Other examples of this kind of lamp come from their *turbes* (funerary monuments) and can be found in the Cinilk Kösk Museum in Istanbul. These two lamps (n. 41.1/2) are decorated in the overelaborate style of manuscripts from the early period of Iznik pottery and, on the lower part, have abstract designs.
The lamp has brackets which are not carved into the neck and body, hence it is possible that the gold decoration has since faded. This type of gilded lamp can also be found in the Istanbul collection. The handles, in the shape of a serpent's head, are very similar to a lamp in the Louvre (n. 5547) which has an identical formal style of painting on the brackets.

Typical of the design repertoire of the first Iznik period are the stylized lotuses and rose-work, the linked cusped leaves and the knot-shaped motifs. The sureness of the drawing leads one to think that it was the work of a craftsmen who was more familiar with manuscript illustration than ceramic decoration. The fact that this lamp is hung from the top section of the funeral chamber explains the significance of the elaborate decoration on the base.
(*John Carswell*)

225
Turkey

Iznik
Candlestick, approx. 1525
Glazed ceramic, 21.2 cm;
diameter 15.5 cm
London, British Museum,
Henderson bequest,
78. 12-30. 522
Bibliography: ATASOY-RABY
1989, figs. 302 and 123

A ceramic candlestick, painted with cobalt before glazing and overlaid with scale shapes and floral and striped motifs.
The shape of the candlestick is very common among Islamic metal objects from the twelfth century, but virtually unknown in ceramics. This particular candlestick could have been inspired by the Chinese porcelain copies of the Islamic copper candlesticks made in the fifteenth century for the Middle East market.
Candles were a luxury item in the Middle East where the heat of the summer made it

necessary to use beeswax, more expensive but less prone to melting than tallow. The cost of the candles meant that the candlesticks were of an equally valuable material, which in itself is proof that Iznik pottery was highly valued during this epoch.
Moreover, the small size of the candlestick indicates that it was destined for private use, since the metal ones found in the mosques and Ottoman tombs are generally very large.
(*Rachel Ward*)

226
Egypt

Mamluk period
Goblet, end of 15th century
Glazed and multicolored ceramic, 13 cm;
diameter 9 cm
Cairo, Museum of Islamic Art, 5592

A ceramic goblet with a cone shaped body and slightly widened base. The relatively thick sides are made of white clay. Part of the body of the cup was broken and lost and was subsequently restored with white pâte. The inside of the cup was not decorated, whereas the external surface beneath the transparent glaze was painted. On the main strip is a simple geometric design of horizontal lines broken by blue and white colours. The section of the upper strip which has been conserved has a very simple blue and white pattern, which echoes the foliated Kufic characters which evolved during the fanida

period (986-1171). Beneath this strip there is a collar which juts out slightly. The style and techniques used reveal the influence of blue and white china pieces which the Egyptians successfully copied at the end of the Mamluk period.
(*Farouk S. Asker*)

227
Damascus

Candlestick, approx. 1480
Brass plate, 47 cm;
diameter 37 cm
From the tomb of the great
mosque of Medina
Inscription: on the body:
"Glory be to our lord the
sultan, the king, the
defender of the faith, sultan
of Islam and the Muslims,
al-Malik al-Ashraf Abül-Nasr
Qa'it Bay"; on the base:
"Glory be to our lord the
sultan, al-Malik al-Ashraf
Abül-Nasr Qa'it Bay, may
his victory be glorious"
Cairo, Museum of Islamic
Art, 4072
Bibliography: WIET 1932, pl.
XXXIII; LONDON 1976, n. 226

This candlestick, which was
one of the two presented by
Qaitbey to the Mamluk Sultan
of Syria and Egypt in H 887
(1482) at the tomb of the
Prophet, was part of the new
furnishings which adorned the
great mosque of the Medina

after the restoration carried
out around 1480. The purpose
of these repairs was mainly
political and religious since, as
a result, the Mamluk control of
Islam's two holy cities, Medina
and Mecca, was reestablished.
The candlesticks were positioned around the mihrab,
where their inscriptions were
a continuous reminder of the
power of sultan Qa'it Bay. The
tradition of placing them
alongside the Mihrabs still
continues in Turkish mosques.
The candlestick has a truncated cone-shaped form with
pairs of projecting arms made
of brass plate and is engraved
with splendid inscriptions of
the name and royal titles of
the sultan. The piece is in the
tradition of the candlesticks
made in Damascus during the
Mamluk period. Research on
this kind of object suggests
that the sultans frequently
commissioned candlesticks in
Damascus, together with elaborately decorated candles, in
order to give them as presents

in Cairo or to send them
abroad as gifts. The inscription
includes the Qa'it Bay coat of
arms: a shield with three fields
with the name and royal titles
of the ruler, in other words a
coat of arms similar to that of
a state official of the 15th cen-

tury, which consisted of a coat
of arms with three fields each
with different symbols specif-
ying the position he or she
held.
(*James W. Allan*)

299

228
Egypt

Mamluk period
Bowl, end of the 15th
century
Turned, incised and glazed
ceramic, 17 cm; diameter
of base 11 cm; diameter
of lip 12.5 cm
Inscriptions: "One of the
objects made for his noble
excellency, the heavily
escorted and well-served
house of Azdagiya
al-Aidakiyya, be there
eternal glory throughout the
long life of its owner,"
written in Nasji
Cairo, Museum of Islamic
Art, 2712

This deep ceramic bowl, in
the shape of a truncated cone
and with a low base, strongly
resembles those popularized
by the Mamluk artisans working in metal. The outer surface
is decorated with wide strips,
the largest of which has a votive inscription in *tuhluth* of
the titles of its owner. The en-

gravings were done with
white slip applied before the
glaze and coloured with chest-
nut-brown, green and yellow.
These pieces were frequently
made as a result of individual
commissions. The inscriptions
were their main decorative
feature and usually depicted
the coat of arms and titles of
the Mamluk officials. A series
of engraved objects date from
the Mamluk period which, because of their form and decoration, appear to have been
a cheap substitute for metal
objects with higher quality in-
laying, which were much rarer
in this era. This type of ceramic bowl was normally used
for everyday purposes in the
kitchen.
Unfortunately, the Mamluk
person bearing the name of
Azdagi or Aydakin does not
appear to have done anything
of significance during the
Mamluk dynasties.
(*Nimat M. Abu Bakr*)

229
Turkey

Mosque lamp, approx. 1510
Ceramic, 27.6 cm
Instanbul, Archaeological
Museum
Bibliography: Atasoy-Ruby
1989

An Iznik ceramic mosque
lamp, decorated in blue and
white, dating from the reign of
sultan Bayazid, in the style of
the second phase of the *Rumi-
Hatayi* school, founded by
Bba Nakkas of Dr. Raby.
The lamp, along with other
similarly decorated pieces, belonged to an artisan workshop
which was known as the
"Circle of the master of knots,"
because of the themes which
appeared on the top and on the
bracket attachments which surround the cursive epigraphy, in
which we can also see an
example of the evolution of the
Ottoman epigraphists under
sultan Bayazid.
The lamp is decorated in a
series of horizontal stripes. The

ring has two geometric and ornamental braid friezes, the
lower one consists of a curved
line whereas the upper one has
a zig-zag shape.
Emerging lengthways from the
middle section of the body are
brackets with dark blue dots on
a blue background on which
the epigraph, "Allah Muhammad Ali" is visible, and is similar
to the bracket of another lamp
from the tomb of Bayazid II.
Between the brackets are small
palm trees formed by wavy
stems, from which sprout well-
shaped palm leaves drawn in
dark blue lines. On the upper
section of the body three small
handles serve as hooks for the
chains used to hang the lamp.
White in colour, the tall,
tapered neck has cloud patterns with palm leaves drawn
inside in dark blue and in tones
resulting from the points of the
Kufic epigraph which, in turn,
surrounds another inscribed
bracket.
(*Purificación Marinetto Sánchez*)

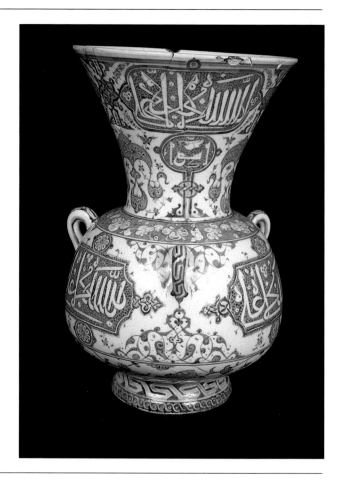

230
Islam

Abd al-Khalil Qutb al-din
Jug, 1495
Bronze, 13 cm; diameter
of the mouth 8.5 cm; diameter
of the base 7.6 cm
Surrey, Keir Collection, n. 145
Bibliography: Fehérvári 1976,
n. 145; Komaroff 1979-1980,
fig. 6

A cast bronze jug (missing the
handle and lid) engraved with
scroll-shaped leaves and inscriptions and damascened in
gold and silver. The inscriptions on the body and neck
are lines of Persian poetry. An
inscription on the base of the
jug indicates that it was made
by Abd al-Khalil Qutb al-din
during the month of Ramadan
of H 901 (May-June 1495).
There are a large number of
jugs similar in size and decoration in existence, some of
which are signed and dated by
the craftsmen who made
them. The nisbas-names
derive from the place of origin

of the artisans and suggest that
the jugs were made in Kho-
rasan, probably Herat, the
capital of Timur. On the other
hand the dates are evidence
that they were produced con-
tinuously throughout the fifteenth century and well into
the sixteenth. Similar jugs
were made in other materials
such as jade and ceramic. The
Ming porcelain objects with
the same form, with blue and
white decoration, were probably destined for export to the
Middle East.
(*Rachel Ward*)

231
Egypt

Mamluk period
Bowl, end of the 15th century
Beaten, engraved and etched
brass, diameter 41.5 cm.
Inscriptions on the rim
dedicated to the Mamluk emir
Aq-bardy ibn Alí Bay, written
in Nasji
Cairo, Museum of Islamic Art,
15191

Inscribed on this brass bowl,
typical of the style of metal objects made at the end of the
15th century, is the name Ag-
Bardy ibn Ali Bay, one of sultan Qa'it Bay's emirs. Ag-
Bardy held the post of *dawa-
dar*, the inkstand carrier for
the sultan in H 897 (1491).
Its exterior consists of twelve
panels which, starting at the
base, end in a pointed arch. A
combination of Y-shaped frets
and floral scrolls, with a naturalism characteristic of the age,
provide the decorative features of these arches.
The side is decorated with
an enla which appears with
inscriptions in Nasji, broken
by six coats of arms consisting of a circular shield
divided into three sections.
The upper part includes the
coat of arms of the serviette,
whilst the cup is in the
middle as well as the feather
holder flanked by two horns
of power. A cup is also included in the lower section
of the coat of arms. This emblem with six heraldic symbols was used by the Sultan
and his Emirs, as well as the
ladies at the court of Qa'it
Bay.
Written in Nasji, the inscription on the side reads: "One
of the objects made for the
most noble excellency, the
generous, the grand emir,
the master, the wise, the just,
the conqueror, the warrior,
the defender of the faith,
lord, our follower, the magis-
terial official Ag-Bardy, the
great secretary to the king,
the honourable."
(*Nimat M. Abu Bakr*)

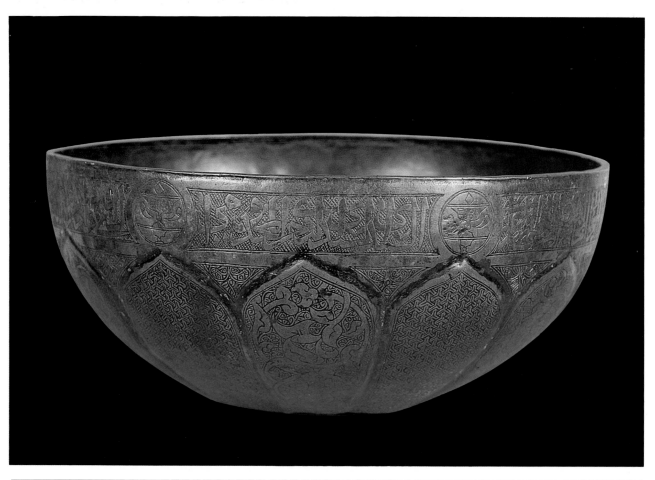

232
Thailand

Ayudhya
Vishnu, 15th century
Sculpture, bronze
with gilding, 9,5 cm
London, Victoria and Albert
Museum, IM 38-1928
Bibliography: Le May 1962,
fig. 295; Subhadradis Diskul
1990

Traditionally, Thailand is generally known as a Buddhist country and it is somewhat surprising to discover the existence of Hindu deities alongside those of a Buddhist character. Since it is founded at the end of the 13th or beginning of the 14th century, Thailand has been devoted to Buddhist teachings. Beginning with the portrayal of statues – some of which are on a monumental scale – it is, however, obvious that the Hindu religion was also practised. Inscriptions dating from this epoch mention that Hindu brahmins served at the Thai courts of Sukhothai and Ayudhya as both spiritual advisers and in secular roles. It seems likely that these deities were set up in Hindu altars for their use. Moreover, in Thai Buddhist cosmology Hindu gods such as Brahma formed part of the Buddhist pantheon. The majority of the statues were kept in the Brahminical temple (brahminist) in Bangkok before being transferred to the National Museum. It is believed that they originate from the ruins of the ancient capital of Sukhothai during the reign of king Rama (1782-1806) or later. This statue probably represents Vishnu, a Hindu deity, in spite of the fact that the absence of four of its arms makes it difficult to identify. The conical crown (*kirita-makuta*) and the sacred thread (*vajnasutra*) which crosses his breast diagonally are associated with Vishnu. The treatment of the diadem which carefully surrounds the face and on which the crown rests is typical of the Hindu and Buddhist

statues of the Ayudhya period. The complex treatment of the robes, covered with braid and sashes and the tassels flapping in the wind, seem to have been reserved for Thai sculptures of Buddhist statues.
(*John Guy*)

233
Tibet

Vajradhara, 15th century
Sculpture, bronze with silver
and copper inlaid work
London, British Museum,
1979. 5-14.1
Bibliography: Zwalf 1985

Vajradhara is one of the cosmic
invocations of the supreme
Buddha or Adi Buddha, and as
such is a symbol of the total
transcendence of all reality or
unreality which can be attained
in Buddhism. Adi Buddha is
from the sect of the lamas of the
Yellow Hat and from the bka'-
rgyud-pa. Adi Buddha always
wears a crown, as in this case,
and holds a *vajra* or thunder-
bolt and a *ghanta* or bell in his
hands. His arms are crossed at
the wrists, a gesture which sig-
nifies the sound *ohm*. The figure is richly adorned as was the
custom with Vajradhara statues,
in this example the inlaid work
is in silver. The face is gilded,
the eyes are of silver, the lips of
copper and the hair is painted

blue. This statue of Buddha,
seated on a double lotus
throne, resembles the bronzes
in the Chinese-Tibetan style
made in the 15th century.
(*J.R. Knox*)

234
Tibet

Mahasiddha Avadhutipa
Sculpture, brass with silver
and copper inlaid work,
17.8 x 12.3 cm
London, Victoria and Albert
Museum, IS 12-1971
Exhibitions: Paris, 1977
Bibliography: Lowry 1973,
n. 10; Beguin 1977, n. 151;
Von Schroeder 1981, pl. 131 I.

Mahasiddha is one of the mystical characters who has attained supernatural powers
through the perfection of the
tantric rituals. The *siddha* of
Tibetan Buddhism belong to
the tradition of religious mendi-
cants who hope to obtain spiritual and supernatural powers
by practising yoga and meditation. Throughout history the
term *siddha* defines those who
have attained the powers of the
magician, a step on the path towards achieving spiritual freedom. The eighty-four original
mahasiddhas of Tibetan Buddhism symbolize those who

have reached complete illumination in only one lifetime, by
means of an apprenticeship in
the teachings of Buddha. The
deeds of the Tibetan *mahasiddhas* were documented for
the first time in the 12th century
in the Vajryana text *Caturasiti-
siddha-pravrtti*.
The sculpture has an inscription in Tibetan which reads,
"Worship Avadhutipa." This
mahasiddah, known as Tilopa,
was a spiritual adviser to the
court of southern India. He renounced his post and retired to
a cemetery close to Kanchipu-
ram, where he attained *siddhi*
(complete understanding of
the supernatural forces). As
was typical of many of the *mahasiddhas*, he is portrayed with
long hair, gathered at the top of
the head and adorned with
flowers, and in an attitude of
prayer sitting on a meditation
mat made of animal skin. One
of the characteristics common
to many of these statues which
is worth mentioning, including
this example, is the portrait

style of representation. Traditionally, they are remembered
as very respected persons, despite the fact that their social and
moral conduct would eventually be described as scanda-
lous. Only by using these
human qualities they did

achieve their spiritual goals
which, for other human beings,
were unattainable.
(*John Guy*)

235
India

Venugopala (Krishna), 15th or 16th century
Sculpture, bronze,
68.5 x 40.5 x 23.5 cm
New Delhi, National
Museum, 47.109/18

Krishna is one of the incarnations of the god Vishnu. His followers, however, regard him as the complete manifestation of the essence of Vishnu. He is worshipped in a variety of ways, for instance among the most well-known are as Balakrishna (a mischievous child crawling on all fours with a lump of butter in his hands), as Venugopala (a young cowherd playing the flute, friend and lover of the *gopis*), as Kaliyamardan Krishna (a child overpowering the snake kaliya), as Govardhanadri (raising mount Govardhana), in addition to being worshipped as the supreme reality, creator, destroyer and controller of all

things. In his human form, Krishna was born into a royal family and is usually portrayed with their consorts.

This beautiful bronze sculpture depicts him in the role of Venugopala, delighting the hearts of the shepherds, *gopis* and cows with his enchanting music. He appears standing up, with his legs crossed on a lotus pedestal which is set on a square base. Krishna is normally portrayed with two arms, however, here he appears to have eight, illustrating his supreme reality: in his right hands he holds the discus, arrow and sword; in the right hands, a shell, bow and shield. The two remaining hands are holding a flute as if he were playing it. The latter is the feature which determines his form.

The head of the statue is adorned with a *kirita mukuta*, a listel and a *fillak* on his forehead, whilst on his chest and arms are necklaces, the sacred thread, armbands, bracelets

and wristbands. His clothing consists of short trousers tied at the waist with a belt. In addition to his attractive face and

sweet smile, all these features illustrate the youthful image of a cowherd.
(*Shashi Astana*)

236
China

Ming dynasty (1368-1644)
Beijing (Tibetan-Chinese)
Sceptre (Khatvanga),
1403-1424
Steel with silver and gold inlaid work, 44 cm
Inscriptions: mark from the reign of emperor Yongle (1403-24)
London, British Museum,
OA 1981.2-7.1
Bibliography: ZWALF 1981;
ZWALF 1985

A khatvanga is a type of sceptre used in the rituals of Lamaist Buddhism. The handle is composed of various symbols: the vessel of life, an inclined head, another head which is decomposing and a skull. In this example the vessel of life is finely decorated with inlays of lotuses, chrysanthemums and peonies and surrounded by four vertically positioned leaves. There are two *vajras* (thunderbolts) at each end of the sceptre,

whilst in the middle there are two crossed *vajras* which emerge from animal masks. This khatvanga sceptre would have been used in a ritual associated with a specific deity.
(*J.R. Knox*)

237
Tibet

Lama Seated in an Attitude of Teaching, 15th century
Sculpture, brass with silver and copper inlaid work,
35.5 cm
London, British Museum,
OA 1979.7-26.1
Bibliography: ZWALF 1985

Portraits of well-known people, normally with their name inscribed on them, were very popular in Tibet, and metal sculptures and painted portraits have been found which date from very early periods. The characters depicted were part of the Buddhist pantheon, such as the case of Padmasambhava (8th century A.C.) who spread Buddhism in Tibet, or Milarepa (1040-1123), the great holy man of Tibet. Many portraits of these people and hundreds of other holy lamas, abbots from monasteries or Buddhist sages were made in Tibet, usually after their death.

This statue, with a prominent jaw and the hands in the *mudra dharmacakra* or a teaching attitude, has no inscription but resembles another lama in bronze belonging to the British Museum's collection. There is no doubt that it is the same person and from the inscription on the second piece he can be identified as Phyogs-las rnam-rgyal of Bodong (1306-1386). The man was a renowned member of the Jo-nang-pa philosophical school, and recognised for his extensive literary output and for his leadership of various monasteries.

The statue is made of three cast pieces. The original head and the upper section of the torso were restored and enlarged when they were originally cast, as can be seen from the two additions to the lower section.
(*J.R. Knox*)

238
India

Vijayanagar
Vishnu Anantapadmanabha,
15th century
Stone, 183 x 82 x 52 cm
Hampi, Vijayanagar
Museum, 329
Bibliography: GOPINATHA RAO 1971; LONGHURST 1981

Located in one of their temples of worship, this statue of Vishnu is one of the best examples of the period. Immersed in deep sleep, Vishnu lies on the original waters supported by Adisesha, his snake. At his feet the waves of the sea contrast with the five heads of Adisesha on the upper section, which coils itself in two circles to make space for the deity, whose rigid legs and feet are curled up naturally. Vishnu, with four hands, holds a bow in his right hand, while his palm holds the crown, positioned on the head of the holy man. The completely outstretched left hand touches

the breast of Bhudevi, the goddess of earth and one of Vishnu's consorts, who sits cross-legged holding a water lily. The goddess's right hand rests on Vishnu's thigh, whilst Sri Devi, another of his consorts and the goddess of plenty and good fortune stands beside his knee. Sri Devi is holding a lotus stalk and wears a close-fitting sash across her breast; both con-

sorts are wearing identical crowns, elaborate earrings, necklaces encrusted with precious stones, bracelets and wristbands. Their iconography is based on the stipulations of the *Varkhanasa agama.*
Vishnu is portrayed with the typical and heavy *karanda-muta*, and wears jewellery on his large ear lobes and necklaces, one with a precious stone and the other with a

gem set into it. The birth of Trimukha Brahma, creator of the universe, is illustrated extremely well by an image of Brahma seated inside a lotus, emerging from the navel. The temples in southern India devoted to this deity are called Sri Ranganatha.
(*I.K. Sarma*)

Vijayanagar
Siva Veerabhadra,
16th century
Sculpture, stone, 140 x 82 cm
Hampi, Vijayanagar Museum,
202

306

Veerabhadra is considered as a significant manifestation of Siva between *ghora* or *samhara-murtis* (the destroyer). Indeed Veerabhadra was created by Siva to get rid of *Daksha yajña*. Daksha would later become a follower of Siva and was made leader of the *ganas*. The image of Veerabhadra can frequently be found in Hampi, both in stone and on stucco work, and the cult to this deity thrived throughout the Vijayanagar empire.

The inscriptions on the hill of Matanga which refer to this image of the deity date from the 14th century.

The statues depicting this deity standing up usually have two or four hands. There are many examples in the local museum, near Noble Palace and on the hill north of Zanana. Although the head and hands are broken, the statue still has the robust and majestic posture of a warrior god. All of this is surrounded by a *prabha* which in the upper section culminates in a *kirtimukha* or lion's head. Despite the fact that this part is broken, the base of the stand points to the presence of this structure. This version of Siva with four arms is standing in the *abhanga* position, leaning forward slightly. The left and right hands are holding a bow ad arrow. The lower right hand normally has hold of a curved sword or *khadja*, whilst the lower left hand rests firmly on a large rectangular shield which has an ornamental ivy plant engraved on the front. Daksha, with his head of spikes, is in the *samabhanga* position. In addition to the jewels which adorn his neck and arms, the torso is strung with a large garland of skulls, as a godly attribute, and he wears daggers in his belt.
(*I.K. Sarma*)

240
India

Vijayanagar
Bhudevi, 15th century
Sculpture, stone,
88.5 x 39.5 x 23 cm
New Delhi, National
Museum, 59.153/81

Bhudevi, also called Bhumi
Devi, means the goddess of
earth and she is understood to
be one of Vishnu's consorts.
This association of the goddess with Vishnu is probably
due to his famous incarnation
as a wild boar, when he rescued her from the demon's
clutches. She does not normally appear alone and is habitually accompanied by Sri
(or Lakshmi), Vishnu's other
consort.
This statue of Bhudevi belongs to a group which includes Vishnu and Sridevi, positioned to the left of Vishnu
as indicated by his seated position. In the left hand she
holds a lotus flower, whilst the
outstretched right hand rests
on the pedestal with the palm
facing inwards.
Richly dressed in a *karanda
mukuta*, she is bejewelled
with necklaces, bracelets and
wristbands and wears a sari
with folds hanging down her
left leg.
(*Shashi Astana*)

241
India

Vijayanagar
Vishnu, 15th century
Sculpture, stone,
138 x 62 x 39 cm
New Delhi, National
Museum, 59.153/80

Vishnu is the principal deity of
dharma or virtue and the re-
storer of moral order. In the
Hindu trinity, consisting of
Brahma, Siva and Vishnu, the
latter, being the protector of
the universe, is seated in the
middle with Brahma on his
right and Siva on the left.
The most common form of
Vishnu is with four arms,
seated in *sukasana* with the
left leg hanging and the right
leg bent on a raised ornamental pedestal. In his upper
hands he holds a discus and
conch, whilst the lower right
is in the *mudra abhaya* position and the lower left in the
mudra abuyavarada posi-
tion. Vishnu is adorned with a
kirita mujuta, a listel decorated with precious stones
and a *tilaka* on his forehead.
In accordance with icono-
graphic norms, the pedestal
includes two lions and is decorated with floral and geometric designs.
(*Shashi Astana*)

242
India

Vijayanagar
Parvati, 15th century
Sculpture, stone,
150 x 64 x 28 cm
New Delhi, National
Museum, 59.153/168

Among the many forms of Devi, the goddess par excellence, described in ancient Hindu literature and in the *silpa* texts, the place occupied by Parvati is unique. She plays a very important role in the Sakti cult, given that many other goddesses emanate from her since Parvati is regarded as the supreme source. She is frequently represented alongside Siva, although in some instances she has been depicted alone. The sculpture portrays the goddess Parvati with four arms, standing on a circular base in the *samabhanga* position. Only the upper left hand holding a lotus bud has been conserved. Normally the lower hands show an *abhaya*, granting freedom in the face of fear, and the *varada*.

She is dressed in a sari, which has a beautiful series of horizontal folds, and is tied at the waist with a belt, both sides of which have been decorated with precious stones and has tassels hanging from the middle section. Her necklaces and shoulder and arm adornments add to her beauty. The hair is tied up artistically in the *Jata mukuta* style and is embellished with a crest. A listel and a third eye add the finishing touches to her face.
(*Shashi Astana*)

243
India

Vijayanagar
Sri Devi, 15th century
Sculpture, stone,
95 x 35 x 23 cm
New Delhi, National
Museum, 59.153/79

Sri Devi is the goddess of wealth, plenty, good fortune and beauty. She is identified with Lakshmi who, according to widely received legends, rose from the ocean when it turned stormy in order to obtain ambrosia from the gods, and assumed the status of one of Vishnu's consorts, hence she sits on his right hand side. He safeguards her, like a treasure, on the right side of her master's large chest. She is also known as Sri, Lakshmi, Pada and Kamala and as a consequence appears in numerous texts, such as the Amsumadbhedagama, Vishnudharmottara and Silparatna. Normally she is depicted in a seated position or standing on a lotus flower, holding one or two lotuses in her hands.

A significant number of sculptures representing Vishnu, flanked by Sri and Bhudevi, were made in the south of India, of which this is an example. Sri Devi is seated on a pedestal with her right leg resting on a lotus, whilst the left leg is raised and bent at the knee. Like Bhudevi, a crown rests on her head, from which hang jewels which become part of her necklaces, bracelets and wristbands.

Although the face appears somewhat static, the shape of her body, with a thin waist and full breasts, represents the ideal of female beauty.
(*Shashi Astana*)

244
Spain

Unknown Spaniard
The Archangel Saint Michael, after 1480
Oil on canvas, 242 x 153 cm
From Zafra
Madrid, Museo del Prado,
1326

The canvas, which was stuck on to panel, depicts an armed archangel wearing a red cloak and holding a sword in his right hand to fight off the dragon, while in his left hand he holds a shield portraying the image of the donor, between the devil and his guardian angel. The struggle between the good angels and the fallen angels, who can be seen on the lower section and have been converted into devils, is narrated on both sides.

There is an inscription on the sword which was traditionally regarded as the armourer's signature.

The painting has been attributed to the painter Juan Sánchez de Castro or one of the masters associated with him. It was purchased for the Museo del Prado by their board of trustees, in 1924, from the Hospital de San Miguel in Zafra (Badajoz). (*Museo del Prado*)

Man the Creator

The thematic essence of *Art and Culture around 1492* explores two of the great privileges of the human being: the privilege of creation (works n. 245-283) and the privilege of sight (works n. 284-331). In every culture man has created beautiful forms; forms that can be useful in both daily life and sacred ritual, but above all forms that surprise by their beauty. The works which allude to the "privilege of creation" show the search for the idea of perfection that confounds the human being; they indicate his anxiety to dominate the expression of colour, to achieve geometric equilibrium, to combine the regular with the irregular, to convert the inert into the dynamic, to achieve a work of art which simulates time and space. Such works show, ultimately, man's will to turn himself into the maker of beautiful objects. The first reference to that beauty is man himself, an image present throughout the whole of the exhibition; the second, the exterior world. Through the privilege of sight, the human being seeks to discover the environment in which he lives and, when he discovers it, to represent it. Nature, the countryside, flora and fauna become inexhaustible sources of reflection and creation; through sight man finds his place in the world.

245
Germany

Double goblet, approx. 1500
Gilded silver, engraved on the
rim, total height 44.6 cm
Leipzig, Museum des
Kunsthandwerks, V 414 a/b
Exhibitions: Leipzig, 1907;
Vienna, 1989-90

A bell-shaped goblet with four circular-shaped lines and an ogee form. A fluted handle which ends in a cylindrical form in the middle of the base; filigree work in the form of plants decorates the main section. The base has a multifoliated stand on which seven semispheres are positioned. The goblet is finished with a braided moulding and a smooth cylindrical rim to which another identical goblet has been joined. The rim of the second is visible and has been engraved with plant motifs. This double goblet has a Buckelpokal *doppelter* – circular shape or a double goblet with a convex form and bears the mark of Nuremberg, in addition to a coat of arms and the word Leipzig engraved on the base. The goblet was part of Leipzig's municipal property. The municipal records register a purchase by Kilian Rudolf, a silver merchant from Nuremberg, but not the maker, of two gilded goblets in 1513 and a dish and bottle in the following year, which was exchanged in 1521 for another goblet. The piece we are discussing is definitely one of the objects bought at that time which, judging by its style, could be dated from some time just before 1500. The circular or convex structure was one of the most commonly used during the German late gothic period, but especially for goblets, whether they were single or double versions, and can also be seen in chalices and monstrances. Goblets of this type can often be found in paintings and in a number of drawings by famous artists. There are variations in the details, although not in the overall shape: a

bell-shaped body, a decorated top section of stem and a multifoliated base. The majority of the pieces conserved up to date are single goblets with lids, but there are also several versions of the double goblet in existence. Very similar to the one from Leipzig is the goblet in the Museum of Karlsruhe's collection, also marked in Nuremberg, dating from 1519 and which has a slightly deformed stem and lower section. The period in which this double goblet was made was one of the most

prosperous periods for silver-making in the middle ages in Nuremberg, where there were dozens of practising silver-smiths and work was exported to many cities, as happened with the present piece. The style was encoded and the technical skill reached high levels as a result of a strictly monitored apprenticeship.
(José Manuel Cruz Valdo-vinos)

246
Germany

Hans Greiff
Goblet with lid, approx. 1480
Partially gilded silver and
enamelled, 32.5 cm;
diameter 13 cm
Munich, Bayerisches
Nationalmuseum, MA. 3635
Exhibitions: Ingolstadt, 1988,
p. 102, n. 6
Bibliography: Müller 1974,
pp. 7-36; Fritz 1982, p. 274

A goblet with an inverted cone-
shaped body, although the
upper half is virtually cylindrical; the exterior is decorated
with horizontal lines with a
globe-shaped form and with an
ogee outline. Rough leaves alternate with intertwined braid,
which are part of the fourth
line. The base consists of a
frieze with wavy stems and finished with flowers and ornamental cresting above and
below, and has three feet in the
form of knights who are driving
their swords into winged dragons. The lid also has a globe-
shaped surface and cresting on
the edge similar to the base; A
cone-shaped pedestal rises
from the middle and sup-
ports a small leafy tree with a
pyramid-shaped top. The coat
of arms on the goblet belongs
to the Gläzl family from Ingolstadt. One of its members,
Hans, who died in 1494, was
involved with the City Council
from 1453 onwards. As the
piece originates from the municipal stock of silver it is
possible that the coat of arms
corresponds to the latter. In addition, the goblet has a regional
stamp which was already in use
in 1486 when the city's silversmiths draughted their first
statutes. Another almost identical piece, also with the Ingolstadt stamp, can be found in the
Metropolitan Museum of New
York. It has a similar structure,
including the middle strip and
the frieze on the base, the
knight-shaped feet and the
small tree, but the body and the
lid are smooth and have engraved decorations. Müller believed – as did Hernmarck and
Fritz – that it was the work of

313

Hans Greiff, whose Saint Anne
locket, dated 1472, has been
conserved in the Cluny Museum, as well as a miniature
portrait, dated 1492, in a privileged manuscript from the municipal archives of Ingolstadt.
Greiff died in 1516. Although
his status has been proved, we
do not know whether more
than four or five silversmiths
were working in Ingolstadt at
the time and comparison with
the locket in Paris does not verify its author. Even acknowledging the different character
of both pieces, only the design

of the cresting and the pyramid
shape are the same, neither of
which are very significant.
Therefore, we can accept the
attribution but with reservations. This type of goblet with
lid – known in German as a
pokal – was very common in
Germany, at least in the 14th,
15th and 16th centuries. The
overall shape of these objects is
the same: a very flat and slightly
convex lid with cresting on the
edge, a conical body and a lack
of decoration and almost cylindrical at the bottom, cresting
and an ornamental frieze on the

base and three tall sections
composed of small figures.
However, certain features distinguish this piece from the Munich museum and only the one
in the Metropolitan approaches
it in similarity. Hence the top of
the small tree, the cresting on
the lid, the extraordinary likeness of middle strip, the ornamental frieze and the cresting and the use of statuettes for
feet. The globe shape is typically German and continued to
be used in many pieces throughout the 16th century. (*José Manuel Cruz Valdovinos*)

247
Sierra Leone

Sapi-Portuguese culture
Salt cellar, approx. 1490-1530
Carving, marble, 43 cm
Rome, Museo Nazionale
Preistorico Etnografico
L. Pigorini, 104079
Exhibitions: Washington, 1991
Bibliography: Ryder 1964, V,
pp. 363-365; Dittmer 1967,
XV, pp. 183-238; Grottanelli
1975, VIII, pp. 14-23; Teixeira
Da Mota 1975, XXX,
pp. 580-589; Grottanelli 1976,
I, pp. 23-58; Bassani-Fagg 1988

Today about a hundred pieces remain from the original output of carved marble objects from Sierra Leone between the 15th and 16th centuries: goblets or saltcellars, spoons, hunting horns, manufactured articles of a functional nature with a sophisticated, rich and complex ornamentation.

The iconographic repertoire, which frequently makes use of themes obviously originating in the western world – such as functional aspects – and the fact that there has been no modern production of marble which could be described as the natural successor of a traditional art from this region have, in the past, contributed to spreading the notion among scholars that what is being dealt with here is a hybrid art, done exclusively by African artists and always commissioned and according to Portuguese designs, hence the name Afro-Portuguese marbles.

More recent studies have shown that it is an art which had matured and was refined before the arrival of the Europeans; nor do the forms, erroneously regarded as of western origin, such as in the case of the goblets, have an absolute resemblance to the style, structure and materials of the Renaissance, but, on the contrary, reveal structural and stylistic similarities to a series of African prototypes from the Gulf of Guinea, although in general they were made from different materials.

This piece is, without doubt, one of the most remarkable, not only because of its extraordinary size but also because of the delicacy of the work and the sophistication of its forms. This work belongs to the sculptural tradition of the Bulom from Sierra Leone or, as has recently been suggested by Ezio Bassani and William Fagg, of the Sapi (Capes, Sapi), a collective ethnic name adopted by the Portuguese to describe a group of people, among whom are the Bulom, the Temne and other neighbouring races.

The cup shown here is of the type with a hollow cylindrical base and has figurative details carved in relief within a kind of architectural structure. Four human figures, alternately male and female, seated on the edge of the base, are combined with a series of six vertical elements, some of which are decorated with crocodiles in low relief, hence varying the sculptural rhythm of the whole piece, which sits on a base of rectangular sections. On a formal level the architectural whole is lightened by a clever variation of mass and empty space, aimed to produce a piercing effect. The lid of the cup, supported by the base, is elaborately decorated with an execution scene, the formal structure of which and the original iconographic theme are combined and make this saltcellar a unique object within the sphere of this style of sculpture making. Because of its sophisticated design and form – note the elegant alternation of sculptural masses, smooth and flat surfaces decorated with simple geometric incisions – the work is evidently a masterpiece by an artist who knew how to interpret a rhythmic modulation of volumes with an artistic rigour and with surprising effects of balance, energy and intrinsicality, using the most significant morphological features of the great tradition of African sculpture.
(*Egidio Cossa*)

248
China

Ming dynasty (1368-1644)
Plate, 1488-1505
Ceramic, yellow porcelain,
4.4 cm; diameter of rim
21.5 cm; diameter of base
13.1 cm
Inscriptions: mark from the reign of the emperor Hongzhi (1488-1505)
Shanghai, National Museum, 36785

The application of the colour yellow onto a porcelain body can be done using two techniques: either colouring the paste by means of an application of antimony oxide varnish baked at high temperatures, or with enamels baked twice, once high (1280 ˚C) and once low (850-900 ˚C). At the beginning of the Ming dynasty the reintroduction of the technique of applying yellow began, although production was always minimal and mostly limited to the imperial household. In the 15th century the double baking method came into use, in order to achieve these yellow tones, alternating them with rims in faded white.

On the base there is a six character stamp which reads: "made during the reign of the emperor Hongzhi of the great Ming dynasty."
(*Zhu Shuyi*)

249
China

Ming dynasty
Plate, 1488-1505
Yellow porcelain, 4.6 cm;
diameter of rim 21.7 cm;
diameter of base 12.9 cm
Inscriptions: mark from the
reign of emperor Hongzhi
(1488-1505)
London, Percival David
Foundation of Chinese
Art, 599
Bibliography: MEDLEY 1973;
MEDLEY 1989

The yellow monochrome of
this simple piece is a pale
shade of lemon which com-
pletely covers the light and
resonant porcelain. In the
reign of Hongzhi, the transparent, brilliant and at times
slightly iridescent antimony
covered the whole range of
yellows, depending on the
thickness of glaze applied.
The traditional mark of
Hongzhi appears on the base,
with six characters painted in
cobalt blue, inside a double
circle and reads: Da Ming
Hongzhi Nian Zhi (made in
the reign of Hongzhi of the
great Ming dynasty). However,
unusually, there is also another character, Tian (sky), on
the outer section of the base,
a raw mark seen through the
glaze, which is probably to indicate that it was destined for
the palace or to stress its exquisite quality.
The plate has a feldspathic
coating, which reveals the
whiteness of the porcelain and
helps to increase the paleness
of the yellows during the second firing. Two coats and two
consecutive firings were applied and its porcelain paste is
of exceptional quality and
strength. Monochrome ce-
ramics have a long and prestigious tradition in the history
of Chinese pottery. They have
been regarded as the out-
standing classical pieces since
the time of the Song dynasty
(960-1279 A.D.), when they
were consecrated as ritual objects with the name Qingzhi or
"porcelain with the colour of
nature", and incorporated into
Taoist aesthetics. Their watery
and undefinable colours gradually increased in vivacity until
they achieved the colourful
decorative effect which characterizes the pottery of the
Ming dynasty.
(*Carmen García Ormaechea*)

250
China

Ming dynasty
Bowl, 1426-1435
Ceramic, porcelain, 4.4 cm;
diameter of rim 19.9 cm;
diameter of base 12.4 cm
Inscriptions: mark from the
reign of emperor Xuande
(1426-1435)
London, Percival David
Foundation of Chinese Art,
A519
Bibliography: MEDLEY 1973;
MEDLEY 1989

Judging by the scarcity of imperial marks and the limited
number of examples in the palace collections it would seem
that only the most beautiful
monochrome pottery aroused
the interest of the Ming court.
However, this humble bowl,
barely the size of a saucer,
bears the mark of the emperor
Xuande (1426-1435) on its
base. It consists of six characters, written in a double circle,
which reads: Da Ming Xuande
NianZhi (made during the
reign of Xuande of the great
Ming dynasty). The elegance
of its slightly sinuous shape
was ideal for the light porcelain paste of which it is made.
But its excellence stems from
the red copper glaze of the exterior, becoming whiter at the
edge and turning to a pale
grey around the base. The
"red copper" technique, the
most famous of all the monochrome ceramics in China,
was not perfected until the
Ming dynasty, since the difficulties during the firing process were only solved by strict
control of timing, temperature
and the reducing atmosphere
of the kiln. Up until then, the
colour red used to fade to a
shade of dirty reddish brown;
the Ming potters of the 15th
century mastered the "red
copper" technique and it became the leading figure within
the large family of mono-
chrome ceramics.

"Red copper" is a copper oxide
glaze which is very volatile and
hard to manage when firing,
since it always tends to spread
and overflow and the desired
ruby sheen becomes blurred by
shades of grey and brown. Although the collectors from the
west give these monochromes
the absurd title of "bulls blood",
the Chinese potters call them
"Xianhung" or "fresh red" and
also "baoshihung" or "precious
red stone."
Despite the fact that all current
scientific research rejects any
pigment that does not derive
from copper, the Chinese
tradition, and widespread opinion, has up to now always
appreciated this colour, in particular because it is composed
of ruby and cornelian powder.
(*Carmen García Ormaechea*)

317

251
Korea

Choson dynasty (1392-1910)
Kang Hui-an (1419-1464)
Bowl, 15th century
Ceramic, porcelain,
11.2 x 21.2 x 8.2 cm
Inscriptions: dai
Seoul, Horim Museum

This bowl is glazed with a
cloudy white colour and has a
wide and open rim. Its base is
formed by a concave circle
and the stand was fired in the
kiln with sandy soil.
A Chinese character, dai or
large, can be seen on the base,
indicating that this piece was
reserved for the royal palace.
The shape of the bowl and the
application of the white glaze
over the whole surface would
suggest that it was made in a
royal kiln in Osanri and/or
Kwaneumri, situated in
Kwangju in the Kyunggi province.
(*Horim Museum*)

252
China

Ming dynasty (1368-1644)
Wine jug, beginning of the
15th century
Ceramic, earthenware,
33.5 cm; maximum diameter
of rim 14 cm; maximum
width 31.6 cm; diameter
of base 19.4 cm
From the Imperial Palace
collection, Beijing
Inscriptions: on the body it
reads, "Made for use in the
Interior Palace"
London, Percival David
Foundation of Chinese Art,
London, 518
Exhibitions: 1935-1936

The Guan type of wine vessel
is a good example of how the
symbolic forms of Chinese ritual receptacles have evolved
towards greater functionalism
since the neolithic age.

From a ceramic point of view
this Guan is of great value,
since the formal robustness is
complemented by vivid colours and a coarse earthenware, blending form with decoration and technique. It is a
polished and vigorous
example which persistently
evokes the use for which it
was destined. We know that it
is an imperial piece because,
although it has no mark, the
inscription of the four characters *nei-fu gong-yong* (made
for use in the Interior Palace),
tells us for what use it was
made. In addition, the turquoise blue glaze of this large
Guan is exceptional for such
an early period, and the strip
of gilded copper around the
rim, common on pieces from
palace collections, guarantee
its imperial standing. The high
artistic standards of Ming
monochrome pottery is consistent with the technical expertise achieved by the Jingdezhen potters (the province
of Jiangxi). The ostentatious
turquoise blue of this piece
was achieved by mixing copper oxide with an alkaline
glaze; for the surface to vitrify
so fluidly and brightly, a firing
at a lower temperature, normally used for earthenware,

was required. As a result, this
Guan did not have to undergo
the complex process of at least
two firings.

Controlling alkaline turquoise
in the kiln is complicated,
since it needs exactly the right
temperature to achieve the fusion of paste with glaze; perhaps for this reason this form
of monochrome pottery was
not widely used during the
Ming dynasty, but it was to figure prominently in the Quing
monochromes of the 18th century.

(*Carmen García Ormaechea*)

253
Italy

Michelangelo Buonarroti
(Caprese, 1475-Rome, 1564)
Study of Door, 16th century
Drawing, black pencil and
gouache on paper,
39.9 x 26.9 cm
Florence, Casa Buonarroti,
73 A bis
Bibliography: Dussler 1959;
Barocchi 1962; Barocchi
1964[a]; Barocchi 1964[b]; Berti
1965; Hartt 1971; Tolnay
1975; Tolnay 1975-1980;
Berti 1985

It is thought that this drawing
belongs to Michelangelo's late
period and that it was one of
the artist's numerous prelimi-
nary studies for the construction of the Pia door, which
was carried out between 1561
and 1565, on the orders of
Pius IV.
Judging by the content of the
drawing it was obviously not
used for the construction of
the door, although there are a
series of modified elements
which appear in it. Thus, the
use of columns on the sides
was rejected in favour of pillars, the Roman arch was lowered and the trapezoidal
pediment was in the end supported on its base.
Although this sketch was
never used, the layout of the
doorway is clearly outlined
and is related to its architectural designs, eliminating the
possibility that the facade
might be diminished when
viewed from a distance. In
short, with this doorway he
aimed to achieve a sceno-
graphic effect, whose final result depended on the design
of the facade in which the
doorway was to be placed.
(*Enrique Valdivieso*)

320

254
Italy

Michelangelo Buonarroti
(Caprese, 1475-Rome, 1564)
*Ground plan for San Juan de
los Florentinos*, 16th century
Drawing, black pencil and
gouache on paper,
28.4 x 21.1 cm
Florence, Casa Buonarroti, 121
Bibliography: Dussler 1959;
Barocchi 1962; Barocchi
1964[a]; Barocchi 1964[b]; Berti
1965; Hartt 1971; Tolnay
1975; Tolnay 1975-1980; Berti
1985

This is one of the most detailed original ground plans of
all those preserved from the
Italian Renaissance. In the
drawing we can observe the
combination of two fun-
damental geometric elements,
the square and the circle,
which at the time were considered as the essential starting
points for undertaking any
construction.
By studying Michelangelo's
ground plan, it has been u-

nanimously recognised that its
surrounding square exterior
was conditioned by the surviving foundations of an earlier
building, into which he incor-
porates a circle which, in turn,
was to form a cupola.
In the circular area of the
ground plan there are two
naves formed by a row of columns which follow the line of
the walls, and two side por-
ticos. These features illustrate
Michelangelo's extensive
architectural training and especially his studies on classical
architecture and his remarkable knowledge of late Roman
and paleo-christian buildings,
since obvious parallels with
the basilicas of Santa Costanza
and Santo Stefano Rotondo
can be seen in this building.
The structure also illustrates
Michelangelo's tendency to
give architectural forms a
sense of precision and order
which gives them a serious-
ness imbued with great solemnity.
(*Enrique Valdivieso*)

255
Italy

Michelangelo Buonarroti
(Caprese, 1475-Rome, 1564)
*Pilaster base for the New
Sacristy, fragment of the
ground-plan for the convent
of San Lorenzo*, 16th century
Drawing, sanguine and pen
on paper, 28.3 x 21.4 cm
Florence, Casa Buonarroti,
10 A
Bibliography: Dussler 1959;
Barocchi 1962; Barocchi
1964[a]; Barocchi 1964[b]; Berti
1965; Hartt 1971; Tolnay
1975; Tolnay 1975-1980; Berti
1985

An interesting aspect of this
drawing is that it contains a
paragraph of written text by
Michelangelo in which he reflects on the construction process of the Medicea chapel,
also called the New Sacristy of
San Lorenzo.
The drawing of the bases,
concise and meticulous in
spite of the apparent careless-
ness of his sketch, show Mi-

chelangelo's desire to capture
even the most minute details
of the building, and also the
high standards of his creative
work.
Michelangelo's involvement in
this project began in 1520, on
the orders of Pope Leon X,
and was intended to house the
sepulchres of his brother Julián and his nephew Lorenzo.
Michelangelo designed the
space within a square ground
plan which was covered with
a cupola, giving the whole interior a solemn and serious
feeling which was perfectly
suited to its funereal ends.
(*Enrique Valdivieso*)

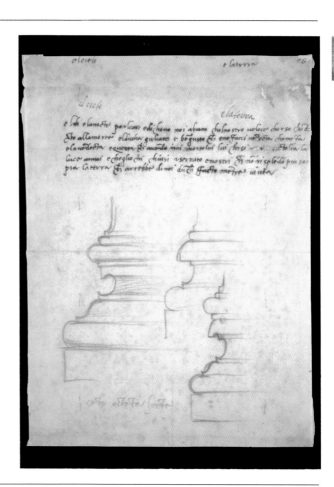

256
Nigeria

Edo culture
Plaque depicting three servants of the court,
end of the 16th century
Bronze sculpture, 49 cm
From Benin, Nigeria
Lagos, National Museum, 50-30-6
Bibliography: Eyo 1974; Eyo 1976, VI, pp. 37-58; Eyo 1977; Eyo-Willet 1980

Benin, the capital of the Edo people, is 115 km to the south of Owo and 196 km southeast of Ife. The best-known and most numerous bronze sculptures of Africa originate from Benin. It is a court art since the Oba or king had a monopoly on all the work and was also the richest person in the kingdom. The tributes paid to him allowed him to maintain a special guild of artists who worked in bronze, wood, marble and earthenware. In fact the Bronze moulders were forbidden, on threat of death, to make pieces for other people. Scientifically speaking, the pieces cast in Benin were not really in bronze, but the term has been universally accepted when referring to all these copper alloys.

Several theories suggest that Benin art may have derived from Ife art and they are supported by documents from Benin and Ife oral traditions. However, others maintain that, except for the use of works of art for the veneration of their kings and deities and the immortalisation of their dead royal ancestors, these two artistic styles followed different paths and only the early Benin art bore any resemblance to that of the Ife. There are also conflicting opinions as to where the "bini" learnt bronze casting. Some believe that it was the Portuguese who were the first Europeans to make contact with the kingdom of Benin (1485). Others expound the theory that the technique of casting was adopted from the Yoruba. Ekpo Eyo in *Two Thousand Years of Nigerian*

Art (1977), pointed out that there was insufficient information on both artistic centres to draw any definitive conclusions.

Benin art can be divided into three periods or phases. The first was around 1400 and was characterised by heads with a very thin casting due to the scarcity of copper before the arrival of the Portuguese. The thicker heads, plaques and leopards date from an intermediary period, around 1500 and, finally, there was a decadent phase around the year 1650, during which enormous gaudy heads were made. The end came in 1897, after the dethroning of the Oba and his subsequent exile. Nevertheless, after five centuries (15th-19th) of working exclusively

for the royal house, Benin's artists have contributed to the imperial splendour with works that are astounding because of the perfection of the casting techniques and their delicate form.

The Benin plaques, which date from the end of the 16th century and the beginning of the 17th, were used to decorate the wooden columns holding up the roof of the Oba's palace. The holes used to hang them are clearly visible on the plaques. It has been said that their rectangular shape, which very rarely appears in African art, except for the sculpted doors, was based on illustrations that the Bini saw in European books. Many plaques depict scenes of life at court. This plaque portrays three servants of the court wearing loincloths knotted at the waist and necklaces on their arms and necks. They are probably holding a medicine bag in their right hands. In the lower left corner the registration number of the British Museum can still be seen, a reminder of the punitive exhibition by the English in 1897, during which they took away the majority of Benin's works of art. After the second world war, the Nigerian government made great efforts to recover the works, and currently have the third most important collection of Benin art in the world.
(*V.K. Agili*)

257
Italy

Bartolomeo Suardi known as "il Bramantino" (Milan, approx. 1465-1530)
Piety, approx. 1513
Painting, Oil on canvas, 193 x 152 cm
From the Werner Collection
Milan, Castello Sforzesco, 1462
Bibliography: DE PAGAVE, ms. S 157 sup. Biblioteca Ambrosiana (ed. Suida 1953), p. 220; SUIDA 1953, pp. 110, 126, 220, 223; LONGHI 1955, p. 59; BERENSON 1968, p. 61; MULAZZANI 1978, p. 94

The first reference to this painting was made in 1513 in De Pagave's manuscript, which mentions a painting located in the sacristy of San Barnaba in Milan.

We do not have precise information on the original location of the work, although it is assumed that it was in the old church dedicated to San Barnaba, which was subsequently replaced by the Alessi building (1561).

Bramantino returned to the *Piety* theme on other occasions. The painting in Vienna (Artaria collection), the one in Bucarest and the one in the parish church at Mezzana, together with the one from the Castello Sforzesco – which precedes them chronologically – show the always different but always intensely dramatic approaches to this distressingly emotional theme, a theme that was closely related to Bramantino's strict religious beliefs.

This is a key piece in the artists' development: his interest in architecture determines his monumental vision of space; the figures assembled around the inert body of Christ show a contained sorrow, typical of the extreme sensibility of the great artist of Lombardy.
(*Maria Teresa Franco Fiorio, Mercedes Garberi*)

258 and 260
Italy

Pier Antonio degli Abbati (active between 1462 and 1504)
Urban Perspective (G and K), between 1474 and 1507, the year of the consecration of the church of Sant'Andrea of Ferrara
Marquetry, 125 x 66 x 5 cm
From the choir stalls of the Augustinian church of Sant'Andrea of Ferrara
Ferrara, Museo Schifanoia, tarsia G and K
Exhibitions: Ferrara, 1988; Ferrara, 1991
Bibliography: SCALABRINI 1779, p. 301; GRUYER 1897, I, p. 563; VARESE 1979, pp. 24-27; FERRETTI 1982, XI, p. 105; BAGATIN 1990, p. 210, fig. 197; BAGATIN 1991, pp. 89-104, p. 58, fig. 34

The charm of these urban landscapes is not just the result of the interplay of woods, as in a perfect mosaic, but stems from the magical composition of the perspective, a new Renaissance secret for representing space, and from the magic of a rigorous, synthetic and clear reproduction. The historical background of landscape marquetry is linked to the influence of Piero della Francesca on Canozzi, and is particularly common in Ferrara, where the great painter worked and left a profound mark around the middle of the 15th century, more specifically in 1449. The technique of marquetry, in this example as well as in the work by other artists from Lendinara, combines perfectly with the vision of the perspective. The decomposition of the visual pyramid in proportional sections is indicated by means of the layout of the lines cut on the wooden base, following the original outline of the board. Great skill and a profound pictorial sense thus come together in the choice of the teseras of the different woods: the poplar and linden are easy to recognise, although there is no lack of the strange and exotic variety, sometimes the consequence of a fortuitous recovery of debris from ships which had sailed around the world. The results are quite different to the ordinary wood joinery that could be achieved by a good cabinetmaker. Science and poetry find a unifying expression through the work of these artists. In the marquetry portraying a view of the Sant'Andrea church, using the "space" of an imaginary architecture – that roman arch behind which one imagines the viewer – there is frequently a fleeting cityscape. In this case, as in others, the view is broken by the raised walls of the neighbouring houses so that a continuity of space and perhaps of events can be imagined, which goes beyond that which can be conferred on the view. It represents "another place," silent, made of a nameless architecture, a calm synthesis between a medieval past and a present Renaissance, in which the presence of figures is unnecessary since it is satisfactory in itself.

The G marquetry depicts a small Romanic church with a saddle roof, a facade separated by projections in three areas corresponding to the three naves, and the vertical arched crenellations which provide light, with three circular rose windows, creating a bleak and pious interior. The doorways, except for the one on the side, have a rigid architrave which moderates the interplay of the curves of the doorway arches of the flat-roofed gallery of the palace on the right, in which we find the first two visual elevations of the three dimensional composition, which can be regarded as genuine scenic frames. Next, our eye follows the line of the back street leading to the white building in the background, opened out by severe sash windows and a portico area which, despite the fact that it only shows the two arches, makes us think of a long horizontal sequence of openings, as can be found in several of the palaces in Ferrara. The K marquetry depicts another view of the same city: sober palaces, long paths in the Venetian tradition, rectangular windows which break up the interaction of the curved outlines, and a hesitant background of hills. What is clear are the intersections, corresponding to the pavements, at the base of the first building on the edge of the canal and then in the passage beneath the portico, along the line of the water which scarcely touches the other bank where other horizontal lines multiply. In this case, the vanishing point of the perspective is on the left, following the line of the moat, crossed diagonally by a footbridge. The divergence of the perspective of this marquetry with that of the G marquetry, could reveal the original sequence of the panels which, according to a common horizon line, should lead the viewer to a panoramic view, in rotation with a graded development of line which relates to the vanishing point of the perspective. There should be inlays on the right side of the semicircular chancel, as in G, pointing perspectively to the right, and on the left hand side should be those, as in K, which point to the left. The middle panels are less directional, although they should always be placed according to the general orientation. As to whether the work is attributable to Pier Antonio degli Abbati, an artist linked to the Canozzi, there are clear similarities to the marquetry he undertook for the chancel of the temple of Santa Corona, in Vicenza (Bagatin 1991). In this sense, the traditional opinion that this is the work of other artists, all of whom worked in the same area as Canozzi, for instance Rizzardi, or Bernadino and Daniele da Lendinara, has no real basis.
(*Chiara Toschi Cavaliere*)

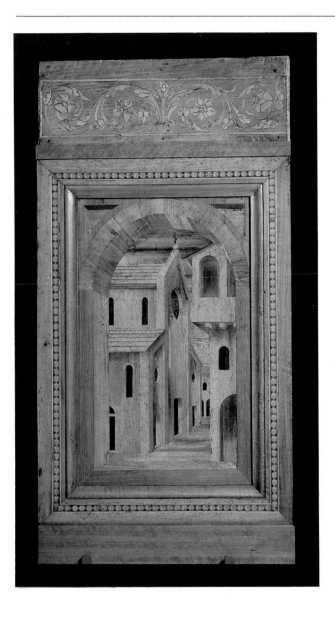

259
Italy

Bartolomeo Montagna
(Orzinuovi, Brescia,
approx. 1450-Vicenza, 1523)
*Saint Peter Benedicting and
Presenting*, approx. 1505
Oil painting on panel,
60 x 39 cm
Inscriptions: ESTO FIDELIS,
on the piece of paper the
small dog holds in its mouth
Venice, Gallerie
dell'Accademia, 1343
Exhibitions: Padua, 1976, n. 27
Bibliography:
CROWE-CAVALCASELLE 1911-1912,
vol. II pp. 12 and 70;
MOSCHETTI 1922; MOSCHETTI
1927, pp. 71-75; BERENSON
1957, p. 120; PUPPI 1962,
pp. 50 and 117; NEPI
SCIRÉ-VALCANOVER 1985, n. 101.
p. 113, with previous
bibliography

The *Saint Peter benedicting
and presenting* by Bartolomeo
Montagna was mentioned for
the first time by Crowe-Cavalcaselle as a work belonging to
the Papafava de Padua collection, where it remained until
1971, the year in which it was
purchased by the Italian state
for the Gallerie dell'Accademia
in Venice. The painting was du-
biously ascribed to Squarcione,
pointing to the evidence of stylistic forms related to Jacopo da
Montagna and Bartolomeo
Montagna. In 1922, A. Mo-
schetti wrote an article address-
ing the "dipinto di Casa Papafava attribuito a Jacopo da
Montagnana", in an attempt to
establish a link with the work of
a follower of Francesco del
Cossa. The definitive attribution to Bartolomeo Montagna
was made by B. Berenson in
1957 and it was soon taken up
by the scholars, among them L.
Puppi, researching into the
painter from Vicenza.
The work is a kind of summary
and a synthesis of the pictorial
style of Montagna, incorporating Venetian influences from
Vivarini to Giovanni Bellini,
from Antonello of Mantegna
and even from the Lombardy
school. In this sense, its comparison with *The Virgin with

*Child and Musical Angels, be-
tween Saint John and another
Saint,* from the charterhouse of
Pavía, is eloquent enough.
The figure of Saint Peter
stands majestically, erect and
powerful in front of a wall
with two large arches which
make, if this is possible, the
image of the saint seem even
stronger. The arches open out
onto a landscape with a lake
stretching to the left and right
in a very varied way. On the
left hand side, the diagonals of
the embankment mark the
vanishing points of several fa-
cades which were treated as
though they were intarsia.
This obvious relationship was
pointed out by Magagnato and
more recently by M. Ferretti ("I
maestri della prospettiva," in
Storia dell'Arte Italiana,
Torino 1982, vol. 11, p. 508-
509) when referring more gen-
erically to the intarsia by Pier
Antonio degli Abbati in
Vicenza; on the right, although
the landscape has a sense of
continuity, is a view of a city
between water and mountain,
in which he aimed to differen-
tiate the facade from the dome
of Vicenza. It is to some extent
a representation of two different kinds of reality, separated
by the figure of Saint Peter.
If the architectural presence is
very obvious, from the ground
to the landscape, no less so is
the treatment of the light
which emphatically modulates
the volumes, giving a marked
accentuation to the contrast of
light and shade. The dim-
inished presence of the donor
and of the dog holding a piece
of paper which reads ESTO
FIDELIS, seem a little strange in
front of this construction.
Neither one nor the other enables us to situate the work
chronologically, which some
scholars have put it at around
1495, that is, during the most
productive artistic phase of
Bartolomeo Montagna, and
others, alluding to the relationship of the work with murals
in the Santi Nazzario and
Celso church in Verona, put it
back almost a decade.
(*Joan Sureda i Pons*)

261
Egypt

Late Mamluk period
Bowl, end of the 14th century
Beaten brass, engraved and
scored, diameter 31 cm
Inscriptions: written in Nasji,
the name of the Sultan of
Mamluk, Abu al-Saadat
Mohammed, son of Qa'it Bay
Cairo, Museum of Islamic Art,
15052

This bowl is typical of the style
of metal objects made at the
end of the 15th century. The
slender rim is skillfully decorated with an engraved strip of
floral scrolls. The exterior is
divided into twenty-four rectangular panels, engraved and
printed with floral motifs and
epigraphs. Inserted between
each three panels with a floral
and geometric design is a panel
with an epigraph. The panels
form triangles both on the
upper and lower sections. The
inscription in Nasji on the panels says, "Made by order of our
lord the Sultan, the royal, the

king al-Nasir Abu al-Saadat Mohammed, the shadow of the
Sultan on earth, on whom de-
pend those who suffer injus-
tices." For the first time an additional title for the sultan appears, that of "the shadow of
the Sultan on earth," in other
words, "the shadow of law and
justice." The central section of
the base is a flower with twelve
petals, surrounded by curved
ribs which resemble the
Chinese *tschi-tschi*. A number
of these types of bowls were
made by the artisans of the
court during this period, and
were normally used for
carrying food to the place of
honour of the sultan's table.
Sultan Abu al-Saadat was fourteen years old when he acceded to the throne, after the
death of his father Qa'it Bay in
1496. His reign lasted two years
and three months, in two
periods separated by an inter-
val of five days, and he was
eventually dethroned after
being assassinated by Tumanbay. (*Nimat M. Abu Bakr*)

262
Egypt

Mamluk period
Goblet,
end of the 15th century
Glazed and polychrome
ceramic, 13 cm; diameter
10 cm
Inscriptions: written in Nasji,
"Eternal glory and prosperity"
Cairo, Museum of Islamic
Art, 5591

This ceramic goblet has a
cone-shaped body and a widened base. The interior of the

goblet has no decoration,
whilst the external surface is
decorated with Nasji writing in
black and white, on a background of stylised painted
scrolls beneath a transparent
glaze.
This type of decoration
denotes the influence of the
Chinese blue and white artistic
tradition which was greatly
imitated in this period. The
main strip has the traditional
votive statement, which reads,
"Eternal glory and prosperity."
(*Farouk S. Asker*)

263
Spain

Manises
Ceramic dish, 15th-16th
century
Ceramic with stanniferous
enamelling and gilding,
diameter 36.5 cm; height 5 cm
Granada, Museo Nacional
de Arte Hispanomusulmán,
3.947
Bibliography: BERMÚDEZ PAREJA
1968; FLORES ESCOBOSA 1982;
FLORES ESCOBOSA 1983-1985

The piece is made of turned earthenware using the habitual technique of three firings. The first is made after the modelling and the second after it has been covered with creamy-white stanniferous enamelling. Both firings are carried out in an oxidizing atmosphere at high temperature. The last firing is for the copper-coloured gilding, applied by brush on both surfaces. The last phase is carried out in a reducing atmosphere.

Typologically, this piece belongs to the group called "Plat de tetó," because of the umbo in the middle of the obverse, the rounded and uneven sides which form the rim, defined by an internal edge, and also because of the slightly dropped finish of the rim, which is thicker on the concave and non-circular base of the exterior.

These pieces were very decorative and were not necessarily made for use on the table. The decoration on the obverse of this example is separated into two sections. There is a quadripartite composition on the concave area, the centre of which is the umbo itself, decorated with a fish and enclosed by a nobleman's coat of arms, which is surrounded by a gilt strip and small wheels in negative. The rest of the sections are covered with double leaves, silhouetted against a background of small plant motifs of small flowers and spikelets.

On the rim there are gilded strips of different thickness, the most outstanding being the strip composed of alternate asterisk and R shapes. The main composition is an ovolo frieze painted in spiral shapes, with the small flowers and spikes being alternated with "lace" patterns. These detailed motifs appeared at the end of the 15th century and were developed throughout the 16th century, as can be seen, for example, on the piece in the Museo Civico of Bologna. The central theme of this piece is the coat of arms of pope León X (1513-1521), which is surrounded by decorative features similar to those mentioned earlier.

On the reverse of the dish, the decoration is centred around the middle section and consists of curved rib rosettes, and on the rim there is a frieze formed by "feathers," surrounded by stalks which are joined together by small sashes.

(*Isabel Flores Escobosa*)

264
Turkey

Muhammad b. Ibrahim al-ghori or Muhammed b. Shamsuddin al-ghuri
Jug, 1497
Cast bronze with inlaid gold and silver, 12.5 cm; diameter of the mouth 8.6 cm; diameter of the base 7.6 cm
Inscriptions: on the base: a dedication to sultan Husayn Bayqara, signed by Muhammad b. Ibrahim al-ghori 903 H (11 April 1497): "amal al-abd al-faqir al-haqir Muhammad b. (...) al-Awrani fi awsat shahr shaban al-mu azz sana al-thalath wa this mia"
London, British Museum, 1962, 7-18.1
Bibliography: GRUBE 1974, fig. 76-77; LENTZ-LOWRY 1989, cat. n. 151

This cast bronze jug, whose handle and lid are missing, is engraved with scroll-shaped leaves and inscriptions and damascened in silver and gold. The inscription, a collar shaped strip, bears the name and titles of the Timurí governor Abu al-Ghazi Sultán Husayn (1470-1506). Under this great Maecenas of the arts, Herat became an important artistic and intellectual centre. He himself wrote poetry and among his courtiers was the mystic poet Rumi. Their contemporaries described banquets with performances of music, poetry recitals, literary discussions and riddle competitions; all of which were accompanied by an abundance of wine. Illustrations from Timurí manuscripts depict the jugs that were used at such feasts. The pleasures of wine are mentioned in Persian verse, which also appears on many of the jugs which have been conserved and would therefore have been particularly appropriate for such occasions.
An inscription on the base indicates that it was made halfway through the month of Sh'ban of H 903 (April 1498) for Muhammad ibn Shamsi

(Shams al-Din) al-Ghuri. The *nisba* – the names derived from the place of origin – of the artisan, al-Ghuri, suggests that it came from Ghur, a mountainous region to the east of Herat.
(*Rachel Ward*)

265
Spain

Al-Andalus, Nasrid period
Drinking fountain, 15th
century
Moulded ceramic with
a layer of stanniferous
enamelling and gilding,
diameter 10 x 35.2 cm
From the convent of Zafra
Granada, Museo Nacional
de Arte Hispanomusulmán,
7.298
Bibliography: Marinetto
Sánchez-Flores Escobosa 1991

This ceramic drinking fountain has an oval-shaped interior and a flat rim with an undulating due to the manual flattening of the edge. The interior shows the remains of its vitreous layer of gold on the edge. The ovolos are on the outside and in this case are painted as far as the base in a dark copper-coloured gold.

For practical purposes, it has a hole in the middle of the base to let water in and two pairs of small perforations, just beside the edge, for drainage. Its rich vitreous finish in gold which gave it a metallic effect has become worn through use.

Very few of these ceramic drinking fountains have been conserved and even fewer have this ovolo shape, a reminder of those made in marble. However, there are several fragments which have rotated ovolos and the inside decorated with blue fish blue, as a reminder of the fact that they were used for water. Water-related themes such as fishes, turtles and algae can be traced back to the Califal period, depicted on drinking fountains of the Almanzor period, and also appear in the eastern Selyuqí culture, on enamelled glass and ceramic objects, and would appear again in Mamluk art, on metal pieces with fishes decorating the centre.

These small ceramic drinking fountains, part of the architectural ceramic group, are related, even more so because of their size, to the type of domestic drinking fountain or large plates from the Nasrid school of ceramics. This pottery is decorated in white, blue and gold and was painted in a similar fashion to those with moulded ovolos, with each space carefully decorated with palm leaves or epigraphs, sometimes with the ovolos in the normal position or, as in this type of drinking fountain, with rotated versions, of which there are numerous examples in the Museo Nacional de Arte Hispanomusulmán.

The decorative themes on these oval-shaped drinking fountains made their appearance in the Hispano-Muslim world during the Califal epoch, and important examples, varying in size and style of ovolo, were made throughout the Nasrid period.
(*Purificación Marinetto Sánchez*)

266
Spain

Al-Andalus, Nasrid period
Gorronera, 14th century
Polychrome muqarnas in
wood, 40 x 45 cm
From the door of the
courtyard of the Cuarto
Dorado of the Alhambra
Granada, Museo Nacional
de Arte Hispanomusulmán,
n. 3,972

This wooden gorronera comes from the central arched doorway of the Cuarto Dorado (Golden Court), from the exterior facade below and the lattices, as is usual for maintaining a constant flow of air when the doors are closed. There is now no sign of it in its place of origin, although we know where it was located before being deposited in the Museo Nacional de Arte Hispanomusulmán from photographs.

Nothing remains of the original doors which were destroyed by the shock wave from an explosion in the workshop of a gunpowder maker between Guadix gate and the river Darro near San Pedro. According to Juan de la Vega, surveyor of the royal works, in a report to the governor of the Alhambra written on 18 February 1590, the main door was blown open and smashed to pieces.

In the middle sixties it was decided to restore the north facade of the Cuarto Dorado to its original appearance by knocking down the arcade dating from the 16th century and revealing the original arcade in all its magnificence. It was also decide to make copies of the doors modelled on the ones which had been preserved at the entrance to the Hall of the Two Sisters, adapting them for size, and to make use of the preserved original gorroneras. This work was carried out by the master carpenter of the Alhambra, Joaquín Vera Medina. The gorroneras were later removed from their place of origin.

This gorronera, like the other,

is made of wood and is decorated with three levels of toothing stone of different sizes which project from a somewhat rectangular base and end in a similar one with a projection towards the upper part, between ten and twenty centimeters higher.

The toothing stones are joined by T irons and also display fine wooden bolts. Inside, the toothing stones are spread out and their ends are rounded at different levels.

The beautiful finish of the muqarnas is completed with a layer of red paint which serves as the base for the definitive polychroming in black and white alternating with a pearled border which has circular knots in the upper panel in the key, which are arched in the alfiz style, joining with the upper part.

The patillas and guillillo of the first and second levels are painted completely black and display flowers with four petals formed by small circles, one central and four at the sides. The lower part reveals marks from the opening and closing of the door.

The tradition of the gorronera in Hispano-Muslim art is known from the caliphal period in Madinat al-Zahra', when the Classical and Visigothic tradition was revived. It was in the Nasrid period that they reached their greatest size in relation to the hinging posts and were used as an element of decoration and construction in the muqarnas, which was also decorated with polychrome, as is the case here, carvings on the wood, with epigraphs, and vegetal and geometric motifs, as in the examples which are found in the entrance to the Hall of Comares. Although the wood seems to be most used in gorroneras, they are also found in white marble, like those in the Casa del Chapiz in Granada currently in the Museo Nacional de Arte Hispanomusulmán (n. 2872-2873), which have an independent cyma decorated with the motto of the Nasrid dynasty as if they were capitals.

(*Purificación Marinetto Sánchez*)

267
Turkey

Iznik, Ottoman period
Water jug, 1510
Ceramic, 17 cm; diameter
of mouth 6.9 cm; diameter
of base 7.2 cm
Inscriptions: Armenian
inscription with the date
H 959
London, British Museum,
Godman Legacy, G. 1983.1
Bibliography: ATASOY-RABY
1989, fig. 96

A small water jug with pourer
and handle in the form of a
dragon's head – possibly in
imitation of an Italian prototype in metal – painted with
cobalt applied before glazing,
with floral and other motifs.
The most important characteristic of this water jug is an Armenian inscription on the
base which reveals that it was
made for Abraham of Kutahya
in H 959 (1510). Few of such
pieces are dated and this is
why this water jug provides
important information on the
development of Turkish ceramics. Indeed, due to this inscription, a whole group of ceramics painted with cobalt before glazing produced be-
tween approximately 1470
and 1525 has been named
"Abraham of Kutahya."
The name of the jug's owner,
Abraham of Kutahya, a member of a religious minority and
apparently not a member of
the court, also suggests that
Turkish ceramics – which had
arisen at the end of the 15th
century to supply the demand
of the court – were favoured
by the growth of a much
wider market around 1510.
(*Rachel Ward*)

268
Turkey

Iznik
Pot, approx. 1510-1520
Ceramic, 24.5 cm; diameter
of the mouth 15.6 cm;
diameter of the base 14.4 cm
London, British Museum.
Henderson Legacy, G. 1983.6
Bibliography: ATASOY-RABY
1989, n. 297

A large ceramic pot painted in
cobalt before glazing with floral motifs. This pot reveals the
great technical virtuosity of the
potters of Iznik in the first half
of the 16th century. The size,
the whiteness of the background, the richness of the cobalt blue, the clarity of line,
the well-performed glazing
without fissures all combine to
create a pot which emulates
the quality of the Ming china
which was very popular in the
Ottoman court.
The pottery of Iznik was
priced more than anything by
size, which means that this pot
must have been amongst the
dearest made there. The big
flowers in the form of volutes
are closely related to the decoration of other materials such
as cloths and seem to be inspired by the motifs created by
the court workshop in Istanbul. The pot must have been
used to hold food. Pots of a
similar size are represented on
the shelves of a fruit seller's
shop in the manuscript *Surname* of the sultan Murad III
(approx. 1582) (Atasoy-Raby
fig. 10). It was necessary to
store the food in ceramic containers to prevent mice getting
at it – a cat which appears in
the illustration was presumably one more means of deter-
ring them.
(*Rachel Ward*)

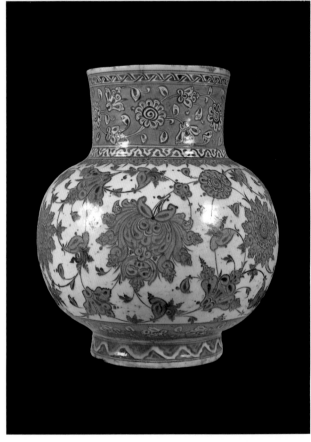

269
Italy

Master of 1473 and assistant
The Miracles of Saint
Bernardino of Siena: the
Miracle of the Stillborn
Child, approx. 1473
Tempera on panel,
79 x 57 cm
From the sacristy of the
former monastery of San
Francesco al Prato, Perugia
Perugia, Galleria Nazionale
dell'Umbria, 222
Bibliography: SANTI 1977,
pp. 49-53; BELLOSI 1975, 3,
pp. 50-60; VASCO 1974,
XXV, 1-2, pp. 64-67;
SCARPELLINI 1984, p. 92

This panel formed part of a
group of eight representing
the miracles of Saint Bernardino of Siena known as the
"Saint Bernardino niche." This
was completed with a standard depicting the saint by the
Perugian painter Benedetto
Bonfigli and a niche in the
Bernardinian trigram inserted
in the sculpted wreath. It was
located in the small chapel
dedicated to him in San
Francesco al Prato in Perugia.
It has proven quite difficult to
reconstruct the first structure.
None of the hypotheses produced so far (altar, niche, or
cupboard) seems completely
convincing.
It is certain that the eight panels were placed in two
groups of four and that they
were materially divided on a
second occasion.
The panel in question depicts
the story of the stillborn child
of Margaret of Basel who was
brought back to life through
the intercession of the saint.
This occurrence, which is set
in a courtyard with architecture reminiscent of that of the
ducal palace of Urbino is articulated around various moments in the life of the youth.
A cornice imitating a bronze
decoration with pearls and
precious stones extends
around it. The painting, with
its evident references to the
culture of Ferrara has, like the
group as a whole, been attributed to various different
painters, making it one of the
most intricate points in the history of Umbrian painting at
the end of the *Quattrocento*.
Initially attributed to Pisanello,
in 1838 Pavant ascribed to it
to the Umbrian Fiorenzo di
Lorenzo. In 1912 Bombe set
research in another direction
by adding the names of
Francesco di Giorgio (for the
architectural scenes), Pinturic-
chio and Perugino.
In 1913 Venturi ascribed a
dominant role to the latter,
identifying him as the father of
the idea of the architectural
backgrounds and the painter
of two of the panels. Van
Marle opposed this idea in
1923, rightly calling the painter
the "Master of 1473." It was
impossible to more clearly
identify the artist with Florentine influences who worked
with the assistance of Pinturic-
chio and another anonymous
artist on this work.
Santi (1985) made an important contribution to clarifying
which artists were responsible
for certain basic aspects, confirming that the re-sizing in the
two single panels was by Perugino, that the complex abstract architecture was by "intellectual" painter, probably
Urbino, the presence of Pintu-
ricchio and Bonfigli in the
work, and the influence of artists from Ferrara and Padua.
Such points of view have also
been put forward by Scarpellini, who also notes express-
ionistic aspects which would
stem from an artist close to
Bonfigli and Caporali.
Perhaps we should also consider the name of Bartolomeo
della Gatta as advanced by
Bellosi and confirmed by Scarpellini.
(*Vittoria Garibaldi*)

270
Turkey

Iznik
Writing case, approx. 1510
Ceramic with silver
mounting, 29.6 x 6.3 cm
London, British Museum,
Godman Legacy, G. 1983.7
Inscriptions: ornamental
Cufic inscriptions and an
inscription in Nasji script
from the Koran (sura LXI.13)
"aid of God and victory is
close"
Bibliography: ROGERS-WARD
1988, n. 2; ATASOY-RABY 1989,
fig. 87: 8

A ceramic writing case painted
in cobalt before glazing, with
decorations of leaves and
bands of clouds in the Chinese
style. The silver lids of the case
and of the inkwell are from a
later date; the former carries
the tughra of Selim III (1789-
1807). This is one of the three
known writing cases made in
the workshops of Iznik. It may
have been modelled on a

Chinese porcelain prototype
since decorated porcelain
writing cases were made during the Ming dynasty in Jingdezhen, China, for export to
the Middle East. One of them
is still in the treasury of the
Topkapi palace. Its damascene of golden thread, with its
inset rubies and emeralds
demonstrate the great value of
Chinese porcelain at the Ottoman court.
The writing case was an important accessory in the Islamic world where calligraphy
was held in high respect. They
were generally made of metal
or wood, but richly decorated
examples in a great variety of
materials were also produced.
The treasury of the Topkapi
palace of Istanbul possesses
various 16th century writing
cases in gold, jade and rock
crystal, all of them decorated
with precious stones.
(*Rachel Ward*)

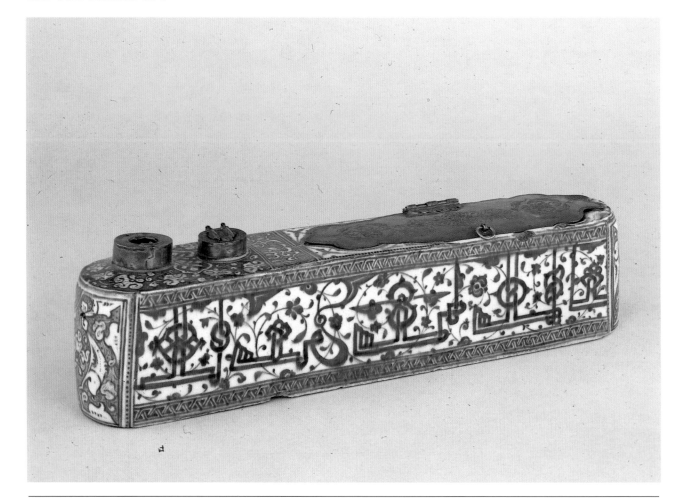

271
Spain

Al-Andalus, Nasrid period
Box, 15th century
Inlaid wood,
21 x 20 x 21 cm
Granada, Museo Nacional
de Arte Hispanomusulmán,
1.598

Amongst the few surviving pieces of furniture from the Nasrid period of Hispano-Muslim art is a series of decorated household accessories made in inlaid wood. The importance of geometry of previous periods is adapted to this technique, producing works as meticulous as those of the cupboard doors of the palace of Los Infantes in the Calle Cetti Merien, which are kept in the Museo Nacional de Arte Hispanomusulmán, or the writing case of the Museo Arqueológico Nacional of Madrid, amongst others. This jewelry box has a rectangular form and is made of wood, with small inlaid drawers and a small metal handle for carrying which is joined to the box with a piece in the form of small four-petalled flowers. The marks of the metal fasteners used to close the box still remain. Two rose from the base of the interior like hinges to close a lost lateral door, whilst another set closed the box at the top and prevented its drawers from being opened in the style of a tiny *bargueño*. When the box was closed it displayed a smooth wooden surface which was decorated simply with a few laths framing each side.

The lateral door opens to reveal seven small drawers with inlays fixed to parchment before being set on the wood; the same solution is seen in the fortress of Marrakus (cloth), and the minbar of the Bu-naniyya of Fez (leather), where a flexible base which is fixed to the wooden structure is employed. The decoration consists of interlaced wheels made out of small pieces of bone, wood in various tones and green-coloured bone. The wheels are contained in octagons, with four-pointed stars set between them. The wheels are not complete in some cases at the ends of each side, their size not having been correctly judged, thereby necessitating cutting. The drawers and the laths separating them are decorated with herringbone which goes in different directions. A small handle hangs from a ring in the centre of each drawer. The mixture of colours of the different inlays created a mosaic effect which Ferrandis connected with the impression of the mosaics of the mihrab of the Córdoba mosque, but in these late examples, where the central ornamental theme is centered on geometry, the decoration stands in direct relation with the colour effect of the glazed tiling.

When the decoration is removed, the joinery of the drawers and the nails which hold the external structure together can be seen.
(*Purificación Marinetto Sán-chez*)

335

272
India

Kerala
Siva Chandrashekhar,
15th century
Bronze sculpture,
72 x 34.5 x 26.5 cm
New Delhi, National
Museum, 47.109/11

Siva is one of the three major gods of the Hindu pantheon, the others being Vishnu and Brahma. Siva is also called Chandrashekkar, which means "he who has the moon as a decoration on his head". This form of Siva is described in the well-known treatises on iconography of the *Amsumadbhedagama* and the *Uttarakamikagama*. Siva Chandrashekkar is represented standing in the *samabhanga* posture on a lotus mounted on a square base. This posture expresses the *rajo guna*. It is said that *rajas* is the cause of activity in living beings. Siva has four arms: in his upper pair he brandishes an axe and an antelope in the *Kartaribasta* attitude, whilst in the lower pair he holds his right hand in the *abhaya* position of protection and the left hand in the *Varada* position, or attitude of charity.

Siva wears a crown, a narrow band, necklaces, *skandhamala*, armbands and bracelets. The dress is a *dhoti* that is sustained on the front of the figure by a little lace. Both his garments and his jewelry have been treated with great meticulousness, with fluid and free-flowing lines which create an attractive sensation of smoothness.

The slender profile of a crescent moon situated to the left of Siva's crown underlines the image of Chandrashekhar. The moon is symbolic of cyclic time and the vessel of *Soma*, the drink of immortality or water of life.
(*Shashi Astana*)

273
Italy

Pierino da Vinci (Vinci, Florence, approx. 1530-Pisa 1554)
Holy Family, 16th century
Wax (or terracotta), diameter 38 cm
Florence, Collezione Carlo Loeser
Bibliography: LOESER 1922; LENSI 1934, p. 39

This tondo of the *Holy Family* from the Palazzo Vecchio in Florence reveals how the contemporaries and followers of Michelangelo could be influenced by his creations but still produce very different results. According to Loeser this wax "è senza dubbio la prima versione della composizione che Michelangelo fece poi nel tondo di marmo del Bargello." Later critics have not agreed with Loeser. Although Lensi enters the tondo under Michelangelo in his commentary on the donation, in his analysis he puts it down to a follower such as Pierino da Vinci or Silvio Cosini. The composition is undoubtedly inspired by the "Pitti tondo" (Florence, Museo Nazionale del Bargello) produced by Michelangelo for Bartolomeo Pitti. The composition is similar, although in the wax model we see St. Joseph, who is not in the Michelangelo marble, probably appearing to some extent in order to compensate for the infant Saint John. This scheme was not necessary in Michelangelo's composition since the masses of the three figures balanced each other out; but the greater rigidity of the wax, which acquires neither the ductility nor the monumentality of the original, makes it necessary to incorporate the fourth figure, also leading to a break with the typical High Renaissance iconography of the Virgin with Jesus and the infant Saint John.

Rather than seek the author of this work in Silvio Cosini, who was especially influenced by Andrea Sansovino and Francesco Rustici, we should turn our attention to skillful followers of Michelangelo such as Pierino da Vinci, who nonetheless normally worked in marble. This is not to say that Pierino da Vinci was a secondary artist. Vasari cites this cousin of Leonardo da Vinci as one of the greatest of his age, and is fulsome in his praise, considering that only his early death prevented him from producing more outstanding works. Vasari also mentions that he produced a wax copy of Michelangelo's *Moses* for Luca Martini, who was one of his patrons.
(*Joan Sureda i Pons*)

274
India

Vijayanagar
Ardhanarisvara, 15th century
Bronze sculpture,
77.5 x 31.5 x 25.5 cm
New Delhi, National
Museum, 47.109/13

Ardhanarisvara is one of the composite figures of Siva, where he appears with a body which is half male and half female. Siva represents the masculine principle and Parvati the feminine. The mythological explanation for this figure is found in texts such as the *Amsumadbhedagama, Kamikagama, Suprabhedagama, Karanagam, Silparatna*, and *Siva Purana.*

According to the *Siva Purana*, Brahma created a series of male beings known as the Prajapatis and ordered them to create further beings, but they failed in their mission. Unable to understand his error, Brahma began to worship Siva, who appeared to him in the form of Ardhanarisvara. This guided him to understanding, the idea underlying this story being that only the union of the masculine and feminine principles leads to creation.

Other mythological stories relate this form to Bhringi's desire to worship only Siva. This provoked the anger of Parvati, who reduced him to a skeleton. Siva, however, gave him a third leg which allowed him to survive. At the same time he appeared in the form of Ardhanarisvara in order to save Parvati's honour, Bhringi being obliged to pay homage to her as well.

Sometimes Siva Ardhanarisvara is represented with four arms, and sometimes with three. He is always represented standing on his vehicle, the bull Nandi. The right-hand side represents the male body of Siva, and the left-hand side, with its prominent breast, the female body.

This magnificent bronze sculpture is a four-armed image of Ardhanarisvara. It

stands, with the triple flexion or *abhanga*, on a lotus pedestal, holding an axe, now lost, in its upper right hand, and supposedly resting its lower hand on Nandi. The upper hand of its female side holds a lotus petal whilst the lower one rests gracefully on the waist in the *katyavalambita* posture.

Both Siva's large crown and Uma's beautiful hair, which are represented as one on his head, are richly decorated. The male half of the body wears a short pair of breeches and the female half a sari.
(*Shashi Astana*)

275
Italy

Anonymous, Italian school,
Florence
*Madonna and Child and
Angels*, 16th century
High relief in Carrara
marble, 36.5 x 18.8 x 8 cm
Rome, Musei Vaticani, 44089

Lombard sculpture of the first
half of the 16th century is
dominated by the figure of
Agostino Busti, "il Bambaja"
(Busto Arsizio, 1483-Milan,
1548). Trained in the Lombard
tradition of Giovanni Antonio
Amadeo and Briosco, Bam-
baia endowed his works with
a Classicism full of formal
elegance which also reveals
the influence of Leonardo da
Vinci. The richness of Mi-
lanese sculpture in this period
and the fact it does not represent a nodal point in the evolution of Italian sculpture during the *Cinquecento* has
meant that only in recent years
has the figure of Bambaja
been studied in depth and
some of his works attributed
to other sculptors such as
Marco Sanmicheli recon-
sidered. Following the suggestion of Andrea de Marchi, Giovanni Agosti has added the
*Madonna and Child and
Angels* of the Musei Vaticani to
this list (Agosti 1990, p. 193, n.
49). The association is plausible, although the *Madonna*
displays greater formal rigidity
than Bambaja and more of da
Vinci's influence along with a
volumetry in which there are
echoes of Bramante and the
Bramantino. This is perhaps a
relationship which becomes
more patent in the field of
painting, not only in Lombardy but also in artists who
left there to work in Rome and
especially in Naples. All this
allows us to locate the *Madonna and Child and Angels*
in the early years of the 16th
century, which undoubtedly
complicates its attribution to
Bambaja.
(*Joan Sureda i Pons*)

276
India

Vijayanagar
Kali, 15th century
Basalt sculpture, 24 cm
Paris, Musée Guimet, 3391

Tantric philosophy, which seeks the way to truth rather than to define it, has been adopted as a way of knowledge by many religions. In Tantric Hinduism the goddess Kali represents the power of overcoming suffering, of converting bad into good. This is why she is always represented with such a fearful look in the iconography, with her decrepit body, her bloody fangs, the violence of her movement and the skulls she wears as ornaments.

However, the Vijayanagar sculptural style softens the features of this Kali, endowing her with a healthy body and a distant, dignified attitude which is not at all terrifying. This image for worship represents the goddess as the feminine energy of the god Siva, mastering life and death. In her right hand she holds a tambour, the symbol of creation, and in her left hand fire, the symbol of destruction and incineration, which allow the soul to reincarnate and obtain a purer existence.

The rich "Renaissance" eclecticism which dominates Vijayanagar art makes the image less dramatic, increasing its splendour and softening even the monsterous aspect of the image of the child trampled under her right foot, symbolising ignorance.

The mastery of this statue lies in the exceptional nature of its iconography and the ease with which basalt can be sculpted, necessitating no great effort in the detailing of the body of the goddess and the splendour of her jewels.

In 1336 the Vijayanagar ("City of Victory") dynasty created an empire in the south as a last bastion against the devastating and increasingly frequent incursions of the Muslims which threatened to wipe Hindu culture off the entire face of the subcontinent. The artistic splendour of Vijayanagar is undoubtedly due to the arrival of many Hindu artists from the north, where independent sultanates had already been established.

(*Carmen García Ormaechea*)

277
Italy

Luca Signorelli (Cortona 1445/1450-1523)
Pentecost, 1494
Tempera on canvas,
156 x 104 cm
From the fraternity of the Holy Spirit in the church of St. Lucy of Urbino
Urbino, Galleria Nazionale delle Marche
Exhibitions: Japan, 1990-1991; Torre dei Passeri, 1991
Bibliography: SALMI 1953, p. 33; RAGGHIANTI 1954, pp. 96-97; SCARPELLINI 1964 pp. 33, 122; LENZINI MORIONDO 1966, pp. 14, 25-26 (with preceding bibliography)

The lack of documentary evidence for the year of Luca Signorelli's birth (Vasari gives no definite date) causes a certain amount of confusion, although it is generally accepted as being between 1445 and 1450. After an initial influence from Piero della Francesca which can be seen in the Brera panels depicting the *Flagellation* and the *Madonna of the Milk* (around 1480), Signorelli was more decisively influenced by Florence, and in particular by Pollaiolo, whose approach, along with the influence of Perugino, can be seen in the frescos of the basilica of Loreto (1470-1480). We can also see this influence in the large fresco of *The Testament and Death of Moses* in the Sistine Chapel (1482). This is one of the few testimonies of his youth, since his first works have been lost. His mature work belongs to the last decade of the *Quattrocento*. These include the medallion of the *Madonna and Child* (Florence, Uffizi), *The Annunciation* (Volterra, Galleria Comunale) and the magnificent *Adoration of the Magi* (Paris, Louvre). All of these paintings are characterised by the grandeur and plasticity of the composition of the sketch, which is energetic but careful, and the variety and strength of the colours.

The frescos of the cloister of Monteoliveto, which depict the *Story of Saint Benedict* in which Signorelli assumes a vivacious, narrative tone, are dated around 1497-1498. Only a few years later, around 1502, did the painter execute a more laboured effort: *The Story of the Antichrist* and *The Final Judgement* in the chapel of San Brizio in Orvieto cathedral. The dramatic effect obtained with the contrasts of mass and the extraordinary vigour and clarity of the chiaroscuro give the scene great vitality. However, the high level achieved in these works is not seen in all the paintings of his later career, and sometimes they fall into mediocrity.

His work in the Marche region and his stays in Umbria and Tuscany reveals the maturity of his expressive models and the deepening of his search for monumental forms, which was also helped by his contact with Florentine culture. This resulted in works of great corporeity which reveal a deep moral yearning.

His paintings of the *Crucifixion* and the *Pentecost*, which originally constituted the front of a small standard for processions belong to this period. The painter was commissioned to do them in 1494 by Filippo Gueroli by the fraternity of the Holy Spirit of Urbino. Both were damaged at the time of their separation in the 18th century.

Almost all the commentators from Venturi to Salmi agree on the dating of these works, although Berenson (*Italian Pictures of the Renaissance*, 1932) argues that the two canvases were painted a few years after 1494.

With a mottled red and blue border, the paintings reveal the deep spiritual solemnity of this period in the painter's career. In the *Pentecost* was seen an absolute simplification of space with the presentation of a scene which is bleak and enclosed, dominated by the lead grey of the walls.

The concept of space differs from that used by Piero della Francesca, with the perspective marked by the coloured rectangular tiles of the floor converging on the vanishing point of the Virgin and three female figures seated behind her. The intimacy of the walls, the door and the small closed windows build up a mysterious atmosphere of expectation and spiritual suspense where the reddish glow which surrounds the apparition of the Holy Spirit erupts unexpectedly at the highest point of the vault.

The solid, elegant architectonic forms lead us to think of iconographical sources more recent than those of Piero della Francesca, more in contact with Francesco di Giorgio Martini, Ercole de Roberti and the culture of Ferrara. Signorelli reveals himself as someone who knew about the crisis in *Quattrocento* painting, displaying the sense of inner peace and the permanent search for new sources of inspiration which characterise the artistic culture of the following century.
(*Claudia Caldari Giovannelli*)

278
Spain

Juan de Carrión (active around 1470)
The Assumption of the Virgin, signed "Iohan de Carion," 1470
Choirbook, grisaille on parchment,
74 x 112 x 16 cm (open);
70 x 54 x 16 cm (closed)
From the cathedral of Avila
Avila, Museo Catedralicio
Exhibitions: Avila, 1990
Bibliography: MAYER 1926, n. 275, XLVIII, p. 104, fig. A; DOMÍNGUEZ BORDONA 1929, pp. 151-152, n. 86; DOMÍNGUEZ BORDONA 1930, n. VI, pp. 17-20, fig. 7; DOMÍNGUEZ BORDONA 1932, p. 22; DOMÍNGUEZ BORDONA 1933, 1, pp. 1-3, fig. 11; DOMÍNGUEZ BORDONA 1957, CXL, p. 85; DOMÍNGUEZ BORDONA-AINAUD DE LASARTE 1962, XVIII, pp. 195-196, fig. 256; CAMÓN AZNAR 1966, XXII, p. 625, fig. 626; YARZA 1980, II, p. 423; DE LAS HERAS-CARLOS MARTÍN 1981; GONZÁLEZ-SOBRINO 1981, p. 73, fig. 71; SILVA MAROTO 1982, pp. 55-56, fig. 1; GÓMEZ MORENO 1983, pp. 119-120, pl. vol. I, n. 177; SEBASTÍAN 1986, pp. 9-12; VALLADOLID 1988, pp. 317-318

The hymns of the cathedral of Avila are written in black Gothic letters with headings in red, and set out in pages of twenty-four lines. The musical score is set down in lines of four ruled in red. Apart from the the border illustrations, which include rich vegetal motifs and occasional human figures, there are only nine illustrations. According to Gómez Moreno (with whom certain other specialists disagree) their order is as follows. In volume I, *Lettering with David* (fol. 1); *Adoration of the Child* (fol. 80), with the name "Carion" written on a parchment held by one of the *putti*; *Epiphany* (fol. 102), with an inscription in the margin below: "Johan de Carion me fecit". In volume II, the *Resur-*

rection (fol. 1); with an inscription at the bottom of the text to the effect that Juan Carion did the lettering for all the books. In volume III, the *Ascension* (fol. 1); *Pentecost*, with the name "Carion" in the text (fol. 30). The theme of volume IV is the *Assumption* (fol. 3). In volume 5 the *Martyrdom of St. Stephen* (fol. 7) is depicted, and finally, in volume VI, the *Annunciation* (fol. 1). The collection was brought to light by Gómez Moreno in his catalogue of the province of Avila written in 1902. Although it was not published until 1983 it has always been easily available to researchers. It was included in the 1924 exhibition of manuscripts in Madrid, after which the specialists devoted a number of works to Juan de Carrión, the author of some of the illustrations. Gómez Moreno established a rather imprecise chronology for this miniaturist, establishing only that it must date before 1494; Domínguez Bordona tried to make it more precise, taking the tenures of the bishops Francisco Sánchez de Toledo (1493-1496) and Fernando de Talavera (1485-1493) as reference. But it was Silva Maroto who published the only definite information we have so far, dating the hymn book to between 1470 and 1472. We are told that Juan de Carrión was paid six thousand maravedis for two pieces of lettering, and another six thousand on another occasion for the lettering of the Resurrection and the Assumption. On both occasions another five hundred maravedis were added for expenses. There is also information about his brother, Pedro de Guemeres, who received two thousand maravedis for the lettering of the Spiritus Domini and two other pieces, and three hundred for expenses. Two years later, in 1472, he received two thousand five hundred for the lettering of an unspecified text and two hundred for expenses.

Domínguez Bordona believes that all the illustrations are the work of a single but highly versatile artist. The documents published by Silva Maroto credit the illustrations to at least the two brothers, although she also distinguishes a new painter to whom the *Annunciation* must be attributed. Following the documents and the signatures, we can definitely attribute the *Epiphany*, *Resurrection*, and *Assumption* to Juan de Carrión. Pedro de Guemeres was paid for two pieces of lettering, but whilst only the *Pentecost* is specified, he must also be the author of the *Annunciation* since the name "Carrión" that figures there is the same as in the previous work. The remaining illustrations can only be classified by stylistic analysis, and this is quite difficult due to the lack of certain references for the identification of a style containing many common elements from the same studio. Despite this, the

experts disagree on the identifications given above.
Juan de Carrión was the master of a studio, and had a definite German-Flemish training. The Italianisms noted by Bordona and Silva Maroto are nothing more than the fruit of the broad "international" lexicon of the last quarter of the 15th century. The brother's surname of Guemeres could perhaps indicate they were members of a Flemish family who adopted the Spanish name of Carrión in that generation.

(Isidro G. Bango)

279
Netherlands

Censer, approx. 1500
Silverwork, 23.5 cm;
diameter of body 13 cm;
diameter of stand 11.5 cm
Haarlem, Episcopal Palace
Exhibitions: Amsterdam,
1958; Paris 1988

A censer with eight main faces which divide in two slanting inwards at the top; the surface is divided into pointed arches, with the upper ones fitting into the lower ones, decorated with interior tracery. The star-studded stand rises in the centre, with a perforated surface. The body is shaped like a pyramid and structured with a double row of crossed ogee arches with interior tracery ending in rosettes with various peaks and in one upper one. On the lower edge of the body are four nude children holding rings for the chains. The maniple is studded with stars which alternate between four points and four lobes and rises with a sinuous profile and a bulbous form.

This tiny censer comes from the church of Edamen in Holland, but it is difficult to pinpoint its place of origin, and it is not even certain that its maker was Dutch. We know that this peculiar model coincides almost exactly with the one in an engraving signed by Martin Schongauer (Bartsh, n. 107; *Exhibition of the Petit Palais, Paris*, 1991, n. 69).

Various hypotheses have been formed around Schongauer's engraving. Lehrs and Baum consider that the censer, the support and the engravings of decorations are models which he produced whilst training in his father's workshop; in contrast, Flechig argues that it is a study of a piece of silverware since the detail of his figures would make it impossible for any silversmith to copy. In the catalogue of the recent Schongauer exhibition in Paris, Sophie Renouard de Busierre did not side with either of these arguments.

The censer of the chapel of the Episcopal Palace of Haarlem is not always mentioned in works on Schongauer's painting and engravings. Although we do not know the origin of the censer, it is more logical to assume that the engraving reached Haarlem or Amsterdam, where a Dutch silversmith copied it with a few variations, than to think that Schongauer had produced it before it arrived in Holland – the distance between Haarlem and Colmar is considerable.

The silversmith has eliminated the angels from the upper part of the body – they are easy to draw, but not so easy to execute in silver – and has added the figures of children, who do not pose any problems and are used to hold the rings for the chains. Schongauer did not represent the maniple but rather a sort of decoration which combined with the chains, and the silversmith has to invent one. If Schongauer had copied a real

censer he would have represented the maniple, which is one more argument to think that the engraving preceded the censer.

Despite this, the complexity of the silverwork and the difficulty of executing Schongauer's drawing must be emphasised. No known censer of the time displays such an exuberant design, although the crossed ogee arches are used in another. Even with the model in front of him, the anonymous silversmith demonstrated rare ability.

(*José Manuel Cruz Valdovinos*)

280
China

Ming dynasty (1368-1644)
Censer (Ding), 1465-1488
Bronze with incrusted gold,
9.5 x 14 cm
Inscriptions: "Made for the
Wan family during the reign
of the emperor Chenghua
of the Great Ming Dynasty"
Paris, Musée Cernuschi,
Fondes Henri Cernuschi,
M.C. 171
Exhibitions: London, 1958
Bibliography:
Carrington-Goodrich 1976,
pp. 1335-1337, II

A censer on a tripod, or Ding,
inspired by the ancient bronze
forms used for ritual purposes.
The body is of reddish bronze
coated in silver and incrusted
with gold. The decoration of
the rim and base is distributed
in frets, with vegetal motifs on
the rim and floral motifs on
the base and the two handles
at the sides. On the main body
of the censer there are six
large Sanskrit characters incrusted in gold alternating
with the eight Buddhist emblems, including the jewel, the
wheel, and a leaf.

Four characters incrusted in
gold and distributed in two
columns appear in the centre,
bearing the inscription "Made
for the Wan family during the
reign of the emperor Chenghua of the Great Ming Dynasty." The Wan family in
question is directly related to
that of Wan Guifei (1430-
1488), the famous imperial
concubine.
(*Marie-Thérèse Bobot*)

281
Syria

Censer, end of 15th century
Perforated bronze engraved
with gold and silver
damascene, diameter 13.4 cm
London, British Museum,
82.3-21.19
Bibliography: Ward 1991,
fig. 12

A two-piece bronze censer.
One part was originally fitted
to a bowl which was kept in
balance by suspension from a
cardan joint with two metal
rings. This meant that the
bowl could be kept in a vertical position whilst the recipient was on the floor. The
bowl would have contained
burning coals and incense, or
possibly a perfumed candle,
which would have meant less
risk of fire and have illuminated the perforated decoration. Similar objects are
known from the Tang period
in China, although these were
hung, but it does not appear
that they were introduced into
the Middle East until the mid-
12th century.

Many of the censers, like other
objects made in Damascus,
were exported to Europe.
They were mentioned in
various European inventories
in the 15th and 16th centuries
amongst other pieces of me-
talware from Damascus and
were ususally used by priests
to warm their hands at the
altar during the mass. The decoration of all these objects is
similar: the interlacing, the
leaves in the form of volutes,
and the ornamental inscriptions were especially popular.
Many of them carry European
coats of arms.
(*Rachel Ward*)

282
Iran/Afghanistan

Alí al-Katib (calligrapher);
Bihzad (illustrator)
Bustan of Sacdi, 1488
Miniature, opaque
watercolour, ink, gilt on
paper, 30.5 x 21.5 cm
Cairo, General Egyptian
Book, 908
Bibliography: ETTINGHAUSEN
1960, p. 1212; LENTZ-LOWRY
1989, p. 359, cat. 146

A calligraphy copy from an
exquisite monumental dictionary decorated with geometric
carvings, gilded on the outside
and coloured on the inside.
The two sides of the covers
are engraved with beautiful
geometric designs, with colours between the different
lines, using golden ink. The
rest of the pages are gilded between the lines and in the corners with golden and blue
inks. Written by the famous
calligrapher Haraqui Sultán
Ali, "the Writer", known in his
time as "the king of calligraphers"; it is indicated at the
end that the document was
written at the end of the
month of Rajab in the year H
893 (1488).
It has 55 pages, each of 23
lines. At the end of the document there is a poem with five
different rhymes (*nizam*) with
beautiful calligraphy. There is
also a royal seal under the
name of Abbas, perhaps
Abbas Ibn Khadd Safoui who
was reigning in the year H 995
(1586).
The document contains six
paintings, four by the famous
painter Bihzad (1450-1535).
These paintings are con-
sidered the most beautiful
produced by the artist for the
clarity of their unique style.
The document carries the
dates H 894 (1488-1489), in
the fifth painting, and H 893
(1488) in the sixth painting. It
is understood that the six
paintings were done over the
two years by various artists,
even though the document
was written in Rajab H 893
(1488).
(*Lalia Hemeda*)

Alonso Berruguete (Paredes de Nava,
approx. 1486-Toledo, 1561)
Saintly Bishop, 1527-1533
Sculpture, polychrome wood carving, 102 x 36 x 25 cm
From the altarpiece of the main altar of the monastery of San Benito, Valladolid
Valladolid, Museo Nacional de Escultura, 271
Exhibitions: Madrid, 1961
Bibliography: Arfe 1585 (1979 ed.), II, fol. 2v.; Bosarte 1804, pp. 156, 359; Llaguno y Amirola 1829, I, p. 11; Martí-Monso 1901, p. 137; Agapito y Revilla 1910, p. 542; Agapito y Revilla 1913, p. 226; Agapito y Revilla 1920-1929, I, p. 85; Agapito y Revilla 1926, p. 81; García Chico 1941, p. 12; Gómez Moreno 1941, p. 159; Candeira Pérez 1945, p. 15; Azcárate 1958, p. 146; Candeira Pérez 1959; Wattenberg 1963, p. 107; Wattenberg 1966, p. 29; Camón Aznar 1967, p. 178; Zaragoza Pascual 1976, p. 222; Martín González 1977, p. 27; García de Wattenberg 1978, p. 11; Camón Aznar 1980, p. 62; Rodríguez Martínez 1981, p. 231

The figure of a bishop who it is thought might represent St. Augustine, although there is no supporting evidence. The absence of a beard is curious. This work is not generally paid much attention, but it has some highly interesting features. The extremely long form is intensified by the verticality of the work, which is revealed both in the general pose and the abundance of parallel folds in the inner garments; this abundance of folds contrasts with the simplicity of the cloak, which envelops the forms as if encapsulating them and is prolonged by the mitre, which is small and fixed firmly to the head. This play on form turns the figure into one of Alonso Berruguete's most distinguished works.
(*Luis Luna Moreno*)

Giovanni Neri (active in Bologna in the second half of the 16th century)
Peruvian Sunflower in Full Flower, after 1558
Colour drawing, watercolour and tempera on white paper, 47 x 36 cm
From the manuscript collection of Ulisse Aldrovandi (1522-1605)
Bologna, Biblioteca Universitaria, Museo Aldrovandiano
Exhibitions: Bologna, 1991; Bologna, 1992
Bibliography: BATTISTI 1962, pp. 266-269; OLMI 1977, III, pp. 142-143

The *Chrysanthemy Peruniani maximus flos* forms part of a collection of colour drawings of plants, flowers and fruits.
This drawing of a *helianthus* (sunflower) follows the rules for illustrating nature conceived by Aldrovandi. In a letter to cardinal Gabriele Paleotti on 20 January 1581 (ms. Aldrov. 6, vol. II cc. 119r-128v), Aldrovandi explains his ideas on the painting of plants. In order to arrive at a perfect understanding of them they should be painted at three stages: when they only have leaves, when they have leaves and flowers, and then in their periods of decline when they bear fruits and seeds.
The sunflower is thus represented in different states, as in a photographic sequence: first the leaf alone; then complete, with roots, leaves and flowers; then in full flower; and finally with the white, black and ash-grey seeds falling (volume I of the plants, cc. 74r-77r).
This drawing would appear to be the work of Giovanni Neri, who produced a great number of illustrations for Aldrovandi, and who was also nicknamed Giovanni degli Uccelli ("of the birds") for his great ability to paint miniatures of birds (Masini, *Bologna perlustrata*, Bologna, 1666, I, p. 628). However, the most direct sensation

transmitted by these images is the magic of their colours. For Aldrovandi, the existence of colours in nature is the first condition for seeing: "nothing can be seen unless it has colour" (Battisti 1962, p. 270).
(*Irene Ventura Folli*)

285
Peru

Department of Cuzco
Inca culture
Strip of fabric with tocapus,
second half of 15th
century-first half of 16th
century
Vegetable fibre, 122 x 20 cm
Madrid, Museo de América,
14636
Exhibitions: Madrid, 1935;
Vienna, 1986; Budapest,
Cologne, 1987
Bibliography: MADRID 1935,
pl. L; COSSÍO DEL POMAR 1971,
p. 215; CUESTA DOMINGO 1980,
p. 392; RAMOS GÓMEZ-BLASCO
BOSQUED 1980, pp. 185, 186,
and 188; VIENNA 1986,
p. 315, n. 3,139

A fragment of reversible fabric,
complete in the direction of the
weft (122 cm), but cut in the direction of the warp (20 cm). A
series of lines of continuous
colours form a decorative grid
decorated with geometrical
figures, or *tocapus*, which in
turn give rise to slanting bands.
The fabric is coloured red, violet, blue, green, yellow, and
white. The warp and the weft
are interwoven at a rate of one
to one. The decoration is produced partially by means of dis-
continuous threads, which produce slanting openings made
invisible by the pressure of the
fabric. Fabrics were very important since the beginning of
Andean civilisation, but it was
during the Inca period that
mass production arose. Enormous quantities of all kinds of
fabric left the monasteries of
the Sun, most of them of incomparable fineness and lightness.
Before the 70s the geometric
designs known as *tocapus*
were not considered purely
decorative elements, but it was
Thomas Barthel of the University of Tübingen who gave birth
to the idea that they might be an
embryonic system of writing.
Working on the decorative
motifs on fabrics and wooden
goblets (*keros*), he registered
more than 400 sign-drawings,
opening up an interesting new
field of enquiry in the study of
the *tocapus*. (*Felix Jiménez*)

286
Italy

North-central school
Remora, approx. 1565
Colour drawing, tempera
on white paper, 47 x 37 cm
From the manuscript
collection of Ulisse
Aldrovandi (1522-1605)
Bologna, Biblioteca
Universitaria, Museo
Aldrovandiano
Exhibitions: Bologna, 1991;
Bologna, 1992
Bibliography: CAPRATTI 1980,
p. 35, f. 12, fig. 48;
LAURENCICH MINELLI-SERRA
1987-1988, IV, pp. 221-228

The *Reversus Indicus alius
anguilli formis. Guaiacanus
dicitur Hispanis* forms part of
a collection of colour drawing-
s of animals and monsters.
This fish, drawn face upwards,
can be identified with the
Remora remora, and is cited in
important studies of the New
World (P. Martire d'Anghiera, F.
Colombo, S. Grynaeus and L.
Anania). The scene repre-

sented by the drawing is very
simple, although it becomes
more complex when we at-
tempt to describe details such
as those of the garments of the
fishermen. This illustration was
published in 1560 in Zurich in
Konrad Gesner's *Nomenclator
aquatilium animantium*,
p. 92. Contrary to usual practice, Gesner does not make any
reference to the source of the
picture in his accompanying
note, stating: *Figura hac de-
sumpta est ex tabula quadam
descriptionis orbis terrarum.*
The fish had drawn the attention of travellers and naturalists
due to the use the natives of
Cuba made of it as bait. The
picture portrays the fish in a
somewhat fantastic light, although it does not totally forget
the scientific character and an-
thropological curiosity of the
man who commissioned it.
(*Irene Ventura Folli*)

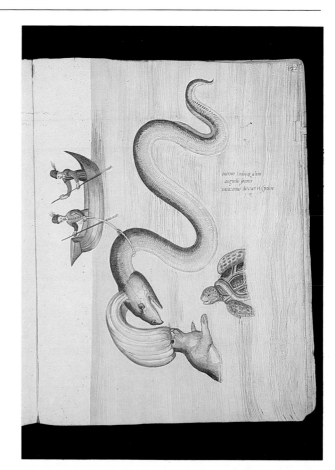

349

287
Antilles

Taina culture
Anthromorphic Pounder,
15th century
Carving in basalt rock,
15.6 x 10 cm
Santo Domingo, Museo del
Hombre Dominicano

The upper part represents a
crouching man. His large,
prominent ears, with studs
and decorations on the lobes,
constitute one of the most
characteristic decorative traits
of the Taina Indians. The
handle is conical and its base
bell-shaped.
Taina pounders were usually
made from hard rocks in order
to make the instrument dur-
able and resistant. They exist
in many forms and for many
uses, from simple instruments
for domestic use to others
with outstanding pieces of
symbolic and decorative carving. Votive functions are attributed to the latter type.
This sort of pounder displays

beautiful and well finished figurative carvings, usually of an
anthropomorphic or bird-like
nature; they were used for
crushing hallucinogenic plants
for the *coboba* ritual or in the
curative magic of the *behiques*
or Taino witchdoctors.
(*Manuel Antonio García Arévalo*)

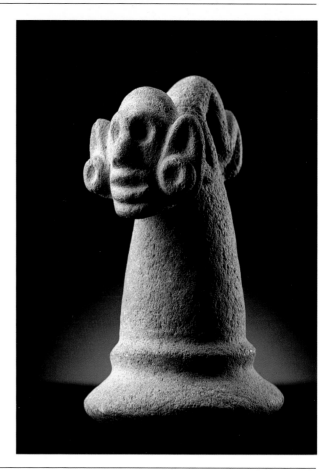

288
Guatemala

Postclassical Mayan culture
Efigy-vessel, 1250-1500
Ceramic, 17.8 cm; diameter
of the opening, 8 cm
From Asunción Mita, Jutiapa
Guatemala, Museo Nacional
de Arqueología y Etnología,
4409

"Tohil" plumbake ceramic piece which combines, in a semiglobular shape with a medium-sized neck, a modelled decoration with incisions representing a cat. The way in which the vessel was fired gives it a lustrous, black finish. "Tohil" plumbake ware is the most important feature of the early post-classical period (1000-1250) in the Guamatemalan highlands, and can be considered as one of the main elements in defining the cultural horizon at this stage. Although it has not been possible to determine their precise place of origin, the manufacture of plumbake ware began around the year 600 in some area of the southern border of Chiapas with Guatemala. Recent evidence suggests that they are derived from an even older vessel known as a Tiquisate, which was particularly popular during the early classical period (300-600) on the south coast of Guatemala. Around the year 600, a very fine clay ceramic began to be manufactured, which included ferrous materials and silica to remove grease and was covered with an engobe of a reddish orange colour. The most common forms were bowls with a plain or composite outline, glasses and pots with a medium-sized neck. This is the "San Juan" type plumbake ware, which was widely distributed during the late classical period in the Pacific coastal plain and in the high plateau. At the end of the period, around the year 900, a change occurred – technological, decorative and formal – which culminated in the appearance of the "tohil" plumbake ware which, as pointed

out earlier, is characteristic of the early postclassical period in the region.

From a technological point of view, the inclusion of ferrous materials is less frequent, these being substituted by volcanic ash and rock crystal to remove grease. Greater control is achieved in firing, with an incipient vitrification process when temperatures of more than 950° are reached, unusual in American ceramics, and a variety of surface colours which range from shining black and metallic grey – hence the name plumbake – to reddish orange.

Formally, they follow the style of the earlier stage, but with the addition of new forms such as jars with three hollow legs and pear-shaped glasses on pedestals or supporrts. However, the most relevant feature of these ceramics is the ornamentation which, by means of modelling, incision or moulding, introduces the depiction of animals which reflect the wildlife of the region, such as dogs, turkeys, coatis, tepezcuintle or jaguars; anthropomorphic subjects such as eagle-warriors, the heads of old men; and of the gods Tlaloc, Xipe Totec, Xochipilli, Ehecatl and Xicuhtecuhtli.
(*Andrés Ciudad*)

289
Guatemala

Late postclassical Mayan
culture
Funerial urn, 1250-1500
Ceramic, 36.3 cm; diameter
of the mouth 14.7 cm
From Gumarcaj, Quiché
Guatemala, Museo Nacional
de Arqueología y Etnología,
10435

At the beginning of the late
postclassical period (1250-
1521) – usually referred to in
the Guatamalan highlands as
the protohistoric period – cremation or incineration became
the funeral system in general
use among the ruling classes,
doubtless as a consequence of
the Quiché superposition. The
ashes were kept in urns situated at strategic positions in
public squares, altars and
temples in the most important
townships of the upper plateau.

The vessels used to this end
were jugs which contained
such remains as whole bones,
offerings such as obsidian
knives and objects made of
shell, turquoise and metal.
This method of burying high-
ranking individuals also involved the use of two pots,
which would always appear in
conjunction with other elements of mexicanized Quiché
culture: "white fortress on red"
and "polychrome chinautla."
The "white fortress on red"
type, pertaining to the jug
shown here, is widely found
at strategic defence points in
the north and west of the Guatemalan highlands, hence the
name "fortress." Its distribution coincides with the ethnic,
linguistic and cultural expansion of the Quichés, and it is
for this reason that it is
thought to be related to the
evolution of this group.
From 1250, in all the townships between lake Atitlán,
Utatlán, Zaculeu and the
southern slopes of the western
high plateau, the appearance
of bowls with three legs –
some with efigies –, semispheres and jars or jugs with
a high neck became common-

place. These ceramics, with a
red engobe, were decorated
with white paint in geometric
patterns such as lines, borders,
spirals, triangles which combine lines and dots, and even
very stylised representations
ofjaguars. On occasions, as in
this case, the human form appears modelled on the neck of
the cremation urns, or the
jaguar as the nocturnal sun,
one of the principal deities of
night, which acts directly on
the dead with whom it is associated.
(*Andrés Ciudad*)

290
Japan

Muromachi period
(1333-1573)
Birds and Flowers
Painting, ink on paper,
122.9 x 269.3 cm
Tokyo, Museum of Fuji Art

Originally, screens were used in the home as pieces of furniture for dividing the living-space, serving both as protection from the wind and as a decorative objects to be contemplated. "Birds and Flowers" constitutes one of the most popular subjects in Japanese art, and began to stand out as such at the end of the 13th century. In this work, the artist has succeeded in producing one of the finest examples of the genre, combining birds, flowers and vegetation in a background landscape setting. These motifs are divided into three major blocks, establishing the characteristic composition of decorative painting.
(*Museum of Fuji Art*)

291
Japan

Muromachi period
(1333-1573)
The Construction of a Boat
Painting, ink and paint on paper, 136.8 x 314 cm
Tokyo, Museum of Fuji Art

Scenes depicting the construction of boats are frequently represented in Chinese art. They were carried out in memory of Kateki (Huo-di), whose reputation as a boat-builder became legend. This iconographic subject, together with many others, was introduced to Japan by monks and scholars who visited the continent. Due to the fact that various works on the same subject are known, all showing great similarity in the positions of the figures and in overall structure, it is extremely likely that all of them were reproductions of an original work brought from China. The scene of the painting depicts several men working on

the construction of two boats, the front of which are decorated with the heads of the flying fish and the dragon, both animals that protect seamen. The figure in the centre of the composition is associated with Kateki.
(*Museum of Fuji Art*)

292
Egypt

Mamluk period
Bowl with pedestal, 14th century
Thrown ceramic with fired painting, incisions and glazed, 25 cm diameter
Inscriptions: on the pedestal, dedicated to an unknown Mamluk emir, in Nasji script
Cairo, Museum of Islamic Art, 5927

Ceramic bowl with slightly concave sides and a high pedestal base. The interior is decorated with a thick white barbotine under a brown glaze. In a central medallion a very elegantly drawn bird can be seen, perhaps representing a pelican or goose, painted on a background of dots and stylised leaves. The interior borders are decorated with six registers separated by pairs of lines. On a background of dots, an inscription written in Nasji may be read which says: "By order of the emir."

The decoration of this bowl, intended for everyday use, recalls a type of drawing used frequently during the period of Ayyubid and Seljuk. This type of decoration remained in use during the 14th century in pieces painted in cobalt and black from Syria, Persia and Turkey.
(*Nimat M. Abu Bakr*)

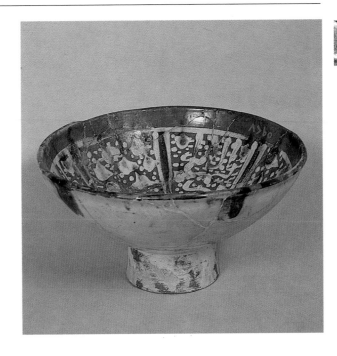

293
Egypt

Late Mamluk period
Washbasin, 15th century
Beaten and engraved brass with incisions, 23 cm; diameter 51 cm
Inscriptions: on the sides eulogies and wishes for victory to the sultan Qa'it Bay, in Nasji script
Cairo, Museum of Islamic Art, 15099

This brass washbasin, with straight sides and an extended border, has its interior divided into rectangles in which the name of the Mamluk sultan, Qa'it Bay, can be read, along with his titles and the habitual votive formula written in Nasji on a background of arabesques based on vegetable and lotus flower motifs. The top part of the border, decorated with oval-shaped medallions shows inscriptions in Nasji with very emphasized letters. This decoration has alternating cartuches in which the name Qa'it Bay appears, with expressions of praise dedicated to him and a desire for his victory, together with other panels with interlaced drawings. The lower part of the border is decorated with complicated interlaced drawings on a background of dots. The interior of the base is decorated with arabesques and a broad band of interlacing drawings of knots. Most of these metal objects from the middle of the 15th century which have managed to survive to the present day are no longer decorated with inlays. The decline in the decoration of these objects began in the first half of the century. Their production was revitalised under the patronage of Qa'it Bay, who had achieved a situation of relative peace and prosperity for the Mamluk empire. A few brass pieces with gold and silver inlays were made for his court, although the majority were engraved and had bitumen prints applied to the ground. (*Sibam Al-Mahdi*)

294
Egypt

Ornamental tile, latter part of the 15th century
Polychrome glazed ceramic, 19.2 x 18 cm
Cairo, Museum of Islamic Art, 4583

This hexagonal tile shows how the glazed tiles of the 15th century had come to be influenced by Chinese themes. The blue floral decoration on a white background appears under a transparent glaze. The black lines at the corners are framed by a band of turquoise. A bunch of flowers combining three large jagged leaves along with four others which are more stylised ascend from the base. From the lower part a long stem rises from which two large lotus flowers sprout among the petals. In this piece, elements and techniques may be discerned from both Chinese and the indigenous culture. Evidence of this adaptation is es-

pecially clear in the ceramics produced in Egypt and Syria. The Chinese influence started to become evident in the works of the Mamluk period in the 14th century. The excavations carried out in the Fustat area to the south of Cairo and in Harna, Syria, have brought to light a large number of china pieces decorated in black and white which served as a model for the Mamluk potters. The similarity between Egyptian tiles and those which were produced during the same period in Syria indicates that Egyptian and Syrian potters were following the same models.
(*Yehya M. Al-Shayb*)

295
Iran or Central Asia

Glass decorated with lotus leaves, second half of the 15th century
Jade, engraved decoration, diameter 64 x 14.5 cm
Inscription: poetic, not deciphered
Paris, Musée du Louvre, MR 199
Exhibitions: Paris, 1971; Paris, 1977; Washington D.C.-Los Angeles, 1989
Bibliography: PARIS 1971, n. 104; BARBET DE JOUY 1967, n. E 176; GRUBE 1974, I, p. 255, figs. 113-114

The sides of the glass are slightly broader than the rim. It is supported on a small angular base, adorned with a simple groove. Along the edge runs a poetic inscription in Persian, as yet not deciphired, divided into three elongated cartuches with lobular ends, between which figures comprised of four lobes adorned with rosettes are inserted. A

subtle ornamentation of curves and countercurves based on plant forms, of the most extreme elegance and delicacy, appear on the main body of the piece.
The lotus flowers, the broad leaves which recall the acanthus, the rosettes of six lobes and the leaves of three lobes are typical features of miniature work. The Timurid princes, who introduced this extravagant technique in Central Asia and Iran, had no doubt been inspired by Chinese jade crockery. Jade was not in fact known in the first centuries of Islamic culture, although the great and erudite sage Al-Biruni (973-1040), informs us that the Turks of the steppes awarded it magical powers and that this offerred protection against thieves, as well as thunderclaps and rain.
The glass was worked from an extremely dark green jade, almost black in the light, which was the most well-known type

of jade during the Timurid epoch. The delicacy of its ornamentation is proof of the artistic refinement that distinguished this magnificent period in all areas.
(*Marthe Bernus-Taylor*)

296
Spain

Manises
Plate with bull, first quarter
of the 16th century
Ceramic, thrown
stanniferous earthenware
with cobalt and
gold-coloured glazes,
diameter, 43.5 cm
Madrid, Instituto Valencia
de Don Juan, 345
Bibliography: GONZÁLEZ MARTÍ
1944; AINAUD DE LASARTE 1952;
LLUBIÁ MUNNÉ 1967; MARTÍNEZ
CAVIRÓ 1983; MARTÍNEZ CAVIRÓ
1991

In spite of the generalized rejection of figurative subjects in
Muslim art, these frequently
adorn numerous sumptuary
pieces, both in Al-Andalus and
in the rest of the Islamic
world. We need only think of
the ivories, the miniatures, the
bronzes, the textiles, the ceramics, etc. In Abbasid golden
earthenware wildlife and an-
thropomorphical subjects are
a constant feature, as in all
other Muslim areas, from the
Seljuks and Fatimids to the Ottomans.
The Spanish golden earthenware produced in Malaga at
the time of the Nazrids are
also adorned sporadically with
zoomorphic subjects. The
most beautiful example in the
world is found in the gazelles
on the glass from the Alhambra in the Museo Nacional de
Arte Hispanomusulmán, in
Granada.
Figurative subjects were also
frequent in the Mudejar pottery workshops in Manises.
However, when the later
series emerged, those we refer
to as Moorish, the zoomorphic
motifs, although still in evidence, are not so frequent, especially during the 16th century, having to wait until the
17th and 18th centuries with
the triumph of the Valencian
"pardalots."
For this reason, this gold-coloured plate with bull is exceptional, with its vigorous cobalt
lines, accompanied by large
leaves, also outlined in blue,
standing out against the milky

stanniferous background. The
centre of both the leaves and
the bull consists of characteristic "inlay," the motifs included in the group of so-
called unimportant subjects.
The rest of the background is
covered with little flowers and
leaves, also a typical feature in
the world of the Moorish gold-
en earthenware from Manises.
(*Balbina Martínez Caviró*)

297
Portugal

Salver with stand, first third of the 16th century
Embossed and engraved gilt silver and polychromatic enamels, diameter 27.7 cm
Lisbon, Museo Nacional de Arte Antiga, 806
Exhibitions: London, 1955-1956, n. 64; Luxembourg-Lisbon, 1988, n. 13
Bibliography:
Couto-Gonçalves, 1960; Orey 1984; Orey 1988, n. 1, pp. 20-21

This fruit bowl or salver (a word which is derived from the verb "salvar" – or "save" – in the sense of tasting the food of a high-ranking personage to prevent his being poisoned) is typical of 16th and even 17th century Portugese gold and silver work. It follows the normal typology in utensils of this kind: concentric bands enclosing a circular space, possibly containing the arms of the chief family, an allegorical scene or, as in this case, a decorative heraldic motif in various carefully chosen colours.

The central band, rather than showing narrative scenes, normally contains ornamentation based on plant forms, with the exterior being used for the depiction of episodes which tend to be interpretations of imaginary events experienced by the Portugese conquistadors in far off lands, in which fantasy is normally combined with an attempt at realism, and which are almost always handled with a certain ingenuity.

The salver, in addition to the thick foliage which only serves to demonstrate the *horror vacui* of gold and silver work, depicts a world in which the conquistadors are having an adventure protagonized by "wild men: standing up to animals both fantastic and real."

These salvers, which on occasion also depict ancient tales and myths, were the product

of the gold and silversmith workshops of Lisbon, although they were also produced in various other areas under Portuguese domination.
(*Joan Sureda i Pons*)

298
Thailand

Naga, 15th century
Ceramic, 48 x 26 cm
Singapore, National Museum,
C1453
Bibliography:
STRATTON-MACNAIR-SCOTT 1987;
SWAN 1987; 1981; GUY 1989

Thai artisans such as the Mon
and the Khmer liked to adorn
the finials of their architecture
with animal figures from the
world of their mythology.
Among these, the most popular
were the *shinga* (lion), the *ma-
kara* (an aquatic reptile similar
to the crocodile), the *naga* (a
divine serpent), and *yaksha* (an
earth spirit). All of these figures
have their origin in India, having been introduced to Thailand by the Khmers and Mons,
who continued to associate
them with the earth and the
sky. The appearance of the four
together is taken as a reference
to ancient fertility beliefs concerning the regulation of the
rains and the reaping of a boun-

tiful harvest. The *Nagas*, popular throughout southeast Asia,
are considered guardian spirits,
and were frequently used to
adorn the temple entrances, in
the form of roof finials, or
through other architectural elements.
The Nagas are represented
with multiple heads as a reference to their power. It is said
that they posess the power to
take human form, to change
into an attractive young man or
a beautiful woman, with the
object of confounding mortals.
The three principal centers of
ceramic craftsmanship which
existed in Thailand during both
the Sukhothai period (1250-
1438) and in the reign of Ayut-
thaya (1438-1569), were: Ban
Ko Noi, Pa Yang, and Tukuta.
Their production was known
by the generic name Sawankhalok. Of these, the kiln of Pa
Yang distinguished itself for the
making of painted and varnished pieces destined for use in
architectonic ornamentation.
(*Isabel Cervera*)

299
Vietnam

Jar (kendi), 15th century
Ceramic, blue and white
porcelain, 18.2 cm
Singapore, National
Museum, C1232

The *kendi* is the name given to
a type of ceramic and porcelain
water jar that originated in
southeast Asia. Shaped like a
squat round body, they are distinguished by their long neck,
wide, opened lips, and a bulky
side handle, in the form of a
breast. In some cases, especially with those from the kilns
of Sawankhalok, Thailand,
they take zoomorphic forms.
The kendi originate from a
certain type of bottles and jars
called *kundika*, which have a
more elongated form, and
were introduced to Cambodia,
Vietnam, and Thailand by Indian merchants.
The introduction of decorative
motifs applied with subdued
blue pigments proceeds from
the Chinese ceramic tradition

of the Yuan and Ming dynasties. The different parts that
make up the kendi jars, present a well proportioned decoration, with vegetable
shaped neck, lips, and base,
arranged radially, marking the
horizontality of the piece,
while the central body takes
up a much looser composite
scheme, showing various
scenes from the natural world.
(*Isabel Cervera*)

300
Cambodia

Buddhist Lion, 15th-16th century
Sculpture, bronze, 15.8 cm
Paris, Musée Guimet, 850

From the year 260 B.C., three centuries after Buddhism was founded by the prince Siddharta Gautama of the Sakya dynasty, it was used to serve as a vehicle of political unification for the first Indian empire of the Maurya. Along with the prestige of the empire, appeared the first Buddhist iconography, created by the emporer Ashoka, who chose the lion, an emblematic animal of the Sakya, as a symbol of the Buddha. It is logical that as an emporer of royal blood, Ashoka would elect an aristocratic symbol, since he was interested in giving emphasis to the Buddha's princely origins. In spite of the fact that Buddhist iconography would by degrees abandon the heraldic language in which it was created, converting to a more popular and customary didacticism, the forms of the lion of Buddha would always be shaped by its hierarchical and sensational origins.

From the second century A.D. Buddhism spread from India throughout all of Asia, first by land along the silk road towards China, and through searoutes reaching to southeast Asia, and would come to constitute the principal font of artistic inspiration of such outstanding cultures as the Khmer of the Cambodian empire.

Although the image of expanding Buddhism as a protagonistic cult lies with the anthropomorphic figure of Buddha, austere, atavistic, and monklike, the lion would continue to be the most diffuse symbol. While the Far East is home to the fantastic figure of the Chinese dragon, Cambodian art, nevertheless, simplified its zoomorphic appearance, although it wasn't able to completely eliminate its heraldic symbolism.

The Cambodian Empire of the

Khmer flourished in the 12th and 13th centuries around its capital, Angkor, where its principal temples and palaces mark the stylistic evolution of its art. This gilded bronze piece, doubtless belongs to a Buddhist altar, and shows the characteristics of the late Banyan style, typical of the 15th century.

(*Carmen García Ormaechea*)

301
Korea

Choson dynasty, (1392-1910)
Kang Hui-an (1419-1464)
*Wise Man Resting
on a Rock*, 15th century
Painting, ink on paper,
23.4 x 15.7 cm
Inscriptions: In-jae (Kang
Hui-an)
Seoul, National Museum
of Korea, Pon. n. 2504
Exhibitions: London, 1984;
Washington, 1991
Bibliography: San Francisco
1979

Kang Hui-an was an eminent scholar from the early period of the Choson dynasty who occupied important posts at court. His official work does not overshadow his great natural gifts as a painter, poet and calligraphist.

In this small painting, done in the format of an album page, Kang Hui-an divides the composition into two planes. The fluvial current of the foreground, indicated by horizontal lines, is observed by a scholar in the act of meditation. Without a doubt these two elements constitute the central focus of the composition. In the background a rocky wall, emphasized by means of heavy brush strokes, marks the contrasting verticality.

All of these composite elements, as well as the use of loose, rapid calligraphic brushstrokes, proceed from Chinese painting that was done in the course of the Song dynasty of the South. These principles were also developed during the Ming dynasty in China, and form the basis of a tradition that would continue through the Choson and Koryo dynasties.
(*National Museum of Korea*)

359

302
Korea

Choson dynasty (1392-1910)
Ahn Kyon (attributed)
Landscapes of the Four Seasons, 15th century
Paint, ink and colors on silk,
35.2 x 28.5 cm
Seoul, National Museum
of Korea, Duk n. 3144
Exhibitions: San Francisco,
1981; London, 1984
Bibliography:
GOEPPER-WHITFIELD 1984

On an album page from the 15th century, Ahn Kyon represented the four seasons, delicately expressing the changes within nature. The Spring, in which all of creation is mistily reborn, is expressed with soft brushstrokes, while the winter is cold and desolate, with strong linear traces and marked contrasts in the tones of the ink.

The whole work possesses a sense of unity, harmonizing each one of the landscapes in a manner that stands out more for its visual composition than for its thematic coherence. Each panel has been structured with an unbalanced composition, which is one-sided, thus requiring the panels to be placed together in pairs in order to make the group symmetrical.

In each one the spatial element is enriched by the emptiness of the middleground between the river that flows in the foreground and the high mountains.

These spatial and structural characteristics are those of landscape painting from the school of Ahn Kyon, and were developed during the 15th and 16th centuries, and had great influence in the Shuubun school and the Japanese landscape paintings of the Muromachi period in Japan.
(*National Museum of Korea*)

360

303
Nigeria

Igbo Laja
Yoruba culture
*Hand Holding an Akoko
Leaf*, 15th century
Sculpture, fired clay, 11 cm
Igbo Jaga origin, from Owo,
Nigeria
Lagos, Onikan National
Museum, 73.2.47
Exhibitions: North
America-Canada-Europe,
1980-1985; Lagos, 1985 until
the present
Bibliography: EYO 1974; EYO
1976, VI, pp. 37-58; EYO 1977;
EYO-WILLET 1980

This clay hand with triangular nails holds an akoko leaf between its fingers.

The leaves and branches of certain types of trees are considered sacred to the Yoruba culture, and the leaves of the akoko (*Newbouldia laevis*), a tree famous for its longevity, are used, especially in their coronation ceremonies for kings and chiefs. When a king is crowned, he is given some akoko leaves in order to wish him a long life. The base of these trees was often used as an open altar for praying and offering sacrifices. The excavations at Igbo Laja, have discovered many works of art that show similarities, not only to the art of the Ife, but also to that of Benin. The ancient Yoruban city of Owo, is situated approximately 130 kilometres to the Southeast of Ile-Ife and some 110 kilometres to the North of Benin in Nigeria. According to oral tradition, Owo was founded by immigrants from Ile-Ife. The immigration was led by Ojugbelu, the youngest of the sixteen sons of Oduduwa, founder of Ife, who was not mentioned in his father's will. The findings at Owo, which date from the 15th century, have affinities with the art of Ife. Uncertainty still exists as to whether the objects in the Ife style were brought or traded from this city, or if they were made in the Owo region. So the influence of Benin in Owo can be appreciated as much in the sculpture as in the architecture, this last being very common in the striated walls in the houses of nobles in both of the cities. Politically both cities possessed similar titles as tribal headquarters, and they both practiced the same Igue religious ritual. This influence also affected royalty. The *Olowo* (king) of Owo wore a crown of coral beads, in place of one of multi-colored beads, which are found among most other Yoruban kings. They also used a ceremonial sword with a heavy grip equal to that of the *Oba* of Benin. It is probable that in the 15th century, Owo fell under the feudal sovereignty of the Benin empire. The date of the excavated material in Owo, between 1435-1465, clearly confirms this last influence; it was during the middle of the 15th century that the Benin empire expanded westward. toward the west. (*V.K. Agili*)

304
Nigeria

Igbo Laja, Owo
Yoruba culture
Hand Holding an Animal,
15th century
Terracota, width 16.1 cm
Lagos, Onikan National
Museum, 73.2.43
Exhibitions: North
America-Canada-Europe,
1980-1985; Lagos, 1985
Bibliography: EYO 1974; EYO
1976, VI, pp. 37-58; EYO
1977; EYO-WILLET 1980

Sacrificial themes appear frequently in the art of the city of
Owo. This hand is offering up
a lizard or a rat. It has a ring
on the thumb, and its nail is
triangular. The wrist is decorated with three rows of
beads.
Other examples of ringed
fingers have been found in Ife,
but none in Benin. Nevertheless the beads were often used
as necklaces in the dress, or in
the crown of the Oba, the king
of Benin. Rarely have they

been seen to appear on the
arm, a trait unique to the cities
of Ife and Owo. The triangular
shape of the fingernails is
characteristic of Owo art and
also appears among the art of
the Nok, the oldest known
Nigerian culture, between 500
B.C. and 200, suggesting a
possible connection between
the two cultures.
Even though the works of
Owo help to relate the cities
of Ife and Benin, they possess
certain characteristic traits, the
most surprising being the
great variety of their sacrificial
offerings.
(*V.K. Agili*)

305
Peru

Cuzco Department
Inca culture
Ceremonial cup (kero), late
15th century-first half
of 16th century
Polychromatic wood and
lacquer, 19 cm; maximum
diameter: 15 cm
Madrid, Museo de América,
7507
Exhibitions: Paris, 1933;
Madrid, 1935; Alicante,
1988-Murcia, Cádiz, 1989
Bibliography: PARIS 1933,
n. 11; MADRID 1935, pl.
XLVIII; TRIMBORN-FERNÁNDEZ
VEGA 1935, n. 11; CUESTA
DOMINGO 1980, pp. 297, 346;
MARTÍNEZ 1988, p. 156

Conical ceremonial cup in the
form of a jaguar's head with
the mouth open, revealing
fangs. The head is decorated
with vertical bands of ellipsoi-
dal motifs which cover the
face and neck, configuring the
spots of the animal's coat.
The forward part of the neck

houses a network of rhom-
buses.
The representation of a
jaguar's head is not unusual
on the kero, the conical-based
Incan ritual cup. This design is
still found in use among the
Quechua-speaking peasants
of the Andes. The jaguar is related to power: the power of
the Shaman, of the priest, of
the warrior, of the governor,
and the power of reproduction. It is also identified with
the mythic ancestors and in-
mortals, the holders of the absolute authority over that
which they have created. It is
likely that this cup was related
to ancestral rites, and even to
the high Incan; perceived as
the absolute governor, supreme priest, God himself,
son of the solar divinity, or of
some member of his lineage.
(*Paz Cabello*)

306
Peru

Incan culture
Zoomorphic figure, late 15th century-first half of 16th century
Gold melted in wasted wax, 5.9 x 5.2 cm
Madrid, Museo de América, 7401
Exhibitions: Paris, 1933; Madrid, 1935; Alicante, 1988; Murcia-Cádiz, 1989
Bibliography: Paris 1933, n. 527; Madrid 1935, n. 315; Cuesta Domingo-Rovira Llorens 1982, n. 329; Martínez 1988, p. 119

This is a solid zoomorphic figure representing a male llama. This type of object formed part of ritual offerings given to temples, buried below the foundations of houses or public buildings, or used as funeral dowry in the tombs of people of standing in Inca society.
The Andes were the most ancient and most important center of metallurgy in the pre-Colombian Americas. Probably originating between Panama and Equador, in what is present-day Colombia, reached its zenith in Peru.
The most frequently used manufacturing method was the "lost wax" process, which consisted in modelling the desired object in wax. The model would then be covered in thick clay. When the clay hardened it would be exposed to heat in a kiln and the melted wax would escape through an opening in the gangue, and be replaced by molten metal. Once the metal cooled, it was only necessary to break the clay, retrieve the object, take off the rough edges and polish it.
Metallurgy played an important propagandistic role during the expansion of the Inca empire. The metal objects that travelled from the Andes to the Amazon, the "Chaco," and the Pampa, were a testament to the Incas' immense power;

they spread throughout the entire continent, where the art of sculpture was still confined to the working and polishing of stone.
(*Félix Jiménez*)

307
Germany

Albrecht Dürer (Nuremberg, 1471-1528)
Lily, early 16th century
Painting, watercolor on paper fixed to wood, 57 x 17 cm
A version of the *Lily* of the Kunsthalle of Bremen (approx. 1503)
Madrid, El Escorial, Monasterio de San Lorenzo el Real, Palacio de los Austrias, Despacho de Felipe II, 100344
Bibliography: Tietze-Tietze Conrat 1928-1938; Zarco Cuevas 1930; Panofsky 1955; Sala 1964, II; Viñas Torner 1972, n. 31

Not all historians and critics attribute this drawing to Dürer. E. Panofsky, while appreciating its qualities, is not fully convinced of its authenticity, and the Tietze consider it to be from Dürer's workshop, or perhaps the work of an unknown imitator who was close to the master.
It has been linked to the same theme that appears in the pictoral composition, from about 1508, known as *Virgin with Child* (or *Virgin of the Lily*) from the Cook collection at Richmond, which was added to the collection at the National Gallery in London in 1945. Notwithstanding, such acceptance of a well-known piece is no guarantee of certainty; because of the way in which it reflects different elements from different stages in the painter's career, it has been questioned whether this painting was really done by Dürer. The implication is that whoever did this painting, chose random motifs from Dürer's work, while ignoring its chronological consistency, and his personal and aesthetic evolution.
The lily represents a sword that will pierce the soul of the Virgin, a way of directly alluding to the Passion of Christ, and its effect on the Mother of God. Dürer's skill as an illustrator reveals his gifts of observation, as well as his command of color and draughtsmanship; at the same time he copied the natural world accurately, and expressed himself with a not unpoetic sincerity, anticipating many of his successors in this genre.
(*Juan José Luna*)

308
England

Coconut cup, approx. 1490
Silver, partially gilded,
coconut, 20.5 cm
Exposition: Washington,
1911, n. 11
Oxford, New College
Bibliography: JACKSON 1911,
2, p. 649; OMAN 1979,
p. 296, fig. 71; GLANVILLE
1987, p. 21, fig. 4

A hollowed out coconut forms the goblet's cup, which is adorned with six silver boughs of oak leaves at the rim of the mouth; it is supported below by a thick trunk with pruned boughs, decorated with an interlaced band formed by the letter D. The circular base has various grooved holes, and is encircled by a low rim.

In an inventory of the property of the New College there are seven coconut goblets, two of them without lids. This one has been preserved, along with another less ornate one. The letter D, on the band which encircles the trunk, has been interpreted as corresponding to Robert Dalton, who came to the college in 1472, left in 1485, and who became the prebend of Chichester, among other things.

The exceptional decoration on this coconut goblet does not appear on any of the other known goblets. It has been decorated naturalistically, as if it were a tree, imitating the trunk, and the trimmed boughs – similar to the Castilian crosses made of broken twisted branches. More surprising still is the base, with its rim, and its imitation of a piece of earth with burrows; the various scholars who have studied this cup believe that it once sported little rabbits, which have since disappeared.

Glanville notes that late medieval documents mention pieces from both England and France that showed enamelled green fields, with small birds and animals, but practically no piece remains which is com-

parable to the outstanding naturalism of this coconut goblet. It is an object realized with imagination, coinciding in its aesthetic vision with the work of painters and sculptors during the flood of realism in the late Gothic period.
(*José Manuel Cruz Valdovinos*)

309
Turkey

Tile, 1560-1565
Ceramic, 24 x 23.6 x 1.6 cm
Istanbul, Archaeological
Museum

This is a tile which formed part of a larger composition, with a background of white and dark blue, decorated with green stalks with red and blue flowers. Part of it carries medallion motifs, with floral themes, of peonies, carnations, and between those, on a white background, boughs of plum trees that come together in small bouquets of waving stalks. From its decoration and because of its similarity to other examples, we would date it roughly between 1560-1565.
(*Purificación Marinetto Sánchez*)

310
Turkey

Tiles for border work,
1575-1580
Ceramic, 16 x 62 x 1.9 cm
Istanbul, Archaeological
Museum

This is a pair of tiles that form part of a lengthwise border with a theme of two undulating interwoven vines from which peonies and chrysanthemums bloom, separated by a small butterfly with plum blossoms in its centre.
The background is blue and white is kept for ornamental themes which are completed in turquoise and red. The upper and lower parts show an interwoven cord.
The tiles' decoration, typical of the third style as classified by professor Lane, gives an approximate dating of 1575-1580.
(*Purificación Marinetto Sánchez*)

311
Spain

Al-Andalus, Nasrid period
Fabric, 15th century
Silk, 25 x 25 cm
Granada, Museo Nacional
de Arte Hispanomusulmán,
3.914

This fabric has a network of pointed arches formed by two lanceolate palms, outlined on a red background. Their undulating profile is trimmed, with the upper part of the palms inclined towards the stems. These grow smaller towards the lower part where they unite to form a pineapple, from whose base two other palms sprout, while asymmetrical leaves shoot from the two stems. All of these ornamental elements are dark green, wrapped in white. Within the lancet arches there are rampant crowned lions facing the pineapple, representing the tree of life. The lions are in profile, with the head in a frontal position, done in yellow and wrapped in dark green, with white crowns. Below the arches are small inverted palm fronds which remind one of the parsley leaf so often used in the 15th century gilded pottery from Manises. In this fabric the traditional Muslim decoration is combined with a gothic design which, according to Shepherd, was made in Granada by Mudejar weavers after the city was taken, commissioned by new Christian customers. The fabric can thus be dated from between the late 15th century and the beginning of the 16th. There must have been a large and disparate community of Mudejar weavers, to go by the various examples of their work preserved in the Instituto Valencia de Don Juan in Madrid, and in the Victoria and Albert Museum in London, where the composite scheme is repeated with light variations. This would appear to be quite normal, as has been remarked in the studies carried out by May. (*Cristina Partearroyo*)

312
China

Ming dynasty (1368-1644)
Censer, 15th century
Septate enamel, 10.9 cm;
diameter of mouth 11 cm
Shanghai, National Museum,
7718

This tripod censer, made of copper covered with gold, has a bulky body supported by three feet around which are sculpted animal faces, a thin neck, and a round mouth, with two symmetrical handles. The top part has golden circles on a red background, and on the lower part, over a celestial background, eight lotus flowers of differing sizes in red, yellow, white, and green. Within the enamel work two decorative elements can be made out: septate enamel and paint. The art of septate enamel was introduced to China from parts of Arabia during the Yuan dynasty, and was developed in the Ming and Qing dynasties, the main manufacturing centers being Beijing, Yangzhou, and Guanzhou. The septate technique consists of the application of strands of soldered copper to form the design, over which the variously colored enamels are applied. After the color is applied, the piece is bathed in gold. This enamelling technique has been applied to all kinds of objects, such as censers, vessels, tea pots, wine glasses, and boxes. The value of these works of art lies in their decorative character. (*Lu Minghua*)

313
China

Ming dynasty (1368-1644)
Plate (pan), 1488-1505
Ceramic, polychromate
porcelain, 4.8 cm;
upper diameter: 18 cm;
lower diameter 10.7 cm
Inscriptions: mark of the
reign of the emperor
Hongzhi, 1488-1505
London, Percival David
Foundation of Chinese Art,
A724
Exhibitions: London,
1935-1936, n. 2054; USA,
1989-1990, n. 43
Bibliography: MEDLEY 1978,
n. 21; ; SCOTT 1989

Chinese porcelain impressed
Europeans with its durability,
fineness, lightness, whiteness,
transparency, sonorousness,
impermeability, and dec-
orative qualities. Porcelain
was discovered by the
Chinese ceramicists of the
Tang dynasty (618-907 A.D.).
After many centuries of experimentation it reached its
zenith during the Ming dynasty, whereas Europe did not
discover porcelain until the
early 18th century.
This classic plate, with regular
lines and a level base, is made
of excellent porcelain from
Jingdezhen, the famous
Chinese pottery city, where
the main imperial kilns were
to be found, which met the
demands of the Ming court.
On the base are brushstrokes
in a subdued cobalt-blue
covering. Between a double
circle are the six characters
which allow the piece to be
dated to the years of the
Hongzhi kingdom (1488-
1505): Da Ming Hongzhi Nian
Zhi Hongzhi (made in the
Kingdom of Hongzhi of the
great Ming dynasty).
The best pieces of the
Hongzhi kingdom are, in
general, monochromes, particularly whites and yellows,
which appear decorated with
a simple dragon, cut lightly
into the clay, and colored in
green directly over the clay,
not over the crystalline covering; this produces not only a
chromatic contrast, but also a
tactile contrast. The technique
consists of modeling the dragon while the clay is still wet,
taking care that the crystalline
finish which covers the entire
piece does not run into the
etched decorative motif when
the piece is fired. Once fired,
the dragon is colored green
with a very fluid, lead-based
enamel, and fired a second
time at a low temperature.
This piece is typologically exceptional, there being two
other dragons in varnish, one
yellow, one purple, which
adorn the outside of the plate.
Curiously, the five claws on
each foot, which identify the
dragon as a symbol of the Emperor, have not been detailed
here, making this a rather controversial piece.
(*Carmen García Ormaechea*)

314
Japan

Muromachi period
(1333-1573)
Kano Motonobu (1476-1559)
Mountain Landscape
Folding screen,
152.80 x 339.70 cm
Inscriptions: seal of
Motonobu
Tochigi, Museum
of the Prefecture

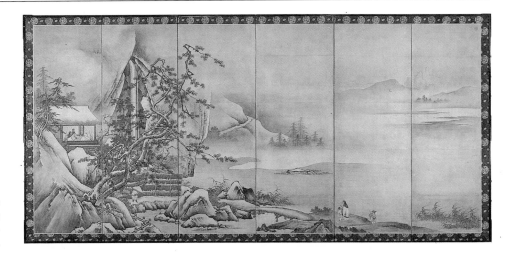

This work, which belonged to
the Arima family, lords of the
Kyushu region, is a sober
mountain landscape in-
fluenced by Chinese artistic
tradition. The care shown in
the drawing of the pine
boughs, together with the detailed depiction of the texture
of the rocks, is indisputably a
copy of the style of Ba En Ma
Yuan (circa 1190-1230), a famous Chinese painter belonging to the Northern school.
Through the use of different
planes, and the gradation of
ink tones, Montonobu shaped
the perspective, faithfully reflecting the immensity of the
landscape, and the spatial
depth. In general, the screens
of Montonobu, or his dis-
ciples, are characterized by
the placing of the points closest to the viewer on the far
sides of the screen. In this
case, nevertheless, we observe
that on both sides the foreground of the landscape is
placed to the far left of the
screen, moving inwards, from
center to right. The artist's seal
is on the far left.
Along with this work, which
illustrates the seasons of
autumn and winter, there was
apparently another screen by
the same artist, whose two
decorated faces corresponding to spring and summer.
On the far left of the screen
appears the seal of the artist.
This work belongs to Arima
family, master of Kyushu region.
(*Hideo Kitaguchi*)

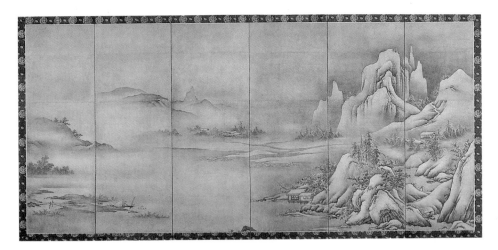

315
Japan

Muromachi period
(1333-1575)
Shoei Kano (1519-1592)
*Painting of Birds and
Flowers*
Painting, silk, and colors,
156.5 x 350.5 cm
Tokyo, Agency of Cultural
Affairs

The various motifs of birds, flowers, and herbs, in this work, placed together in perfect harmony, symbolise the four seasons of the year. To the right, appears the Spring, represented by the plums and the violets, the Summer by the jasmine. To the left the flowers of life indicate the Autumn, while the winter is symbolised by the snow that covers the hills in the background. Although the illustrations of birds and seasonal flowers appear frequently on the screens of the Muromachi period, the peacocks and golden roosters, like the waterfalls, were adopted as central motifs by the painters of the Kano school, starting with the works of Motonobu Kano (1476-1559). The artists belonging to this school, (considered to be the official art school of the Muromachi shogun), are characterized by their formalism, and by the importance they attached to the general balance of the composition.

Shoei Kano (1519-1592), who painted this screen, was the third son of Masanobu Kano, founder of the school of the same name. His son, Eitoku Kano (1543-1565) was at the same time a representative painter of the Momoyama period (late 16th approx.-early 17th approx.). Although Shoei followed his father's expressive style, one can see the spirit of the new age in the vitality of his brushstrokes.
(*Agency of Cultural Affairs*)

316
Japan

Muromachi period
(1333-1573)
So-Ami (attributed)
Mount Fuji
Painting, ink on paper,
210 x 65 cm
Tokyo, Fuji Museum of Art

The colossal outline of Mount Fuji rises up on the horizon beyond the mountain chain in the middle distance. The smooth shape of the mountain peaks and the correct use of ink give this painting a tone of peaceful moderation. A bridge and vague silhouettes of travellers are near a small village in the foreground. The almost imperceptible shadows of the sails on a boat in the bay complete this scene of serenity, in which a balanced integration of nature and human life can be appreciated.
The majesty of the composition and the lyricism of the subject lead us to think that this could be a painting from the Ami school at the end of the Muromachi period. Although this attribution cannot be confirmed, it seems that the author could have been So-Ami, one of the greatest exponents of *suibokuga* art, or Japanese monochrome painting.
(*Fuji Museum of Art*)

317
Japan

Muromachi period
(1333-1573)
So-Ami (attributed)
Mount Fuji
Painting, ink on paper,
210 x 65cm
Tokyo, Fuji Museum of Art

The *kakemono*, or vertical scrolls used for interior decoration, were introduced into Japan from China. Landscapes, portraits of ancient masters or the motifs of Chinese calligraphy are the main subjects of these paintings, which were used to decorate the *tokonama*, the main room in Japanese homes.
This landscape is somewhat smaller and of simpler composition compared to other views of Mount Fuji attributed to the same author. In the foreground we can appreciate the vague outlines of a village and a small boat floating on the waters of the bay. Mount Fuji lies majestically in the background. This work was probably intended to decorate the *tokonoma*, the part of the home used for the tea ceremony. People who attended these elegant gatherings used to talk about the aesthetic qualities of the objects used in the ceremony, and about the paintings decorating their environment.
(*Fuji Museum of Art*)

318
China

Ming dynasty (1368-1644)
Wu school, Shen Zhou
(1427-1509)
Landscape in the Style of Da Chi, 1494
Painting, ink and colour on paper, vertical scroll,
115.5 x 48.5 cm
Inscriptions: stamps, Hongzhi, Jinyin, Qiu Bayu, Zhen Zhou, Lin Da Chi, Bao ren bi Yi; stamps, Hongzhi, Zhen Zhou, Shen Shi Qi Nan, Bei Shi Weng, Zai Ming
Shanghai, National Museum, 3831

Shen Zhou, also known as Qinan and Shitian, was born in Wu, in the province of Jiangsu. Apart from being a painter, he was a well-known calligrapher and poet. He followed Huang Tingjian's style of calligraphy and that of Bai Juyi, Su Shi and Lu Yu in poetry. He acquired his painting technique from the works of Dong Yuang, Ju Ran and Li Cheng; in middle age he preferred the techniques of Huang Gongwan and those of Wu Zhen in old age.

Many of his paintings were landscapes and gardens of southern Changjiang (River Yangtze), and dealt with aspects of every day scholarly life. Apart from landscapes, Shen Zhou liked painting flowers and plants, using soft colours and very pale ink. This works describes a hermit's visit to a friend. There is a craggy mountain furrowed by a tortuous winding path in the background. Various hangings can be seen between the mountain peaks, while in the foreground an old man is crossing a bridge on a donkey, guided by a young boy carrying a musical instrument. Shen Zhou combined different brushstrokes to achieve the different qualities of the elements in the painting, with vigorous strokes characteristic of Dong Gongwang for the rocks; and brushstrokes full of ink, similar to those used by Wu Zhen, for the leaves on the trees and the moss on the rocks.
(*Shan Guolin*)

319
Japan

Muromachi period
(1333-1573)
Koetsu
*Pear Tree Branches with
Wagtail*
Painting, ink and colour
on silk, 77 x 22.5 cm
Osaka, Masaki Museum
of Art

Nature is one of the traditional
subjects of Japanese painting.
Flowers and birds, in this case
a branch of a pear tree in blossom together with a wagtail in
flight, comprise the two single
elements of this composition.
According to the *Honcho
Gashi*, an official biographical
history of Japanese artists,
Koetsu was one of the most
outstanding painters in the
"birds and flowers" genre,
having learnt the technique
from Shubun. After a detailed
study of his works, however,
it seems more feasible to affirm that Koetsu belonged to
the Kamakura school, created
around the great painter of the
Shokei period.
(*Noriko Takahashi*)

320
Japan

Muromachi period
(1333-1573)
Mountain Landscape
Painting, ink on paper
79.2 x 31.8 cm
Inscriptions: Banri Shukyu
Osaka, Masaki Museum
of Art

Drawn with dark toned ink,
the foreground of the landscape appears in the lower
right hand part of the work. A
rocky precipice projects diagonally across the middle distance. The silhouette of a boat
can be seen with a fisherman
peacefully fishing. The lake's
surface extends around the
precipice to the scene's background. The landscape in the
distance is drawn with soft ink
tones.
A poem written by Banri Shu-
kyi in the upper part of the
work, extols the scene's
beauty. Banri was a priest-
painter who was also known
to be a friend of Sesshu.
(*Noriko Takahashi*)

321
Spain

Cardinal Juan de Cervantes's Gospel Book, approx. 1440
Gold ware, engraved gilted silver, and translucent enamel, 29 x 20 x 10 cm
From Avila Cathedral
Avila, Museo Catedralicio
Exhibitions: Valladolid, 1988
Bibliography: ALCOLEA 1975, XX, pp 166, figs. 191-192; DE LAS HERAS-MARTÍN 1981; GÓMEZ MORENO 1983, I, pp. 126, 203; VALLADOLID 1988, p 316

This *codex* contains the gospel book texts for mass on religious festivals, which were written on parchment and finished in 1345. Its heavy covers date from the same period as this personage, who became a cardinal in 1426 at the insistence of Martín V. Juan de Cervantes was Bishop of Túy, Segovia, Burgos, and of Avila between 1436 and 1444, and Archbishop of Seville, where he died in 1453. His tumulus-shaped tomb is in the Chapel of San Hermenegildo, in Seville Cathedral, and was finished by Lorenzo Mercadante de Bretaña in 1458.

Binding, an art linked inevitably to book production, was needed to provide them with suitable protection to ensure their conservation. During the Middle Ages, when books used to remain on a desk, table or altar, book binders concentrated on strengthening the covers and adorning the most highly valued books with gold ware, ivory or enamel. This book is an example of the so-called "rich bindings", or "altar bindings", which were used particularly for books of praise, giving them a fine aesthetic quality matching other objects used in worship. The covers of this book are an outstanding example of this genre, and are thickly decorated with gilded silver, applied uniformly to the rectangular surface, with rhombi surrounding the main subjects in the centre, which have now almost completely disappeared leaving the engraving uncovered. This is in accordance with the artistic taste prevailing at the time. The ornamental features are underlined with bands of Gothic decoration, and particularly with beautiful flamboyant tracings based on sinuous lines and a "bubble" motif, which allow for multiple combinations, like those in numerous Spanish choir stalls and pulpits of the time.

The *Resurrection of Christ* appears at the centre of one of the covers, and is presented in the Italian style. It is similar to the one which appears in the paten of the San Segundo chalice, also in Avila Cathedral Museum, which was done by the Siena goldsmith Andrea Petrucci in the 16th century. With the solemnity and monumentality of a Pantocrator, Christ appears as a sacred image, and only the strength of his left leg indicates that he has emerged with the standard from his tomb, which is presented as an altar. The figure is depicted with detailed clothing and conventional anatomy.

The soldiers are asleep, representing the contrast between mankind and the dramatic moment of salvation. The lines of a mound in the background converge towards Christ's head, and serve to balance his figure. This, combined with the simplicity of the landscape, confers a sensation of detention and immobility.

Juan de Cervantes was the patron of this work, and his coat of arms appear on the other cover. This shows two hinds, one in the upper section, passing by, and one below, grazing. The shield is crowned by an episcopal hat with tassels with the colour (red) representing his status as a cardinal and the number (four) for Archbishop.

Nobody knows who the author of this work is, although it is assumed that it could have been by a Spanish goldsmith from the studio in Avila around 1440. Finally, it should be mentioned that the Bishops of Avila swore on this book in their inaugural ceremony.

(*José María Martínez Frías*)

322
Germany

Stephan Lochner (Meersburg, approx. 1410-Cologne, 1451)
Presentation of Jesus in the Temple, and the Stigmatization of Saint Francis, 1445
Painting, egg tempera and oil on wood, 35.5 x 22.5 cm
Lisbon, Museu Calouste Gulbenkian, 272
Exhibitions: London, 1936-1950; Washington 1950-1960; Paris, 1960; Lisbon, 1961-1963; Orejas, 1965
Bibliography: BALDAS 1933-1934, p. 233; FÖRSTER 1938, pp. 23, 150, 175-176; WELLESZ 1967

Stephan Lochner was without doubt the most notable Cologne artist of the 15th century. Nevertheless, after his death, his name was soon forgotten, and only Romanticism rescued it from silence. It was Schlegel, who by comparing him with Raffaello, placed him among the highest artistic echelons: "As Raffaello is for the Italians the painter of tenderness and grace, so is Lochner for the Germans"; Goethe knew perfectly how to measure Lochner's relevance to the development of painting. Goethe commented: "The painting of the cathedral of Cologne, "with strokes that are today Byzantine in composition, demonstrate nevertheless, an obvious similarity with portrait-painting. In this picture, the artist has mastered nature. This work deserves attention: one can only hope that sweet and overdone praises for it be not raised to an enthusiastic and mystical interpretation that the experts would dislike."
Little is known of Lochner's origins in his native land, Upper Swabia, but it is possible that he developed his style during a stay in the Netherlands (from 1430 on), where he became familiar with the art of Robert Campin, and doubtless, that of Van Eyck. Nevertheless his compositions have the gilded backgrounds demanded by local tradition, and show little concern for landscape or for spatial problems.

Lochner's interest centers on the human figure, as both Goethe, and probably Dürer pointed out, the latter in Cologne when he asked permission and paid to see the altarpiece which *Meister Stephan zu Köln* had painted for the city's chapel, in other words, the one Goether describes as having seen in the cathedral. While it is true that through some works, such as the "Master of Saint Veronica," Lochner can be linked to other Cologne artists, his painting focuses more on faces and dress, without going beyond the limits of a moderate expressiveness which led him, on occasion, to paint compositions of great subtlety. The panel in Gulbenkian, for many years attributed to Meister Wilhelm, probably forms part of a small devotional tryptich, based on the vision and the *Virgin and the Child*. Dated 1445, the work is placed chronologically between the altarpiece called *Our Lady*, in the Munich Art Gallery and the painter's most important work: *The Adoration of the Magi*. Painted for Cologne's City Council, it was moved in 1810 to the cathedral.
On the front side of the panel one sees the *Presentation in the Temple*, in a beautiful architectural setting with an altar in the center, which shows a concern for perspective and spatial composition – not always present in Lochner's paintings – as is shown by the transparent lamp which hangs from the center of the arched vault.
On the reverse side, which has a reddish background, Lochner's workshop painted *Saint Francis receiving the stigmata*; the composition of this episode is simpler than the other, but works to great effect, as much for the chromatism as for the treatment of the mountains and the folds of the saint's habit, which lend a certain dramatic character to the overall effect.
(*Joan Sureda i Pons*)

323
Korea

Choson dynasty (1392-1910)
Vase, 15th century
Ceramic, blue and white
porcelain, 25 cm; diameter
of body 22 cm; diameter of
mouth 9.3 cm
Seoul, National Museum of
Korea, Duk 1224

The technique of blue varnish finishing was introduced to China during the Yuan dynasty (1268-1344), and was perfected during the Ming dynasty (1368-1644). From China it passed through the normal channels to Korea, where not only the technical aspects but also the decorative themes were imitated. The vases come from the Chinese *meiping* shape or "plum tree bottles," with a wide base and a vertical body the upper part of which widens out.
Bird and flower decorations made up one of the most popular genres in this type of piece, and were done by ap-

plying light brushstrokes to the vase while the clay was still soft. Once the decoration was finished the piece was fired a second time at high temperature which gave a fine, transparent covering of white engobe under which the decorative motifs stood out.
(*National Museum of Korea*)

324
Korea

Choson dynasty (1392-1910)
Water container, 15th
century
Ceramic, blue and white
porcelain, 7.7 cm; diameter
of body 11.7 cm; diameter
of base 6.35 cm
Seoul, National Museum
of Korea, Shin 955
Exhibitions: San Francisco,
1979; London, 1984
Bibliography: SAN FRANCISCO
1979, n. 174;
GOEPPER-WHITFIELD 1984,
n. 193

The ink, inkpot, paper, and the artist's brush were the "four precious objects" on the desks of poets, painters, and calligraphers. They were made of ceramic, porcelain, wood or metal, making them artistic as well as practical. Artists used porcelain containers, like the one here, to dilute their ink with water. This one is in the form of a peach, with a light blue finish, and dec-

orated with pine and plum tree motifs. There is an arm on one side for pouring the water, and the upper part has a small opening to let air in.
(*National Museum of Korea*)

325
Korea

Choson dynasty (1392-1910)
Bottle, 15th century
Ceramic, porcelain,
30.6 x 9.6 cm
Seoul, National Museum of
Korea, Dong-won 550

376

The globe shaped body of this
bottle has a tall base, and thins
at the neck before widening
out at the opening. The entire
bottle is varnished with a fine
finish, showing carved decoration, which shows the original
color of the ceramic. The main
motif is marked by two horizontal lines which contrast
with the bottle's uprightness.
Although the other motifs are
based on floral designs, they
tend to be abstract, and fill the
piece's central section.
(*National Museum of Korea*)

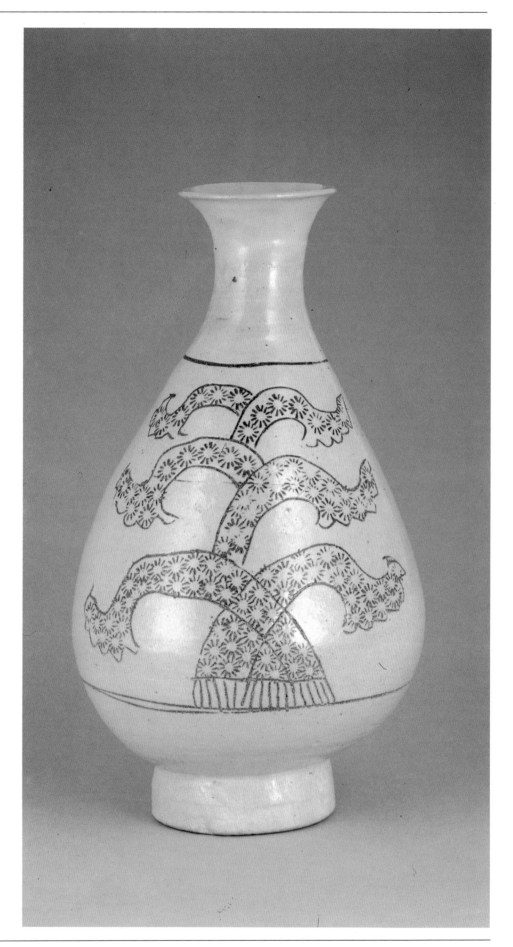

326
Korea

Choson dynasty (1392-1910)
Bowl, 15th century
Ceramic, porcelain,
7.7 x 16.7 cm
Seoul, National Museum
of Korea, Duk 6098

Korean pottery follows traditional Chinese pottery styles,
both in everyday pieces and
those made for the royal court.
The bowls meant for food or
drink are decorated with floral
motifs painted under a fine
finish of transparent varnish
through which the dark colors
stand out. This piece has the
lotus flower as its main motif,
which undulates around the
outside of the bowl. This type
of pottery comes from the
kilns of either Osanri or Byun-
cheonri, in the province of
Kyunggi.
(*National Museum of Korea*)

The Beginnings of a New World

As a colophon to *Art and Culture around 1492*, five works symbolize both its content and its meaning: a chain of visual experiences of different cultures which, as a whole, have transported the visitor to the world of five hundred years ago, a world which he may not be able to understand in all its complexity, but which he will surely, through the physical creations left by man in his journey through that moment in history, have come to see as his own, from which the trace of time have been erased.

Taina culture
Cemi of the Cohoba,
15th century
Carved Granite, 45 cm;
base width, 21 cm
Santo Domingo, Museo del
Hombre Dominicano

This sculpture shows a male figure squatting. The head is supported by the hands, which appear to be holding a mask which covers his face. Shown in relief on the arms and legs are simulations of the characteristic bands which the Taino aborigines used as decorative garments.

On the head is a circular receptacle or saucer, used by the Tainos to hold the hallucinogenic powder which they inhaled during their religious ceremonies, through a Y-shaped tube, as illustrated by Gonzalo Fernandez de Oviedo in his *Historia General y Natural de las Indias.*

The chroniclers of the Indies, Christopher Colombus among them, explain that the one who used the hallucinogenic powder of the *cohoba* to enter into a trance was believed to be in communication with the god, receiving revelations from him.

The *cohoba* gods were guardian deities carved in wood, and sometimes in stone. They are generally anthropomorphic, with the figure in a ritual squatting position.

These idols represent various mythical personalities or divinities that inhabit the sky, or the *Turey,* the indigenous animist pantheon, the main divinity of which was Yócahu Bagua Maórocoti, the supreme being, protector of the Taino people.

The *cohoba* idols, like the three-pointed icons, were highly esteemed among the natives of the West Indies. The tribal chiefs sought to glorify themselves by possessing finer idols than the others. One of these idols, by way of an apocalyptic prediction, foretold the disappearance of the

Taino village and its traditional ways of life; a sad omen for a happy people who ruled the island paradise the West Indies used to be.
(*Manuel Antonio García Arévalo*)

328
China

Ming dynasty (1368-1644)
Plate, 1465-1487
Blue and white Jingdezhen porcelain, 11.3 cm; diameter 19.2 cm; diameter of base 11.7 cm
Inscriptions: *Daming Chenghua Nian Zhi* (Made in the great Ming dynasty); mark of the reign of the emperor Chenghua (1465-1487)
Shanghai, National Museum

This plate is made of fine white high-quality porcelain. It is shallow, with a wide mouth and a thin base. The outer rim of the base is concave, while the inner rim is vertical. The surface is so smooth and clear that it can reflect an image. Highlights in a dark shade of green can be seen on the white base. The overall design has a dark blue finish, with some black markings, characteristic of the blue and white pieces of the period of the emperors Yongle (1403-1424) and Chenghua (1465-1487).

During the reign of Chenghua the color blue, was produced in Leping, in the province of Jiangxi, a city famous for the quality of its production; the blue pigment on this piece, however, was imported.

The decoration on the inside and outside recalls the "eight precious objects" of Buddhism: the wheel, the snail, the bell, the parasol, the flower, the fish, the vessel, and the bow, around a lotus flower, made of copper strands. The symbolism of this decoration has its origins in Tibetan Lamaism; it first appeared, with no apparent or established order, in the Yuan dynasty. During the Ming dynasty all these symbols began to be grouped together, and associated within Lamaism. With time the fish and the vessel changed their place in the group, but the other six symbols kept their order and significance.

In pieces designed for ritual use, the "eight precious objects" were usually shown in connection with the lotus flower. On the base is the seal which authenticates the piece: six characters inscribed in a double circle on the blue finish reading: "Made during the great Ming dynasty in the reign of the Emperor Chenghua."
(*Zhou Lili*)

329
Egypt

Mamluk period
Panel, late 15th century
Ivory and carved/engraved
wood, 31 x 9.4 cm
Inscriptions: Nasji script, in
relief: "Our Lord the sultan,
the honorable king Qa'it
Bay, may his victory be
glorious."
Cairo, Museum of Islamic
Art, 2334

This rectangular ivory panel
was discovered framed in
wood inlaid with fine pieces
of ivory. The panel is
covered with nashji inscriptions in relief over a background of simple foils and
boughs. The legend bears
the name of the Mamluk sultan Qa'it Bay, who died in
1496.

From the protectorate of Qa'it
Bay, various objects have
been preserved, which in-
clude manuscripts, candlesticks, lanterns, marble jars,
etc. During his long reign the
sultan also ordered the construction of various civic and
religious buildings; mosques,
irrigation canals, *Sabil-kuttabs*
(schools with public fountains), doors, houses, and *wa-
kalas*.

This panel was originally in
his great mosque, built in
Cairo (1472-1474). It probably
formed part of some door,
window, or mimbar.
(*Nimat M. Abu Bakr*)

330
Sierra Leone

Sherbro-portuguese culture
Hunting horn (oliphant),
approx. 1500
Carved ivory, 63.5 cm
Los Angeles, The Paul and
Ruth Thisman Collection of
African Art, Walt Disney Co.
Exhibitions: New
York-Houston-Baltimore,
1989; Washington
D.C.-Richmond, Va-Kansas-
Paris, 1989-1990; Washington
D.C., 1991-1992
Bibliography: Vogel 1981,
p. 64

The so-called Sape peoples of
the 15th century, which include the Sherbro or Bulom,
and the Temne, manufactured
most of the ivory artefacts. In
the 16th century, visitors from
Portugal commissioned the
Sherbro and Bini artisans to
make works of art for the European market.
The *Afro-Portuguese* ivories
are European type objects; oliphants, spoons, and ornamental saltcellars, carved by African artisans in a style which
represents a combination of
the two cultures before the
slave trade provoked barbaric
and inhuman warring be-
tween Africans and Euro-
peans. Of all the Sherbro-Portuguese oliphants, the piece
we see here, and another by
the same artist, in Drummond
Castle, are the most richly decorated, and have been the
most fully documented.
(*Van A. Romans*)

331
Germany

Martin Waldseemüller
(Radolfzell, approx.
1470-Saint-Dié, 1518-1521)
Cosmographiae introductio,
25 April, 1507
Book, 20 x 15 x 1.5 cm
From the library of the
humanist Beatus Rhenanus
(1485-1547)
Selestat, Humanist Library,
F. 67600
Bibliography: Ronsin 1979;
Ronsin 1991; Kubler 1992,
n. 115, pp. 9-15

This book is a prologue or an accompanying book of cartographic documents: planispheres, globes with spherical lunes, and a map drawn by Martin Waldseemüller. The book is entitled: *Cosmographiae introductio cum quibusdam geometriae ac astronomiae principiis ad eam rem necessariis in super quatuor Americi Vespucii navigationes. Universalis Cosmographiae descriptio tam in solido quam in plano eis etiam insertis quae Ptholomaeo ignota a nuperis reperta sunt.* (An introduction to cosmography with some elements of geometry and astronomy necessary for the comprehension of this science, such as the four voyages of Amerigo Vespucci and the reproduction of the entire world in both spherical and flat projection, including the regions ignored by Ptolomy and which have only recently been discovered.)

This book was published for the first time on April 25th, 1507 in Saint-Dié, France. It consists of fifty-three folio pages, printed in Roman characters. On the reverse side of the title page appears the dedication of Mathias Ringman using the pseudonym Philesius Vogesigena, to the emperor Maximillian I: an elegaic poem of ten verses. On the following page, marked by "Aij," the prologue of Martin Ilacomilus places the work under the Emperor's protection. The index is on the reverse side of the folio. On the page "Aiij," is the text proper, which is composed of two parts.

In the first part the authors have published a treatise on cosmography in which they explain the principles of spherical geometry, of the circles of heaven, of the globe, of the celestial zones, the parallels, the climates, the winds, and the divisions of the Earth. The authors allude several times to the discoveries of Amerigo Vespucci. In the chapter dealing with the divisions of the Earth, on page 32, one finds a paragraph called *The Baptism of America.* In the margin is printed the word "America," and the text says: *Nunc vero et haec partes sunt latius lustratae, et alia quarta pars par Americum Vesputium (ut in sequentibus audietur) inventa est, quam non video cur quis jure vetet ab Americo inventore, sagacias ingenii viro Amerigen quasi Americi terram, sive Americam dicendam: cum et Europa et Asia a mulieribus sua sortita sint nomina. Ejus sintum et gentis mores ex bisbinis Americi navigationibus quae sequuntur liquide intelligi datur.* (In the present day, these regions [Europe, Africa, and Asia] have been completely explored, and a fourth part has been discovered by Amerigo Vespucci, as will be later discussed, and as Europe and Asia, received women's names, I see no reason why this other part should not be called Amerige, that is to say land of Americo, or America, in honor of the sagacious man who has discovered it. We shall have more information about the situation of this land and about the customs of its inhabitants from Amerigo's next four voyages).

The second part of the book begins on the reverse side of the folio "bij," with a poem of twenty-two verses by Mathias Ringman, which was first printed in the author's *De Ora Antartice,* published in 1505. This piece is followed by the part titled *Quatuor Americi Vesputii Navigationes,* which begins with other poems of ten verses from the Ringman folio "biij." The folios from twenty-three to fifty-three consist of an account of the voyages to "the islands recently discovered during his four voyages," the text written by Vespucci in Lisbon on September 4th, 1504.

This text had been translated into Latin by Jean Basin de Sandaucourt starting with a text in French that was at the time a translation of the original text in Italian.

The book ends on page fifty-three with the typographic mark, a wood engraving showing a globe crowned by a cross of Lorena on a black background, with the initials, S.D. (Sanctus Deodatus), G.L. (Gualterus Lud), N.L. (Nicolas Lud), M.I. (Martinus Ilacomylus). Below this is the date of the edition's completion: *Finitum VII kl Septembris anno supra sesqui millesimum VII* (finished the 4th of the calends of September 1507, which corresponds to the 25th of April, 1507).

The final page pays homage to the members of the Gymnase Vosgien de Saint-Dié, particularly to Gualterus and to Nicolaus Lud, owners of the printing press, and active members of the humanist group of Saint-Dié. The important work of the cartographer Martin Waldseemüller is also commented on. Because the text is not explicitly signed, the dispute over the author remains open. The most likely hypothesis is that the maps are the work of Martin Waldseemüller, while the text was composed by Mathias Ringman, who had been a student of the latin school of Sélestat. These two scholars were contracted by the printers for this edition of the work.

The copies of this edition which have been preserved are very rare. The edition preserved in the Sélestat comes from the personal library of Beatus Rhenanus (1485-1547) as can be read in the lower part of the title page of the *ex libris* manuscript: *Sum beati Rhenani Selestatini M.D.X.*

(Hubert Meyer)

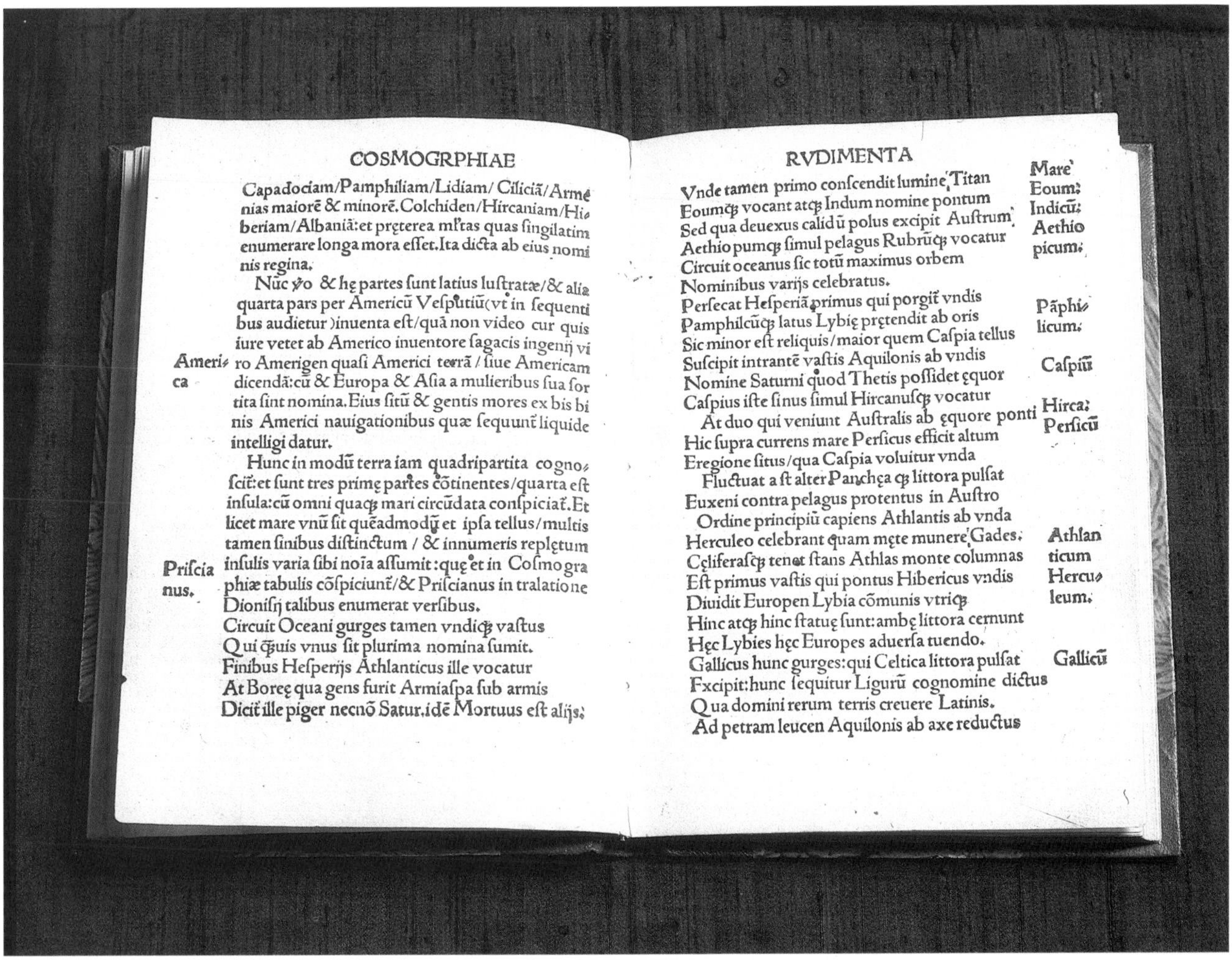

Capadociam/Pamphiliam/Lidiam/ Ciliciã/ Armé
nias maiorē & minorē. Colchiden/Hircaniam/Hi⸗
beriam/Albaniã: et preterea młtas quas singilatim
enumerare longa mora esset. Ita dicta ab eius nomi
nis regina.

Nũc vo & hę partes sunt latius lustratæ/& alia
quarta pars per Americũ Vesputiũ (vt in sequenti
bus audietur) inuenta est/quã non video cur quis
iure vetet ab Americo inuentore sagacis ingenij vi
Ameri⸗ ro Amerigen quasi Americi terrã / siue Americam
ca dicendã: cũ & Europa & Asia a mulieribus sua sor
tita sint nomina. Eius situ & gentis mores ex bis bi
nis Americi nauigationibus quæ sequunt liquide
intelligi datur.

Hunc in modũ terra iam quadripartita cogno⸗
scič: et sunt tres primę partes cõtinentes/quarta est
insula: cũ omni quacż mari circũdata conspiciač. Et
licet mare vnũ sit queãadmodũ et ipsa tellus/multis
tamen sinibus distinctum / & innumeris replętum
Priscia insulis varia sibi noĩa assumit: quę et in Cosmo gra
nus. phiæ tabulis cõspiciunł/& Priscianus in tralatione
Dionisĳ talibus enumerat versibus.

Circuit Oceani gurges tamen vndicż vastus
Qui ǫuis vnus sit plurima nomina sumit.
Finibus Hesperijs Athlanticus ille vocatur
At Boreę qua gens furit Armiaspa sub armis
Diciț ille piger necnõ Satur. idẽ Mortuus est alijs;

Vnde tamen primo conscendit lumine Titan
Eoumcż vocant atcż Indum nomine pontum
Sed qua deuexus calidũ polus excipit Austrum.
Aethiopumcż simul pelagus Rubrũcż vocatur
Circuit oceanus sic totũ maximus orbem
Nominibus varijs celebratus.
Persecat Hesperiã primus qui porgit vndis
Pamphilcũcż latus Lybię pretendit ab oris
Sic minor est reliquis/maior quem Caspia tellus
Suscipit intrantē vastis Aquilonis ab vndis
Nomine Saturni quod Thetis possidet equor
Caspius iste sinus simul Hircanuscż vocatur
At duo qui veniunt Australis ab equore ponti
Hic supra currens mare Persicus efficit altum
Eregione situs/qua Caspia voluitur vnda
Fluctuat a st alter Panchea cż littora pulsat
Euxeni contra pelagus protentus in Austro
Ordine principiũ capiens Athlantis ab vnda
Herculeo celebrant quam męte munere Gades.
Celiferascż tenet stans Athlas monte columnas
Est primus vastis qui pontus Hibericus vndis
Diuidit Europen Lybia cõmunis vtricż
Hinc atcż hinc statuę sunt: ambę littora cernunt
Hęc Lybies hęc Europes aduersa tuendo.
Gallicus hunc gurges: qui Celtica littora pulsat
Fxcipit: hunc sequitur Ligurũ cognomine dictus
Qua domini rerum terris creuere Latinis.
Ad petram leucen Aquilonis ab axe reductus

Marginal notes (right column):
Mare
Eoum;
Indicũ;
Aethio
picum;

Paphi⸗
licum;

Caspiũ

Hirca;
Persicũ

Athlan
ticum
Hercu⸗
leum.

Gallicũ

Appendix

388

Europe around 1492

M. Batllori, *Humanismo y Renacimiento, Estudios hispanoeuropeos*, Barcelona 1987.

E. Battisti, *L'Antirinascimento*, Milan 1962.

O. Benesch, *The Art of the Renaissance in Northern Europe*, London 1985.

V. Borghesi, *Il Mediterraneo tra due rivoluzioni nautiche (secc. XIV-XVII)*, Florence 1977.

F. Braudel, *Civilisation matérielle, économie et capitalisme (XVe-XVIIIe siècles)*, Paris 1979.

P. Bressi, *Il dissolversi del mondo medioevale*, Rome 1973.

J. Burkhardt, *Die Kultur der Renaissance in Italien. Ein Versuch*, Basel 1860.

D. Cantimori, *Umanesimo e religione nel Rinascimento*, Turin 1975.

F. Cardini, *Europa 1492. Ritratto di un continente cinquecento anni fa*, Milan 1989.

E. Cassirer-P.P. Kristeller-J.H. Randall, *The Renaissance Philosophy of Man*, Chicago 1948.

A. Chastel, *Art et humanisme à Florence au temps de Laurens le Magnifique*, Paris 1961.

A. Chastel-R. Klein, *L'Age de l'humanisme*, Paris 1963.

H. Damisch, *L'Origine de la perspective*, Paris 1987.

J. Delumeau, *La Civilisation de la Renaissance*, Paris 1967.

G.R. Elton, *The Reformation Era 1520-1559*, Cambridge 1958.

W.K. Fergusson, *The Renaissance in Italy*, London 1875-1876.

R.J. Forbes, *Man the Maker*, New York 1960.

F. Gaeta, *Il Rinascimento e la Riforma*, Turin 1976.

E. Garín, *La Cultura del Rinascimento*, Bari 1967.

M.P. Gilmore, *The World of Humanism*, New York 1952.

J. Huizinga, *Herfsttij der Meddleeuwen*, Haarlem 1919.

V. Nieto Alcaide-F. Checa Cremades, *El Renacimiento. Formación y crisis del modelo clásico*, Madrid 1980.

H.A. Oberman, *Masters of Reformation*, Cambridge 1981.

G.R. Potter, *The Renaissance 1493-1520*, Cambridge 1957.

G. Ritter, *Die Neugestaltung Europas im 16. Jahrhundert*, Berlin 1950.

R. Romano-A. Tenenti, *Die Grundlegung der modernen Welt*, Frankfurt am M.-Hamburg 1967.

A. Rupert Hall, *The Revolution in Science. 1500-1750*, London 1983.

G. Simonici, *Città e Società nel Rinascimento*, Turin 1974.

J. Sureda, *El Renacimiento. Siglo XV*, Barcelona 1988.

A. Symons, *Renaissance in Italy*, London 1875-1876.

P.E. Taviani, *Cristoforo Colombo. La genesi della grande scoperta*, Novara 1982.

M. Wackernagel, *The World of the Florentine Renaissance Artist*, Princeton 1981 (reed.).

R. Weiss, *The Renaissance Discovery of Classical Antiquity*, Oxford 1969.

W.P. Wightman, *Science and the Renaissance*, Aberdeen 1962.

The Muslim World in 1492

R. Arié, "Quelques remarques sur le costume des musulmans d'Espagne au temps des nasrides", *Arabica*, XII, 3, 1965.

R. Arié, *L'Espagne musulmane au temps des nasrides (1232-1492)*, Paris 1990.

R. Arié, "Apuntes sobre la Granada nazarí", *500 años de la Toma de Granada, Ideal*, XX, 1992.

N. Atasoy-J. Raby, *The Pottery in Ottoman Turkey*, London 1989.

C. Bernis, "Modas moriscas en la sociedad cristiana española del siglo XV y principios del XVI", *Boletín de la Real Academia de la Historia*, LXLIV, Madrid 1959.

D. Cabanelas, *El techo del salón de Comares en la Alhambra. Decoración, Policromía, Simbolismo y Etimología*, Granada 1988.

M. Cruz Hernández, "La significación social del final del poder islámico de al-Andalus", *500 años de la Toma de Granada, Ideal*, XVIII, 1992.

J.C. Garcin-B. Maury-J. Revault-M. Zakariya, *Palais et Maisons du Claire, I, Epoque Mamelouke (XIIIe-XVIe siècles)*, Paris 1982.

M. Goméz-Moreno, *Guía de Granada*, Granada 1892 (1982).

B. Gray, *Persian Miniatures*, New York 1962.

J.D. Hoag, *Architecture islamique*, Paris 1982.

E. Hühnel, "Losa Hispanoárabe excavada en Oriente" *Al-Andalus*, Madrid 1942.

D. Kuban, *L'Architecture ottomane*, Fribourg 1981.

E. Kühnel, *Islamic Art and Architecture*, London 1966.

M.A. Ladero Quesada, *Granada. Historia de un país islámico (1232-1571)*, Madrid 1979.

A. Lane, *Later Islamic Pottery. Persia, Syria, Egypt, Turkey*, London 1971.

F.M. Pareja, *Islamología*, Madrid 1952-1954.

C. Partearroyo Lacaba, "Textiles. Telas, alfombras, tapices" *Historia de las artes aplicadas e industriales en España*, Madrid 1987.

M. Rogers, "The Gorgeous East: Trade and Tribute in the Islamic Empires", *Europe and the Mediterranean World*, Washington 1991.

L. Seco de Lucena, *La Granada nazarí del siglo XV*, Granada 1975.

L. Seco de Lucena, "Panorama político del Islam granadino durante el s. XV", *Miscelánea de estudios árabes y hebraicos*, Granada 1960.

B. Spuler, *The Muslim World*, Leiden 1969.

L. Torres Balbás, "Las alhóndigas hispanomusulmanas y el Corral del Carbón de Granada", *Al-Andalus*, Madrid 1946.

L. Torres Balbás, *Arte Almohade. Arte Nazarí. Arte Mudéjar*, Ars Hispaniae, Madrid 1949.

The Far East around 1492

J. Brijbhushan, *The World of Indian Miniatures*, Tokyo 1979.

J. Cahill, *The Distant Mountains (Ming Dynasty)*, New York 1982.

F. Carycao-Blanchard, *L'Asie du Sud-Est* (2 vols.), Paris 1970.

I. Cervera, *La vía de la caligrafía*, Madrid 1988.

A. Coomaraswamy, *History of Indian and Indonesian Art*, New York 1965.

M.G. Cosgrove, *The Enamels of China and Japan*, London 1974.

E. Fenollosa-E. Pound, *El carácter de la escritura china*

como medio poético, Madrid 1977.

L. Frederic, *The Art of Southeast Asia. Temples and Sculptures*, New York 1975.

R. Goepper-R. Whitfield, *Treasures from Korea*, London 1984.

J. Gómez-Rea-S. Deudan, *Himalaya*, Madrid 1985.

R.S. Gupte, *Iconography of the Hindus, Buddhists and Jains*, Bombay 1980.

F.G. Gutiérrez, *El arte del Japón*, "Summa Artis", Madrid 1967.

E.R. Heinz-Martin, *El arte tibetano*, Barcelona 1980.

J. Hutt, *Understanding far Eastern Art (China, Korea, Japan)*, Oxford 1987.

T. Itoh, *The Gardens of Japan*, Tokyo 1985.

E. Kidder, *El arte del Japón*, Madrid 1984.

Y.K. Lee, *Oriental Lacquer Art*, New York 1972.

D. Lion-Goldschmidt- J.C. Moreau-Gobard, *Arts de la Chine* (3 vols.), Fribourg 1985.

A.H. Longhurst, *Hampi Ruins*, Madras 1990.

D. Mazzeo-Ch. Antonini, *Civilización kbmer*, Valencia 1975.

M. Medley, *The Chinese Potter*, Oxford 1980.

S. Nandanjeet, *Los tesoros del Himalaya*, Barcelona 1968.

J. Needham, *De la ciencia y de la tecnología chinas*, Madrid 1978.

K. Okakura, *El libro del té*, Barcelona 1978.

P. Pal, *Art of Nepal*, Los Angeles 1985.

P. Pal, *Art of Tibet*, Los Angeles 1990.

L. Racionero, *Textos de estética taoista*, Madrid 1987.

Ph. Rawson, *The Art of Southeast Asia*, London 1967.

Ch. Reinolds, *Sri Lanka*, Madrid 1985.

H. Rousset, *Arts de la Corée*, Fribourg 1977.

G. Rowley, *Principios de la pintura obina*, Madrid 1981.

R. Sewell, *Forgotten Empire (Vijayanagar)*, Madras 1988.

C. Sivaramamurti, *El arte de la India*, Barcelona 1975.

C. Sivaramamurti, *South Indian Bronzes*, New Delhi 1981.

K.V. Soundararajan, *Ahmadabad*, New Delhi 1980.

D.T. Suzuki, *Budismo Zen*, Barcelona 1986.

Various Authors, *Masterworks of Chinese Art in the National Palace Museum*, (20 vols.), Taipei 1970.

A. Volwahsen, *Living Architecture Islamic Indian*, London 1970.

W. Watson, *L'Art de l'ancienne Chine*, Paris 1979.

H. Zimmer, *Filosofías de la India*, Buenos Aires 1965.

America around 1492

J. Adánez, "Sociedad y cultura de los indios de Norteamérica", *Las Américas*, 19, Madrid 1991.

J. Alcina Franch, "Ingapirca: arquitectura y áreas de asentamiento", *Revista Española de Antropología Americana*, 8, Madrid 1978, S. 127-146.

J. Alcina Franch, "Religiosidad, alucinógenos y patrones artísticos taínos", *Boletín del Museo del Hombre Dominicano*, X, 17, Santo Domingo, 1981, S. 103-117.

J. Alcina Franch, "La cultura Taína como sociedad en transición entre los niveles tribal y de jefatura", *La Cultura Taína*, Madrid 1983, S. 67-80.

J. Alcina Franch, "Evolución social de los pueblos indígenas en América", *Etnica*, 20, Barcelona 1984, S. 7-35.

J. Alcina Franch, "Los indios Cañaris de la Sierra sur del Ecuador", *Miscelánea Antropológica Ecuatoriana*, 6, Guayaquil 1986, S. 141-188.

J. Alcina Franch, "Patrones de asentamiento en la América Precolombina: impacto urbanístico y demográfico a la llegada de los europeos", *La Ciudad iberoamericana*, Madrid 1987.

J. Alcina Franch, "Los aztecas", *Biblioteca Histórica. Historia*, 16, Madrid 1989.

J. Alcina Franch, "El problema de las 'jefaturas' de la costa Noroeste a la luz de los primeros informes españoles del siglo XVIII", *Culturas de la Coste Noroeste de América*, Madrid 1989, S. 33-49.

J. Alcina Franch, *El complejo "santuario-mercado-festival" y el origen de los centros ceremoniales en el Area Andina Septentrional. Homenaje a Richard P. Schaedel*, Austin TX (in print).

R.I. Cameiro, "The Chiefdom: Precursor of the State", *The Transition of the Statehood in the New World*, Cambridge 1981, S. 37-79.

B. de las Casas, *Obra indigenista*, ed. Madrid 1985.

G.W. Conrad-A. Demarest, *Religion and Empire. The Dynamics of Aztec and Inca Expansionism*, Cambridge 1984.

M.H. Fried, *The Evolution of Political Society*, New York 1975.

G. Gasparini-L. Margolles, *Arquitectura Inca*, Caracas 1977.

W. Knickeberg, *Etnología de América*, Mexico 1946.

M. León-Portilla, *Trece poetas del mundo azteca*, Mexico 1967.

J.V. Murra, *Formaciones económicas y políticas del mundo andino*, Lima 1975.

J. Palop, "Los Cayapas en el siglo XVI", *Arqueología y Etnohistoria del Sur de Colombia y Norte de Ecuador*, (Alcino Moreno eds.) Guayaquil 1986.

E. Pasztory, *Aztec Art*, Mew York 1983.

L. Pericot, *América Indígena*, Barcelona 1961.

W.T. Sanders-B.J. Price, *Mesoamérica. The Evolution of a Civilization*, New York 1968.

E.R. Service, *Primitive Social Organizacion*, New York 1962.

J.H. Steward, "Handbook on South American Indians", *Bureau of America: Ethnology*, Bulletin 43, Smithsonian Institution, Washington 1946-1950.

N. Wachtel, "La reciprocidad y el espacio inca: de Karl Polanyi a John V. Murra", *Sociedad e ideología*, 59-78, Lima 1973.

Related Exhibitions

390

Alicante/Murcia/Cádiz, 1988-89
Piedras de Oro. El arte en el imperio de los Incas.

Antwerp, 1960
Henri le navigateur.

Antwerp, 1975
Afrikaanse Beeldhouwkunst.

Antwerp, 1991
Feitorias.

Bologna, 1985
Leonardo e il Codice Hammer.

Bologna, New York, Washington, 1986
Nell'età del Correggio e dei Carracci.

Boston, 1985
Life at Court, Art for India's Rules 16th-19th Centuries.

Brussels, 1963
Le siècle Bruegel.

Brussels, 1977
Le voyage de Dürer dans les Pays Bas.

Brussels, 1987
Cadeaux à la Cour Impériale de Vienne.

Budapest, 1924
Magyar Szónyegkereskedök Egyesületének Régi Keleti Szónyeg Kiállitása.

Budapest, 1962
Keleti szönyegek Iparmüvészeti Múzeum.

Budapest, 1986
500 év oszmán-török szöyegmüvészeti Iparmüvészeti Múzeum.

Cáceres, 1984-1985
Muestra de cultura precolombina y colonial.

Cairo, 1935
Art Persan.

Celle, 1947
Islamische Kunst Schloss Celle.

Coimbra, 1940
Exposição de ouriversaria portuguesa dos séc. XII a XVII. Comemorações Nacionais de 1940.

Córdoba, 1953
V Centenario del nacimiento del Gran Capitán.

Darmstadt, Düsseldorf, Munich, 1965
Türkische Kunst.

Düsseldorf, 1967
Preußischer Kulturbesitz.

Eger, 1982
Kora-oszmán szönyegek.

Essen, Stockholm, Zürich, 1961
5000 Jahre ägyptische Kunst.

Ferrara, 1972
Ceramica nelle civiche collezioni.

Ferrara, 1981
Libri manoscritti e a stampa da Pomposa all'Umanesimo.

Ferrara, 1983
Esposizione della pittura ferrarese del Rinascimento.

Ferrara, 1985
Le arti figurative a Ferrara nel Secondo Rinascimento.

Ferrara, 1988
Ferrara 1474: miniatura, tipografia, committenza; Il "Decretum Gratiani Roverella".

Ferrara, 1988-1989
A tavola con il Principe. Materiali per una mostra su alimentazione e cultura nella Ferrara degli Estensi.

Ferrara, 1989-1990
Ceramiche a Ferrara in età estense dalla Collezione Pasetti.

Ferrara, 1989-1990
Terre ed acqua. Le bonifiche ferraresi nel delta del Po.

Ferrara, 1991
Arte del legno. La tarsia rinascimentale a Ferrara.

Florence, 1986
Donatello e i suoi. Scultura fiorentina del primo Rinascimento.

Florence, 1990
Pittura di luce.

Gent, 1991
Aux confins du Moyen Age.

Granada, 1992
Al-Andalus. Arte islámico de España.

Graz, 1974
Alte Anatolische Teppiche: Ausstellung im Steiermärkischen Landesmuseum Joanneum Abteilung für Kunstgewerbe.

Houston, 1989
Africa and the Renaissance.

Huelva, 1981
Arte Precolombino.

Humlebaek, 1987
Art from the World of Islam.

Ingolstadt, 1974
Goldschmiedearbeiten in und aus Ingolstadt.

Istanbul, 1989
Iznik Ceramics.

Japan, 1989
The Ancient Art of Nigeria.

Japan, 1989
Masterpieces from the Vatican.

Japan, 1990-1991
L'Arte di Corte a Urbino e a Pesaro (dai Montefeltro ai Della Rovere).

Kansas, 1989-1990
Sounding Forms: African Musical Instruments.

Lagos, 1985
Treasures of Ancient Nigeria. Legacy of Two Thousand Years.

Leitmeritz, 1989
Master of the Litomerice Altar.

Linz, 1988
Kaiserliche Geschenke

Lisbon, 1882
Exposição Retrospectiva da Arte Ornamental Portuguesa e Hespanhola.

Lisbon, 1940
Primitivos portugueses 1450-1550.

Lisbon, 1958
A Rainha D. Leonor - Mosteiro Madre de Deus.

Lisbon, 1983
XVII Exposição de Arte, Ciencia e Cultura do Conselho da Europa.

Lisbon, 1983
Os descobrimentos portugueses e a Europa do Renascimento.

Lisbon, 1985
Gahtan.

Lisbon, 1989
O vidro em Portugal.

Lisbon, 1990
Convento de Jesús. 500 años.

Lisbon, Abrantes, 1971
Mestres do Sardoal e Abrantes.

Lisbon, June 1988
XVII Exposição Europeia de Arte Ciencia e Cultura - As Descobertas e o Renascimento, Formas de coincidencia e de Cultura.

Lisbon, June 1988
Le Langage des Orfevres da Portugal.

London, 1935-1936
International Exhibition of Chinese Art.

London, 1955-1956
Portuguese Art 800-1800.

London, 1957
Arts of the Ming Dynasty.

London, 1958
Exposition des bronzes Ming.

London, 1978
A King's Good Servant: Sir Thomas More.

London, 1980
A Hundred Masterpieces of Chinese Ceramics from the Percival David Collection.

London, 1982
The Art of the Book in India.

London, 1983
The Genius of Venice 1500-1600.

London, 1984
From Borso to Cesare d'Este. The School of Ferrara 1450-1628.

London, 1984
Treasures from Korea.

London, Amsterdam, Florence, 1961-1962
Bronzetti Italiani del Rinascimento.

Los Angeles, 1989
Timur and the Princely Vision: Persian Art and Culture in the Fifteenth Century.

Luxembourg, 1988
Le Langage des Orfevres de Portugal.

Madrid, 1892
Exposición histórico americana de Madrid.

Madrid, 1935
Arte Inca (Colección Jaun Larrea).

Madrid, 1961
Conmemorativa del IV Centenario de la muerte de Alonso Berruguete.

Madrid, 1972
San José en el arte español.

Madrid, Seville, Cádiz, Santillana del Mar, Barcelona, 1985
Culturas indígenas de los Andes Septentrionales.

Mantua, 1974
Tesori d'arte nella terra del Gonzaga.

Modena, 1925
Libro emiliano nella R. Biblioteca Modenese.

Modena, 1954
Codici emiliani miniati.

Modena, 1971
La ceramica graffita in Emilia Romagna.

Munich, 1910
Meisterwerke Muhammedanischer Kunst.

Naples, 1983
Leonardo e il Leonardismo a Napoli e a Parma.

New York, 1985
India: Art and Culture, 1300-1900.

New York, 1988
Africa and the Renaissance: Art in Ivory.

New York, 1989-1991
Yoruba, Nine Centuries of Art & Thought.

New York, Nuremberg, 1986
Gothic and Renaissance Art in Nuremberg 1800-1550.

Padua, 1970
Dopo Mantegna.

Padua, 1988
La Quadreria Emo Capodilista.

Palencia, 1991
Antología de Alonso Berruguete.

Paris, 1933
Art des Incas.

Paris, 1935
L'art italien de Cimabue à Tiepolo.

Paris, 1971
Les Arts de l'Islam des origines à 1700.

Paris, 1977
Dieux et Démons de l'Himalaya.

Paris, 1977
L'Islam dans les collections nationales.

Paris, 1990
Soliman le Magnifique.

Perugia, 1945
Quattro secoli di pittura in Umbria. Mostra celebrativa del V centenario della nascita di Pietro Perugino.

Pesaro, 1991
Signorelli e Dante.

Prague, 1935
Madonna. Religious Painting and Sculpture in the Time 1350-1550 from Church and Private Property.

Prague, 1978
Master from the Litomerice Altar.

Rome, 1953
Mostra storica nazionale della miniatura.

Rome, 1966
Dipinti fiamminghi di collezioni romane.

Rotterdam, 1969
Erasmo da Rotterdam.

Salerno, 1987
Tavole restaurate del Museo Diocesano di Salerno.

San Francisco, 1979
5000 Years of Korean Art.

San Lorenzo, 1986 (Kartanse San Lorenzo)
Andrea da Salerno nel Rinascimento meridionale.

Santillana del Mar, Zamora, 1982-1983
Arte y Cultura del Cuzco.

Setúbal, 1960
Arte sacra.

Setúbal, 1969
Manuelina.

Setúbal, 1969
Exposição manuelina 1469-1969.

Setúbal, 1989
Convento de Jesús. 500 años.

Setúbal, 1990
Convento de Jesús. 500 años

Setúbal, 1991
Santa Casa da Misericordia de Setúbal. Historia e arte.

Seville, 1929
Exposição de Sevilha Ibero-Americana. Pavilhao Portugués com a exposição "Epoca dos Descubrimientos".

Seville, Granada, 1982
Escultura castellana.

Skzekszárd, 1975
Régi török szónyegek.

Tokyo, 1990
I tesori di arte antica della Regione Emilia Romagna.

Tokyo, Nagoja, 1991
Firenze: Arte del Rinascimento e Restauro.

Toledo, 1958
Carlos V y su ambiente: exposición homenaje en el IV Centenario de su muerte (1558-1958).

Toledo, 1991
Damasquinado en Toledo.

Turin, 1977
Valle di Susa, Arte e storia dall'XI al XVIII secolo.

Turin, 1988
Dipinti e sculture del Museo Civico d'Arte Antica in Galleria Sabauda.

Turin, 1989
Gotico e Rinascimento in Piemonte.

Venice, 1946
I Capolavori dei Musei Veneti.

Vienna, Budapest, Cologne, 1986-1987
Gold und Macht. Spanien in der Neuen Welt.

Vila Viçosa, 1986
D. Fernando II/Rei-Artista.

Washington, 1988-1989
A Jeweleler's Eye.

Washington, 1989
Sounding Forms: African Musical Instruments.

Washington, 1989
Timur and the Princely Vision: Persian Art and Culture in the Fifteenth Century.

Washington, 1991
Circa 1492. Art in the Age of Exploration.

General Bibliography

*Compiled by Joan Sureda i Pons
and Isabel Cervera*

392

Acosta 1956
J.R. Acosta, *El enigma de los Chac Mooles de Tula. Homenaje a Manuel Gamio*, Mexico 1956.

Agapito y Revilla 1910
J. Agapito y Revilla, "Alonso Berruguete", *Boletín de la Sociedad Castellana de Excursiones*, IV, Valladolid 1910.

Agapito y Revilla 1913
J. Agapito y Revilla, "Los Retablos de San Benito el Real", *Boletín de la Sociedad Castellana de Excursiones*, IV, Valladolid 1913

Agapito y Revilla 1920-1929
J. Agapito y Revilla, *La obra de los maestros de la escultura castellana*, Valladolid 1920-1929.

Agapito y Revilla 1926
J. Agapito y Revilla, "Los restos del retablo mayor de San Benito", *Boletín del Museo Provincial de Bellas Artes*, Valladolid 1926.

Agosti 1990
G. Agosti, *Bambaia e il classicismo lombardo*, Turin 1990.

Ainaud de Lasarte 1952
J. Ainaud de Lasarte, *Cerámica y vidrio*, 1952.

Al Basha 1965
H. Al Basha, *Al-Funun al Islamyya wal-wazaif...*, I, II and III, Cairo 1965.

Al Basha 1978
H. Al Basha, *Al-Alqab al Islamyya...*, Cairo 1978.

Al-Hatib 1901 (1975)
I. Al-hatib, *Ihata*, Cairo 1901 (1975 edition).

Alcolea 1975
S. Alcolea, "Artes decorativas en la España Cristiana", *Ars Hispaniae*, Madrid 1975.

Allende Salazar 1915-1916
J. Allende Salazar, "La familia Berruguete (Noticias inéditas)", *Boletín de la Sociedad Castellana de Excur-*

siones, VII, 1915-1916, pp. 194-198.

Almeda y Vives 1933
F. Almeda y Vives, "Vocabulario de la Cerámica de manises", *Boletín de la Sociedad Castellonense de Cultura*, Castellón 1933.

Alvarez Ossorio 1925
F. Alvarez Ossorio, *Una visita al Museo Arqueológico Nacional*, Madrid 1925.

Andres Ordax et al. 1989
S. Andres Ordax, *Castilla y León /1. La España Gótica*, Madrid 1989.

Angulo Iñiguez 1953
D. Angulo Iñiguez, "La Virgen con el Niño de Berruguete en la colección del Vizconde de Roda", *Archivo Español de Arte*, XVI, 56, 1953, pp. 111-115.

Angulo Iñiguez 1954
D. Angulo Iñiguez, "Pintura del Renacimiento", *Ars Hispaniae*, Madrid 1954.

Angulo Iñiguez 1954
D. Angulo Iñiguez, "Pintura del s. XVI", *Ars Hispaniae*, XII, Madrid 1954.

Anonymous 1877
Anonymous, "Legado del Sr. Martínez Vallejo al Museo Provincial", *Diario de Las Provincias*, 9. November 1877.

Arfe 1585 (1979)
J. Arfe y Villafañe, *De varia commesvracion para la escvlptvra y architectvra*, Seville 1585 (1979 edition).

Arias de Miranda 1843
J. Arias de Miranda, *Apuntes históricos sobre la Cartuja de Miraflores de Burgos*, Burgos 1843.

Arié 1990
R. Arié, *L'Espagne musulmane au temps des Nazarides*, Paris 1990.

Atasoy-Raby 1989
N. Atasoy-J. Raby, *Iznik. The*

Pottery of Ottoman Turkey, London 1989.

Atil 1980
E. Atil, *Turkish Art*, 1980.

Atil 1981
E. Atil, *Art of the Mamluks*, 1981.

Avena 1914
A. Avena, "Catalogo della Pinacoteca Monga", *Madonna Verona*, VIII, 1914, Nos. 2-3.

Avena 1947
A. Avena, *Capolavori della pittura veronese*, Verona 1947.

Avril 1989
F. Avril, "Le maître des heures de Saluces: Antoine de Lonhy", *Revue de l'Art*, No. 85, 1989, pp. 9-34.

Azcárate 1958
J.M. Azcárate, "Escultura del siglo XVI", *Ars Hispaniae*, XIII, Madrid 1958.

Bacci 1966
M. Bacci, *Piero di Cosimo*, Milan 1966.

Badin 1909
J. Badin, *La Manufacture de Tapisserie de Beauvais*, Paris 1909.

Baer 1967
E. Baer, "The Suaire of St. Lazare. An Early Datable Hispano-Islamic Embroidery", *Oriental Art*, XIII, 1967.

Bagatin 1990
P.L. Bagatin, *L'arte dei Canozi Lendinaresi*, Trieste 1990.

Bagatin 1991
P.L. Bagatin, *La tarsia rinascimentale a Ferrara*, Florence 1991.

Baldas 1933-1934
L. Baldas, *Wallraf-Richartz Jahrbuch*, Cologne 1933-1934.

Bange 1922
E.F. Bange, *Reliefs und Plaketten*, Berlin-Leipzig 1922.

Barbet de Jouy 1967
H. Barbet de Jouy, *Musée Impérial du Louvre: Galerie*

d'Apollon, Notice des Gemmes et Joyaux, 176, 1967.

Barbieri 1962
F. Barbieri, *Il Museo Civico di Vicenza*, Vicenza 1962.

Barbosa-Baptista Pereira 1984
P.G.E. Barbosa-F.A. Baptista Pereira, "Iconografía da morte e ressurreição de Cristo", *Prelo. Revista da Imprensa Nacional-Casa da Moeda*, 2, Lisbon 1984.

Barocchi 1950
P. Barocchi, *Il Rosso Fiorentino*, Rome 1950.

Barocchi 1962
P. Barocchi, "Michelangelo e la sua scuola. I disegni di Casa Buonarroti e degli Uffizi", *Accademia Toscana di Scienze e Lettere "La Colombaria", Studi*, VIII, Florence 1962.

Barocchi 1964[a]
P. Barocchi, *Michelangelo. Mostra di disegni, manoscritti e documenti*, Florence 1964.

Barocchi 1964[b]
P. Barocchi, *Michelangelo e la sua scuola. I disegni dell'Archivio Buonarroti*, Florence 1964.

Barros 1983
C.V. Barros da Silva, *O vitral em Portugal séculos XV-XVI*, Lisbon 1983.

Barthhold 1928
W. Barthhold, *Turkistan Down to the Mogol Invasion*, Oxford 1928.

Bashir Hecht 1985
H. Bashir Hecht, "Die Paradieslandschaft bei Dante und Botticelli", *Kunst*, 97, 1985.

Bassani 1985
E. Bassani, "Scheda", *Introduzione al Museo Medievale*, 49, Bologna 1985, pp. 79-80.

Bassani 1986
E. Bassani, "La saliera Bulom-Portoghese del Museo Civico di Bologna. Contributo allo studio degli avori afro-portog-

hesi", *Critica d'Arte*, LI, 9, 1986, pp. 46-56.

Bassani-Fagg 1988
E. Bassani-W. Fagg, *Africa and the Renaissance. Art in Ivory*, Munich-New York 1988.

Batard 1952
Y. Batard, *Les Dessins de Sandro Botticelli pour la Divine Comédie*, Paris 1952.

Battisti 1962
E. Battisti, *L'antirinascimento con una appendice di manoscritti inediti*, Milan 1962.

Beaulieu 1953
M. Beaulieu, "Nouvelles attributions à Pierre Bontemps", *La Revue des Arts*, 1953, p. 88.

Beaulieu 1978
M. Beaulieu, *Description raisonée des sculptures du Musée du Louvre. Renaissance française*, Paris 1978.

Beccherucci 1944
L. Beccherucci, *Manieristi Toscani*, Bergamo 1944.

Begemann 1952
E. H. Begemann, "Juan de Flandes y los reyes Católicos", *Archivo Español de Arte*, XXV, 1952.

Begni Rodona 1988
P.V. Begni Rodona, *Alessandro Bonvicino il Moretto*, 1988.

Beguin 1977
G. Beguin, *Dieux et Démons de l'Himalaya*, Paris 1977.

Belem 1750-1755
Fray J. de Belem, *Chronica da Orden Serafica de Santa Provincia dos Algarves*, Lisbon 1750-1755.

Bellosi 1975
L. Bellosi, "La Mostra di Arezzo", *Prospettiva*, 3, 1975, pp. 55-60.

Benkard 1907
E.A. Benkard, *Die venezianische Frühzeit des Sebastiano del Piombo*, Heidelberg 1907.

Berenson 1897
B. Berenson, *The Central Ita-*

lian Painters of the Renaissance, New York 1897.

Berenson 1899
B. Berenson, *The Venetian Painters of the Renaissance*, London 1899.

Berenson 1907
B. Berenson, *The North Italian Painters of the Renaissance*, New York-London 1907.

Berenson 1932
B. Berenson, *Italian Pictures of the Renaissance*, Oxford 1932.

Berenson 1936
B. Berenson, *Pitture italiane del Rinascimento*, Milan 1936.

Berenson 1957
B. Berenson, *Italian Pictures of the Renaissance, Venetian School*, London 1957.

Berenson 1958
B. Berenson, *Pitture italiane del Rinascimento. La scuola veneta*, London-Florence 1958.

Berenson 1968
B. Berenson, *Central Italian and North Italian Schools*, London 1968.

Bermejo 1962
E. Bermejo, *Juan de Flandes*, Madrid 1962.

Bermejo-Portus 1988
E. Bermejo-J. Portus, *Juan de Flandes*, Madrid 1988.

Bermejo-Vandevivere 1986
E. Bermejo-I. Vandevivere, *Juan de Flandes*, Madrid 1986.

Bermúdez Pareja 1968
J. Bermúdez Pareja, "Ultimas adquisiciones del Museo de la Alhambra", *Cuadernos de la Alhambra*, 4, Granada 1968.

Bernardini 1902
G. Bernardini, *La collezione dei quadri nel Museo Civico di Verona*, Rome 1902.

Bernardini 1908
G. Bernardini, *Sebastiano del Piombo*, Bergamo 1908.

Bernasconi 1865
C. Bernasconi, *Catalogo degli oggetti d'arte e d'antichità del Museo Civico di Verona*, Verona 1865.

Bernini Pezzini 1985
G. Bernini Pezzini, *Il fregio dell'arte della guerra n. 1, Palazzo Ducale di Urbino*, Rome 1985.

Bernis 1956
C. Bernis, *Indumentaria medieval española. Artes y Artistas*, Madrid 1956.

Bernis 1959
C. Bernis, *Modas moriscas en la sociedad cristiana española del siglo XV y principios del XVI*, Madrid 1959.

Bernis 1979
C. Bernis, *Trajes y modas en la España de los Reyes Católicos*, Instituto Diego Velázquez, Madrid 1979.

Bertaux 1911
E. Bertaux, "La Renaissance en Espagne et au Portugal", *Histoire de l'Art depuis les premiers temps chrétiens jusqu'à nos jours*, IV, Paris 1911.

Berti 1965
L. Berti, "I disegni", *Michelangelo Artista Pensatore Scrittore*, Novara 1965.

Berti 1985
L. Berti, *Michelangelo. I disegni di Casa Buonarroti*, Florence 1985.

Beyer 1955
H. Beyer, "La Procesión de los Señores", *El México Antiguo*, vol. 8, Mexico 1955, pp. 8-42.

Blunt 1970
A. Blunt, *Art and Architecture in France, 1500 to 1700*, Hardmondsworth, Middlesex 1970.

Bobeli 1954
C. Bobeli, *Il Moretto*, Brescia 1954.

Boccia 1984
L.G. Boccia, *Museo Bardini, Le Armi*, Florence 1984.

Boisselier 1990
J. Boisselier, *Majapahit*, Paris 1990.

Bokotopoulos 1990
P. Bokotopoulos, *Imagenes de Korfú*, Athens 1990.

Bombosi 1943
G. Bombosi, *Moretto da Brescia*, Basel 1943.

Bonet Correa 1982
A. Bonet Correa, *Historia de las Artes Aplicadas e Industriales en España*, Madrid 1982.

Bora 1982
G. Bora, "Battesimo di Cristo", *Zenale e Leonardo*, Milan 1982.

Borba 1975
J. Borba Moniz, "Fragmento de vitral (datado) da igreja de Jesús de Setúbal", *Setúbal Arqueológica*, 1, Setúbal 1975, pp. 227.

Borba 1976-1977
J. Borba Moniz, "Os sinos medievais da igreja de Jesús de Setúbal", *Setúbal Arqueológica*, 2-3, Setúbal 1976-1977, p. 477.

Bordeaux 1968
Tapisseries, Maisons royales d'Espagne, 1968.

Bosarte 1804
I. Bosarte, *Viaje artístico a varios pueblos de España*, Madrid 1804.

Bosch 1991
L.M.F. Bosch, *Los manuscritos abulenses de Juan de Carrión*, 1991.

Boschini 1660
M. Boschini, *La carta del navegar pittoresco*, Venice 1600.

Boschini 1674
M. Boschini, *Le ricche miniere della pittura veneziana*, Venice 1674.

Bottari 1942
S. Bottari, *Leonardo*, Bergamo 1942.

394

Bottari 1963
S. Bottari, *Tutta la pittura di Giovanni Bellini*, Milan 1963.

Brabantini 1933
N. Brabantini, *Esposizione della pittura ferrarese del Rinascimento*, Ferrara 1933.

Brandi 1949
C. Brandi, *Quattrocentisti senesi*, Milan 1949.

Bray 1977
W. Bray, "Maya Metalwork and its External Connections", *Social Process in Maya Prehistory*, New York 1977.

Brice 1684 (1713)
G. Brice, *Description de la ville de Paris*, Paris 1684 (second edition 1713).

Briganti 1938
G. Briganti, "Su Giusto di Gand", *Critica d'Arte*, 1938, 104.

Brisch-Hauptmann-Gladiss-Kröger-Spuhler-Zick-Nissen 1979
K. Brisch-A. Hauptmann-V. Gladiss-J. Kröger-F. Spuhler-J. Zick- Nissen, *Museum für islamische Kunst*, no. 575, Berlin 1979.

Budapest 1962
Keleti szönyegek: Iparmüvészeti Muzeum (Eastern Carpets. An Exhibition in the Budapest Museum of Applied Arts), Budapest 1962.

Budapest 1974
Alte Anatolische Teppiche aus dem Museum für Kunstgewerbe in Budapest. Ausstellung im Steiermärkischen Landesmuseum Joanneum, Abteilung für Kunstgewerbe (Old Anatolian Carpets, from the Collection of the Museum of Applied Arts, Budapest, an Exhibition in the Landesmuseum Joanneum), Budapest 1974.

Budapest 1979
Az Iparmuvészeti Múzeum gyüjteményei (The Collections of the Budapest Museum of Applied Arts), Budapest 1979.

Budapest 1985
A Jubilee Exhibition for the 75th Anniversary of the Budapest Museum of Fine Arts, Budapest 1985.

Budapest 1986
500 év oszman-török szönyegmüvészete: Iparmüvészeti Múzeum (Five Hundred Years in the Art of Ottoman-Turkish Carpetmaking, an Exhibition in the Budapest Museum of Applied Arts), Budapest 1986.

Budapest 1987
Spanyolok Az Uyvilagban. A Madridi Amerika Múzeum Aranykincsei es mutargyai, Budapest 1987.

Buscaroli 1931
R. Buscaroli, *La pittura romagnola del Quattrocento*, Faenza 1931

Buscaroli 1955
R. Buscaroli, *Melozzo e il melozzismo*, Bologna 1955.

Cabello Carro 1981
P. Cabello Carro, *Arte precolombino. Jade, cerámica, piedra, plata y madera*, Madrid 1981.

Cabello Carro 1989
P. Cabello Carro, *Coleccionismo americano indígena en la España del siglo XVIII*, Madrid 1989.

Cabello Carro 1991
P. Cabello Carro, "Las colecciones peruanas en España y los inicios de la arqueología andina en el siglo XVIII", *Los Incas y el antiguo Perú. 3000 años de historia*, Madrid 1991.

Cáceres 1984
Various Authors, *Muestra de arte precolombino y colonial*, Cáceres 1984.

Cairo, 1932
Catalogue du Musée Arabe du Cairo. Objects en Cuivre, Cairo 1932.

Camesasca 1958
E. Camesasca, *Tutta la pittura di Raffaello. I Quadri*, Milan 1958.

Camón Aznar 1966
J. Camón Aznar, "La Pintura medieval española", *Summa Artis*, Madrid 1966.

Camón Aznar 1967
J. Camón Aznar, "La escultura y la rejería española del siglo XVI", *Summa Artis*, XVIII, Madrid 1967.

Camón Aznar 1970
J. Camón Aznar, "La pintura española del siglo XVI", *Summa Artis*, XXIV, Madrid 1970.

Camón Aznar 1980
J. Camón Aznar, *Alonso Berruguete*, Madrid 1980.

Campana 1966
M. Campana, *Tappeti d'Occidente*, Milan 1966.

Campori 1870
G. Campori, *La raccolta di Cataloghi e inventari*, Modena 1870.

Candeira Pérez 1945
C. Candeira Pérez, *Guía del Museo Nacional de Escultura de Valladolid*, Valladolid 1945.

Candeira Pérez 1959
C. Candeira Pérez, *Alonso Berruguete en el Retablo de San Benito el Real de Valladolid*, Valladolid 1959.

Capratti 1980
E. Capratti, *Mostri, draghi e serpenti nelle silografie dell'opera di Ulisse Aldrovandi e dei suoi contemporanei*, Milan 1980.

Carli 1955
E. Carli, *La peinture siennoise*, Paris 1955.

Carli 1980
E. Carli, *Gli scultori sienesi*, Milan 1980.

Carrillo 1616
F.J. Carrillo, *Relación histórica de la Real Fundación del Monasterio de las Descalzas de Santa Clara de la Villa de Madrid*, Madrid 1616.

Carrington Goodrich 1976
L. Carrington Goodrich, *Dictionary of Ming Biography*, New York-London 1976.

Carrol 1966
E.A. Carrol, "Drawings by Rosso Fiorentino in the British Museum", *Burlington Magazine*, CVIII, 1966, pp. 168-180.

Carswell 1985
J. Carswell, *Blue and White Chinese Porcelain and its Impact on the Western World*, Chicago 1985.

Carucci 1982
A. Carucci, "Salerno. Museo el Duomo", *Guida alla storia di Salerno e della sua provincia*, Salerno 1982.

Castañeda-Mendoza 1933
D. Castañeda-V.T. Mendoza, *Los Percutores Precortesianos*, vol 8, nos. 2 and 4, Mexico 1933.

Castillejo et al. 1984
D. Castillejo et al., *El corral de Comedias. Escenarios Sociedad. Actores*, Madrid 1984.

Caturla 1942
Mª L. Caturla, "Fernando Yañez no es leonardesco", *Archivo español de Arte*, 49, 1942, pp. 35-49.

Cean Bermúdez 1980
J.A. Cean Bermúdez, *Diccionario Histórico de los más ilustres profesores de las Bellas Artes en España*, Madrid 1980 (reprint of Madrid 1965)

Chastel 1954
A. Chastel, "Les capitanines antiques affrontés dans l'art florentin du XVème siècle", *Mèmoires de la Societé Nationale des Antiquaries de France*, III, 1954, pp. 279-289.

Chatzidakis 1956
M. Chatzidakis, *The painter Eufrosunos*, 1956.

Chatzidakis 1969
M. Chatzidakis, *Musée Byzantin d'Athenes. Ikones*, 1969.

Chatzidakis 1970
M. CHATZIDAKIS, *Museo Bizantino de Atenas, Ikones*, 1970.

Chaves de Almeida 1947
L. CHAVES DE ALMEIDA. "Um túmulo de rara importancia Arqueológica da Escola Coimbra", *Arquivo do Distrito de Aveiro*, XIII, 1947.

Chirol 1952
E. CHIROL, *Le Château de Gaillon*, Paris-Rouen 1952.

Christiansen-Kanter-Brandon Strehlke 1988
K. CHRISTIANSEN-L.B. KANTER-C. BRANDON STREHLKE, *Painting in Renaissance Sien: 1420-1500*, New York 1988.

Ciardi Dupré Dal Poggetto-Dal Poggetto 1983
M.G. CIARDI DUPRÉ DAL POGGETTO-P. DAL POGGETTO, *Urbino e le Marche prima e dopo Raffaello*, Florence 1983.

Clark 1976
K. CLARK, *The Drawing for Dante's Divine Comedy by Sandro Botticelli*, London 1976.

Clark 1989
N. CLARK, *Melozzo da Forlì, Pictor papalis*, Faenza 1989.

Combe-Sauveget-Wiet 1931
ET. COMBE-J. SAUVEGET-G. WIET, *Répertoire chronologique d'épigraphies Arabe*, Cairo 1931.

Company i Climent 1987
X. COMPANY I CLIMENT, *La pintura del Renaixement*, Valencia 1987.

Coo-Reynaud 1979
J. DE COO-N. REYNAUD, "Origen del retablo de San Juan Bautista atribuido a Juan de Flandes", *Archivo Español de Arte*, 206, 1979, pp. 125-144.

Coor 1961
G. COOR, *Neroccio de' Landi, 1447-1500*, Princeton 1961.

Correia 1921
V. CORREIA, "A pintura quatrocentista e quinhentista em

Portugal", *Boletim do Arte e Arqueología*, LX, 1921.

Corrozet 1586
G. CORROZET, *Les Antiquités, croniques et singularités de Paris*, Paris 1586.

Cossio del Pomar 1971
F. COSSIO DEL POMAR, *Arte del Antiguo Perú*, Barcelona 1971.

Courajod 1878-1887
COURAJOD, *Alexandre Lenoir...*, Paris 1878-1887.

Couto 1927
J. COUTO, "Os Calices na ouriversaria portuguesa do século XII", *Revista Esmeralda*, 5, Lisbon 1927, pp. 24, 25, 26, 27, 45.

Couto 1938
J. COUTO, "O calvário, painel do políptico da igreja do convento de Jesús de Setúbal", *Boletim da Academia Nacional de Belas-Artes*, IV, Lisbon 1938.

Couto 1940
J. COUTO, "A data num painel da Igreja da madre de Deus", *Boletim do Museu Nacional de Arte Antiga*, I, 3, 1940.

Couto 1941
J. COUTO, "A colecção de pratas religiosas e profanas no Museu das Janelas Verdes", *Boletim do Museu Nacional de Arte Antiga*, II, 2, Lisbon 1941, p. 9.

Couto 1946
J. COUTO, "Alguns tipos de porta-paz nas colecçoes do Museu das Janelas Verdas", *Boletím do Museu Nacional de Arte Antiga*, I, 1, Lisbon 1946, pp. 15-23 and 57.

Couto 1961
J. COUTO, "O Museu de Setúbal", *Coloquio*, I serie, 1961, pp. 13, 15-23 and 163.

Couto-Gonçalves 1960
J. COUTO-A.M. GONÇALVES, *Ouriversaria em Portugal*, Lisbon 1960.

Crowe-Cavalcaselle (1871), 1911-1912
J.A. CROWE-G.B. CAVALCASELLE, *A History of Painting in North Italy*, London (1871), 1911-1912.

Crowe-Cavalcaselle 1876
J.A. CROWE-G.B. CAVALCASELLE, *Geschichte der italienischen Malerei*, 1876.

Crowe-Cavalcaselle 1879
J.A. CROWE-G.B. CAVALCASELLE, *A History of Painting in North Italy*, London 1879.

Crowe-Cavalcaselle 1884-1891
Y.A. CROWE-G.B. CAVALCASELLE, *Raffaello, la sua vita e le sue opere*, Florence 1884-1891.

Cuéllar 1981
A. CUÉLLAR, *Tezcatzoncatl escultórico*, Mexico 1981.

Cuesta Domingo 1980
M. CUESTA DOMINGO, *Arqueología andina: Perú*, Madrid 1980.

Cuesta Domingo-Rovira Llorens 1982
M. CUESTA DOMINGO-S. ROVIRA LLORENS, *Los trabajos en metal en el área andina*, Madrid 1982.

Cuppini 1981
M.T. CUPPINI, "L'arte a Verona tra i secoli XV e XVI", *Verona e il suo territorio*, Verona 1981.

D'Achiardi 1908
P. D'ACHIARDI, *Sebastiano del Piombo*, Rome 1908.

D'Agostino 1972
G. D'AGOSTINO, "Il governo spagnolo nell'Italia meridionale. Napoli dal 1503 al 1580", *Storia di Napoli*, Naples 1972.

Da Ponte 1898
P. DA PONTE, *L'opera del Moretto*, Brescia 1898.

Darcel 1878
A. DARCEL, "Le Moyen Age et la Renaissance au Trocadero", *Gazette des Beaux Arts*, 1878.

De Dominici 1743 (1742-1745)
B. DE DOMINICI, *Vite dei pittori,*

scultori e architetti napoletani, Naples 1743 (1742-1745).

De las Heras-Carlos Martín 1981
F. DE LAS HERAS-G. CARLOS MARTÍN, *La catedral de Ávila*, Ávila 1981.

De Rinaldis 1927
DE RINALDIS, *Pinacoteca di Napoli*, Naples 1927.

De Vecchi 1968
P. DE VECCHI, *La obra pictórica completa de Rafael*, Madrid 1968.

Del Bravo 1962
C. DEL BRAVO, "Francesco Morone", *Paragone*, 1962.

Del Bravo 1964
C. DEL BRAVO, "Pier Giovan Francesco Caroto", *Paragone*, 173, 1964, pp. 3-23.

Del Vecchio 1972
E. DEL VECCHIO, *I Farnese*, Città di Castello 1972.

Delange 1967
J. DELANGE, *Arts et peuples de l'Afrique noire*, Paris 1967.

Delmarcel-Brown 1988
G. DELMARCEL-C.M. BROWN, "Les Jeaux d'Enfants tapisseries italiennes et flamandes pour les Gonzague", *Racar, revue d'art canadienne*, XV, 2, 1988, pp. 109-121, 170-177.

Devakunjari 1983
DEVAKUNJARI, *Hampi*, New Delhi 1983.

Dezallier D'Argenville 1749
DEZALLIER D'ARGENVILLE, *Voyage pittoresque de Paris*, Paris 1749.

Di Carpegna 1965
N. DI CARPEGNA, *Catalogo della Galleria Nazionale*, Rome 1965.

Di Carpegna 1969
N. DI CARPEGNA, *La Galleria Nazionale di Palazzo Barberini*, Rome 1969.

Diamand 1964
M.S. DIAMAND, "Two Fifteenth Century Hispano-Moresque

396

Rugs", *Museum of Art Bulletin*, New York 1964.

Dimier 1900
I. Dimier, *Le Primatice*, Paris 1900.

Dittmer 1967
K. Dittmer, "Bedeutung, Datierung und kulturhistorische Zusammenhange der 'prähistorichen' Steinfiguren aus Sierra Leone und Guinée", *Baesser-Archiv.*, 15, 1967, pp. 183-238.

Djuric 1972
V.J. Djuric, *La peinture murals de Resava en l'école de la Morava et son Temps*, Symposium de Rosava 1968, Belgrade 1972.

Dodds 1992
J. Dodds, "La pila de Játiva", *Al-Andalus, las Artes Islámicas en España*, The Metropolitan Museum of Art, Madrid 1992.

Domínguez Bordona 1929
A.J. Domínguez Bordona, *Catálogo de la exposición de códices miniados españoles*, Madrid 1929.

Domínguez Bordona 1930
A.J. Domínguez Bordona, "Las miniaturas de Juan de Carrión", *Archivo Español de Arte y Arqueología*, VI, 1930, pp. 17-20.

Domínguez Bordona 1932
A.J. Domínguez Bordona, *El arte de la miniatura española*, Madrid 1932.

Domínguez Bordona 1933
A.J. Domínguez Bordona, *Manuscritos con pinturas*, Madrid 1933.

Domínguez Bordona 1957
A.J. Domínguez Bordona, "Diccionario de iluminadores españoles", *Boletín de la Real Academia de la Historia*, CXL, 1957, pp. 49-110.

Domínguez Bordona-Ainaud de Lasarte 1962
A.J. Domínguez Bordona-J. Ainaud de Lasarte, "Miniatura. Grabado. Encuadernación", *Ars Hispaniae*, XVIII, Madrid 1962.

Drow-Kelch-Van Thiel 1991
C. Drow-J. Kelch-P. van Thiel, *Rembrandt: the Master and his Workshop. Paintings*, New Haven and London 1991.

Dussler 1935
L. Dussler, *Giovanni Bellini*, Frankfurt 1935.

Dussler 1942
L. Dussler, *Sebastiano del Piombo*, Basel 1942.

Dussler 1959
L. Dussler, *Die Zeichnungen des Michelangelo*, Berlin 1959.

Edgell 1932
G.H. Edgell, *History of Sienese Painting*, New York 1932.

Erdmann 1940
K. Erdmann, *Ars Islamica 7*, 66, 22, 1940.

Erdmann 1966
K. Erdmann, *Siebenhundert Jahre Orientteppich 94*, 1966.

Erfa 1946
H. von Erfa, "A Tombstone of the Timurid Period in the Gardner Museum of Boston", *Ars Islamica*, XI-XII, 1946.

Erfa 1976
H.M. von Erfa, "Dier Nürnberger Stadtpatron auf Italieschen Gemälden", *Mitteilungen des Kunsthistorisches Institutes in Florenz*, Florence 1976.

Essenwein 1881
A. von Essenwein, "Die Ervealoing der fürstlich Sulkowskischen Sammlung für das germanische Museum", *Anzeiger des Germanisches Nationalmuseums 1881*, 1881.

Essenwein 1887-1889
A. von Essenwein, "Die Erwerbung der fürtslisch Sulkowskischen Sammlung für das Germanische Nationalmuseum", *Anzeiger des Germanischen Nationalmuseums*, II, 1887-1889, pp. 216-222.

Estrada 1984
J. Estrada, *La Música de México*, Mexico 1984.

Ethé 1903
H. Ethé, *Catalogue of the Persian Manuscripts in the Library of the India Office*, no. 2775, Oxford 1903.

Ettinghausen 1960
R. Ettinghausen, "Bilzard", *Enciclopedia del Islam*, I, Leiden 1960.

Ettinghausen 1966
R. Ettinghausen, *Los tesoros de Turquía*, Geneva 1966.

Eyo 1974
E. Eyo, *Recent Excavations at Ife and Owo and their Implications for Ife, Owo and Benin Studies*, Ph. D. Thesis University of Ibadan, 1974.

Eyo 1976
E. Eyo, "Igbo' Laja, Owo Nigeria", *West African Journal of Archaeology*, 6, 1976, pp. 37-58.

Eyo 1977
E. Eyo, *Two Thousand Years of Nigerian Art*, Lagos 1977.

Eyo-Willet 1980
E. Eyo-F. Willet, *Treasures of Ancient Nigeria*, New York 1980.

Fagg 1959
W.B. Fagg, *Afro-Portuguese Ivories*, London 1959.

Falke 1922
D. von Falke, *Historia del Tejido de seda*, Barcelona 1922.

Fehérvári 1976
G. Fehérvári, *Islamic Metalwork of the Eighth to the Fifteenth Century in the Keir Collection*, 145, London 1976.

Fernández Puertas 1973
A.Fernández Puertas, "En torno a la cronología de la torre de Abul l-Hayyay", *Actas del XXIII C.I.H.A.*, Granada 1973.

Fernández Puertas 1980
A. Fernández Puertas, *La fachada del Palacio de Comares. Situación, Función y Génesis (The Facade of the Palace of Comares, Location, Function and Origins)*, Granada 1980.

Fernández Vega 1935
P. Fernández Vega, "Dagas granadinas", *Anuario del Cuerpo Facultativo de Archiveros, Bibliotecarios y Arqueólogos*, 1935.

Fernández y González 1872
Fernández y González, *Espadas hispanoárabes. Espadas de Abindarraez y de Aliatar. Espada de hoja tunecina atribuida vulgarmente a Muhammad Boaddeli (Boabdil)*, Museo Español de Antigüedades 1872.

Fernández y González 1875
F. Fernández y González, *Espadas hispano-árabes*, Museo Español de Antigüedades, V, 1875.

Ferrandis Torres 1940
J. Ferrandis Torres, *Muebles hispanoárabes de taracea*, 1940.

Ferrandis Torres 1943
J. Ferrandis Torres, "Espadas granadinas de la jineta", *Archivo español de arte*, XV, 1943.

Ferrara 1972
L. Reggi, *Ceramica nella pittura ferrarese del Rinascimento*, Ferrara 1972.

Ferrara 1988
G. Mariani Canova, *Ferrara 1474: miniatura, tipografia, committenza. Il "decretum Gratiani" Roverella*, Florence 1988.

Ferrara 1989
A tavola con il Principe. Materiali per una mostra su alimentazione e cultura nella Ferrara degli Estensi, Ferrara 1989.

Ferrari 1963
M.L. FERRARI, "Ritorno a Bernardo Zenale", *Paragone*, 157, 1963, pp. 14-29.

Ferreira Neves 1938
F. FERREIRA NEVES, "O túmulo de João de Alburquerque", *Arquivo do Distrito de Aveiro*, IV, 1938.

Ferreira Neves 1946
F. FERREIRA NEVES, "A trasladação do túmulo de João de Alburquerque", *Arquivo do Distrito de Aveiro*, XII, 1946.

Ferretti 1982
M. FERRETTI, "I maestri della prospettiva", *Storia dell'Arte Italiana*, XI, 1982, p. 105.

Ferris i Soler-Catala i Jimeno 1987
V. FERRIS I SOLER-J. CATALA I JIMENO, *La cerámica de Manises: els seus vocables y locucions*, Valencia 1987.

Fiocco 1913
G. FIOCCO, "Appunti d'arte veronese", *Madonna Verona*, 1913.

Fiocco 1915
G. FIOCCO, "Introduzione, Note e Bibliografía", G. VASARI, *Vita di fra Giocondo e d'altri veronesi*, Florence 1915.

Fiocco 1939
G. FIOCCO, *Giovanni Antonio Pordenone*, Udine 1939.

Fiocco 1948
G. FIOCCO, "Un'opera giovanile del Moretto", *Bollettino d'Arte*, 1948, p. 334.

Fischel 1948
O. FISCHEL, *Raphael*, London 1948.

Florence 1940
VARIOUS AUTHORS, *Mostra del Cinquecento toscano*, Florence 1940.

Florence 1956
U. BALDINI, *Mostra del Pontormo e del primo manierismo fiorentino* (catalogue by de L. Berti), Florence 1956.

Florence 1980
Mostra di Firenze e la Toscana dei Medici nell'Europa del Cinquecento. Il primato del disegno, Florence 1980.

Florence 1986
F. ABATE, *Andrea da Salerno nel Rinascimento Meridionale*, Florence 1986.

Florence 1986
A.P. DARR-G. BOSANTI, *Donatello e i suoi. Scultura fiorentina del primo Rinascimento*, Milan 1986.

Florence 1990
L. BELLOSI, *Pittura di luce*, Florence 1990.

Flores Escobosa 1982
I. FLORES ESCOBOSA, *Estudio y catalogación de la loza dorada de Manises de los fondos del Museo Nacional de Arte Hispanomusulmán*, Granada 1982.

Flores Escobosa 1983-1985
I. FLORES ESCOBOSA, "Algunas consideraciones sobre la loza dorada de Manises", *Anales del Colegio Universitario de Almería*, V, Almería 1983-1985.

Flores Escobosa 1988
I. FLORES ESCOBOSA, *La colección de loza dorada de Manises del Museo de arte Hispanomusulmán de Granada, Estudios dedicados a Don Jesús Bermúdez Pareja*, Granada 1988.

Fogg 1967
W. FOGG, *El arte del Africa central*, Mexico 1967.

Folch y Torres 1928
J. FOLCH Y TORRES, "La decoració dels reversos en els plats daurats de manises", *Gaseta de les Arts*, Barcelona 1928.

Folsach 1990
K. VON FOLSACH, *Islamic Art. The David Collection*, Copenhagen 1990.

Fornari-Schianchi 1983
L. FORNARI-SCHIANCHI, *La Galleria Nazionale di Parma*, Parma 1983.

Fornari-Schianchi 1986
L. FORNARI-SCHIANCHI, *Nell'età del Correggio e dei Carracci*, Bologna-Washington-New York 1986.

Förster 1938
O.H. FÖRSTER, *Stefan Lochner*, 1938.

Forti Grazzini 1982
N. FORTI GRAZZINI, *Gli arazzi dei Mesi Trivulzio: il committente, l'iconografia*, Milan 1982.

Franco Fiorio 1971
M.T. FRANCO FIORIO, *Giovan Francesco Caroto*, Verona 1971.

Franco Fiorio 1987
M.T. FRANCO FIORIO, "Una traccia per la sezione di pittura e qualche proposta", *Disegni e dipinti leonardeschi dalle collezioni milanesi*, Milan 1987.

Frangi 1991
F. FRANGI, "Qualche considerazione su un leonardesco eccentrico: Francesco Napoletano", *I Leonardeschi a Milano*, Milan 1991.

Fray 1974
R. FRAY PANÉ, *Relación acerca de las Antigüedades de los Indios*, Mexico 1974.

Freedberg 1961
S. FREEDBERG, *Painting of the High Renaissance in Rome and Florence*, Cambridge 1961.

Fritz 1965
J.M. FRITZ, *Gestochene Bilder, Gravierungen auf deutschen Goldschmiedearbeiten der Sätgotik*, Cologne-Graz 1965.

Fritz 1982
J.M. FRITZ, *Goldschmiedekunst der Gotik in Mitteleuropa*, München 1982.

Fritz Volbach-Lafontaine-Desoque 1968
W. FRITZ VOLBACH-J. LAFONTAINE-DESOQUE, *Byzanz und der Christliche osten, Propyläen Kunstgeschichte*, Berlín 1968.

Frizzoni 1891
G. FRIZZONI, *Arte italiana del Rinascimento*, Milan 1891.

Frulli 1987
C. FRULLI, "Ghirlandaio", *La Pittura in Italia, Il Quattrocento*, Milan 1987.

Gamba 1934
C. GAMBA, "Un quadro e un ritratto di Gaspare Sacchi", *Rivista d'Arte*, XVI, 1934, pp. 380-386.

Gamba 1937
C. GAMBA, *Giovanni Bellini*, Milan 1937.

Gamba 1949
C. GAMBA, *Pittura umbra del Rinascimento*, Novara 1949.

Garavaglia 1967
N. GARAVAGLIA, *L'opera completa del Mantegna*, Milan 1967.

García Chico 1941
E. GARCÍA CHICO, *Documentos para el estudio del Arte en Castilla. Escultores*, Valladolid 1941.

García de Wattenberg 1978
E. GARCÍA DE WATTENBERG, *Guía del visitante. Museo nacional de Escultura de Valladolid*, Valladolid 1978.

García Fuentes 1969
J.M. GARCÍA FUENTES, "Las armas hispanomusulmanas al final de la Reconquista" *Chronica Nova*, 3, 1969, pp. 7-38.

Garín Llombart 1980
F.V. GARÍN LLOMBART, *Breve visita al Museo de Bellas Artes de Valencia*, Valencia 1980.

Garín Ortiz de Taranco 1955
F.M. GARÍN ORTIZ DE TARANCO, *Catálogo-Guía del Museo Provincial de Bellas Artes de San Carlos*, no. 457, Valencia 1955.

398

Garín Ortiz de Taranco 1964
F.M. GARÍN ORTIZ DE TARANCO, *El Museo de Valencia*, Madrid 1964.

Garín Ortiz de Taranco 1978
F.M. GARÍN ORTIZ DE TARANCO, *Yañez de la Almedina: Pintor español*, Ciudad Real 1978.

Garín Ortiz de Taranco 1987
F.Mª GARÍN ORTIZ DE TARANCO, "El Renacimiento", *Historia del Arte Valenciano*, Valencia 1987.

Garrison 1926
F.H. GARRISON, *Principles of Anatomic Illustration before Vesalius*, New York 1926.

Gatti Grazzini 1958
G. GATTI GRAZZINI, *L'arazzo*, Florence 1958.

Gesner 1560
K. GESNER, *Nomenclator aquatilium animantium*, Zurich 1560.

Ghidiglia Quintavalle 1965
A. GHIDIGLIA QUINTAVALLE, *La Galleria Nazionale di Parma*, Milan 1965.

Giardini 1990
C. GIARDINI, *L'Arte di corte ad Urbino e Pesaro*, Tokyo 1990.

Gillón 1989
W.GILLÓN, *Breve historia del arte africano*, 1989.

Giusti-Leone de Castris 1985
P. GIUSTI-P. LEONE DE CASTRIS, "Foresteri e regnicoli", *La pittura moderna a Napoli nel primo Cinquecento*, Naples 1985.

Gnoli 1915
U. GNOLI, "Documenti inediti sui pittori perugini", *Bollettino d'Arte*, 5, 1915, p. 309.

Gobel 1923
H. GOBEL, *Die Wandteppiche*, vol. II, Leipzig 1923.

Goepper-Whitfield 1984
R. GOEPPER-R. WHITFIELD, *Treasures from Korea*, London 1984.

Goffen 1989
R. GOFFEN, *Giovanni Bellini*, New Haven-London 1989.

Golombek 1969
L. GOLOMBEK, "The Timurid Shrine at Gazur Gak", *Art and Archaeology Occasional Paper*, 15, Toronto 1969.

Gombosi 1933
G. GOMBOSI, "Piombo, fra Sebastiano del, propriamente Sebastiano Luciani o de' Lucianis", THIEME-BECKER, *Allgemeines Lexikon der bildende Künstler*, XXXVI, Leipzig 1933.

Gómez Moreno 1924
M.Gómez MORENO, *Cerámica medieval española*, Barcelona 1924.

Gómez Moreno 1941
M. GÓMEZ MORENO, *Las Águilas del Renacimiento Español*, Madrid 1941.

Gómez Moreno 1982
M. GÓMEZ MORENO, *Guía de Granada*, Granada 1982.

Gómez Moreno 1983
M. GÓMEZ MORENO, "Arte cristiano entre los moros de Granada", *Estudios de Erudición Oriental*, Zaragoza 1904.

Gómez Moreno 1983
M. GÓMEZ MORENO, *Catálogo Monumental de la provincia de Ávila*, Ávila 1983.

González Martí 1914-1915
M. GONZÁLEZ MARTÍ, "De la historia artística de Valencia: las tablas de los pintores Llanos y Almedina del siglo XVI", *Museum*, IV, 2, 1914-1915, pp. 379, 402.

González Martí 1944
M. GONZÁLEZ MARTÍ, "La loza", *Cerámica del Levante español*, 1944.

González Mena 1976
GONZÁLEZ MENA, *Catálogo de encajes del Instituto Valencia de Don Juan*, Madrid 1976.

González-Sobrino 1981
N. GONZÁLEZ, T. SOBRINO, *La Catedral de Ávila*, León 1981.

Gopinatha Rao 1971
T.A. GOPINATHA RAO, *Elements of Hindu Iconography*, I, New Delhi 1971.

Gorostizaga 1896
A. GOROSTIZAGA, "Tesoro de los Quimbayas", *Revista de Archivos, Bibliotecas y Museos*, Madrid 1896.

Gould 1969
C. GOULD, "The Pala of S. Giovanni Crisostomo and the later Giorgione", *Arte Veneta*, 1969.

Gould 1975
C. GOULD, *The Sixteenth Century Italian Schools, National Gallery Catalogues*, London 1975.

Gray 1961
B. GRAY, *Persian Painting*, Geneva 1961.

Gray 1979
B. GRAY, *The Arts of the Book in Central Asia, 14th and 16th centuries*, London, Paris and Boulder 1979.

Gronau 1922
G. GRONAU, "Uber bildnisse von Giovanni Bellini", *Jahrbuch der preussischen Kunstsammlungen*, 1922.

Gronau 1930
G. GRONAU, *Giovanni Bellini*, Berlin 1930.

Grottanelli 1975
V.L. GROTTANELLI, "Discovery of a Masterpiece: A Sixteenth Century Ivory Bowl from Sierra Leone", *African Arts*, 8, 1975, pp. 14-23.

Grottanelli 1976
V.L. GROTTANELLI, "Su un'antica scultura in avorio della Sierra Leone", *Quaderni Poro*, 1, 1976, pp. 23-58.

Grube 1974
E.J. GRUBE, "Notes on the Decorative Arts of the Timurid Period", *Studi in onore di Giuseppe Tucci*, Naples 1974, p. 255, fig. 76-77, 113-114.

Gruyer 1897
G. GRUYER, *L'Art Ferrarais à l'Epoque des Princes d'Este*, I, Paris 1897.

Guazzoni 1981
V. GUAZZONI, *Moretto, il tema sacro*, Brescia 1981.

Guerreiro 1966
G. GUERREIRO, "Tapeçarias da Colecçao Calouste Gulbenkian", *Colóquio*, 41, diciembre 1966.

Guerreiro 1970
G. GUERREIRO, "Some European Tapestries in the Caloustre Gulbenkian Collection in Lisbon", *The Connoisseur*, April 1970, p. 229.

Guerrini 1986
S. GUERRINI, "Note e documenti per la storia dell'arte bresciana dal XVI al XVIII secolo", *Brixia sacra*, XXI, 1986.

Guiffrey 1880-1881
J.J. GUIFFREY, *Nouvelles Archives de l'Art Francais*, VIII, 1880-1881.

Guiffrey 1886
J. GUIFFREY, *Historie de la Tapisserie*, Tours 1886.

Guiffrey 1911
J. GUIFFREY. "Les Tapisseries du XIIe à la fin du XVIe siècle", *Histoire Génerale des Arts Appliqués à l'Industrie*, Paris 1911.

Guilhermy 1852
F. DE GUILHERMY, en *Annales Archélogiques*, 1852, II, pp. 90-91.

Gusmao 1960
A. GUSMAO, "O Mestre da Madre de Deus", *Nova Colecção de Arte Portuguesa*, Lisbon 1960.

Gutierrez Solana Kelly 1983
N. GUTIERREZ SOLANA KELLY, *Objetos ceremoniales en piedra de la cultura mexicana*, Mexico 1983.

Guy 1989
J. GUY, *Ceramic Traditions of South-East Asia*, Singapore 1989.

Guy 1990
J. Guy, *Ceramic Traditions of South-East Asia*, Singapore 1990.

Habese 1980
G. Habese, *A Hundred Masterpiece of Chinese Ceramics from the Percival David Collection*, London, Tokyo 1980.

Halden 1927
D. von Halden, "Two Portraits by Giovanni Bellini", *The Burlington Magazine*, LI, 1927, pp. 4-7.

Hartt 1958
F. Hartt, *Giulio Romano*, New Haven 1958.

Hartt 1961
F. Hartt, "New Light on the Rossellino Family", *Burlington Magazine*, CIII, 1961, pp. 385-392.

Hartt 1971
F. Hartt, *The Drawings of Michelangelo*, London 1971.

Hautecoeur 1926
L. Hautecoeur, *Musée National du Louvre, catalogue des peintures exposées dans les galeries II, école italienne et école espagnole*, Paris 1926.

Heinemann 1962
F. Heinemann, *Bellini e i belliniani*, Venice 1962.

Heinz 1963
D. Heinz, *Europäische Wandteppiche. I. Von den Anfängen der Bildwirkerei bis zum Ende des 16. Jahrhunderts*, Braunschweig 1963.

Helsinky 1988
Museum of industrial design in Helsinky, Helsinky 1988.

Heredia y Lozano 1983
M. Heredia y Lozano, *El Museo del Ejército*, Madrid 1983.

Herreman-Holsbeke-Van Alphen 1991
F. Herreman-M. Holsbeke-J. van Alphen, *Le Musée d'Ethnographie d'Anvers*, Brussels 1991.

Herrero 1992
C. Herrero, *Al-Andalus las Artes Islámicas en España*, The Metropolitan Museum of Art, Madrid 1992.

Hetherington 1950
A.L. Hetherington. "The David Collection", *The Antique Collector*, Sept.-Oct., 1950, p. 190.

Hill 1930 (1984)
G.F. Hill, *A corpus of Italian Medals of the Renaissance before Cellini*, London 1930 (an. repr. Florence 1984).

Hill 1976
E.G. Hill, *The Story of the Seven Princesses*, Oxford 1976.

Hobson 1934
R.L. Hobson, *A Catalogue of Chinese Pottery and Porcelain in the Collection of Sir Percival David Bt., F.S.A.*, London 1934.

Hollande 1936
E. Hollande, "Une erreur au Musée du Louvre concernant la maison de Savoie", *Mémories de la Societé Savoisienne d'histoire et d'archéologie*, 73, 1936, pp. 11-13.

Huse 1972
N. Huse, *Studien zu Giovanni Bellini*, Berlin-New York 1972.

Ingoldstadt 1988
Goldschmiedearbeiten in und aus Ingolstadt, Ingolstadt 1988.

Ishikawa-Ch. Garrido 1987
Ch. Ishikawa-C. Ch. Garrido, "Cambios de composición en el retablo de Isabel la Católica, de Juan de Flandes", *Reales Sitios*, XXIV, 94, 1987.

Janneau 1947
G. Janneau, *Evolution de la tapisserie*, Paris 1947.

Jarry 1971
M. Jarry, "Jeux d'amours...jeux d'enfants", *L'Oeil*, 204, décembre 1971, pp. 2-9, 52.

Jenkins 1983
M. Jenkins, "Islamic Pottery a Brief History", *Metropolitan Museum of Arts Bulletin*, Spring 1983.

Jenyns-Atson 1963
R.S. Jenyns-W. Atson, *Chinese Art, the Minor Arts*, II, London 1963.

Jerusalem 1988
Israel Museum in Jerusalem, Jerusalem 1988.

Johnson-Martini 1986
C. Johnson-R. Martini, *Catalogo delle medaglie, I-Secolo XV*, Civiche Raccolte Numismatiche, Milan 1986, p. 88, nos. 389-390.

Jubinal-Sensi 1839
A. Jubinal-G. Sensi, *L'Armeria Real ou Collection des principales pièces de la galerie d'armes anciennes de Madrid*, I, Paris 1839.

Justi 1887
K. Justi, "Juan de Flandes. Ein nieder ländischer Hofmaler Isabella der Katholisoher", *Jahrbuch der Königlich Preussischen Kunstammlungen*, 1887, VII, pp. 157-169.

Justi 1908
L. Justi, *Giorgiones*, 1908, I, 1926, II, 1936, III, Berlín.

Kalbi 1965
L.G. Kalbi, *Andrea da Salerno*, Salerno 1965.

Kendrich 1930
A.F. Kendrich, "Art Notes", *Collector*, XI, 1930.

Khandalavala-Chandra 1969
K. Khandalavala-M. Chandra, *New documents of Indian Painting, a Reappraisal*, Bombay 1969.

Komaroff 1979-80
L. Komaroff, "Timurid to Safavid Iran: Continuity and Change", *Marsyas XX*, 1979-80, fig. 6.

Kris 1929
E. Kris, *Meister und Meisterwerke der Steinschneidekunst in der Italienischen Renaissance*, Vienna 1929.

Kubler 1992
M. Kubler, "Matthias Ringmann nommé l'Amerique", *Saisons d'Alsace*, 1992.

Kubler-Soria 1959
J. Kubler-M. Soria, *Art and Architecture in Spain and Portugal (1500-1800)*, London 1959.

Kühnel 1925
E. Kühnel, *Islamische Kleinkunst*, 167, 1925.

Kühnel 1963
E. Kühnel, *Islamic Arts*, London 1963.

Kusenberg 1931
K. Kusenberg, *Le Rosso*, Paris 1931.

Laclotte-Thiebaut 1983
M. Laclotte-D. Thiebaut, *L'Ecole d'Avignon*, Paris 1983.

Landolt-Ackermann 1991
E. Landolt-F. Ackermann, *Sammeln in der Renaissance. Das Amerbach-Kabinett. Die Objekts im Historischen Museum Basel*, Basel 1991.

Lane 1957
A. Lane, "The Ottoman Pottery of Isnik", *Ars Orientalis*, II, 1957, pp. 247-281, fig. 22.

Lane 1971
A. Lane. *Later Islamic Pottery. Persia, Syria, Egypt, Turkey*, London 1971.

Lane-Poole 1925
S. Lane-Poole, *The Nohammadan Dynasties*, Paris 1925.

Laude 1968
J. Laude, *Las artes del Africa negra*, Barcelona 1963.

Laurencich Minelli-Serra 1987-1988
L. Laurencich Minelli-M. Serra, "Tra museo e biblioteca. Un esempio del metodo di lavoro di Ulisse Aldrovandi 'americanista'", *Museología scientifica*, IV, 3-4, 1987-1988, pp. 221-228.

Lausanne 1969
Tapisseries anciennes des XVI, XVII et XVIII siècles provenant

400

du Musée des Arts Decoratifs de Budapest, Lausanne 1969.

Le May 1938
R. Le May, *A Concise History of Buddhist Art in Siam*, 1938.

Le May 1962
R. Le May, *A Concise History of Buddhist Art in Sian*, Tokyo 1962.

Lédacs-Kiss-Szütsné Brenner 1963
A. Lédacs-Kiss-K. -Szütsne Brenner, *Ismerjük meg a keleti szönyegeket (Let us Get Acquainted with Oriental Carperts)*, Budapest 1963.

Lensi 1934
A. Lensi, *La donazione Loeser in Palazzo Vecchio*, Florence 1934.

Lentz-Lowry 1989
T.W. Lentz-G.D. Lowry, *Timur and the Princely Vision: Persian Art and Culture in the Fifteenth Century*, Los Angeles 1989.

Lenzinger 1976
E. Lenzinger, *Arte del África negra*, Barcelona 1976.

Lenzini Moriondo 1966
M. Lenzini Moriondo, *Signorelli*, Florence 1966.

León-Portilla 1985
M. León Portilla, *Tonalamah de los Pochtecas*, Mexico 1985.

Lion-Goldschmidt 1957
D. Lion-Goldschmidt, *Les Poteries et Porcelanes Chinoises*, Paris 1957.

Lion-Goldschmidt 1978
D. Lion-Goldschmidt, *Ming Porcelain*, London 1978.

Lisbon 1882
Exposição Retrospectiva de Arte ornamental Portuguesa e Hispanhola, no. 109, Lisbon 1882.

Lisbon 1938
Catálogo Guía do museu das Janelas Verdes, Lisbon 1938.

Lisbon 1963
Arte do oriente Islâmico Co-

lecção da Fundação Calouste Gulbenkian Museu Nacional de Arte Antiga, Lisbon, May 1963.

Lisbon 1965
Obras Primas da Pintura estangeira no M.N.A.A., Lisbon 1965.

Lizardi Ramos 1944
C. Lizardi Ramos, "El Chacmool mexicano", *Cuadernos Americanos*, Mexico 1944.

Llaguno y Amirola 1829
E. Llaguno y Amirola, *Noticias de los arquitectos y arquitecturas de España*, Madrid 1829.

Llubiá Munné 1967
L.M. Llubia Munné, *Cerámica medieval española*, 1967.

Loeser 1922
Ch. Loeser, "Disegni di Piero di Cosimo e Filippino Lippi", *Disegni della R. Galleria degli Uffizi*, Florence 1922.

Londres 1932
Ch. Sterling, *Exhibition of French Art*, London 1932.

Londres 1935
Various Authors, *International Exhibition of Chinese Art Catalogue*, London 1935.

Londres 1976
"The Art of Islam", *The Art Council of Great Britain*, London 1976.

Londres 1983
The Genius of Venice, 1500-1600, Royal Academy of Arts London 1983.

Londres 1984
E. Mattaliano-P. Mattiesen, *From Borso to Cesare d'Este, the Scool of Ferrara 1450-1628*, London 1984.

Longhi 1953
R. Longhi, "Comprimari spagnoli della maniera italiana", *Paragone*, 43, luglio 1953, pp. 3-15.

Longhi 1979
R. Longhi, *Opere complete di Roberto Longhi. Arte italiana e arte tedesca con altre con-*

giunture fra Italia e Europa, Florence 1979.

Longhurst 1981
A.H. Longhurst, *Hampi Ruins*, New Delhi 1981.

López 1991
C.E. López, *Asentamientos arqueológicos en el Magdalena Medio*, Bogotá 1991.

López Austin 1973
A. López Austin, *Hombre-Dios. Religión y política en el mundo náhuatl*, Mexico 1973.

Losty 1982
J.P. Losty, *The Art of the Book in India*, London 1982.

Lowry 1973
J. Lowry, "Tibetan Art", *HMSO*, 10, 1973.

Lozoya 1940
el Marques de Lozoya, *Historia del Arte Hispánico*, III, Barcelona 1940.

Lucco 1980
M. Lucco, *L'opera completa di Sebastiano del Piombo*, Milan 1980.

Lukens-Swietochowski 1979
M. Lukens-Swietochowski, "The School of Herat from 1450 to 1506", *The Arts of the Book in Central Asia, 14th-16th Centuries*, London, Paris and Boulder 1979, pp. 206-209.

Luna Moreno 1982
L. Luna Moreno, *Escultura castellana*, Seville 1982.

Madrid 1892
Catálogo de los objetos que presenta el Gobierno de Colombia a la exposición americana de Madrid, Madrid 1892.

Madrid 1893
Joyas Artísticas de la Exposición Histórico-Europea de Madrid, Madrid 1893.

Madrid 1898
Valencia de don Juan, *Catálogo Histórico-descriptivo de la Real Armería de Madrid*, Madrid 1898.

Madrid 1933
Catálogo de la Exposición de alfombras antiguas españolas, Madrid 1933.

Madrid 1935
Arte peruano. Colección Juan Larrea, 26th International Congress of the Americanists, Madrid 1935.

Madrid 1985
Culturas indígenas de los Andes Septentrionales, National Commission of 5th Centennial, Madrid 1985.

Malle 1963
L. Malle, *I dipinti del Museo d'Arte Antica*, Turin 1963.

Maltese 1966
C. Maltese, "Francesco di Giorgio", *I maestri della scultura*, 51, Milan 1966, pp. 5-6.

Maltese 1969
C. Maltese, "Il protomanierismo di Francesco di Giorgio", *Storia dell'Arte*, 4, 1969, pp. 440-446.

Mancinelli 1983
F. Mancinelli, "Melozzo da Forlì, Affreschi distaccati raffiguranti figure di angeli e teste di Apostoli", *Bollettino Monumenti Musei e Gallerie Pontificie*, IV, 193, 1983, p. 49.

Mantua 1974
Tesori d'arte nella terra dei Gonzaga, Milan 1974.

Marcos Vallaure 1901
E. Marcos Vallaure, *Estudios Histórico- Artísticos*, Valladolid 1901.

Margherini 1897
G. Margherini, *L'arte a Città di Castello*, 1897.

Marias 1989
F. Marias, *El largo siglo XVI*, Madrid 1989.

Marinelli 1983
S. Marinelli, *Museo di Castelvecchio, Verona*, Venice 1983.

Marinelli 1990
S. Marinelli, "Verona", *La pittura nel Veneto. II Quattrocento*, Milan 1990.

Marinelli 1991
S. Marinelli, *Castelvecchio a Verona*, Milan 1991.

Marinetto Sánchez-Flores Escobosa 1991
P. Marinetto Sánchez-I. Flores Escobosa, *Estudio tipo cronológico de la cerámica nazarí. Elemento de Agua y Fuego*, Rabat 1991.

Markl-Baptista Pereira 1986
D. Markl-F.A. Baptista Pereira, *História de Arte em Portugal. O Renascimento*, VI, Lisbon 1986.

Marlier 1954
G. Marlier, *Erasme et la peinture flamande de son temps*, Damme 1954.

Martín-Arnold 1926
F.R. Martín-R.W. Arnold, *The Nizami ms: Written in 1495 for Sultamn Ali Mirza Barlas, Ruler of Samarqand, in the British Museum (Or.6810)*, Vienna 1926.

Martín González 1977
J.J. Martín González, *El Museo Nacional de Escultura de Valladolid*, León 1977.

Martin Mery 1952
G. Martin Mery, *Les primitifs mediterranées XIVème et XVème siècles*, Bordeaux 1952.

Martínez 1988
C. Martínez-P. Cabello, "El arte inca epigonal", *Piedras y oro. El arte en el imperio de los incas*, Alicante 1988.

Martínez Caviró 1983
B. Martínez Caviró, *Artes del tiempo y del espacio. La loza dorada*, Madrid 1983.

Martínez Caviró 1991
B. Martínez Caviró, *La cerámica hispanomusulmana. Andalusí y mudéjar*, 1991.

Martínez del Romero 1849
A. Martínez del Romero, *Catá-logo de la Real Armeria*, Madrid 1849.

Martini 1872
P. Martini, *La Pubblica Pinacoteca*, Parma 1872.

Masini 1666
A. Masini, *Bologna perlustrata*, Bologna 1666

Matos Moctezuma 1988[a]
E. Matos Moctezuma, *Obras maestras del Templo Mayor*, Mexico 1988.

Matos Moctezuma 1988[b]
E. Matos Moctezuma, *Ofrendas del Templo Mayor*, Mexico 1988.

Matthiae 1935
G. Matthiae, *Inventario degli oggetti d'arte d'Italia*, VI, Provincial Administration of Mantua, Rome 1935.

Mattioli 1972
M. Mattioli, *Contributi dell'Istituto di Storia dell'Arte*, II, Milan 1972.

May 1957
F.L. May, *Silk textiles of Spain*, New York 1957.

Mayer 1926
A.L. Mayer, "Miniatures by Juan de Carrión in the British Museum", *Burlington Magazine*, 275, XLVIII, 1926.

Mayer 1933
L.A. Mayer, *Saracenic Heraldry*, Oxford 1933.

Mayer 1958
L.A. Mayer, *Islamic Woodcarvers and their Works*, 1958.

Mazzini 1982
F. Mazzini, *I Mattoni e le Pietre di Urbino*, Urbino 1982.

Meco 1985
J. Meco, *Azulejaría portuguesa*, Lisbon 1985.

Medley 1973 (1989)
M. Medley, *Ming and Ch'ing Monochrome*, London 1973 (Revised edition 1989).

Medley 1976
M. Medley, *The Chinese Potter*, London 1976.

Medley 1978
M. Medley, *Ming Polychrome Wares*, London 1978.

Medley 1989
M. Medley, *Ming and Qing Monochrome Wares*, London 1989.

Millet 1927
G. Millet, *Monuments de L'Athos II. Les peintures*, Paris 1927.

Millet-Frolov 1962
G. Millet-A. Frolov, *La peinture du Moyen Age en Yugoslavie*, III, Paris 1962.

Milstein 1978
A.R. Milstein, *The Paintings of Girolamo Mazzola Bedoli*, New York-London 1978.

Modena 1971
G.L. Reggi, *La ceramica graffita in Emilia-Romagna dal secolo XIV al secolo XIX*, Modena 1971.

Molinier 1884
J. Cavalucci-E. Molinier, *Les Della Robbia. Leur vie et leur oeuvre*, Paris 1884.

Molinier 1886
E. Molinier, *Les plaquettes*, Paris 1886.

Monzo Tormo-Sánchez Cantón 1919
E. Monzo Tormo-F.J. Sánchez Canton, *Los tapices de la Casa del Rey N.S.*, Madrid 1919.

Moschetti 1922
A. Moschetti, "Di un dipinto di casa Papafava attribuito a Jacopo da Montagnana", *Bollettino del Museo Civico di Padova*, 1922.

Moschetti 1927
A. Moschetti, "Un dipinto di Francesco da Ponte il Vecchio", *Bollettino del Museo Civico di Padova*, 1927.

Moschetti 1938
A. Moschetti, *Il Museo Civico di Padova*, Padua 1938.

Moschini 1815
G.A. Moschini, *Guida per la città di Venezia*, Venice 1815.

Moschini 1943
V. Moschini, *Giambellino*, Bergamo 1943.

Moschini Marconi 1962
S. Moschini Marconi, *Gallerie dell'Accademia. Opere d'Arte del secolo XVI*, Rome 1962.

Moscow 1988
Museo de los Pueblos de Oriente en Moscú, Moscow 1988.

Mossetti 1985
C. Mossetti, "Pittori del Quattrocento tra Novalesa e Torino", Various Authors, *Ricerche sulla pittura del Quattrocento in Piemonte*, Turin 1985.

Mulazzani 1969
G. Mulazzani, *Mostra di opere d'arte restaurate*, Urbino 1969.

Müller 1974
T. Müller, "Das Ratssilber", *Ingoldstadt*, Ingolstadt 1974, pp. 7-36.

Muntz 1879-1884
E. Muntz, *Histoire Générale de la Tapisserie. Italie*, Paris 1879-1884.

Muntz 1882
E. Muntz, *La Tapisserie*, Paris 1882.

Muntz 1897
E. Muntz, *Les Tapisseries de Raphaël au Vatican*, Paris 1897.

Naldi 1986
R. Naldi, "Un'ipotesi per l'affresco di Pedro Fernández in San Domenico Maggiore a Napoli", *Prospettiva*, 42, 1986.

Naples 1933
S. Ortolani, *Catalogo della mostra salernitana d'arte*, Naples 1933.

Nardini 1778
A. Nardini, *Series historico-chronologica praefectorum qui ecclesiam titulo S. Demetrï Mar. Thessalonicensis fondatam, deinceps S. Bartholomei Apostoli de Rivoalto repara-*

402

tam rexerunt ab ecclesia condita..., Venetiis 1778.

Navarrete 1962
C. Navarrete, "La cerámica de Mixco Viejo" *Cuadernos de Antropología,* I, Guatemala 1962.

Navarro 1982
F. Navarro, "Lo pseudo Bramantino. Proposta per la ricostruzione di una vicenda artistica", *Bollettino d'Arte,* LXVII, 14, 1982, pp. 37-68.

Navarro 1985
F. Navarro, "Una nuova opera di Pedro Fernández del tempo di Genova", *Prospettiva,* 42, 1985, pp. 62-64.

Neff-Bishop 1988
H. Neff-R.L. Bishop, "Plumbate Origins and Development", *American Antiquity,* 53 (3), Washington 1988.

Nepi Sciré-Valcanover 1985
G. Nepi Sciré-F. Valcanover, *Le Gallerie dell'Accademia,* Milan 1985.

New York 1982
F. Mancinelli, "Melozzo da Forlì", *The Vatican Collections. The Papacy and Art,* New York 1982.

New York 1989-1991
Yoruba, Nine Centuries of Art & Thought, New York 1989-1991.

New York-Nuremberg 1986
Various Authors, *Gothic and Renaissance Art in Nuremberg,* 1300-1500, Munich 1986.

Nicholson 1983
H.B. Nicholson, *Art of the Aztecs. Treasures of Tenochtitlan,* Washington 1983.

Nicolaisen 1986
J. Nicolaisen, *Art Africain,* Paris 1986.

Olderogge 1969
D.A. Olderogge, *El Arte Negro,* Mexico 1969.

Oliver Hurtado 1875
J.M. Oliver Hurtado, *Granada y sus monumentos árabes,* Málaga 1875.

Olmi 1977
G. Olmi, "Osservazione della natura e raffigurazione in Ulisse Aldrovandi (1522-1605)", *Annali dell'Istituto storico italo-germanico in Trento,* III, 1977, pp. 142-143.

Orey 1984
L. d'Orey, *Ouriversaria Portuguesa no Museu de Arte Antiga,* Lisbon 1984, p. 11.

Orey 1986
L. d'Orey, "Ouriversaria Portuguesa-Outra forma de contar a historia", *Revista Clube Ediçoes de Arte,* 1, Lisbon, 1986, pp. 10 and 23.

Orey 1988
L. d'Orey, *Le Langage des Orfèvres du Portugal, (A Linguagem dos nossos Ourives),* Lisbon, May 1988.

Orey 1988
L. d'Orey, "Ouriversaria Portuguesa – Outra forma de contar a história", *Revista Cea,* 1, Lisbon 1988, pp. 20-21.

Orey 1991
L. Orey, *Feitoiras,* Antwerp 1991.

Ortolani 1945
S. Ortolani. *Raffaello,* Bergamo 1945.

Ottino dalla Chiesa 1967
A. Ottino dalla Chiesa, *L'opera completa di Leonardo pittore,* Milan 1967.

Pagliaro-Bausani 1960
A. Pagliaro-A.Bausani, *Storia della letteratura persiana,* Milan 1960.

Pallucchini 1935
A. Pallucchini, "La formazione di Sebastiano del Piombo", *La Critica d'Arte,* 1935, pp. 41-42.

Pallucchini 1941
A. Pallucchini, "Vicende delle ante d'organo di Sebastiano del Piombo per San Bartolomeo a Rialto", *Le Arti,* 1941, pp. 448-456.

Pallucchini 1944
A. Pallucchini, *Sebastian Viniziano (Fra Sebastiano del Piombo),* Milan 1944.

Pallucchini 1947
R. Pallucchini, "Capolavori della pittura veronese", *Arte Veneta,* 1947, p. 236.

Pallucchini 1947
R. Pallucchini, *Trésors de l'art vénitien,* Brussels-Milan 1947.

Pallucchini 1959
A. Pallucchini, *Giovanni Bellini,* Milan 1959.

Pallucchini 1966
A. Pallucchini, "La Carta del Navegar Pittoresco. 1600", *Civiltà veneziana. Fonti e Testi,* 7, Venice 1966.

Panofsky 1955
E. Panofsky, "The History of the Theory of Human Proportions as a Reflection of the History of Styles", *Meaning in the Visual Arts,* Princeton 1955.

Panvini Rosati 1968
Panvini Rosati, *Medaglie e placchette dal Rinascimento al XVIII secolo,* Rome 1968.

Papadopoulo 1977
A. Papadopoulo, *El Islam y el arte musulmán,* Barcelona 1977.

París 1933
Art des Incas. Catalogue de l'Exposition de la collection J.L. au Palais du Trocadéro. Musée d'Ethnographie. Musée National d'Histoire Naturelle, Paris 1933.

Paris 1965-1966
Le Seizième Siècle Européen. Tapisseries, Paris 1965-1966.

París 1968
Rome à Paris, Petit Palais, Paris 1968.

París 1971
Arts de l'Islam des origines à 1700, Paris 1971.

Paris 1972-1973
L'Ecole de Fontainebleau, Paris 1972-1973.

Paris 1977
L'Islam dans les collections nationales, Paris 1977.

Paris 1990
Various Authors, *Soliman le Magnifique,* Galerie Nationale du Grand Palais, Paris 1990.

Partearroyo 1982
C. Partearroyo, "Tejidos, alfombras y tapices", *Historia de las artes aplicadas e industriales en España,* Madrid 1982.

Partearroyo 1992
C. Partearroyo, "Tejidos almorávides y almohades", *Al-Andalus, las Artes Islámicas en España*", The Metropolitan Museum of Art, Madrid 1992.

Passavant 1839-1858
J.D. Passavant, *Raphael von Urbino und sein Vater Giovanni Santi, 3,* Leipzig 1839-1858.

Passoni 1986
R. Passoni, "Pittura del Quattrocento in Piemonte e Valle d'Aosta", Various Authors, *La pittura in Italia, Il Quattrocento,* Milan 1986.

Pasztory 1983
E. Pasztory, *Aztec Art,* New York 1983.

Pavón Maldonado 1973
B. Pavón Maldonado, "Una silla de taracea del reinado de Muhammad VII de Granada", *Boletín de la Asociación Española de Orientalistas,* Madrid 1973.

Pavón Maldonado 1977
B. Pavón Maldonado, "Estudios sobre la Alhambra", *Cuadernos de la Alhambra,* 1977.

Pavone 1982
M.A. Pavone, "Correnti pittoriche dal Cinque al Settecento", *Guida alla Storia di Salerno e della sua provincia,* Salerno 1982.

Pazzi 1928
G. Pazzi, "Amor degli Arazzi",

Ospitalità Italiana, 5, 1928, pp. 67-69.

Pedretti 1953
C. PEDRETTI, *Leonardo a Bologna e in Emilia*, Bologna 1953.

Pedretti 1983
C. PEDRETTI, *Leonardo e il leonardismo a Napoli e a Parma*, Florence 1983.

Pereira 1985
F.A.B. PEREIRA, "Pintura antigua do convento de Jesús (Historia de uma colecção, séc. XV e XVI)", *Movimento Cultural, revista dos Municipios do Distrito de Setúbal*, 1, 1985, pp. 29-38.

Pereira 1989
F.A.B. PEREIRA, *Retabulo da igreja de Jesús de Setúbal*, Lisbon 1989.

Pereira 1990
F.A.B. PEREIRA, *O Museu do Convento de Jesús de Setúbal*, Lisbon 1990.

Pérez de Barradas 1966
J. PÉREZ DE BARRADAS, *Orfebrería prehispánica en Colombia: Estilos Quimbaya y otros*, Bogotá 1966.

Pérez Villanueva 1933-1934
J. PÉREZ VILLANUEVA, "Una escultura de Berruguete: El Ecce Homo del retablo de la Mejorada en Olmedo", *Boletín del Seminario de Estudios de Arte y Arqueología*, II, Valladolid 1933-1934.

Perugia 1945
Quattro secoli di pittura in Umbria, Mostra celebrativa del V centenario della nascita di Pietro Perugino, Perugia 1945.

Piganiol de la Force 1765
PIGANIOL DE LA FORCE, *Descripción de la ville de Paris*, Paris 1765.

Pignatti 1969
T. PIGNATTI, *L'opera completa di Giovanni Bellini detto Giambellino*, Milan 1969.

Pigorini 1887
L. PIGORINI, *Catalogo della regia Pinacoteca di Parma*, Parma 1887.

Pinedo-Vizcaino 1977
C. PINEDO-E. VIZCAINO, *La cerámica de Manises en la Historia*, León 1977.

Piña Chan 1977
R. PIÑA CHAN, *Quetzcóatl. Serpiente emplumada*, Mexico 1977.

Pistolesi 1829
E. PISTOLESI, *Il Vaticano descritto ed illustrato da Erasmo Pistolesi*, Rome 1829.

Planischig 1942
L. PLANISCHIG, *Bernardo und Antonio Rossellino*, Vienna 1942.

Polidori 1956
G.C. POLIDORI, *Musei Civici di Pesaro*, Genova 1956.

Pollard 1984
J.G. POLLARD, *Medaglie Italiane del Rinascimento*, Florence 1984.

Pollard 1986
J.G. POLLARD, "Medaglie Italiane del Rinascimento", *S.P.E.S.*, 27, Florence 1986.

Ponz 1776-1794 (1947)
A. PONZ, *Viaje a España en que se da noticia de las cosas más apreciables y dignas de saberse que hay en ella*, Madrid 1776-1794 (repr. 1947).

Pope-Hennessy 1947
J. POPE-HENNESSY, *Sienese Quattrocento Painting*, London 1947.

Pope-Hennessy 1969
J. POPE-HENNESSY, "The Virgin with the Laughing Child", *Essays on Italian Sculpture*, London 1969, pp. 72-77.

Pope-Hennessy 1980
J. POPE-HENNESSY, "The Altman Madonna by Antonio Rossellino", *The Study and Criticism of Italian Sculpture*, New York 1980.

Pope-Hennessy 1980
J. POPE-HENNESSY, *Luca Della Robbia*, Oxford 1980.

Pope-Hennessy 1985
J. POPE-HENNESSY, *Italian Renaissance Sculpture*, New York 1985.

Pophan 1967
A.E. POPHAN, *Italian Drawings in the British Museum*, London 1967.

Post 1966
CH.R. POST, *A History of the Spanish Painting*, XIV, Cambridge 1966.

Post 1970
CH.R. POST, "The Valencian School in the Early Renaissance", *A History of Spanish Painting*, New York 1970, pp. 212, 213.

Prats Rivelles 1983
R. PRATS RIVELLES, "La entrada de la plástica leonardesca en España: 'La Resurrección' de Yáñez", *Diario Levante*, 24. July 1983.

Premuda 1957
L. PREMUDA, *Storia dell'iconografia anatomica*, Milan 1957.

Propping 1892
F. PROPPING, *Die Künstlerische Laufbahn des Sebastiano del Piombo bis zum Tode Raphaels*, Leipzig 1892.

Proto Pisani, 1980
R. PROTO PISANI, *Il primato del disegno*, Florence 1980.

Puppi 1962
L. PUPPI, *Bartolomeo Montagna*, Venice 1962.

Puppi 1976
L. PUPPI, *Dopo Mantegna, Arte a Padova e nel territorio nei secoli XV e XVI*, 27, Milan 1976.

Putelli 1935
R. PUTELLI, *Vita, storia ed Arte mantovana nel Cinquecento: I: Inventari d'arredi sacri*, Mantua 1935.

Quintavalle 1939
A.O. QUINTAVALLE, *La Galleria Nazionale di Parma*, Rome 1939.

Quintavalle 1939
A.O. QUINTAVALLE, "La testa leonardesca di fanciulla", *Emporium*, 1939, pp. 273-280.

Quintavalle 1943
A.O. QUINTAVALLE, "Nuovi ritratti farnesiani...", *Aurea Parma*, 1943, pp. 59-89.

Quintavalle 1948
A.O. QUINTAVALLE, *Dipinti noti e ignoti della Galleria Nazionale di Parma*, Parma 1948.

Raby 1982
J. RABY, "Venice, Dürer and the Oriental Mode", *The Hans Huth Memorial Studies*, I, London 1982.

Rachewiltz 1966
B. DE RACHEWILTZ, *Introduction to African Art*, London 1966.

Ragghianti 1954
C.L. RAGGHIANTI, "Catalogo della mostra di Luca Signorelli", *Critica d'Arte*, I, 1954.

Ramírez 1843
L.M. RAMÍREZ, *Varias antigüedades de Córdoba*, 1843.

Ramos de Castro-Redondo Cantera 1988
G. RAMOS DE CASTRO-REDONDO CANTERA, *Las Edades del Hombre. El arte de la Iglesia de Castilla y León*, Valladolid 1988.

Ramos Gómez-Blasco Bosqued 1975
L. RAMOS GÓMEZ-C. BLASCO BOSQUED, "Materiales líticos taínos en el Museo de América", *Cuadernos Prehispánicos*, 3, pp. 19-52, Seminar on American studies, University of Valladolid, Valladolid 1975.

Ramos Gómez-Blasco Bosqued 1980
L. RAMOS GÓMEZ-C. BLASCO BOSQUED, *Los tejidos Prehispánicos del Area Central Andina en el Museo de América de Madrid*, Madrid 1980.

404

Raunie 1899
RAUNIE, *Epitaphier du Vieux París*, Paris 1899.

Reales Sitios 1969
"Las tablas del oratorio de Isabel la Católica del Palacio de Oriente", *Reales Sitios*, VI, 1969, pp. 14-26.

Reis Santos 1943
L. REIS SANTOS, "Reconstituição do antigo poliptico da paixão da igreja de Jesús de Setúbal", *Estudios de Pintura Antiga*, 1943, pp. 147-155.

Reis Santos 1957
L. REIS SANTOS, *Os primitivos portugueses*, Lisbon 1957.

Reis Santos 1958
L. REIS SANTOS, "Painéis de Metsys em Portugal, anteriores ao retábulo de Lovaina", *Belas Artes*, II Série, 12, Lisbon 1958.

Reis Santos 1960
L. REIS SANTOS, *Cristovao de Figuereido*, Lisbon 1960.

Reis Santos 1961
L. REIS SANTOS, "Retábulo Joanino da Madre de Deus", *Boletim Academia Nacional de Bellas Artes*, 16-17, 1961.

Reis Santos 1966
L. REIS SANTOS, *Jorge Afonso*, Lisbon 1966.

Reynaud 1967
N. REYNAUD, "Le Couronnement de la Vierge de Michel Zitow", *Revue du Louvre*, XVII, 6, 1967, pp. 345-352.

Ricci 1896
C. RICCI, *Catalogo della Regia Pinacoteca di Parma*, Parma 1896.

Ricci 1911
C. RICCI, *Melozzo da Forlì*, Rome 1911.

Ricci 1913
S. DE RICCI, *Description raisonnée des peintures du Louvre, I, Italie et Espagne*, Paris 1913.

Riccomini 1985
E. RICCOMINI, *Leonardo e il Codice Hammer e la mappa di Imola*, Bologna 1985.

Richter 1937
G.M. RICHTER, *Giorgio da Castelfranco, called Giorgione*, Chicago 1937.

Rico de Estasen 1973
J. RICO DE ESTASEN, "En el Museo Provincial de Bellas Artes de Valencia: un lienzo de excepción que reproduce el misterio de la Resurrección del señor", *Diario de Las Provincias*, 22. April 1973.

Ring 1949
G. RING, *A Century of French Painting, 1400-1500*, London 1949.

Ring 1949
G. RING, *La peinture française du XVème siècle*, London-Paris 1949.

Ritter 1927
H. RITTER, *Über die Bildersprache Nizamis*, Berlin, Leipzig 1927.

Robertson 1954
G. ROBERTSON, *Vincenzo Catena*, Edinburgh 1954.

Robertson 1968
G. ROBERTSON, *Giovanni Bellini*, Oxford 1968.

Robinson 1967
B.W. Robinson, *Persian Miniature Painting from Collections in the British Isles*, Geneva 1967.

Rodríguez Lorente 1963
J.J. RODRÍGUEZ LORENTE, "Las dagas o puñales de oreja. Su origen hispanoárabe", *Archivo español de Arte*, XXXVI, 1963, pp. 119-130.

Rodríguez Lorente 1964
J.J. RODRÍGUEZ LORENTE, *The 15th Century Ear Dagger. Its Hispano Moresque Origin*, 1964.

Rodríguez Martínez 1981
L. RODRÍGUEZ MARTÍNEZ, *Historia del Monasterio de San Benito el Real de Valladolid*, Valladolid 1981.

Rogers 1986
J.M. ROGERS, *Hülyetezcan,*

Selma Delibas, Topkapi. Costumes, Embroideries and other Textiles*, London 1986.

Rogers-Ward 1988
J.M. ROGERS-R.M. WARD, *Süleyman the Magnificent*, London 1988.

Rogers-Ward 1990
J.M. ROGERS-R.M. WARD, *Süleyman the Magnificent*, London 1990.

Rojas de Perdomo 1979
L. ROJAS DE PERDOMO, *Manual de Arqueología Colombiana*, Bogotá 1979.

Romano 1977
G. ROMANO, *Valle di Susa, arte e storia dell'XI al XVIII secolo*, Turin 1977.

Romano 1989
G. ROMANO, "Sur Antoine de Lonhy", *Revue de l'Art*, 85, 1989, pp. 35-44.

Romano 1991
G. ROMANO, *Dal Trecento al Seicento. Le arti a paragone*, Turin 1991.

Romano-Macco 1988
G. ROMANO-M. DI MACCO. *Monumenti del Quattrocento a Chieri*, Turin 1988.

Romero 1975
M. ROMERO, "Evocación histórica de la seda", *Telas con história*, 1975.

Ronsin 1979
A. RONSIN, *Découverte et baptême de l'Amérique*, Montreal 1979.

Ronsin 1991
A. RONSIN, *La fortune d'ún nom: America, le baptême du Nouveau Monde à Saint-Diedes-Vosges. Cosmographiae Introductio suivi des Lettres d'Amerigo Vespuci*, Grenoble 1991.

Rosemberg 1908
A. ROSEMBERG, *Raffael. Des Meisters Gemälde*, Stuttgart, Berlin, Leipzig 1908.

Rosemberg 1909
A. ROSEMBERG, *Raffael*, Stuttgart and Leipzig 1909.

Rotondi 1948
P. ROTONDI, *Guida del Palazzo Ducale di Urbino e della Galleria Nazionale delle Marche*, Urbino 1948.

Rotondi 1950
P. ROTONDI, *Il Palazzo Ducale di Urbino*, Urbino 1950.

Rovira LLorens 1990
S. ROVIRA LLORENS, *La metalurgia americana: Análisis tecnológico de materiales prehispánicos y coloniales*, Madrid 1990.

Roy 1921
M. ROY, "Le Monument funéraire d'Albert Pie de Savoie, compte de Carpi (1531-1535)", *Bulletin de la Societé de l'historie de l'art français*, 1921, pp. 33-47.

Roy 1929
M. ROY, "Le Monument funéraire d'Albert Pie de Savoie, comte de Carpi (1531-1535)", *Monuments de la Reinaissance*, Paris 1929, pp. 138-147.

Rubiera Mata 1977
Mª J. RUBIERA MATA, "Ibn Zamrek, su biógrafo Ibn Ahmar y los poemas epigráficos de la Alhambra", *Al-Andalus*, 1977.

Ruiz García 1980
A. RUIZ GARCÍA, *La cerámica doméstica nazaría en vidriado verde en el Museo Nacional de Arte Hispanomusulmán*, Granada 1980.

Rusk Shapley 1979
F. RUSK SHAPLEY, *National Gallery of Art. Catalogue of the Italian Paintings*, Washington 1979.

Ryder 1964
A.F.C. RYDER, "A Note on Afro-Portuguese Ivories", *Journal of African History*, 5, 1964, pp. 363-365.

Sala 1964
X. SALA, "Pintura española y

flamenca en las colecciones escurialenses", *El Escorial, IV Centenario*, II, 1964.

Salgado 1986
H. SALGADO, *Asentamientos prehispánicos en el noroccidente del Valle del rio Cauca*, Bogotá 1986

Salmi 1938
M. SALMI, "Melozzo e i suoi rapporti con la pittura toscana e umbra", *Melozzo da Forlî*, 1938.

Salmi 1949
M. SALMI, "Il Palazzo Ducale di Urbino e Francesco di Giorgio", *Studi Artistici Urbinati*, I, Urbino 1949, pp. 11-55.

Salmi 1953
M. SALMI, *Luca Signorelli*, Novara 1953.

San Francisco-Seoul 1979
5000 Years of Korean Art, San Francisco 1979.

Sánchez Cantón 1923
F.J. SÁNCHEZ CANTÓN, *Fuentes literarias para la historia del arte español*, I, 1923.

Sánchez Cantón 1930 and 1931
F.J. SÁNCHEZ CANTÓN, "El retablo de la Reina Católica", *Archivo Español de Arte y Arqueología*, VI, 1930, pp. 97-152 and VII, 1931, p. 151.

Sánchez Cantón 1950
F.J. SÁNCHEZ CANTÓN, *Libros tapices y cuadros que coleccionó Isabel la Católica*, Madrid 1950.

Sánchez Ferrer 1986
J. SÁNCHEZ FERRER, *Alfombras en la provincia de Albacete*, Madrid 1986.

Sangiorgi 1982
F. SANGIORGI, *Iconografía federiciana*, Urbino 1982.

Santi 1977
F. SANTI, "Ancora sulle architetture dei 'Miracoli' del 1473 e sui rapporti tra l'ambiente urbinate e la scuola perugina", *Rapporti artistici tra le Mar-*

che e l'Umbria*, Perugia 1977, pp. 55-60.

Santi 1985
F. SANTI, *Dipinti, sculture ed oggetti dei secoli XV-XVI*, Rome 1985.

Santillana del Mar 1982-Zamora 1983
Arte y Cultura del Cuzco, Santillana del Mar 1982.

Santos Simoes 1990
J.M. SANTOS SIMOES, *Azulejaría em Portugal nos séculos XV e XVI*, Lisbon 1990.

Sarre 1906
FR. SARRE, *Erzeugnisse islamischer Kunst I, Metall*, 1906.

Sarre 1912
FR. SARRE, *Die Ausstellung von Meisterwerken muhammedanischer Kunst in München III*, 1912.

Saulnier 1982
A. SAULNIER, "Oeuvres inedites de l'enlumineur Juan de Carrion", *Revue de l'Art*, no. 57, 1982.

Sauvaget 1945-1946
J. SAUVAGET, "Une ancienne représentation de Damas au Musée du Louvre", *Bulletin d'études orientales*, Institut Français de Damas, 11, 1945-1946, pp. 5-12.

Sauval 1724
SAUVAL, *Histoire et recherches des antiquités de la Ville de Paris*, Paris 1724.

Scalabrini 1779
G.A. SCALABRINI, *Memorie storiche delle chiese di Ferrara e de' suoi borghi*, 301, Ferrara 1779.

Scanelli 1657
F. SCANELLI, *Il Microcosmo della pittura*, Cesena 1657.

Scarpellini 1964
P. SCARPELLINI, *Luca Signorelli*, Milan 1964.

Scarpellini 1984
P. SCARPELLINI, *Perugino*, Milan 1984.

Schiavo 1977
A. SCHIAVO, "Melozzo a Roma", *Presenza Romagnola*, I, 1977, pp. 89-110.

Schroeder 1981
U. VON SCHROEDER, *Indo-Tibetan Bronzen*, I, Hong Kong 1981.

Schubring 1907
P. SCHUBRING, *Die plastik Sienas in Quattrocento*, Berlin 1907.

Scott 1989
R.E. SCOTT, *Imperial Taste: Chinese Ceramics from the Percival David Foundation*, Seattle 1989.

Sebastian 1986
S. SEBASTIAN, *El Fisiólogo atribuido a San Epifanio*, Madrid 1986.

Séjourné 1962
L. SÉJOURNÉ, *El Universo de Quetzalcóal*, Mexico 1962.

Serra 1930
L. SERRA, *Il Palazzo Ducale e la Galleria Nazionale di Urbino*, Urbino 1930.

Serra 1934
L. SERRA, *L'Arte nelle Marche*, II, Rome 1934.

Sgulmero 1899
P. SGULMERO, *Il Moretto a Verona*, Verona 1899.

Shaw 1987
J.C. SHAW, *Introducing Thai Ceramics also Burmese and Khmer*, Bangkok 1987.

Shephard 1948
A.O. SHEPHARD, *Plumbate. A Mesoamerican trade ware*, Washington 1948.

Shepherd 1978
D. SHEPHERD, "A Treasure from a Thirteenth-Century Spanish Tomb", *The Bulletin of the Cleveland Museum of Art*, Cleveland 1978.

Sherril 1974
S.B. SHERRIL, "The Islamic Tradition in Spanish Rug Weaving", *The Magazine Antiques*, 1974.

Silva Maroto 1982
M. D.P. SILVA MAROTO, "La miniatura hispano- flamenca en Avila. Nuevos datos documentales", *Miscelanea de Arte*, Madrid 1982, pp. 55-56.

Singer 1957
C. SINGER, "The Confluence of Humanism Anatomic and Art", *Melanges F. Saxi*, London 1957.

Skelton 1958
R. SKELTON, "The Ni'mat Nama: a Landmark in Malwa Painting", *Marg*, 12, Bombay 1958.

Skrobucha 1961
H. SKROBUCHA, *Meisterwerke der Ikonenmalerei*, Recklinghausen 1961.

Smith 1968
R. SMITH, *The Art of Portugal, 1500-1800*, New York 1968.

Soler 1992
A. SOLER, "Armas y armaduras", *Las Artes Islamicas en España*, Madrid 1992.

Sotiriou 1924
G. SOTIRIOU, *Guía del Museo Bizantino de Atenas*, Athens 1924.

Sotiriou 1931
G. SOTIRIOU, *Guía del Museo Bizantino de Atenas*, Athens 1931.

Sourdel-Thomine-Spuhler 1973
J. SOURDEL-THOMINE-SPUHLER, *Die Kunst des Islam*, Berlin 1973.

Soustiel 1985
J. SOUSTIEL, *La céramique Islamique: La Guide du Connaisseur*, Freibourg 1985.

Spuhler 1987
F. SPUHLER, *Die Orientteppiche im Museum für Islamische Kunst*, 63, Berlin 1987.

Sricchia Santoro 1988
F. SRICCHIA SANTORO, *Da Sodoma a Marco Pino, pittori a Siena nella Prima metà del Cinquecento*, Siena 1988.

Sricchia Santoro 1990
F. SRICCHIA SANTORO, *Domenico*

406

Beccafumi e il suo tempo, Milan 1990.

Stadtner 1991
D.M. STADTNER, "A Fifteenth-Century Royal Monument in Surma and the Seven Stations in Buddhist Art", *The Art Bulletin,* LXXIII, 1, 1991.

Stchoukline 1950
N. STCHOUKLINE, *Les peintures de la Khamseh de Nizami du British Museum,* Syria, 27, 1950.

Stchoukline 1954
N. STCHOUKLINE, *Les peintures des manuscrits timurides,* Paris 1954.

Sterling 1945
CH. STERLING, "Saint Sebastian Interceding for the Plague Stricken", *The Art Quaterly,* 1945.

Sterling 1972
CH. STERLING, "Etudes savoyardes II: le Maître de la Trinité de Turin", *L'Oeil,* 215, 1972.

Stratton-Macnair-Scott 1987
C. STRATTON-A. MACNAIR-M. SCOTT, *The Art of Sukhothai,* Singapore 1987.

Subhadradis Diskul 1990
M.C. SUBHADRADIS DISKUL, *Hindu Gods at Sukhodaya,* Bangkok 1990.

Suida 1929
W. SUIDA, *Leonardo und Sein Kreis,* Munich 1929.

Szmodis-Eszláry 1981
E. SZMODIS-ESZLÁRY, "Relief en cristal de roche d'un maître vénitien du debut du XVIème siècle", *Bulletin du Musée Hongrois des Beaux-Arts,* Budapest 1981, pp. 97-104.

Taja 1750
A. TAJA, *Descrizione del Palazzo Apostolico Vaticano,* Rome 1750.

Tavares da Silva-Baptista Pereira 1989
C. TAVARES DA SILVA-F.A. BAPTISTA PEREIRA, *Convento de Jesús-500*

anos-Arqueología e Historia, Setúbal 1989.

Teixeira da Mota 1975
A. TEIXEIRA DA MOTA, "Gli avori africani nella documentazione portoghese dei secoli 15-17", *Africa,* 30, 1975, pp. 580-589.

Tempestini 1992
A. TEMPESTINI, *Giovanni Bellini. Catalogo completo dei dipinti,* Florence 1992.

Thiery 1787
THIERY, *Guide des amateurs et des étrangers à París,* Paris 1787.

Thirion 1971
J. THIRION, "Rosso et les Arts décoratifs", *Revue de l'Art,* 13, 1971, p. 47.

Thomas-Gamber 1976
B. THOMAS-ORTWIN GAMBER, *Katalog der Leibrüstkammer, 1 Teil: Der Zritraum von 500-1530,* (Führer durch das Kunsthistorische Museum, no. 13), Vienna 1976.

Titley 1977
N.M. TITLEY, *Miniatures from Persian Manuscripts: A Catalogue and Subject Index of Painting from Persia, India and Turkey in The British Library and British Museum,* London 1977.

Titley 1983
N.M. TITLEY, *Persian Miniature Painting and its Influence on the Art of Turkey and India,* London 1983.

Tokio 1989
The Ancient Art of Nigeria, Tokyo 1989.

Toledo 1991
Damasquinado en Toledo, Toledo 1991.

Tolnay 1975
CH. DE TOLNAY, *I disegni di Michelangelo nelle collezioni italiane,* Florence 1975.

Tolnay 1975-1980
CH. DE TOLNAY, *Corpus dei disegni di Michelangelo,* Novara 1975-1980.

Tormo y Monzo 1932
E. TORMO Y MONZO, *Valencia: Los Museos. Guías-Catálogo,* Madrid 1932.

Torres Balbás 1935
L. TORRES BALBÁS, "Hojas de puerta de una alacena en el Museo de la Alhambra de Granada", *Al-Andalus* (A.A), III, 1935.

Torres Balbás 1931
L. TORRES BALBÁS, "Paseos por la Alhambra. La Torre del Peinador de la Reina o de la Estufa", *Archivo español de Arte y Arqueología,* Madrid 1931.

Torres Balbás 1949
L. TORRES BALBÁS, "Arte almohade. Arte nazarí. Arte mudéjar", *Ars Hispaniae,* IV, Madrid 1949.

Tramoyeres y Blasco 1915
L. TRAMOYERES Y BLASCO, *Guía del Museo de Bellas Artes de Valencia,* Valencia 1915.

Trecca 1912
G. TRECCA, *Catalogo della Pinacoteca comunale di Verona,* Bergamo 1912.

Trenti Antonelli 1991
M.G. TRENTI ANTONELLI, "Il ruolo della medaglia nella cultura umanistica", *Le muse e il principe,* Modena 1991.

Trimborn-Fernández Vega 1935
H. TRIMBORN-P. FERNÁNDEZ VEGA, *Catálogo de la Exposición de Arte Inca, (Colección Juan Larrea),* Biblioteca Nacional, Madrid 1935.

Trizna 1976
J. TRIZNA, *Michel Sittow,* Brussels 1976.

Tulli 1932
A. TULLI, "La Sala di Melozzo nella nuova Pinacoteca Vaticana", *L'Illustrazione Vaticana,* 1932, pp. 5-6.

Tzeutschler Lurie 1976
A. TZEUTSCHLER LURIE, "Birth and Naming of St. John the Baptist. Attributed to Juan de Flandes.

A Newly Discovered Panel from a Hypothetical Alterpiece", *The Bulletin of the Cleveland Museum os Art,* LXIII, 5, 1976, pp. 118-135.

Valsecchi 1973
M. VALSECCHI, *Tesori in Lombardia, Avori e oreficerie,* Milan 1973.

Van Marle 1935
R. VAN MARLE, *The Development of the Italian Schools of Painting,* The Hague 1935.

Varese 1979
R. VARESE, *Donazione e restauri,* Bologna 1979.

Varese 1980
R. VARESE, *Ferrara-Palazzina Marfisa,* Bologna 1980.

Varese 1983
R. VARESE, "Il libro come 'locus memoriae': una ipotesi di lettura", *Notizie da palazzo Albani,* 12, 1-2, Urbino 1983, pp. 18-31.

Various Authors 1856
Catálogo de los objetos que contienen el Real Museo Militar a cargo del Cuerpo de Artillería, Madrid 1856.

Various Authors 1914
VARIOUS AUTHORS, *De oude Kerkelijke Kunst in Nederland,* 's Hertogenbosch 1914.

Various Authors 1951
VARIOUS AUTHORS, *Roteiro das pinturas, Museu Nacional d'Arte Antiga,* Lisbon 1951 and 1956.

Various Authors 1953
VARIOUS AUTHORS, *The Nederlandse Monumenten van Geschiedenis en Kunst,* VIII, Den Haag 1953.

Various Authors 1953
VARIOUS AUTHORS, "Oriental Islamic Art", *Collection of the C. G. F.,* Lisbon 1953.

Various Authors 1955
VARIOUS AUTHORS, *Boletins do M.N.A.A.,* III, 1, Lisbon 1955.

Various Authors 1957
VARIOUS AUTHORS, *Roteiro das*

pinturas, Museu Nacional d'Arte Antiga, Lisbon 1957.

Various Authors 1969
VARIOUS AUTHORS, *Islamic Art in Egypt*, 1969.

Various Authors 1971-1979
Katalog des Museums für Islamische Kunst, no. 558, Berlin 1971-1979.

Various Authors 1976
VARIOUS AUTHORS, *Jewellery through 7000 Years*, London 1976.

Various Authors 1981
VARIOUS AUTHORS, *El arte hispano árabe y su decoración floral*, Madrid 1981.

Various Authors 1981
VARIOUS AUTHORS, *Esplendores del Imperio Vijayanagara; Hampi*, Bombay 1981.

Various Authors 1981
VARIOUS AUTHORS, *Museo Nacional de Arte Hispano Musulmán de la Alhambra*, Madrid 1981.

Various Authors 1983
VARIOUS AUTHORS, *Vijayanagara, Proceso de la Investigación, 1979-83*, XVIV-a, b, Mysoore 1983.

Various Authors 1985
VARIOUS AUTHORS, *Le arti figurative nel secondo Rinascimento*, Ferrara 1985.

Various Authors 1985
VARIOUS AUTHORS, *Vijayanagara, Proceso de la Investigación 1983-1984*, LXXIX-a, LXXVI - LXXVIII, LXXX, XCCI, XCII, XCVI-a and XCVI-b, Mysoore 1985.

Various Authors 1987
VARIOUS AUTHORS, "Art from the World of Islam", *Louisiana Revue*, 27, 3, cat. 186, 218, 1987.

Various Authors 1987
VARIOUS AUTHORS, *La Pittura in Italia. Il Cinquecento*, I, Milan 1987.

Various Authors 1989
VARIOUS AUTHORS, *Arte de la*

Tierra. Muiscas y Guanes, Colección Tesoros Precolombinos, Bogotá 1989.

Various Authors 1989
VARIOUS AUTHORS, *A Guide to the Percival David Foundation of Chinese Art*, Hong Kong 1989.

Various Authors 1990
VARIOUS AUTHORS, *Arte de la Tierra. Quimbayas*, Colección Tesoros Precolombinos, Bogotá 1990.

Various Authors 1990
VARIOUS AUTHORS, "Artesonados Museo Hispano Musulmán", *Intervenciones en el Patrimonio Arquitectónico (1980-1985)*, Madrid 1990.

Various Authors 1991
VARIOUS AUTHORS, *Arte de la Tierra. Taironas*, Colección Tesoros Precolombinos, Bogotá 1991.

Various Authors 1991
VARIOUS AUTHORS, *Enciclopedia del Islam*, Paris 1991.

Various Authors 1991
VARIOUS AUTHORS, *Guía de los Museos de la Comunidad Valenciana*, Valencia 1991.

Vasari-Milanesi 1878
G. VASARI, *Le vite de' piú eccellenti pittori, scultori e architettori*, edited by G. Milanesi, Florence 1878.

Vasco 1974
S. VASCO, "Le tavolette di S. Bernardino a Perugia", *Commentari*, XXV, 1-2, 1974, pp. 64-67.

Vasconcelos 1914
VASCONCELOS, *Arte Religiosa em Portugal*, Porto 1914.

Vavra 1982
E. VAVRA, *800 Jahre Franz von Assisi. Franziskische Kunst und Kultur des Mittelaltera*, Vienna 1982.

Venice 1946
R. PALLUCCHINI, *I capolavori dei Maestri Veneti*, Venice 1946.

Venice 1949
R. PALLUCCHINI, *Mostra di Giovanni Bellini*, Venice 1949.

Venturi 1891
A. VENTURI, *Le Gallerie Nazionali Italiane, Notizie e documenti*, 1891.

Venturi 1900
A. VENTURI, *La miniatura ferrarese nel secolo XV e il 'Decretum Gratiani'*, Rome 1900.

Venturi 1901-1902
A. VENTURI, "Un bronzo del Verrocchio", *L'Arte*, 5, 1902, pp. 43-44.

Venturi 1904
A. VENTURI, "Di alcune opere di scultura a Parigi", *L'Arte*, VII, 1904, pp. 469-477.

Venturi 1908
A. VENTURI, *Storia dell'Arte italiana*, VI, Milan 1908.

Venturi 1913
L. VENTURI, *Giorgione e il giorgionismo*, Milan 1913.

Venturi 1914
L. VENTURI, "Nella Galleria Nazionale delle Marche", *Bollettino d'Arte*, VIII, 1914, 10. pp. 316-319.

Venturi 1914
L. VENTURI, "Studi sul Palazzo Ducale di Urbino", *L'Arte*, 1914, p. 439.

Venturi 1924
A. VENTURI, "Leonardiana", *L'Arte*, 1924, pp. 55-57.

Venturi 1925
A. VENTURI, "Francesco di Giorgio Martini scultore", *L'Arte*, 1925, pp. 197-228.

Viale Ferrero 1963
M. VIALE FERRERO, *Arazzi del Cinquecento*, Milan 1963.

Viale Ferrero 1982
M. VIALE FERRERO, "Arazzo e pittura", *Storia dell'Arte italiana*, III, IV, Forme e modelli, Turin 1982, pp. 133-134.

Viale Ferrero 1984
M. VIALE FERRERO, "Arazzi", *Musei e Gallerie di Milano.*

Museo Poldi Pezzoli. Arazzi, tappeti, tessuti copti, pizzi, ricami, ventagli, Milan 1984, pp. 15-40.

Vieira Santos 1955
A. VIEIRA SANTOS, *Primitivos portugueses do Museu de Setúbal*, Lisbon 1955.

Vienna 1986
Gold und Macht. Spanien in der Neuen Welt, Vienna 1986.

Vilchez Vilchez 1983
C. VILCHEZ VILCHEZ, "Los restos conservados del Palacio de los Alijares", *Andalucía Islámica*, Granada 1983.

Villot 1849
VILLOT, *Notice des tableaux exposés dans les galeries du Musée National du Louvre, 1ère partie, écoles d'Italie et d'Espagne*, Paris 1849.

Viñas Torner 1972
V. VIÑAS TORNER, "Restauración de tres obras de Alberto Durero conservadas en El Escorial", *Reales Sitios*, 31, 1972.

Visser Travagli 1989
A.M. VISSER TRAVAGLI, "Ceramiche a Ferrara in età estense dalla Collezione Pasetti", *Quaderni dei Musei Ferraresi*, V, 1989, 24, p. 50.

Vitry 1900
P. VITRY, *Michel Colombe et la sculpture de son temps*, Paris 1900.

Vitry 1922
P. VITRY, "Les accroissements du département des sculptures au Musée du Louvre", *Gazette des Beaux-Arts*, 1, 1922, pp. 13-19.

Vitry 1934
P. VITRY, *La sculpture française classique*, Paris 1934.

Vogel 1981
S. VOGEL, *For Spirit and Kings: African Art from the Tishman Collection*, New York 1981

Ward 1991
A. WARD, "Incense and Incense Burners in Mamluk Egypt and

408

Syria", *Transactions of the Oriental Ceramic Society*, Londres 1991.

Washington 1953
Catalogue of Spanish Rugs, The Textile Museum, Washington D.C. 1953.

Washington 1991
Circa 1492. Art in the Age of Exploration, Washington 1991.

Wattenberg 1963
F. WATTENBERG, *Museo nacional de Escultura de Valladolid*, Madrid 1963.

Wattenberg 1966
F. WATTENBERG, *Museo nacional de Escultura de Valladolid*, Madrid 1966.

Wauchope 1970
R.L. WAUCHOPE, *Protohistoric Pottery of the Guatemalan Highlands. Monographs and Papers in Maya Archaeology*, Cambridge 1970.

Weiss 1953
R. WEISS, "The Castle of Gaillon in 1509-1510", *Journal of the Warburg Institute*, XVI, 1953, pp. 1-12 and 351.

Weller 1943
A.S. WELLER, *Francesco di Giorgio*, Chicago 1943.

Wellesz 1967
E. WELLESZ, "Lochner", *The Masters*, London 1967.

Wickhoff 1908
F. WICKHOFF. "Die Sammlung Tucher", *Munchner Jahrbuch der bildenden Kunst*, 1908.

Wiet 1935
G. WIET, *Exposition d'Art persan*, Cairo 1935.

Wilder 1933
J. WILDER, "Die Probleme um Domenico Mancini", *Jahrbuch der Kunsthistorischen Sammlungen in Wien*, 1933, p. 116.

Wilder 1974
J. WILDER, *Venetian Art from Bellini to Titian*, Oxford 1974.

Willers 1978
J.K.W. WILLERS, "Historische Waffen-und Jagdaltertümer", *Das Germanische Nationalmuseum 1852-1977*, Munich and Berlin 1978, pp. 833-859.

Willers 1986
J.K.W. WILLERS, *Gothic and Renaissance Art in Nuremberg 1300-1450*, Munich 1986.

Wilson 1951
A. FROTHINGHAM WILSON, *Lustware of Spain*, New York 1951.

Wingfield Digby 1959
G. WINGFIELD DIGBY, "Tapestries by the Wauters Family of Antwerp for the English Market", *La tapisserie flamande aux XVIIème et XVIIIème siècle*, Internacional Colloquium, 1959, p. 233.

Wingfield Digby-Hefford 1980
G. WINGFIELD-W. HEFFORD, *Victoria and Albert Museum. The Tapestries Collection, Medieval and Renaissance*, London 1980.

Wurtenberger 1962
F. WURTENBERGER, *Der Manierismus*, Vienna 1962.

Xigopoulos 1957
A. XIGOPOULOS, *Los Monumentos de los Serbios*, Athens 1957.

Yarza 1980
J. YARZA, "La Edad Media", *Historia del Arte Hispánico*, Madrid 1980.

Zaki 1961
A.R. ZAKI, "Introduction to the Study of Islamic Arms and Armour", *Gladius*, 1961.

Zamboni 1968
S. ZAMBONI, *Ludovico Mazzolino*, Milan 1968.

Zamboni 1978
S. ZAMBONI, "Ludovico Mazzolino: una primizia e altri inediti", *Prospettiva*, XV, 1978.

Zamrak 1971
I. ZAMRAK, Degree Thesis of Tawfiq al-Nayfar, Faculty of Letters, University of Tunis, 1971.

Zanetti 1771
A.M. ZANETTI, *Della pittura veneziana e delle opere pubbliche de' veneziani maestri*, Venice 1771.

Zaragoza Pascual 1976
E. ZARAGOZA PASCUAL, *Los Generales de la Congregación de San Benito de Valladolid, II. Los Abades trienales*, Silos 1976.

Zarco Cuevas 1930
ZARCO CUEVAS, *Inventario de alhajas, pinturas, objetos de valor*, Madrid 1930.

Zeri 1953
F. ZERI, "Alonso Berruguete: una Madonna con San Giovannino", *Paragone*, 43, 1953, pp. 49-51.

Zeri 1962
F. ZERI, "Eccentrici fiorentini", *Bollettino d'Arte*, 1962.

Zeri 1988
F. ZERI, *La collezione Federico Mason Perkins*, Turin 1988.

Zwalf 1981
W. ZWALF, *Heritage of Tibet*, London 1981.

Zwalf 1985
W. ZWALF, *Buddhism, Art and Faith*, London 1985.